THE
SYSTEM OF THE VEDANTA

THE
SYSTEM OF THE VEDANTA

DR. PAUL DEUSSEN

GYAN

Published by

Gyan Publishing House
5, Ansari Road
Daryaganj, New Delhi-110002
Phone: 011-47034999, 9811692060
E-mail: books@gyanbooks.com

Distribution Network
gyanbooks.com
India, USA, Canada, UK, Australia

ISBN: 978-93-6780-040-9 (HB)

First Published, 1912

2nd Impression 2024

Printed at: Gyan Press, Delhi.

THE SYSTEM OF THE VEDANTA
Author: DR. PAUL DEUSSEN

THE
SYSTEM OF THE VEDÂNTA.

THE

SYSTEM OF THE VEDĀNTA

According to Bādarāyaṇa's Brahma-Sūtras and Śaṅkara's Commentary thereon set forth as a Compendium of the Dogmatics of Brāhmanism from the standpoint of Śaṅkara

Dr Paul Deussen
Professor of Philosophy, Kiel University

AUTHORIZED TRANSLATION
By

Charles Johnston
Bengal Civil Service, Retired

MOTILAL BANARSIDASS
DELHI . VARANASI :: PATNA

Translator's Preface.

My dear Professor Deussen,

When, writing to me of your pilgrimage to India and your many friends in that old, sacred land, you suggested that I should translate *Das System des Vedânta* for them, and I most willingly consented, we had no thought that so long a time must pass, ere the completed book should see the light of day. Now that the period of waiting is ended, we rejoice together over the finished work.

I was then, as you remember, in the Austrian Alps, seeking, amid the warm scented breath of the pine woods and the many-coloured beauty of the flowers, to drive from my veins the lingering fever of the Ganges delta, and steeping myself in the lore of the Eastern wisdom: the great *Upanishads*, the *Bhagavad Gîtâ*, the poems of Çañkara, Master of Southern India.

Your book brought me a new task, a new opportunity. For in it I found, most lucidly set forth, the systematic teaching of the Vedânta, according to its greatest Master, with many rich treasures of the *Upanishads* added.

Shall we say that the great *Upanishads* are the deep, still mountain tarns, fed from the pure water of the everlasting snows, lit by clear sunshine, or, by night, mirroring the high serenity of the stars?

The *Bhagavad Gîtâ* is, perhaps, the lake among the foothills, wherein are gathered the same waters of wisdom, after flowing through the forest of Indian history, with the fierce conflict of the Children of Bharata.

Then, in the *Brahma Sûtras*, we have the reservoir, four-square, where the sacred waters are assembled in ordered quiet and graded depth, to be distributed by careful measure for the sustenance of the sons of men.

What shall we say, then, of the Master Çañkara? Is he not the Guardian of the sacred waters, who, by his Commentaries, has hemmed about, against all impurities or Time's jealousy, first the mountain tarns of the *Upanishads*, then the serene forest lake of the *Bhagavad Gîtâ*, and last the deep reservoir of the *Sûtras*; adding, from the generous riches of his wisdom, lovely fountains and lakelets of his own, the *Crest Jewel*, the *Awakening*, the *Discernment*?

And now, in this our day, when the ancient waters are somewhat clogged by time, and their old courses hidden and choked, you come as the Restorer, tracing the old, holy streams, clearing the reservoir, making the primal waters of life potable for our own people and our own day; making them easier of access also, and this is near to both our hearts, for the children's children of those who first heard Çañkâra, in the sacred land where he lived his luminous days.

So the task is done. May the Sages look on it with favor. May the sunlit waters once more flow in life-restoring streams, bringing to the world the benediction of spiritual light.

Believe me, as ever,

Cordially yours

CHARLES JOHNSTON.

Contents.

INTRODUCTION.

page

I. Literary Notes . . . . 3—46

1. The Name Vedânta, p. 3.—2. Some Remarks on the Veda, p. 5.—3. The Philosophical Systems, p. 19.—4. Form of the Brahma-sûtras; Çañkara's Commentary, p. 25.—5. The Quotations in Çañkara's Commentary, p. 29.—6. Some Remarks on Çañkara, p. 35.—7. Analysis of the Contents of the Brahmasûtras with Çañkara's Commentary according to *adhyâya*, *pâda* and *adhikaraṇam*, p. 39.

II. Aim of the Vedânta: The Destruction of an innate error . . . . 47—59

1. The fundamental Thought of the Vedânta and its previous History; a Glance at allied Theories in the West, p. 47.—2. Analysis of Çañkara's Introduction p. 53.

III. Who is called to the Study of the Vedânta? 60—76

1. The indispensable Condition, p. 60.—2. Exclusion of the Çûdras, p. 60.—3. Admission of the Gods; their Rôle in the Vedânta System, p. 65.—4. Episode: on the Vedântic Philosophy of Language, p. 72.

IV. Qualifications of those called to the Study of the Vedânta . . . . 77—87

1. The Study of the Veda, p. 77.—2. The four Requirements, p. 79.—3. Relation of the System to that of Justification by Works, p. 82.—4. Liberation through "the Grace" of Knowledge, p. 85.

V. Source of the Vedânta . . . . 88—96

1. General Remarks on the Indian Pramâṇas or Canons of Knowledge, p. 88.—2. Insufficiency of the secular Canons of Knowledge, p. 89.—3. The Revelation of the Veda, p. 94.

page

VI. Exoteric and Esoteric Vedânta Doctrine . . 97—115

1. Justification of Exoteric Metaphysics, p. 97.—2. Exoteric and Esoteric Form of the Vedânta, p. 98.—3. Appendix: Çañkara's Esoteric Philosophy, translated from 4, 3, 14, (a) Do the liberated go to Brahman? (b) Esoteric Cosmology. (c) Esoteric Psychology. (d) Esoteric Morality. (e) Esoteric Eschatology. (f) Esoteric Theology, p. 109.

FIRST PART:

THEOLOGY OR THE DOCTRINE OF BRAHMAN.

VII. Prefatory Remarks and Arrangement . . . 119—122

1. On the Names of God, p. 119.—2. Arrangement of the Theology, p. 120.

VIII. Proofs of the Existence of God . . . . . 123—128

1. Prefatory Remark, p. 123.—2. Definition of the Brahman, p. 123.—3. Cosmological Proof, p. 124.—4. Physico-theological Proof, p. 125.—5. Psychological Proof, p. 126.—6. *Cogito, ergo sum*, p. 127.

IX. The Brahman in itself . . . . 129—144

1. Brahman as the non-Existent, p. 129.—2. Brahman as the primordial Light, p. 130.—3. Brahman as the last, unknowable Origin of the Existent, p. 131.—4. Brahman as pure Intelligence, p. 134.—5. Brahman as Bliss, p. 137.—6. Brahman as Free from all Evil, p. 140.—7. Brahman as Free from Causality and Affliction, p. 141.

X. The Brahman as Cosmic Principle . . . . . 145—151

1. Brahman as Creator of the World, p. 145.—2. Brahman as Ruler of the World, p. 148.—3. Brahman as Destroyer of the World, p. 150.

XI. The Brahman as Cosmic and at the same time Psychic Principle . . . . 152—171

1. Brahman as the very Small and very Great, p. 152.—2. Brahman as Joy (*kam*) and as Amplitude (*kham*), p. 164.—3. Brahman as the Light beyond Heaven and in the Heart, p. 167.—4. Brahman and the Soul dwelling together in the Heart, p. 170.

page

XII. The Brahman as Soul . . . . 172—197

1. Brahman as the Self (*âtman*), p. 172.—2. Brahman as *Prâṇa* (Breath, Life), p. 177.—3. Brahman as the Soul in deep Sleep, p. 183.—4. Brahman as the Soul in the State of Liberation, p. 188.

XIII. The Brahman as the highest Goal . . . . 198—204

1. Brahman as Object of Meditation, p. 198.—2. Brahman as the Place of the Liberated, p. 200.—3. Brahman as Attainment of absolute Unity, p. 201.

XIV. Esoteric Theology . . . . 205—215

1. Preliminary Remark, p. 205.—2. The differentiated and undifferentiated Brahman, p. 206.—3. Characteristics of the esoteric Brahman, p. 210.—4. On the Possibility of Knowing the esoteric Brahman, p. 213. —5. On certain figurative Expressions used of Brahman, p. 214.

SECOND PART:

COSMOLOGY OR THE DOCTRINE OF THE WORLD.

XV. Preliminary Remarks and Arrangement . . 219—221

XVI. Brahman as Creator of the World . . . . 222—229

1. The Motive of Creation, p. 222.—2. Brahman is the efficient and at the same time material Cause of the World, p. 223.—3. Brahman creates without Instruments, p. 225.—4. Brahman and the Powers of Nature, p. 227.

XVII. The exoteric Picture of Creation . . . . 230—249

1. General, p. 230.—2. The Origin of Space (*Âkâça*), p. 232.—3. The Origin of Air, Fire, Water, Earth, p. 235.—4. Incidental Remark on the Destruction of the World, p. 237.—5. Organic Nature, p. 238.—6. Physiological Remarks, p. 240.—7. The Controversy with the Buddhists concerning the Reality of the outer World, p. 241.

XVIII. Cosmological Problems . . . . . . , . 250—254

1. The Problem of Causality, p. 250.—2. The Problem of the One and the Many, p. 252.—3. The Moral Problem, p. 252.

page

XIX. The Idea of Causality . . . . 255—260

1. The Cause persists in the Effect, p. 256.—2. The Effect exists before its Manifestation, namely, as Cause, p. 256.—3. What is the Difference between the Effect before and after Manifestation? p. 257.—4. The Effect is prefigured in the Cause, p. 257.—5. The Activity of becoming manifest must have a Subject, p. 258.—6. The Activity of the Agent is not superfluous, p. 258.—7. Generality of the Identity of Cause and Effect, p. 258.—8. The Activity of the Agent must have an Object, p. 259.—9. Result, p. 259.—10. Illustrative Examples, p. 259.

XX. The Doctrine of Identity . . . . 261—272

1. Introductory, p. 261.—2. "*Tat tvam asi*"—That art thou, p. 262.—3. The Doctrine of Identity in the Vedânta System: a) The Extinction of Plurality in Brâhman, p. 267.—b) The Relation of Unity to Plurality, p. 268.—c) How is the Knowledge of Unity possible, from the Standpoint of Plurality? p. 270.—d) The Value of the Doctrine of Unity, p. 271.—e) Criticism of Anthropomorphism, p. 271.

XXI. Solution of the Cosmological Problems . . 273—281

1. The Problem of Causality, p. 274.—2. The Problem of the One and the Many, p. 277.—3. The Moral Problem, p. 278.

THIRD PART:

PSYCHOLOGY OR THE DOCTRINE OF THE SOUL.

XXII. Proofs of the Immortality of the Soul . . 285—292

1. Preliminary Remarks on Psychology, p. 285.—2. Arguments of the Materialists against the Immortality of the Soul, p. 287.—3. Proofs of the Immortality of the Soul, p. 288.—4. On the Doctrine of Immortality in general, p. 290.

XXIII. Origin and Nature of the Soul . . . . 293—296

1. Origin of the Soul, p. 293.—2. Nature of the Soul, p. 295.

page

XXIV. Relation of the Soul to God . . . . . 297—305

1. Non-Identity and Identity, p. 297.—2. Illusion of all Pain, p. 299.—3. Subjection to and Freedom from Law, p. 300.—4. How are the individual souls separated from each other? p. 301.—5. Brahman and the Upâdhis, p. 302.

XXV. Relation of the Soul to the Body . . . . 306—314

1. The Opinion of the *Jainas* that the Soul is as large as the Body, p. 306.—2. The Opinion that the Soul is of minute (*aṇu*) size, p. 308.—3. The Soul is infinitely great (*vibhu*), p. 310.—4. Connection of the Soul with the Intellect (*buddhi*), p. 312.

XXVI. Relation of the Soul to its Actions . . . 315—323

1. Preliminary, p. 315.—2. Reasons for Supposing the Soul to be essentially an Agent (*i. e.* exercising Volition), p. 316.—3. The Soul is naturally not an Agent (exercising Volition), p. 317.—4. Freedom of the Will and Determinism, p. 321.

XXVII. The Organs of the Soul . . . . . . 324—341

1. Preliminary Survey, p. 324.—2. Origin and Nature of the Organs of Life (*prâṇa*), p. 327.—3. The System of the conscious Life: Organs of Relation, p. 329.—4. The System of the unconscious Life: Organs of Nutrition, p. 333.—5. Mutual Relation of the Systems of the conscious and unconscious Life, p. 336.—6. The Cooperation of the Gods, p. 337.—7. Retrospect, p. 338.

XXVIII. Special States of the Soul . . . . . 342—354

1. Dream-Sleep, p. 343.—2. Deep Sleep, p. 346.—3. Swooning, p. 352.—4. Metaphysical Significance of Death, p. 353.

FOURTH PART:

SAṂSÂRA OR THE DOCTRINE OF THE TRANSMIGRATION OF THE SOUL.

XXIX. The Eschatology of the Vedânta . . . . 357—360

1. The main Phases of Indian Eschatology, p. 357.—2. Exoteric and Esoteric Eschatology, p. 358.—3. No Transmigration from the Esoteric Standpoint, p. 359.

page

XXX. The Vedic Doctrine of the Five Fires . . 361—366

1. Introduction, p. 361.—2. The Five Sacrificial Offerings, p. 361.—3. The Path of the God (*devayâna*), p. 362.—4. The Path of the Fathers (*pitṛiyâna*), p. 363. —5. The third Place, p. 364.—6. Epilogue (only in Châṇdogya-Up.), p. 364.—7. On the two Recensions of the Doctrine of the Five Fires, p. 365.

XXXI. The Passing of the Soul from the Body . 367—380

1. The Vedic Basis, p. 367.—2. The Involution of the Organs, p. 367.—3. The subtle Body, p. 370.—4. Moral Determination of the transmigrating Soul: a) Prefatory Remark, p. 374.—b) The *Karma-âçraya*, p. 375.—c) *Vidyâ-karma-pûrvaprajñâ*, p. 376.—d) The *Apûrvam*, p. 377.—e) The *Çraddhâ*, p. 378.—5. The Path into the Beyond, p. 379.

XXXII. The Destinies of the Soul in the Body . 381—386

1. Contradictions of the Vedic Texts, p. 381.—2. The Punishments of Hell, p. 382.—3. The Third Place, p. 383.—4. Felicity on the Moon, p. 385.

XXXIII. The Cause of the Return to Earthly Existence . . . . 387—393

1. Prefatory Remark, p. 387.—2. In Retribution a Residue remains (*anuçaya*), p. 387.—3. How is this Residue to be conceived? p. 389.—4. Ritual and Moral Work, p. 390.

XXXIV. The Descent of the Soul for a new Embodiment . . . . 394—398

1. The Stages on the Way, p. 394.—2. Duration of the Descent, p. 394.—3. The Soul sojourns in the various Stages only as a Guest, p. 395.—4. Retrospect, p. 396.

FIFTH PART:

MOKSHA OR THE TEACHING OF LIBERATION.

XXXV. The Path of Liberation . . . . 401—417

1. Definition of Liberation, p. 401.—2. Liberation impossible through Works, p. 402.—3. Liberation impossible through moral Improvement, p. 403.—4. Knowledge without Works liberates, p. 405.—5. How is this

page

saving Knowledge brought about? p. 408.—6. Works as Means to Knowledge, p. 411.—7. Devout Meditation (*upâsanam*) as Means to Knowledge, p. 413.

XXXVI. Condition of the Sage in this Life . . 418—426

1. Characteristics of the Sage, p. 418.—2. The Destruction of Sin, p. 421.—3. Destruction of Good Works also, p. 423.—4. Why the Body, in spite of Liberation, still continues to exist, p. 424.

XXXVII. The dying Sage . . . . 427—431

1. His Soul does not depart, p. 427.—2. The Dissolution of the Psychic Apparatus, p. 428.—3. Can the Liberated assume a new Body? p. 430.

XXXVIII. Condition of the Sage after Death . . 432—435

1. Entrance into the highest Light, p. 432.—2. Characteristics of him who has obtained absoluteness, p. 433. —3. The *Unio mystica*, p. 434.

XXXIX. The Passing of the Pious to Brahman . 436—443

1. The Characteristics of the Pious, p. 436.—2. The Departure of the Soul of the Pious, p. 439.—3. The Stages on the Path of the Gods, p. 440.—4. Brahman as Goal of the Path, p. 442.

XL. Heavenly Lordship and Final Liberation of the Pious . . . . 444—448

1. Lordship (*aiçvaryam*), p. 444.—2. The Existence of those who have obtained Lordship, p. 445.—3. Limits of Lordship, p. 446.—4. Final Liberation of the Pious, p. 447.

Concordance 449

APPENDIX.

I. Short Survey of the Vedânta System . . . . 453—478

1. Introductory, p. 453.—2. Theology, p. 455.—3. Cosmology, p. 459.—4. Psychology, p. 467.—5. Transmigration, p. 471.—6. Liberation, p. 474.

II. Index of all Quotations in Çaṅkara's Commentary on the Brahmasûtras . . . . 479—500

III. Index of the proper names in Çaṅkara's Commentary . . . . 501—504

IV. Terms of the Vedânta . . . . 505—513

Upanishad Passages Quoted.

The numbers on the right are those of the present work.

Bṛih. 1, 1 = 8
„ 1, 3, 28 = 82
„ 1, 5, 3 = 331
„ 2, 4 = 172 ff.
„ 2, 4, 5 = 52
„ 3, 2, 13 = 375
„ 3, 4—5 = 141 ff.
„ 3, 7 = 149
„ 3, 8 = 132
„ 4, 3—4 = 188 ff.
„ 4, 4, 23 = 80
„ 4, 5 = 172 ff.
„ 6, 2 = 361 ff.
Chând. 1, 6 = 140
„ 1, 8, 9 = 145
„ 1, 11, 5 = 147
„ 3, 12—13 = 167
„ 3, 14 = 50. 152
„ 4, 1—2 = 61 ff.
„ 4, 4 = 63 ff.
„ 4, 5—9 = 64
„ 4, 10—15 = 64. 164 ff.
„ 5, 3—10 = 361 ff.
„ 5, 11—24 = 156
„ 6, 1, 4 = 52
„ 6, 1—7 = 262 ff. 230
„ 6, 8—16 = 263 ff.
„ 7 = 201 ff.
„ 8, 1—6 = 159 ff.
„ 8, 6, 6 = 379 ff.
Chând. 8, 7—12 = 51. 183 ff. 432
„ 8, 14 = 146
Kâṭh. 2, 23 = 409
„ 2, 24—25 = 150
„ 3, 1 = 170 ff.
„ 4, 10—11 = 52 ff.
„ 4, 12—13 = 155
„ 5, 1—3 = 50
„ 5, 7 = 373
„ 6, 1 = 148
„ 6, 17 = 155
Muṇḍ. 1, 1, 5 = 131
„ 2, 1, 1 = 131. 291
„ 2, 2, 5 = 200
„ 2, 2, 8 = 200 ff.
„ 2, 2, 10 = 130
„ 3, 1, 1 = 171
„ 3, 2, 8 = 201
Praçna 5 = 198
„ 6, 5 = 429
Taitt. 2, 1—7 = 51 ff. 129. 137
„ 2, 1 = 230
Ait. 1, 1 = 230
Kaush. 3 = 177 ff.
„ 4 = 181 ff.
Kena 11 = 408
Îçâ 1, 6 = 52
Çvet. 1, 11 = 87
„ 3, 8 = 313
„ 4, 3 = 298

INTRODUCTION.

I. Literary Notes.

1. The Name Vedânta.

Vedânta means literally "the end of the Veda" and signifies originally the theologico-philosophical treatises which appear as the closing chapters of the single Brâhmaṇa's of the Veda, and which are afterwards generally called *Upanishad*, that is, "(secret) séance," "secret doctrine."[1]—Further on, the

[1] Vedânta may originally mean either 1. "End of the Veda," or 2. "Dogmas of the Veda" (cf. *siddhânta, râddhânta*), or 3. "Final Aim of the Veda." Max Müller declares himself in favor of the latter view (Upanishads I, p. LXXXVI N.); but this presupposes an appreciation of the dogmatic at the expense of the ritual part, which it is difficult to accept for the time at which the word arose (we find it already rigidly fixed in TÂ. p. 817, 2 = Muṇḍ. 3, 2, 6 = Kaiv. 3 and Çvet. 6, 22). Hence the view given above (for which we must of course not rely on TÂ. p. 820, 1) recommends itself as the simplest and most natural. The remarkable circumstance that the etymological meaning of both *vedânta* and *upanishad* cannot be proved by quotations may be explained, if we assume that both were originally popular terms in the language of the pupils, and first received a definite sense when they were transferred to the language of the higher style. After the Brahmacârin had learnt the formulas of prayer (*mantra*) necessary for his future calling, and the manner of their application in the cult (*bandhu, brâhmaṇam*), at the conclusion of the course (Ind. Stud. X, 128 cf. Chând. 4, 10—15;— a chapter like Bṛih. 6, 4 was of course possible only at the end of a period of study) the Guru might communicate to him certain things easy to misinterpret, and therefore secret, concerning the metaphysical power of the prayer (*brahman*) which supported and maintained the gods, and the resulting superiority of the own Self of the knower (*âtman*) over all the powers of nature, whence in course of time arose the Brahmavidyâ, Âtmavidyâ, which the pupils might joyfully hail and greet as the *Vedânta*, that is, as "the end of the studies," and of the (not seldom severe [Mahâbhâratam I, 745]) period of pupilage. These communications to the Antevâsin took place in a confidential séance, that is (in contrast with

name Vedânta in the sense of "Final Aim of the Veda" is applied to the theologico-philosophical system founded on the Upanishad's, which may fitly be termed the Dogmatics of Brahmanism, and the exposition of which is to occupy us here. In order not to mix things historically distinct, we base this exposition exclusively on the standard work of the Vedânta School, the *Çârîraka-mîmâṅsâ-sûtra*'s of Bâdarâyaṇa together with Çañkara's Commentary thereon. As for the present a separate treatment of these two authors does not yet seem practicable, we consider the work as an indivisible whole for the purpose of our systematic exposition, and shall quote it in the sequel either with three numbers according to *adhyâya*, *pâda* and *sûtram* or with two numbers according to page and line in the edition of Roer and Râma Nârâyaṇa Vidyâratna in the Bibliotheca Indica, Calcutta, 1863.[2]

To characterise the position of this work and its two authors in Sanskrit Literature, it may be well to recall briefly certain facts.[3]

---

parishad, saṃsad), in an *upanishad*, an expression which then adopted the meanings of "secret meaning, secret name, secret teachings" just as the word "Collegium" adopted in German has been transferred from the idea of "assembly" to that of an "object of study" which can be "read" or "heard."

[2] Unfortunately no translation of this work exists as yet, (1883) since neither the aphorisms of the Vedânta by Ballantyne (Mirzapore, 1851) nor the translation by Banerjea (Calcutta, 1870), nor that in the *Shaḍdarçana-cintanikâ* (Bombay, since 1877) have up to the present got beyond the beginning. A Dutch rendering by A. Bruining in the "Bijdragen tot de Taal-, Land- en Volkenkunde van N.-Indie" only goes as far as the end of the first Adhyâya.

[The whole work has now been translated: into German by the author of the present work (Leipzig 1887), and into English by G. Thibaut (Oxford 1890—96)].

[3] Cf. with the following: Colebrooke, On the Vedas or sacred writings of the Hindus, As. Res., VIII, 369—476; On the philosophy of the Hindus, Transact. of the R. As. Soc., I, 19—43. 92—118. 439—461, II, 1—39, I, 549—579 (in the Misc. Ess.[3], II, 8ff., 239ff.); A. Weber, Indische Litteraturgeschichte[2], 1876, S. 8ff., 249ff., where the literature up to the most recent times (1878) is to be found brought together in the notes and supplements; Max Müller, A History of Ancient Sanskrit Literature[2], 1860.

2. Some Remarks on the Veda.

a) General view.

The great and not yet fully accessible complex of writings which bears the name of *Veda*, that is, "(theological) knowledge," and whose extent exceeds that of the Bible more than six times over, falls in the first place into four divisions, the *Ṛigveda, Sâmaveda, Yajurveda* and *Atharvaveda*; in each of these four Vedas we have to distinguish between three different classes of writings, according to content, form and age: 1) The *Saṃhitâ*, 2) The *Brâhmaṇam*, 3) The *Sûtram*; moreover the greater part of these twelve divisions exists in different, more or less divergent recensions, as used by the different schools for whose study they served, and these are commonly spoken of as the *Çâkhâ*'s, that is, "the branches," of the Veda-tree. For an understanding of this complicated organism it will be useful to distinguish between the form in which the Veda exists at present, and the historical development through which it has grown to this form.

b) The literary materials of the Veda.

In the first place the four Vedas, in the form in which they come to us, are nothing else than the Manuals of the Brahmanical Priests (*ṛitvij*), providing them with the materials of hymns and sentences necessary for the sacrificial cult, as well as teaching them their right use. To each complete sacrificial ceremony belong, in fact, four chief-priests distinguished according to their courses of studies, and their functions: 1) the Hotar, who recites the verses (*ṛic*) of the hymns, in order to invite the gods to the enjoyment of the Soma or other offerings, 2) the Udgâtar, who accompanies the preparation and presentation of the Soma with his chants (*sâman*), 3) the Adhvaryu, who performs the sacred rite, while he mutters the corresponding verses and sacrificial sentences (*yajus*), 4) the Brahmân, to whom is confided the superintending and guiding of the whole. The canonical book for the Hotar is the Ṛigveda (though the Ṛigveda-saṃhitâ has from the outset a wider import, not merely ritual but also literary), that for the Udgâtar is the Sâmaveda, that for the Adhvaryu the Yajurveda, while on the contrary the Atharvaveda has nothing to do with the Brahmân,[4] who must know all the three Vedas, and to whom the Atharvaveda is only referred for the sake of appearance, in order to help to raise it to the dignity of a fourth Veda, which was for a long time refused to it.[5] It finds its practical application on the one hand in the domestic cult (birth, marriage, burial, sicknesses, blessing the harvest, incantations over cattle and so forth), on the other hand in certain official acts (inauguration of the king, blessing before a battle, cursing of the enemy and so on); in the latter aspect it is the Veda of the Kshatriya caste, as the three others are of the Brahman caste,[6] and might stand in the same relation to the *Purohita* (prince's family priest) as that which the others hold to the *Ṛitvij*'s (cf. Yâjñavalkya 1, 312).

Each of the priests named required in his duties, first, a collection of prayer-formulas (*mantra*) and, second, directions for the right liturgical and ritual application of these (*brâhmaṇam*). With the exception of the black Yajurveda, we find these two more or less completely separated and relegated to two different divisions.

I. The SAṂHITÂ of each Veda, as the name indicates, is a "collection" of the Mantra's belonging to it, which are either verses (*ṛic*) or chants (*sâman*) or sacrificial sentences (*yajus*).

---

[4] Âpastamba-çrauta-sûtram 24, 16—19: *ṛigvedena hotâ karoti. sâmavedena udgâtâ, yajurvedena adhvaryuḥ, sarvair brahmâ.*—Madhusûdana (Ind. Stud. I, 16, 8): *tatra hautra-prayoga' ṛigvedena, âdhvaryava-prayogo yajurvedena, audgâtra-prayogaḥ sâmavedena, brâhma-yâjamâna-prayogau tu atra eva antarbhûtau; atharvavedas tu, yajña-anupayuktaḥ. çânti-paushṭika-abhicâra-âdi-karma-pratipâdakatvena atyanta-vilakshaṇa' eva.*

[5] Gopatha-brâhmaṇam I, 2, 24: *ṛigvidam eva hotâraṃ vṛiṇîshva, yajurvidam adhvaryuṃ, sâmavidam udgâtâram, atharvâñgirovidam brahmâṇam.*—Atharva-pariçishṭam 1 (Ind. Stud. I, 296, 28): *rakshâṅsi rakshati brahmâ, brahmâ tasmâd atharvavit.*—Cf. Vishṇupurâṇam III, 4 (p. 276, Wilson).—An indirect acknowledgement of the fourth Veda by Çañkara is found on p. 239, 2.

[6] It is perhaps to be understood in this sense, when Bṛih. 5, 13 (Çatap. Br. 14, 8, 14) *kshatram* appears as fourth along with *uktham*, *yajus* and *sâman*.

Thus the Ṛigveda-saṃhitâ consists of 1017 hymns in 10580 verses; from which the Hotar has to select the required invocation for the purpose in view; the Sâmaveda-saṃhitâ contains a selection of 1549 verses (or with repetitions 1810), either from the Ṛigveda-saṃhitâ, or from the materials on which it is based; all these excepting only 75, are also found in the Ṛigveda. They are modulated in numerous ways, for the purposes of the chant (*sâman*); the Samhitâ of the white Yajurveda contains both prose sacrificial sentences (*yajus*) and verses, the latter of which are in great measure taken from the materials of the Ṛigveda; on the other hand, the Atharvaveda-saṃhitâ consists merely of 760 Hymns, only about one sixth of which are common to it and the Ṛigveda, while the remainder occupy an independent and in many respects quite peculiar position in the total of the Vedic Mantra literature, of which later. Each of these four Saṃhitâs, according to the *Çâkhâ*'s or Schools, in which it is studied, is extant in different recensions, which, however, do not, as a rule, differ materially from one another. It is otherwise, as will presently be shown, with the second division of Vedic literature.

II. The BRÂHMAṆAM, whose most direct purpose generally is, to teach the practical use of the materials presented in the Saṃhitâ, in its widest scope often goes far beyond this immediate purpose, and draws within its sphere what (with Madhusûdana) we may include in the three categories of *vidhi*, *arthavâda* and *vedânta*. 1) As *vidhi* (*i. e.*, precept) the Brâhmaṇam enjoins the ceremonies, explains the occasions of their use, as well as the means for carrying them out, and finally describes the process of the sacred rite itself. 2) With this, under the name of *arthavâda* (*i. e.*, explanation) are linked the most various discussions, whose purpose is, to support the content of the precept by exegesis, polemic, mythology, dogma and so forth. 3) The consideration of the subject here and there rises to thoughts of a philosophical character, which, as they are found for the most part towards the end of the Brâhmaṇa's, are called *vedânta* (*i. e.*, Veda-end). They are the chief content of the appendixes to the Brâhmaṇa's which are called *Âraṇyaka's*, and whose original purpose (though not strictly maintained) was to serve for the life in the forest (*araṇyam*), which was enjoined upon the Brahmans in old age, to serve as a substitute for the ritual which, if not completely left behind, was yet very much limited. However this may be, it is the fact that in them we meet abundantly a wonderful spiritualising of the sacrificial cult: in place of the practical carrying out of the ceremonies, comes meditation upon them, and with it a symbolical change of meaning, which then leads on farther to the loftiest thoughts.[7]

[7] Let the opening passage of the Bṛihad-âraṇyakam (which is intended for the Adhvaryu), in which the Horse Sacrifice is treated, serve as an example:

"Om!—Dawn verily is the head of the sacrificial horse, the sun "is his eye, the wind his breath, his mouth is the all-pervading fire, the "year is the body of the sacrificial horse; heaven is his back, space is his "belly, the earth is his foot-stool (Çaṅk.). The poles are his loins, the "intermediate quarters are his ribs, the seasons are his limbs, months and "half-months are his joints, day and night are his feet, the stars are his "bones, the clouds are his flesh. The deserts are the food which he con"sumes, rivers are his entrails, the mountains his liver and lungs, plants "and trees his hair; the rising sun is his forequarters, the setting sun is "his hindquarters; when he yawns, that is the lightning, when he neighs, "that is the thunder, when he waters, that is rain; his voice is speech. " Day verily arose after the horse as the sacrificial vessel, which stands "before him: its cradle is in the eastern ocean; night verily arose as the "sacrificial vessel, which stands behind him: its cradle is in the western "ocean; these two sacrificial vessels arose to surround the horse. As a "racer he carried the gods, as a war-horse the gandharvas, as a steed the "demons, as a horse mankind. The ocean is his companion, the ocean his "cradle."

Here the universe takes the place of the horse to be offered, perhaps with the thought in the background, that the ascetic is to renounce the world (cf. Bṛih. 3, 5, 1. 4, 4, 22), as the father of the family renounces the real sacrificial gift. In just the same way, the Chândogya-Upanishad (1, 1) which is intended for the Udgâtar, teaches as the true *udgîtha*: to be recognised and honoured the syllable "om," which is a symbol of Brahman (*paramâtma-pratîkam*); and the *uktham* (hymn) which belongs to the Hotar is subjected to a like transformation of meaning in Aitareya-âraṇyakam (2, 1, 2).—Compare Brahmasûtra 3, 3, 55—56, where the thought is developed that symbolical representations (*pratyaya*) of this kind have validity not only within the Çâkhâ, in which they are found, but also in general.

The most important parts of these Âraṇyaka's were later detached from them under the name Upanishad, and were brought together from the different Veda's into a single whole; but originally, as we must admit, each Vedic school had its special ritual textbook, and together with this a more or less rich dogmatic textbook, and if there were in reality, as the Muktikâ-Upanishad (Ind. St. III, 324) affirms, 21 + 1000 + 109 + 50 = 1180 Çâkhâ's, it follows that there must have been 1180 Upanishad's. In reality, however, the matter is much simpler, since the number of the Çâkhâ's, which we really know, is limited for each Veda to a very small number, whose textbooks present the common ritual and dogmatic material in differing order, treatment and elaboration. Thus we are acquainted with only two Çâkhâ's of the Ṛigveda, that of the *Aitareyin*'s and that of the *Kaushîtakin*'s, each of which possesses one *Brâhmaṇam* and one *Âraṇyakam*, the latter containing the Upanishad of the school.—For the Sâmaveda we know up to the present for the Brâhmaṇa section only one Çâkhâ accurately and completely, that of the *Tâṇḍin*'s, to which belong the following writings: a) the *Pañcaviṅça-brâhmaṇam*; b) the *Shaḍviṅça-brâhmaṇam*, whose name already characterizes it as an addition to the former; c) we must also attribute to the school of the Tâṇḍin's the hitherto incompletely known *Châṇdogya-brâhmaṇam*, since Çaṅkara under this name quotes a passage, p. 892, 9, which according to Râjendralâla Mitra (The Châṇdogya-Up., Introduction, p. 17 N.) forms the beginning of the Châṇdogya-brâhmaṇam; d) finally Çaṅkara repeatedly quotes the *Châṇdogya-upanishad* as belonging to the Tâṇḍin's; thus Châṇd. 3, 16 (quoted p. 889, 10. 890, 8) 8, 13, 1 (p. 899, 3. 907, 7. 908, 5) 6, 8, 7 (p. 923, 8).—A second independent book of ritual for the Sâmaveda is possibly the *Talavakâra-brâhmaṇam* of the Jaiminîya-çâkhâ (cf. Çaṅkara's statement on Kena-Up., p. 28, and those of Burnell in Müller's Upanishad's I, p. XC), according to Burnell in five Adhyâya's, the last but one of which contains the well-known short *Kena-Upanishad* (quoted p. 70, 1. 4. 10. 163, 3. 808, 10), while the last consists of the *Ârsheya-brâhmaṇam* (quoted p. 301, 8). The four remaining Brâhmaṇa's of the

Sâmaveda (*Sâmavidhâna, Vaṅça, Devatâdhyâya, Saṃhitopanishad*) can make no claim to the name of independent textbooks of the school.—For the Yajurveda we have to distinguish two forms, the black (that is, unarranged) and the white (arranged) Yajurveda. The former contains Brâhmaṇa-like materials mingled with the Mantra's in the Saṃhitâ; in this form the schools of the *Taittirîyaka*'s (whose Brâhmaṇam and Âraṇyakam are merely continuations of the Saṃhitâ), the *Kaṭha*'s and the *Maitrâyaṇîya*'s have handed the Yajurveda down to us. The Taittirîya-âraṇyakam contains at its close two Upanishad's, the *Taittirîya-Upanishad* (Book VII. VIII. IX) and the *Nârâyaṇîya-Upanishad* (Book X). To the school of the Kaṭha's belongs the *Kâṭhaka-Upanishad,* which we now possess only in an Atharvan recension, whereas in Çaṅkara's time it seems to have formed a whole with the other texts of the Kaṭha's, of which more will be said later; under the name *Maitri-Upanishad* we have received a late product of very apocryphal character;[8] the name of a fourth Çâkhâ of the black Yajurveda, the *Çvetâçvatara*'s, is that of a metrical Upanishad of secondary origin, which, however, is largely quoted by Çaṅkara as "*Çvetâçvatarâṇâṃ mantropanishad*" (p. 110, 5, cf. 416, 1. 920, 4) and seemingly also already by Bâdarâyaṇa (1, 1, 11. 1, 4, 8. 2, 3, 2).

In contrast to the Çâkhâ's of the black Yajurveda, the *Vâjasaneyin*'s, the chief school of the white Yajurveda, separated the Mantra's and Brâhmaṇa's after the manner of the remaining Veda's; the former are collected in the Vâjasaneyi-saṃhitâ, the latter form the content of the *Çatapatha-brâhmaṇam*, the concluding part (B. XIV) of which contains the greatest and most beautiful of all the Upanishad's, the *Bṛihad-âraṇyakam.* A piece closely related to it (probably only on account of its metrical form) has been added to the Vâjasaneyi-saṃhitâ as Book XL, and is called, from its first word, the *Îçâ-upanishad*; in the version of Anquetil Duperron four ad-

[8] Çaṅkara nowhere quotes it (*Maitreyî-brâhmaṇam* p. 385, 8. 1006, 5 means the section Bṛih. 2, 4 = 4, 5); moreover the term *Sushumnâ* (Maitr. 6, 21) is not yet to be found in the Commentary to the Brahmasûtra's.

ditional sections of the same Saṃhitâ, *Çatarudriyam* (B. XVI), *Purushasûktam* (XXXI), *Tadeva* (XXXII), and *Çivasaṃkalpa* (XXXIV, the beginning) are classed as Upanishad's.—Besides the Vâjasaneyin's Çañkara thirteen times quotes an other school of the White Yajurveda, the *Jâbâla*'s; nine of these quotations (p. 222, 8. 223, 1. 417, 11. 988, 8 = 991, 4. 999, 6. 1000, 1, 3. 1025, 8) are found, with important variants, in the *Jâbâla-Upanishad*, which is to-day included among the Atharva-Upanishad's, four others (924, 7 = 1059, 1. 931, 4 = 933, 4) are not, so that, as it seems, Çañkara had a more complete work of this school before him. Whether Bâdarâyaṇa quotes the same work (1, 2, 32. 4, 1, 3) remains uncertain.[9]—To the Atharvaveda belongs the *Gopatha-brâhmaṇam*, a work which has preponderatingly the character of a compilation and is without close relation to the Atharva-Saṃhitâ. We find no quotations from it in Çañkara; the circumstance that at 3, 3, 24, p. 889 ff., he does not also consider Gopatha-br. II, 5, 4, increases the probability that he did not know or did not recognize this work. Finally, to the Atharvaveda, which could most probably not be guarded against new invasions by supervision of the guild as were the other Veda's, has been attached a long series of Upanishad's for the most part short, many of which have a wholly apocryphal character and are nothing more than the textbooks of later Indian sects. Two Upanishad's of the Atharvan are of special significance for the Vedânta, the *Muṇḍaka-* and the *Praçna-Upanishad,* both of which are frequently quoted by Bâdarâyaṇa and Çañkara, while we strangely find no certain quotation from the *Mâṇḍûkya-Upanishad* which is so abundantly used in the Vedântasâra.

III. A third and last stage of the Vedic literature is formed by the SÛTRA's, likewise divided according to Veda's and Çâkhâ's (whose relations however seem to be somewhat un-

---

[9] Çañkara understands 1, 2, 32 as the Jâbâlopanishad 2, p. 439 and 4, 1, 3 as a text of this school unknown to us; on the other hand according to the *Vedânta-çaiva-bhâshyam* (Pandit, June 1872, p. 19) 1, 2, 32 and according to the *Vedânta-kaustubha-prabhâ* (Pandit, August 1874, p. 55) 4, 1, 3 are not to be referred to the Jâbâla's.

fixed); they bring together the contents of the Brâhmaṇa's, on which they are based, condensing, systematizing and completing them, for the purpose of practical life, in very compendious form, and in the lapidary style which is often quite incomprehensible without a commentary, a style to which also the grammatical, and, as we shall shortly see, the philosophical literature of India has adapted itself. There are three classes of Vedic Sûtra's: 1) the *Çrauta-sûtra*'s, which regulate public worship, 2) the *Gṛihya-sûtra*'s, which regulate domestic ceremonies (at birth, marriage, and the funeral), and 3) the *Dharma-sûtra*'s, in which the duties of the Castes and Âçrama's are set forth in detail, and from which the later lawbooks of Manu and so on are derived. As the Çrauta-sûtra's are based on the *Çruti* (that is, Divine Revelation), the two other classes in like manner rest on the *Smṛiti* (that is, Tradition) and *Âcâra* (that is, Custom); more will be said further on of the meaning of these expressions in the terminology of the Vedânta.

c) Of the Genesis of the Veda.

The most ancient monument in this extensive circle of literature (and perhaps also the most ancient literary monument of the human race) is formed by the Hymns of the Ṛigveda, since, as regards the great bulk of them, they go back to a time when their possessors were not yet in the valley of the Ganges, but lived among the tributaries of the Indus, had as yet no Castes, no privileged worship, no Brahmanical system of government and life, but belonged to small tribes (*viç*) under kings most of whom were hereditary, tilling their fields, pasturing their herds, fighting among themselves, and enjoying a primitive life. The Hymns of the Ṛigveda unfold a graphic picture [10] of all these relations, but especially we can follow in them the genesis of the primitive nature

---

[10] Cf. on this point the mutually supplementary works: Zimmer, Altindisches Leben, Berlin 1879; Ludwig, Die Mantra-Litteratur und das alte Indien (in the third volume of Ludwig's Ṛigveda), Prague 1878; Kaegi, Der Ṛigveda, Leipzig 1881; Oldenberg, Die Religion des Veda, Berlin 1894; Hillebrandt, Vedische Mythologie, Breslau 1891—1902.

religion of India through its different phases, in part even from the moment when the gods are crystallizing under the hand of the poet out of the phenomena of nature, to the point at which belief in them for the thinking part of the nation begins to grow dim,[11] and is being replaced by the first stirrings of philosophical speculation, the latter especially in the later hymns chiefly found in the last Maṇḍala, many of which, as for example the Hymn of Purusha, Ṛigv. 10, 90 (VS. 31. AV. 19, 6. TÂ. 3, 12), already show an immigration into the Ganges valley with the consequent development of the Caste system.

For after the Indians through many battles and struggles, whose poetical reflections are contained for us in the Mahâbhâratam, had won a permanent dwelling place for themselves in the paradise-like plain between the Himâlaya and the Vindhya, their manner of life took on a form essentially different from the earlier one, owing to its altered external relations: an insurmountable barrier was in the first place erected between the *Çûdra*'s, the repressed population of the aborigines, and the immigrant Aryans; then further, above the *Vâiçya*'s, that is, the collective mass of Aryan tribes, were raised on the one side, as possessors of material might, the *Kshatriya*'s, the warrior-nobility with the kings at their head, and on the other side the real or pretended descendants of the old Vedic poet-families, who called themselves *Brâhmaṇa*'s (offerers of prayer, priests), and succeeded in making their family privilege not only the Vedic hymns and the worship bound up with them, but by and by also the whole national education. It is true that, as before, all members of the three upper castes, so far as they

---

[11] There are hymns in the Ṛigveda which treat religion with open scorn. Thus among others (e. g. Ṛigv. 7, 103) the hymn Ṛigv. 9, 112, which not without humour develops the thought that even the god Indra, like mankind, selfishly follows his own profit; and which very effectively uses a constantly recurring refrain, borrowed apparently from a religious hymn, "*indrâya indo parisrava.*" It is true that Grassman has omitted this refrain, in which the whole point lies.—The "Liturgy of the Dogs" (*çauva udgîtha*) Chând. 1, 12 seems to own its origin to similar motives.

were *Dvija*'s ("twice-born," reborn through the sacrament of the *Upanayanam*, the admission into the Brahmanical church) had to offer, and in part also to perform, sacrifices, but only the Brahmans could eat the sacrificial food, drink the Soma, and receive the sacrificial gift without which the sacrifice was not efficacious; they only could be *Ṛitvij*'s (sacrificial priests for another for hire) and *Purohita*'s (permanent family priests of the princes). Of these caste privileges the Brahmans were able in time to make a more and more extended use. In proportion as, through the consolidation of their settlements, the prosperity of the princes and the people grew, the external pageantry of worship increased; the number of the participating priests augmented, the names Brahman, Hotar, Adhvaryu, Udgâtar, which we see emerging in the Ṛigveda at first sporadically and without strict distinction, were bound up into a system, and by the side of each of these Ṛitvij's at a great sacrifice stood a series of accolytes.

Now the more complex the system of worship became, the more imperatively it demanded a special training, and this practical need was the decisive factor in the arrangement of the Vedic literature,—if indeed this word can be employed for a condition of things in which no written record is to be thought of.[12] Little by little, a firm tradition grew up about the verses and sentences with which the Adhvaryu had to accompany his manipulations (*Yajurveda*), as about the songs which the Udgâtar chanted at the sacred operations (*Sâmaveda*), and lastly it was no longer enough for the Hotar to know the songs hereditary in his own family; the separate

---

[12] Even the Upanishads seem originally to have been handed down only orally. On the one hand we find passages in them which only become intelligible by an accompanying gesture (*e.g.*, Bṛih. 1, 4, 6: *atha iti abhyamanthat*; 2, 2, 4: *imau eva* [the ears] *Gautama-Bharadvâjau, ayam eva Gautamo, 'yaṃ Bharadvâjaḥ*, and so on); on the other hand, *e.g.*, Chând. 8, 3, 5 *satyam* is treated as a trisyllable, Bṛih. 5, 14, 1, *bhûmir antarikshaṃ dyauḥ* and 5, 14, 3 *prâṇo 'pâno vyânaḥ* are treated as eight syllables.—For the rest, the question of a written record in India has not the importance which we, judging by our own position, are inclined to give it.

collections of hymns were gathered into circles (*maṇḍalam*), the circles into a single whole (*Ṛigveda*), which then for a certain further period still remained open for additional new productions.—Not all the old hymns were admitted into this canon; many had to be excluded, because their contents were thought to be offensive or otherwise unsuited; others because, sprung from the people, they were not supported by the authority of some famous bardic family. To these were continually added new blossoms which the old stem of Vedic lyrics bore in the Brâhmaṇa Period, and which bear clear testimony to the altered consciousness of the time. From these materials, which had to be handed down for a long time outside the schools in the mouths of the people (to which fact their frequent and especially metrical negligence bears testimony), there came into being in course of time a fourth collection (*Atharvaveda*), which had to struggle long before gaining a recognition which always remained conditional.

Meanwhile the other older collections had become the basis of a certain course of study, which in course of time took a more and more regular form. Originally it was the father who initiated his son into the sacred lore handed down by the family, as best he could (Bṛih. 6, 2, 4. Chând. 5, 3, 5), soon, through the growing difficulty of understanding the old texts, the more and more complicated form of the ritual, the perpetually extending circle of studies, this became too difficult for him; it became necessary to look for the most approved authorities for each of the theories (*vidyâ*) that had to be learned, travelling scholars (*caraka*) went further afield (Bṛih. 3, 3, 1), çelebrated wandering teachers moved from place to place (Kaush. 4, 1), and to many teachers pupils streamed, "like the waters to the deep" (Taitt. 1, 4, 3). Later custom demanded that every Ârya should spend a series of years (according to Âpast. dharma-sûtra 1, 1, 2, 16 at least twelve) in the house of a teacher, the Brâhmaṇa's, to prepare themselves for their future calling, the Kshatriya's and Vaiçya's, to receive the influences which were to mould their later thought and life. We must assume (even if we have no quotation at hand to prove it) that the imparting of this instruction became in course of time the exclusive privilege of the Brahmans: only thus can be explained the unparalleled influence over the life of the Indian peoples which the Brahmans succeeded in winning and maintaining. As the outward apparel of the scholars of the different castes differed, so also probably did their instruction. As payment for it, the scholars performed the household and field labour of the teacher; they tended the sacred fire (Chând. 4, 10, 1), herded the teacher's cattle (Chând. 4, 4, 5), collected the customary gifts for him in the village and brought him presents at the conclusion of the course. In the time left free by these manifold obligations (*guroḥ karma-atiçesheṇa*, Chând. 8, 15) the Veda was studied. On the whole, it was less a time of study than a time of discipline, as the name *Âçrama* implies, intended for the practice of obedience to the teacher (of which extravagant examples are handed down) and strenuous self-abnegating activity. It was the tendency of Brahmanism to mould the whole life to such an *Âçrama*. Not all, after the termination of the time of study, set themselves to found a family: many remained in the teacher's house to the end of their lives (*naishṭhika*); others betook themselves to the forest to devote themselves to privations and penance; others again disdained even this form of regular existence, and cast away every thing (*saṃnyâsin*), to roam about (*parivrâjaka*) as beggars (*bhikshu*). The different kinds of "*Âçrama*," or "religious exercise," were further bound together in a whole, in which what appears as an abrupt command in St. Matthew's Gospel XIX, 21, seems to have been expanded into a vast system embracing the whole of life. Accordingly the life of every Brâhmaṇa, and even the life of every Dvija,[13] was to be divided into four stages, or *Âçrama*'s; he was (1), as *Brahmacârin*, to dwell in the house of a teacher, then (2), as *Gṛihastha*, to fulfil the duty of founding a family, then (3) to leave it in old age, as a *Vânaprastha* (forest hermit), to give himself up more and more to increasing

[13] A limitation to the Brâhmaṇa caste does not seem to follow with certainty from Manu VI, cf. v. 38. 70. 97 *brâhmaṇa*, v. 29. 32. 93 *vipra*; on the other hand v. 2 *gṛihasthas tu*, and so on; v. 40. 85. 91. 94 *dvija*.

penances, and lastly (4), towards the end of his life, as a *Saṃnyâsin* (*Bhikshu, Parivrâjaka*) to wander free from all earthly ties and live on alms.—We do not know how far the reality corresponded to these ideal claims.

While Brahmanical teaching and conduct of life were surrounding the existence of the Indian peoples in ever denser toils, we see ripening on the branch of Brahmanism itself a world concept which, though outwardly bound up with it, was inwardly opposed to it in its very basis.—Already in the Ṛigveda strong movements of a certain philosophical tendency make themselves manifest. We perceive a special seeking and asking after the Unity which finally lies at the basis of all diversity; we see many attempts being made to solve the riddle of creation; to grasp through the motley changes of the world of appearances, through the more and more richly developed variety of the Vedic pantheon, the one formless principle of all that has form,—until at last the soul finds and lays hold of unity where alone unity is to be found —in the soul itself. Here, in the mysterious depths of his own heart, the seeker, raised above his own individuality by the fervour of aspiration (*bráhman*) discovered a power which he felt to transcend all the other powers of creation, a godlike might which, as he felt, dwells within all earthly and celestial beings as inner ruling principle (*antaryâmin*) on which all worlds and all gods rest, through fear of which fire burns, the sun shines, the storm, wind and death perform their work (*Kâṭh.* 6, 3), and without which not a straw can be burned by Agni, or carried away by Vâyu (Kena 3, 19. 23). A poetic formative power had clothed Agni, Indra and Vâyu with personality; this power it was by which that power of fervour, "that which in the narrow sphere expanding to all sides grows "mightily, as a delight of the great gods, that which extends "as a god to the gods from afar and embraces this universe" (Ṛigv. II, 24, 11) was raised above all gods first in a very transparent personification as *Bṛihaspati, Brahmaṇaspati,* but afterwards more truly, boldly, philosophically as *Bráhman* (prayer), as *Âtman* (Self), and from this power the gods and the whole world besides were derived in endlessly varied play of phantasy.—We may hope that thanks to the wealth of texts preserved in the Ṛigveda, Atharvaveda, and Brâhmaṇa's, we may be able to trace step by step how the sparks of philosophic light appearing in the Ṛigveda shine out brighter and brighter until, at last, in the Upanishad's, they burst out in that bright flame which is able to light and warm us to-day.

Numerous indications intimate that the real guardians of these thoughts were originally not the priestly caste, absorbed in their ceremonial, but rather the caste of the Kshatriya's. Again and again, in the Upanishad's, we meet the situation that the Brahman begs the Kshatriya for instruction which the latter, after several representations of the unseemliness of such a proceeding, imparts to him (cf. Bṛih. 2, 1. Kaush. 4, 1. Bṛih. 6, 2. Chând. 5, 3. Chând. 5, 11. Kaush. 1, 1).—However this may be, the Brahmans appropriated this new teaching of Brâhman and its identity with the Self, and attached it, as best they could, to their own system of justification by works, in a way of which we shall say more in the sequel. Both systems, the ritual and the philosophic, were propagated in the Vedic schools, became inside and outside the school (at public festivals, at the courts of kings and so forth) the subject of keen debate and a not seldom vehement polemic; both suffered manifold transformations and exchanges in these contests and mutual accommodations; at last, as the precipitate of this rich spiritual life, the *Brâhmaṇa*'s and the *Upanishad*'s, in which they issue, were formed and brought into their present shape and finally (probably after their practical meaning had already long been transferred to the Sûtra's) recorded in writing. It is to be hoped that in time it will be possible to reconstruct from them, even if not in every detail, the course of development which found its conclusion in them.

We have already seen how to the older Upanishad's, which are the philosophic text-books of the different Çâkhâ's, were added a long series of younger products of the same name; in these we can follow the further extension of religious concepts, and, hand in hand with it, the development of a special tendency to accomplish even in this life the union with the All-spirit, through a certain practical process (called *Yoga*), down to the time of the Indian sects. These texts, as it seems, have a purely external connection with the Atharvaveda.

3. The Philosophical Systems.

Parallel with this development of the Vedic theories there early arose side by side in India, from the germs contained in the Brâhmaṇa's and older Upanishad's, a whole series of philosophic systems, which stand in very varied, sometimes convergent, sometimes hostile, relations to the Vedas and to each other, and in which we can trace every shade of philosophical concept of the world, from the crass and cynical materialism of the Cârvâka's up to the orthodox faith in the letter of the Vedas. Six among them were able to obtain the reputation of orthodoxy, that is, of a harmony between their teachings and the Vedic faith, or at least an appearance of it; the others, and among them Buddhism, were held to be heterodox and heretical. The six orthodox systems (a name to which, in its full sense, only the two Mîmâṅsâ's can lay claim) are as follows:—

1) The Sâñkhyam of Kapila, which served, as some believe, as the basis of Buddhism, a highly spiritual theory of the unfolding of the world to the end of self-knowledge and thence resulting liberation, which, however, falls into an irreconcileable dualism between the unfolding primitive matter (*prakṛiti, pradhânam*) and an original plurality of individual spirits (*purusha*).

2) The Yoga of Patañjali, which, interpreting the Sâñkhya-system theistically, undertakes to point out the way of attaining a union with God, treating it in four parts, 1. of contemplation (*samâdhi*), 2. of the means of attaining it (*sâdhanam*), 3. of the mastery over nature thereby gained (*vibhûti*), 4. of the condition of absoluteness (*kaivalyam*).[14]

---

[14] The relation of this teaching to the Yoga-Upanishad's has yet to be investigated; in the Saṃkshepa-Çañkara-jaya 1, 21—27 (Gildemeister, Anthologia³, p. 88) are distinguished three parts of the Veda, the *karma kâṇḍa*, *jñâna-kâṇḍa*, and *yoga-kâṇḍa*, to which the three systems of *Jaimini*, *Bâdarâyaṇa* and *Patañjali* refer; the latter appears as an incarnation of *Çesha* (this throws light on Cowell's remark on Colebrooke M. E.³, p. 247, n. 2).

3) The Nyâya of Gotama, a system of logic, which, however, draws within its sphere all the subjects of Indian thought and treats of them under its sixteen categories (*pramâṇam* proof, *prameyam* what is to be proved, *saṃçaya* doubt, and so on).

4) The Vaiçeshikam of Kaṇâda, frequently (*e.g.*, in the Bhâshâpariccheda, in the Tarkabhâshâ) woven together with the Nyâya into a single whole, which teaches the growth of the world from atoms (*paramâṇu*) and undertakes a classification of existence, according to natural science, under the six categories of substance, quality, action, identity, difference and inherence (*dravyam, guṇa, karman, sâmânyam, viçesha samavâya*).

The gradual growth and consolidation of this and other systems may have instigated the stricter adherents of the Veda also, on their side, to a scientific, systematic investigation (*mîmâṅsâ*) into the contents of the Veda, whence arose

5) The *Karma-mîmâṅsâ, Pûrva-mîmâṅsâ*, or, as it is usually simply called, the Mîmâṅsâ of Jaimini, as a system of worship through works, which investigates the duties (*dharma*) enjoined by the Veda, together with the rewards (*phalam*) attached thereto, and

6) The *Çârîraka-mîmâṅsâ, Uttara-mîmâṅsâ*, or, as it is mostly called from its source, Vedânta of Bâdarâyaṇa which unites the contents of the Upanishad's in a theologico-philosophical system.

The two Mîmâṅsâ's may have arisen together, since Jaimini and Bâdarâyaṇa quote each other, often agreeing, often opposing; the two systems complete each other in that together they exhibit the totality of Vedic theology (since in particular the Vedânta holds fast throughout to the system of rewards of the Karma-mîmâṅsâ cf. 2, 3, 42. 3, 1, 25. 3, 2, 9 and p. 1076, 13), and their principles are in a thorough-going antithesis, which has its foundation in the Veda itself. For the Veda falls (as Çaṅkara on Bṛih. p. 4 ff. shows), according to the concept of the Vedânta, into two parts, which show a far-reaching analogy with the Old and New Testaments, a Part of Works (*karma-kâṇḍa*), which includes the Mantra's and

Brâhmaṇa's in general, and a **Part of Knowledge** (*jñâna-kâṇḍa*), which includes the Upanishad's and what belongs to them (*e.g.*, the Agnirahasyam, Çatap. Br. X, for which compare 3, 3, 44—52, p. 943–952). The former enjoins works, such as sacrifices and other ceremonies, promising like the Old Testament, rewards and threatening punishments, with this difference however that, for the most part, by relegating these to the other world, it evades the conflict with experience; the investigation of these circumstances, of the religious works and the merit obtained by them, which enters as a "new moment" (*apûrvam*) into the complex of deeds necessitating a requital in the other world, forms the essential content of Jaimini's Karma-mîmâṅsâ, which precedes the Vedânta not so much in time as in order, and is largely quoted by Çaṅkara in his Commentary on the Vedânta-sûtras as "the first part," "the first book" (*e.g.*, p. 848, 6. 897, 1. 919, 9. 944, 4. 951, 3. 1011, 12). However, as we shall see (Chap. IV, 3), a knowledge of it is not necessary for the study of the Vedânta, which bases itself entirely on the "part of knowledge" of the Veda's, that is, on the Upanishad's. The work of Bâdarâyaṇa stands to the Upanishad's in the same relation as the Christian Dogmatics to the New Testament: it investigates their teaching about God, the world, the soul, in its conditions of wandering and of deliverance, removes apparent contradictions of the doctrines, binds them systematically together, and is especially concerned to defend them against the attacks of opponents. As such appear not only the heterodox philosophers, the **Buddhists** (whose teachings 2, 2, 18—32 in their various forms are examined, and entirely rejected as an outcome of hatred toward the human race p. 581, 2), the **Jaina's** (2, 2, 33—36), the **Pâçupata's** (2, 2, 37—41) and the **Pâñcarâtra's** (2, 2, 42—45), but also the adherents of the other orthodox systems; inasmuch as Bâdarâyaṇa, 2, 1, 11, declares himself fundamentally against any possibility of discovering the truth by means of reflection (*tarka*). This will be further treated in Chap. V, 2.— **For the purpose of fixing Bâdarâyaṇa's time**, it is important to note how he treats the four non-Vedic systems. The **Nyâya** is not mentioned by Bâdarâyaṇa at all, and only twice casually quoted by Çaṅkara (p. 67, 6. 594, 1), but with approbation, perhaps because it lent no support to his polemics (but compare on Bṛih. p. 801, 8); the Yoga appears, as far as we see (1, 1, 19 the word has another meaning), with the exception of 4, 2, 21 (where, however "*Yoginaḥ*" refers in the first place to Bhag. G. 8, 23) only at 2, 1, 3, where it is briefly dismissed with the remark, that what has been said against the Sâṅkhyam applies to it also; the Vaiçeshika-teaching is confuted at 2, 2, 11—17 with the remark that no attention need be paid to it, since no one adopts it (2, 2, 17: *aparigrahâc ca atyantam anapekshâ*), a proof, that in Bâdarâyaṇa's time or country Kaṇâda's teaching was in disrepute. On the other hand, we must conclude from the way in which he treats the Sâṅkhyam that this system (recommended by authorities like Manu and the Mahâbhâratam) was held in high regard in his time. At every opportunity he recurs to it, in part in long discussions (as 1, 1, 5—11. 1, 4, 1—13. 2, 1, 1—12. 2, 2, 1—10), in part in single references (1, 1, 18. 1, 2, 19. 1, 2, 22. 1, 3, 3. 1, 3, 11. 1, 4, 28. 2, 1, 29. 2, 3, 51. 4, 2, 21), to which others are sometimes attached (2, 1, 3 and 4, 2, 21, the Yoga; 2, 1, 29, and 2, 3, 51, the Vaiçeshikam; 2, 1, 4—11, the systems of reflection in general), and repeatedly (1, 4, 28; 2, 1, 12) the remark is made, that with the Sâṅkhya system the others are also dealt with.[15] It is worthy of remark, that Bâdarâyaṇa does not mention by name any of the other systems (except the Yoga, 2, 1, 3 and the Yogin's 4, 2, 21, which in fact stand nearer to the Veda)

---

[15] Cf. Çaṅkara on 1, 4, 28, p. 403: "From *îkshater na açabdam* (1, 1, 5) onwards the teaching of the Pradhânam [primitive matter of the Sâṅkhya's] as the cause of the world has been again and again examined and refuted in the Sûtra's [not only in the Commentary]; for this assertion finds a support in certain passages of the Vedânta [Upanishad's], which apparently speak for it, and this might at first sight deceive the inexpert. Also the said teaching approaches the teaching of the Vedânta, in that it recognises the identity of cause and effect, and is therefore recognised by Devala, and other composers of *Dharmasûtra*'s; therefore so much more effort has been expended on refuting it, than on refuting the atomism [of Kaṇâda] and other teachings."—Cf. p. 440, 6: "The atomic teaching and others [contrary to the Sâṅkhyam], have not even been accepted in part by sages like Manu and Vyâsa."

or any of their founders, and even avoids repeating the usual terms for their chief ideas; so, instead of *pradhânam* (the primitive material of the Sâñkhya's), he says rather *smârtam* (1, 2, 19), *anumânam* (1, 1, 18. 1, 3, 3) *anumânikam* (1, 4, 1) "the traditional," "the hypothetical," while on the other hand *pradhânam* with him 3, 3, 11 means the Brahman. But the more careful he is to allow the names of his opponents to fall into oblivion, the more frequently, for the most part when investigating small differences between them, does he name the teachers of the two Mîmâṅsâ schools. As such appear in his work: *Bâdarâyaṇa* (1, 3, 26. 1, 3, 33. 3, 2, 41. 3, 4, 1. 3, 4, 8. 3, 4, 19. 4, 3, 15. 4, 4, 7. 4, 4, 12). *Jaimini* (1, 2, 28. 1, 2, 31. 1, 3, 31. 1, 4, 18. 3, 2, 40. 3, 4, 2. 3, 4, 18. 3, 4, 40. 4, 3, 12. 4, 4, 5. 4, 4, 11), *Bâdari* (1, 2, 30. 3, 1, 11. 4, 3, 7. 4, 4, 10), *Auḍulomi* (1, 4, 21. 3, 4, 45. 4, 4, 6), *Âçmarathya* (1, 2, 29. 1, 4, 20), *Kâçakṛitsna* (1, 4, 22), *Kârshṇâjini* (3, 1, 9), and *Âtreya* (3, 4, 44).—These are in fact with two exceptions (1, 1, 30. 1, 3, 35), the only proper names that appear in Bâdarâyaṇa's Sûtra's.

As sources of knowledge our author makes use of the *Çruti*, and in the second rank for confirmation and without binding force, the *Smṛiti*; and in doing so he in a very curious way uses the names which serve in the other systems to indicate the natural sources of knowledge, with an altered meaning in his own, so that with him *pratyaksham* (perception) repeatedly stands for Çruti, and *anumânam* (inference) for Smṛiti (1, 3, 28. 3, 2, 24. 4, 4, 20), and this as Çañkara, p. 287, 11 explains, because the latter requires a basis of knowledge (*prâmâṇyam*), and the former not. Under *Çruti* (revelation, holy scripture) Bâdarâyaṇa understands, not only the older Upanishad's, Bṛihadâraṇyaka, Chândogya, Kâṭhaka, Kâushîtaki (2, 3, 41), Aitareya (1, 1, 5), Taittirîya (1, 1, 15) and the rest, but also certain Upanishad's of the Atharvaveda, as especially the frequently quoted Muṇḍaka and Praçna, even products of such late origin as the Çvetâçvatara (1, 1, 11. 1, 4, 8. 2, 3, 22), and perhaps even the Jâbâla Upanishad (1, 2, 32. 4, 1, 3); 3, 3, 25 refers to an unknown Upanishad of the Atharvaveda. It is also worthy of note, that the Sûtra 2, 3, 43 alludes to a verse of the Atharvaveda which is not found in the printed editions. Under *Smṛiti* (tradition) our author, according to Çañkara, on whose explanations we are completely dependent for all quotations, understands the Sâñkhya and Yoga systems (4, 2, 21), the Mahâbhâratam, especially its episode called the Bhagavadgîtâ, the law-book of Manu, and perhaps other books (cf. 4, 3, 11). Beside it appears, 3, 4, 43, custom (*âcâra*; cf. 3, 4, 3; 3, 3, 3). As perfectly known, are mentioned the recensions of the same Çruti work, differing according to the Vedic schools (*çâkhâ*'s): thus Bâdarâyaṇa considers in particular the agreement and divergence in the Kâṇva and Mâdhyandina recensions[16] of the Bṛihadâraṇyaka Upanishad (1, 2, 20 *ubhaye*; 1, 4, 13 *asati anne*), as also the frequently appearing "some" (*eke*) refers for the most part to the differences of the Vedic schools (1, 4, 9. 3, 2, 2. 3, 2, 13. 4, 1, 17, and likewise *anye* 3, 3, 27), but at times also means different passages (4, 2, 13. 2, 3, 43) and teachers of the Mîmâṅsâ (3, 4, 15. 3, 4, 43) and once even (3, 3, 53) something quite different, namely, the materialists.—His own work our author quotes with the words "*tad uktam*" (about this it has been said), by which at 1, 3, 21 he points back to 1, 2, 7, further at 2, 1, 31 to 2, 1, 27, and at 3, 3, 8 to 3, 3, 7, just as through the equivalent "*tad vyâkhyâtam*" at 1, 4, 17 to 1, 1, 31.—But the same formula "*tad uktam*" is further frequently used to indicate the Karmasûtra's of Jaimini, thus 3, 3, 33 (Jaim. 3, 3, 9), 3, 4, 42 (Jaim. 1, 3, 8–9), 3, 3, 26 (p. 903, 9: *dvâdaçalakshaṇyâm*) 3, 3, 43 (p. 942, 5: *sañkarshe*), 3, 3, 44 *tadapi* (Jaim. 3, 3, 14), 3, 3, 50 (p. 951, 3: *prathame kâṇḍe*), from which it may perhaps be concluded that the works of Jaimini and Bâdarâyaṇa, each of whom quotes both himself and the other by name, may have been combined by a later editor into one work, and provided with the additions already mentioned and others.[17] To such an

---

[16] The two are distinguished by Çañkara p. 1098, 14 as different Çâkhâ's, while on the other hand p. 882, 6 Bṛih. 5, 6, 1 in the Kâṇva recension and Çatap. Br. 10, 6, 3, 2 in the Mâdhyandina recension (perhaps identical with the Kâṇva recension?) are quoted as belonging to the same Çâkhâ of the Vâjasaneyin's.

[17] In this unified form the work of Jaimini and Bâdarâyaṇa seems to have been commented on by Upavarsha, on whose work the com-

editor the name *Vyâsa* (the arranger), occurring (according to Colebrooke M. E.[3], p. 352) in connection with Bâdarâyaṇa, would be admirably suited, and he might very well be Vyâsa, the father of Çuka, the teacher of Gâuḍapâda, the teacher of Govinda, the teacher of Çañkara, and thus be 200—300 years older than his commentator, Çañkara (Windischmann, Sanc. p. 85), though Çañkara understands by Vyâsa in all the passages where this name occurs (p. 313, 9. 440, 6. 690, 11. 764, 10 and *Vedavyâsa,* p. 298, 5, cf. Mahâbh. XII, 7660), only the editor of the Mahâbhâratam while he calls the author of the Sûtra's, p. 1153, 8, *bhagavân Bâdarâyaṇa-âcârya.*

4. Form of the Brahma-sûtra's; Çañkara's Commentary.

After these indications, which can only be of use after a determination, only possible later on, of the date when our work was composed, let us turn to a consideration of its form, which is a very singular one. It is composed, as are also the fundamental works of the other Indian philosophic systems, in a series of *sûtra*'s, which word means "thread" (from *sîv* = Lat. *suere*), and is here best understood as the warp of

mentaries of Çabarasvâmin and Çañkara may rest, cf. p. 953, 2: "We "proceed now to an investigation of the immortality of the soul, for the "purpose of the teaching of its bondage and deliverance. For did the "soul not endure beyond the body, the commandments which promise a "reward in another world would not be permissible, and still less could "it be proved that the soul is identical with Brahman. But was not the "existence of the soul beyond the body, and its enjoyment of the fruit "promised in the teaching of the scripture already settled at the beginn-"ing of the book in the first pâda [that is, on Jaim. 1, 1, 5]?—Certainly, but "only by the commentator (*bhâshyakṛit*), and there is no sûtram there on "the continued existence of the soul. Here, on the contrary, its con-"tinued existence is, after previous mention of objections, confirmed by "the composer of the sûtra's (*sûtrakṛit*) himself. It was from here that "the teacher Çabarasvâmin took it and explained it in the Pramâṇa-"lakshaṇam [the first book of Jaimini, at viz. 1, 1, 5 p. 18-24]. The vener-"able Upavarsha also, in the first book, where he declares the continued "existence of the soul, points to this also, since he says: 'In the Çârî-"'rakam [that is, in the Brahmasûtra's] we shall explain it.' And so here, "after consideration of the honours resting on prescription, the continued "existence of the soul is taken into consideration, in order to show that "this teaching is in conformity with the whole of our canon."

threads stretched out in weaving to form the basis of the web, but which will become the web only when the woof is added,[18] just as the Sûtra's become a connected whole only through the explanations interwoven among them by oral or written exposition. For without this the 555 Sûtra's, consisting for the most part of two or three words each, in which our author lays down the whole Vedânta system, are utterly unintelligible, especially as they contain, not so much the leading words of the system, as the catch words, for the memory to grasp, and these seldom exhibit the main matter, but frequently something quite subordinate, have often a quite general, indeterminate form, which fits the most different circumstances and leaves everything to the interpreter. Thus the same Sûtra often recurs: thus for instance *smṛiteç ca* 1, 2, 6. 4, 3, 11; *çruteç ca* 3, 4, 4. 3, 4, 46; *darçayati ca* 3, 3, 4. 3, 3, 22; *sva-paksha-doshâc ca* 2, 1, 10. 2, 1, 29; *ubhayathâ ca doshât* 2, 2, 16. 2, 2, 23; *darçanâc ca* 3, 1, 20. 3, 2, 21. 3, 3, 48. 3, 3, 66. 4, 3, 13, that is, five times, and, in fact, if we are to believe the Commentator (as indeed we must), in different meanings, since *darçanâc ca* generally (3, 2, 21. 4, 3, 13 cf. 1, 3, 30) means "because the scripture teaches it," while in 3, 1, 20. 2, 2, 15 and 4, 2, 1 it means: "because experience shows it," and 3, 3, 48: "because it is perceived (from the indications)." In the same way we twice have the sûtra *gauṇyasambhavât* (2, 3, 3. 2, 4, 2), and this, as Çañkara himself says (p. 706, 9), in quite contrary meanings. Thus *anumânam* generally means "the Smṛiti" (*e.g.* 1, 3, 28. 3, 2, 24. 4, 4, 20), then it is also for a change the synonym of *pradhânam* (primordial matter of the Sâñkhya's) in 1, 3, 3; thus, again, *itara*, 1, 1, 16. 2, 1, 21, means the individual, but, 2, 3, 21, the highest soul, and again, 4, 1, 14, "the good work"; and *prakaraṇât*, 1, 2, 10 and 1, 3, 6, "because it is spoken of," but, 4, 4, 17, "because he is charged with it." This is accompanied by a special leaning to rare words and phrases in which another word is frequently chosen, than that used in the passage of the Upanishad taken for consideration, which is sometimes indicated

---

[18] Cf. p. 622, 2: *tathâ sûtrair ûrṇâ-âdibhiç ca vicitrân kambalân vitanvate.*—Compare also our "text," from *texere*, to weave, and the Chinese *king*, "warp of a web" (Schott, *Chin. Litt.*, p. 3).

only by this word; thus 1, 1, 24 *caraṇa* for *pâda* (Chând. 3, 12, 6); 1, 3, 1 *sva* for *âtman*, *bhû* for *prithivî* (Muṇḍ. 2, 2, 5); 1, 3, 2 *upasarp* for *upa-i* (Muṇḍ. 3, 2, 8); 1, 3, 10 *ambara* for *âkâça* (Brih. 3, 8, 7); 1, 3, 39 *kampana* for *ejati* (Kâṭh. 6, 2); 1, 4, 24 *abhidhyâ* for *akâmayata* (Taitt. 2, 6), *aikshata* (Chând. 6, 2, 3); 4, 2, 4 *upagama* for *abhisamâyanti* (Brih. 4, 3, 38); 4, 3, 2 *abda* for *saṃvatsara* (Chând. 5, 10, 2); 4, 3, 3 *taḍit* for *vidyut* (Chând. 5, 10, 2) and so on.[19]

This condition of the Brahmasûtra's cannot be sufficiently explained either by striving after brevity or a predilection for characteristic ways of expression. Rather must we admit that the composer, or composers, intentionally sought after obscurity, in order to make their work treating of the secret doctrine of the Veda inaccessible to all those to whom it was not opened up by the explanations of a teacher. From such explanations, which conformably to this intention were originally only oral, may in the course of time have arisen the written Commentaries on the work which Colebrooke (Misc. Ess.[1] p. 332, 334) enumerates, and of which only that of Çaṅkara is now accessible to us. We must therefore at present renounce the attempt to keep Bâdarâyaṇa's teaching and Çaṅkara's interpretation of it separate from each other, so that our exposition, strictly taken, is one of the Vedânta system from the standpoint of Çaṅkara only. However, he is nowhere in contradiction to the Sûtra's (if we omit 1, 1, 19, about which we shall treat, Chapter IX, 5, and perhaps also p. 870, 5,

---

[19] As rare, words and phrases in part found nowhere else we note the following: 1, 1, 5 and 1, 3, 13, *îkshati* as substantive; 1, 1, 25 *nigada*; 1, 1, 31 *upâsâ* for *upâsanâ*; 1, 2, 4 *karma-kartri* for *prâpya-prâpaka*; 1, 2, 7 *arbhaka*, *okas*; 1, 2, 26 *drishṭi*; 1, 1, 30 *çâstra-drishṭi*; 1, 3, 4 *prâṇabhrit*, "individual soul;" 1, 3, 34 *çuc*; 2, 1, 16 *avaram* for *kâryam* (effect); 2, 1, 26 *kopa* shaking (of the authority of scripture); 2, 3, 1 *viyat* for *âkâça*; 2, 3, 8 *mâtariçvan* for *vâyu*; 2, 3, 10 *tejas* for *agni*; 2, 4, 9 *kriyâ*, organ, for *karaṇam*; 2, 4, 20 *sañjñâ-mûrti-klipti* for the usual *nâma-rûpa-kalpanam*; 3, 1, 1 *raṅhati*; 3, 1, 8 *anuçaya* "remainder of work" (*bhuktaphalât karmaṇo 'tiriktaṃ karma* Çaṅk. p. 760, 5); 3, 1, 21 *saṃçokaja* for *svedaja*; 3, 1, 22 *sâbhâvya*; 3, 2, 10 *mugdha* for *mûrchita* (faint); 3, 3, 3 *sara*; 3, 3, 25 *vedha*; 3, 3, 57 *bhûman* = *samasta*; 4, 2, 4 *adhyaksha* "individual soul;" 4, 2, 7 *sriti* way; 4, 2, 17 *çesha* consequence; 4, 3, 1 *prathiti* proclamation; 4, 3, 7 *kâryam* for *aparam brahma*.

where *âdhyânâya* is explained by *samyagdarçana-artham*, and p. 908, 12, where the interpreter for *ubhayathâ* substitutes *ubhayathâ-vibhâgena*), although 3, 1, 13, p. 764, 3 we have the strange case that, in considering Kâṭh., 2, 6, Çañkara refers the words *punaḥ punar vaçam âpadyate me*, with Bâdarâyaṇa, wrongly to the penalties of hell, while, in his Commentary on Kâṭh., 2, 6, p. 96, 14, he rightly understands the same words as referring to repeated birth and death. Here and there his explanation of a Sûtram is given with reserve (*e.g.* 2, 4, 12. 3, 2, 33); in the following places he (or the different hands that have redacted them) give a double explanation: 1, 1, 12-19. 1, 1, 31. 1, 3, 27. 1, 4, 3. 2, 2, 39—40. 2, 4, 5—6. 3, 1, 7. 3, 2, 22. 3, 2, 33. 3, 3, 16—17. 3, 3, 26. 3, 3, 35. 3, 3, 64; at 1, 1, 23 he combats (p. 141, 7 ff.) the reference of the Sûtram to Bṛih. 4, 4, 18, Chând. 6, 8, 2 instead of to Chând. 1, 10, 9; at 1, 4, 26 he remarks that many treat it as two Sûtra's; at 1, 2, 26 and 2, 1, 15 he discusses a variant reading of the Sûtram; at 2, 4, 2. 3, 3, 38 and 3, 3, 57 another interpretation of it; 3, 2, 11—21 he treats as connected, and rejects, after a very detailed discussion, the opinion of those who make two sections (*adhikaraṇa*), namely 11—14 and 15—21, of it; yet more remarkable and indicative of profound differences of principle among the interpreters is it, that Çañkara, p. 1124, 9, mentions and further amply refutes, the opinion of others who find the Siddhânta (the final opinion) expressed, not in the concept of Bâdarâyaṇa 4, 3, 7—11, but in the subsequent one of Jaimini, which seems to presuppose that, for them, Bâdarâyaṇa was not the final author of the work, and would be in harmony with the above-mentioned indications of the Karma-mîmâṅsâ as a part of the same work, and of the author as *Vyâsa*.

Çañkara's Commentary has, there is reason to believe, suffered many interpolations, particularly in the first part, where they are generally introduced with the words *apara' âha*. The pursuit of this subject would lead us too far, so that we only name briefly the passages in which we believe ourselves to detect additions from a foreign hand: 1) p. 122, 9—129, 5, which we shall treat of in Chap. IX, 5; 2) p. 141, 7—142, 3, seems to be a polemic addition of another, cf. p. 138, 12; 3) p. 150,

10—151, 5, without doubt an interpolation; 4) p. 153, 5—154, 2 an "*apara*," who took offence at the saying that Brahman is in Heaven instead of beyond Heaven, repeats Çañkara's words, while correcting them; 5) p. 163, 11 there follows, with the words "*athavâ—asya ayam anyo 'rthaḥ*," a quite different explanation of the Sûtram, possibly from a different hand; 6) p. 184, 1—185, 17: an "*apara*" contests the previously made application of the verse Muṇḍ. 3, 1, 1 and explains it in another sense, with an appeal to the Paiñgi-rahasya-brâhmaṇam; here he quotes Bṛih. 4, 5, 15 according to the Mâdhyandinas, while Çañkara is usually wont to quote this passage according to the Kâṇvas (or instead 2, 4, 14 Mâdhy.), p. 111, 4. 199, 12. 393, 3. The motive of this excursus seems to be taken from p. 232, 12; it is ignored at 3, 3, 34, just as much as the addition p. 122, 9—129, 5 at 3, 3, 11—13; 7) p. 228, 2—6 an evident addition of an interpolator, according to whom the bridge "*setu*" in Muṇḍ 2, 2, 5 is the knowledge of Brahman, and not Brahman itself, to which, however, the expression is referred before, p. 227, 10, and again later, p. 834, 11; 8) p. 247, 3 (perhaps only to 247, 7) an "*apara*" asserts that the *jîvaghana* is not the *jîva*, as already explained, but *brahmaloka*. On a fusion of both views seems to rest the apprehension of *jîvaghana* as Hiraṇyagarbha in the Commentary on Praçna 5, 5.

5. The Quotations in Çañkara's Commentary.

It is of special interest to trace back to their sources the numerous quotations, introduced for the most part by a "*çrûyate*" or "*smaryate*" and so on, without further statement of their origin, though in general verbally correct, in which Çañkara's Commentary in all its parts is so rich, partly because a full understanding of the text becomes thereby possible for the first time,[20] partly because an accurate determination of the writings which Çañkara did and did not use may support many

[20] Thus, to give only one example, Banerjea (Transl. p. 34) has completely misunderstood the words p. 87, 11 "*sthita-prajñasya kâ bhâshâ*," because he did not recognise them as a quotation from the Bhag. G. 2, 54, and Bruining (Transl. p. 29) does not make matters better by leaving the passage in question out altogether (cf. further p. 395, 5. 1081, 9).

valuable conclusions as to the genuineness of the other works which are attributed to Çañkara, as to certain interpolations in the Commentary, as to the incorporation of older preparatory works in it, and so forth.

Not without labour, we have prepared an Index of all the quotations occurring in Çañkara's Commentary, together with a statement of their source, which is added at the end of this work, and will serve as a welcome aid to the study of the Brahmasûtra's. However, it is to be used with a certain care; for on the one hand the quotations sometimes show more or less important deviations from their sources, and it cannot in every case be satisfactorily decided whether these deviations are due merely to inaccuracy, or to difference of reading, or, finally, to the fact that Çañkara had before him, not the passage quoted by us, but a parallel passage from another Çâkhâ; on the other hand we must leave a (relatively small) number of quotations undetermined, whether it is that they are taken from lost writings, or that we have not yet come across them, or have overlooked them in the writings which we have. We shall indicate them the more exactly, because the conclusions which can be drawn from the other facts have validity only so far as they are not traversed by the quotations not yet recognised.

According to an estimate, which within certain bounds (according as things connected are joined or separated) is subjective, we count in the whole Commentary, all repetitions and simple references included, 2, 523 quotations, of which 2, 060 are derived from the Upanishad's, 150 from other Vedic scriptures, and 313 from non-Vedic literature.

a) Upanishad Quotations.

The Upanishads, arranged according to the frequency with which they are used, provide quotations in the following numbers: Chândogya (quoted in 8, not in 10 *prapâṭhakas,* p. 106, 1) *810*; Bṛihadâraṇyaka (the fourth Adhyâya of which is quoted, p. 330, 4, as *shashṭha prapâṭhaka,* and as its beginning p. 893, 3, Çatap. Br. XIV, 1, 1, 1, therefore, according to the Mâdhyandina's) *567,* eight of which (p. 198, 8. 366, 9. 385, 3.

677, 7. 682, 12. 685, 10. 893, 3. 1098, 13) are only found in the Mâdhyandina recension (Çatap. Br. XIV), while the others are mostly quoted according to the Kâṇva's, but also sometimes according to the Mâdhyandina's, without showing any fixed principle[21]; Taittirîya (Taitt. âr. VII, VIII, IX), *142;* Muṇḍaka *129;* Kâṭhaka *103;* Kaushîtaki *88* (which agree now with the first, now with the second recension of Cowell, but often diverge from both, as for example Kaush. 3, 3 is quoted p. 140, 15 and again exactly the same p. 299, 7 contrary to both recensions which makes it very probable that Çaṅkara had before him a third recension of this work, which he quotes comparatively seldom; Çvetâçvatara (quoted p. 110, 5 as "*Çvetâçvatarâṇâṃ mantropanishad,*" cf. p. 416, 1. 920, 4) *53* Agnirahasya (Çatap. Br. X) *40* (mostly found on pp. 214—222. 943—952); Praçna *39;* Aitareya (Ait. âr. II, 4—6) *22;* Jâbâla *13,* nine of which (p. 222, 8. 223, 1. 417, 11. 988, 8 — 991, 4. 999, 6. 1000, 1. 3. 1025, 8) are found in the Jâbâlopanishad, but the four others (924, 7 = 1059, 1. 931, 4 = 933, 4) not; Nârâyaṇîyâ (Taitt. âr. X) *9* (890, 2, 13. 891, 1. 5. 6. 10. 892, 1. 998, 2. 998 4); Îçâ (Vâj. saṃh. XL)

---

[21] Very remarkable is the disproportion with which the two great Upanishad's, Bṛihadâraṇyaka and Châdogya, are used. According to the external extent and internal importance of these two works, as well as the treatment which Çaṅkara bestows on them in his Commentaries (where the Bṛih. numbers 1096, the Chând. 628 pages, including the text), one would rather expect a contrary relation of the numbers of quotations. This one-sided preference for the Chând. Up. is in harmony with the leading rôle which it plays in the whole design of the Brahmasûtra's; thus of the 28 Upanishad passages in connection with which the theology in the first Adhyâya is discussed, Chând. provides 12, Bṛih. 4, Kâṭh. 4, Muṇḍ. and Praçna together 4, Taitt. and Kaush. together 4, (on this cf. Chap. VII, 2). In the case of parallel texts, as for example in the Pañcâgnividyâ Bṛih. 6, 2, Chând. 5, 3—10), as a rule, the (mostly secondary) readings of the Chând. are preferred; finally, it is remarkable that where a passage is quoted with the bare addition: "*iti brâhmaṇam,*" "*tathâ brâhmaṇam,*" with two exceptions (p. 1115, 8. 1116, 11) as far as we know, the Chândogya is always to be understood (p. 143, 6. 240, 11. 262, 12. 367, 7. 390, 4. 906, 3. 1014, 11) as though it were the Brâhmaṇam, κατ' ἐξοχήν and even on p. 106, 1 Chând. VI is quoted with the words "*shashṭha-prapâṭhake*" without further addition, as if it were self-evident that it only could be meant.

8 (66, 4. 74, 1. 395, 5. 414, 1. 979, 9. 985, 12. 986, 2. 1126, 10); Paiñgi *6* (184, 2, 7. 185, 4. 889, 10. quoted as *Paiñgi-rahasya-brâhmaṇam*, 232, 12 [= 184, 2] as *Paiñgy-upanishad*, undetermined 903, 3); Kena *5* (70, 1. 4. 10. 163, 3. 808, 10). Besides, p. 892, 7 (perhaps only because the Sûtram required it) an Atharva-Upanishad unknown to me (or the unknown beginning of a known one) is quoted with the words *âtharvaṇikânâm-upanishad-ârambhe*). We leave undetermined the seven times quoted passage: "*âkâçavat sarvagataç ca nityaḥ*" (130, 12 = 172, 5 = 610, 3 = 624, 8 = 652, 7 = 838, 9 = 1124, 12), which, according to the Commentator of Chând. Up. p. 409, 8 is ascribed to the Kâṭhakam (by which he understands the Upanishad [p. 409, 6] as well as the Saṃhitâ [p. 139, 4]), hardly with justice; as also the following Upanishad-like passages: 87, 9. 112, 8 (= 1047, 12 = 1135, 6). 113, 3. 182, 7. 610, 6. 7. 613, 4. 679, 8. 717, 10 (= 719, 8 = 939, 7). 741, 10. 832, 8, and, as especially worthy of notice, 808, 11 and 982, 11. If we overlook these not yet discovered quotations, we can state as result that no Upanishad except those above enumerated occurs; that is, neither Mâṇḍûkya (69, 2. 77, 5 occur also in Bṛih.), nor Maitri nor any of the Âtharvaṇa-Upanishad's, since 810, 1 is indeed to be found in Brahmavindûp. 12, but probably also in Mahâbh. XII, and was taken probably from that work.

b) Other Vedic Quotations.

Ṛigveda-saṃhitâ: Book I) 138, 1. 211, 13. 403, 2. II) 960, 8. IX) 341, 7. X) 151, 13. 208, 13. 211, 11. 215, 6. 298, 3. 304, 4. 426, 12. 495, 7. 716, 7. 764, 7.—*Aitareya-brâhmaṇam*: I) 901, 9. III) 74, 8. 313, 2. V) 43, 2. VII) 990, 10.—*Aitareya-âraṇyakam*: II) 103, 10. 872, 10. 924, 6. 958, 4. 1000, 9. 1002, 9. III) 150, 6. 450, 7. 450, 8. 783, 9. 852, 3.—*Kaushîtaki-brâhmaṇam* perhaps 893, 4. (Under the same name Kâush. Up. is quoted 378, 2. 865, 3: perhaps Çañkara regarded both as a single work).—Perhaps the supplements of the Râṇâyaṇîya's (*khila*), quoted 887, 9, may be counted to the *Sâmaveda-saṃhitâ*.—*Pañcaviñça-brâhmaṇam* X) 319, 9. 319, 10. XXI) 919, 5. 960, 7.—*Shaḍviñça-brâhmaṇam*: I) 892, 9 (cf. Râjendralâla

Mitra, Chând. Up., introd., p. 17 n.)—*Ârsheya-brâhmaṇam*, p. 3 (Burnell): 301, 8.—According to the Glossator 288, 1 also comes from a Brâhmaṇam of the Chandogas (cf. Ṛigv. IX, 62, 1); presumably also the passage quoted with "*iti brâhmaṇam*"; 1115, 6.—*Vâjasaneyi-saṃhitâ*: I) 960, 1? XXI) 960, 5? XXXII) 1123, 7.—*Çatapatha-brâhmaṇam* (besides books X and XIV): I) 1033, 10. VI) 310, 5. 422, 9. 701, 7. 901, 8. VIII) 1098, 3. XI) 320, 7. 749, 1. XII) 980, 1. XIII) 609, 10. 1005, 3.—*Taittirîya-saṃhitâ*: I) 51, 5. 52, 2. 146, 12. 362, 11. 747, 4. 990, 8. II) 311, 12. 412, 8. 704, 3. 858, 5. 858, 6. 941, 9. 942, 1. 975, 4. 992, 5. 1006, 8. 1011, 10. III) 312, 1. 935, 4. 971, 4. 975, 2. V) 709, 5. 6. 12. 711, 15. 712, 3. 951, 12. 1077, 2. VI) 975, 3. VII) 315, 11. 960, 9.—*Taittirîya-brâhmaṇam*: I) 902, 1. II) 289, 6. III) 146, 9. 304, 7. 418, 1.—*Taittirîya-âraṇyakam* (with exception of books VII, VIII, IX, X): III) 111, 8. 390, 6. 454, 14. 686, 9.—*Kâṭhakam*: 311, 5 and 1016, 11. ("*Kaṭhânâṃ saṃhitâyâm*") 859, 12; ("*agnihotra-darça-pûrṇa-mâsa-âdînâṃ kâṭhaka-eka-grantha-paripaṭhitânâm*"), 893, 1 ("*Kaṭhânâm*"); the latter passage belongs to those which according to 893, 10 stand "*upanishad-granthânâṃ samîpe;*" let it be remembered that the Kâṭh. Up. is repeatedly (335, 6. 852, 5. 869, 2) quoted as "*Kâṭhakam*," and it follows almost certainly that for Çaṅkara it still formed a whole with the Kâṭhakam.—*Maitrâyaṇî-saṃhitâ:* 959, 14; 960, 3 (according to the Glossator).—*Atharvaveda-saṃhitâ:* no certain quotation; 171, 4. 686, 7 are far more probably to be referred to Çvet.; the verse 686, 2. ("*âtharvaṇikâ brahmasûkte*") is not found in our recension; for 851, 11 cf. A. V. 10, 9. Kauç. 64ff.—That the *Gopatha-brâhmaṇam* is ignored, we have already seen above, p. 11.—The following brâhmaṇa-like quotations remain undetermined; 43, 1 (= 370, 1 = 483, 1 = 849, 13). 75, 1. 81, 8. 83, 4. 112, 1. 141, 15. (cf. schol. Kâṭy. 7, 1, 4, p. 625, 23). 640, 8. 747, 8. 846, 2. 960, 4. 994, 6. 1001, 4. 1017, 10. Probably many of them may yet be found in the Taittirîya texts.[22]

[22] Çaṅkara quotes, p. 412, 8 not "*Manur vai yat kiñca avadat, tad bhîshajam âsît*" (Kâṭhaka 11, 5. Ind. Stud. III, 463), but "*yad vai kiñca Manur avadat, tad bheshajam*" (Taitt. S. 2, 2, 10, 2);—p. 747, 4 not "*âpo vai çraddhâ*" (Maitrây. S. p. 59, 3 Schröder), but "*çraddhâ vâ' âpaḥ*"

Mention is further made of other Vedic schools, in part with quotations: *Kauthumaka* 846, 1; *Çâṭyâyanaka* **846, 1.** 893, 1. 899, 7 = 907, 8 = 1082, 15. 902, 10; *Bhâllavin* 902, 9. 903, 6; *Ârcâbhin* 903, 4.

From the Sûtra-Literature occur: *Âçvalâyana* 894, 10. 897, 5; *Kâtyâyana* 931, 11. 932, 8. 1020, 1; *Âpastamba* 410, 6. 754, 3. 1026, 7? 1036, 4. 1130, 9.—To the same source may belong: 322, 5. 6. 9. 11. 692, 4. 4. 5. 761, 5. 1016, 6. 1030, 1.

c) Non-Vedic Quotations.

Bhagavadgîtâ in 56 passages; *Mahâbhâratam* (with many variants): I) 310, 4. III) 276, 7. 412, 6. VI) 1107, 14. XII) 133, 5. 213, 12. 283, 9. 288, 6. 288, 10. 298 5. 302, 7. 304, 12. 305, 1. 322, 14. 409, 6. 409, 9. 413, 1. 413, 2. 413, 4. 413, 7. 638, 1. 660, 1. 677, 9. 690, 13. 692, 5. 758, 1. 809, 6. 828, 3. 915, 8. 1025, 5. 1048, 1. 1101, 6. XIII) 338, 12. 1022, 5.—Undetermined, Mahâbhârata-like: 214, 3. 309, 10. 362, 7. 726, 11. 809, 14. 828, 5. 916, 3. 917, 1. (= 1122, 1) 1009, 6. 1041, 8, 12. 1057, 6. 1075, 11. 1101, 9. 15.—*Râmâyaṇam*: 1036, 5.—*Mârkaṇḍeya-purâṇam* XLV) 208, 15. 872, 8.—*Purâṇa*'s: 410, 1. 427, 3 = 482, 6. 495, 10. 633, 12, perhaps 713, 14.—*Manu*: I) 196, 13. 289, 1. 1093, 14. II) 730, 5. 1023, 3. IV) 322, 10. 907, 12. X) 321, 2. 321, 3. 1016, 4. XII) 412, 10. 437, 3.—*Dharmaçâstra*-like: 1024, 4. 1027, 3 = 1030, 6. 1031, 1.

Yâska (p. 31, 15 Roth) 39, 2.—*Pâṇini*: 234, 3. 366, 1.

(Taitt. S. 1, 6, 8, 1);—p. 1077, 2 not "*tarati sarvam pâpmânam*" and so on, (Çatap. Br. 13, 3, 1, 1) but "*sarvam pâpmânam tarati*" and so on (Taitt. S. 5, 3, 12, 1);—p. 709, 5, not "*sapta vai çîrshan prâṇâḥ*" (Ait. Br. 3, 3, 1) or "*sapta çirasi prâṇâḥ*" (Pañc. Br. 22, 4, 3) or "*sapta vai çîrshaṇyâḥ prâṇâḥ*" (Çat. Br. 13, 1, 7, 2), but "*sapta vai çîrshaṇyâḥ prâṇâ, dvâv avâñcau*" (Taitt. S. 5, 3, 2, 5).—A glance at the above comparisons shows further, that (excepting the Upanishad's and what pertains to them). Çañkara quotes from the other Çâkhâ's only occasionally, but from that of the Tâittirîya's constantly. Perhaps in the future, from this fact, and conversely from the above mentioned preference for the Chând. Up. (note 21), which runs through the original web of the work, certain conclusions may be drawn as to its compilation from elements of different character.

399, 10; mentioned as a „*smṛitir anapavadanîyâ*" 416, 6.—*Paribhâshâ* to Pâṇini (8, 3, 82) 1122, 9.

Sâṅkhyâ-kârikâ: 355, 12. 361, 4. 718, 2.—No certain quotation from the *Sâṅkhya-sûtra*'s; cf. however 417, 9. 447, 11. 485, 7.—Other Sâṅkhya quotations are perhaps 345, 10. 346, 1. 420, 13.—*Yogasûtra*'s: 314, 6. 723, 12; not in our text 416, 4; cf. also 1072, 3.—*Nyâyasûtra*'s: 67, 6. 594, 1.—*Vaiçeshikasûtra*'s: I) 539, 13. IV) 525, 1. 534, 5. 534, 7. 535, 2. VII) 524, 1. 524, 2 and again 524, 2.—*Mîmâṅsâsûtra*'s: I) 50, 5. 58, 4. 52, 1, again 58, 4. 80, 1. 61, 7. 89, 2. 285, 3. 411, 2. 1002, 3. 1028, 10. II) 100, 5. 848, 6. III) 897, 1. 944, 4. 919, 10. 995, 1. 1011, 12. VI) 278, 3. 1027, 1; presumably from book XI—XII) 903, 9. 906, 3. 942, 5. 951, 3. Similar: 58, 2. 79, 9. 953, 5. 953, 9. 77, 14.—*Gauḍapâda*: 375, 3. 433, 1.—Unknown 89, 10. 1003, 1.—*Buddhistic*: 555, 6. 558, 7. 563, 4.—*Bhâgavata*'s: 601, 3. 602, 6. 14. 604, 6. 8.—*Svapnâdhyâyavidaḥ*: 783, 11.—*Indian proverbs*: 823, 10 = 825, 5; unknown 978, 3.

To these are added 99 quotations and references to the Sûtra's of Bâdarâyaṇa himself, and eight passages about which it is doubtful if they contain a quotation (61, 8. 157, 10. 238, 4. 301, 6. 367, 9. 369, 9. 1025, 4. 1094, 13), which raises the sum total to 2523 quotations.

6. Some Remarks on Çankara.

The date of Bâdarâyaṇa and the circumstances of his life are entirely unknown to us. Of Çaṅkara it seems to be certain that he lived about 700 or 800 A. D., founded a famous school in *Çriṅgagiri*, where perhaps also he was born, as an ascetic pilgrim (*paramahaṅsa, parivrâjaka*), undertook journeys as far as Kashmir, to work for his doctrine, and died in *Kâñcî*.[23]

[23] Colebrooke, M. E.[1] p. 332; Wilson, Sanskrit Dict.[1] p. XVI ff; Windischmann, Sanc. p. 39—48.—According to the Âryavidyâsudhâkara p. 226 and the quotations there given, Çaṅkara was born in the village of *Kâlapî* in the territory of *Kerala* as son of *Çivaguruçarman* in the year 3889 of the Kaliyuga (which began 18th February 3102 B. C.), in the year 845 of the Vikramâditya era (beginning 56 B. C.), which brings us to 787—789 A. D. as the year of his birth. The passage runs: "*Sâ iyam adhyâtma-vidyâ, Kali-kâla-vaçât kriçatvam âpannâ api, çrîmac-Chaṅkara-âcâryair brahmasûtra-upanishad-bhagavadgîtâ-pramukheshu brah-*

From teaching, by which a new impetus was given to the Vedânta doctrine in India, arose a great number of writings

---

mavidyâ-pratipâdaka-grantheshu bhâshya-âdîn prasanna-gambhîrân mahânibandhân viracya samupabriṅhitâ. Tad anu Viçvarûpâcârya- Vâcaspatimiçra-prabhritibhir âcârya-çishya-praçishya-âdibhir vârttika-vivaraṇa-bhâmatî-pramukhân udâra-nibandha-nicayân âbadhya supratishṭhâpitâ, iti jñeyaṃ. Çaṅkara-âcârya-prâdurbhâvas tu Vikramârka-samayâd atîte (845) *pañca-catvâriṅçad-adhika-ashṭaçatîmite saṃvatsare Kerala-deçe Kâlapî-grâme Çivaguruçarmaṇo bhâryâyâṃ samabhavat. Tathâ ca sampradâya-vida' âhur:*

Nidhi-nâga-ibha-vahny-abde, vibhave, mâsi mâdhave,
Çukle tithau, daçamyâṃ tu Çaṅkara-ârya-udayaḥ-smṛita', iti.

« *Nidhinâgebhavahnyabde* »: (3889) *nava-açîti-uttara-ashṭaçatî-adhika-trisahasrîmite varshe, iti arthaḥ, Kaliyugasya, iti çeshaḥ.—Tathâ Çaṅkara-mandâra-saurabhe Nîlakaṇṭha-bhaṭṭâ' api evam eva âhuḥ:* « *Prâsûta tishya-çaradâm atiyâtavatyâm ekâdaça-adhika-çata-ûna-catuḥsahasryâm* » *iti-âdi.—* « *Tishya-çaradâṃ* », *Kali-yuga-varshâṇâm, iti arthaḥ.*"

„After this science of the highest spirit had suffered diminution "through the sway of the Kali age, it was supplied with new force by "the illustrious Çaṅkara-âcârya, in that he composed luminous and pro- "found commentaries and the like of great compass to the Brahmasûtra's, "the Upanishad's, the Bhagavadgîtâ and other scriptures which handed "down the teaching of Brahman. These were then further fortified by "Viçvarûpâcârya, Vâcaspatimiçra, and other pupils and pupils' pupils of "the master, through the composition of a mass of excellent works, such "as scholia, interprepations, explanations and the like; that is the fact. "The birth of Çaṅkara from the wife of Çivaguruçarman happened in the "territory of Kerala in the village of Kâlapî after the 845th year of the "era of Vikramârka [Vikramâditya] had gone by. And thus the knowers "of the tradition say:

"In the year sea-elephant-mountain-beast-fire,
"In the increasing year, in the month Mâdhava,
"On the tenth day of the bright fortnight,
"There came to the world the noble Çaṅkara.

"In the year sea-elephant-mountain-beast-fire, that is in the year 3889, "meaning, as must be supplied, of the Kali era.—So too says the Master "Nîlakaṇṭha in the work called 'the fragrance of the tree of heaven "Çaṅkara' 'He was born in the myrobalan harvest while the four "thousandth year less a hundred and eleven years was rolling by.' The "myrobalan harvests mean the year of the Kali era."

Further it is circumstantially explained that Mâṇikya (who according to Merutuṅga, lived about 1150 of Vikramâditya's era) in his commentary to the Kâvyaprakâça, quotes Kumârila-bhaṭṭa as a commonly recognised authority; the latter must therefore have lived long before 1150 (= 1094 which bear his name, whose genuineness still remains to be investigated. His master-piece is the Commentary on the Brahmasûtra's, numbering 1155 pages together with the gloss of Govindânanda (for 3, 4 of Ânandagiri) in the Bibl. Ind., which gives a substantially complete and sufficient picture of his system, and from which alone we draw our exposition of it, in order in this way to form a safe standard by which the genuineness of the other works attributed to Çañkara, the minor writings, as well as the Commentaries to the Upanishad's, may subsequently be tested. From the examination of the latter, weighty conclusions can then again be drawn as to the time when the different Upanishad's came into existence, and as to their authority. We believe we have made a contribution toward this in the demonstration, of course still conditional, that has already been given, that Çañkara, in the Commentary to the Brahmasûtra's, used no other Upanishad's except *Aitareya, Kaushîtaki; Chândogya, Kena; Taittirîya, Kâṭhaka, Çvetâçvatara, Îçâ, Bṛihadâraṇyaka; Muṇḍaka, Praçna* (and incidentally *Paiñgi, Agnirahasya, Jâbâla, Nârâyaṇîya* and, once, an Atharva Up.)[24] The Commentaries published in the Bibl. Ind. (Vol. II, III, VII, VIII.) to *Bṛihadâraṇyaka, Chândogya, Taittirîya, Aitareya, Çvetâçvatara, Îçâ, Kena, Kaṭha, Praçna, Muṇḍaka, Mâṇḍûkya,* are handed down under Çañkara's name; it is remarkable that *Kaushîtaki* is not among them.[25] Besides these, he is said to have commented on *Atharvaçikhâ* (Weber, Ind. Stud., II, 53, L, G.[2], p. 182), *Nṛisiñhatâpanîya* (Colebr.[1], p. 96) and *Atharvaçiras* (Ind. St.

A. D.), and therefore also Çañkara, who had a meeting [very problematical, however] with Kumârila-bhaṭṭa in Prayâga.

[24] The *Vâshkala-Upanishad*, still existing in 1656 A. D., he cannot well have known, as otherwise he would quote the Myth of Indra as a ram, p. 310, 2, according to it, and not according to Shaḍv. 1, 1. For the remarkable passage 808, 11, there is no place in the Vâshkala Up., as we know it according to Anquetil Duperron.

[25] According to Weber (L. G.[2], p. 56) he also commented on *Kaushîtaki*; yet this statement must be erroneous, so far as it rests (Ind. St., I, 392) only on the Berlin Manuscripts, No. 83–84 (Chambers, 292*a*, 294*b*, not 262); the Commentary contained in them bears the name of *Çañkara-ânanda*, pupil of the *Ânandâtman*, and is identical with that published by Cowell.

I, 383, L. G.[2], p. 188). Other works going under his name are: *Âptavajrasûcî* (ed. Weber, Berlin 1860) and *Tripurî*, which are both counted as Upanishad's (Weber, L. G.[2], p. 179), *Upadeçasahasrî* (Colebr.[1], p. 335, Hall, Bibliogr. Index, p. 99), *Âtmabodha* (ed. Calc. 1858), *Mohamudgara* (Hall, p. 103), *Bâlabodhanî* (ed. Windischmann in Sanc., Bonn 1833), *Bâlabodhinî* (Berl. Ms. No. 618, 2) and a series of other writings, which will be found enumerated by Windischmann and Hall (cf. Regnaud, Matériaux, p. 34. Weber Verz. der Berliner H. S., p. 180, L. G.[2], p. 205, n. Lassen, *Bhagavadgîtâ*, p. XII).

Characteristic[26] for Çankara's period as well as for his theological conception is a passage of his Commentary on the Brahmasûtra's, p. 313, 8ff., which we translate here:

"For also, what is for us imperceptible was perceptible for "the ancients; thus it is recorded, that Vyâsa [the author of "the Mahâbhâratam] and others used to meet the Gods and "[Rishis] face to face. But if some would assert that, as for those "now living so for the ancients also it was impossible to meet "with gods and the like, they would deny the variety of the "world; they might also maintain that, as at present, so also "in other times, there was no world-swaying prince (*sârvabhau*-"*maḥ kshatriyaḥ*) and thus they would not acknowledge the "injunctions referring to the consecration of kings; they might "further assume that, as at present, so also in other times, the "duties of castes and Âçrama's had no stable rules, and "thus treat as vain the canon of law which provides rules for them. "We must therefore believe that the ancients, in consequence

---

26 As stylistic curiosities from Çankara's Commentary may be quoted: *prathama-tara*, p. 137, 4, 148, 12 (also on Brih. 273, 5); *upapadyate-tarâm* 144, 6; *na-tarâm* 931, 8; *akalpate* 815, 2 and *avyâcakshîta* 819, 8 (a privative with a verb) and, to read it so, also *avirudhyeta* 265, 3; *janimataḥ* 833, 14; *janyate* 844, 7; *akiñcitkaratvât* 141, 5; *arddhajaratîya* 122, 13, 176, 11 (read so); *mukhya' eva prâṇasya dharmaḥ* (for *mukhyaprâṇasya eva dharmaḥ*) 161, 3; *çrutarahasyasya vijñânasya* (for *çruta-rahasya-vijñânasya*) 191, 7. Frequent enough is the use of the 3rd pers. sing. pres. as substantive: *caratiḥ* 762, 4; *srijatiḥ* 707, 10; *dhyâyatiḥ* 1071, 11; *îkshati-âdi-çravaṇam* 109, 7; *karoti-artha* 381, 4; *dhyâyati-artha* 1071, 10; also in the genitive: *sambhavater* 630, 3; *âpnoter* 1132, 9; *tarateḥ prâpnoti-arthaḥ* 834, 14 and even *prapañcayishyater* 99, 5, which is, however, retracted in the Çuddhipatram.

"of pre-eminent merits, held visible converse with Gods and "[Ṛishis]. The Smṛiti also says [*Yogasûtra 2, 44*]: "through "study [is gained] union with the beloved godhead." And "when it further teaches, that Yoga bestows as reward the "mastery of nature, consisting [in the freedom from embodied "being and its laws, and thereby] in the ability to become as "small as an atom and the like [2, to become light, 3, to "become large, 4, to reach everything, 5, to realise every wish, "6, to rule all being with one's will, 7, to possess creative power, "8, to penetrate all, *Gauḍap*, on *Sâñkhyak*. 23, *Vedavyâsa* on "*Yogas. 3, 44*] this is not to be rejected out of hand by a "mere dictatorial sentence."

7. Analysis of the contents of the Brahmasûtra's with Çañkara's Commentary according to adhyâya, pâda and adhikaraṇam.

We conclude with an analysis of the contents of the Brahmasûtra's, which will be useful not only for our exposition of the system, but also in the study of the original work. The work (in which the number four everywhere plays an important rôle, cf. Chap. VII, 2) falls, as we have it, into four Adhyâya's (Lectures) of four Pâda's (Feet or Quarters) each, a division which calls to mind the four fourfold feet of Brahman (Chând. 4, 5-8) and the sixteenfold Spirit (Praçna 6, cf. Chând. 6, 7, Çvet. 1, 4, Bṛih. 1, 5, 15). The numbers at the beginning of the lines indicate the 555 Sûtra's of the work, their unions the Adhikaraṇas or chapters, of which, following the appended Adhikaraṇamâlâ, we count 192 (not with Colebrooke 191).

I, 1.

Introduction: concerning Avidyâ and Vidyâ.

1. Preliminaries to the Vedânta.
2. That, from which the world has sprung, is Brahman.
3. Relation of Brahman to the Veda.
4. Relation of the Vedânta to the Mîmâñsâ.

5—11. The Principle of the world is conscious, not, as the *Sâñkhya's* teach, unconscious.

12—19. The *ânandamaya* Taitt. 2, 5 is Brahman.

20—21. The ***antar âditye*** Chând. 1, 6, 6 is Brahman.

22. The *âkâça* Chând. 1, 9, 1 is Brahman.
23. The *prâṇa* Chând. 1, 11, 5 is Brahman.
24—27. The *paro divo jyotis* Chând. 3, 13, 7 is Brahman.
28—31. The *prâṇa* Kaush. 3, 2 is Brahman.

I, 2.

1—8. The *manomaya prâṇaçarîra* Chând. 3, 14, 2 is Brahman.
9—10. The *attar* Kâṭh. 2, 25 is Brahman.
11—12. The *guhâṃ pravishṭau* Kâṭh. 3, 1 are Brahman and Jîva.
13—17. The *antara* Chând. 4, 15, 1 is Brahman.
18—20. The *antaryâmin* Bṛih. 3, 7, 3 is Brahman.
21—23. The *adreçyam* Muṇḍ. 1, 1, 6 is Brahman.
24—32. The *âtman vaiçvânara* Chând. 5, 11, 6 is Brahman.

I, 3.

1—7. The *âyatanam* Muṇḍ. 2, 2, 5 is Brahman.
8—9. The *bhûman* Chând. 7, 23 is Brahman.
10—12. The *aksharam* Bṛih. 3, 8, 8 is Brahman.
13. The object of *om* Praçna 5, 5 is Brahman.
14—18. The *dahara* Chând. 8, 1, 1 is Brahman.
19—21. The *samprasâda* Chând. 8, 12, 3 refers to Brahman.
22—23. The *na tatra sûryo bhâti* Muṇḍ. 2, 2, 10 refers to Brahman.
24—25. The *aṅgushṭha-mâtra* Kâṭh. 4, 12 is Brahman.
26—33. Claim of the gods to the Vidyâ. Eternity of the Veda.
34—38. Exclusion of Çûdra's from the Vidyâ.
39. The *prâṇa* Kâṭh. 6, 2 is Brahman.
40. The *jyotis* Chând. 8, 12, 3 is Brahman.
41. The *âkâça* Chând. 8, 14 is Brahman.
42—43. The *vijñânamaya* Bṛih. 4, 3, 7 is Brahman.

I, 4.

1—7. The *avyaktam* Kâṭh. 3, 11 is not the Matter of the Sâñkhya's (*pradhânam*) but "the subtle Body" (*sûkshmaṃ çarîram*).
8—10. The *ajâ* Çvet. 4, 5 is not the Sâñkhya Matter but Nature.
11—13. The *pañca pañca-janâḥ* Bṛih. 4, 4, 17 are not the 25 Principles of the Sâñkhyas, but Breath, Eye, Ear, Food and Manas.
14—15. Consistency of the Vedânta. The Nonbeing, from which in Taitt. 2, 7 the world arose, is only relative.
16—18. The *kartar* Kaush. 4, 19 is Brahman.
19—22. The *âtman* Bṛih. 2, 4, 5 is Brahman.

23—27. Brahman is the *causa efficiens* and *causa materialis* of the world,
28. The refutation of the Sâñkhya Matter holds good also for the atomists.

II, 1.

1—2. Why the Sâñkhya's do not mention Brahman.

3. This applied also to the Yoga.

4—11. Brahman is also the *causa materialis* of Nature. Objections of reflection rebutted.

12. This rebuttal extended also to the atomists and others.

13. Subject (*bhoktar*) and Object (*bhogyam*) one in Brahman.

14—20. Identity of Cause and Effect, Brahman and World.

21—23. The Origin of Evil. The soul, although not the author of creation, bears all the guilt for it. Illusory character of the *Saṃsâra.*

24—25. Brahman works without tools, although he is pure Spirit.

26—29. Brahman is transformed into the world, and yet remains whole and undivided, as a dreamer, a magician makes forms and yet remains one.

30—31. Brahman as Creator has many powers and yet remains without difference.

32—33. Motive of creation: Brahman, self-sufficing, creates only for sport.

34—36. Brahman neither unjust nor cruel; inequality of creatures due to themselves by their earlier forms of being. Beginninglessness of the *Saṃsâra.*

37. Recapitulation concerning Brahman as Creator.

II, 2.

1—10. Refutation of the *Sâñkhya*'s. Physico-theological proof.

11. An objection of the Vaiçeshika's answered.

12—17. Refutation of the *Vaiçeshika*'s. Impossibility of the atom.

18—27. Refutation of the *Buddhists of realistic tendency*; persistence of subject and substance.

28—32. Refutation of the *Buddhists of idealistic tendency*; the reality of the outer world demonstrated.

33—36. Refutation of the *Jaina*'s; how great is the soul?

37—41. Refutation of the *Pâçupata*'s.

42—45. Refutation of the *Pâñcarâtra*'s.

II, 3.

1—7. The *âkâça* was evolved. Not so Brahman. *Cogito, ergo sum.*

8. From the *âkâça*, the *vâyu* was evolved;—

9. Brahman was not evolved; cosmological proof;—

10. From the *vâyu*, the *agni* was evolved,

11. From the *agni*, the *âpas*,

12. From the *âpas*, the *annam*, that is, the earth.

13. Not the elements, but Brahman in them is the creating agent.

14. Reabsorbtion of the world in reverse order.

15. Evolution of the soul-organs: *indriya*'s, *manas*, *buddhi*.

16. The individual soul was not evolved. Moral grounds.

17. Counter-reasons weighed. Identity of the soul with the Brahman. Only its *upâdhi*'s are evolved and disappear.
18. The soul is conscious essentially (as the Sâṅkhya's) not accidentally (as the Vaiçeshika's teach).
19—32. Relation of soul to body; it is not *aṇu* but *vibhu*.
33—39. Of the *kartṛitvam* (actorship) of the soul.
40. Its *kartṛitvam* is not *svâbhâvikam*, but *upâdhi-nimittam*.
41—42. The soul is not free and is guided in acting by God (*îçvara*) according to its former works.
43—53. The soul identical and not identical with Brahman. Illusory character of all individual existence and its pains.

II, 4.

1—4. The *prâṇas* (organs of relation) also evolved from Brahman.
5—6. Eleven of them: 5 *buddhi-indriya*'s, 5 *karma-indriya's*, 1 *manas*.
7. On their extension in space.
8. The *mukhya prâṇa* (organ of nutrition) also created.
9—12. Of its nature and five functions.
13. Of its extension in space.
14—16. Connection of the *prâṇa*'s with the soul. Collaboration of the gods.
17—19. Relation of the *mukhya prâṇa* to the other *prâṇas*.
20—22. Relation of the body and its organs to the elements.

III, 1.

1—7. Departure of the soul with its organs after death.
8—11. Why must it re-enter a new body?
12—21. Punishment of evildoers; different destinies of the soul after death. The four classes of (organic) beings.
22. Return through the *âkâça* and other stations. Relation to them that of a guest.
23. Of the duration of the halts at these stations.
24—27. Animation of plants. Return of the soul through plants, food, seed, womb to embodiment.

III, 2.

1—6. Of the nature of dream; difference from waking.
7—8. Nature of deep sleep; it is an entering into Brahman.
9. Why is he who wakes identical with him who went to sleep?
10. The swoon; difference from deep sleep and death. Metaphysical meaning of death.
11—21. Brahman is free from all differences, determinations and attributes.
22—30. Brahman is never object, because eternally subject (*sâkshiṅ*).
31—37. Of certain figurative expressions used of Brahman.
38—41. The fruit of works comes from God, who takes account of former works. On the *apûrvam*.

III, 3.

1—4. There is unity of knowledge in the *Saguṇâ Vidyâḥ* also. Consistency of the Vedânta texts.

5. Union of the different *Vijñâna*'s therefore necessary..

6—8. Of the differences in the *prâṇa-saṃvâda* Chând. 1, 3, Bṛih. 1, 3.

9. Relation between *om* and *udgîtha* Chând. 1, 1, 1.

10. The parallel passages Bṛih. 6, 1, 14. Chând. 5, 1, 13, Kaush. 2, 14 on the *prâṇa-saṃvâda* to be combined.

11—13. Qualities of Brahman of general and those of occasional validity, explained by Taitt. 2.

14—15. In Kâṭh. 3, 10—11 no gradation of powers but only the pre-eminence of *Purusha* is intended.

16—17. To Brahman applies Ait. 1, 1 [or Bṛih. 4, 3, 7—4, 25 and Chând. 6, 8-16].

18. Chând. 5, 2, Bṛih. 6, 1 *vâsovijñânam*, not *âcamanam* is recommanded.

19. The *Çâṇḍilya-vidyâ* of Çat. Br. 10, 6, 3 to be combined Bṛih. 5, 6.

20—22. But Bṛih. 5, 6 *ahar* and *aham* to be separated.

23. Also the *vibhûti*'s in the Râṇâyanîya-Khila's and Chând. 3, 14.

24. Also the *purusha-yajña* of the Tâṇḍin's, Paiṅgin's, and Taittirîyaka's.

25. Different opening passages of the Upanishad's, not part of the Vidyâ.

26. Chând. 8, 13, Muṇḍ. 3, 1, 3 etc. to be completed by Kaush. 1, 4.

27—28. The shaking off of good and bad works at death.

29—30. The *devayâna* valid only in the *saguṇâ vidyâḥ*.

31. But in this universally. Of the difference of *satyam* (Bṛih. 6, 2, 15) and *tapas* (Chând. 5, 10, 1) in the *Pañcâgni-vidyâ*.

32. Possibility of a new body in the case of one liberated, for the purpose of a mission.—Direct certainly of liberation.

33. The passages (Bṛih. 3, 8, 8, Muṇḍ. 1, 1, 6), of *aksharam*, mutually complementary.

34. The passages *ṛitaṃ pibantau* (Kâṭh. 3, 1) and *dvâ suparṇâ* (Muṇḍ. 3, 1) belong to each other.

35—36. Also Bṛih. 3, 4 and 3, 5. Brahman free from (1) causality,—(2) suffering.

37. Brahman and the worshipper separated for the purpose of meditation.

38. Bṛih. 5, 4 and 5, 5 [not Bṛih. 5, 4, 5 and Chând. 1, 6, 7] are one Vidyâ.

39. Unity and difference of Chând. 8, 1, 1. 5 and Bṛih. 4, 4, 22.

40—41. Ritual questions concerning the *Vaiçvânara-vidyâ* Chând. 5, 11-24.

42. Relation of conceptions like Chând. 1, 1, 1 to works.

43. Bṛih. 1, 5, 21-23 and Chând. 4, 3 *adhyâtmam* and *adhidaivam* are to be separated for purposes of adoration.

44—52. In the Agnirahasyam *manaçcit* etc. Çat. Br. 10, 5 belongs to the Vidyâ.

53—54. Episode on the immortality of the soul.
55—56. Conception connected with works like Chând. 1, 1, 1. 2, 2, 1. Ait. âr. 2, 1, 2, 1. Çat. Br. 10, 5, 4, 1 are valid, not only for their own Çâkhâ, but, like the Mantra's etc. generally.
57. Chând. 5, 11-24 the *samasta*, not the *vyasta* is to be worshipped.
58. Passage where unity of dogma, difference of method.
59. For the last, choice, not union holds good.
60. Teachings referring to special wishes can be united.
61—66. For those mentioned 55—56 either union or choice.

III, 4.

1—17. The Upanishad teaching without works leads man to the goal. Position of the sage to works.
18—20. Difference between Jaimini and Bâdarâyaṇa about the *Âçrama*'s.
21—22. Passages like Chând. 1, 1, 3. 1, 6, 1. Çatap. Br. 10, 1, 2, 2. Ait. âr. 2, 1, 2, 1 are not mere *stuti*, but part of the *upâsanam*.
23—24. Limited validily of the legends Bṛih. 4, 5, Kaush. 3, 1, Chând. 4, 1.
25. Resumé of 1—17: knowledge without works leads to the goal.
26—27. *Yajña*, *dânam*, *tapas* etc. as means to knowledge.
28—31. In mortal danger neglect of the laws as to food is lawful.
32—35. He who does not strive after knowledge, must also perform the *âçrama-karmâṇi*, which only further, but do not produce, knowledge.
36—39. Those who through want have no *âçrama* are also called to knowledge.
40. *Character indelebilis* of the *Ûrddhvaretas* vow.
41—42. How far is penance possible for a fallen *Brahmacârin*?
43. Exclusion of him after *mahâpâtaka*'s and *upapâtaka*'s.
44—46. Whether the *upâsana*'s belong to the *yajamâna* or the *ṛitvij*?
47—49. How far Bṛih. 3, 5, 1 are the *Âçrama*'s to be understood?
50. "ἐὰν μὴ γένησθε ὡς τὰ παιδία . . ."—"λάθε βιώσας."
51. Knowledge as fruit of this means follows here, where there is no stronger *atîndriyâ çaktiḥ*, otherwise in the next life.
52. A "more" or "less," according to the different strength of the *sâdhana*'s exists only in the *saguṇâ vidyâḥ*, not in the *nirguṇâ vidyâ*.

IV, 1.

1—2. The *pratyaya* of the *âtman* is to be practised, until Intuition is reached.
3. Then follows identity of self and Brahman; for the awakened there is no evil, no perception, no Veda.
4. "Thou shalt not make to thyself any image (*pratîkam*)!"
5. In Chând. 3, 19, 1 ("*âdityo brahma*") *brahman* is predicated of *âditya*.

6. But Chând. 1, 3, 1 *âditya* is predicated of *udgîtha*.
7—10. *Upâsanam* is to be practised sitting, not lying or standing.
11. Place, time, direction are indifferent, only entire freedom from disturbance necessary.
12. The *upâsana*'s have as aim partly *samyagdarçanam* partly *abhyudaya*; the former are to be practised till the goal is reached, the latter till death.
13. On attainment of knowledge, former sins are destroyed, further sins impossible. (The power of *karman* is paralysed.)
14. Destruction of good works also. Why?
15. Persistence of the body, in spite of liberation, until the extinction of works entered on. Potter's wheel; double moon.
16—17. Sacrifices etc. are not binding for the *Brahmavid*, though they are for the *Saguṇavid*.
18. Purifying effect of sacrifices etc. with, but also without knowledge.
19. After expiation of *karman*: Death and with it *Kaivalyam*.

IV, 2.

1—2. (*Aparavidyâ*.) At death the *indriya*'s enter *manas*,
3. the *manas* enters the *prâṇa*,
4—6. the *Prâṇa* enters the *vijñânâtman* (*jîva*), this enters the elements.
7. Hence the *Avidvân* goes to re-embodiment, the *Vidvân* to immortality: This *amṛitatvam* is *âpekshikam*.
8—11. Persistence of the "subtle body." Its nature described.
12—14. (*Paravidyâ*.) For the *Akâmayamâna* (*Parabrahmavid*) there is no departure of the soul; he is already Brahman.
15. His *prâṇa*'s enter Brahman, the coarse becomes earth etc.
16. His dissolution is without residue, not, as otherwise, with a residue.
17. (*Aparavidyâ*.) The *Vidvân* (he who knows exoterically) goes out through the 101st channel (the others through others);
18—19. Thence by a sun ray, which, by day and night,
20—21. in summer and winter, ever exists. (*Sâñkhya-Yoga* differ.)

IV, 3.

1. Stations on the way: *nâḍî*,—*raçmi*,—*arcis*,—
2. *ahar*,—*âpûryamâṇapaksha*,—*yân shaḍ udañ eti*,—*saṃvatsara*,—*vâyu*,—*âditya*,—
3. *candra*,—*vidyut*,—*varuṇaloka*,—*indra*,—*prajâpati*.
4—6. These are guides of the soul whose organs, as they are enveloped do not act.
7—14. Terminus: *Brahman*, not the all-present *param brahma*, but the, *aparam*, *saguṇam brahman*, which as *kâryam* is transitory. *Kramamukti*.
15—16. But those who worship Brahman under a *pratîkam*, have other rewards.

IV, 4.

1–3. (*Paravidyâ.*) Identity of the liberated soul with the soul bound in ignorance, suffering, perishableness.

4. *Unio mystica.*

5–7. (*Aparavidyâ.*) Characteristics of the (imperfectly) liberated.

8–9. The "wishes" (Chând. 8, 2) of the liberated soul. Then freedom.

10–14. Does the liberated possess organs (*manas* etc.)?

15–16. His wonderful powers; animation of several bodies together.

17–22. His *aiçvaryam* and its limits. Description of *Brahmaloka*. After he has there gained *Samyagdarçanam* he also enters the everlasting, perfect *Nirvâṇam*.

II. Aim of the Vedânta: The destruction of an innate error.

1. The fundamental thought of the Vedânta and its previous history; a glance at allied theories in the west.

IN the introduction which Çankara prefixes (p. 5-23) to his Commentary on the Brahmasûtra's, he introduces us at once to the fundamental concept of the system, declaring all empirical, physical knowledge to be ignorance (*Avidyâ*), to which he opposes the metaphysics of the Vedânta, as knowledge (*Vidyâ*).—Before we approach this thought in detail, let us call to mind certain truths suited to throw light on its philosophic meaning, and thereby on the Vedânta system of which they are the root.

The thought that the empirical view of nature is not able to lead us to a final solution of the being of things, meets us not only among the Indians but also in many forms in the philosophy of the west. More closely examined this thought is even the root of all metaphysics, so far as without it no metaphysics can come into being or exist. For if empirical or physical investigation were able to throw open to us the true and innermost being of nature, we should only have to continue along this path in order to come at last to an understanding of all truth; the final result would be PHYSICS (in the broader sense, as the teaching of φύσις, nature), and there would be no ground or justification for METAPHYSICS. If, therefore, the metaphysicians of ancient and modern times, dissatisfied with empirical knowledge, went on to metaphysics, this step is only to be explained by a more or less clear consciousness that all empirical investigation and knowledge amounts in the end only to a great deception grounded in the nature of our knowing faculties, to open our eyes to which is the task of metaphysics.

Thrice, so far as we know, has this knowledge reached conviction among mankind, and each time, as it appears, by a different way, according to conditions of time, national and individual character; once among the Indians, of which we are to speak, again in Greek philosophy, through Parmenides, and the third time in the modern philosophy through Kant.

What drove the Eleatic sage to proceed beyond the world as "τὸ μὴ ὄν" to the investigation of "the existent" seems to have been the conception, brought into prominence by his predecessor Xenophanes, of the Unity of Being, that is, the unity of nature (by him called θεός), the consequence of which Parmenides drew with unparalleled powers of abstraction, turning his back on nature, and for that reason also cutting off his return to nature.

To the same conviction came Kant by quite another way, since with German patience and thoroughness he subjected the cognitive faculties of mankind to a critical analysis, really or nominally only to examine whether these faculties be really the fitting instruments for the investigation of transcendent objects, whereby, however, he arrived at the astonishing discovery that, amongst others, three essential elements of the world, namely, Space, Time and Causality, are nothing but three forms of perception adhering to the subject, or, if this be expressed in terms of physiology, innate functions of the brain; from this he concluded, with incontestable logic, that the world as it is extended in space and time, and knit together in all its phenomena, great and small, by the causal nexus, *in this form* exists only for our intellect, and is conditioned by the same; and that consequently the world reveals to us "appearances" only, and not the being of "things in themselves." What the latter are, he holds to be unknowable, regarding only external experience as the source of knowledge, so long as we are restricted to intellectual faculties like ours.

These methods of the Greek and German thinkers, admirable as they are, may seem external and cold, when we compare them with the way in which the Indians, as we may assume even in the present condition of research, reached the same concepts. Their pre-eminence will be intelligible when we consider that no people on earth took religion so seriously, none toiled on the way to salvation as they did. Their reward for this was to have got, if not the most scientific, yet the most inward and immediate expression of the deepest secret of being.

How the development which led them to this goal is to be conceived in detail, we cannot yet accurately determine; it seems to us specially matter of question how the historical relation between *Brahman* and *Âtman*, the two chief concepts on which Indian metaphysics grew, and which already in the Upanishad's, so far as we see, are used throughout as synonyms, is to be considered: whether the concept of *Âtman* developed itself from that of *Brahman* through a mere sharpening of the subjective moment lying therein, or whether we have rather to distinguish between two streams, the one, more ecclesiastical, which raised *Brahman* to a principle; the other, more philosophical, which did the same for *Âtman*, until both, closely connected in their nature, were led into a common bed. Putting aside these questions for the present, let us briefly, by a few selected examples, indicate the steps along which the Indian genius probably raised itself to the conception of the world, which we are then to set forth.

1. We have already pointed out how the Indians, setting out from the worship of personified powers of nature, recognised in that raising of the feeling above the consciousness of individual existence which occurs in prayer, that is, in the *Brahman*, the central force in all the forces of nature, the shaping and supporting principle of all Gods and all worlds; the word *Brahman* in the whole Rigveda never meaning anything else than this lifting and spiritualising power of prayer. (With the history of this concept may be compared that of the Logos (Λόγος) of the fourth Gospel, which rests on a similar abstraction and hypostasis.) From the standpoint of this apprehension of the Brahman as a cosmic potency inherent

in the subject, the *Taittirîya-Brâhmaṇam* (2, 8, 9, 6) for example, takes up a question put in the *Ṛigveda* (X, 81, 4) and answers it as follows:—

"Where was the tree and where the wood,
"From which the heaven and earth were shaped?
"Musing in mind seek that, ye wise,
"Whereon the bearer of them stood!" (*Ṛigv.* 10, 81, 4)

"The Brahman was the tree, the wood,
"From which the heavens and earth were shaped,
"Musing in mind, I say, ye wise,
"On Him the bearer of them stood!"

2. To this is joined the idea that Brahman is the innermost and noblest in all the phenomena of the world; it is, as the *Kâṭhaka-Up.* (5, 1—3) expresses it, changing and deepening the sense of the verse *Ṛigv.* 4, 40, 5, the sun in the firmament (*haṅsaḥ çucishad*), the God (*vasu*, the good) in the atmosphere, the Hotar at the altar, the guest at the threshold of the house, it dwells everywhere, is born everywhere,—but he only is free from sorrow and sure of liberation, who honours it, the unborn, unassailable spirit, in "the city with eleven doors" (the body), wherein it dwells, with the powers of life round it,—

"And in the middle sits a dwarf,
"Whom all the godlike Powers adore."

3. Here "in the lotus of the heart" the Brahman is now nothing else than the *Âtman*, that is, the soul, literally "the self." We select an example from *Chândogya-Up.* 3, 14:

"Verily this universe is Brahman; as *Tajjalân* [in it be-"coming, ceasing, breathing] it is to be adored in silence. "Spirit is its material, life its body, light its form; its decree "is truth, its self endlessness [literally æther]; all-working is "He, all-wishing, all-smelling, all-tasting[27] comprehending the "All, silent, ungrieved:—this is my soul (*âtman*) in the inmost "heart, smaller than a grain of rice, or of barley, or of mus-"tard-seed, or of millet, or a grain of millet's kernel;—this is "my soul in the inmost heart, greater than the earth, greater

[27] Otherwise Max Müller and Oldenberg (Buddha[1], p. 31); cf. however Bṛih. 4, 3, 24 and the οὖλος ὁρᾷ, οὖλος δὲ νοεῖ, οὖλος δέ τ' ἀκούει of Xenophanes.

"than the atmosphere, greater than the heaven, greater than "these worlds.—The all-working, all-wishing, all-smelling, all-"tasting, embracing-the-All, silent, ungrieved, this is my soul "in the inmost heart, this is Brahman, into him I shall enter "on departing hence.—He to whom this happens, he, verily, "doubts no more!—Thus spoke Çâṇḍilya, Çâṇḍilya."

4. The last-mentioned entering into the true Self after death presupposes the consciousness of a difference between the empiric self, that is, the bodily personality, and the highest Self (*paramâtman*), which is the Soul, that is, God. This difference is the subject of a lesson, which Prajâpati gives to Indra, *Châṇdogya-Up.* 8, 7—12, and in which he leads him up step by step to ever truer knowledge. To the question: "What is the Self?" comes as the first answer: 1) "The Self is the body, as it is reflected in the eye, in water, in a mirror." To the objection, that then the Self is also affected by the defect and dissolution of the body, follows the second explanation: 2) "The Self is the soul, as it enjoys itself in dream." To the objection that the dreaming soul, if it does not suffer, still believes itself to suffer, it is replied: 3) "When "he who has sunk to sleep has come altogether, fully, and "wholly to rest, so that he beholds no dream,—that is the "Self, the undying, the fearless, the Brahman." To the objection that in this condition consciousness ceases, and that it is like entering into nothing, Prajâpati at last answers: 4) "Mortal, verily, O Mighty one, is this body, possessed by "death; it is the dwelling-place of that undying, bodiless Self. "The embodied is possessed by pleasure and pain, for while "he is embodied, there can be no escaping of pleasure and "pain. But pleasure and pain, do not touch the bodiless one.— "Bodiless is the wind;—clouds, lightning, thunder are bodiless. "Now as these arise from the atmosphere [in which they are "bound, like the soul in the body], enter into the highest light, "and thereby appear in their own form, so also this full rest "[that is, the Soul, in deep sleep] arises from this body, enters "into the highest light and reaches its own form; that is the "highest Spirit."—

In similar fashion the *Taittirîya-Up.* 2, 1—7 leads from the bodily self, by stripping one covering after another off it, at last to the true Self. It distinguishes: 1) the Self consisting of food; in this, as in a case, is held 2) the Self of breath, in this 3) the Self of manas, in this 4) the Self of knowledge, in this finally as innermost 5) the Self of bliss. "Verily, this is the Essence (*rasa*); he who reaches this "essence, is filled with bliss; for who could breathe and who "could live, if this bliss were not in space?—For he it is that "causes bliss; for when one finds peace and support in this "invisible, bodiless, unspeakable, unfathomable one, then has "he entered into peace; but if he in this also [as in the four "first] recognises a hollow, an "other," then he finds unrest; "this is the unrest of him who thinks himself wise."

5. The Self, in this sense, is, according to *Chândogya-Up.* 6, 2, 1 "the existent," "the One without a second," and, answering to this, *Bṛihadâraṇyaka-Up.* 2, 4, 5 refers and limits all investigation to the Self: "The Self, verily, o Maitreyî, must "be seen, heard, thought on, and investigated; he who sees, "hears, thinks on, and investigates the Self, has understood "all this world." "These worlds, these Gods, these beings, all "these are what the Self is." It is the point of union (*ekâyanam*) for all, as the ocean for the waters, the ear for sound, the eye for forms, and so on; all outside it is as devoid of being as the sound that goes out from a musical instrument; he who has laid hold on the instrument has therewith also laid hold on the sounds that spring from it (*loc. cit.*, 2, 4, 6—11). It is, according to *Chândogya-Up.* 6, 1, 4, that from which all the world has come into being, as a mere transformation of it: he who knows this One, therewith knows all, "just as, oh dear "one, by a lump of clay, all that is made of clay is known; "the transformation is a matter of words, a mere name; in "reality it is only clay!"—

6. In conformity with this, the *Içâ-Up.* 1, 6 bids us "sink the whole world in God," that is, in the Self:

> "Who, seeking, finds all being in the Self
> "For him all error fades, all sorrow ends;"

and the *Kâṭhaka-Up.* (4, 10—11) warns us not to admit a multiplicity, anything different (*nânâ*) from the soul:

"For what is here is there, and what is there is here;
"From death to death he hastes who here another knows!
"In spirit shall ye know, here is no manifold;
"From death to death is he ensnared who difference sees."

7. It was a simple consequence of these conceptions when the Vedânta declared the empirical concept which represents to us a manifold existing outside the Self, a world of the Object existing independently of the Subject, to be a glamour (*mâyâ*), an innate illusion (*bhrama*) resting on an illegitimate transference (*adhyâsa*), in virtue of which we transfer the reality, which alone belongs to the subject, to the world of the object, and, conversely, the characteristics of the objective world, *e. g.*, corporeality, to the subject, the Self, the Soul.

Concerning this, let us hear Çañkara himself.

2. Analysis of Çañkara's Introduction (p. 5-23).

"Object (*vishaya*) and Subject (*vishayin*)", he says at the beginning of his work, "having as their province the presen- "tation of the 'Thou' [the not I] and the 'I,'[28] are of a nature "as opposed as darkness and light. If it is certain that the "being of the one is incompatible with the being of the other, "it follows so much the more that the qualities of the one "also do not exist in the other. Hence it follows that the "transfer (*adhyâsa*) of the object, which has as its province "the idea of the 'Thou,' and its qualities, to the pure spiri- "tual subject, which has as its province the idea of the 'I,' "and conversely, that the transfer of the subject and its "qualities to the object, is logically false.—Yet in mankind "this procedure resting on false knowledge (*mithyâ-jñâna-* "*nimitta*) of pairing together the true and untrue [that is, "subjective and objective] is inborn (*naisargika*), so that they

---

28 *Yushmad-asmat-pratyaya-gocara;* Banerjea translates: "*indicated by the second and first personal pronouns,*" and so p. 15, 2 *asmat-pratyaya-vishayatvât: "because it (the soul) is the object of the first personal pronoun,"* which, however, gives us no clear meaning, for only presentations, not pronouns, have objects,—The soul is therefore subject (*vishayin*), yet not (empiric) subject of knowledge as which the *ahampratyayin* (that is, the *manas*, to distinguish from the *ahaṃkartar*) figures, to which the soul again stands opposed as object (*vishaya*); *cf.* the passages in notes 29 and 30, and further in the course of the work (Chap. XXVII, 3).

"transfer the being and qualities of the one to the other, not "separating object and subject, although they are absolutely "different (*atyanta-vivikta*) and so saying, for example: 'This "am I,' 'That is mine.'"[29]

However this transference be defined, (p. 12, 1—14, 3) in any case it comes to this, that qualities of one thing appear in another, as when mother-of-pearl is taken for silver, or when two moons are seen instead of one (p. 14, 3—5). This erroneous transference of the things and relations of the objective world to the inner Soul, the Self in the strictest sense of the word, is possible because the soul also is, in a certain sense, object, namely, object of presentation to the "I," and, as our author here affirms, in no sense something transcendent, lying beyond the province of perception (*paroksham*).[30]

---

[29] By this the objective, *e. g.*, the body, is sometimes treated as subject, sometimes as a quality of it. As explanation the following passage may serve, p. 20, 8: "As one is accustomed, when it goes ill or well with his "son or wife and the like, to say, 'it goes ill or well with me,' and thus "transfers the qualities of outer things to the Self (soul, *âtman*) [cf. p. 689, "3 ff.], in just the same way he transfers the qualities of the body, when "he says: 'I am fat, I am thin, I am white, I stand, I go, I leap,' and "similarly the qualities of the sense organs when he says: 'I am dumb, "impotent, deaf, one-eyed, blind,' and similarly the qualities of the inner "organ [*antaḥkaraṇam* = *manas*, cf. 2, 3, 32], desire, wish, doubt, resolution "and the like;—thus also he transfers the subject presenting the 'I' "(*ahaṃ-pratyayin*) to the inner soul, present solely as witness (*sâkshin*) "of the personal tendencies, and conversely the witness of all, the inner "soul, to the inner organ and the rest" [that is, to the sense organs, the body and the objects of the outer world].

[30] P. 14, 5: "Question: but how is it possible to transfer to the inner "soul, which is no object, the qualities of objects? For everyone transfers "[only] to one object standing before him another object: and of the "inner soul thou maintainest that it is cut off from the idea of 'Thou' "[not-I] and is no object [I read with Govinda: *avishayatvam*]?—Answer: "Not in every sense is it non-object; for it is the object of perception "of the 'I'" [*asmat-pratyaya-vishaya;* taken strictly and according to p. 78, 6, cf. 73, 5. 672, 1, not the *sâkshin*, but only the *kartar*, that is, the individual soul already endowed with objective qualities, is *aham-pratyaya-vishaya*]; "and the [whole] assumption of an inner soul rests "on this, that it is not transcendent (*aparoksha*). It is also not necessary "that the object, to which we transfer another object, should stand before "us; as, for instance, when simple people transfer to space (*âkâça*),

"This transference, thus made, the wise term IGNORANCE "(*avidyâ*), and, in contradistinction to it, they call the accurate "determination of the own nature of things" (*vastu-svarûpam*, of the being-in-itself of things, as we should say) "KNOWLEDGE "(*vidyâ*). If this be so, it follows that that to which a [similar, "false] transfer is thus made, is not in the slightest degree "affected by any want or excess caused thereby" (p. 16, 1—4).

The object of knowledge, the Soul, thus remains, as made clear in these words, entirely unaltered, no matter whether we rightly understand it, or not. From this we must conclude that the ground of the erroneous empirical concept is to be sought for solely in the knowing subject; in this subject the avidyâ, as repeatedly (p. 10, l. 21, 7. 807, 12) asserted, is innate (*naisargika*); its cause is a wrong perception (it is *mithyâ-jñâna-nimitta*, p. 9, 3); its being is a wrong conception (*mithyâ-pratyaya-rûpa*, p. 21, 7);—all these expressions point to the fact that the final reason of the false empirical concept is to be sought—where, however, the Vêdanta did not seek it—in the nature of our cognitive faculty. An analysis of this, as Kant undertook it, would in fact give the true scientific foundation of the Vedânta system; and it is to be hoped that the Indians, whose orthodox dogmatics, holding good still at the present day, we here set forth, will accept the teachings of the "Critique of Pure Reason," when it is brought to their knowledge, with grateful respect.[31]

"which is not an object of perception, the dark colour of the ground, "and the like. In just the same way is it possible to transfer to the "inner soul what is not soul."

[31] Also Kant's axiom that the transcendental ideality of the world does not exclude its empiric reality, finds its full analogy in the concepts of Çañkara: cf. p. 448, 6: "All empiric action is true, so long as the "knowledge of the soul is not reached, just as the actions in dream, "before awaking occurs. As long in fact as the knowledge of unity with "the true Self is not reached, one has not a consciousness of the unreality "of the procedure connected with standards and objects of know-"ledge and fruits of works, but every creature, under the designation of "'I' and 'mine,' takes mere transformations for the Self and for charac-"teristics of the Self, and on the other hand leaves out of consideration "their original Brahman-Selfhood; therefore before the consciousness

On the soil of this natural Ignorance stands according to Çañkara, all human knowledge, with the exception of the metaphysics of the Vedânta; thus, not only the empirical thought, that is, thought by means of the sense-organs, of common life, but also the whole ritual canon of the Veda, with its things commanded and forbidden under promise of reward and punishment in another world (p. 16, 4—17, 1).

The immediate ground on which both worldly and Vedic actions must be referred to the sphere of Ignorance, lies in this, that both are not free from the delusion (*abhimâna*) of seeing the "I" in the body; for neither knowledge nor action is possible unless one considers as belonging to the Self,[32] the sense-organs and the body bearing them, and the ritual part of the Veda also cannot but transfer many circumstances of the outer world erroneously to the Soul.[33]

A further ground for the inadequacy of all empirical knowledge is, that it is only distinguished from that of animals in degree through higher evolution (*vyutpatti*), but is in kind similar to it, so far as, like it, it is wholly subservient

"of identity with Brahman awakes, all worldly and Vedic actions are "justified."

[32] P. 17, 2: "But how is it possible that the means of knowledge, "perception and the rest, and the [ritual] books of doctrine are limited to "the province of Ignorance?—Answer: Because without the delusion that "'I' and 'mine' consist in the body, sense-organs, and the like, no "knower can exist, and consequently a use of the means of knowledge "is not possible. For without calling in the aid of the sense-organs, "there can be no perception, but the action of the sense-organs is not "possible without a resting place [the body], and no action at all is "possible without transferring the being of the Self (the Soul, *âtman*) "to the body, and without all this taking place no knowledge is possible "for the soul, which is independent [reading *asañgasya*] [of embodied "existence]. But without action of knowing, no knowing is possible. "Consequently, the means of knowledge, perception and the rest, as "as well as the books of doctrine [in question] belong to the province "of Ignorance."

[33] P. 20, 5: "For when it is said, for example: 'Let the Brahman "offer', the like ordinances rest on the fact of transferring the castes, "Âçrama's, ages of life and similar differences to the soul; this trans- "ference is, as we have said, the assumption that something is where it "is not."

to egoism, which impels us to seek for what is desired and to avoid what is not desired; and it makes no difference here whether these egoistic aims, as in the case of worldly actions, reach their realisation already in this life, or, as in the case of the works ordained by the Vedas, only in a future existence, thus presupposing a knowledge of it. Quite otherwise the Vedânta, which, on the contrary, leaves the whole sphere of desire behind, turns its back on all differences of position in outer life (even if, as we shall see, not quite consistently), and raises itself to the knowledge that the Soul is in reality not the least involved in the circle of transmigration (*saṃsâra*).[34]

---

[34] The interesting passage which gives us an insight into the Indian idea of the difference between man and animals, reads in its entirety as follows, (p. 18, 4ff.):—"For this reason also" [worldly and Vedic knowledge belongs to the province of Ignorance], "because [thereby] no "difference is made between man and animals. For just as the animals, "when, for instance, a sound strikes their ears, in case the perception of "the sound is disagreeable to them, move away from it, and in case it is "agreeable, move towards it,—as, when they see a man with an upraised "stick before them, thinking: 'He will strike me,' they try to escape, and "when they see one with a handful of fresh grass, approach him [one sees that when the Indian speaks of an animal, he thinks of a cow, somewhat as we think of a dog]: so men also whose knowledge is more "developed (*vyutpanna-cittâḥ*), when they perceive strong men of terrible "aspect, with drawn swords in their hands, turn away from them, and "turn towards the contrary.—Thus with reference to the means and "objects of knowledge, the process in men and animals is alike. Of "course in the case of animals perception, and the like, goes on without "previous (!) judgment (*viveka*); but as can be seen by the resemblance, "even in the case of [spiritually] developed (*vyutpattimatâm*) men, per-"ception and the like for the time [of false knowledge] is the same; and if "according to the spiritual canon the performance of works is permitted "only to one who has gained insight (*buddhi*), and not to one who has not "recognised the connection of the soul with the other world, yet for this "permission it is not imperative that one [should have recognised] the truth "concerning the soul freed from the *Saṃsâra*, to be taught by the Vedânta, "which leaves behind hunger and the other [desires], and turns away "from the difference between Brahmans, warriors and the rest. For this "truth is not implied in the injunction [of the work of sacrifice], but is "rather in contradiction to it. And while the canon of ordinances is "valid [only] for this degree of knowledge of the soul, it does not rise "above the province of Ignorance."

For all those laws of empirical knowledge and action are valid for us only so long as we are influenced by the Ignorance, resting on a false transference, which nature imposes on us, of which it is said in conclusion (p. 21, 7): "Thus it stands "with this beginningless, endless, innate transference, which "in its essence is a false assumption, producing all the con- "ditions of doing and enjoying [or suffering] and forming the "[natural] standpoint of all men. To remove this, the root "of the evil, and to teach the knowledge of the unity of the "soul,—this is the aim of all the texts of the Vedânta."[35]

This aim the Vedânta reaches by separating from the soul (the Self, *âtman*) everything that is not soul, not Self, and is only transferred thereto falsely, thus, in a word, all *Upâdhi*'s, or individualising determinations, clothed (*upahitam* 163, 9. 690, 5. 739, 7) in which the Brahman appears as individual soul. Such Upâdhi's are: 1) all things and relations of the outer world (cf. note 29), 2) the body, consisting of the gross elements, 3) the *Indriya*'s, that is the five sense-organs and five organs of action of the body, represented as separate existences, 4) *Manas*, also called the inner organ (*antaḥkaraṇam*), the central organ for the sense-organs as well as for the organs of action, in the first place closely approaching what we call understanding, and in the latter almost synonymous with, what we call conscious will, the unified principle of conscious life, as 5) the *Mukhya prâṇa* with its five offshoots, is the unified principle of unconscious life, subserving nutrition. —All this, of which more in our psychological part, metaphysics cuts away, in order to retain the soul, that is, the real Self or "I," which is present as spectator (*sâkshin*) of all individual actions, but itself only apparently individualised by the Upâdhi's, is on the contrary in reality indentical with the highest godhead, and, like this, is pure spiritual nature, pure consciousness (*caitanyam*).

---

[35] Cf. for the doctrine of the Avidyâ also the following passages: p. 98, 8. 112, 3. 182, 12. 185, 12. 199, 5. 205, 10. 343, 4. 360, 2. 433, 13. 452, 2. 455, 4. 473, 17. 483, 6. 507, 1. 660, 10. 680, 12. 682, 3. 689, 1. 690, 5. 692, 14. 787, 13. 804, 1. 807, 11. 837, 2. 860, 15. 1056, 1. 1132, 10. 1133, 12. 1133, 15.

And here we touch the fundamental want of the Vedânta system, which, among other things, causes the absence of its proper morality, however near this, in its purest form, lay to its principle.[36] Rightly the Vedânta recognises, as the sole source by which we may reach true knowledge, true apprehension of being-in-itself, our own "I," but it wrongly halts at the form in which it directly appeals to our consciousness, as a knower, even after it has cut away the whole intellectual apparatus, and ascribed it to the "not I," the world of phenomena, just as it has also, very rightly, indicated as the dwelling of the highest soul, not, as Descartes did, the head (about which Bṛih. 2, 2 treats), but the heart.

Meanwhile, as we shall see, the spiritual (*caitanyam*) is, in our system, a potency which lies at the root of all motion and change in nature, which is therefore also ascribed, for example, to plants, and means thus rather the capacity of reaction to outer influences, a potency which, in its highest development, reveals itself as human intellect, as spirit.

---

[36] The command "ἀγαπήσεις τὸν πλησίον σου ὡς σεαυτόν" ["Love thy neighbour as thyself"] is an immediate consequence of the fundamental concept of the Vedânta, as the following verses of the *Bhagavadgîtâ* (13, 27–28) may show:—

"This highest Godhead hath his seat in every being,
"And liveth though they die; who seeth him, is seeing,
"And he who everywhere this highest God hath found,
"Will not wound self through self. . . ."

III. Who is called to the Study of the Vedânta?

1. The indispensable Condition.

The question, who is to be admitted to the saving teaching of the Vedânta, and who is to be excluded from it, is discussed in an episode of the first Adhyâya of the Brahmasûtra's with great fulness (p. 280—323), and the result is, that there are called to knowledge, all those who are reborn (*dvija*) through the Sacrament of the *Upanayanam* (the initiation by a teacher with the solemn investiture with the sacred thread), therefore if they fulfil this condition, all Brâhmaṇa's, Kshatriya's and Vaiçyas, and further also the gods and (departed) Ṛishis; that, on the contrary, the Çûdra's (belonging to the fourth, non-Aryan, caste) are excluded from it.

Both the exclusion of the Çûdra's and the inclusion of the gods, give rise to long and interesting discussions.

2. Exclusion of the Çûdra's.

At first sight it may appear strange considering the principle of the Vedânta, that the Çûdra's are shut out from the path of salvation. Of course birth in a particular caste is not a matter of chance, but the necessary consequence of conduct and works in a former existence; but, as the Vedânta makes no difference between the three higher castes, it should have been a logical consequence of its views (first however drawn by Buddhism), to admit the Çûdra too; for he also has a soul, he also is Brahman, and there is no conceivable reason why he also should not become conscious of this, and thus partake of the saving knowledge, especially as it is recognised that he is in need of it (p. 315, 11. 317, 3), and further the objector's argument of the Çûdra's qualification for knowledge (p. 315, 11) is not contested from a worldly point of view (p. 317, 4), as also his right, admitted by the Smṛiti, to participate in the hearing of the *Itihâsa*'s and *Purâṇa*'s (the epic and mythological poems) is not denied (p. 322, 14).

But the same accommodation to national prejudices which determines the philosophers of the Vedânta to derive all their knowledge, even by the most tortuous procedure from the Veda, makes it also impossible for them to admit the Çûdra; for a condition precedent to the study of the Vedânta, is the study of the Veda and a knowledge of its contents (p. 316, 9), for this again, the *Upanayanam* (initiation by a teacher), to which the Çûdra cannot attain (p. 317, 2, 320, 6), as the law (*smṛiti*) further forbids the reading aloud of the Veda, even in the presence of a Çûdra (p. 322, 2. 6).

With this is connected the discussion of certain cases occurring in the Veda itself, where a doctrine is apparently imparted to a Çûdra, or man of doubtful caste.

The first is that of the *Saṃvarga-vidyâ*, a theory (reminding one of Anaximenes) of *Vâyu* (wind) and *Prâṇa* (breath) as "*saṃvargâḥ*" (absorbers), on the one hand, of the elements, on the other, of the life-organs, which Chând. 4, 1—3 Raikva imparts to Jânaçruti, even after he has previously called him a Çûdra.[37]

---

[37] The wording of this legend, which shows in very drastic fashion that the knower of Brahman, be he ever so wretched, stands higher than the richest and best who does not know it, is as follows (Chând. 4, 1-2): "Jânaçruti, the grandson [of Janaçruta] was a dispenser, giving "much, cooking much. He had houses of rest built on all sides, that "men from all parts might eat with him. Once geese [or flamingoes] "flew past in the night. Then spoke one goose to the other: Ha there! "dim-eyed, dim-eyed [seest thou not] the splendour of Jânuçruti the "grandson is extended like the heaven; approach it not, burn not thyself.'— "To her the other said: 'Who is he of whom thou speakest, as though "he were Raikva with the car!'—'What is this—of Raikva with the "car?'—'As [at dice] to him who has won with the kṛita [the highest] "throw [or perhaps *vijitâya* from *vij*, cf. Ṛigv. I, 92, 10 *vijaḥ*] the lower "throws are also counted with it, so to him [Raikva] comes home all "the good the creatures do; and he who knows what he knows, for him "also is this true.'—This Jânaçruti the grandson over-heard. As soon "as he rose, he spoke to his steward [who praised him in the way the

On the other side, Çaṅkara reminds us firstly that a single case does not make a rule (p. 317, 9), and that what was right in the case of the Saṃvarga-vidyâ need nòt therefore be transferred to all other things (p. 318, 1); but after this both Sûtram and scholion (315, 6. 318, 10) affirm that "Çûdra" in the foregoing case is not to be taken in its tra-

" *Vaitâlika*'s were afterwards wont to do]: 'Thou speakest [of me] as if "I were Raikva with the car.'—'What is this—of Raikva with the car?' "—'As to him who has won with the kṛita throw, the lower throws are "also counted, so to him comes home all the good the creatures do; and "he who knows what he knows, for him also is this true.'—Then went "the steward forth to seek him. He came back and said 'I have not "found him.'—He [Jânaçruti] spoke to him: 'Go seek him where a "*Brâhmaṇa* [in the full sense, as Bṛih. 3, 5, 1. 3, 8, 10] is to be sought "[in solitude, in the forest, on a sandbank, in the river, in a remote "place,—as the scholiast explains].'—There sat one under his car, scratch-"ing his sores. To him he made obeisance saying: 'Art thou, venerable "one, Raikva with the car?'—'I am verily he,' he answered.—The steward "returned and said: 'I have found him.'—Then took Jânaçruti the grand-"son six hundred cows, a golden necklace, and a waggon with mules, "and went to him and said: 'Raikva! here are six hundred cows, here is a "golden necklace, here is a waggon with mules, teach me, venerable one, the "Godhead whom thou worshippest.'—To him answered the other: 'Ha, ha! "for a trinket and a yoke, thou Çûdra! keep them for thyself, with thy "cows.'—Then took Jânaçruti the grandson again a thousand cows, a golden "necklace, a waggon with mules and his daughter; he took them, and went to "him and said: 'Raikva! here are a thousand cows, here is a golden necklace, "here is a waggon with mules, here is a wife, here also is the village in which "thou sittest;—teach me, venerable one!'—Then raised he her face [sunk "in shame] and said: 'He has brought these [cows]; through this face "alone, Çûdra, thou wouldst have made me speak.'—Those are the "[villages] called Raikvaparṇa, in the country of the Mahâvṛisha's, where "he dwelt [at his invitation] and he spoke to him."

Then follows, in the mouth of Raikva, the *Saṃvargavidyâ*, which has, however, not the slightest connection with the foregoing narrative, so that one could substitute for it, quite as suitably, almost any other extract from the Upanishad's. Also the systematising at the beginning, the legend of Kâpeya and Abhipratârin in the middle, with its Trishṭubh verses, and the promise *"ya' evam veda"* at the conclusion, go to show that here, as so often in the Upanishad's, we have to do with two quite independent passages, originally placed side by side only perhaps because the kṛita throw occurs in both, carelessly united by a later editor, and in later times (*e. g.* by Çaṅkara, p. 1006, 7) expressly maintained to be connected with each other.

ditional sense (*rûḍhârtha*), but in its etymological sense (*avayavârtha*); namely because Jânaçruti from sorrow (*çu-câ*) at the humiliating speech of the goose, had run (*du-drâ-va*) to Raikva, this Ṛishi, who, through supernatural knowledge, became aware of what happened, and wished to make this evident, called him "*çû-dra*" (!). A subsequent (p. 319—320) direct proof that Jânaçruti was a Kshatriya, must be termed utterly inadequate, so far as it seeks by all kinds of quibbles to make it probable that the Abhipratârin mentioned in the Saṃvargavidyâ (Chând. 4, 3, 5) was a Kshatriya,—and therefore also Jânaçruti, because he is mentioned in the same Vidyâ (!). It is more arguable, as Çaṅkara insists in this connection, that Jânaçruti must have been a Kshatriya because he had a steward (*kshattar*) (p. 320, 2);—however this may be, the whole zealously prosecuted investigation only proves for us that, for the time of Çankara and also for that of Bâdarâyaṇa, it was by no means held to be self-evident that a man of princely wealth and pomp like Jânaçruti, could not have been a Çûdra, which is interesting from the point of view of the history of culture.

A further case is that of the boy Satyakâma, to whom his mother Jabâlâ declares she cannot tell him from what family (*gotram*) he comes, because in her youth she had had to do with too many; with childlike naiveté, Satyakâma (whose name, as M. Müller fittingly observes, means Φιλαλήθης) repeats this to the teacher who asks him concerning his family; the teacher finds that only a Brahman can be so sincere, and imparts the knowledge to him as such.[38]

---

[38] *Chândogya-Upanishad* 4, 4: "Satyakâma, the son of Jabâlâ, said "to his mother: 'Venerable one, I would enter as a Brahman student; "tell me of what family I am.'—She said to him: 'This I know not, my "boy, of what family thou art: in my youth I went about much as a "maid; there I got thee; I myself know not of what family thou art; "my name is Jabâlâ, and thy name is Satyakâma; so call thyself [instead "of after the father] Satyakâma, son of Jabâlâ.'—Then went he to Hâri-"drumata, the Gautama, and said: 'I would enter with thee, venerable "one, as Brahmacârin, deign to accept me, venerable one!' He said to "him: 'Of what family art thou, dear one?'—He said: 'I know not, oh "master, of what family I am. I asked my mother, and she answered

In this story Bâdarâyaṇa (p. 321, 5) and Çañkara (p. 321, 6) find a confirmation of the rule excluding the Çûdra, because Satyakâma is admitted only "after it is decided that he cannot be Çûdra because he spoke the truth" (! —*satya-vacanena Çûdratva-abhâve nirddhârite,*)—but we might rather conclude from it that in ancient times liberality was greater, and that there was a disposition to let the question of Brahmanhood by birth alone, where a Brahmanhood of heart and mind existed.[39]

However this may be, for our authors, the Çûdra, so long as he has not been raised on the path of transmigration to a higher caste,[40] remains entirely excluded from all share in the teaching of salvation. On the other hand the boundary of admission, which is so ungenerously narrowed below, is very generously widened above, so that not only all men of the three Aryan castes, but also the Gods, and the departed Ṛishis, are called to the study of the saving Brahmavidyâ.

"me: 'in my youth I went about much as a maid; there I got thee; I "myself know not of what family thou art; my name is Jabâlâ, and thy "name is Satyakâma;' so am I called Satyakâma, the son of Jabâlâ, oh "master.'—He said to him: 'only a Brahman can speak so frankly; bring "the fuel, dear one [that is necessary to the ceremony], I will take thee "because thou hast not departed from the truth.'"

In the continuation (Chând. 4, 5-9) Satyakâma while he is keeping cows, is first taught concerning the four four-fold feet of Brahman (4 cardinal points, 4 parts of the world, 4 sources of light, 4 organs of life), in order, by the bull, the fire, the goose and the diver, until he also receives the teacher's doctrine which "brings furthest." In the following section (Chând. 4, 10-15) Satyakâma is in his turn teacher of Upakosala, in whose case the supernatural teachings (like the miracles of Elija in the case of Elisha) are repeated.

[39] Cf. for this especially the Upanishad translated in Anquetil Duperron II, 372-377 under the name of "*Tschhakli*" (according to Stenzler's view = *Châgaleya*) and Weber's analysis of it, Ind. Stud. IX, 42-46.

[40] *Chând.* 5, 10, 7; *Âpastamba-dharmasûtra* 2, 5, 11, 10; ***Manu*** 10, 65.—In our work this one hope for the Çûdra so severily dismissed is, peculiarly enough, nowhere directly proclaimed; ***implicitly*** it is contained in the much used passage, Chând. 5, 10, 7, as also in the Smṛiti passage, Bhag. G. 6, 45, quoted p. 1045, 7.

3. Admission of the Gods; their rôle in the Vedânta system.

One would err if one held the being of the Gods (*deva, devatâ*) to be incompatible with the strict monistic teaching of our system of the Brahman as the Lord (*îçvara*) the omnipresent (*sarvagata*), the one without a second (*ekam eva advitîyam*). On the contrary, they are as real as the rest of the world: the phenomenal existence which the latter has, they also have, and the Gods of the Indian popular creed (whose retention was besides already necessitated by the recognition of the *Karma-kâṇḍa* and the *Karma-mîmâṅsâ* cf. above p. [18ff.]), are as little denied by the Vedânta as the Gods of Greece were by Plato or Epicurus, even if, as in the latter case, they play no particular rôle, and the ideas of them which are occasionally found cannot very well be made to agree.

In general the Gods, at whose head as a rule, *Indra* is mentioned,[41] are, for our authors, still what they were in the Rigveda, personifications of natural forces and natural phenomena; and an attempt to resolve them into the corresponding natural elements[42] is rejected in the following way (p. 309, 11):

---

[41] *Indra-âdayaḥ* p. 281, 8. 9. 282, 5. 7. 287, 4, etc.—From quite different ideas came the sporadically occurring *Hiraṇyagarbha-âdaya' îçvarâḥ*, who at the disappearance of the world do not disappear like the other Gods and beings, but, as it seems, only pass the time in sleep, and at the new creation of the world, help the *îçvara*; p. 300, 3. 4. 9. 301, 1. 303, 9; cf. *Hiraṇyagarbha* as *prathamaja* p. 339, 3, as *adhyaksha* in the lower world of Brahma p. 1121, 13; *mahân* (Kâṭh. 3, 11) as *Hairaṇyagarbhî buddhiḥ* p. 343, 3; *sarva-karaṇa-âtmani Hiraṇyagarbhe brahma-loka-nivâsini* p. 247, 6; *samashṭi-vyashṭi-rûpeṇa Hairaṇyagarbheṇa prâṇâtmanâ* 724, 8; and the (*râja-*)*Vaivasvata-âdaya' îçvarâḥ* p. 397, 8.

[42] (P. 307, 4). "To the disk of light dwelling in the heaven, which "lightens the world, mightily wandering by day and night [and the other "corresponding natural phenomena] apply the words which speak of Gods "as *Âditya* [the sun-god] and the like, as the ordinary use of the word, "as also the consistent sense of the passages shows; and it is not fitting "to ascribe to the light-disk individuality (*vigraha*) with a heart etc., "spirituality and needs and the like, as it is clear that, like the earth etc., "they are without spirit (*cetanâ*). This holds good also for Agni [Fire "and God of fire] and the others."

"The names of the Gods, like *Âditya* and so forth, even if "they refer to light etc., compel us, according to the scriptures, "to assume spiritual beings corresponding [to the elements] "gifted with *aiçvaryam* (ruling power); for they are thus "used in the Mantra's and Brâhmaṇa's; and the Gods have, in "virtue of their *aiçvaryam*, the power of remaining as the "Self (*âtman*) of light etc., or, according to their pleasure, of "taking this or that individuality (*vigraha*); for the scriptures "say, in explaining the *Subrahmaṇyâ* formula [Shaḍviṅça-br. "1, 1]: '*O ram of Medhâtithi*,'—*that is as ram he* [Indra, as "Çaṅkara adds] *once stole Medhâtithi, the scion of Kâṇva*;' and as the Smṛiti relates [Mahâbh. 1, 4397), Âditya, as a man "visited Kuntî; also the earth etc. have, according to the "scriptures, spiritual overseers, for it is said [Çatap. Br. 6, 1, "3, 2. 4] '*the earth said*'—'*the waters said*'; and, even if the "natural elements, as the light in the sun, and so on, are "without spirit, still they have, to judge by the part they play "in the Mantra's and Brâhmaṇa's, God-like beings as their "spiritual overseers."

As such "overseers" and "disposers," the Gods act especially in the life-organs (p. 186, 6: *devatâ-âtmâ indriyasya adhishṭhâtâ*, p. 728, 9: *karaṇânâm niyantrîshu devatâsu*), in which they entered according to Ait. 1, 2, 4, *Agni* as speech, *Vâyu* as breath, *Âditya* as eye, and so on (p. 423, 14); for, though the organs in themselves are capable (*çakta*) of doing their own work, yet they do it only like a cart, which must be drawn by an ox (p. 727, 1); however, the Gods do not therefore take part in the enjoyment [and suffering] which in the body is the lot only of the individual soul (p. 727, 13;—the Gods are only *bhoga-upakaraṇa-bhûta*, the soul alone is *bhoktar*, enjoyer, p. 379, 4), for the soul alone is stained by good and bad, affected by pleasure and pain (p. 728, 3), while the Gods are free from all evil (p. 728, 6); as also at death they do not wander forth with the life organs and the soul, but withdraw their assisting power (p. 745, 8), partly in order to hold intercourse on the moon with the (temporarily) blessed (p. 750, 5), partly, to show the way through the different heavenly regions, to the soul entering into the Brahman (p. 1117, 11).

As for the rest, the Gods dwell in the highest region of sovereignity (*parasmin aiçvarye pade* p. 728, 4), but all their *aiçvaryam* is dependent on the *Parameçvara* (p. 217, 7), the "highest lord," that is the Brahman: this is the *Âtman* (the (Self), as in everything else, so also in the Gods (*Âtmâ devânâm* Chând. 4, 3, 7); it is the *Antaryâmin* (inner ruler), which, according to Bṛih. 3, 7, inwardly rules all beings, all organs, and so also all Gods without their being conscious of it themselves, being for that reason, in this sense, different from their empirical self (*devatâtman*, p. 196, 6). The *Îçvara* (Lord), as the Brahman is called by preference in these exoteric discussions, is further the power that creates Gods, men and beasts, being guided in doing so strictly by the merit and demerit of the soul in a previous existence (p. 492, 12), and in accordance with this, has destined animals to unending suffering, men to a middle state, and the Gods to "unending enjoyment" (p. 491, 6). But this "unending enjoyment," like everything except the Brahman, comes at last to an end; the immortality of the Gods is a relative one (*âpekshikam* p. 326, 4. 241, 14) and means only longevity (p. 193, 12); they are also entangled in the *Saṃsâra* (the circle of transmigration), are mere products (*vikâra* p. 195, 13. 280, 3) doomed to transitoriness and want; for, as the scripture (Bṛih. 3, 4, 2) says: "whatever is different from Him is subject to sorrow" (p. 241, 15), and for this reason the Gods also are called to the saving knowledge, as we shall now consider more closely.

First it is to be noted that the Gods are nowhere in the scriptures excluded from the Brahmavidyâ (p. 281, 1). They have, it is true, no part in the *Upanayanam* (initiation by a teacher), but they do not require this; for the aim of this ceremony is merely admission to the study of the Veda, which is of itself revealed (*svayaṃ-pratibhâta*) to the gods (p. 281, 3). Moreover, there are even instances of gods and Ṛishis becoming Brahman pupils, like Indra of Prajâpati (Chând. 8, 7—12) and Bhṛigu of Varuṇa (Taitt. 3, 1). In the hearts of the Gods too (according to Kâṭh. 4, 12) dwells the *Purusha* (Brahman) "a thumb's breadth in height," for the purpose of knowledge,—

naturally in the case of the gods, we are to understand the breadth of a God's thumb (p. 282, 1).

Moreover, the Gods are capable of liberation, because, according to the witness of the Mantra's, Brâhmaṇa's, Itihâsa's, Purâṇa's and popular belief, they possess individuality (*vigraha-vattvam*) (p. 280, 9), and need liberation, because their power (*vibhûti*) belongs to the sphere of the changeable and is therefore transitory (p. 280, 7).

Now against these two assumptions very serious difficulties are raised.

First objection: The asserted individuality of the gods, says the opponent, is neither real nor possible. It is not real, because, although the gods are present when sacrifices are offered to them, they are not perceived (p. 282, 7), and it is not possible, because individuality cannot be in several places at the same time; but the gods can so, since Indra for instance is often recipient of offerings in several places at the same time (p. 282, 8).

To this it is to be rejoined: The gods are not seen at sacrifices, because they have the power to make themselves invisible (p. 284, 5), and they can be in several places at the same time, because they are able to divide their being (*âtman*) into different forms (p. 284, 4); for if even the *Yogin*, according to the *Smṛiti* (Mahâbhâratam 12, 11062), can multiply his body a thousand-fold, in order to enjoy the things of sense in one form, and to undergo frightful penances in another (p. 283, 9), how much more to the gods, who, according to one Vedic passage (Bṛih. 3, 9, 1), are first counted as 303 and 3003, that is 3306, and then as only 33, with the explanation that the greater number indicates only their powers (*mahimânas*), as the 33 are again reduced to one only, since the being of them all is *Prâṇa*, the Life (that is, here, the Brahman) (p. 283).

Second objection: If the gods are, like ourselves, individuals, they must also, like ourselves, be born and die[43]; now

---

[43] P. 285, 7; a quite correct deduction, which is also not contested by Çaṅkara, but is in another place expressly stated by him (p. 598, 11:

the Veda is eternal (in the spirit of the Creator, who "breathed it out" as the Vedânta affirms, p. 48, 6 after Bṛih. 2, 4, 10), and the Veda speaks of the gods. How is this possible if the gods are not also eternal (p. 285, 8)?

This objection forces the composer of the commentary, and, perhaps, even the composer of the Sûtra's (cf. 1, 3, 30), to a very remarkable theory, which comes very close to Plato's doctrine of ideas; and, as we have no ground at all for supposing that either side has borrowed from the other, this bears witness to the fact, that there is something in the nature of things, which tends towards Plato's teaching, to lead to which the teaching of the Indian can be of use.

It is true, he says, the individual Gods are transitory, and the word of the Veda, which speaks of them, is eternal; but the words of the Veda, for instance the word "cow" occurring in the Veda, does not refer to individuals (to any separate cow), but to "the object of the words: cow etc." (*çabda-artha* p. 286, 6), that is, to the species; and in just the same way the word "Indra" means, not an individual, but a certain position (*sthâna-viçesha*), something like the word "General;" whoever occupies the position, bears the name (p. 287, 5).

Therefore we must make a distinguish between the individuals (*vyakti*, p. 286, 7, and also p. 464, 5, literally: "manifestation"), which are transitory, and the species (*âkriti*, that is "form," "shape," "εἶδος,") which are eternal; p. 286, 7: "For though the individuals, as cows etc. originate, their "species do not thereby originate; for in substances, qualities "and activities originate the individual appearances (*vyakti*), "not the forms of the species (*âkriti*), and only with the species, "not with the individuals are the words [of the Veda] connected, "for with the latter, on account of the eternity [of the Veda],

---

yadd hi loke iyattâ-paricchinnaṃ vastu ghaṭa-âdi, tad antavad drishṭam) with a profound feeling that what is limited in space must be so in time also; of which the sole exception, perhaps is matter (that is) if its quantity in space is limited, (which we do not know), which, however, as such, is an abstraction without individual existence.—Among the Greeks this thought was expressed by Melissos, ap. Simplic. in Aristot. *Phys.* fol. 23b: οὐ γὰρ ἀεὶ εἶναι ἀνυστὸν, ὅ,τι μὴ πᾶν ἐστι.

"no connection can be admitted. Therefore, though the individuals originate, the species, in words like cow etc., are eternal; "therefore there is no contradiction; in just the same way there "is no contradiction in the case of names [of the gods] like "Vasu and the like, because the species of the gods are eternal, "even when an origin is admitted for the individuals."

These eternal species of things, as they are stored up in the Veda as the everlasting repository of all wisdom and knowledge, are, however, for our author not mere forms (*âkṛiti*, εἶδος), but the conception of them, exactly as in Plato (Soph. p. 247 D. ff.) approaches that of the efficient powers (*çakti*, δύναμις), from which the universe, after its disappearance, originates again and again; p. 303, 1: "This world in truth "disappears, but in such fashion that the powers remain, and "these powers are the root from which it comes forth anew; "for otherwise we should have an effect without a cause. Now "it cannot be assumed that the powers [from which the world "comes forth anew] are different in kind [from those from which "it formerly came forth]. Therefore it must be granted that, "in spite of the constantly repeated interruption [of the course "of the world], a necessary determination (*niyatatvam*) exists "in the beginningless Saṃsâra for the [newly] developing series "of worlds, as the earth etc., for the series of groups of living "beings, gods, animals and men, and for the different con-"ditions of castes, Âçrama's, duties and rewards, like the "necessary determination in the correlation of the [five] sense-"organs with the [five] elements: for in the case of these "also, we cannot admit as possible a difference for each new "creation, so that there might be a sixth sense-organ and "element.[44] While therefore the process of the world in all "world-periods (*kalpa*) is similar and makes it possible [in a

---

[44] P. 303, 7: *shashṭha-indriya-vishaya*; in the same way, as an example of impossibility p. 415, 1: *shashṭhasya iva indriya-arthasya.*—Of other scholastic examples, to indicate impossibility, there occur in our work: *bandhyâ-putra* (the son of the barren) p. 570, 12 and *çaça-vishâṇam* (hare's horn) p. 564, 1. 4. 8. 565, 7. Cf. 332, 8: *sa prâçîm api diçam prasthâpitaḥ pratîcîm api diçam pratishṭheta* (for "for him all things are possible"); the same image as Xenoph. *Memorab.* 4, 2, 21.

"new creation] to be guided according to the process in the "former world-period, therefore at every creation the differences "of the same names and forms are present in the mind of the "creators (*îçvarâḥ* cf. n. 41), and in consequence of the likeness "of names and forms it happens that, even if a return of the "world by means of a collective evolution and a collective "disappearance is maintained, yet the authority and so forth "of the word of the Veda suffers no injury."

Thus the word of the Veda, with its whole complex of ideas of the world and its relations, forms an eternal rule of guidance for the Creator, outlasting every disappearance of the world. The Creator "remembers," while he shapes the world, the words of the Veda (p. 297, 10), and thus the world originates with its constant forms (*niyata-âkṛiti*) as the gods and the rest; from the word of the Veda (p. 298, 2). Naturally this coming forth of the gods etc. from the Veda is not, like the evolution from the Brahman, to be taken in the sense of a *causa materialis* (*upâdâna-kâraṇam*), but it means only "a coming forth of the individuals of things in conformity with the use of the words of the scriptures" (*çabda-vyavahâra-yogya-artha-vyakti-nishpattiḥ*, p. 287, 9), which were there before the world, not only according to the witness of scripture and tradition (p. 288), but also because they are the necessary pre-supposition of creation. For if one wishes to make anything, one must first call to mind the word that indicates it (p. 289, 3), and thus also before the creation the Vedic words were present in the spirit of the Creator, and, according to them, he shaped all things (p. 289, 5).

But what are we to understand by "word" in this world-creating sense (p. 289, 9)?—Perhaps we might answer: the concepts corresponding to the words. But this answer the Indian cannot give, because he never reached a conscious separation of concept and perception. He answers in the first place: By word he understands[45] here the *Sphoṭa* (the burst-

---

[45] Who? is not said. It is the opponent, but not Çaṅkara, as Cowell assumes in Colebr. M. E.[3] p. 373 n. 1; what Cowell quotes is only the *Pûrvapaksha*, not the *Siddhânta*, which *Upavarsha* afterwards maintains; probably Çaṅkara took the whole discussion from his commentary (cf. n. 17).

ing forth, the sudden coming to consciousness of the idea on hearing the letters of the word); and this conception leads to a discussion which is not without interest, and which, as a contribution to the Philosophy of Language, we here translate as accurately as possible in the form of an episode.

4. Episode: on the vedântic philosophy of language (translated from p. 289, 10—297, 7).

[The Opponent, who defends the *Sphoṭa*, says:] "An origination "of individuals, such as gods etc., from the eternal words [of the Veda] "is not possible, on the assumption that the letters [of the word are the "bearers of its meaning], for they as soon as they appear, pass away. "Not only so but the letters which pass away as soon as they have "appeared are continually apprehended differently according to their "pronunciation. Thus it is possible, for example, to recognise a man with "certainty, even without seeing him, when we hear him read aloud, by "his voice, and to say 'Devadatta is reading,' or 'Yajñadatta is reading.' "And this diversity of apprehension of the [same] letters is, how- "ever, not based on error, because there is no apprehension which "could refute it.—It cannot, therefore, be assumed at all that the "meaning of a word is recognised [merely] from the letters. For [*firstly*] "it cannot be assumed that each single letter in itself makes known the "sense, because they are different from each other; [*secondly*] [the sense "of the word] is also not [merely] a conception of the sense of the "letters, because they succeed each other [so that the earlier have already "passed away when the latter are pronounced]. It is perhaps [*thirdly*] "that the last letter, assisted by the impression [*saṃskâra*], which the "perception of the preceding letters has produced, makes the sense known? "—This also is impossible. For [only] the word itself, presupposing "the apprehension of the connection [of the letters], makes the meaning "known, as in the case of smoke [whose vanishing and continually "reproduced particles alone are not able to give the conception of smoke]. "Further, an apprehension of the 'last letter, assisted by the impression, "which the perception of the preceding letters has produced,' is not "possible, because the impressions are not [any longer] perceptible.—Is "it then perhaps [*fourthly*] the last letter, assisted by the impressions [of "the preceding] perceived in their after effect, which makes the sense "known?—Not this, either; for the recalling also, as it is the after effect "of the impressions, is again a series [of presentations in time,—which "has already been discussed above, under the second head].—Therefore "it only remains possible that the word [as a whole, that is, its sense] is "a *Sphoṭa* [an outbursting], which, after the percipient has received the "seed of the impression through the apprehension of the single letters, "and has brought it to ripeness by means of the apprehension of the last "letter, flashes before him suddenly in its unity as a single conception. "And this single conception is no reminiscence, referring back to the "letters; for the letters are several, and cannot, therefore, be the object "of the single conception. This [*Sphoṭa*, the soul of the word, as we might "say,] is [only] recognised again, [not produced], on the occasion of its "pronunciation, and is therefore eternal [as well as a unity,] because the "conception of the manifold refers only to the letters. Thus the word, "[that is, its sense] in the form of the *Sphoṭa* is eternal, and from it, "as that which names, goes forth as that which is to be named, the world, "consisting of deed, doer and fruits."

"In reply, the venerable Upavarsha" [an old Mîmâṅsâ and Vedânta "teacher, cf. above, Note 17, and Colebrooke Misc. Ess.[3] I, 332] "main-"tains that only the letters are the word."

[Opponent:] "But I have said, however, that the letters, as soon "they appear, pass away."

[Upavarsha:] "This it not so, because they are again recognised "as the same."

[Opponent:] "That they are recognised again, depends in their case "on the fact that they resemble [the former], somewhat as in the case "of hairs (cf. on Bṛih. 743, 2)."

[Upavarsha:] "O no! For that it is a recognition [of the same, "not merely of like], is not refuted by any other recognition."

[Opponent:] "Recognition is grounded on species (*âkṛiti*)." [When I say *a* repeatedly, it is not the individual *a*, but the species *a*, which recurs in different individuals.]

[Upavarsha:] "No; it is a recognition of individuals. Yes, if in "speech other letters were continually apprehended, as in the case of "other individuals, for example, cows, then recognition would be grounded "on species; but this is not so; for only the individual letters are re-"cognised again in speaking, and [if the same word, for example, 'cow,' "is repeated,] then it is assumed that the word 'cow' has been spoken, "twice, not two words 'cow' [once].

[Opponent:] "But the letters are still [as argued above] apprehended "as different, according to the difference of pronunciation; for when the "reading aloud of Devadatta and Yajñadatta can be recognised by the "tone, merely by hearing them, it results from the fact that a difference "is apprehended." [Therefore the recognition of a letter must be that of the species, not of the individual differing according to pronunciation.]

[Upavarsha:] "Without detriment to the exactness of the recognition "in the case of the letters, letters may be pronounced [more] joined or "[more] separated; hence the different apprehension of the letters is "grounded on the difference of pronunciation, not in the nature of the "letters. Further: he also, who transfers the difference to the individual "letters [instead of the manner of pronunciation], must, if a recognition "is to be possible, [first] settle species for the letters, and then assume, "that these [species] are differently apprehended owing to foreign in- "influences; and here it is preferable to assume, as simpler, that, in the "case of the individual letters, the apprehension of the difference is con- "ditioned by foreign influences, while, on the other hand, their recognition "is conditioned by their own nature. For the assumption that there is "a difference in the letters, is refuted precisely by the fact that a re- "cognition of them takes place."

[Opponent:] "But how can it happen that the sound *ga* which is "one, is at the same time different, when several pronounce it at the "same time, and [likewise] when it is pronounced with the acute, grave, "or circumflex accent, or without the nasal?"

[Upavarsha:] "But this difference of apprehension is not caused "by the letters, but by the tone (*dhvani*)."

[Opponent:] "What is tone?"

[Upavarsha:] "That which reaches the ear, when one hears sounds "from a distance, and does not perceive the difference of the syllables, "and which prompts one sitting near to attribute his own differences of "stupidity and sagacity to the letters [which he hears]. And from this "[the tone] depend attached the differences of accentuation with the "acute etc., and not the nature of the letters. But the letters are re- "cognised just as they are pronounced [independently of the tone]. If "this be assumed, then the perceptions of accentuation have a basis, "otherwise not; for, as regards the letters, they are only recognised "again, and do not differ [in themselves]; therefore we should have to "assume that the differences of accentuation lie in their connection and "separation; but connection and separation are not perceptible, and we "cannot take our stand on them, in order to arrive at an explanation "of the difference of the letters; consequently the perception of accen- "tuation etc. would have no basis [without the assumption of tone].—We "must not fall into that error either that, because the accentuation is "different, the letters to be recognised are also different. For because "one thing shews differences, another, which is not different does not "need to shew them also; as, for example, one does not conclude that "the species is different, because individuals differ among themselves. "And as it is thus possible to recognise the sense from the letters, the "hypothesis of the *Sphoṭa* is unnecessary."

[Opponent:] "But the *Sphoṭa* is no hypothesis, but an object of "perception. For in the understanding (*buddhi*), after it has received "[different] impressions through apprehension of the single letters, [the "sense of the word] flashes out suddenly."

[Upavarsha:] "This is not so: for this understanding [of the sense "of the word] also refers to the letters. For after the apprehension of "the separate letters [of the word 'cow,' for example,] has preceded in "time, there follows this single concept (*buddhi*)—'cow,' whose object is "the totality of the letters and nothing else."

[Opponent:] "How do you prove this?"

[Upavarsha:] "By the fact that with the concept which thus comes "into being [cow], the letters *C* etc., and not the letters *T* etc., are connected; "for if the object of this concept were a *Sphoṭa*, something different "from the letters *C* etc., then the letters *C* etc., would have just as little "to do with it as the letters *T* etc.; but this is not so; and therefore this "simple concept [of the idea] is [not a *Sphoṭa*, but] *only a reminiscence* "*connected with the letters.*"

[Opponent:] "But how is it possible, that the different letters are "the object of the simple concept?"

[Upavarsha:] "To this we answer: a thing which is not simple can "also be the object of a simple concept, as is seen in examples like: series, "forest, army, ten, hundred, thousand, and the like. For the understand- "ing of the word 'cow' as a unity, since it is conditioned by the extract- "ing of one sense from many letters, is a metaphorical one (*aupacârikî*), "just as is the understanding of forest, army, and the like."

[Opponent:] "But if the mere letters, by entering, in their totality, "into the sphere of a simple concept, formed the word, then no difference "would be made between words like *jâ-râ* (paramours) and *râ-jâ* (king), "*ka-pi* (ape), and *pi-ka* [cuckoo), for the letters are the same, yet in a "different connection they give a different sense."

[Upavarsha:] "To this we answer: even when all the letters are "perceived, just as ants can only form our idea of a row, when they are "in a row, so the letters can only form the concept of a word, when they "keep their sequence [this is only an evasion of the opponent's objection] "and there is no contradiction in the fact that, even when there is no "difference in the letters, a difference in the words may be perceived in "consequence of a different order of letters. Therefore since certain "letters perceived in their order etc. are, according to the traditional "usage of language, connected with a given meaning, apprehended "[through them], though they are perceived in their own proper function "as single letters, our unifying understanding becomes conscious of them "simply as this or that, and they thereby convey this or that given sense. "—Therefore the assumption that the letters [are the bearers of the sense] "is the simpler, while the assumption of a *Sphoṭa* leaves the sensible "and hypostatises the supersensible, by which it is assumed that these "given letters, perceived in order, reveal the *Sphoṭa* and this *Sphoṭa* "reveals the sense; which is certainly complicated enough. Admitting "therefore that the letters, according as they are pronounced, are different "in each case, it must yet undeniably be assumed, that as that on which "recognition rests is an identity existing in the letters, and that in the "case of the letters the deliberate design of communicating the sense is "transmitted in this identity."

Author's note. The truth in this controversy probably lies between the two extremes. The Opponent is right, in so far as philosophy cannot dispense with the acceptance of ideas (for ideas are reasonably to be understood by the *Sphoṭa*), and Upavarsha is right, in so far as ideas exist only so far as words exist (retained by memory). Moreover, the relation between idea and word is certainly no mere external, conventional one, but originally inner and organic; but why just these sounds express just this idea, is a problem which philosophy, comparative philology and physiology have hitherto worked at in vain, yet the solution of which can and will never be abandoned by science.

IV. Qualifications of those called to the study of the Vedânta.

1. The Study of the Veda.

An indispensable condition of our science, the impossibility of fulfilling which in the case of the Çûdra, as we saw, (p. 58 ff.) excluded him from the saving doctrine, is the study of the Veda, and this requirement, or at least the appearance of it, seems to have been continually more exaggerated in course of time. Thus it is said in *Sadânanda's Vedântasâra*, a later compendium of the Vedânta, § 5: "He who is called to the study must have regularly studied the Veda and the Vedângas (that is, the six subsidiary sciences of the Veda: phonetics, grammar, etymology, metre, ritual and astronomy, as they are already enumerated Muṇḍ. 1, 1, 5) so, that he may be able to understand the full sense of the Veda *ex tempore (âpâtataḥ)*,"—a requirement which, considering the extent of the Veda[46] and the great difficulty of many Vedic texts, in the strict sense of the word no one except Brahmán can have fulfilled, while men must have satisfied themselves, in the case of each hymn for instance, with imprinting accurately on their memories the metre, poet, deity and ritual purpose, and at the same time, perhaps, also understanding something of the sense.[47] Of such exaggerations we find no trace in Çañ-

---

[46] There is no question of a limitation to one's own *çâkhâ* (cf. p. 979, 4: *samasta-veda-artha-vijñânavataḥ*), and such a limitation would also not include all the Upanishad texts presupposed by the Vedânta.

[47] Cf. Colebrooke, Misc. Ess.[1] p. 20, and in Çaṅkara's work (p. 301, 8) the quotation from the *Ârsheya-brâhmaṇam* p. 3: "For whoever employs a hymn for sacrifice or study without knowing the Ṛishi, Metre, Godhead, and ritual use of it, knocks against the trunk of a tree, or falls into a pit."

kara: he contents himself with simply indicating the study of the Veda and a knowledge of its contents as an indispensable condition (p. 24, 4. 316, 9); what he actually presupposes apart from the occasional quotations of other Vedic texts (cf p. 32), is hardly more than an accurate knowledge of the eleven older, or, as we might almost say, of the genuine Upanishad's (*Aitareya* and *Kaushîtaki*; *Chândogya* and *Kena*, *Taittirîya*, *Kâṭhaka*, *Çvetâçvatara* and *Brihadâraṇyaka* with *Îçâ*; *Muṇḍaka* and *Praçna*), with quotations from which he everywhere deals very liberally; generally quoting only the opening words with the "etc." which is unfortunately so common in Indian texts, and which sometimes slips from him even where there is nothing more to follow (cf. p. 269, 4), and greatly injures the precision of treatment. As we cannot in general assume in our readers such an acquaintance with the Upanishad texts as the Indian could in his, we shall interweave in our presentation an anthology embracing a series of the most beautiful and important passages of the Upanishad's, even if we do not select them according to a standard of our own, but in accordance with the texts of the scriptures employed by Bâdarâyaṇa and Çaṅkara.[48]

---

[48] The most important part of what has already been done for the Upanishad's, excepting editions of texts (by Roer, Weber, Cowell, Polcy and others) is as follows: Anquetil Duperron, *Oupnek'hat*, Argentorati 1801–1802, a Latin translation of 50 Upanishad's from the Persian into which Sultan Daraschakoh, 1656 A.D., had had them translated, contains: Vol. I, p. 15 *Tschehandouk*, 98 *Brehdarang*, 294 *Mitri*, 375 *Mandek*, 395 *Eischavasieh*, 400 *Sarb;* Vol. II, p. 1 *Naraïn*, 5 *Tadiw*, 12 *Athrbsar*, 27 *Hensnad*, 35 *Sarbsar*, 68 *Kok'henk*, 94 *Sataster*, 128 *Porsch*. 152 *Dehian band*, 157 *Maha oupnek'hat*, 162 *Atma pra boudeh*, 165 *Kioul*, 171 *Schat roudri*, 197 *Djog sank'ha*, 200 *Djogtat*, 204 *Schiw Sanklap*, 207 *Abrat (athrb) sak'ha*, 213 *Atma*, 217 *Brahm badia*, 221 *Anbrat bandeh*, 229 *Tidj bandeh*, 232 *Karbheh*, 241 *Djabal*, 249 *Maha naraïn*, 266 *Mandouk*, 271 *Pankl*, 274 *Tschehourka*, 279 *Pram hens*, 286 *Arank*, 291 *Kin*, 299 *Kiouni*, 328 *Anandbli*, 338 *Bharkbli*, 346 *Bark'heh soukt*, 351 *Djounka*, 355 *Mrat lankoul*, 358 *Anbratnad*, 366 *Baschkl*, 372 *Tschhakli*, 378 *Tark*, 380 *Ark'hi*, 387 *Pranou*, 403 *Schavank*, 412 *Nersing'heh atma;* for the corresponding Sanskrit names see below. A German translation of this translation of a translation has appeared Dresden 1882.—Ram Mohun Roy, Translation of several principal books, passages and texts of the Veds, ed. II, London 1832 (contains *Muṇḍaka*, *Kena*, *Kâṭhaka*,

2. The four Requirements.

As further conditions for the study of the Vedânta, Çañkara mentions (p. 28, 3), in conformity with the Vedântasâra, the four requirements which we shall now consider more closely.

Îçâ).—Colebrooke, Misc. Ess.[1] I, p. 47–54. 62–71. 76–79. 83–88. 91–98. 110–113.—F. W. Windischmann, Sancara, Bonnae 1833, p. 49–186.—The same in his father's "Philosophie im Fortgange der Weltgeschichte," Bonn, 1832–34, p. 1388–90. 1448–49. 1540. 1585–91. 1595–98. 1613–23. 1655–60. 1673–76. 1689–1719. 1737–40.—Poley, *Kâṭhaka*-Oupanichat (with *Muṇḍaka*) translated into French, Paris 1837.—Roer, the *Taittirîya, Aitareya, Çvetâçvatara, Kena, Îçâ, Kaṭha, Praçna, Muṇḍaka* and *Mâṇḍûkya* Upanishads, translated, Bibl. Ind., Calcutta 1853.—The same, the *Bṛihadâraṇyaka* Up. transl. Calc. 1856.—Râjendralâla Mitra, the *Chândogya*-Up., transl. Calc. 1862.—Cowell, the *Kaushîtaki*-brâhmaṇa-upanishad, ed. with an Engl. Transl., Calc. 1861.—The same, the *Maitri* Up., Calc. 1870.—A. Weber, Analyse der in Anquetil Duperron's Übersetzung enthaltenen Upanishad, Ind. Stud. I, p. 247–302. 380–456. II, 1–111. 170–236 IX, 1–173, Berl. 1849. 1853. Leipz. 1865; the only thorough treatment of the material existing up to the present (1883). An index (wanting in the Ind. Stud.) is added here for more convenient reference: Vol. I: p. 254 *Chândogya*, 273 *Bṛihadâraṇyaka*, 273 *Maitrâyaṇî*, 279 *Muṇḍaka*, 298 *Îçâ*, 301 *Sarvopanishatsâra*, 380 *Nârâyaṇa*, 381 *Tadeva*, 382 *Atharvaçiras*, 385 *Haṅsanâda*, 387 *Sarvasâra* (Aitareya-Up.), 392 *Kaushîtaki*, 420 *Çvetâçvatara*, 439 *Praçna*; Vol. II, p. 1 *Dhyânavindu*, 5 *Mahâ*, 8 *Âtmaprabodha*, 9 *Kaivalya*, 14 *Çatarudriyam*, 47 *Yogaçikshâ*, 49 *Yogatattva*, 51 *Çivasaṃkalpa*, 53 *Atharvaçikhâ*, 56 *Âtma*, 57 *Brahmavidyâ*, 59 *Amritavindu*, 62 *Tejovindu*, 65 *Garbha*, 71 *Jâbâla*, 78 *Mahânârâyaṇa*, 100 *Mâṇḍûkya*, 170 *Çâkalya* (?), 170 *Kshurikâ*, 173 *Paramahaṅsa*, 176 *Âruṇika*, 181 *Kena*, 195 *Kâṭhaka*, 207 *Ânandavallî* (= Taitt. 2), 230 *Bhriguvallî* (= Taitt. 3); Vol. IX, p. 1 *Purushasûkta*, 10 *Chûlikâ*, 21 *Mrityulâṅgûla* (?), 23 *Amritanâda*, 38 *Vâshkala*, 42 *Châgaleya* (?), 46 *Târaka*, 48 *Ârsheya* (?), 49 *Praṇava*, 52 *Çaunaka* (?), 53 *Nrisiṅha*.—The same, Die *Vajrasûcî* des Açvaghosha, Berl. 1860.—The same, Die *Râmatâpanîya* Up., Berl. 1864.—The same, Ind. Lit.[2], p. 54–57. 77–81. 103. 106–109. 139–154. 170–190.—A. E. Gough, The Philosophy of the Upanishads, Calcutta Review, CXXXI, 1878–1880. —P. Regnaud, Matériaux pour servir à l'histoire de la philosophie de l'Inde, Paris 1876–78; cf. Weber's Critique of the first part, Jenaer Liter.-Z. 1878 Nr. 6, p. 81ff.—F. Max Müller, The Upanishads, translated, part. I, Oxford 1879 (Sacred Books of the East, Vol. 1); the first volume includes the Introduction and *Chândogya, Kena, Aitareya, Kaushîtaki, Îçâ*; the second (Vol. XV, 1884) contains *Kâṭhaka, Muṇḍaka, Taittirîya, Bṛihadâraṇyaka, Çvetâçvatara, Praçna, Maitrâyaṇa*. For

1) The first is "discerning between eternal and non-eternal substance" (*nitya-anitya-vastu-viveka*); by eternal substance Brahman is meant, and by non-eternal every thing else. As this discernment in the full sense of the word is really the last result of our science, we are to understand by it here, where it appears as condition precedent, only the general metaphysical disposition in virtue of which one has a consciousness of an unchanging being, in contrast with the changeableness of all worldly things and relations; in this sense the said condition of the Vedânta agrees exactly with the question with which Plato begins his exposition of metaphysics, and which also pre-supposes the consciousness of the same difference: "τί τὸ ὂν ἀεί, γένεσιν δὲ οὐκ ἔχον, καὶ τί τὸ γιγνόμενον μὲν ἀεί, ὂν δὲ οὐδέποτε" (Tim. p. 27 D).

2) The requirement which Çankara, and (better, because without *artha*) Sadânanda, mention in the second place, gives us a high conception of the earnestness of Indian thought: it is "Renunciation of the enjoyment of reward here and in the other world" (*iha-amutra-[artha-]phala-bhoga-virâga*). Only as far as we pursue philosophy without the consciousness of following material aims at the same time, do we pursue it worthily and rightly,—and he only can hope to find an explanation of the highest questions of being who has learned to raise himself above all hopes and longings of the heart to pure objectivity of spirit.

3) There is more misgiving about the third requirement, as which Çankara gives "the attainment of the [six] means, peace, restraint, etc." (*çama-dama-âdi-sâdhana-sampad*). This is based on a passage in the Bṛih. Up., where, at the end of a wonderful description of the *Akâmayamâna,* that is, the man who already in this life, through the power of knowledge, has reached freedom from all desires, it is said in conclusion (Bṛih. 4, 4, 23): "Therefore he who knows this is "peaceful, restrained, resigned, patient and collected; only in "the Self he sees the Self, he beholds all as the Self (the Soul,

---

further refs. cf. now my "Sechzig Up. des Veda übersetzt mit Einleitungen und Anmerkungen, Leipzig 1897."

"*âtman*); evil vanquishes him not, he vanquishes evil; evil burns "him not, he burns evil; free from passion and free from "doubt, he becomes a Brâhmaṇa, he whose world is the "Brahman." Fitting as all this is, when said of the saint who has overcome the world, it is strange when the Vedântists, relying on the passage, enumerate the possession of the following six means as conditions precedent to knowledge:—

1. *Çama* Tranquillity,
2. *Dama* Restraint,
3. *Uparati* Renunciation,
4. *Titikshâ* Resignation,
5. *Samâdhi* Concentration,
6. *Çraddhâ* Belief.

The explanation of these conceptions by Çañkara (on Bṛih. loc. cit.), Govindânanda and Sadânanda, with numerous divergencies in detail, amounts to this, that, under No. 4, they all understand an apathy towards contraries like heat, cold, and the rest, in the sense of the Stoics; under Nos. 1, 2, 3, 5, on the other hand, an inner concentration along with a full withdrawal of the senses from the objects of the outer world. Neither of these will fit the picture that we form of the true philosopher to-day. In contrast to the Stoic sages (whose model was certainly not Heraclitus, the real father of the Stoic doctrine), we imagine the philosophic genius rather as a profoundly excitable, nay, even passionate nature; and, in spite of all concentration and meditation, we demand from him, as from the empiric investigator, a full interest in the visible world and its wonderful phenomena, only that he must see them with other eyes than the empiric, in a word, to use an expression of Plato's (Scholia in Ar. ed. Brand., p. 66 B 48), not only with the eye which sees the ἵππος, but also with that which sees the ἱππότης. And just as little will the requirement demanded from the pupil under No. 6 commend itself to us, since we have learnt from Descartes, that the beginning of wisdom consists in this, *de omnibus dubitare.*

4) As fourth and last requirement for the study of the Vedânta, Çañkara and Sadânanda name *Mumukshutvam*, "the

longing for liberation." And rightly so. For he who enjoys the day of life with childlike, Hellenic, cheerfulness, however high a flight his genius may take in other respects, will only touch in passing the last and highest problems of being, as did the Greeks; to seize them fully and clearly requires a deep feeling of the vanity and nothingness of all this life, and a corresponding longing to pass "*from the non-existent to the existent,* "*from darkness to light, from death to immortality*" (Bṛih. 1, 3, 28), a longing by which, as the passage quoted leads us to believe, the Indians were inspired even in ancient times, and which remained the true motive principle of their philosophy; so that, exceptions apart, the question of liberation forms the corner-stone of all the philosophic systems of India.

3. Relation of the System to that of Justification by Works.

The already enumerated requirements in the elect are, according to Çañkara, the only ones which are indispensable. As soon as (*anantaram*) they are fulfilled, the "investigation of the Brahman" can begin (p. 29, 4); and it is not necessary that the "investigation of duty," that is, the study of the Mîmâṅsâ of Jaimini (cf. above p. 20), should precede it (p. 28, 4); on the contrary it may just as well follow as go before (p. 25, 1), since the contents and aim of the two systems are independent; the investigation of duty demands observance, as Çañkara (p. 27) remarks; and refers to a future, dependent on the action of men, and has, as its fruit, *abhyudaya* (going upward, happiness, both transitory in heaven, and also earthly in a future birth), but the investigation of the Brahman, on the contrary, has as its fruit *niḥçreyasam* (literally: *quo nihil melius, summum bonum*), that is, liberation; it refers to a something which has always existed, not dependent on the action of men; it does not command, like the other, but only teaches, "as if, in teaching concerning any thing, it is brought before the eyes" (p. 28, 1, cf. 818, 7); therefore all imperatives, even if they are taken from the scriptures, are, when directed to the knowledge of Brahman, as blunt as a knife with which one would cut a stone (p. 76, 3); therefore also all the commands of the scripture, that we should investigate the Brahman, have only the meaning that they turn the thoughts from their natural tendency towards outward things (p. 76, 6) and the egoistic aims bound up with them (p. 76, 7), through which the eternal goal of mankind is not reached (p. 76, 8), and give them a direction towards the inner soul, in order then to teach them about the existence of the soul (p. 77); as also further, for him who knows the Brahman, all commands and prohibitions cease to be in force: "for this is our ornament and pride (*alaṃkâra*), that after the knowledge of the soul as the Brahman all obligation of action ceases, and all past actions are annihilated" (p. 77, 7).

However freely, as is visible in these quotations, our science raises itself above the whole legal system with which the Brahmans had succeeded in fettering the spirit of the Indian peoples, yet it hardly ventures at all to carry this into practice. Only for him who has won the knowledge of the Brahman, as we shall see further on more in detail, do all laws cease[49]; but, as long as this point is not reached, the four *Âçramas*, or stages of practice in which, according to Brahmanical law, the life of each twice-born has to traverse the steps of Brahman pupil, householder, hermit and beggar (above p. 15 ff.), along with the works prescribed in them, remain in force (p. 1008, 5): "For [only] full-grown knowledge requires "nothing else for the perfecting of its fruit [liberation]; yet it "certainly requires other things, in order that it may first "grow. Why? Because of the passage of scripture which "speaks of sacrifice and so forth. For thus says the scripture "(Bṛih. 4, 4, 22): 'The Brahmans seek to know this [the "'highest spirit], by reading the Veda, by sacrifice, by gifts, "'by penances, by fasts'; and this passage shows that sacrifice "&c. are a means of knowledge; and, as it is therein said, "'they seek to know,' therefore this limits them to being a

[49] p. 1007, 1: "For knowledge [alone] is the cause through which the goal of man is reached; therefore, after this goal has been gained through knowledge, the works of the *Âçramas*, such as kindling the fires &c., are not [further] to be observed."

"means for the growth [of knowledge]." In the same way, by the passages Chând. 8, 5, 1, Kâṭh. 2, 15 and others it is "shown that the works of the *Âçramas* are a means of knowledge" (p. 1009, 4). Their difference from the means, tranquillity &c., enumerated above, consists only in this, that the latter continue even for those who have gained knowledge, and thereby form the more immediate (*pratyâsanna*) means, while sacrifice &c. are to be considered as the external (*vâhya*) means, since they exist only for those who are striving after knowledge (p. 1012, 4). These external means, sacrifices, gifts, penances, fastings, are to be followed by every one with the exception of those who have reached knowledge, whether desiring liberation or not (p. 1017, 9); in the latter case the obligation to fulfil them lasts the whole life, in the former, for a time only (p. 1019, 2), since they are only helpful in gaining knowledge, but, this once gained, become superfluous. For thus teaches scripture (p. 1008, 9. 1019, 4), it also shows, how he who possesses the means of Brahma-scholarship &c., will not be overcome by affections (*kleça*), such as love [and hate] (p. 1021, 3). In what their collaboration towards knowledge further consists, is not more definitely determined; according to p. 1044, 4, they are to collaborate towards the knowledge which arises from the hearing of the scriptures, by destroying the hindrances which may exist; these hindrances consist in this, that other works of a former birth may come to ripeness, whose fruit may be a hindrance to knowledge; if the power of the stated means be the stronger, it overcomes the other fruits of works, and knowledge is gained (p. 1043, 4); but if, on the other hand, the hindrances are stronger, the pious practices, in virtue of the metaphysical power (*atîndriyâ çaktiḥ*) which dwells in them, as in all works (p. 1044, 1), bring forth knowledge in the next birth, in which, as was the case, for instance, with *Vâmadeva* (Ait. Up. 2, 5. Bṛih. 1, 4, 10), it may occasionally exist even from the mother's womb (p. 1044, 10).

But how stands it with those who, on account of wretched circumstances, lack of means and the like, cannot fulfil the religious duties of the *Âçramas*, and thus stand, as it were, in the middle,[50] between the twice-born and the Çûdras (p. 1021, 8)? They also, thus declares the answer, as is seen, for instance, in the case of *Raikva* (cf. n. 37), are called to knowledge (p. 1022, 1), although it is better to live in the *Âçramas* (p. 1024, 2). For those whose condition is wretched, we must admit that, either on the ground of ordinary human actions, such as repetition of prayers, fasts, worship of the gods (p. 1023, 1), or also in consequence of the works of the *Âçramas* performed by them in a former birth, the grace (*anugraha*) of knowledge is bestowed on them (p. 1023, 6). And here we touch a very remarkable conception, concerning which we shall try further on to reach perfect clearness, but the material for which we shall introduce here, in order to direct the reader's whole attention to it.

4. Liberation through "the Grace" of Knowledge.

How is the knowledge that leads to liberation, that is, the recognition of the Brahman, produced in men? To begin with, we must remember that it is not a question of gaining something which we did not possess; to gain it is impossible, since the Brahman is actually nothing else than our own self (p. 71, 7). But what have we to do, in order to become conscious of this? This is briefly answered by the passage, p. 69, 7: "The knowledge of the Brahman is not dependent "on the action of man, but on the contrary, just like the "knowledge of a thing which is an object of perception and "other means of knowledge this also depends only on the "object [that is, on the Brahman]." One must also not think that the recognition of the Brahman is an effect of the action of investigating (p. 69, 10), or of worshipping (p. 70, 3); and even the scriptures are its source only so far as they destroy Ignorance concerning the Brahman (p. 70, 7), just as they have no further significance for the state of awakening (*prabodha*) (p. 1060, 11); nay (p. 70, 10), all investigation and

[50] *Antarâ* 3, 4, 36, explained by Çañkara as *antarâle;* if we understand the expression rightly, it means, what we were before (n. 13) not able to conclude with certainty from Manu, that the *Âçramas* were obligatory on all three *Dvija* castes.

knowledge, so far as subject and object are thereby separated, is a direct hindrance to the recognition of the Brahman, as says the scripture (Kena-Up. 2, 11, recalling the Gospel according to Matthew, XI, 25):

"Who doth not know, he knoweth it
"And he who knoweth it, doth not;
"Unknown it is to him who knoweth
"And known to him who doth not know."

Under these circumstances, according to the mode of expression of the exoteric, theological teaching, in which the philosophy of our system is framed,[51] the birth of knowledge and the liberation connected with it, appears as a grace of God (literally: of the Lord *îçvara*), as becomes clear from the two passages which we here quote:

P. 682, 3: "For the individual soul, which is impotent, in "the condition of Ignorance, to distinguish [from the soul] "the aggregate of the organs of activity [appearing as the "body], and is blind through the darkness of Ignorance, from "the highest soul, the overseer of the work; the onlooker "dwelling in all being, the Lord who is the cause of spirit, "from him, by his permission, comes the Saṃsâra, consisting "in the states of doing and enjoying (suffering), and through "his grace, is caused knowledge, and, through this, "liberation."

P. 786, 7: "Granted, that the soul and God are related "as the part and the whole, yet it is evident that the soul "and God are of different character. How stands it, then, "with the identity of God and the soul? Does it exist, or "does it not?—In truth it exists, but it is hidden; for Ignorance "hides it. But, although it is hidden, yet, when a creature

[51] That in the conception of grace (as in general in the whole apprehension of *Brahman* as *Îçvara)* we have to do only with an exoteric personification, which is not to be taken strictly, becomes also clear from the fact that p. 1023, 9 the *Saṃskârâḥ* (moral purifications) are likewise spoken of personified, as *anugrahîtâro vidyâyâḥ*. Cf. on the teaching of grace, besides the two above quoted chief passages, also p. 662, 1, where the *para âtman* is spoken of as *cakshur-âdi-anavagâhya* and *jñâna-prasâda-avagamya*; to the teaching of creation refers the *parameçvara-anugraha* p. 300, 3. 301, 2. There are no further passages as far as we know, in which the conception of grace occurs.

"thinks on and strives towards the highest God, just as the "faculty of sight in one who has become blind, after the "darkness is shaken off by the power of remedies, in him, in "whom the grace of God perfects it, does it become mani-"fest, but not naturally in any being whatsoever. Why? "Because through him, through God as cause, the binding "and loosing of the soul are accomplished, binding when it "does not recognise the essence of God, and loosing, when it "does. For thus says the scripture (Çvet. 1, 11):

"When God is known, all fetters fall away,
"All torments cease; birth is no more nor death;
"And he who knows him, when his body dies,
"Has for his lot blest freedom and release."

V. Source of the Vedânta.

1. General Remarks on the Indian Pramâṇas or Canons of Knowledge.

WHAT are the sources from which we draw our knowledge? This question, of which every philosophy has to give an account, meets us in the Indian systems largely in the form of a consideration of the *Pramâṇas*, literally, "measures" or "canons," of our knowledge; in which, therefore, not the concept of a source from which we draw is the basis, but on the contrary that of a means of control, by which we are to measure the knowledge already existing in us, and test its correctness, a concept which is explained by the fact that Indian philosophy did not start, as far the most part the Grecian did, from an investigation, free of assumptions, into "the existent," but rather, like modern philosophy, from the critical analysis and testing of a complex of knowledge handed down (through the Veda)[52]. As such *Pramâṇas*, or canons of knowledge, the systems, as a rule, enumerate: 1) *Pratyaksham*, also called *dṛishṭam*, the sensuously perceptible, as it is known to us by direct perception; 2) *Anumânam* "the measuring after something," inference, by which that part of "the existent" which does not fall within direct perception,[53] becomes acces-

---

[52] An essential difference consists in modern philosophy in its fundamental character, even up to to-day, being a toilsome struggle and gradual shaking off of the fetters of mediæval scholasticism,—while the Indian philosophy through all time has been the better, the more closely it has adhered to the basis laid down in the Vedic Upanishads. But in truth this basis is also of an eminently philosophical character.

[53] By this is explained the fundamental proposition of the theory of knowledge, that where *Pratyaksham* exists, there is no *Anumânam* p. 657, 9: *pratyakshatvâd anumâna-apravṛitteḥ.*

sible; we know of it only because the perceptible points to something else, not perceptible, with which it is connected. This connection can be threefold, according as the element to be inferred is either the cause of the element perceived, or its effect, or as, thirdly, the two stand in a relation which does not fall under the conception of causality, for example, in that of analogy.

These two spheres of knowledge, the perceived and the inferred, embrace naturally the whole complex of "the existent." The position of the Cârvâkas (materialists) who will only allow validity to the first is crude but correspondingly little objection can be raised, when the Vaiçeshikas and Bauddhas (Buddhists) will not go further than these two *pramâṇas.* For it is very strange that the Sâṅkhyas and others add to these also 3) *Âptavacanam,* that is "right communication," which then, again, according as it is understood, means secular or religious tradition. For the former goes back again to *Pratyaksham* and *Anumânam* and the latter is, in philosophy, no legal component, and is one of the means by which the Sâṅkhyas and others, with all their heresy, were yet able to keep up an appearance of orthodoxy. Through further splitting up of *Anumânam,* not to the advantage of clearness, the adherents of the Nyâya reached four, the Mîmâṅsakas of the school of Jaimini six, and others even nine Pramâṇas (cf. Colebr. *Misc. Ess.*[1] p. 240, 266, 303-304, 330, 403).

2. Insufficiency of the secular Canons of Knowledge.

Like the *Pûrva-mîmâṅsâ,* the *Vedânta* also accepts six canons of knowledge, according to Colebrooke (*loc. cit.* p. 330), who appeals for support to the (modern) *Vedântaparibhâshâ.* As far as our Vedânta-sûtras are concerned, there is, neither in the text nor in the Commentary, any discussion of the Pramâṇas at all; on the contrary they are everywhere presupposed as well known, and set aside as inadmissible for the metaphysics of the Vedânta,[54]—and in reality a fundamental ac-

[54] p. 49, 2: "Only from the canon of scripture as means of knowledge "is the Brahman known as the cause of the coming into being and "[existence and passing away] of the world;" p. 488, 1: "only through

count of the fact that metaphysics attains its contents only through a right use of the natural means of knowledge, is very difficult, and presupposes a greater ripeness of thought than we find in the Vedânta, which helps itself out of the difficulty by the short cut of substituting a theological for the philosophical means of knowledge, as we shall now further show.

As for Bâdarâyaṇa, he expresses his rejection of the secular means of knowledge, *Pratyaksham* and *Anumânam* with the drastic brevity which characterises him, in this, as we have already remarked (above p. 23), that he uses the two words to indicate something altogether different, namely the *Çruti* and *Smṛiti*; thus in the Sûtras 1, 3, 28. 3, 2, 24. 4, 4, 20 (supposing, naturally, that Çaṅkara has explained them correctly). The *Çruti*, therefore, the holy scriptures, in the narrower sense the Brâhmaṇas and Upanishads, but also the Mantras presupposed by them, that is, hymns and formulas,[55] are for Bâdarâyaṇa the *Pratyaksham*; the revealed is for him self-evident, needing no further authority. It is otherwise with the *Smṛiti*,[56] under which name Çaṅkara quotes testimonies from the Sâṅkhya and Yoga systems, from the law-book of Manu, from the Mahâbhâratam and Purâṇas, as also from the Vedic Sûtra literature. For while the *Veda*, like the sun, which has its own light, possesses unconditional authority (*nirapeksham prâmâṇyam* p. 414, 6), the *Smṛiti* is called *Anumânam* because, as Çaṅkara, p. 287, 11, explains, for its support another basis of authority (*prâmâṇyam*) is necessary. As, namely, the secular

"the scripture can one plunge into this deepest, highest Brahman; one "cannot plunge into Him by reflection." Of passages where the *Pramâṇas* are mentioned, we have noted, besides these the following: the *pramâṇâni, pratyaksha-âdîni* are *avidyâvad-vishayâṇi* (p. 17, 13); they are frail (p. 448, 1); are common to us and animals (p. 19, 6): *pratyaksham* is *rûpa-âdi, anumânam* &c. is *liṅga-âdi* (p. 426, 8. 438, 1); of different character is *anubhava*, permissible, according to 42, 4, in the investigation of Brahman, cf. 419, 2 *anubhava-avasânam brahma-vijñânam*; the monstrosity of an absolute perception (subject without object) occurs on p. 671, 2; cf. 96, 5.

[55] Thus, for example, passages of the Ṛigveda-Saṃhitâ are quoted as Çruti p. 208, 13. 212, 1. 304, 4; on the contrary the *mantra* is opposed to the *çruti*, p. 308, 4.

[56] As also with the *Âcâra* (above p. 24); cf. p. 990, 1: *smṛiti-âcârâbhyâm, na çruteḥ*.

Anumânam rests on the *Pratyaksham*, and only has the force of proof so long as it is rightly inferred therefrom, the *Smṛiti* also is only so far valid as an authority, as it confirms the Çruti by its testimony, and completes it by right inference. Therefore it is frequently quoted in confirmation, but not seldom also rejected; as for instance 4, 2, 21, in reference to the departure of the soul, the ideas of the *Smṛiti* (Bhagavadgîtâ 8, 23) are only so far rejected as they are in contradiction to the *Çruti* (p. 1109, 5). For the rest Bâdarâyaṇa declares himself, 2, 1, 11, as opposed in principle to any possibility of basing the metaphysical verities on reflection (*tarka*), which is commented on by Çañkara as follows (p. 435, 11):—"And, therefore, mere reflection (*kevalas tarkaḥ*) must not be quoted in opposition in a matter which is to be known by [sacred] tradition (*âgama*); for reflections which, without [sacred] tradition, rest only on the speculation (*utprekshâ*) of men, are untenable, since this speculation is unbridled. For instance the reflections thought out by some experts after great trouble are recognized by others, still more expert, as [merely] apparent, and those of the latter in the same way by others. Therefore one cannot rely on it, that reflections have stability, because the opinions of men vary. But [it may be objected], when there is a man of recognised greatness, a *Kapila* or another, who has made a reflection, one could at least rely on it as well-founded. Even here a sound foundation is lacking, since even the recognised pioneers (*tîrthakara*) such as *Kapila*, *Kaṇâda* and the like, openly contradict each other." To this the opponent objects: "Yet one can, perhaps, come to a well-founded reflection, in reflecting in a different way, for that there can be no well-founded reflection at all is in itself a law based on reflection alone (p. 436, 7); and because one reflection is false, the other need not also be false; the opinion that all reflection is unreliable, would make an end of all worldly action resting thereon (p. 436, 10)." Reflection, he says, might have in view the consideration of the words of scripture, in order to reach in this way the full truth (p. 437, 1); even *Manu* (12, 105) recommends, besides the tradition of scripture, perception and inference; and the excellence of reflection is precisely this, that, unbound by previous reflections, in case they are untenable, other reflections may be made (p. 437, 7). To this Çañkara replies (p. 437, 10): "Even though it appear that in many provinces reflection is well-founded, yet, in the province here spoken of, reflection cannot be freed from the reproach of baselessness; for it is impossible to know at all this extremely profound essence of being *(bhâva-yâthâtmyam)*, without the [sacred] tradition, connected with liberation; for this subject does not fall within the province of perception *(pratyaksham)*, because it is without form and the like, and therefore also not within the province of inference *(anumânam)* and the other [Pramâṇas], because it has no characteristics [*liñgam*] and the like." Here, as our author further develops the question, where the full truth and the liberation which results from it—as all admit—are being considered, the subject of knowledge must be identical, and the knowledge of it uncontradictable. But reflections do not fulfil these conditions, because they contradict each other, and what the one maintains, another overthrows, and what the latter puts in its place, yet another overthrows (p. 438, 9). Besides, the Sâñkhya system is not in any way recognised by everyone as the highest, and in any case it is impossible to bring together all the thinkers of all lands and times, to establish firmly the final truth of reflection among them. But, on the other hand, the Veda, as a source of knowledge, is eternal; its subject stands fast; the full knowledge of it formed therefrom cannot be turned aside by all the reflecters of the past, present and future (p. 439, 5). By this the full validity of the Upanishad teaching is proved, and by this it is established, "in virtue of the [sacred] tradition and the reflection which follows it" that (which was to be proved) the spiritual Brahman is at once the *causa efficiens* and the *causa materialis* of the world (p. 439, 7).

Çañkara expresses himself even more strongly in discussing the same point in another place. To the objection that the Brahman can only be *causa efficiens* and not also *materialis*, because experience (*loka*) shows that only a *causa efficiens*, as for instance, the potter, can be endowed with knowledge, he answers (p. 403, 7): "It is not necessary that it should be here the same as in experience; for this subject [Brahman] is not known by inference (*anumânam*), but only by revelation (*çabda*), and it is therefore [only] necessary here that [which is to be proved] it should be in accordance with revelation, and this shows that the knowing *Îçvara* (Lord) is the *causa materialis* [of the world]" (cf. p. 1144, 13).

In these circumstances it is possible occasionally to make such statements about the Brahman as would be, according to worldly standards, absolutely contradictory; for example, that the Brahman does not wholly enter into the phenomenal world, and yet is without parts: (p. 481, 13) "in the scripture the Brahman is rooted; in the scripture it has its ground of knowledge, not in sense-perception and the like; therefore it must be taken as scripture gives it; and scripture teaches of the Brahman both that it is not wholly [used up in forming the world of appearances], and that it is yet without parts. Nay, even in the case of worldly things, such as amulets, spells, drugs and the like, it happens that, in virtue of difference of place, time, and cause, they manifest powers with various contradictory effects, and even these cannot be known by mere reflection without instruction, nor can it be determined, what powers, with what accompaniments, referring to what, for what available, a given thing may have,—how can it then be possible to know the nature of the Brahman, with its unthinkable perfections of might, without the scripture?"

This advantage, however, of being allowed occasionally to ignore experience, holds good only in the case of the Vedânta teacher, but not of his opponent (p. 595, 8): "The follower of the Brahman investigates the being of the cause [of the world] and the like, relying on the [sacred] tradition, and it is not unconditionally necessary for him to accept every thing in accordance with perception (*na avaçyam tasya yathâ-drishṭam eva sarvam abhyupagantavyam*); but the opponent, who investigates the being of the cause [of the world] and the like, relying on the examples of experience (*drishṭânta*), must accept everything according to experience,—that is the difference."

3. The Revelation of the Veda.

To mitigate the severity of these declarations, we must call to mind the details given in Chap. II, 2 (reading especially the passage in n. 32, above p. 56), according to which all empirical means of knowledge, and all the world produced by them, belong to the realm of *Avidyâ*, as also, on the other hand, that in the Veda, especially in the Upanishads, there are philosophic conceptions which have their like neither in India, nor, perhaps, anywhere else in the world. Therefore we can well understand our author's view that the Veda is of superhuman origin (*apaurusheya* p. 170, 2); that it is infallible (p. 618, 1); that, as we saw above p. 69ff., the Gods are created, but the Veda, on the contrary, is ever-present in the spirit of the creator of the world, as the timeless rule of being; that it was "out-breathed" by him[57], concerning which the two chief passages are (p. 47, 2): "The great canon of scripture beginning with the Ṛigveda, which, enforced by many branches of knowledge, lights all things like a lamp, and in a certain measure is omniscient, has the Brahman as its origin and cause. For such a canon as the Ṛigveda and the rest, which is endowed with the quality of omniscience, can come from none but an omniscient source." And further (p. 48, 4): "The great being which, according to the scripture [Bṛih. 2, 4, 10] brought forth unwearying in sport, like the outbreathing of a man, the Ṛigveda and the rest, as a mine of all knowledge, which is the basis of the division into Gods, animals, men, castes, Âçramas and the like, this being must possess an unsurpassable omniscience and omnipotence."

As the Brahman itself is free from all differences, so also is the knowledge of the Brahman, as we gain it from the

[57] We have thus in India, as analogy of our Inspiration, an Expiration, through which the Vedic texts were revealed to their composers, who are therefore called *Ṛishis*; the Mantras and Brâhmaṇas "appear" (*pratibhânti*) to them, are "seen" (*drishṭa*) by them; cf. p. 301, 6: "Çaunaka and the other [composers of Prâtiçâkyas] teach, that the Decades [of the Ṛigveda] were seen by ***Madhucchandas*** [the composer of the opening hymns of the Ṛigveda] and the other *Ṛishis*." In the same way, according to p. 314, 13, the Brâhmaṇas were also seen by the *Ṛishis*: ***rishîṇâṃ mantra-brâhmaṇa-darçinâm***; cf. p. 119, 3: ***mantra-brâhmaṇayoç ca ekârthatvaṃ yuktam, avirodhât.***

Upanishads, uniform throughout and without contradiction (p. 834, 4): "Has it not been established that the Brahman, the object of knowledge, is free from all differences, as before, behind, and the like, uniform, and, like the lump of salt [Brih. 4, 5, 13], of one taste? How, then, can the thought arise of a difference or non-difference of knowledge? For that, like the variety of [pious] works, a variety with reference to the Brahman could be taught by the Vedânta, can by no means be affirmed, since the Brahman is one and uniform. And if the Brahman is uniform, then the knowledge of the Brahman cannot be manifold; for the assumption that the subject can be one thing and the knowledge of it another, is necessarily erroneous. And if, on the other hand, there were to be taught different doctrines of the one Brahman in the Vedânta, of which some were true and others false, we should have the case of disbelief in the Vedânta [that is, the Upanishads] [cf. p. 104, 1],— therefore one cannot assume that there are in the Vedânta differences in the knowledge of Brahman." In conformity with this principle, the numerous contradictions in the Upanishads are explained away (1, 1, 27 may serve as an example), or hidden under the broad mantle of exoteric doctrine, of which we shall speak in the next Chapter. However, occasionally minor contradictions in the parallel texts of the Upanishads are admitted with the remark, that they are not important.[58] Where the sense of the scripture is doubtful, the rule of experience (*laukiko nyâyaḥ*) decides, p. 1064, 5: "But still it is unseemly to check the view of the scriptures "by a rule of experience? To this we answer: this is so, where "the sense of the scripture is certain; but where it is doubt-"ful, it is permissible to have recourse to a rule of experience, "for the sake of clearing up the question;"—as generally the the worldly means of knowledge are helpful to the investigation of the sense of the scriptures (p. 40, 6): "The knowledge of "the Brahman is gained by the sense of the word of the Veda

[58] For example p. 222, 2. 849, 11. 855, 6: *na hi etâvatâ viçesheṇa vidyâ-ekatvam apagacchati.*—418, 12 *çrutînâm paraspara-virodhe sati, ekavaçena itarâ nîyante.* This especially holds good in the case of contradictions in things where the aim of man (*purusha-artha*) does not come into question, p. 374, 7.

"being considered and determined; it is not gained by other "means of knowledge, such as inference (*anumânam*) &c. But "although it is the Vedânta texts which inform us of the "cause of the world's coming into existence &c., yet, to make "sure that we have grasped their sense [correctly], an inference "which does not contradict the words of the Vedânta is not "excluded as a means of knowledge. For by the scripture "itself [Bṛih. 2, 4, 5. Chând. 6, 14, 2] reflection is called in as "a help."—(p. 42, 3): "For in the investigation of the Brahman, "the scripture is not, as in the investigation of duty [the *Pûrva-"mîmâṅsâ*], the exclusive authority, but the authorities here "are, according to circumstances, the scripture and the [inner] "perception (*anubhava*) and the like. For the knowledge of "the Brahman reaches its final point in perception, as far as "it refers to a really existing subject."—(p. 44, 6): "But does "not the Brahman, so far as it is something really existing, "alone belong to the province of other means of knowledge, "and is not the consideration of the words of the Vedânta "consequently aimless? By no means the Brahman, for, as "it is not an object of sense, the [causal] connection with "the world would not be grasped [with certainty]. That is to "say, the senses, according to their nature, have as their object "external things, and not the Brahman. If the Brahman were "an object of sense, then the world might be grasped as an "effect connected with Brahman. Now, we only perceive the "effect, so that [without revelation], it cannot be decided whether "the world is connected with Brahman [as cause], or with "something else [for the same effect can have different causes]."

Of the possibility here suggested, of bringing in reflection as an aid, our author makes a far more extensive use than might appear from these expressions. Since this side of Çaṅkara's work has for us the chief interest, we will, as far as possible, pass over his endless quotations from the Veda, but, on the other hand, bend our whole attention to the philosophic reflection. The perfection of the latter, as it meets us in Çaṅkara's Commentary, may itself speak for the fact that we have to do here with a monument of Indian antiquity not merely theological, but also in the highest degree philosophical.

VI. Exoteric and Esoteric Vedânta Doctrine.

1. Justification of Exoteric Metaphysics.

ALL metaphysics has to battle with the great difficulty, unique in the whole province of science, that it must think in conceptions and express in words what is properly contrary to their nature, since all words and conceptions at last spring from that very base of empiric reality which metaphysics undertakes to transcend, in order to lay hold on the "Self" (*âtman*) of the world, the "ὄντως ὄν" the "thing in itself," which finds its expression and manifestation in all empiric reality, yet without being identical with it.

So far, then, as metaphysics adapts itself to the form of empirical knowledge, in order thereby to express its own content, it necessarily assumes an allegorical, more or less mythical character; and, as this is the only form in which it can be grasped by the people, standing in need of it (ἐκείνοις δὲ τοῖς ἔξω ἐν παραβολαῖς τὰ πάντα γίνεται, St. Mark, IV, 11), is called exoteric metaphysics. So far as, on the other hand, it adheres to the path of exact science, in order to attain to a Whole, thoroughly demonstrable in all its parts, and equal to any opposition, metaphysics must often choose difficult bypaths, turning conceptions through many shades of meaning, with all kinds of reservations, and in many cases entirely renounce results that can be clearly represented.—And all this demands a great power and habit of abstraction, attainable only by few; therefore for this form of our science the name of esoteric metaphysics is to be taken.

2. Exoteric and Esoteric form of the Vedânta.

a) General Survey.

In accordance with what has been said, the metaphysics of the Vedânta also has two forms, a theological, exoteric, and a philosophical, esoteric form; both are present in the work which we have to analyse, running parallel, and being present in all the five provinces of the Vedânta teaching, namely, the theology, cosmology, psychology, the doctrine of transmigration, and that of liberation; they stand in a continuous contradiction which is necessitated by the nature of the matter. But the great difficulty for the philosophic understanding of the Brahmasûtras lies in the fact, that neither in the text nor in the commentary are the two conceptions clearly separated from each other, but rather meet us everywhere interwoven with each other, in such sort that the fundamental texture of the whole consists of a representation of the exoteric, or, as we may also call it (with an extension of the conception, whose justification will be given in what follows) the lower doctrine (*aparâ vidyâ*), which, however, is penetrated in every province by the esoteric or higher doctrine (*parâ vidyâ*), standing in contradiction to it, a relation which compels us to justify our general view here at the outset.

As is shown by the analysis of contents at the conclusion of our first chapter, the doctrine of the Vedânta consists properly in a richly coloured picture of the world on a mythological ground. The first part contains, in Adhyâya I, the theology, which on the basis of seven times four passages of the Upanishads, discusses the essence of the Brahman, its relation to the world as creator, ruler and destroyer, its relation to the soul, and its various names and attributes. This is followed, in Adhyâya II, by the cosmology which is concerned with the relation of the world to the Brahman as cause, its gradual evolution from and re-absorption in it, and, from II, 3, 15 on, the psychology, in which are thoroughly discussed the nature of the soul and its organs, its relation to God, to the body, and to its own deeds. In Adhyâya III comes first the doctrine of transmigration, then a supplement to the psychology (III, 2, 1—10), another to the theology (III, 2, 11—41); the rest of the Adhyâya contains a miscellaneous assemblage of discussions, for the most part exegetic in character, as the chief content of which we can, in any case, with Çañkara (p. 1049, 3), consider the teaching of the means (*sâdhana*) to attain the higher and lower doctrine, that is the knowledge and worship of the Brahman. For the most part these discussions deal with the strange question whether certain passages of the Veda are to be comprehended in one "Vidyâ," or to be separated, a question which has a meaning only for the lower doctrine, with its aim of worship. Finally, the conclusion of the work, Adhyâya IV, contains the eschatology; it sketches in detail the departure of the soul after death, and how some souls follow the way of the Fathers (*pitṛiyâna*) to a new incarnation, while, on the contrary, others, the worshippers of the Brahman, are led along the way of the gods (*devayâna*) higher and higher upwards to the Brahman, "whence there is no return"—according to the Upanishads, but not without further conditions, according to the reasoning of our system: for this Brahman is only the "lower" Brahman, that is, as considered as possessing attributes (*guṇa*), it is the object of worship, and not of "perfect knowledge" (*samyagdarçanam*); only after this latter, that is, the esoteric doctrine, is imparted to the pious in the world of Brahman, is he also liberated; until then, although he is in the world of Brahman, and a partaker of Lordship (*aiçvaryam*), "his darkness is not yet driven away" (p. 1154, 9), "his ignorance not yet destroyed" (p. 1133, 15), that is, he possesses only the lower doctrine (*aparâ vidyâ*), whose content consists of all that has hitherto been mentioned, not the opposed higher doctrine, the *parâ vidyâ* or *samyagdarçanam*, that is, the pure philosophic, esoteric doctrine, which, in every part of this picture of the world with its empiric colouring, crops up in contradiction with it, and whose results, according to the metaphysical standpoint which we occupy, we may find strange, or admirable. In the department of Theology it teaches that the Brahman is not thus or thus, but altogether without attributes (*guṇa*), distinctions (*viçesha*) and limitations (*upâdhi*), and therefore in no way capable of being defined or conceived. And this Brahman, devoid of all limitation, is the only being, outside which nothing is; therefore, in the department of Cosmology, there can be as little question of the origin of the world as of its existence, but only of there being neither anything different (*nânâ*) from the Brahman, nor any plurality of things (*prapañca*), and that the world extended in names and forms is non-existent (*avastu*), is only a glamour (*mâyâ*) which Brahman, as master-magician (*mâyâvin*), projects (*prasârayati*), as the dreamer projects dream forms (p. 432, 8). In the same way all further Psychology falls away, after the saying "*tat tvam asi*" (that thou art), is comprehended according to which the soul of each human being is not an emanation, not a part of the Brahman, but fully and completely the Brahman. For him who knows this, there is no more migration of the soul, nor even liberation; for he is already liberated; the continued existence of the world and of his own body appears to him only as an illusion, the appearance of which he cannot remove, but which cannot further deceive him, till the time when, after the decease of the body, he wanders not forth, as the others, but remains where he is and what he is and eternally was,—the first principle of all things, "the originally eternal, pure, free Brahman."

This is the *Samyagdarçanam*, the *Vidyâ* in the stricter sense of the word, distinguished on the one side from empiric cosmology, and psychology, *Avidyâ*, and on the other from the doctrine of the *aparam, saguṇam brahma*, of its worship and the entering into it by the way of *devayâna*; this is the *aparâ vidyâ, saguṇâ vidyâ*, whose possessor can, however, also on occasion be called *vidvân* (p. 1095, 11. 1134, 11). Strictly viewed, this *aparâ vidyâ* is nothing but metaphysics in an empiric dress, that is *Vidyâ* as it appears, considered from the standpoint of *Avidyâ* (the realism innate in us). This definition is not, however, found in Çañkara, as in general the distinction of the esoteric and exoteric doctrine and the inner connection of the latter, as well as of the former, does not attain the clearness with which we express it and must express it here, unless we have to renounce a full comprehension of the system. What prevented our author from connecting together—as he did in the case of the *parâ vidyâ*—the *aparâ vidyâ* also, with his doctrine of the creation of the world and Saṃsâra, in the unity of an exoteric system, was firstly the excessive attention which, in Indian fashion, he paid to theological and eschatological questions, and, on the other hand, the apprehension of injuring the letter of the Veda, in which esoteric and exoteric teaching are interwoven, by a recognition of the contradictions between them. For this reason, for instance, he takes endless pains to maintain the teaching of the creation of the world through the Brahman, and to unify it with his better insight into the identity of the two, by trying to show that cause and effect are identical, and then constantly (*e.g.*, p. 374, 12. 391, 10. 484, 2. 491, 1) asserting that the doctrine of creation had only the aim of teaching this identity of the world with the Brahman, a view which cannot be brought into harmony with the ample and realistic treatment which he himself bestowed on it.

Naturally we shall do no violence to our author, and where, in the organism of his system, we note a false connection, we shall only indicate it, and not remedy it; but, on the other side, we have the right to exercise philosophic criticism and this will be the better, the more it is done entirely from within, that is, from the principles of the system itself. For in every philosophical system lies something more than its originator put into it; the genius reaches further than the individual, and it is the task of the historian to indicate where the thinker has lagged behind the full scope of his thoughts.

To this end we must be allowed here, at the outset of our exposition of the system, to bring together the passages which justify our general view of it; they will form the beacons to which we have to look for guidance on our laborious and dangerous journey, and from them we shall take the standard to test where our author has fallen short of the greatness of his own point of view.

b) Exoteric and Esoteric Theology.

Quite clearly and consciously, if not everywhere carried out in detail, do we find the contrast made between exoteric and esoteric doctrine in the province of Theology, under the names of the lower, attribute-possessing (*aparâ, sagunâ*), and the higher, attributeless doctrines (*parâ, nirguṇâ vidyâ*); the former is the doctrine of the lower, attribute-possessing Brahman, the latter of the higher, attribute-free Brahman (*aparam, saguṇam, saviçesham*, also *kâryam, amukhyam brahma*, and *param, nirguṇam, nirviçesham*, also *avikṛitam, mukhyam, çuddham brahma*); the former is the object of worship, the latter of knowledge; in the case of the former doctrine the fulfilment of duties is commanded; but not in the latter (p. 1077, 7); the former has many different rewards, the only fruit of the latter is deliverance.

The most important passages are as follows:

(p. 111, 3:) "The Brahman is known in two forms, [1.] as "qualified by limitations (*upâdhi*) which are derived from the "multitude of his metamorphoses in respect of names and forms, "and [2.] on the contrary as free from all limitations."

(p. 803, 3:) "There are passages of twofold character (*liṅgam*) "referring to the Brahman; the one, as *e. g.* 'all-working, all-wish- " 'ing, all-smelling, all-tasting,' etc. [Chând. 3, 14, 2, cf. p. 50 above] "indicate that it is affected by difference (*viçesha*); the others, "*e. g.*, 'not coarse, not fine, not short, not long,' etc. (Bṛih. "3, 8, 8), indicate its freedom from all differences . . . But "it is not admissible to assume from the passages of twofold "character that the highest (*param*) Brahman has itself "(*svatas*) this double nature; for one and same thing cannot "in itself be affected by differences such as form, etc., and "not be affected by them, for this is a contradiction . . . And "by being connected with limitations (*upâdhi*) a thing of a "one kind cannot assume another nature; for when rock crystal "is transparent, it does not become opaque by being connected "with limitations such as red colour and the like; on the con- "trary it is only an illusion (*bhrama*) that opaqueness per- "meates it; what adds the limitations to it is ignorance "(*avidyâ*). Therefore, whichever character is assumed, the

"Brahman must be conceived as unchangeably free from all "differences, and not the reverse. For everywhere in the "scriptures where it is a question of teaching the proper "nature of the Brahman, it is taught by such passages as "'not to be heard, not to be felt, without form, eternal' "(Kâṭh. 3, 15), that the Brahman is completely above all "change.[59]

(p. 133, 7:) "For where in teaching the nature (*rûpam*) of "the highest Lord all differences are excluded, the scriptures "use such expressions as: 'not to be heard, not to be felt, "'without form, eternal' (Kâṭh. 3, 15). Because the highest "Lord, however, is the cause of all, He is exhibited to us as "distinguished by certain qualifications of the changeable world "[of creation, which is a transformation of Him], when we "read 'all-working, all-wishing, all-smelling, all-tasting' (Chând. "3, 14, 2); and the case is the same when He is termed 'the "'[man in the sun] with the golden beard' (Chând. 1, 6, 6), etc."

(p. 1121, 1:) "As the lower (*aparam*) Brahman is closely "connected with the higher (*param*) Brahman, it is no con-"tradiction to apply the word Brahman to the former also. "For the fact of the matter is this: the higher Brahman it-"self is the lower Brahman, so far as it [the former] is now "and again for the purpose of worship described as possess-"ing certain qualities of the changeable world, such as 'Manas "'is what it is formed of' (Chând. 3, 14, 2) etc., qualities which "depend on the ascription to it of pure limitations (*viçuddha-"upâdhi*)."

(p. 867, 12:) "These qualifications too [from Taitt. 2, 5: "'Love is his head' etc.] are only assumed in the highest "Brahman as a means of turning the thoughts to it (*citta-"avatâra-upâya-mâtratvena*), not with a view to knowledge . . . "and this rule [that such qualifications have only local not "general validity] is applied elsewhere, when it is a question

---

[59] Cf. p. 806, 9: "Therefore the Brahman must in these passages ac-"cording to the Scriptures be regarded as quite without form (*nirâkâram*); "but the other passages which refer to the Brahman as possessing form "(*âkâravat*) are not concerned with it but with the enjoining of wor-"ship (*upâsanâ*)."

"of certain qualities of the Brahman which are inculcated for "the purpose of worship ... For a 'More' and 'Less' of "attributes in which continues the [empirical] action of the "manifold (*sati bheda-vyavahâre*) exists in the attribute-possess-"ing (*saguṇam*) Brahman, not in the attribute-less (*nirguṇam*) "highest Brahman."

(p. 112, 2:) "In a thousand passages the scripture teaches "the double nature of the Brahman, distinguishing between "it when it is the object of knowledge and ignorance (*vidyâ-"avidyâ-vishaya*). From the standpoint of ignorance (*avidyâ-"avasthâyâm*) all occupation with Brahman has the distinguish-"ing mark that it, as object of worship, and its worshipper "are distinguished; and in this case certain ways of worship-"ping the Brahman have as their end an exaltation (*abhyud-"aya*); the end of others is gradual deliverance (*kramamukti*); "others again have as their aim the success of the work of "sacrifice;[60] and they vary according to the attributes (*guṇa*), "differences (*viçesha*) and limitation (*upâdhi*). Now though "the God to be honoured, the highest Âtman, distinguished "by this or that attribute and difference, is one, still the "rewards [of worship] are different according to the attributes "worshipped."

(p. 148, 2:) "For where the highest Brahman (*param brahma*), "free from all connection with differences, is indicated as soul, "there is, as is to be seen [from the scripture], only one single "fruit, namely liberation; where, on the contrary, the Brahman is "taught in its connection with different attributes (*guṇa-viçesha*), "or in its connection with different symbols [*pratîka-viçesha*, "on which 4, 1, 4. 4, 3, 15—16], there are produced high and "low rewards only limited to Samsâra (*saṃsâra-gocarâṇi eva*)."[61]

---

[60] Cf. p. 815, 5: "The fruit of the same [the worship of the *saguṇam* "*brahma*] varying with the instruction, is sometimes annihilation of sin, "sometimes attainment of [heavenly] lordship (*aiçvaryam*), sometimes "gradual deliverance; so it is to be understood. It is thus correct to "assume that the words of the scripture about worship and the words "about the Brahman [as object of knowledge] have not a single but "different purposes."

[61] Cf. p. 1047, 7: "Where no difference of teaching exists, there cannot

c) Exoteric and Esoteric Eschatology.

As already made clear by the passages quoted, this two-fold nature of the lower Brahman, as the object of worship, and of the higher, as the object of knowledge, corresponds exactly to the two-fold eschatological theory of our system. The names *parâ* and *aparâ vidyâ* comprehend, for Çañkara, not only the philosophical and theological theories of the Brahman, but also the doctrine of the destiny of those who adhere to the one or the other; the *parâ vidyâ* teaches how he who knows the *param brahma*, by this very knowledge, becomes identical with it, and accordingly stands in need of no departure of the soul and further advance towards it, in order to reach it; on the other hand the *aparâ vidyâ* comprehends the theory of the Brahman as object of worship, and at the same time the theory of the rewards which fall to the lot of the worshipper; these are, as we saw, partly temporal, partly celestial, partly even the gradual liberation of the *Devayâna*, but always limited to the *Saṃsâra* (p. 148, 5), from which it follows that, like the *Pitṛiyâna*, the *Devayâna* also belongs to the Saṃsâra, namely, as its termination. According to this, as we are expressively assured, the whole teaching of the *Devayâna* (the ascent of the pious to the Brahman) belongs to the *aparâ vidyâ* (p. 1087, 3); to the attribute-possessing worship (*saguṇâ upâsanâ*) of the Brahman, not to the *Samyagdarçanam* (p. 909, 8. 10); heaven and the like, with its lordship (*aiçvaryam*) is the ripened fruit of the *saguṇâ vidyâḥ* (p. 1149, 13); for him who, on the contrary, knows the *param brahma*, as is developed in the episode

"be, as in the case of fruit of works, a difference of fruit either. For in "the case of that doctrine [the *nirguṇâ vidyâ*], which is the means of "liberation, there is no difference as in the case of works. On the con-"trary, in the case of attribute-possessing doctrines (*saguṇâsu vidyâsu*), "as, for example, 'Manas is his material, Prâṇa his body' (Chând. 3, 14, 2), "and so on, there exists a difference, in consequence of the admixture or "separation of attributes, and accordingly, as in the case of the fruit of "works, a difference of fruit according to the given peculiarity. And a "token of this is the scripture, when it is said: 'whatever he adores him "'as, that he becomes;' but it is not so in the case of the attributeless "doctrine (*nirguṇâyâṃ vidyâyâm*), because [in it] no attributes exist."

concerning the *parâ vidyâ* 4, 2, 12—16 (*prâsañgikî paravidyâ-gatâ cintâ* p. 1103, 12), there is no more departure from the body, nor any entering into the Brahman (p. 1102, 1).

d) Exoteric and Esoteric Cosmology and Psychology.

At first sight, the matter stands somewhat differently in the province of Cosmology and Psychology. The question is here no longer the contrast between *aparâ* and *parâ vidyâ*, but another, the contrast between two standpoints, which, p. 456, 1, are distinguished as the standpoint of worldly action (*vyavahâra-avasthâ*) and the standpoint of the highest reality (*paramârtha-avasthâ*). The former is that of the *Avidyâ* (p. 455, 6), the latter that of the *Vidyâ*. The former teaches a creation of the world by the Brahman who is endowed with a plurality of powers (*çakti*), and the existence of a plurality of individual souls, for whose activities and enjoyments it is the stage from the latter standpoint, the possibility of a creation and a transmigration ceases along with plurality, and in place of both comes the doctrine of the identity of Brahman with nature and with the soul.

(p. 491, 1:) "This scripture-doctrine of the creation does "not belong to the highest reality (*paramârtha*), for it lies in "the province of worldly action (*vyavahâra*) in name and form "admitted by *Avidyâ*, and has, as its highest aim, to teach "that the Brahman is the soul; this must not be forgotten!"

(p. 473, 13:) "When, through declarations of identity like "'*tat tvam asi*' (that thou art), identity has become known, "then the soul's existence as wanderer, and Brahman's "existence as creator have vanished away.

That the *paramârtha-avasthâ* of Cosmology and Psychology forms a whole with the *parâ vidyâ* of Theology and Eschatology, may be concluded from the explanations of Çañkara himself, in the single passage in which he lays down the esoteric teaching connectedly, and which is translated at the end of this chapter. Here we will prove only, what Çañkara was not so clearly conscious of, that, quite analogously, the *vyavahâra-avasthâ* of the doctrines of creation and transmigration are to be connected with the *aparâ vidyâ* of an attribute-possessing, that is, to speak in our language, of a personal God and a soul which departs to him after death, in the unity of an exoteric metaphysics, which treats of the Beyond from the standpoint of innate realism (*avidyâ*), since the *aparâ vidyâ* cannot exist without the *vyavahâra-avasthâ*, nor the *vyavahâra-avasthâ* without the *aparâ vidyâ*.

1) The *aparâ vidyâ* cannot exist without the *vyavahâra-avasthâ*; for the *devayâna* of the *aparâ vidyâ* demands, as its complement, the *pitṛiyâna*; but this is the path of *Saṃsâra*, and Çañkara himself has told us (above p. 106), that the reality of *Saṃsâra* and the reality of the creation stand and fall together; therefore the *aparâ vidyâ* demands, as its complement, the realism of the doctrine of creation; as also, conversely, the *devayâna*, and, along with it, the *aparâ vidyâ*, disappear only for him who has recognised the unity of his *Âtman* with *Brahman*, and therewith the illusion of the manifold world and the wandering soul.

2) In exactly the same way the *vyavahâra-avasthâ* of the teaching of creation cannot exist without the *aparâ vidyâ* of *saguṇam brahma*; for, in order to create, Brahman requires a plurality of *çaktis*, or powers (p. 342, 6. 486, 10); but these stand in contradiction (p. 1126, 2) to a *nirviçesham brahma*, from which it follows that only a *saguṇam*, *saviçesham*, not a *nirguṇam*, *nirviçesham brahma* can be a Creator.

The inner necessary connection between the *vyavahâra-avasthâ* and the *aparâ vidyâ*, here demonstrated, often enough comes more or less clearly to Çañkara's consciousness: thus, when he describes the *saguṇam brahma* as *avidyâ-vishaya* (p. 112, 2), for which the *bheda-vyavahâra* exists (p. 868, 7); when he views the *upâdhis* attributed to it as resting on *avidyâ* (p. 804, 1); when he explains the fruit of its worship as *saṃsâra-gocaram* (p. 148, 5), the *aiçvaryam* of the *apara-brahmavid* as *saṃsâra-gocaram* (p. 1133, 14) and those who have entered into the lower Brahman as still subject to *Avidyâ* (p. 1154, 9. 1133, 15), that is, with the same word with which he everywhere else describes the realism of the doctrine of creation and transmigration. And on occasion he expresses it openly, that the cosmological distinction of *îçvara* and *prapañca* belongs to the *saguṇâ upâsanâ* (p. 456, 10), and, conversely, that the teaching of *saguṇam brahma* presupposes the *prapañca* (p. 820, 12).

From these facts we justify the weaving together of the teaching of the *saguṇam brahma*, of a world thereby created and of an individual soul which moves in this world, and finally enters into that *brahma*, into a whole of exoteric metaphysics. And Çañkara also, if we were to ask him—"Is, then, "that *saguṇam brahma* and the *devayâna* leading thither real, "although from the standpoint of the highest truth neither "exists?" He would certainly answer: "They are precisely as "real as this world; and only in the sense that the *prapañca* "and *saṃsâra* are unreal, are the *saguṇam brahma* and the "*devayâna* unreal; both are the *aparâ vidyâ*, that is Vidyâ "as it appears from the standpoint of Avidyâ" (*avidyâ-avasthâyâm* p. 112, 3. 680, 12. 682, 3).[62]

But it must still be borne in mind that Çañkara did not reach full clearness as to the necessary connection of the exoteric doctrines, and this will often become clear enough from his discussions, which we shall reproduce faithfully and unaltered; but, as regards the esoteric doctrine, on the contrary, there is found at the end of his work a passage from which his consciousness of its inner necessary connection comes out as clearly as possible, and which, as a compendium *in nuce* of Çañkara's Metaphysics, and, at the same time, as an example of the style and character of thought of the work with which we are occupied, we here translate word for word.

---

[62] The thought that the exoteric doctrine aims at accommodating the truth to the comprehension of the masses, can also be pointed out in Çañkara; thus the spatial conception of the Brahman is formed *upalabdhi-artham*, p. 182, 8. 193, 4; the measurement of Brahman is *buddhi-artha'*, *upâsana-arthaḥ*, 835, 4; *na hi avikâre 'nante brahmaṇi sarvaiḥ puṃbhiḥ çakyâ buddhiḥ sthâpayitum, manda-madhya-uttama-buddhitvât puṅsâm, iti*, 835, 6. The propædeutic character of the exoteric doctrine is very clearly laid down in the Commentary to Chând. 8, 1, p. 528, and this passage (which we shall translate in Chapter XI, 1, d) is before all to be considered, when the rightness of our comprehension of the Vedânta system comes in question.

3. Appendix: Çañkara's Esoteric Philosophy, translated from 4, 3, 14 (p. 1124, 10—1134, 3).

a) Do the liberated go to the Brahman?

"Some maintain that the passages of scripture as to going [to the "Brahman] refer to the higher [not to the lower, attribute-possessing "Brahman]. This cannot be, because a going to the Brahman is im-"possible. For to the all-present highest Brahman, inmost of all, who "is the soul that is within all, of whom it is said: 'like the ether [p. 1125] "'omni-present, eternal' (cf. above p. 32, l. 9)—'the perceptible, not super-"'sensible Brahman, that as Self is the innermost being of all' (Bṛih. "3, 4, 1),—'Self only is this universe' (Chând. 7, 25, 2),—'The Brahman "'only is this universe, the most excellent' (Muṇḍ. 2, 2, 11),—to this "Brahman whose character is determined by passages of scripture like "these, there cannot now or ever be a going in. For we cannot go to "a place where we already are; but on the contrary, according to com-"mon acceptation, only to another place. It is true experience shews, "that we can also go to that, in which we are already, so far as we dis-"tinguish different places in it. Thus a man is on the earth, and yet "goes to it, in so far as he goes to another place. So also the child is "identical with itself, and yet reaches puberty, which is its own self, "separated by time. In the same way, one might think, there may be a "way of going to the Brahman, so far as it is endowed with all kinds "of powers (*çakti*). But this is not so; on account of the negation of all "differences (*viçesha*) in Brahman: 'Without parts, without action, rest-"'ful, faultless, stainless' (Çvet. 6, 19),—'Nor gross nor fine, nor short nor "'long' (Bṛih. 3, 8, 8),—'For he, the unborn, is without and within' (Muṇḍ. "2, 1, 2),—'Verily this great unborn soul (*âtman*), that neither grows old "'nor fades nor dies, that is without fear, is the Brahman' (Bṛih. 4, 4, 25), "—'He is not thus, not thus' (Bṛih. 3, 9, 26);—according to these rules of "scripture and tradition no connection of the highest soul with spatial, "temporal or other differences can be assumed, so that one could go to "it as to a part of the earth or to an age of life; but a spatially and "temporally [p. 1126] determined going to the earth and to the age is "possible[63] because they are differentiated by locality and circumstances."

[63] It is in the highest degree attractive and instructive, to observe, how here and elsewhere the spirit of man in antiquity toils and struggles to reach the eternal fundamental truth of all metaphysics, which it was reserved for the genius of Kant to set forth in perfect clearness and to prove beyond contradiction: the truth that Being-in-itself must be spaceless and timeless, because space and time are nothing else but subjective forms of our intellect.—As here *space* and *time* are denied for the Brahman, so in the sequel will causality of creation be interpreted as identity.

b) Esoteric Cosmology.

"If you assert, that the Brahman must have manifold powers (*çakti*), "because, according to the scripture, it is the cause of the creation, sub- "sistence and extinction of the world, we say no! for the passages of "scripture which deny differences to it can have no other sense [but the "literal one]. But the passages of scripture about the creation and so on "can likewise have no other sense?—This is not so; for their aim is "[only] to teach the identity [of the world with Brahman]. For when "the scripture, by the examples of lumps of clay and the like,[64] teaches "that 'the Existent", the Brahman, alone is true, but that [its] trans- "formation [into the world] is untrue, it cannot have the aim of teach- "ing a creation and the like.—But why should the passages of scripture "about the creation and the like be subordinated to those about the "negation of all differences, and not conversely the latter be subordinated "to the former?—To this we answer: because the passages of scripture "about the negation of all differences have a meaning which leaves nothing "more to be wished for. For after the unity, eternity, purity, and the "like, of the soul are recognised, nothing more remains to be desired, "because thereby the knowledge, which is the aim of man, has been ob- "tained: 'where can error or sorrow be, for him who beholds unity?' "(Îçâ 7)—'Fearlessness, verily, o Janaka, hast thou attained' (Bṛih. 4, 2, "4),— 'The wise has no fear of any one at all' (Taitt. 2, 9),—'Him verily "'the question troubles not, what good he has not done [p. 1127], what "'evil he has done' (ibid.),—thus teaches the scripture. And while in "this way it shews that the wise are conscious of satisfaction, it also for- "bids the untrue assertion of a transformation [creation], since it says: "'From death to death he is ensnared who difference sees' (Kâṭh. 4, 10). "Consequently it cannot be assumed that the passages of scripture which "deny difference are to be subordinated to the others. Not so is it with "the passages of scripture about creation and the like. For these are "not able to teach a sense which leaves nothing more to be wished for. "On the contrary, it is evident, that these have another aim [than that, "immediately put forward, of teaching a creation]. For after it is first "said (Chând. 6, 8, 3): 'Of this growth which has spring up, dear one, "'learn that it cannot be without a root,'—the scripture in the sequel "teaches, how the one thing, which is to be known, is 'the Existent', as "the root of the world. And thus it is also said: 'That, whence these "'beings come forth, whereby they, coming forth, live, wherein they, "'departing hence, enter again, that seek, for that is the Brahman' (Taitt. "3, 1). Thus the passages of scripture about the creation &c., have the "aim of teaching the unity of the Âtman, so that no connection of the

---

[64] Chând. 6, 1, 4: "Just as, dear one, by a lump of clay everything "that consists of clay, is known; resting on words is the transformation, "a mere name, in truth it is only clay," etc.

"Brahman with manifold powers [is to be assumed], and consequently a "going to it is impossible. And also the passage: 'His vital spirit with- "'draws not, Brahman is he, and into Brahman he is resolved' (Bṛih. 4, "4, 6), forbids us to think of an end to the higher Brahman (*param* "*brahma*). This we explained in discussing [Sûtram 4, 2, 13] 'clearly "'according to some' [passage], it is the body, not the individual soul, "out of which he who has reached liberation withdraws]."

c) Esoteric Psychology.

"Further, when a going to the Brahman is assumed, the Jîva (the "individual soul) which goes is either [1.] a part of the Brahman, or [2.] "a modification, or [3.] different from the Brahman. For in the case of "absolute identity with him, a going is impossible. If this be so, which "of them is right?—We answer: if [according to 1.] that [Jîva] is a part "[literally: a separate place] [in the Brahman], then he has already reached "that [Brahman] consisting of the parts, and consequently even in this "case a going to the Brahman is impossible. [p. 1128] But the assumption "of parts and of that which is composed of them has no application to "the Brahman, because, as everybody knows, the Brahman is without "members. It is much the same if [according to 2.] we assume a modi- "fication. For the modification is also already in that from which it is "modified. For a vessel of clay cannot exist, if it ceases to be clay; if "this happened, it would cease to exist. If we could understand [the "soul] as a modification or member [of the Brahman], the soul must "remain inherent [in the Brahman], and a going of the wandering soul "[reading *saṃsârigamanam*] to the Brahman is absurd. But perhaps "[according to 3.] the Jîva is different from the Brahman? Then it "must be either [a.] the size of an atom, or [b.] all-pervading, or [c.] of "middle size. If it is [according to b.] all-pervading, no going can be "possible. If it is [according to c.] of middle size, it cannot [cf. above "p. 68, note 43] be eternal [which was, however, proved 3, 3, 54]; if it is "[according to a.] the size of an atom, then it is inexplicable that sen- "sation exists throughout the whole body. We have moreover proved "above [2, 3, 19—29] fully, that it can neither be of the size of an atom "nor of middle size. But that the Jîva is different from the Highest is "altogether contrary to the canonical words: '*tat tvam asi*' ('That thou "art,' Chând. 6, 8, 7). The same error occurs, if we assume that it [the "Jîva] is a modification or a part of it [the Brahman]. If you assert, "that the error does not occur, because a modification or a part is not "separate from that of which they are [modification or part], we contest "this, because the unity in the main point would be wanting. And in "the case of all these assumptions, you cannot get over it that either no "cessation of transmigration is possible, or that in case it ceases, the soul, "unless its Brahman-selfhood be assumed, must perish."

d) Esoteric Morality.

"But there are some who come and say: 'Suppose someone practised "'the regular and occasional [good] works, in order to escape the fall "'[into transmigration], and avoided at the same time those springing "'from the desire [for reward], as also the forbidden [works] in order "'to go neither to heaven nor hell, and exhausted the works [of his "'former existence] which are to be expiated in the present body [p. 1129] "'by the expiation itself, there would thus, after the dissolution of the "'present body, exist no further cause for incurring a new body; and "'thus the liberation of such a one, being only a continuation in his "'own essence, would be reached even without identification with Brah- "'man.'—But this is not so; for there is no proof of it. Because by no "canonical scripture is it taught, that he who seeks liberation should "proceed in this wise. On the contrary, they have evolved it out from "their own intellects, thinking thus: because Saṃsâra is caused by the "works [of an earlier existence], therefore it cannot exist, where there is "no cause. But the calculation falls to the ground, because the non- "existence of the cause cannot well be known [cf. the detailed statements "p. 673, 9 ff.]. For of each single creature it must be admitted, that it "has accumulated many works in an earlier existence, which ripen to "desirable and undesirable fruits. As these bring contrary fruits, they "cannot both be expiated at the same time; therefore some of them [the "works] seize the opportunity and build up the present existence, others, "on the contrary, sit idle and wait until space, time and cause come for "them. As these which remain over cannot be exhausted by the present "expiation, it cannot therefore be determined with certainty, that, for "one who leads his life in the prescribed way, after the dissolution of "his present body, no further cause should exist for another body; on "the contrary the existence of a residuum of works is proved by passages "of the Çruti and the Smṛiti like (Chând. 5, 10, 7): 'Those whose conduct "'here is fair,' and as it is further said ['for them there is the prospect "'that they enter a fair womb, a Brahman womb, or Kshatriya womb, "'or Vaiçya womb;—but those whose conduct here is foul, for them is "'the prospect of entering a foul womb, a dog's, or pig's, or Çaṇḍâla's "'womb'].—But if this be so, still [p. 1130] those [residual fruits of works] "can be got rid of [*kshepakâṇi*; perhaps here and in the sequal *kshapa-* "*kâṇi*, *kshapya*, etc. 'exhausted' would be better; cf. p. 909, 12] by regular "and occasional good works?—That cannot be; because no contrast "[between them] exists. For if they were contraries, then the one might "be wiped out by the others; but between the good works heaped up in "an earlier existence and the regular and occasional [ceremonies] there "is no contrast, because the one and the other are of morally meritorious "nature. In the case of evil works, since they are of immoral nature; "the contrast exists indeed, and accordingly a wiping out might very "well take place; but still it will not result in there being no cause for "a new body. For in case of the good works, it still happens that they "remain as cause, and for the evil works, it cannot be ascertained that "they have been completely paid for [by pious ceremonies]. It can also "not be proved that by performing the constant and occasional [cere-"monies] only avoidance of the descent [into transmigration] and no "other fruits besides are obtained; for it is quite possible, that yet other "fruits result therefrom, in addition. At least *Âpastamba* [*dharma-sûtra* "1, 7, 20, 3] teaches: 'For, as in the case of the mango-tree, which is "'planted for the sake of the fruit, also shadow and sweet scent result as "'well, so also, when duties are performed, other beneficial ends also spring "'therefrom.' Moreover no man, who has not *Samyagdarçanam* (perfect "knowledge), can be sure that, with his whole self, from birth to death, "he has avoided all forbidden practices and those aiming at enjoyment "for, even in the most perfect, small lapses can be perceived. But even "if we could be in doubt about this, in any case it cannot be known "that no cause [for a new birth] exists. And without the Brahman-hood "of the soul having been brought to consciousness, by the way of know-"ledge, the soul, whose nature it is to act and enjoy, cannot reach liber-"ation, for it cannot renounce its own nature, any more than fire can "[cease to be] hot.—[p. 1131] This may be, it may be objected, but the "evil lies only in the acting and enjoying as effect, not in its potentiality "[in the deeds, not in the will, from which they proceed], so that, even "while the potentiality remains in existence, liberation is possible through "avoiding the effect. But this also cannot be the case. For if the poten-"tiality remains in existence [reading: *çakti-sadbhâve*], it cannot possibly "be prevented from producing its effect.—But it might still be, that the "potentiality, without any further causal moment, [the will without an "efficient motive] may not produce any effect; hence [the potentiality] "by itself, even when it remains in existence, commits no transgression. "—This also cannot be; for the causal moments are always connected "[with the potentiality] by a connection referred to the potentiality.[65] "So long, therefore, as the soul possesses the natural tendency to act "and enjoy, and so long as the Brahman-hood of the soul, which is to "be gained by knowledge, is not attained, there is not the faintest prospect "of liberation. And the scripture also, when it says: 'There is no other

---

[65] *çakti-lakshaṇena sambandhena nityasambaddha*; whether the sense of these rather obscure words has been caught above, or not, in any case it is clear that our author misses the main point of the matter, so far as he does not see that the real guilt lies only in the quality of the *çakti* (that is, the will), it being all the same, whether the will, instigated by the chance occurrence of *nimitta* (motive), unfolds its being in deeds, or whether this unfolding remains latent.—To have recognised this clearly and expressed it, is the service which Jesus has rendered to philosophy; compare Matthew v, 21 ff., xii, 33 ff.

"'way to go' (Çvet. 3, 8), admits no other way of liberation but the way "of knowledge.—But from the fact that the Jîva is identical with the "Brahman, will not all worldly action be annihilated, since the means of "knowledge, like perception etc., cannot be employed?—Not so; on the "contrary, it goes on just as well as the action in dreams before awaking "[cf. above p. 55, note 31]. And the canon also, when it says: 'For where "'there is a duality, as it were, one sees the other' and so on (Bṛih. 4, 5, "15), explains with these words the action of perception, and the like, "for the unawakened, as valid, but on the other hand declares it as not "valid for the awakened; for it is said further: 'But when for anyone "'all has become as his own self, how should he then see any other?' "and so on. Therefore because for him who knows the highest Brahman, "the idea of going and the like has ceased entirely, any going [to the "Brahman after death] is quite impossible for him."

e) Esoteric Eschatology.

"But where do the passages of scripture belong which speak of a "going [to the Brahman]?—[p. 1132] Answer: they belong to the region "of the attribute-possessing doctrines (*saguṇâ vidyâḥ*). Accordingly a "going is spoken of partly in the doctrine of the five fires (Chând. 5, "3–10. Bṛih. 6, 2), partly in the doctrine of the throne (Kaush. 1), partly "in the Doctrine of the All-soul (Chând. 5, 11–24). But where in reference "to the Brahman a going is spoken of, for example, in the passages: "'The Brahman is life, the Brahman is joy, the Brahman is amplitude' "(Chând. 4, 10, 5; translated Chap. XI, 2, below p. 164) and 'Here in this "'city of the Brahman [the body] is a house, a small lotus blossom' "(Chând. 8, 1, 1; translated Chap. XI, 1d, below p. 160)—there also, in "consequence of the attribute 'bringing love' and so on (Chând. 4, 15, 3) "and 'having true wishes' and so on (Chând. 8, 1, 5) it is only a question "of worshipping the attribute possessing [Brahman], and therefore a go- "ing is in place; but nowhere is a going taught with reference to the "highest Brahman (*parabrahman*). As therefore in the passage: 'His "'vital spirits withdraw not' (Bṛih. 4, 4, 6; translated Chap. XII, 4), a "going is denied, as also in the case of the words: 'The knower of the "'Brahman reaches the Highest' (Taitt. 2, 1); for even if the word "'reaches' implies a going, yet it indicates here, where, as shewn, a "reaching of another place cannot be understood, only the entering into "one's own being, with regard to the annihilation of the extension of "names and forms ascribed by Ignorance [that is, empirical reality]. "'Brahman is he, and into the Brahman is he resolved' (Bṛih. 4, 4, 6); "this saying must be kept in sight. Further: if the going had reference "to the highest [Brahman], it might be taught either for the purpose of "attracting or for meditation. Now an attraction through the mention "of the going [p. 1133] cannot happen in the case of those who know the "Brahman; for he becomes this solely because, through knowledge, his "unveiled original selfhood comes to consciousness; and a meditation on "the going also has not the slightest reference to the knowledge which "is conscious of an eternally perfected bliss, leaving no further goal to "be reached. Consequently the going refers to the lower [Brahman]; "and only so far as the difference between the higher and lower Brahman "is not kept steadily in view, will the passages of scripture concerning a "going referring to the lower Brahman be falsely made to refer to the "higher."

f) Esoteric Theology.

"Are there then two Brahmans, a higher and a lower?—There are "certainly two; as is seen from the words: 'In truth, o Satyakâma, this "'sound *Om* is the higher and the lower Brahman' (Praçna 5, 2).—What "then is the higher Brahman, and what the lower?—To this we answer: "Where, by discarding the differences of name, form and the like, ascribed "by Ignorance, Brahman is indicated by the [purely negative] expressions "'nor gross [nor fine, nor short, nor long]' and so on (Bṛih. 3, 8, 8) it is "the higher. But where, on the contrary, exactly the same [reality], for "the purpose of worship, is described as distinguished by some difference "or other, for example, in words like: 'Spirit is his material, life his "'body, light his form' (Chând. 3, 14, 2), it is the lower.—But does that "not contradict the word of the scripture, that it is 'without a second' "(Chând. 6, 2, 1)?—Not at all! [The contradiction] disappears, because "ascribed limitations like name and form spring from Ignorance. But "the fruit of the worship of this lower Brahman is, according to the "context 'If he desires the world of the fathers' and so on (Chând. 8, "2, 1) a world-lordship *(jagad-aiçvaryam)* belonging to Saṃsâra, since "Ignorance is not [yet] destroyed. Now this [fruit] [p. 1134] is connected "with a given place; therefore a going, in order to gain it, is no con-"tradiction. It is true the soul is all-present; but as space [ether] enters "into the vessel and the like, it also enters into connection with ascribed "limitation (*upâdhi*) like Buddhi and the rest, and so far a going is "assumed for it, concerning which we have spoken, with reference to the "Sûtra: 'because it [the soul in the condition of Saṃsâra] is the nucleus "'of its [Buddhi's] qualities [love, hate, desire, sorrow, etc.]' (2, 3, 29)."

THE FIRST PART OF THE VEDÂNTA SYSTEM:

THEOLOGY

OR

THE DOCTRINE OF BRAHMAN.

VII. Prefatory Remarks and Arrangement.

1. On the names of God.

THE doctrine, which we here undertake to set forth, is not seldom included under the general conception of Pantheism; this expression (like the corresponding: Theism, Atheism and the like) not only means very little, but also, seems actually inexact in its application to our system, as well in its exoteric and lower, as in its esoteric and higher form. For in the lower doctrine the Theology of the Vedânta should on the contrary be described as Theism, as is shown by the expressions for God, *Îçvara*, the Lord, *Purusha*, the Man, the Spirit, *Prâjña*, the wise, and the like; in the higher doctrine on the contrary, it is something that rises above all such catch words, and resists all attempts to include it in the accepted schemes, however, convenient such inclusion might be. In any case the name *Bráhman*, which, in the work which we are to analyse, is used only as a neuter,[66] indicates something impersonal, only in the sense, however, that its being is raised far above all personality. This word does not originally mean "the liberated," "the Absolute," from *barh*, *separate*, as the Vedântins derive it (p. 33, 2, and also perhaps already Kâṭh. 2, 13. 6, 17 *pravṛihya, prahvṛihet*) but rather from *barh*, *swelling*, that is (above pp. 17, 49) "prayer," conceived not as a wishing

[66] The Brahmán (m.) of Indian mythology appears quite exceptionally p. 913, 10 *Vasishthaç ca Brahmaṇo mânasaḥ putraḥ* and in the formula p. 61, 11 *brahmâdi-sthâvarânta*, p. 604, 2 *brahmâdi-stambaparyanta*; also in the quotations p. 209, 1. 301, 4. 338, 12. 339, 1. 998, 2, where he is usually explained as *Hiraṇyagarbha* (p. 301, 1. 339, 3). In the Vedânta it is frequently the custom, which we shall occasionally follow, to connect a *pronoun of masculine gender* (he, his and the like) with Brahman in the *neuter*.

(εὔχεσθαι) or wording (*orare, precari*) or demanding (*bidjan*) or softening (*молиться*) or offering incense (עָתַר), but as the will of man striving upwards towards the holy, the divine; in accordance with this, the designation of God as ***Brahman*** would arise from a concept which finds and grasps the Divine where it is preeminently to be sought and found. The other designation of God as *Âtman*, that is, "the Self," or "the Soul" also points us to our inner life (cf. p. 100, 18: ***âtmâ hi*** *nâma svarûpam*); but when this is distinguished from "the living Self," the individual soul (***Jîvâtman, Jîva***) as "the highest Self" (***Paramâtman, Mukhyâtman, Aupanishadâtman***), these expressions admonish us to distinguish two sides in our own selves, of which this whole empirical form of existence is only one, while the other, lying behind it, rests in the bosom of the deity, is even identical with it.

This is not the place to follow up further the designations of God as *Brahman, Âtman, Purusha,* ***Îçvara*** and the profound views which they open up; to this end the first steps of our knowledge must first be exhibited from the Veda more clearly than has hitherto been done. Here we must restrict ourselves to developing the Theology of Bâdarâyaṇa and Çañkara, looking at the Upanishads only with their eyes; but even in this scholastic form, the ideas of the Godhead show a loftiness the like of which cannot easily be found elsewhere.

2. Arrangement of the Theology.

Apart from casual phrases scattered through the whole work, the doctrine of the Brahman is dealt with in two parts of the Brahmasûtras; that is, in the first Adhyâya, which lays down the Theology on the basis of a series of scripture texts, in a general way, and without developing the difference between Saguṇâ and Nirguṇâ Vidyâ,[67] and in an appendix to this, in

[67] Such a difference seems to be kept in view, judging from the introductory discussions p. 111—114; but in the development of the question whether *saguṇam* or *nirguṇam brahma* is to be understood, another question is generally substituted, that is, whether the text cited refers to the highest self or to the individual self. The threefold antithesis of *param brahma*, 1) to the forms as which it is presented

Adhyâya III, 2, 11—41, which contains the esoteric theology. We shall follow this twofold division; but within the first Adhyâya, in order to gain a clear idea of the matter, we cannot adhere to the order maintained in the Sûtras, since they bring together the most heterogeneous material in the strangest manner, and, on the other hand, widely separate passages naturally belonging to each other. To justify our transpositions it may be useful to explain as far as possible the principle of arrangement which governs the first Adhyâya of the Brahmasûtras.

To begin with, the first Adhyâya is divided as we have it (cf. table of contents at the end of the first chapter, above p. 39), into forty, that is, ten times *four* Adhikaraṇas (Chapters). *Four* of these chapters separate themselves naturally from the rest: the two last 1, 4, 23—27 and 1, 4, 28 which belong to the following cosmological section, and 1, 3, 26—33. 1, 3, 34—38, which contain an episode already treated in chap. III. Of the remaining Adhikaraṇas, the *four* first form the Introduction, *four* others (1, 1, 5—11. 1, 4, 1—7. 1, 4, 8—10. 1, 4, 11—13) combat the Sâñkhya doctrine. After deducting these, we have seven times *four* Adhikaraṇas, which consist of an exegetical and dogmatic discussion of the same number of passages from the Upanishads. Of these, *four* are taken from Bṛihadâraṇyaka-Up., *four* from Kâṭhaka-Up., *four* from Atharvan Upanishads (three from Muṇḍaka, one from Praçna), *four*, that is two each, from Taittirîya and Kaushîtaki, and the remaining three times *four* from Chândogya-Upanishad.

The following scheme shews their order:

1) 1, 1, 12—19 Taitt. 2, 5
2) —, 20—21 . . . . Chând. 1, 6, 6.
3) —, 22 . . . . Chând. 1, 9, 1.
4) —, 23 . . . . Chând. 1, 11, 5.
5) —, 24—27 . . . . Chând. 3, 13, 7.
6) —, 28—31 Kaush. 3, 2
7) 1, 2, 1—8 . . . . Chând. 3, 14, 1.
8) —, 9—10 . . . . Kâṭh. 2, 25
9) —, 11—12 . . . . Kâṭh. 3, 1

(*saguṇam brahma*), 2) to the forms in which it is manifested, that is, the world, 3) to the individual soul, is not sharply distinguished and preserved by Çañkara; we shall recur to this in Chapter XIV, 1.

10) —, 13—17 . . . . Chând. 4, 15, 1
11) —, 18—20 . . . . Bṛih. 3, 7, 3
12) —, 21—23 . . . . Muṇḍ. 1, 1, 6
13) —, 24—32 . . . . Chând. 5, 11—24
14) 1, 3, 1—7 . . . . Muṇḍ. 2, 2, 5
15) —, 8—9 . . . . Chând. 7, 23
16) —. 10—12 . . . . Bṛih. 3, 8, 8
17) —, 13 . . . . Praçna 5, 5
18) —, 14—18 . . . . Chând. 8, 1, 1
19) —, 19—21 . . . . Chând. 8, 12, 3
20) —, 22—23 . . . . Muṇḍ. 2, 2, 10
21) —, 24—25 . . . . Kâṭh. 4, 12
22) —, 39 . . . . Kâṭh. 6, 1
23) —, 40 . . . . Chând. 8, 12, 3
24) —, 41 . . . . Chând. 8, 14
25) —, 42—43 . . . . Bṛih. 4, 3, 7
26) 1, 4, 14—15 Taitt. 2, 6
27) —, 16—18 Kaush. 4, 19
28) —, 19 22 . . . . Bṛih. 4, 5, 6

As this survey shews, the order of the passages, as they occur in the different Upanishads, is rigidly preserved. But apart from this, these passages are interwoven in a way for which we only here and there seem to recognise a reason. Possibly this enigmatic relation points to preparatory exegetical works within the different Çâkhâs, which were then gradually united in a single whole.

However this may be, this much is clear, that this principle of arrangement is in fact an external one. Therefore, in our statement of the doctrine, we ignore it altogether, in order, after producing certain proofs of the existence of God (Chap. VIII), to treat of the Brahman on the basis of the material in question, first in itself (Chap. IX), then as a cosmic principle (Chap. X), again as a cosmic and at the same time psychic principle (Chap. XI), lastly as the soul (Chap. XII), and as the highest end (Chap. XIII). The investigation of the esoteric (*nirguṇam*) Brahman will form the conclusion of the Theology (Chap. XIV).

VIII. Proofs of the Existence of God.

1. Prefatory Remark.

In the course of the work, with which we are concerned, we several times come across discussions, which have a certain likeness to the proofs of the existence of God that figure in the modern pre-Kantian philosophy. We give them here under the names in use among us, as a comparison of the arguments on both sides is not without historical interest. There can be no question of mutual dependence, since proofs like the cosmological and physico-theological lie in the nature of man's processes of thought; as it appears, the Indians were never ensnared into an ontological proof; on the other hand, we find a new proof, which we may call the psychological, and in which the concept of God blends with the concept of the soul. We begin with a short and provisional definition of the Brahman, and then introduce the passages which occur under the titles mentioned, without meaning to maintain that their entire contents are suited to these titles chosen for the sake of comparison.

2. Definition of the Brahman.

(p. 38, 2:) "The cause, from which [proceeds] the origin or "subsistence, and dissolution of this world which is extended "in names and forms, which includes many agents and enjoyers, "which contains the fruit of works specially determined according to space, time and cause, a world which is formed after "an arrangement inconceivable even for the spirit, this omniscient "and omnipotent cause is the Brahman."

(p. 90, 3:) "Brahman is the omniscient and omnipotent cause "of the origin, persistence and passing away of the world."

3. Cosmological Proof.

Under this title we translate Sûtram 2, 3, 9 with Çañkara's explanation (p. 627—628).

Sûtram: "*But* [there is] *no origin of 'the Existent,' on* "*account of the impossibility.*" Explanation: "After anyone "has been taught from the scripture, that also ether [or: "space] and air have originated, although we cannot conceive "their coming into being, he might come to think that the "Brahman also originated from something, for when he per-"ceives how from the ether and the like, which are still only "modifications, yet other modifications arise, he might conclude "that the ether also sprang into being from the Brahman, as "if from a mere modification. The present Sûtram "*But* [there "is] *no-origin*" etc., serves to remove this doubt; its meaning "is: but one must not think that the Brahman, whose essence "is Being (*sad-âtmaka*), could have originated from anything "else; why? '*owing to impossibility.*' For Brahman is pure "Being. As such it can [*firstly*] not have sprung from pure "Being, because [between the two] there is no superiority, so "that they cannot be related [to each other] as original and "modified;—but also [*secondly*] not from differentiated Being, "because experience contradicts this; for we see that from "homogeneity differences arise, for example, vessels from clay, "but not that homogeneity arises from differences;—further "[*thirdly*] also not from non-Being,[68] for this is essenceless "(*nirâtmaka*); and because the scripture overthrows it, when "it says (Chând. 6, 2, 2): 'How should the Existent come from "the non-Existent?' and because it does not admit a producer "of the Brahman, when it is said (Çvet. 6, 9):

> "Cause is He, Master of the Sense's Lord,
> "He has no Lord, and no Progenitor."

"For ether and wind on the contrary an origin is shewn, "but there is none such for the Brahman, that is the difference. "And because it is seen how, from modifications, other modi-"fications arise, there is no necessity for the Brahman also

---

[68] The similarity of this demonstration with that in the Parmenides v. 62 ff., is conspicuous; Zeller, Philosophie der Griechen I³, p. 471.

"to be a modification. For were this so, then we should come "to no primordial nature (*mûlaprakṛiti*) but should have a "*regressus in infinitum* (*anavasthâ*). What is assumed as the "primordial nature,—just that is our Brahman; there is thus "perfect agreement."[69]

4. Physico-theological Proof.

(p. 500, 3:) "When the matter is considered with the help "of examples only, it is seen that in the world no non-intelligent "object without being guided by an intelligence brings forth "from itself the products which serve to further given aims "of man. For, *e. g.*, houses, palaces, beds, seats, pleasure-"gardens and the like are [only] contrived in life by intelligent "artists in due time for the purpose of obtaining pleasure and "averting pain. Exactly the same it is with this whole world. "For when one sees, how, for example, the earth serves the end "of the enjoyment of the fruit of the manifold works, and how, "again, the body within and without by possessing a given "arrangement of parts suitable to the different species and "determined in detail that it may form the place of the en-"joyment of the fruit of the manifold works,—so that even "highly skilled artists full of insight are unable to comprehend "it through their understanding,—how should this arrangement "proceed from the non-intelligent original-matter [of the Sâñ-"khyas]? For lumps of earth, stones and the like are in "no wise capable of this? Clay also, for example, is formed, "as experience teaches, to different shapes [only] so long as "it is guided by the potter, and exactly in the same way must "matter be guided by another intelligent power. He, there-"fore, who relies on the material cause only as clay, etc., "cannot rightly maintain, that he possesses the primordial "cause; but no objection meets him who, besides it [the clay], "relies on the potter etc. as well. For when this is assumed

[69] In the last phrase, the relationship between the Indian and the western cosmological proof, as well as the inadequacy of both, comes out very clearly; since considered empirically nothing stands in the way of a *regressus* from the effect to the cause, from this again to its cause, etc. *in infinitum*.

"there is no contradiction, and at the same time the scripture, "which teaches an intelligent power as cause, is thereby re-"spected. So that, as the arrangement [of the Kosmos] would "become impossible, we may not have recourse to a non-"intelligent power as the cause of the world."

5. Psychological Proof.

(p. 32, 4:) "Is the Brahman which is to be investigated "known or unknown? If it is known, we do not need to in-"vestigate it; if it is unknown, we cannot investigate it!— "Answer: That Being which of its own nature is eternal, "pure, wise, free, all-knowing, almighty is Brahman. For from "the etymology of the word Brahman the meanings 'eternal, "pure' etc. are reached, according to the meaning of the root "*barh* ['to separate;' see above, p. 119]. But the existence of "the Brahman is demonstrated by the fact that it is the Self "(Soul, *âtman*) of all. For everyone assumes the existence of "himself, for he cannot say: "I am not." For if the existence "of Self were not demonstrated, then all the world could say "'I am not.' And the Self is the Brahman.—But if the "Brahman is universally demonstrated because it is the Self, "then it is known, and the objection that it need not be in-"vestigated, recurs?—Not so! For with reference to its "characteristics there is contradiction. For the common people "and the materialists [*Lokâyatika*: 'those who follow the world'] "assert: 'the Self is only the body invested with intelligence;' "—others again: "the Self is only the [naturally] intellectual "organs of sense;'—others: 'it is the understanding (*manas*);' "—yet others: 'it is only the perishable intellect;'—others: "'the Void;'—others again: 'it is the [individual soul] extend-"ing beyond the body, wandering, acting, and suffering;'—some: "'it is only the sufferer, not the agent;'—some: 'it is the "all-knowing, almighty Lord, who extends beyond this [world];' "—still others: 'it is the Self of him who suffers [or: enjoys] "there.'—Thus many oppose each other, and rely on arguments "and passages [of Scripture] or their appearance. He, there-"fore, who inconsiderately assumes the one or the other, may "compromise his salvation and come to destruction. Therefore, "because they set forth the investigation of the Brahman, the "consideration of the Vedânta [Upanishad] texts, supported "by non-contradictory reflexion, is recommended as a means "of salvation."

(p. 78, 6:) "For the eternal Spirit (*purusha*) different from "the agent [the individual soul], which is the object of the "presentation of I, dwelling as witness (*sâkshin*) in all being, "uniform, one, the highest, is not apprehended by anyone from "the Section of Works [of the Veda] or from any book based "on reflexion; he, who is the soul of all. And therefore none "can deny him, or make him an element of the Section of "Works; for he is even the Self (soul) of him who denies "him; and because he is the Self of all, it is therefore im-"possible either to flee from him or to seek him. For every-"thing that passes away, came into existence and passes away "through modification, because it finds its end in the spirit; "but the spirit is imperishable, because there is no cause of "perishableness in it, and because there is no cause of change "in it, therefore is it raised [above change], and eternal, and "for this very reason in its own nature eternal, pure and free "[or: freed]."

Now in so far as God is the (metaphysical) I of man himself, his existence cannot be proved at all, but also it does not need to be proved, because he is that which is alone known directly, and thereby the basis of all certainty, as is developed in the following most remarkable passage.

6. *Cogito, ergo sum.*

(p. 619, 8:) "For if the Self [that is, Brahman] also [like "ether, wind, fire, water, earth] were a modification, then, "since the Scripture teaches nothing higher above it, every "effect from ether downwards would be without Self (*nirât-*"*maka*, soulless, essenceless), since the Self [also] would be "[only] an effect; and thus we should arrive at Nihilism "(*çûnya-vâda*). Just because it is the Self, it is not possible "to doubt the Self. For one cannot establish the Self [by "proof] in the case of anyone, because in itself it is already "known. For the Self is not demonstrated by proof of itself.

"For it is that which brings into use all means of proof, such "as perception and the like, in order to prove a thing which "is not known. For the objects of the expressions ether etc. "require a proof, because they are not assumed as known of "themselves. But the Self is the basis (*âçraya*) of the action "of proving, and consequently it is evident before the action "of proving. And since it is of this character, it is therefore "impossible to deny it. For we can call in question some-"thing, which comes to us (*âgantuka*) [from outside], but not "that which is our own being. For it is even the own being "of him who calls it in question [cf. p. 79, 1. 823, 2]; fire cannot "call its own heat in question. And further, when it is said: "'It is I, who now know what at present exists, it is I, who "knew the past, and what was before the past, it is I, who shall "know the future and what is after the future,' it is implied "in these words that even when the object of knowledge alters, "the knower does not alter, because he is in the past, future, "and present; for his essence is eternally present (*sar-"vadâ-vartamâna-svabhâvatvâd*); therefore, even when the body "turns to ashes, there is no passing away of the Self, for its "essence is the present, yea, it is not even for a moment "thinkable, that its essence should be anything else than this."

IX. The Brahman in itself.

1. Brahman as the non-Existent.

Sûtram 1, 4, 14—15.

It is asserted, Çaṅkara says (*loc. cit.*), that the Vedânta texts referring to the derivation of the world from Brahman, as well as those referring to the nature of Brahman itself, are frequently contradictory; in the former case, sometimes the ether, sometimes fire, sometimes breath is named as the first created, while in the latter, Brahman is in some passages described as the "non-Existent," in others as the "Existent." With regard to the first point, he says, it will be discussed further on (cf. Chap. XVII, 1); here we have only to do with the latter. It is true that it is said (Taitt. 2, 7):

"Non-Existent was this in the beginning, thence the Existent arose"

while on the other hand it is said (Chând. 6, 2, 1): "Existent "only, dear one, was this in the beginning, alone and without "a second. Some, verily, say: non-Existent was this in the "beginning, alone and without a second; from this non-Existent "arose the Existent. But how could this be, dear one? How "could the Existent arise from the non-Existent."

Here, in the one passage, as in the other, the all-knowing, almighty, all-animating Being without a second is indicated as the cause of the world (p. 372, 7); and if the Taitt. Up. speaks of a non-Existent, it is not an essenceless non-Existent that is to be understood, as the preceding verse (Taitt. 2, 6) proves:

"He is but non-Existent[70] who knows Brahman as non-Existent;
"He who knows Brahman as Existent becomes himself by this Existent."

The word "Existent" is commonly used to indicate the

---

[70] Çaṅkara always reads: *asann eva sa bhavati*, p. 375, 13. 124, 9. 128, 7. 823, 4.

world extended in names and forms; now in order to suggest, that this development did not exist before the creation, it is metaphorically said of Brahman which alone is: it was, as it were, a non-Existent (p. 376, 7).

2. Brahman as the primordial Light.

Sûtram 1, 3, 22—23.

Muṇḍ. 2, 2, 10 (= Kâṭh. 5, 15 = Çvet. 6, 14) says:

"There shines not sun nor moon nor stars, nor shine these "lightnings, far less earthly fire: after Him the shining One, "all shines, from His light is lighted this whole world."

In this passage, as Çañkara explains, it is not some kind of light-element that is to be understood, but the highest Âtman, of which Chând. 3, 14, 2 says: "Light is his form, truth his resolve" (p. 272, 9), and which is spoken of (p. 274, 2) in what goes before (Muṇḍ. 2, 2, 5. 9). A Light-element is not to be thought of, because from such an element the sun etc. [hence the moon also!] cannot borrow their light, since they are themselves just as much light-elements (p. 272, 11); but they can all very well borrow their light from the Brahman, for a borrowing can also take place in the case of things of different kinds, as a glowing ball of iron burns after the fire, and as the dust blows after the wind (p. 273, 2); moreover, besides the light-elements named, the sun etc., no other exists (p. 274, 8).—From the shining of the Âtman "all this" would borrow light, that is, either: the sun, etc., in the sense in which Bṛih. 4, 4, 16 says: "Him the Gods honour as immortal Life, as the light of lights," or it means: this whole world-development, as it has arisen in names and forms as "the reward of works to the doer" (*kriyâ-kâraka-phala*, p. 273, 12; the same formula p. 291, 6. 447, 3. 987, 6), has as cause the light-nature of the Brahman, just as the revelation of all forms has as its cause the light-nature of the sun (p. 273, 13). All that is perceived, is perceived through the Brahman as light, but the Brahman is perceived through no other light, because its own being is to be Self-shining, so that the sun etc. shine in him (*tasmin*). For the Brahman reveals the other, but the Brahman is not revealed by the other (p. 275, 1).

3. Brahman as the last, unknowable origin of the Existent.

a) Sûtram 1, 2, 21—23.

In the Introduction of the Muṇḍaka-Upanishad two doctrines are distinguished (in another sense than above, p. 98 ff.), a lower, which, as Çaṅkara remarks, has as its fruit ascent (*abhyudaya*, cf. p. 82), and a higher, which has as its fruit salvation (p. 203, 5). Under the lower the four Vedas besides the six Vedâṅgas (Phonetics, Grammar, Etymology, Metre, Ritual and Astronomy) are enumerated, and then it is said further, Muṇḍ. 1, 1, 5:

"But the higher is that through which that Imperishable "is known: the invisible, intangible, unoriginated, colourless, "without eyes and ears, without hands and feet, the eternal, "all-pervading, all-present, very subtle, this is the Unchanging "which the wise know as the womb of beings. As the spider "puts forth [the threads] and draws them back again, as herbs "grow up upon the earth, as from a living man the hair on "head and body, so from this Imperishable arises all the "world."

Here, as Çaṅkara develops it, the highest God is to be understood, not primordial matter or the individual soul. For though the examples brought forward, the spider's body and the man's body, are only directed by an intelligent power, but are themselves non-intelligent (p. 200, 12), yet these are only comparisons, which must not be pressed too far (p. 204, 14); that an intelligent original Being is to be understood, is proved by what immediately follows, and is therefore to be applied here, "he who understands all, who knows all" (Muṇḍ. 1, 1, 9), which cannot be applied to a non-intelligent primordial matter (p. 201, 3).—One might also think of the individual soul, because it certainly according to its moral nature (p. 201, 9) conditions what arises as being, but what follows further on, shews clearly that only the highest Brahman can be meant. For it is said further, Muṇḍ. 2, 1, 1:

"This is the truth:—As, from a well lit fire, sparks, of "like nature to it, arise thousandfold, so, dear one, from the

"Imperishable go forth manifold beings, and return into it "again. For divine is the spirit (*purusha*), the formless, who "is within and without, unborn, breathless, wishless, pure, yet "higher than the highest Imperishable. From him arises "breath, the understanding with all the senses, from him arise "ether, wind, and fire, the water, and earth the support of "all. His head is fire, his eyes the moon and sun, the cardinal- "points are his ears, his voice is the revelation of the Veda. "Wind is his breath, his heart the world, from his feet the "earth;—he is the inner Self in all beings."

From this passage, says Çañkara, it is clear, that neither the individual soul, to which such majesty of body does not belong, nor primordial matter is to be thought of, because it is not the inner Self in all beings (*sarva-bhûta-antarâtman*). (p. 207, 12). If at the same time an individualised form is attributed to the invisible womb of beings, this is not in order to ascribe to it a real individuality, but only to make it clear that it is the Self of the universe (*sarva-âtman*) (p. 208, 1).— A difficulty is caused by the fact that the Âtman, which (above p. 131) is called "the Imperishable," is here spoken of as "higher than the highest Imperishable." The way in which Çañkara tries to solve this difficulty, by here understanding the "Imperishable as the undeveloped subtle body [Chap. XXXI, 3], "forming the seed-power for names and forms, which serves as "the ground-work for the Lord, and is only a limitation (*upâdhi*) "ascribed to himself" (p. 206, 1), as well as the opinion of some, considered by Çañkara (p. 208), that in the concluding words of the text Prajâpati (a cosmogonic personification of Brahman) is to be understood, we may very well pass by.

b) Sûtram 1, 3, 10—12.

In the Bṛihadâraṇyaka-Upanishad (3, 8) Gârgî, the daughter of Vacaknu (not the wife of Yâjñavalkya, as Colebrooke, M. E.[1] p. 343 erroneously supposes) asks Yâjñavalkya in what is woven and interwoven that which exists above heaven, beneath the earth, and between heaven and earth, in what the past, the present, and the future, and receives as answer: in the ether (space) all this is woven and interwoven.—"But in what," she asks further, "is ether (space) then woven and interwoven?" —To this Yâjñavalkya:

"It is that, o Gârgî, which the Brahmans call the Im-"perishable (*aksharam*); it is neither gross nor fine, nor short "nor long, nor red [like fire] nor adhering [like water], not "shady nor dark, not wind nor ether, not sticky [like gum], "without taste, without smell, without eye or ear, without "voice, without understanding, without vital-force, and without "breath, without mouth and without measure, without inner or "outer; nothing whatsoever does it consume, nor is it consumed "by any. At the bidding of this Imperishable, o Gârgî, sun "and moon are kept asunder from each other; at the bidding "of this Imperishable, o Gârgî, heaven and earth are kept "asunder from each other; at the bidding of this Imperishable, "o Gârgî, the minutes and the hours, the days and nights, "the half-months, months, the seasons, and the years are kept "asunder. At the bidding of this Imperishable, o Gârgî, the "streams run downward from the snowy mountains some to "the east, some to the west, and whithersoever each one goes; "at the bidding of this Imperishable, o Gârgi, men praise "the generous man, gods strive for the sacrificer, the fathers "for the offerings for the dead. Verily, o Gârgi, he who "knows not this Imperishable, though in this world he offers "and has offerings made, though he suffers penance many a "thousand years, gains an unenduring [reward]; but he who "knows not that Imperishable, o Gârgî, and departs from this "world, he, indeed, is miserable; but he who, o Gârgi, know-"ing this Imperishable, departs from this world, he, indeed, "is a Brâhmaṇa. Verily, o Gârgî, this Imperishable is see-"ing, not seen, hearing, not heard, understanding, not under-"stood, knowing, not known. For outside him there is no "seer, outside him there is no hearer, outside him there is "none with understanding, outside him there is none with "knowledge. In this Imperishable, verily, o Gârgî, is the ether "woven and interwoven."

In this passage, as Çañkara explains, the Imperishable (*aksharam*) means not "the syllable," as usually is the case, generally the sacred syllable "*om*," of which it is said (Chând.

2, 23, 4) "the sound *om* is all this," but the highest divinity (p. 242, 10); for of it only is it true that in it the ether and thereby the universe is woven (p. 242, 14), as even in the passage mentioned (Chând. 2, 23, 4) the sound "*om*" signifies Brahman (p. 243, 3), whose properties of eternity and all-permeation are signified etymologically by *aksharam* (*na ksharati, açnute ca*, p. 243, 4). Primordial matter can also not be understood as the Imperishable, for it is said: "at the bidding of this Imperishable," and "this is seeing not seen" etc., which must refer to an intelligent power (p. 243, 12. 244, 8); but it cannot refer to the individual soul, because in the words: "without eye and without ear" etc., all limitations (*upâdhi*) are excluded, and without these the individual soul cannot exist (p. 244, 13).

All the properties of the Brahman, which we have dealt with hitherto, were (so far as they are not to be taken figuratively) purely negative; now we turn to the two positive determinations of the being of the Godhead, which show it as 1) pure intelligence, 2) pure bliss.

4. Brahman as pure Intelligence.

Sûtram 1, 1, 5—11.

Prefatory Remark. When we consider the weakness and frailty of man's intellect, we can only wonder at the unanimity with which, in Indian, Greek and modern philosophy, Intelligence is ascribed as an essential attribute to "the Thing-in-itself." It is well worth while to follow out the motives which have led the thinkers of ancient and modern times to declare so feeble a faculty, which works only intermittently, is bound up with organic life and perishes with it, to be the essence of the being of Beings. These motives are especially clearly seen in the deeply founded structure of the Vedânta philosophy. Metaphysics must above all seek a firm and immovable point of certainty, in order to attack the subject, and this can only be found in the consciousness of the philosophising subject; hence the Cartesian: *cogito, ergo sum*, and the corresponding statement of our work, which we have given above p. 127 ff. Here, within our own Self, we gain an infallible guide to the absolute Being which we are seeking: that which cannot be laid aside must also be the imperishable, the unchangeable must also be that which lies at the basis of every thing changeable, a conviction, which is most clearly expressed by calling the Principle of all Being the *Âtman*, that is, the Self. We reach it as, in the manner described above p. 58, and in note 29, we gradually separate from our "I" everything which is "not-I," hence not only the outer world, the body and its organs, but also the whole apparatus of *Buddhi* or intellect (the *indriyas* and the *manas*). What remains, should consequently be spoken of only as unconscious; but they could not go so far, without removing the whole phenomenon from the region of perceptibility. Consciousness, therefore, in which all this process of elimination proceeds, was left as the terminus, so that not only was the necessity avoided of abandoning, along with the organs of perception, their function also,—perception,—but also the very noteworthy objections of the adversary, which we shall presently detail, were set at defiance.

Many times, as Çañkara says in the passage, with which we are concerned, intellect is ascribed to the Principle of world-creation in the Veda. So when it is said: "He designed (*aikshata*): I will become many, I will procreate" (Chând. 6, 2, 3);—"He designed: I will create worlds" (Ait. 1, 1, 1);—"He formed the design, then he created Breath" (Praçna 6, 3. 4);—"He who knows all, understands all" etc. (Muṇḍ. 1, 1, 9).—From this it follows that we must ascribe to the Brahman omniscience, absolute, unlimited knowledge, that, as a later passage (3, 2, 16) explains, Brahman is pure spirituality (*caitanyam*) and this alone.—Against these arguments the Sâñkhyas raise the following objections:

First Objection: An eternal cognition in Brahman would take away the freedom of Brahman with reference to the action of cognition (p. 93, 1).—To this Çañkara replies: to begin with, it is to be held that only an eternal actual, and not a potential, cognition (such as the Sâñkhyas ascribe to the *sattva-guṇa* of their primordial matter) satisfies the demands ot omniscience.[71] A cognition of this kind does not take away the freedom of Brahman; for in the case of the sun also, although it continually gives forth heat and light, we say "it warms," "it shines" and thereby indicate that it does this of itself, of its own accord [p. 95, 16; that is to say: the following out of the law of its own nature does not take away the freedom of a being].

Second Objection: a cognition is only possible, if there is also an object of perception (*karman*, literally "a product," in contrast to *karaṇam*, organ), which was not the case before the creation (p. 96, 1).—Answer: as the sun also shines, when there is nothing for it to shine on, so Brahman might know without having an object of cognition (cf. p. 649, 10). Yet one existed, even before the creation. What is this pre-cosmic object?—It is (p. 96, 6) "the Names and Forms which are neither "to be defined as beings nor as the opposite, which are not "evolved, but striving towards evolution (*avyâkṛite. vyâcikîrshite*), "the Names and Forms" of the world [which as the words of the Veda, as we saw above p. 71, hovered before the spirit of the Creator before the creation].

Third Objection: Cognition cannot proceed without organs of perception, body, senses, etc. (p. 93, 4. 96, 11).—Answer: because cognition inheres in Brahman, as shining in the sun, as an eternal law of its nature, it requires no organs to this end, like the individual soul (p. 97, 1), which, as is provisionally set forth on p. 98, is nothing but the Brahman itself, limited by the *Upâdhis* like the body etc., and therefore only separate from the Brahman from the standpoint of Ignorance (cf. above p. 58ff.). The individual soul (p. 100—101) is the Self of Brahman, and the Brahman is the Self of the individual soul; for of Brahman it is said: (Chând. 6, 3, 2) "this "divinity designed: good! I will enter into these three divinities "[Fire, Water, Earth] with this living self!" and again it is said (Chând. 6, 8, 7): "whose being is this universe, that is the

---

[71] p. 95, 10. The passage seems corrupt; it would be a help if we might read: *kathaṃ nitya-jñâna-akriyatve asarvajñatva-hânir*, by which what follows becomes consistent.

"Real, that is the soul (the Self), that art thou, o Çveta-"ketu!"—That Self means the own nature; a spiritual power, like the individual soul, cannot have an unspiritual as its own nature (p. 100, 18. 104, 9).—On this ground, which for our authors is unassailable, they take their stand further on, when, to prove the spirituality of the Existent or the Godhead, they refer to two phenomena, that of liberation, and that of dreamless sleep. Liberation is a return into Brahman (p. 102, 8); and from another point of view it is only a coming to consciousness of one's own Self (p. 103, 7), it follows, therefore, that Brahman is simply this Self, and therefore spiritual. As Liberation is an eternal union with the Existent, that is, with Brahman, the cause of the world, so deep, dreamless sleep according to the scripture (Châṇd. 6, 8, 1) is a temporary union with the Existent (p. 109, 2); the word "he sleeps" (*svapiti*) means, however, "he has entered into himself" (*svam apîta*); a spiritual power, like the individual soul, cannot enter into an unspiritual as into its own self (p. 108, 10).

5. Brahman as Bliss.

Sûtram 1, 1, 12—19; cf. 3, 3, 11—13.

Brahman is the inmost essence of man.—This thought is exhibited in the second part of the Taittirîya Upanishad by the theory (which plays a large part in the later Vedântasâra, but not yet in Bâdarâyaṇa and Çañkara) of the different coverings (*koça*), by which our Self is surrounded, and through which we must break, in order to reach the inmost essence of our nature, and thereby the Brahman.

After Taitt. 2, 1 has briefly explained, how from the Âtman the ether proceeded, from this the wind, from this the fire, from this the waters, from these the earth, from this plants, from these food, from this seed, from this man, and further it is said: this man consists of food (*annarasamaya*), in this self of food indwells, another, filling it, the Self of breath (*prâṇamaya*), in this again the self of understanding (*manomaya*), in this the self of intellect (*vijñânamaya*), in this lastly, as inmost, the self of bliss (*ânandamaya*). For each of these five sheath-like selves, indwelling one in the other, are distinguished and specified (perhaps while the form of a bird is present to the thought) the head, the right and left sides (wings), the body, and "the support (literally: the tail), the base." In the case of the self of food, these parts are formed by the parts of the body, in the case of the self of breath, by the vital spirits with the ether (in the heart) and the earth, for the self of understanding by the four Vedas and the Upanishads (*âdeça*), for the self of intellect by faith, truth, right, piety (*yoga*) and lordship; for the self of bliss it is said finally: "Love [literally: what is dear] is his head, joy "his right side, rejoicing his left side, bliss his body, Brahman "his support, his base" (Taitt. 2, 5).

In this passage, according to Bâdarâyaṇa's Sûtras and the accompanying interpretation, by the "self of bliss" we are to understand Brahman; as is proved p. 116 from the connection of the passage, and from the frequent description of Brahman as bliss in the Taitt. Up. and elsewhere (Bṛih. 3, 9, 28), and finally, because it is spoken of as the innermost of all. The word "of bliss" do not here mean "made of bliss," but indicate only the fulness of the bliss of Brahman (1, 1, 13 p. 117), which is the source of all bliss (1, 1, 14 p. 118). Neither the individual soul (1, 1, 16—17 p. 119—120) nor the primordial matter of the Sâñkhyas (1, 1, 18 p. 121) can be understood here, from the connection of the whole; moreover the union of the individual soul with the being "of bliss" is required (1, 1, 19, p. 121—122) in the words of Taitt. Up. 2, 7: "For "when one finds his resting-place and peace in this invisible, "bodiless, ineffable, unfathomable [literally: baseless], then he "has entered into peace; but if on the contrary, he assumes "a hollow in this [as in the four others]—[Commentary: if he "makes a difference between himself and this], then has he "unrest; it is the unrest of him, who thinks himself wise."

But in direct contradiction to this interpretation, (which is to be applied when the subject is resumed 3, 3, 11—13) another explanation of the Upanishad passage is introduced at the end of our extract by the words: "Here, however, the following is to be noted," (p. 122, 9) explaining that the interpretation of *-maya* as "consisting of" and then as "having the fulness," is as inconsequent as if one had only half-digested his food,[72] and then, entering into the discussion, declares that it is not by the "self of bliss" that Brahman is to be understood, but only by that which is indicated as "its support, its basis;" the self of bliss is not yet the kernel, but only the inmost shell, of which, therefore, we should have counted not four but five (p. 123, 10: *annamaya-âdaya' ânandamaya-paryantâḥ pañca koçâḥ kalpyante*). In conclusion, the representative of this opinion gives an explanation—extremely forced—of the sûtras in his sense.

As both interpretations agree in recognising Bliss (*ânanda*) as the being of Brahman, this difference is of no particular consequence for our purpose. But it is interesting for the literary character of our work, as well as for the history of the Vedânta, that here in Çañkara's commentary two opinions stand side by side, of which, as it seems to us, the former alone corresponds to the text of the Upanishads and Bâdarâyaṇa's Sûtras, while on the side of the latter are ranged the Commentary to the Taittirîya-Upanishad, which goes under Çañkara's name, as well as the Vedântasâra, which likewise interprets the self of bliss as only a shell (Vedântasâra, § 56, ed. Boehtl.) and thus counts five shells on which, in combination with the three Guṇas of the Sâñkhya Philosophy, the whole of its psychology is built up.

Either the latter interpretation is due to a later interpolator, not to Çañkara, in which case the Commentary to the Taittirîya-Upanishad also must not be attributed to him (cf. in it p. 25, 14 *sushumnâ*, and above note 8);—or it is Çañkara's: in the latter case, we may suppose that he copied the first interpretation given to the separate Sûtras from an earlier commentator (a possibility, which would be of great importance for the character of his whole work, cf. notes 17. 45), or we can also suppose, that Çañkara disagrees with Bâda-

---

[72] p. 122, 13: *arddha-jaratîya-nyâyena*; similarly p. 176, 11: *na tatra arddha-jaratîyam* (with this reading) *labhyam*. Differently and very naïvely Govinda explains the latter passage: *arddham, mukhamâtram, jaratyâ vṛiddhâyâḥ kâmayate, na añgâni, iti, so 'yam arddhajaratîya-nyâyaḥ*.

râyaṇa here, that he therefore interprets the Sûtras first in Bâdarâyaṇa's sense, and then rejects this interpretation, in order to give another in its place in the sense of which he finally interprets the Sûtras as the standard authority of the school, consciously changing their original meaning.

6. Brahman as Free from all Evil.

Sûtram 1, 1, 20—21.

As is well known, the hymns of the Sâmaveda, with but few exceptions (above p. 5) rest on those of the Ṛigveda. The composer of the Chândogya-Upanishad (which belongs to the Sâmaveda) takes advantage of this circumstance, to show how, in the provinces of cosmology and psychology, certain phenomena rest on others, while on the contrary Brahman, which is symbolically represented as the man in the sun and the man in the eye, is raised above everything else, and free from all evil.

As the Sâman rests on the Ṛic (so is explained Chând. 1, 6), so fire rests on earth, wind on atmosphere, the moon on the stars, on the clear light of the sun rests the black, very dark in it (which, according to the scholiast, is seen by looking very intently at the sun; possibly: the sun-spots are to be understood?). "But the golden man (*purusha*) who is "seen in the interior of the sun with golden beard and golden "hair, to the tips of his nails all golden,—his eyes are like "the flowers of the Kapyâsa-lotus, his name is "high" (*ud*), "for high above all evil is he; he raises himself high above "all evil, who thus knows;—his songs (? *geshṇau*) are Ṛic and "Sâman, therefore [it is said] the high-song (*ud-gîtha*), there-"fore also the high-singer (*ud-gâtar*), for he is his singer; the "worlds, which lie upwards from the [sun],—over these he "rules, and over the wishes of the gods."

What is here set forth in the province of cosmology (*adhidaivatam*), is then developed in that of psychology (*adhyât-mam*). As the Sâman rests on the Ṛic, so rests breath on speech, the image (*âtman*) on the eye, understanding on the ear, the black, very dark on the bright appearance in the eye. "But the man who is seen in the interior of the eye, "he is this Ṛic, this Sâman, this praise, this sacrificial sentence, "this prayer (*brahman*). The form which the former has, this "also has the latter, the songs of the former are his songs, "the name of the former is his name; the worlds which lie "beneath him,—over these he rules, and over the wishes of "men. Therefore those who sing here to the lute, sing him, "therefore good is their lot."

Here, explains Çañkara, we must by no means understand by the man in the sun and in the eye, an individual soul raised through knowledge and works (p. 130, 3), but Brahman; for when form and position are attributed to him (p. 130, 6. 9), and the boundaries of his might are spoken of (p. 130, 13), all this happens only for the sake of worship (p. 133, 10. 13. 15), since we are dealing here with the attribute-possessing Brahman, not with the attribute-free (p. 133, 7). Of Brahman alone it can be said that he is "high above all evil" (p. 131, 10), and that he, the all-animating, is indicated as the subject of spiritual as well as of secular songs (p. 132, 1. 8). For of him it is said in the Bhagavadgîtâ (10, 41):

"All that has might and beauty, vital force,
"Know thou that of my power 'tis a part."

We must distinguish between this sun-purusha and the individual soul embodied in the sun (p. 134, 2; cf. above p. 66); for thus says the scripture: (Bṛih. 3, 7, 9) "He who, dwelling "in the sun, is different from the sun, whom the sun knows "not, whose body is the sun, who rules the sun within,—he is "thy soul, thine inner ruler, the immortal."

7. Brahman as Free from Causality and Affliction.

Sûtram 3, 3, 35—36.

Just as *Kant* declares theoretical speculation insufficient, and turns the human soul with its demands away from speculation back to the practical way, so already did *Yâjñavalkya*, in a highly remarkable passage in the Bṛihadâraṇyaka Upanishad 3, 4—5, the consideration of which we shall transfer from 3, 3, 35—36 into the present connection.

(Bṛih. 3, 4:) "Then asked him Ushasta, the descendant of "Cakra. 'Yâjñavalkya,' said he, 'the immanent, non-transcen-

"'dent Brahman, which as soul is innermost of all, that shalt "'thou declare to me.'—'It is thy soul, which is innermost of "'all.'—'Which, o Yâjñavalkya, is innermost of all?'—'That "'which inbreathes by inbreath that is thy soul, the inner- "'most of all, that which outbreathes by outbreath that is "'thy soul, the innermost of all, that which interbreathes by "'interbreath that is thy soul, the innermost of all, that which "'upbreathes by upbreath that is thy soul, the innermost of "'all,—this is thy soul, which is innermost of all.'—Then said "Ushasta, the descendant of Cakra: 'It is only indicated by "'this, as when one says: that is a cow, that is a horse; but "'the immanent, non-transcendent Brahman, the soul, which is "'innermost of all, that shalt thou declare to me!'—'It is thy "'soul which is innermost of all.'—'Which, o Yâjñavalkya, is "'innermost of all?'—'Thou canst not see the seer of seeing, "'nor canst thou hear the hearer of hearing, nor canst thou "'understand the understander of understanding, nor canst "'thou know the knower of knowing. He is thy soul, which "'is innermost of all.—What is different from him is afflicted.' "—Then Ushasta, the descendant of Cakra, was silent."

(Bṛih. 3, 5:) "Then asked him Kahola, the descendant of "Kushîtaka. 'Yâjñavalkya,' said he, 'even that immanent, "'non-transcendent Brahman, which as soul is innermost of "'all, that shalt thou declare to me.'—'It is thy soul which "'is innermost of all.'—'Which, o Yâjñavalkya, is innermost "'of all.'—'That which overcomes hunger and thirst, affliction "'and madness, age and death.—Truly, after they have found "'[Çaṅk.: recognised] this soul, the Brahmans cease from long- "'ing after children, and longing after possession, and longing "'after the world, and wander about as beggars. For the "'longing after children is a longing after possessions, and "'the longing after possessions is a longing after the world; "'for both are mere longings.—Therefore after the Brahman "'has put off his erudition, let him abide in childlike sim- "'plicity; and after he has put off both his learned and his "'childlike estate, then he becomes a silent one (*Muni*); after "'he has put off keeping silence and not keeping silence, then "'he becomes a Brâhmaṇa.—By what does this Brâhmaṇa "'live?—By whatever it may be, by that he lives.—Whatever "'is different from him is afflicted.'—Then Kahola, the descen- "dant of Kushîtaka, was silent."

Çañkara's remarks on this passage are limited to showing that both extracts belong to the unity of the same Vidyâ (cf. above p. 99), which appears from the beginnings and endings containing the same words (p. 923, 14), from the use of the particle *eva* "even" (p. 923, 16) as introductory conjunction of the second piece, as also from the fact that in both cases the inner soul is treated of (p. 922, 7), as there are not two inner souls, but one (p. 922, 9). The repetition is due to the difference of the instruction (p. 923, 7): the first time the Âtman is depicted as lying beyond cause and effect (*kârya-kâraṇa-vyatirikta*), the second time as overcoming hunger and the other qualities of Saṃsâra (*açanâyâ-âdi-saṃsâra-dharma-atîta*) (p. 924, 2. 3).

That the two extracts make up a harmonious whole is evident from their parallel construction; moreover a comparison of them may teach us whether, with our recollections of Kant, we have rightly hit the central thought. The Brahman, so teaches the first extract, is theoretically unknowable: for because, in all knowing, it is the knowing subject, it can never be an object of knowledge for us. To the mind which, not resting content with this, puts forward the same question anew, it is, in the second extract, pointed out that Brahman is to be grasped practically. This happens as one raises oneself step by step from the estate of erudition (*pâṇḍityam*) to that of childlike simplicity (*bâlyam*, cf. Matth. 18, 3), from this to the state of the *Muni*, from this to that of the *Brâhmaṇa* [in its emphatic meaning, as Bṛih. 3, 8, 10. Chând. 4, 1, 7], who renounces family, possessions and worldly pleasure, because these are different from the Brahman, and therefore subject to affliction.

Touching the nature of the steps mentioned, and especially the meaning of Bâlyam one may compare the investigations in 3, 4, 47—50 (p. 1034—1041), from which we take only the following beautiful passage of Smṛiti (p. 1041, 8):

"Whom no one knows as high nor lowly born,
"No one as erudite nor yet not erudite,
"No one as of good deeds nor evil deeds,
"He is a Brâhmaṇa, in very truth!
"Given up to hidden duties well fulfilled,
"In secrecy let all his life be spent;
"As he were blind and deaf, of sense bereft,
"Thus let the truly wise pass through the world."

X. The Brahman as Cosmic Principle.

1. The Brahman as Creator of the World.

The creative activity of the Brahman is one of the fundamental ideas concerning it, which recurs in most of the Vedic texts to be considered. We here discuss only a few passages, which cannot conveniently be introduced elsewhere and refer for further information to the texts as well as to our cosmological section (chaps. XVI, XVII). The passages in question teach us to know the Brahman from two sides: (a) as that which conditions the spatial extension of beings (Brahman as *Âkâça*, that is, "Ether" or "Space" of which later),—(b) as that which fills and animates the spatially extended (Brahman as *Prâṇa*, that is, "Breath" or "Life").

(a) The Brahman as *Âkâça*. Sûtram 1, 1, 22 and 1, 3, 41.

1. In the Chândogya-Up. 1, 8—9 there is a dialogue between three men, in which is investigated the point of departure (*gati*), of the Sâman (song). The Sâman, so it is said in the course of the dialogue, goes back to the Tone, the Tone to Breath, Breath to Food, Food to Water, Water to the celestial world, which has, however, as its basis the terrestrial world. But the terrestrial world also is finite, and goes back to the Ether (or space).

"Now it is the Ether from which all these beings arise, "and into which they return; the Ether is older than them "all, the Ether is the highest goal. This most excellent of "all is the Udgîtha [song of the Sâman], it is the endless."

Even though, Çañkara remarks on 1, 1, 22, it would be most natural in the case of the word Ether to think of the so-called element, yet what is said here of the Ether cannot apply to the element, but only to the Brahman (p. 136, 5).

For even if the other beings (elements) have arisen directly and immediately from the ether-element, yet it is said here that "all beings," therefore the ether also, arose from, and return to that which is here, as frequently in the scripture, symbolically called the Ether, that is the Brahman (p. 136, 9). Moreover this only could be meant by the oldest (p. 136, 11), according to the Scripture (Chând. 3, 14, 3) which calls it "older (greater) than the earth, older than the atmosphere, "older than heaven, older than all these worlds;" and only the Brahman can be the highest goal (p. 136, 14), according to the words (Bṛih. 3, 9, 28, where Çañkara, with the Mâdhyandinas, reads *râter*):

"Brahman is bliss and knowledge, the highest aim of the sacrificer
"And of him who desists and knows."

2. Towards the end of the Chândogya-Up. (8, 14) there is found a remarkable saying (perhaps a blessing for the departing pupil), which runs thus: "The Ether it is, which extends "Names and Forms; that in which these two are [or: that "which is in these two], that is the Brahman, that is the im-"mortal, that is the soul. I go forth to the hall of the lord "of creation, to his house [I enter the world]; I am the glory "of Brahmans, the glory of warriors, the glory of cultivators; "to glory following after have I come; let me the glory of "glories not enter into the grey, the toothless, the toothless, "the gray, the slimy [into the womb for a re-birth; or: into "grey old age?]."

In this passage also, according to Çañkara on 1, 3, 41, by the Ether is to be understood the Brahman, chiefly because it is distinguished from Names and Forms,[73] which embrace everything created, everything that is not Brahman itself (p. 329, 7).

(b) The Brahman as *Prâṇa*. Sûtram 1, 1, 23.

Between the two great Upanishads, Bṛihadâraṇyaka, which serves as text-book for the students of the (white) Yajurveda,

[73] p. 329, 5 *antarâ* "different," as at p. 454, 12, where it is explained by *anya*, while the Commentator on Chând. and according to all appearances also Bâdarâyaṇa 1, 3, 41 understand it as "inside."

and Chândogya, which serves for the students of the Sâma-veda, are to be observed many, often verbal agreements, but, side by side with these, certain traces of a thorough-going polemic, which is shown, among other things, by the fact that teachers, who appear in the one Upanishad as the highest authorities, occupy only a subordinate position in the other. Thus, for example, *Ushasta*, the descendant of *Cakra*, whose doctrine in Bṛih. 3, 4 is subordinate to that of Yâjñavalkya (cf. above p. 141), while, in Chând. 1, 10—11, under the name of *Ushasti*[74] it is true, he plays the leading rôle. In the legend, which is here recounted of him, he appears as completely destitute, and yet, notwithstanding his poverty, proud, since he begs food from a rich man, but refuses the drink offered with it, because he can get water to drink without begging. It is further related of him how he betakes himself to a sacrifice, and embarrasses the priests who have been engaged for it by his questions. The king, who is offering the sacrifice, notices him, and, after hearing his name, transfers to him the functions of the other priests. Now it is their turn to examine Ushasti, and the first question in this colloquy runs thus: "Which is the Godhead to which the *Prastâva* (the "introduction to the song of the Sâman) refers?"—To this Ushasti answers (Chând. 1, 11, 5):

"It is the Life (or the Breath, *prâṇa*); for all these beings "enter into Life, and to Life (*prâṇam*, probably better: *prâṇâd*, "from Life) do they arise."

Here, according to Çaṅkara, we must not, by Life, understand the vital force, into which, according to Çatap. 10, 3, 3, 6, the organs enter in sleep, and from which, on awaking, they are born again, but Brahman, because according to the words of the text not only the organs, but all beings arise from it and return to it again (p. 140, 10); and if it be objected that Ushasti's other two answers, as which "the Sun" and "Food" follow, cannot apply to Brahman (p. 139, 13), it may be answered that this is not at all necessary (p. 141, 5).

---

[74] Çaṅkara calls him *Ushasti* also in quoting Bṛih. 3, 4 (p. 922, 3).

2. The Brahman as World-ruler.

(a) Sûtram 1, 3, 39.

In the Kâṭhaka-Upanishad (6, 1) the world is likened to an inverted *Açvattha* (ficus religiosa) whose one root is above (Brahman), and whose manifold branches are below (the beings of the world). Thus Brahman is indicated as the Essence of the Universe, on which all worlds rest, and which penetrates and rules them as the Breath of Life (*prâṇa*):

"The root above, the branch below,
"This fig-tree stands from ancient days:—
"This is the pure, the Brahman this,
"And this is the Immortal called.
"This is the resting-place of worlds,
"By none can this be e'er surpassed.
"This [world] is truly that [the Brahman]!

"This is the Life in which the world,
"Which sprung from it, moves tremblingly,
"Fearful is this, a threatening flash,
"Who knows this, his is immortality.

"From fear of this burns the Fire, from fear of this the Sun,
"From fear of this run Indra and Vâyu, and Death the fifth of them."

In this passage, says Çañkara, by Life (or Breath, *prâṇa*) we are to understand, not the fivefold Vital-breath (Chap. XXVII, 4) or the wind, but Brahman, as is clear from the context (p. 324, 7). To this alone can apply the passage about the trembling of the whole world (p. 325, 2) as also what is said of the lightning-flash; "for just as a man thinks: 'the "'threatening lightning-flash could strike my head if I did not "'fulfil his [Indra's?] bidding;' and impelled by this [and "similar] fear performs the command of a king etc., so the "whole world, fire, wind, sun etc., from fear[75] of Brahman "necessarily perform the duties which are assigned to them" (p. 325, 11). Moreover, proceeds Çañkara, it is only the knowledge of Brahman, through which immortality is ours (p. 326, 2), for thus says the Scripture (Çvet. 3, 8 = Vâj. S. 31, 18; cf. Taitt. Âr. 3, 13, 1):

[75] Cf. Psalm 104, 7 and Heraclitus': ἥλιος οὐχ ὑπερβήσεται μέτρα, εἰ δὲ μή, Ἐρινύες μιν Δίκης ἐπίκουροι ἐξευρήσουσιν.

"Who knoweth him, hath triumphed over death,
"And he who seeks this goal, this path must tread."

As the last words show, by immortality (*amṛitatvam*), in the case of the Indians, we are not so much to understand the western idea of an indestructibility by death, but rather a liberation from the necessity of dying again and again.

(b) Sûtram 1, 2, 18—20.

In the Bṛihadâraṇyaka-Upanishad *Yâjñavalkya* is asked by *Uddâlaka* the son of *Aruṇa* (the father and teacher of *Çvetaketu* in Chând. VI, cf. Chap. XX, 2) concerning "the "inner ruler (*antaryâmin*), which inwardly rules this world, "and the other world, and all beings," and thereupon answers (Bṛih. 3, 7, 3):

"He who, dwelling in the earth, is different from the earth, "whom the earth knows not, whose body is the earth, who "inwardly rules the earth, this is thy soul, thine inner ruler, "the immortal."

What is said here of the earth, is further, by a stereotyped repetition of the same formula, transferred to water, fire, the atmosphere, the wind, sky, the sun, the cardinal points, moon and stars, the ether, darkness, light; then to all beings; then to breath, speech, the eye, the ear, the mind, the skin, knowledge [according to the *Kâṇva*-, "the self" according to the *Mâdhyandina*-Recension] and seed.—In conclusion it is said (3, 7, 23):

"He is seeing, not seen, hearing, not heard, understanding, "not understood, knowing, not known; outside him there is none "that sees, that hears, that understands, that knows; he is thy "soul, thy inner ruler, thy immortal;—what is different from "him, is afflicted."

Here, as Çañkara shows, by the "inner ruler" the highest Âtman is to be understood; for it is his quality to rule all that exists from within; he has the power to do this, because he is the cause of all that exists (p. 195, 13); and in this he makes use of the organs of the beings in question (p. 196, 7). That he is different from beings, is evident from the fact that these beings do not know him; for the said beings know themselves, as, for example the deity earth knows: "I am the earth" (p. 196, 4).—We must not think of the primordial matter of the Sâñkhyas, because although it is true of this, that it is said to be "not seen" etc., it is not true that it is "seeing" etc. (p. 197, 5).—Just as little can the individual soul be meant, because this is enumerated among the things ruled by it, in the passage, where the *Kâṇvas* read "knowledge," and the *Mâdhyandinas* "the self." Both mean the individual soul (p. 198, 7). Besides the difference between the Brahman and the individual soul is not, in the highest sense, real, but only the work of *Avidyâ*, which perceives the highest soul by means of the ascribed limitation (*upâdhi*) as individual soul (p. 199, 5), and on which the separation of subject and object, the empirical means of knowledge, Saṃsâra and the Vedic Canon rest (p. 199, 9). In truth there is only one inner soul, and not two (p. 199, 7).

3. Brahman as Destroyer of the World.

Sûtram 1, 2, 9—10.

In the Kâṭhaka-Upanishad it is said (2, 24—25):

"Not he who ceases not from deeds of violence,
"Nor he who has a restless, wandering mind,
"Nor he who has not peace within his heart,
"By knowledge can that highest Spirit gain.
"To whom the priest and warrior are bread
"Which he besprinkles with the sauce of death—
"Who that hath done these deeds can find him out."

Of the three objects, says Çañkara, of which the Kâṭhaka-Upanishad treats, fire, the individual and the highest soul, only the last can be understood here under that which consumes food. It is true that fire also consumes; it is also true that it is said of the individual soul (Muṇḍ. 3, 1, 1): "The one eats the sweet berry," and the following words "the other looks on, not eating," refer to the highest soul (cf. on this below p. 171); but this is to be understood of the enjoyment of the fruit of works, which comes only to the individual, not to the highest soul (p. 178, 13). In our passage, on the contrary, it is a question of the devouring of all things movable [men and beasts] and immovable [plants], for which priest and warrior, as the noblest, are quoted as examples (p. 178, 11). This devouring of all that lives, after it has been sprinkled with the condiment of death, belongs only to the Brahman in its character of Destroyer of the World (p. 178, 7).

XI. The Brahman as Cosmic and at the same time Psychic Principle.

THE Brahman is identical with the soul;—the power which creates and supports all the worlds, the eternal principle of all Being lives whole and undivided in each one of us. This doctrine of the Vedânta, great and worthy of admiration as it is (cf. St. John 14, 20. Gal. 4, 19. 2, 20), is expressed in a further series of Vedic texts cited by Bâdarâyaṇa, which we bring together in this chapter.

1. Brahman as the very Small and very Great.

(a) Sûtram 1, 2, 1—8.

The section Chând. 3, 14 (cf. Çatap. Br. 10, 6, 3) contains the much quoted "Doctrine of Çâṇḍilya" (*Çâṇḍilya-Vidyâ*). which runs as follows:

"Verily this universe is Brahman; as *Tajjalân* [in it be-"coming, ceasing, breathing] it is to be worshipped in silence."

"Truly of Will (*kratu*) is man formed; according as his "will is in this world, after its likeness is born the man, when "he has departed hence; therefore should a man strive after "[good] Will."[76]

"Spirit is its material, life is its body, light its form; "its resolve is truth, its self is endlessness [literally: the ether];

[76] *Kratu* p. 168, 1 is explained by *saṃkalpa, dhyânam*, in the Commentary to Chând. 3, 14, 1 by *niçcaya, adhyavasâya, avicala pratyaya*, to Bṛih. 4, 4, 5 by *adhyavasâya, niçcayo yad-anantarâ kriyâ pravartate*; cf. Bṛih. 4, 4, 5: "Man is altogether formed of desire (*kâma*); according as "his desire is, so is his will (*kratu*), according as his will is, so he does "the work (*karman*), according as he does the work, so does it befall "him."

"all-working is he, all-wishing, all-smelling, all-tasting, comprehending the All, silent, ungrieved:—this is my soul (*âtman*) "in the innermost heart, smaller than a grain of rice, or of "barley, or of mustard-seed, or of millet, or a grain of millet's "kernel;—this is my soul in the innermost heart, greater than "the earth, greater than the atmosphere, greater than the "heaven, greater than these worlds.—The all-working, all-wishing, all-smelling, all-tasting, embracing the all, silent, ungrieved, this is my soul in the innermost heart, this is Brahman, into Him shall I enter on departing hence.—He who "has gained this, he, verily, doubts no more."

"Thus spoke Çâṇḍilya, Çâṇḍilya."

In this passage, as Çaṅkara at great length explains, the highest Âtman is spoken of, as whose being the ether is mentioned, because, like the ether, He is omnipresent (p. 170, 12). Because He is the being of all, for this reason the qualities belonging to the individual soul, Spirit (*manas*), Life, etc. are ascribed to him (p. 171, 2), just as the Scripture says (Çvet. 4, 3 = A. V. 10, 8, 27):

> "The woman thou art, and the man,
> "The maiden and the boy,
> "And born thou growest everywhere,
> "As old man on a staff."

which refers to Brahman (p. 171, 3). For, so far as He is represented as possessing attributes (*saguṇam*), such individual properties as wish, breath and the like can be ascribed to Him, while of the attributeless Brahman it is said (in the passage quoted above p. 132) "the breathless, wishless, pure" (p. 171, 7). Although in our passage it is said of Brahman that He is also in the body, yet the individual soul is not therefore to be understood, for it is distinguished from Brahman by being only in the body (p. 172, 6). A distinction is pointed out between them in our passage by the words: "Into "Him shall I enter" (p. 172, 12), as also in the parallel passage Çatap. Br. 10, 6, 3, 2, where in the words "thus lives this golden spirit in the inner soul" the highest soul stands in the nominative, the individual in the locative (p. 173, 5); as also in the Smṛiti passage Bhag. G. 18, 61. Of course only the highest soul really exists, and only the ignorant conceive it as limited by Upâdhis: body, senses, Manas, and Buddhi, that is, as the individual soul, just as space, in the vessels, limited through the Upâdhis [of the sides of the vessels] is apparently different from cosmic space. Yet the illusion only endures until identity with the highest soul is known by the sentence "*tat tvam asi*," whereby the whole standpoint of practical life with bondage and liberation [destroying bondage] comes to an end (p. 173, 16).—The objection that the human heart is too narrow a dwelling for the highest soul, is not valid; what is in one particular place cannot be everywhere, but what is everywhere can also be in one particular place (cf. p. 1060, 2: the soul is God, but God is not the soul); he who is lord of the whole earth, is lord also of the city of *Ayodhyâ* (p. 174, 12). Therefore, as space is also in the eye of a needle, so is Brahman also in the heart (p. 175, 2), and is specially there pointed out, in order to concentrate attention upon Him; as Vishṇu is in a Çâlagrâma stone (p. 174, 16; the same comparison also p. 188, 12. 253, 12; cf. 860, 10. 1058, 13. 1065, 12. 1059, 6). If anyone should here object, that Brahman, if He dwells in the different hearts, as parrots in different cages, must Himself be either manifold or divided, he may be reminded that the relations here spoken of have no reality in the highest sense (p. 175, 5). In this also lies the answer to the objection, that the Brahman, if He dwells in the heart, must also take part in pleasure and pain: this is precisely the difference between the individual and the highest soul, that the former is the doer of right and wrong, the enjoyer of pleasure and pain, (p. 176, 2), while the latter, on the contrary, is free from all evil, and although present when one suffers, has as little share in the suffering as space has in the burning, when bodies filling it burn (p. 176, 5). Certainly the scripture teaches the identity of the individual soul with Brahman, but for him who has perfectly, and not only half, understood this teaching, with the entrance into full knowledge, the enjoyments and sufferings of the individual soul also cease (p. 176, 12), since both rest only on a vain illusion (p. 177, 3).

(b) Sûtram 1, 3, 24—25.

In the Kâṭhaka-Upanishad (4, 12—13) it is said:

"And in the midst, a thumb-breadth high,
"The Spirit (*purusha*) in the body dwells,
"Lord of the past, and what shall be,
"Therefore no fear approaches him,
"Verily, this is that."

"The Spirit (*purusha*), but a thumb-breadth high,
"Is as a flame devoid of smoke,
"Lord of the past and what shall be,
"To-morrow even as to-day.
"Verily, this is that."

Here, says Çañkara, where a certain measure is given, it would certainly be simplest to think of the individual soul, of which the Smṛiti, (Mahâbh. 3, 16763) relates, that *Yama* (the god of death) "tore it forth, of the length of a thumb, by force from the body" of *Satyavant* (p. 276, 8); however, not it but Brahman is to be understood here, because it is said "the lord of all that was, and is to be," and also because of the words *etad vai tad* "verily, this is that" [occurring as a refrain, and with the same meaning as the recurring *tat tvam asi* in Chând. VI], that is, this [the world, the soul] is that Brahman, of which thou hast asked me, in the words (Kâth. 2, 14):

"From good and evil free, free from effect and cause,
"From past and future free,—that tell me, what it is."

The Paramâtman seems here limited, just as limitless space is, when anyone says: "the space in this tube is an ell long" (p. 277, 8); and this, because it is necessary to direct people's attention to it (p. 278, 1). It is true that the Spirit thumb-breadth high is first of all the individual soul, but it is precisely the aim of the Vedânta to teach this,—on the one side, the being of Brahman, and, on the other, its identity with the individual soul (p. 279, 2). The latter doctrine occurs in the Kâṭhaka-Upanishad, as is to be seen from its concluding words (6, 17):

"A thumb-breadth high, in every creature's heart,
"The Spirit ever dwells as inner soul;
"Then from the body draw it forth with care,

"As from the reed bank one draws forth a reed,
"This know thou as the immortal, as the pure."

(c) Sûtram 1, 2, 24—32.

To the attempt to transform the names and cult of the old Vedic nature-gods into the religion of Brahman, belongs the Doctrine of *Âtman vaiçvânara* in Chândogya-Up. 5, 11—24. —*Vaiçvânarâ* "who dwells in all men" is originally an epithet of *Agni*, but here becomes a name of the all-animating Brahman, and, in conformity with this, in the place of the fire-sacrifice (*agni-hotram*) offered to *Agni* and through him to the gods, stands a sacramental feeding of one's own body, in which Brahman dwells.

Six rich and learned Brahmans are engaged on the question: "What is our soul, what is Brahman?" and go with it to king *Açvapati*, who, when he rises in the morning, can say:

"In all my kingdom not one thief,
"None covetous, no drunkard dwells,
"Not one who sacrifice or knowledge shuns,
"And none who breaks the holy marriage vow."

He begins to teach his guests, who ask him to impart to them the doctrine of *Âtman vaiçvânara*, by asking what they imagine *Âtman* to be. The answers in order are, that *Âtman* is heaven, the sun, the wind, the ether, the water, the earth. After the king has pointed out the insufficiency of these ideas of *Âtman*, since heaven is only its head, the sun its eye, the wind its breath, the ether its body, the water its belly, the earth its feet, he says to all his six pupils: "As individual, as "it were (*prithag iva*), ye all know the *Âtman vaiçvânara*, "and eat your food; but he who knows this Âtman thus,—as "a span long,—and adores it as immeasurably great,[77] he eats "food in all worlds, in all beings, in all bodies." Then after

---

[77] ***Abhivimâna***; as the different attempts at explanation p. 223, 3 shew, the scholiasts themselves no longer knew what this word meant. The above explanation, suggested by the Petersburg Dictionary in accordance with the etymology, is acceptable from the habit of the Upanishads to emphasize the greatness side by side with the smallness of Brahman. Perhaps, as Weber suggests, we should read *ativimâna*. For a different opinion cf. our Upanishads, p. 145 ff.

the above named divisions of nature have further been mentioned as parts of the Âtman under mystical names, as also the sacrificial bed, the sacrificial grass, and the three sacrificial fires, there follows an interpretation which substitutes, for the cult of the fire-sacrifice, the feeding of the body as a sacrifice for the Âtman; this feeding is divided into five offerings, by which the five vital spirits, and through them the five organs of sense (the fifth is omitted), five pairs of nature-gods and nature-elements, with all that lies under their sovereignty, and lastly the person of the offerer, are satiated. "He who, not "knowing this, offers the fire-sacrifice, with him is it as though "he had raked the coals away, and sacrificed in the ashes; "but he who knowing this thus offers the fire-sacrifice [that "is, the substitute mentioned], he has sacrificed in all worlds, "in all beings, in all bodies. As the pith of a rush, thrown "into the fire, burns away, so burn away all the sins of him, "who, knowing this, consummates the fire-sacrifice. And should "he who knows this give what remains over even to a Caṇḍâla, "he [*asya*, by the Commentator less suitably joined to *âtmani* "*vaiçvânare*] would thereby have offered it in the *Âtman vaiçvânara*. This is said by the verse:

> "As hungry children round their mother sit,
> "All beings sit around the sacrifice."

It is true, says Çañkara, that the words *âtman* and *vaiçvânara* have many meanings. *Vaiçvânara* can mean fire, as in Ṛigv. X, 88, 12, or, as in Ṛigv. I, 98, 1, the God of fire, or, as in Bṛih. 5, 9, 1, the fire of digestion in the body; in the same way by *Âtman* can be understood as well the individual as the highest soul (p. 211—212). Here only the latter is to be understood by *Âtman vaiçvânara*, for the reason that to it only can apply the saying that heaven is its head, etc., and at the same time that it is the inner soul (p. 213, 1), and that the sins of him who knows it are burnt away (p. 213, 6); also it only is the subject of the question raised at the beginning (p. 213, 7). The fire-element cannot be thought of, because its being is limited to burning and lighting (p. 217, 4); nor the god of fire, because his power depends on that of the highest God (p. 217, 7). The fire of digestion also, as such, cannot be meant, on account of the indication that heaven is its head (p. 216, 2), and because in the parallel passage Çatap. Br. 10, 6, 1, 11 the *Âtman vaiçvânara* is termed "the *Purusha* (spirit) in the inward part of the *Purusha* (man)," (p. 216, 6).— Therefore the highest Âtman is to be understood here, whether in the quality or under the symbol of the fire of digestion (p. 215, 13. 217, 10), or, with *Jaimini*, directly and without symbols. It is called *Vaiçvânara*, which means the same as *Viçvânara*, like *Râkshasa* and *Rakshas*, *Vâyasa* and *Vayas* (p. 219, 3), because He is common to all men, or all men are common to Him (p. 219, 1), in that He animates all. The Vedânta teachers are not at one as to why it is said to be "a span long;" *Âçmarathya* believes it is to indicate the heart as the place of the perception (p. 219, 11), *Bâdari*, because it is an object of memory for *Manas*, which dwells in the heart a span large (p. 220, 2); *Jaimini*, because it is true of it, that it is a span large, in that Çatap. Br. 10, 6, 1, 10—11 from the point of view of psychology (*adhyâtmam*) compares its parts with those of the face, allegorically (p. 221, 1), as, lastly, the *Jâbâlas* (Jâbâla-Up. 2, p. 438 ff., ed. Bibl. Ind.) give, as the dwelling place where it is enthroned, the point of union between the nose and eyebrows (p. 223, 1).

(d) Sûtram 1, 3, 14—18.

After the esoteric teaching has been put forward in the sixth and seventh parts of Chândogya-Up., there follows, at the beginning of the eighth part, a kind of direction for the teacher, as to how he is to help pupils who hold the exoteric standpoint. This is introduced by Çañkara in his Commentary on Chândogya-Up. with the following words:

"Even though Brahman has been recognised as free from "spatial, temporal and other distinctions, in the sixth and "seventh lectures, by the words: 'Being is it, One only and "'without a Second,' (Chând. 6, 2, 1)—'Soul only is all this "'world' (Chând. 7, 25, 2), yet the intellect (*buddhi*) of the "slow spirits is such that it perceives Being as affected with "differences of space etc., and cannot be brought immediately "to an intuition of the highest reality. Now as without know-

"ledge of Brahman the goal of man cannot be reached, there-"fore Brahman, in order to be known, must be spatially "pointed out in the lotus of the heart. For even if the essence "of Âtman consists of Being, as it alone is object of the "perfect knowledge and without attributes, yet, because the "slow spirits demand that it shall be possessed of attributes, "it is to be taught with the attributes 'wishing truth' etc. "Further, even if the knowers of Brahman of themselves ab-"stain from objects of sensual enjoyment, as women etc., yet "the thirst (*trishṇâ*) caused by being addicted to sensuality in "different births cannot at once be converted, and therefore "the different means, such as life as Brahman pupils [in a "condition of chastity] etc., are to be applied. Further: if "even for those who know the unity of the Âtman, no goer, "or going, or object to which one goes, exists [cf. above p. 109], "and on the other hand, after the cause for the persistance "of a residuum of Ignorance etc. [in them] has been removed, "liberation is only an entering into one's own Self, like light-"ning in atmosphere, or the wind which has risen [cf. Chând. "8, 12, 2, translated above p. 51], or the fire, when the wood "is burnt out, yet for those whose understanding is saturated "with ideas of goer, going etc., and who adore Brahman as "spatial in the heart, and possessed of attributes, a going to "Brahman through the carotid artery (*mûrdhanyâ nâḍî*) is to "be taught. To this end serves this eighth part. For a "Brahman that is free from space, attributes, going, rewards, "and differences, in the highest sense Being and without a "second, seems to the slow spirits no more than non-Being. "Therefore the scripture thinks: let them first find themselves "on the path of 'the Existent,' then I shall gradually bring "them also to an understanding of 'the Existent' in the "highest sense."

With these words, in which perhaps more clearly than anywhere else, the motive of the exoteric teaching is disclosed, Çaṅkara goes on to consider the following passage (Chândogya-Up. 8, 1):

The Master speaks:

"Here in this city of Brahman [the body] is a house, a "small lotus-flower [the heart]; therein is a small space; what "is in this must be investigated, this, verily, should one seek "to know."

The Pupil speaks:

"Here in this city of Brahman is a house, a small lotus-"flower; therein is a small space; what is then in this, that "must be investigated, that one should seek to know?"

The Master speaks:

"Verily, as great as the Universe, so great is this space "inwardly in the heart; in it both heaven and earth are in-"cluded; both fire and wind, both sun and moon, the lightning "and the stars, and what is in the world, and what is not in "the world [past and future], all that is included therein."

The Pupil speaks:

"If all this is included in the city of Brahman, and all "beings and all wishes,—if now old age overtakes it, or cor-"ruption, what then remains over from it?"

The Teacher speaks:

"This in us ages not with old age; nor is it reached by "weapons; it is the true city of Brahman, in it are the wishes "included; that is the Self (the soul), the sinless, free from "age, free from death, free from suffering, without hunger and "without thirst; its wish is true, true is its resolve."

"For just as mankind here below, as though by command, "aim at the goal, that each one strives after, whether it be "a kingdom or a field, and only live for that—[thus in striv-"ing after heavenly reward, are they also the slaves of their "wishes;] and just as here below the enjoyment, which has "been won by work, vanishes away, thus also in the Beyond "vanishes away the reward that is won by good works."

"Therefore he who departs hence, without having known "the soul and those true wishes, in all worlds his part is a "life of unfreedom; but he who departs hence, after he has "known the soul and those true wishes, in all worlds his part "is a life of freedom."

As the context of this passage shews, the Ignorant is called unfree, because he is dependent on his wishes. In contrast to this heteronomy stands the autonomy of him who knows. He is free, because he knows in himself the Âtman, which embraces the world, and with it the totality of all desires. Therefore, as is stated more fully in the sequel (Chând. 8, 2) the sage possesses and enjoys within himself the fulfilment of every wish. Should he long for intercourse with the departed, with fathers, mothers, brothers, sisters, friends, if his senses demand sweet savours and garlands, food and drink, song, music or women,—"whatsoever goal he longs for, whatever he "may wish, that arises for him at his wish, and becomes his "share, in which he rejoices."

In contrast with the nothingness of all satisfactions brought to men from without, the wishes of him who has become conscious of his "I" as the totality of all Being, are called "true" or "real" (*satya*). In reality this is true of all men, only that, with the exception of those who know, they are not conscious of it, since their true wishes are "covered up" by untruth, that is, by the outer world and the pursuit of it, as is profoundly developed in the sequel.

"These true wishes are covered up by untruth, [in the "Ignorant]. They are there, in truth, but untruth covers "them over; and when one of his friends departs hence, the "man sees him no more. But [it is so in truth, that] all his "friends, who are alive here, and those who have departed, "and whatever else he longs for and reaches not,—all this "he finds when he enters here [into his own heart]; for here "his true wishes are, which untruth covered up.—But just as "he who knows not the place, finds not a hidden treasure of "gold, even though he should walk over it many times, so all "these creatures find not this world of Brahman, although "they daily enter it [in dreamless sleep]; for by untruth are "they forced away.—Truly this Âtman is in the heart! And "this is the interpretation of it: *hṛidi ayam* (in the heart is "he) therefore it is called *hṛidayam* (the heart). Verily, he "who knows this, daily enters into the heavenly world.— "And what this perfect peace is (*saṃprasâda*), that rises from "this body, ascends to the highest light, and appears in own "form; that is the soul,—thus the Master spoke,—that is the "immortal, the fearless, that is Brahman."

In what follows, Brahman is explained with reference to the name *Satyam* (the Real) in its etymological meaning, as that which binds the mortal and immortal together; then again as the bridge (the boundary, *setu*) which keeps asunder the two: "The Âtman is the bridge (the boundary), which keeps "these worlds asunder that they may not blend. This bridge "day and night traverse not, nor old age, nor death, nor "sorrow, nor good work, nor evil work, all sins turn back from "it, for sinless is that world of Brahman. Therefore, verily, "he who being blind has crossed over this bridge, regains his "sight, he who is maimed, becomes whole again, he who is "sick, becomes well. Therefore, verily, night, when it passes "this bridge, changes into day, for, once and for all, this "world of Brahman is light."

After this the different obligations of the Brahmans (sacrifice, offerings, the great Soma festival, silence, fasts, life in a hermitage) receive a new etymological interpretation in the sense of the Brahmavidyâ which leads to Brahmaloka and the renunciation (*brahmacâryam = strî-vishaya-tṛishṇâ-tyâga*) connected with it, there follows at the end of the section the doctrine, indicated by Çaṅkara in the introduction to the section as wholly propaedeutic, of the entering of the soul of him who dies as *Saguṇa-vid* (knowing exoterically) into Brahman through the carotid artery and the sun, which are united by a sunbeam, as two cities by a road. Of this further in our last part (Chap. XXXIX, 2).

It might be thought, so Çaṅkara says in the Commentary to the Brahmasûtras on this passage, that by the "small "space in the lotus of the heart," space properly so called is to be understood (p. 249, 12), or perhaps the individual soul, because to it belongs the "city of Brahman," that is the body, since it has acquired this body through its works (in an earlier existence), (p. 250, 6), because the heart is commonly held to be the seat of ***Manas***, which is a limitation of it (p. 250, 9), because it is called Çvet. 5, 8 "large as the point of an awl" (p. 250, 10), or because, what is in it is still distinguished from the space, that is, the highest soul is still different from the individual soul (p. 250, 13).-- But the natural space is not to be thought of here, because making the space in the heart equivalent to cosmic space would not agree with this (p. 251, 10), and just as little would it suit the individual soul limited by Upâdhis (p. 253, 2). On the contrary everything points to the fact that, by the small space in the heart, the highest soul, and nothing else, should be understood. The description of God as space (ether) is also found elsewhere (p. 258, 11), while it never occurs in the case of the individual soul (p. 258, 13). It is true that God is also called "greater than space" (Çatap. Br. 10, 6, 3, 2), (p. 252, 4), but here it was only intended to accentuate His greatness in the universe in contrast with His smallness in the heart (p. 252, 6). Of Him alone can it rightly be said that he is sinless, without age, death, etc. (p. 252, 9), and the city of Brahman, the body, is, indeed, the dwelling in which he can be perceived (p. 253, 9), in which sense he is called (Praçna 5, 5. Bṛih. 2, 5, 18) the *purusha puriçaya* (p. 253, 10); with Him only, also, can truly be connected the promises, which, in our passage, are connected with a knowledge of Him (p. 254, 5). But concerning the subtle expression of the Opponent, that it is not the small space, but what is in it, that is enquired about, it is to be remarked that in it are in fact heaven and earth, but that it is not about these, but precisely about the small space that the question is raised (p. 254, 14). To Brahman we are also pointed by the expression, that all beings enter day by day the world of Brahman, to wit, in deep sleep; of whoever is in this condition it is said, even popularly: "he is with Brahman," is *brahmîbhûta, brahmatâṃ gata* (p. 256, 6). The "world of Brahman" is not the world of Brahman the popular god (*Kamalâsana*), but "Brahman as the world," for only of the latter can it be said that it is entered day by day (p. 256, 11). Also the term the bridge, which keeps asunder the world and its content, such as castes, Âçramas, etc., that they may not blend, suits Brahman only (p. 258, 1). On the other hand, Perfect Peace (*samprasâda*) in our passage means, not the condition of deep sleep, but the individual soul when in that condition, and, thus, entering into the highest Brahman as into its own proper nature (p. 259, 6); but the individual soul, as already remarked, is not to be understood by space (p. 260, 1).

2. Brahman as Joy (*kam*) and as Amplitude (*kham*).

Sûtras 1, 2, 13—17.

Not gloomy asceticism characterises the knower of Brahman, but the joyous hopeful consciousness of unity with God. —This appears to be the fundamental thought of the *Upakosalavidyâ* in Chând. 4, 10—15, which runs as follows:

"Upakosala, the son of Kamala, lived as pupil (*brahma-* "*cârin*) with Satyakâma, the son of Jabâlâ [cf. note 38]. "Twelve years had he tended for him the sacrificial fires; "then he dismissed the other pupils, but him he would not "dismiss. Then his wife said to him: 'The pupil grieves; he "'has tended the fires well; look to it, that the fires do not "'speak to him instead of thee [Comm.: speak evil of thee], "'teach him the doctrine.'—But he would not teach it to him, "but set out on a journey. Then the pupil fell ill, and would "not eat. Then the teacher's wife said to him: 'Eat, pupil; "why eatest thou not?'—But he said: 'Alas! In men there "'are so many desires! I am quite full of disease; I care "'not to eat.'—Then the fires said among themselves: 'The "'pupil grieves, yet he has tended us well. Come then! let "'us teach him the doctrine!'—And they said to him: 'Brah- "'man is Life, Brahman is Joy, Brahman is Amplitude.'— "But he said: 'I know that Brahman is Life; but the Joy "'and the Amplitude know I not.'—But they said: 'Verily, "'the Amplitude is the Joy, and the Joy is the Amplitude.' "And they explained to him how Brahman was the Life and "wide space.

"Then the fire, that is called *Gârhapatya*, taught him: "'The earth, fire, food, and the sun [are my forms]. But the "'man who is seen in the sun, I am he, and he is I.' [Chorus "of the Fires:] 'He who, knowing this, worships this [Fire], "'he puts away evil deeds, he becomes world-possessing, he "'comes to full age, he lives long, his race fails not, him help "'we in this world and in the other world, who, knowing this "'fire worships it.'

"Then the second fire, which is called *Anvâhâryapacana,* "taught him: 'The water, the regions of the world, the stars "'and the moon [are my forms]. But the man who is seen "'in the moon, I am he, and he is I.' [Chorus of the Fires:] "'He who, knowing this fire worships it,' etc., as before.

"Then the third fire, which is called *Âhavanîya,* taught "him: 'Breath, the ether, heaven, the lightning [are my forms]. "'But the man who is seen in the lightning, I am he, and he "'is I.' [Chorus of the Fires:] 'He who, knowing this fire "'worships it' etc., as before.

"And they said to him: 'Now knowest thou, Upakosala, "'dear one, the doctrine about us, and the doctrine about the "'Âtman. But the way to Him will the teacher point out "'to thee.'

"Now, his teacher when he returned, spoke thus to him: "'Upakosala!'—And he answered and said: 'Master!'—But he "said: 'Thy face shines, dear one, as the face of one who "'knows Brahman. Who, then, has taught thee?'—And he "answered evasively: 'Who should teach me? Of a truth "'these here look as they do, and also differently;' thus he "spoke, pointing to the fires.—'What have they said to thee, "'dear one?'—And he answered him: 'Thus and thus.'—Then "the teacher said: 'They have only told thee its dwelling- "'places; but I will tell thee its own self; as the water clings "'not to the lotus-petal, so no evil deed clings to him who "'knows this.'—And he said: 'Let the master teach it to me!' "And he said to him: 'The man who is seen in the eye, he "'is the Âtman, said he, he is the immortal, the fearless, he "'is Brahman. Therefore also, when grease or water comes "'into the eye, it flows off to the edges. Him they call love's "'treasure, for he is a treasure of what is dear. He is a "'treasure of what is dear, who knows this. He is also called "'the prince of love [literally: the herald of love], for all that "'is dear, he leads; he leads all that is dear, who knows this. "'He is also called the prince of radiance, for he is radiant "'in all worlds; in all worlds is he radiant, who knows this. "'Therefore [when such as these die], whether funeral rites "'are performed or not, they enter into a flame [of the funeral "'fire], from the flame into the day, from the day into the "'light half of the month, from the light half of the month "'into the half-year in which the sun goes northwards, from "'that half-year into the year, from the year into the sun, "'from the sun into the moon, from the moon into the light- "'ning;—there is a man who is not as a human being; he "'leads them in to Brahman. That is the way of the Gods, "'the way of Brahman. They who go that way, for them "'thus is no returning to the earth, no returning.'"

In this narrative, so explains Çankara, by "the man who is seen in the eye," neither a form mirrored in the eye, nor the individual soul, nor the god of light, but the highest Brahman is to be understood, for this only is, in a true sense, "the Âtman," only this is "the immortal, the fearless," who is spoken of here (p. 187, 8). To Brahman only can refer the unstained purity, which is expressed by the grease and water flowing to the edges (p. 187, 10), as also the names "love's treasure," "love's herald," "prince of radiance" (p. 187, 12 ff.). We should not stumble at the fact that a place of Brahman is spoken of; this could only be objected to, if Brahman were said to be in this place only, and not, by other passages of scripture, in many other places as well (p. 188, 3). But as a matter of fact, to the end of the worship of the attribute-possessing Brahman, manifold places, names, and forms are ascribed to it, although it is in reality without attributes or any of these (p. 188, 10). This happens, in order to make it perceptible, like Vishṇu in a Çâlagrâma stone (p. 188, 12). Also only in Brahman can be found the union of joy and amplitude. In the case of amplitude alone, it is true, we might think of space, as the symbol of Brahman (p. 189, 6), in the case of joy alone, of sensual pleasure (p. 189, 9), but in conjunction the two ideas mutually particularise each other (*itara-itara-viçeshitau*) and mean that Brahman which in its own nature consists of pleasure (*sukham*), (p. 189, 12). Also the fact that the fires say that they have not only explained the teaching about themselves, but also that about Âtman (p. 190, 6), so that no sin attaches to him who knows this, as no water clings to the lotus-petal (p. 191, 1), can only apply to Brahman, the entering into which, for him who has heard the Upanishad, by the way of the gods, is set forth at the conclusion (p. 191, 6). In our passage, the form mirrored in the eye cannot be understood, because it is not always in it (p. 192, 13), and precisely at the time of worship, is not there (p. 192, 16), and because according to Chând. 8, 9, 2 it passes away with the body (p. 192, 18); nor the individual soul, either because it has its dwelling, not in the eye only, but in the whole body (p. 193, 3), because not it but the highest soul is "immortal and fearless," in that ignorance of it imposes mortality and fear (p. 193, 7), and because it does not possess lordship (*aiçvaryam*), so that the names "love's treasure," "love's herald," "prince of radiance" cannot apply to it (p. 193, 8); lastly it is also not the deity of the sun either although according to Bṛih. 5, 5, 2 it rests in the eye by means of the rays (p. 193, 9), because it is not the Âtman, but an outer form (p. 193, 10), and because it is not immortal, for the immortality of the gods means only existence for a long time (p. 193, 12), just as their *aiçvaryam* is not self-dependent, but depends on the *Îçvara*, through fear of whom they perform their duties (p. 193, 14).

3. Brahman as the Light beyond Heaven and in the Heart.

Sûtras 1, 1, 24—27.

With strange allegorical embroidery the theme of the present chapter is treated in the section Chând. 3, 12—13, which compares the world, the macrocosm, to the body as microcosm, and this again to the heart, on the basis of the harmony ruling in all three, as which Brahman is regarded in all three, and that by means of the symbol of the *Gâyatrî*,

—a Vedic metre, consisting of three feet, to which, as we shall see, yet a fourth, imaginary foot is added. In order to grasp this glorification of Brahman as *Gâyatrî*, we must remember the eternity and original dignity of the Word of the Veda (discussed above p. 71). As this is, as it were, borne and controlled by the metre, as representative of which the *Gâyatrî* appears here, so Brahman, as the earth, bears and controls all beings, as the organs of sense (*prâṇa*) the body, as vital spirits (*prâṇa*, unless there is a mistake in the repetition of the same word) the heart (the principle of life).

Thus we are to understand, when, in the text, on the basis of the common bearing and controlling of beings, sense-organs, and vital spirits, it is said: "What the earth is, the body is, "what the body is, the heart is." For this reason also the Gâyatrî is called *sixfold*, because it symbolically represents the three things named and their respective contents (cf. p. 149, 8 *bhûta-prithivî-çarîra-hṛidaya-vâk-prâṇa* and on Chândogya-Up. p. 184, 10: *vâg-bhûta-prithivî-çarîra-hṛidaya-prâṇa*). But further it has *four feet*, that is, the three actual and a fourth, imagined, which is also mentioned Bṛih. 5, 14.[78] For the rest, the Bṛihadâraṇyakam *loc. cit.* follows its own course; how, in our passage, the four feet are to be understood, must be deduced from the verse (Ṛigv. X, 90, 3) quoted on this occasion:

"However great is Nature's majesty,
"The Spirit is yet higher raised by far,
"Of it, but one foot do all beings make,
"Three feet are immortality in heaven."

It would be simple to conclude that, for the author of our Chândogya-passage, the three immortal feet or quarters of *Purusha* are represented by the three real feet of the *Gâyatrî*,

---

[78] As in this passage the right of each of the three first feet to the necessary eight syllables is vindicated, we must not with the "*apara*" (Brahmasûtra p. 150, 10), and *Max Müller* (Upanishads I, p. 45) divide the 24 syllables of the Gâyatrî into four times six, in order to explain the *catushpadâ shaḍvidhâ gâyatrî*.

the beingless phenomenal world, on the contrary, by its imaginary foot. With this agrees what immediately follows:

"Therefore, verily, that which is called Brahman, that is "certainly that which this space outside the man is; but the "space which is outside the man is certainly that which this "space inside the man is; but this space inside the man is "certainly that which this space inside the heart is: this is "that Perfect, Unchangeable [a definition, which Bṛih. 2, 1, 5 "is found to be inadequate]; perfect, unchangeable happiness "he gains, who knows this."

Further on, the five gates of the gods in the heart, or, as they later appear personified, "the five warriors of Brahman and doorkeepers of the heaven-world" are described, as which, corresponding to the triplicity running through the whole passage, appear five vital spirits, five sense-organs, and five nature-gods, of which one vital spirit, sense-organ and nature-god are always put as identical.[79] Then it is said further:

"Now, however, the light that gleams there beyond the "heavens, at the back of all, at the back of each, in the "highest world, the highest of all, that is certainly this light "inward here in man; its perception is, that when anyone "here in the body feels it, he perceives a warmness; its audition "is, that when anyone thus [note 12] closes his ears, he hears, "as it were, a humming, as though it were the noise of a "burning fire. This is to be honoured as its perception "and audition. He will be perceived and heard, who knows "this."

Against the objections of the Opponent, who wishes to understand by "the light beyond the heavens" the natural light (p. 142, 11), by "the light inwardly in man" the light of the belly (that is, probably, the fire of digestion), (p. 144, 7) Çaṅkara proves that the one and the other can only mean Brahman, on account of the feet, which cannot be attributed to any natural light (p. 145, 5), but, in harmony with the verse quoted from the Ṛigveda, can be attributed to Brahman

---

[79] In the last Triad *âkâça* should be omitted and before *vâyu* an organ, probably *tvac*, inserted.

(p. 146, 1), who is likened to light, because, in virtue of His spirituality, He lightens the whole world (p. 147, 2); that a place beyond the heavens is ascribed to Him, is done for the purpose of worship (p. 147, 6), just as Brahman is elsewhere indicated locally in the sun, in the eye, in the heart, although He is spaceless (*nishpradeça*), (p. 147, 8); and He also is to be understood by the symbol of the light of the belly (p. 147, 14). That the fruits of this worship mentioned at the end are only slight, is no obstacle to its referring to Brahman; only the knowledge of the attributeless Brahman has, as its one fruit, liberation (p. 148, 4), while the fruit of worship by means of attributes or symbols is manifold, although limited to Saṃsâra (p. 148, 5). That Brahman is indicated as the *Gâyatrî* happens (so Çañkara says, departing from the interpretation which we have set forth above), in order to fix the thoughts on Him (p. 149, 16); the metre itself, as a mere grouping of syllables (p. 150, 1) is not to be thought of here, because it is said: "this world is the *Gâyatrî*" and because beings etc. are indicated as its feet,[80] and also because our passage expressly names Brahman and the warriors of Brahman (p. 152, 4). That it is first said *paro divas* (beyond heaven) and then again *divi* (in heaven) is no contradiction: just as one can say of a falcon, which is sitting upon a tree, he is sitting "on the top of the tree," and he is sitting "on the tree" (p. 153, 4).

4. Brahman and the Soul dwelling together in the Heart.

Sûtras 1, 2, 11—12.

The transition to the Chapter which is to teach us to know Brahman as the Soul itself, may be formed by an isolated passage, in which the highest and the individual soul appear as united together in the heart; it is found in the Kâṭhaka-Up. 3, 1:

---

[80] The Sûtram 1, 1, 26 has *bhûta-âdi-pâda*, that is, beings and the three heavenly feet, while Çañkara (evidently falsely and not in conformity with p. 149, 8) understands: beings, earth, body and heart (p. 151, 8).

"Drinking fulfilment of their deeds in life,
"The two have gone into the secret cave,
"In the highest, that one half is of the highest [that is in the heart];
"He calls these Light and Shade who Brahman knows."

For the theme of the Kâṭhaka-Up. Çañkara firstly infers that by "the two" here either the organs of knowledge with Buddhi at their head and the individual soul, or the individual and the highest soul are to be understood (p. 179—181), then, that only the latter is permissible; for that which drinks fulfilment for its previous deeds, is undoubtedly the individual soul; and side by side with it only a kindred nature, therefore the highest soul, could be mentioned (p. 182, 3); that this dwells in the heart, is so often said in other places (p. 182, 5); that of it also it is said, it drinks, must not be taken literally, just as if it were said: "the people are carrying a parasol," when only one of them is carrying it (p. 180, 12. 182, 9, and 3, 3, 34, p. 921, 7, where the subject is once more explained); they are called shadow and light, because the one is subject to Saṃsâra, the other being free from it, Saṃsâra itself existing only through Ignorance (p. 182, 11). The same contrast is found again not only in other passages of the Kâṭhaka-Up., but also in the verse [taken with changed meaning from Ṛigv. 1, 164, 20] of the Muṇḍaka-Up. 3, 1, 1 (= Çvet. 4, 6. 7):

"Know thou two friends fair-feathered,
"Tied to a single tree;
"One eats at the sweet berry,
"Not eating, one looks on."

Here, by the one that eats, the individual soul is to be understood, by the one that looks on, the highest soul (p. 183, 12), as also in the verse that follows:

"To such a tree sunk down, the spirit
"Is perplexed and sorrowful, without a lord;
"But when the lord is sought and found by him
"In majesty, then sorrow flees away."

In conclusion Çañkara mentions a view of the *Paiñgi-rahasya-brâhmaṇam* (also quoted p. 889, 10, and, as *Paiñgi-Upanishad*, p. 232, 12) according to which by the two are to be understood the *sattvam* (that is, the *antaḥkaraṇam*) and the individual soul, the latter, however, so far as it is raised above Saṃsâra and has gained unity with Brahman (p. 184—185).

XII. The Brahman as Soul.

1. Brahman as the Self (*âtman*).

Sûtras 1, 4, 19—22.

No man, whatever he may do, can get out of his own Self; everything in the world can only arouse our interest, nay, only exists for us, in so far as, affecting us, it enters the sphere of our "I," and so, as it were, becomes a part of us. Therefore our own Self with its content is the first, and in a certain sense the only object of philosophical investigation.

This thought may prepare us for the consideration of one of the most remarkable passages in the Upanishads, the conversation between *Yâjñavalkya* and his spouse *Maitreyî*, which exists in two recensions, Bṛih. 2, 4 and Bṛih. 4, 5, and in both according to the reading of the *Kâṇvas*, as well as (in Çatap. Br.) according to that of the *Mâdhyandinas*; in all, therefore, in four forms. Çañkara quotes, if we leave out of the question passages which are identical, sometimes the recension in Bṛih. 2, 4 (for example p. 385, 10. 392, 8), sometimes that in Bṛih. 4, 5; and the latter as well in the *Kâṇva* form (p. 199, 1. 11. 399, 4. 613, 2. 648, 6. 674, 9. 930, 5. 974, 7. 1142, 6) as in the *Mâdhyandina* form (p. 185, 15. 386, 7. 387, 3. 392, 10. 794, 14. 983, 4). Also the quotation 646, 9 – 647, 1 is according to the *Mâdhyandinas*, borrowing *imam*, however, instead of *idam* from the *Kâṇvas*; the quotation p. 388, 9 is divergent from both, and the same again in another form p. 391, 8;—this seems to shew, that Çañkara is wont to quote the Upanishads chiefly from memory, which might serve him here, where four recensions interfere with one another, less faithfully than usual. In what follows, we analyse the passage according to Bṛih. 2, 4 and introduce the divergencies in Bṛih. 4, 5 only so far as seems interesting.

(Addition in Bṛih. 4, 5: "Yâjñavalkya had two wives, Mai-"treyî and Kâtyâyanî; of these Maitreyî was conversant with "Brahman, Kâtyâyanî on the contrary knew only what women "know [cf. St. Luke X, 38—42]. Now Yâjñavalkya wished to "pass to the other condition of life [from the condition of "householder to that of hermit]). Then said Yâjñavalkya: "'Maitreyî! I will now give up this condition [of householder]. "'Therefore will I make partition between thee and Kâtyâ-"'yanî.'—Then spoke Maitreyî: 'If indeed to me, Master, this "'whole earth with all its riches belonged, should I thereby "'be immortal?'—'By no means!' said Yâjñavalkya, 'but as "'the life of those who prosper, so would thy life be; but "'there is no hope of immortality through riches.'—Maitreyî "spoke: 'What shall I do with that, whereby I become not "'immortal? Share with me rather, Master, the knowledge "'which thou possessest.'—Yâjñavalkya spoke: 'Dear to us, "'verily, art thou, and dear is what thou sayest. Come, seat "'thyself, I will explain it to thee, but do thou mark well "'what I tell thee.'"—

The teaching which now follows begins with the sentence: "Verily, not for the sake of the husband is the husband dear, "but for the sake of the Self is the husband dear." What is here said of the husband, is further, with continual repetition of the same formula, declared of the wife, children, power, Brahmanhood, warriorship, worlds, gods, beings, and finally of all that exists;—all this is not dear for its own sake, but for the sake of the Self.—Apparently nothing more can be found than the thought expressed by us in introducing this chapter; Çañkara, on the other hand, on Bṛih. p. 448, 7 explains that here renunciation (*vairâgyam*) is taught as the means to immortality. And indeed, when everything only serves the purpose of gratifying the Self, it is further the question, what then is our true and real Self? And here the Indian consciousness is led quite of itself by the word *Âtman* (Self, Soul, God) to find in God our own real "I," and in a withdrawal to him the satisfaction which we seek in all relations of life.

Therefore the real *nervus probandi* lies here in the use of the word *Âtman* which arises from deeper philosophical insight: —what we long for, is everywhere and always only the satisfaction of our own Self; but our Self is identical with the highest Godhead and only apparently different from Him; he who sees the illusory nature of this appearance, who has become conscious of God as his own Self, has and possesses the perfect satisfaction, which he has sought in vain in striving after the outward. In this sense it is further said: "The Self, "verily, o Maitreyî, is to be seen, heard, meditated on and "investigated; he who sees, hears, meditates on and investigates "the Self, has understood this whole world."—He who has understood this, knows himself as one with all Being; he who has not understood it, for him all beings are foreign and hostile; this is expressed by the sequel, in which it is explained that Brahmans and warriors, worlds, gods, and beings, all abandon or exclude (*parâdât*) him who regards all these things as different from himself.—Not in its void appearances can the Self be grasped, but in that which produces these appearances; he who has understood this, has understood appearances along with it; this thought is contained in the following images: when a drum is beaten, a shell blown, a lute played, the tones going out from them cannot be grasped; but if the instrument or the player are grasped, then the tones are grasped at the same time.—As from damp wood, when it burns, clouds of smoke go forth, so from this great Being all Vedas and (as Bṛih. 4, 5 adds) all worlds and creatures are breathed forth.—The Âtman is the point of union (*ekâyanam*) for all beings, as the ocean for all waters, the skin for all sensations of touch, the tongue for all tastes, the nose for all smells, the eye for all forms, the ear for all tones, etc.—But why do we not see the Âtman, who alone really is, but only its void appearances? To this replies the following image guaranteed as genuine by Chând. 6, 13, but on account of its being dogmatically exceptionable, already quite altered in the late recension Bṛih. 4, 5: "'As a lump of salt, thrown into "'water, dissolves in the water, so that it cannot be taken "'out, but wherever it is tasted, it is everywhere salt,—thus, "'verily, also this great, endless, shoreless Being which is "'knowledge through and through: from these creatures it "'rises [as knowing spirit] and with them it perishes again; "'after death there is no consciousness! thus verily I tell thee!' "Thus spoke Yâjñavalkya. Then Maitreyî spoke: 'By this, O "'Master, hast thou perplexed me, that thou sayest, there is "'no consciousness after death.' But Yâjñavalkya spoke: "'Nothing bewildering truly speak I; what I said, suffices for "'the understanding, for where there is a duality, as it were, "'there the one sees the other, there the one smells, hears, "'speaks to, thinks of, knows the other; but where, for a man, "'all has become his own Self, how should he there see any- "'one, how should he there smell, hear, speak to, think of, "'know anyone? That through which he knows all this, how "'should he know that, how should he know the Knower?'"— (Addition in Bṛih. 4, 5: "'Now knowest thou the doctrine, O "'Maitreyî; this truly suffices for immortality.' Thus spoke "Yâjñavalkya and departed.")

The remarks of Bâdarâyaṇa and Çankara on this passage are of special interest, in that they allow us to penetrate into certain differences of principle within the Vedânta school, in which *Âçmarathya* and *Auḍulomi*, each in his own way, represent the rationalistic, exoteric understanding, while *Kâçakṛitsna* represents the mystical and esoteric.—As is usual, the question is raised, whether in the passage the individual or the highest soul is to be understood by the "Self" (p. 385, 13); what distinguishes the two, is only the limitations (*upâdhi*), that is, the body, organs of sense and action, Manas and Buddhi, clothed in which the highest soul appears as the individual soul; on them it depends, that it is enjoyer (or sufferer, *bhoktar*) and actor (*kartar*), from both of which conditions the highest soul, that is, Brahman, is free. Now in our passage there are certain unmistakable features, which only suit the individual soul; thus the introduction, in which, the soul's love of things is spoken of, which can only be understood of the enjoyer (p. 386, 5); thus too the doctrine that the soul rises out of these creatures and again perishes with them (p. 386, 9); thus finally, the expression "Knower," which indicates an actor (p. 386, 11). On the other hand, the whole context (p. 386, 15), compels us to think of the highest soul: a knowledge of it only, secures the immortality which Maitreyî strove after (p. 387, 4); only of it is it true, that, when it is known, all is known (p. 387, 6); so also the proposition, that all things exclude him, who believes them to be outside the soul, can only be understood of the highest soul which includes all (p. 387, 13); this is especially true of the similes of the drum and the rest (p. 387, 14) and of the passage, where the soul is indicated as the cause of the Veda etc. (p. 388, 1) and as the point of union of all that is (p. 388, 4). If consequently only the highest soul is to be understood, then we must ask, how are we to deal with the above mentioned features which only suit the individual soul? *Âçmarathya* sees in them a guarantee of the promise, that with the Âtman all is known; if he grasp all, he grasps the individual soul also (p. 388, 8 ff. 390, 10. 391, 12). As this view, not quite clear in spite of repetitions, amounts to understanding the soul as a part of Brahman, and therefore the relation between them as spatial, so *Auḍulomi* sets up a temporal relation: because the soul is temporarily (in deep sleep) one with Brahman, therefore in the passage in question it appears as found in unity with Brahman (p. 389. 390, 12. 392, 1). In opposition to both, *Kâçakṛitsna*, whose view Çankara adheres to, as being in conformity with scripture (p. 390, 14. 393, 11), establishes the doctrine of Identity, in virtue of which the highest soul exists whole and undivided in the form of the individual soul (p. 390, 2. 392, 3); the annihilation of knowledge after death means only that of individual knowledge (*viçesha-vijñânam*), (p. 392, 7) and the description of God as the "Knower" indicates no actorship, but only a consisting of the pure substance of consciousness (p. 393, 9), as also the reality of liberation consists in the irrefragable certainty of the knowledge that God and the soul are one, and the absolute satisfaction therefrom resulting (p. 395, 3).—

Similar considerations of the fact that the difference between God and the soul is a mere appearance, while liberation is a seeing through this appearance, will be met with many times in the sequel; but all altempts of this kind to grasp liberation as a new form of knowledge, do not give, and cannot give, any satisfactory conclusion as to its nature (as it appeared to the Indian in examples and appears to us), so long as it is not supplemented by the idea of the moral transformation, which is so strongly accentuated by Christianity, but remained foreign to Indian thought. This seems to have been felt in the Vedânta schools also;—against those who could acquiesce in the solution of the question sought in the region of intellect only, the words of Çañkara at the end of our extract seem to be directed: "But those who are stubborn, and force the "sense of the scripture, therewith force also the perfect know-"ledge which leads to salvation, hold liberation to be some-"thing made and [therefore] transitory, and do not follow "after what is lawful" (p. 396, 3).

2. Brahman as *Prâṇa* (Breath, Life).

(a) Sûtras 1, 1, 28—31.

Brahman as the principle of life is the subject of the third Adhyâya of the Kaushîtaki-Upanishad, which in Cowell's edition exists in two recensions p. 73—102 and p. 129—134,[81] and the actual contents of which are as follows:

1. *Pratardana* comes to the abode of *Indra*, who allows him to choose a boon. Pratardana begs the god to choose for him what he deems to be the best thing for mankind. After some hesitation Indra speaks: "Then know me; for this "I deem to be the best thing for a man, that he should "know me.... Who knows me, his place [in heaven] is not "diminished by any deed, neither by theft nor by slaying the

[81] Çañkara appears, as we found above (p. 31) to follow a third recension whose readings in general agree with those of Cowell's first; yet he reads 3, 2 p. 78, 4 with the second *prajñâtmâ tam* (p. 151, 8); 3, 5 p. 89, 3 he has contrary both recensions, *adûduhat* (p. 164, 2); at 3, 3 p. 83, 1 he remarks that some read *imam çarîram* (p. 161, 6), which would be an instance of *çarîra* as masculine, as Çañkara's construction *imam* (*jîvam*), *parigrihya çarîram*, *utthâpayati* is hardly possible. Çañkara has a very noteworthy reading 3, 2 p. 82, 2, where he reads *astitve ca* instead of *asti tv eva* (p. 158, 7).

"fruit of the body, nor by matricide nor by parricide; and "even if he has committed (*cakrusho*) evil [previously, before "the knowledge of Brahman], yet the colour fades not from "his face [no fear makes him pale]."

2. "I am the breath (*prâṇa*), I am the Self of knowledge "(*prajñâtman*); as this, as immortal life worship me. Life is "breath and breath is life; for as long as the breath remains "in this body, so long remains the life; only through breath "is immortality [continuance of life] gained in this world, and "through knowledge, true wishes [wishes that are directed to "the Eternal, cf. above p. 161]. He who worships me as im-"mortal life, comes to full life in this world, he gains im-"mortality, imperishability in the [heavenly world."—Further it is developed that all the life-organs (speech, ear, eye, etc.) go back to a unity (*ekabhûyaṃ gacchanti*), through the power of which each organ performs its function, so that, in each special manifestation of life, all organs [in virtue of their centralisation in life] work together. "Thus it is," adds Indra, confirming the theory quoted, "and the well-being of the life-"organs lies in what they are [*astitve*, that is, in Brahman, "not in what they do]."

3. "The organs are not essential to life; for the dumb, "blind, deaf, imbecile (*bâla*) and crippled live; but verily the "life only, the Self of knowledge, surrounds the body and "supports it (*utthâpayati*, literally: raises it up), therefore it "is to be worshipped as the support (*uktham*, literally: hymn). "This is the penetration of all [organs] in the life. Verily, "life is knowledge, and knowledge is life."—According to this identification, carried out all through, of life (*prâṇa*) and knowledge (*prajñâ*)), which is based on the fact that Brahman, as the principle of life, as shewn above (p. 134 ff.), must also be pure intelligence, are depicted the nature of deep sleep and death. In both, the life-organs (speech, eye, ear, etc.), along with the things and relations of the outer world dependent on them (name, form, tone, etc.), enter into the life; on awaking, as sparks arise from the fire, so the organs arise from the life, from them the gods (that is, the powers of nature), and from the gods the worlds, go forth again; in

death, on the contrary, life, with the organs merged in it, wanders forth from the body.

4. It is further shewn how all external relations are poured (*abhivisrijyante*) into the life, by means of the life-organs (as speech, eye, ear, etc.).

5. The life-organs, as separate members or parts, are drawn out of the life [*udûḷham*; or with Çañkara *adûduhat*, the organs each milk a part out of the life]; but the things of the outer world are only the element of being of the organs projected outwards (*parastât prativihitâ bhûtamâtrâ*).

6. By means of intellect [*prajñâ*, which was identified above with life] the man mounts the organs [like a car] and so reaches outer things.

7. For in themselves and without intellect (*prajñâ*) the organs cannot know and notify outer things. (In this passage *prajñâ* takes the place of *manas*, which elsewhere appears as the central organ of the life-organs, but is here ranged along with them.)

8. Not objects, but the subject, should be investigated, not speech, smell, form, tone, etc., but that which speaks, smells, sees, hears, etc.—"The ten elements of being are related to "Cognition, and the ten elements of Cognition to being; for "if the elements of being were not, then the elements of "Cognition also would not be, and if the elements of Cognition "were not, then the elements of being would not be either. "For through the one [without the other] no appearance "(*rûpam*) comes into existence; yet this is not a plurality [of "outer things and organs], but as, in the case of a car, the "felloes are fastened to the spokes, and the spokes to the "nave, so these elements of being are fastened to the elements "of Cognition, and the elements of Cognition to the *Prâṇa* "(Life). This *Prâṇa* alone is the self of Cognition (*prajñâ-"tman*), and bliss, it does not grow old and dies not. He "becomes not higher through good works, or lower through "evil [abstains from all works], for He alone causes him to "do good works, whom He will raise above these worlds, and "He alone causes him to do evil works, whom He will lead "downwards; He is the guardian of the worlds, the ruler of

"the worlds,—He is my soul, this is to be known, He is my "soul, this is to be known!"

In this section of the Kaushîtaki-Upanishad, as Çañkara develops it, by *Prâṇa* neither breath, nor the god Indra, nor the individual soul are to be understood, although there are characteristics which point to all three of them, but on the contrary the highest Brahman (p. 155, 2 read: *param brahma*), for of it only can it be said, that a knowledge of it is the highest good for man (p. 156, 2), and that he who has known it is stained by no sins, in that, after knowledge of Brahman, all works vanish away (p. 156, 7); only to Brahman applies the description as Self of Cognition,[82] as bliss, as also that it does not grow old and dies not, performs no works and predestines the deeds of beings (p. 156, 8—17).—The god Indra, in whose mouth the whole dissertation is placed, is not to be thought of, because in this passage occur a mass of relations, those mentioned and many others, which compel us to understand the highest soul (p. 158, 2), with which Indra is here identified, just as Vâmadeva is with Manu and Sûrya (Ṛigv. 4, 26, 1; cf. Bṛih. 1, 4, 10), in virtue of a gift of seership extending to the life before birth, occurring in the canon of scripture;[83] therefore also the heroic deeds of Indra are only mentioned to the end of glorifying the knowledge of Brahman, connected with them, because he who possesses this knowledge, remains unscathed like Indra in all his battles (p. 160, 5).—No more than Indra can the individual soul or the *Mukhya prâṇa* (the

---

[82] As Kaush. 3, 2 so in Çañkara's work also *prajñâtman* means only the highest (p. 156, 8. 157, 12. 158, 5; on the other hand = *jîva* p. 161, 8 in the Pûrvapaksha), and *vijñânâtman* means only the individual soul (p. 134, 7. 181, 12. 182, 13. 16. 183, 2. 12; 120, 15. 388, 14. 393, 11). In the same way, *prâjña*, for Bâdarâyaṇa (1, 4, 5. 2, 3, 29) and Çañkara (p. 273, 7. 8. 275, 4. 331, 5. 9. 347, 4. 5. 14. 350, 10. 14. 351, 11. 12. 352, 1. 9. 353, 6. 13. 354, 2. 475, 1. 662, 12. 780, 5. 6. 10. 785, 1. 8. 793, 11. 828, 13. 829, 3. 8) and also *prâjña âtman* (p. 271, 12. 272, 7. 9) always means the highest soul.—This is the more to be accentuated, as in the Vedântasâra, § 53 ff., *prâjña* has become a term for the individual soul.

[83] *ârsheṇa darçanena yathâçâstram*, as Çañkara p. 159, 9 explains the *çâstradrishṭi* of the Sûtram; cf. however *drishṭi* in the Sûtram 1, 2, 26 with Çañkara's interpretation p. 215, 11.

central organ of unconscious life) be understood, although to the former would apply the distinction between subject and object (p. 160, 13), to the latter, the support of the body (p. 161, 3), while the indication as Self of knowledge and the separation between *prâṇa* and *prajñâ* would lend itself to this interpretation (p. 161, 8. 11). The most essential reason why not these but Brahman are to be understood, lies in the words of the Sûtram 1, 1, 31: *upâsâtraividhyâd, âçritatvâd, iha tad-yogât,* which either mean: "because, if *Jîva* and *Mukhya* "*prâṇa* as well as Brahman were to be understood, a triplicity "of worship would of necessity arise (p. 161, 15); because "elsewhere also the word *Prâṇa* refers to Brahman (p. 162, 7); "and because here it is connected with marks of Brahman "(p. 162, 8),"—or, according to another explanation of the Sûtram: "Brahman is to be understood, because a triplicity "of worship of Brahman, namely as *prâṇa*, as *prajñâ*, and as "*brahman* is taught here (p. 164), because elsewhere also a "worship of Brahman is taught by means of limiting qualities "(*upâdhi-dharma*) (p. 165, 5), and this is taking place here also "(p. 165, 6)."

(b) Sûtras 1, 4, 16—18.

As a variation of the theme just treated of, we may consider the conversation between *Gârgya*, the son of *Balâka*, and *Ajâtaçatru*, which forms the fourth Adhyâya of the Kaushîtaki-Upanishad, and, with important divergencies in detail, recurs in Bṛih. 2, 1. Çañkara adheres to the Kaushîtaki recension,[84] according to which the main contents are as follows.

Gârgya, a renowned authority on the Veda, comes to king *Ajâtaçatru* and offers to explain Brahman to him. After he has determined Brahman in a series of sixteen definitions, as the spirit (*purusha*) in the sun, in the moon, in lightning, etc., and these explanations have one after the other been rejected

---

[84] Here also Çañkara's readings diverge in many ways from both forms in which the text is printed by Cowell; thus he reads (p. 380, 7) *saṃvadishṭhâḥ* instead of *saṃvâdayishṭhâḥ* and *samavâdayishṭhâḥ* Kaush. 4, 19, p. 117, 3 and 138, 20.

by *Ajâtaçatru* as inadequate, *Gârgya* becomes silent, and the king speaks to him: "In vain therefore hast thou challenged "me to a disputation, in order to explain Brahman to me "for, verily, he who has made those spirits [named by thee] "and whose work this [world] is, he, verily, is to be investigated.' —Now *Ajâtaçatru* undertakes to teach *Gârgya.* He leads him to one in deep sleep, who does not wake when they speak to him, but only after they have pushed him with a stick *Ajâtaçatru* asks *Gâryya*: "Where lay this spirit, where was "he, whence did he come?"—As *Gârgya* does not know it the king explains to him how, in deep sleep, all organs, together with the corresponding things of the outer world, enter into the life (*prâṇa*) and dwell with it in the arteries that go out from the heart and surround the pericardium; on awaking, as sparks rise from the fire, so from the *Âtman* the organs go forth, from them go forth the gods (who rule them) and from them the worlds. "This *Prâṇa*, the *Prajñâtman* "has entered into the body as into its Self, even to the hair "even to the nails. As a knife pushed into the sheath, or "fire into a fire-vessel, so has the *Prajñâtman* entered into "the body as into its own Self, even to the hair, even to the "nails. On this Self depend those selves [the organs] as a "people on their chief. As the chief nourishes himself (*bhuñkte*) "through his people, as the people nourish (*bhuñjanti*) the "chief, so does this Self of Cognition nourish itself through "those selves, so do those selves nourish this Self of Cognition... "All evil he puts away, chieftainship over all beings, indepen-"dence, sovereignty does he gain, who knows thus."

In this passage, as Çañkara explains, not the *Mukhya prâṇa* or the individual soul, but Brahman is to be understood, since at the very beginning it is said: "I will explain "Brahman to thee" (p. 380, 5); in harmony with this, in the case of the words "whose work this is," we are not to think of the nutrition of the body, which is the work of the *Mukhya prâṇa* (p. 378, 6), or of good and bad works, as they are performed by the individual soul (p. 379, 2), but of this world which was made by Brahman (p. 381, 5). To the objection that marks of the *Mukhya prâṇa* and *Jîva* (the individual soul) are also met with, a reply is to be made in the words of the Sûtram 1, 1, 31: *upâsâtraividhyât* etc. (explained by us in the preceding section, above p. 181) (p. 382, 8). For that only Brahman can be meant, appears from the concluding words, and from the unsurpassable fruit promised in them (p. 382, 13).—To this is added, as *Jaimini* remarks, that in the passage concerning deep sleep, in both question and answer, the individual soul is distinguished from Brahman, into which it enters, and from which it comes forth again (p. 383, 10), and in the Vâjasaneyi recension (Bṛih. 2, 1, 16) on this occasion it is expressly indicated as the *vijñânamayaḥ purushaḥ* (p. 384, 9); from this it is clear, that that from which it goes forth, must be something different from itself, namely the highest Brahman (p. 385, 4).

3. Brahman as the Soul in deep Sleep.

Sûtras 1, 3, 19—21 and 1, 3, 40.

The passage which we considered Chap. XI, 1, d (above p. 158 ff.) follows in Chând. 8, 7—12, the teaching of Indra by Prajâpati (a mythological personification of the creative force, which here stands for Brahman) concerning the nature of the Self.

"Prajâpati said: The Self, the sinless, free from old age, "free from death, and free from sorrow, without hunger and "without thirst, whose wishes are true, whose resolve is true, "this Self is to be investigated, this you should seek to know. "He wins all worlds and all wishes, who has found this Self "and knows it!"—In order to gain knowledge of the Self, the gods send Indra, the Asuras (Demons), Virocana, to Prajâpati. —The three successive answers, which Prajâpati gives to the question, what the Self is, represent three stages of knowledge, in virtue of which the Self is seen either in the body, or in the individual soul, or in the highest soul. The first answer to the question: "What is the Self?" runs thus: "The Self in "the body (literally, the person, *purusha*), as it is represented "in the reflection in the eye, in water, in a mirror."—Whoever, like Virocana and the Asuras, is satisfied with this view, will see in sensual enjoyment and in the care of the body the highest goal of being, and even after death will deck the corpse with all kinds of trumpery adornments (*bhikshâ*), with garments and decorations,—in order to gain by this means a life in the Beyond.[85]—Virocana is satisfied with this answer. But Indra, knowing that, if the Self be the body, then the Self must be equally affected by the injury and destruction of the body, returns to Prajâpati, who gives him the second answer: "The Self is the soul as it enjoys itself in dream." But this answer is also unsatisfying. The dream-soul is, it is true, free from the injury of the body, yet it is as though it were slain or persecuted, and is therefore not free from suffering. With this doubt Indra returns a second time to Prajâpati and now receives the third explanation: "When one has "fallen asleep, and entered altogether wholly and completely "into rest, so that he beholds no dream image,—that is the "Self, that is the immortal, the fearless, Brahman."—To the objection of Indra, that in this condition consciousness of one's self, and of other things also, ceases, so that it is, as it were, an entering into nothingness, Prajâpati finally answers: "Mortal, "verily, O mighty one is this body, possessed of death; it is "the dwelling-place of that immortal, bodiless Self. The em- "bodied is possessed by desire and pain; for because he is "embodied, no turning away from desire and pain is possible. "But the bodyless are not moved by desire and pain.—Body- "less is the wind; the clouds, the lightning, the thunder are "bodyless. Therefore as these rise out of the universe [in "which they are bound, as the soul is, in the body], and enter "into the highest light, and thereby stand forth in their own "form, so also this perfect peace [that is, the soul in deep "sleep] rises out of this body, and enters into the highest "light, and thereby stands forth in its own form: that is the "highest spirit, which wanders there, sporting and playing and "delighting himself, whether with women or with chariots or

---

[85] He who holds the body to be the Self, cannot believe in any life after death. Probably the passage, as also what goes before (*Asurâṇâṃ hi eshâ upanishad*) is to be understood ironically.—Çañkara's view, of which below, we cannot agree with.

"with friends [cf. above p. 161], and thinks no longer of this "servile body, to which the Prâṇa is yoked as a beast of "draught to the car.—When the eye is directed to the uni-"verse, this [the Prâṇa] is the spirit in the eye, the eye [it-"self] is [only] the means; and he who wishes to smell, is the "Âtman, the nose is only the means; and he who wishes to "speak, is the Âtman, the voice is only the means; and he "who wishes to hear, is the Âtman, the ear is only the means; "and he who wishes to understand, is the Âtman, the under-"standing is his godlike eye [embracing past and future]; with "this godlike eye, the understanding, he beholds those delights "and enjoys them. Those gods [who were taught like Indra] "in the world of Brahman worship him as the Self; therefore "possess they all worlds and all wishes. He gains all worlds "and all wishes, who has found this Self and knows it. Thus "spoke Prajâpati."

In contrast with our view of this passage, which would recognise in the three chief answers of Prajâpati (at least, as they are understood by the questioners) the expression of three philosophical standpoints, the materialistic, for which the Self is the body, the realistic, for which it is the individual soul, and the idealistic, denying all plurality, for which it is the highest soul,—in contrast to this, the only view as it appears to us, which fits the whole context, Çañkara adheres to the view that, already in the first answer, the beholding, individual self which dwells in the eye is to be understood (p. 261, 2), so that "the man (or spirit), who is seen in the eye," becomes a man "who sees in the eye." He expressly rejects the view, that the picture mirrored in the eye is meant, because otherwise Prajâpati would not have told the truth (p. 266, 13); but it is not necessary to assume with him, "that Prajâpati, if in "each answer we were to understand something different, would "be an imposter" (p. 268, 8); for the formula with which he each time introduces his explanation: "this will I further ex-"plain to thee," suits well a view of the Self which grows deeper step by step.—In the third answer also, as Çañkara develops it, the individual soul is to be understood, yet as it passes over to another condition (p. 261, 5), namely, as, rising out of the body, it becomes the highest spirit (p. 262, 3), so its true nature is revealed (p. 262, 6), according to which it is not individual, but the highest Brahman itself (p. 263, 2). "This in fact is, according to passages of scripture like 'that "thou art' (Chând. 6, 8, 7), the real nature (*pâramârthikaṃ* "*svarûpam*) of the individual soul, not the other, which is "formed through limitations (*upâdhi*). So long, therefore, as "one does not put aside the Ignorance which affirms plurality, "which is like taking the trunk of a tree for a man [p. 263, "5; the same image p. 44, 2. 86, 12. 448, 2: cf. Platon, Phileb., "p. 38 D], so long as one has not reached the highest, eternal "Self, appearing according to its own nature, by the know-"ledge that 'I am Brahman' (Bṛih. 1, 4, 10), so long the in-"dividual soul is individual. But if a man rises above the "aggregate of body, senses, Manas and Buddhi and has been "taught, by the scripture, that man is not an aggregate of "body, senses, Manas and Buddhi, not a wandering soul, but "on the contrary that of which it is said (Chând. 6, 8, 7), "'that is the real, that is the soul'—consisting of pure in-"telligence, 'that thou art,' then he knows the highest eternal "Self which appears according to its own nature; as by this "means he raises himself above the illusion of this [reading "*asmât*] body etc., he goes to that very highest, eternal Self "which appears according to its own nature; for thus says "the scripture (Muṇḍ. 3, 2, 9): 'Verily, he who knows this "'highest Brahman, himself becomes Brahman'" (p. 263, 4 to 264, 3). As such the soul stands forth "in its own form," as gold, when by corroding materials it is freed from the addition of other substances (p. 264, 5), or as the stars, when the day which overpowered them is gone, stand forth by night in their own form (p. 264, 8). However the eternal, spiritual light is never overpowered by anything; on the contrary, like space, it does not come in contact with the sensual world, and stands in contradiction to it (p. 264, 10). The individual soul, so long as it has not been raised above the body [which is what happens in deep sleep], is seeing, hearing, thinking, knowing. Were it so also, after being lifted above the body, then the contradiction [just stated] would not exist [p. 265, 3;

I read *avirudhyeta*, optative with *a privativum*]. Therefore the position of things is such that we must distinguish between the condition of the soul *before* its separation from the limitations, body, senses, Manas, Buddhi, sensibility to pain and object, and its condition *after* separation from them. Before the separation it is apparently affected by the Upâdhis, as the crystal is by the colour outside it; after the separation, it stands forth in its own nature, as the crystal, after the colour is put away (p. 265). Thus the embodiment or bodilessness of the soul only depends on whether one does or does not distinguish it from the Upâdhis (p. 266, 2), and the distinction of the individual and the highest soul rests only on false knowledge, not on an action of things, which is not possible, because the soul, like space, does not adhere to them (p. 266, 8). Only the knowledge of these, only the (individual) knowledge of differences (*viçesha-vijñânam*) is removed in deep sleep, not knowledge in its entirety (p. 267, 7); for the scripture says (Bṛih. 4, 3, 30): "For the knower there is no interruption of knowing."—Some try to evade this identification of the individual with the highest soul, against the context of the passage; but rather is it the case that after the removal of Ignorance, as the imagined serpent becomes a rope, so also the not truly real individual soul, which is stained by doing and suffering, love and hate and other imperfections, and is subject to much that is evil, is transferred through wisdom. to the sinless essence of the highest God, opposed to all these imperfections (p. 268, 10).—Yet others, and some of our Vedântins among them, (realistically) take the individual nature of the soul to be absolutely real; against these the *Çârîrakam* (Bâdarâyaṇa's Sûtras) is directed, in order to shew, that "the alone, supreme, eternal, highest God, whose being "is knowledge, through the glamour (*mâyâ*) of Ignorance, like "a magician, appears manifold, and that there is no other "element of knowledge outside him" (p. 269, 1). Therefore it is true that God is different from the individual soul [so long as such a soul is spoken of], but the individual soul is not different from God [cf. p. 816, 7: the *prapañca* is *brahman*, but *brahman* is not the *prapañca*; and p. 1060, 2: the *saṃsârin* is *îçvara*, but *îçvara* is not the *saṃsârin*], except from the standpoint of Ignorance (p. 269, 10). In waking, the soul is the onlooker in the cage of the body and organs, in dream it lingers in the arteries and looks at the dream-pictures built up of the ideas of the waking state; in deep sleep it enters into the highest light, that is, into Brahman (p. 270, 7). For that Brahman is the highest light, follows from the context (p. 327, 8) and from the above mentioned incorporeality, which belongs to Brahman alone (p. 328, 3), as also from the words "that is the highest spirit" (p. 328, 4).

4. Brahman as the Soul in the State of Liberation.

Sûtras 1, 23, 42—43.

The section Bṛih. 4, 3—4 (p. 705—919), whose main theme, according to Çaṅkara, is the above, unfolds a picture of the condition of the soul before and after death, which for richness and warmth, is unique in the literature of India, and perhaps in the literature of the world. We translate the passage with some abbreviations and omissions, which will justify themselves, remarking, however, that much, especially in the first part, remains problematic.

(a) Introduction (4, 3, 1—9).

To *Janaka*, king of the *Videhas*, comes *Yâjñavalkya*, in order to discourse with him.[86] The king raises the question: "What serves the man [*purusha*] as light?"—The first answer

---

[86] *Sam enena vadishya', iti*; this is not *"an ingenious conjecture"* of Regnaud in *"his excellent work on the Upanishads"* (as may appear from Max Müller, Upanishads I, p. LXXIII ff.), but a variant, which Dvivedagaṅga had already mentioned in his commentary (p. 1141, 13, ed. Weber); Weber adopted it in his edition of the Çatapathabr. (14, 7, 1, 1), and again recalled the fact in his critique of Regnaud's work (Jenaer Literaturz. 1878, 9. Feb., No. 6), to which Regnaud also refers at the beginning of the Errata.—What Max Müller observes as against this reading, can be explained quite as well in the opposite sense: precisely because Yâjñavalkya intends to discourse with the king, the narrator finds it necessary to give a new motive for the fact that not he, but the king, speaks first. [For another view compare my Sixty Upanishads p. 463.]

runs thus: "The sun serves him as a light; for in the light "of the sun he sits and moves about, carries on his work and "returns home."—"But what serves him as light when the "sun is set?"—"The moon."—"And when sun and moon are "set?"—"Fire."—"And when sun and moon are set, and the "fire has gone out?"—"Voice; therefore, when a man cannot "distinguish his own hand, and a voice is raised [reading "*uccarati*] somewhere, he goes towards it."—"But when sun "and moon are set, and the fire is gone out, and the voice "is dumb, what then serves the man as a light?"—"Then his "own self (*âtman*) serves him as a light."—"What is, then, "this Self?"—"It is that among the life-organs which con-"sists of knowledge, as the spirit shining inwardly in the heart. "This remaining the same, wanders through both worlds [this "world in waking and in dream, the other in deep sleep and "death]; it is as though he meditated, as though he wavering "moved [in reality Brahman is without individual knowledge "and motion]; for when he has become sleep (*svapno bhûtva*), "then [in deep sleep] he transcends this world, the forms of "death [all that is transitory, evil]. For, when this spirit is "born, when he enters into the body, he is flooded with evil; "but when he departs, when he dies, he leaves evil behind. "Two conditions are there of this spirit: the present and that "in the other world; a middle condition, as third, is that of "sleep. While it lingers in this middle condition, it beholds "both those conditions, the present [in dream] and that in the "other world [in deep sleep]. And according as he has access "to the condition in the other world, he proceeds and beholds "both, evil [this world, in dream] and bliss [the other world, "in deep sleep]."

(b) Dreamsleep (4, 3, 9—14. 16—18).

"But when he sinks to sleep, then he takes from this all-"embracing world the wood (*mâtrâm*, *materiem*), fells it him-"self and himself builds it, in virtue of his own radiance, "his own light;—when he so sleeps, then this spirit serves "as its own light. There are no chariots, nor teams, nor "roads there, but he forms for himself chariots, and teams, "and roads; there is neither bliss, joy, nor pleasure, but he "creates for himself bliss, joy, and pleasure; there are no "springs, and ponds, and rivers, and but he forms for himself "springs, and ponds, and rivers,—for he is the Creator. On "this subject are these verses:

"Putting aside in sleep the bodily (*çarîram*)
"Sleepless the sleeping organs he beholds;
"Then borrowing their light goes back again
"The golden Spirit, only wandering bird.
"He leaves the Life to guard the lower nest
"And soars immortal from the nest himself,
"Immortal, moving wheresoe'er he wills,
"The golden Spirit, only wandering bird.
"In dream, the Spirit upward, downward moves,
"And, as a God, creates Him many forms,
"Now with fair women sporting joyously,
"And now beholding sights that make him fear.
"His playground canst thou see, but not himself,"—

"therefore it is said: 'let him not be wakened suddenly,' for "hard is one to heal, back to whom the Spirit does not find "its way. Therefore it is said also: 'for him it [sleep] is "'only a state of waking,' for what he sees in waking, the "same also he sees in sleep. Thus therefore this man serves "as a light to itself . . . Thereon, after he has enjoyed him-"self and wandered forth in dream, and beheld good and evil, "he hastens back, according to his entrance, according to his "place, to the condition of waking; and by all that he beholds "in this he is not touched, for to this Spirit nothing adheres; "—and again, after he has taken delight and wandered forth "in the waking state, and after he has beheld good and evil, "he hastens back, according to his entrance, according to his "place, to the condition of dream. And like as a great fish "glides along both banks, on this side and on that, so glides "the Spirit along both conditions, that of dream and that of "waking [without being touched there]."

(c) Deep Sleep (4, 3, 19. 21—33).

"But like as in yon space a falcon or an eagle, after he "has hovered, wearily folds his pinions, and sinks to rest, thus "also hastens the Spirit to that condition in which, sunk to "sleep, he feels no more desire, nor beholds any more dreams. "That is his form of being, wherein he is raised above long-"ing, free from evil and from fear. For, like as one whom "a beloved woman embraces, has no consciousness of what is "without or what is within, so also the Spirit, embraced by "the Self of knowledge [the Brahman], has no consciousness "of what is without or what is within. That is his form of "being, wherein his longing is stilled, himself is his longing, "he is without longing, and freed from grief. Then the father "is not father, nor the mother, mother, nor the worlds, worlds, "nor the gods, gods, nor the Vedas, Vedas; then is the thief "no thief, the murderer no murderer, the Câṇḍâla no Câṇḍâla, "the Paulkasa no Paulkasa, the ascetic no ascetic, the penitent "no penitent; then he is unmoved by good, unmoved by evil, "then he has vanquished all the torments of the heart."

"If then he sees not, yet he is seeing though he does not "see; since, there is no interruption of seeing for the seeing "one, because he is imperishable; but there is then outside "him no second, no other different from him whom he could "see. So too if then he smells not, nor tastes, nor speaks, "nor hears, nor thinks, nor feels, nor knows, yet is he a "knower, even though he does not know; since, for the knower "there is no interruption of knowing, because he is imperish-"able; but there is then no second outside him, no other "different from him, whom he could understand. For only "where, as it were, another is, can one see, smell, taste, address, "hear, think of, feel and know another."

"He stands in the tumultuous ocean [cf. Çvet. 6, 15] as "beholder, alone and without a second, he whose world is the "Brahman. This is his highest goal, this is his highest joy, "this is his highest world, this is his highest bliss; through "a little part only of this bliss, other creatures have their "life."

"When among men one is fortunate and rich, king over "the others and loaded with all human enjoyments, that is "the highest joy for man. But a hundred of these human "joys are but one joy of the fathers, who have conquered "heaven, and a hundred joys of the fathers who have con-

"quered heaven, are but one joy in the world of the Gan-"dharvas, and a hundred joys in the world of the Gandharvas "are but one joy of the Gods through works, who by their "works have attained to godhead, and a hundred joys of the "Gods through works are but one joy of the Gods by birth, "and of one learned in the scripture and without falseness "and free from desire; and a hundred joys of the Gods by "birth are but one joy of Prajâpati's world and of one learned "in the scripture and without falseness and free from desire: "and a hundred joys of Prajâpati's world are but one joy of "the Brahman-world, and of one learned in the scripture and "without falseness and free from desire. And this is the "highest joy, this is Brahman-world."

(d) Death (4, 3, 35—4, 4, 2).

"As a cart, when it is heavily laden, creaks as it goes, so "also this bodily Self, burdened by the Self of knowledge, "goes croaking [rattling], when one is lying at death's door. "And when he falls into weakness, whether it be through old-"age or sickness that he falls into weakness, then, as a mango-"fruit, a fig, a berry, lets go its stalk, so the Spirit lets go "the limbs and hastens backward, according to his entrance, "according to his place, back into the Life . . . And like as "to a king, when he will forth, the chiefs, and officers, and "charioteers, and rulers of villages gather together, so also, "at the time of his end, to the soul all life-organs come to-"gether, when one is lying at death's door. When, therefore, "the soul falls into swoon, and is as if it had lost all sense, "even then these life-organs gather themselves together to the "soul; and it takes up these force-elements into itself and "withdraweth to the heart; but the Spirit, which dwells in "the eye, returns outwards [to the sun, whence it descends, "cf. above p. 66]; then recognises he no more forms. Because "he has come to unity, therefore he sees not, thus it is said, "because he has come to unity, therefore he smells not, tastes "not, speaks not, hears not, thinks not, feels not, knows not. "Then the point of the heart becomes luminous; from it, after "it has become luminous, the Soul departs, whether it be "through the eye, or through the skull, or through any other "part of the body. As it departs, the Life also departs; as "the Life departs, all the life-organs depart with it. It is of "the nature of knowledge, and what is of the nature of know-"ledge, departs after it."

(e) The unliberated Soul after Death (4, 4, 2—6).

"Then knowledge and works take it [the soul] by the hand "and their newly gained experience" [if we may read *apûrva-prajñâ*].—

"As a caterpillar, after it has reached the end of the leaf, "lays hold of another beginning and draws itself over to it, "so also the soul, after it has shaken off the body and let "Ignorance go, lays hold of another beginning, and draws "itself over to it."

"As a goldsmith takes the material of one piece of work, "and out of it hammers another, newer, more beautiful form,[87] "so this soul also, after it has shaken off the body and let "Ignorance go, shapes itself another, newer, more beautiful "form, whether of the Fathers or the Gandharvas or the "Gods or Prajâpati or the Brahman or other beings."

"Verily, this Self is the Brahman, consisting of Intelligence, "of Manas, of Life, of eye, of ear, consisting of earth, of "water, of wind, of ether, consisting of fire and not of fire, "of pleasure and not of pleasure, of anger and not of anger, "of righteousness and not of righteousness, consisting of all. "And according as anyone consists of this or of that, accord-"ing to his deeds and conduct, according to that is he born; "he who does good will be born as a good man, he who does "evil will be born as an evil man, holy he becomes through "holy work, evil through evil. For verily it is said: 'Man is "'altogether formed of desire (*kâma*); and according as his "'desire is, so is his will (*kratu*), and according as his will

---

[87] Compare Pythagoras in Ovid. Met. XV, 169 seq.:
Utque novis facilis signatur cera figuris,
Nec manet ut fuerat, nec formas servat easdem,
Sed tamen ipsa eadem est, animam sic semper eandem
Esse, sed in varias doceo migrare figuras.

"'is, so performs he the work (*karman*), according as he per-"'forms the work, so it befalls him.'—Thereon is this verse:

"That he pursues, and strives by deeds to reach,
"Toward which his character and longing is.—

"After he has received reward
"For all that he has here performed,
"He comes back from that other world
"Into this world of deeds below."

"Thus is it with him who desires (*kâmayamâna*)."

(f) Liberation (4, 4, 6—23).

"Now as to him who desires not (*akâmayamâna*)":

"He who is without desire, free from desire, whose desire "is stilled, who is himself his desire, his vital spirits do not "depart; but Brahman is he and into Brahman he resolves "himself. On this is this verse:

"When every passion utterly is gone,
"That lurks and nestles in the heart of man,
"Then finds this mortal immortality,
"Then has he reached the Brahman, the Supreme."

"As the slough of a snake lies dead and cast away on an "ant-heap, so lies this body then; but the bodiless, the im-"mortal, the Life is Brahman only, is light only."—

"On this are these verses:

"A narrow path and old it is, which I have found and trod;
"The sage, released, upon his way to heaven taked this road.
"Whatever name you give to it, white, black, brown, red, or green,
"This is the only path for those who have the Brahman seen;
"On this he goes, who Brahman knows,
"And does the right, in form of light.

"The man who lives in Ignorance moves on to blindest gloom;
"To blinder still goes he who would by works escape his doom.
"Yea joyless is this world for man and hidden in black night:
"And to it after death he goes who hath not learned the right.

"But he whose mind the inner Self in Thought hath learned to grasp,
"Why should he longer seek to bear the body's pain and woe?
"For when a man in spite of all the stains of mortal sin,
"The great awakening to the Self hath won, and learned to see,
"Him as creator of the worlds, almighty shalt thou know,
"His is the universe, because the universe is he.

"And while we yet are here below, may we this knowledge gain,
"If not, illusion cleaves to us, brings ruin in its train.
"For they who have the knowledge are immortal though they die,
"But they who have not gained it must return to misery.

"He who God's very self in his own bosom sees—
"Lord of what was and is to come—no more he flees.

"Him 'neath whose feet the mighty tide of days and years rolls past,
"In whom the fivefold host of things and space itself stands fast,
"Whom gods as light of lights adore, as immortality,
"The Brahman know I as my deathless Self, for I am he.

"Breath of the breath and very mind of mind,
"Ear of the ear, and apple of the eye,
"Who knoweth him as this hath truly seen
"Old Brahman, who is from eternity.

"Musing in spirit shall ye see:
"That here is no plurality,
"Their never ending death they weave,
"Who here a manifold perceive.

"The Âtman is unchangeable, immense, a unity,
"High above space and stain of sin, unchanging, great is he.

"Muse upon him if thou wouldst wisdom find,
"Use but few words.—They're weariness of mind."

"Truly this great, unborn Self is that among the life-"organs which consists of knowledge [as the spirit shining "inwardly]! Here, inwardly in the heart is a space, therein "he lies, the lord of the universe, the ruler of the universe, "the prince of the universe; he grows not higher through "good works, nor less through evil works; he is the lord of "the universe, the ruler of beings, the guardian of beings; he "is the bridge, which holds these worlds asunder, that they "blend not [cf. above p. 162]."

"Him the Brahmans seek to know through Vedic studies, "through offerings, alms, penances, and fasts; who knows him, "becomes a *Muni.* To him the pilgrims go in pilgrimage, "when they long for home (*loka*)."

"This knew those of old, when they longed not for descen-"dants, and said: 'Why should we wish indeed for descendants, "'we whose self is this universe?' And they ceased from the "longing after children, from the longing after possessions, "from the longing after the world and wandered forth as "beggars. For longing for children is longing for possessions, "and longing for possessions is longing for the world; for one "like the other is merely longing."

"But He, the Âtman, is not thus nor thus. He is incomprehen-"sible, for He is not comprehended, indestructible, for He is "not destroyed, unaffected, for nothing affects Him; He is "unfettered, He trembles not, He suffers no hurt."

"[He who knows thus,] is overcome by neither, whether "he has therefore [because he was in the body] done evil or "whether he has done good; but he overcomes both; he is not "burned by what he has done or not done. This also says "the verse:

"This is the eternal majesty of Brahman's friend,
"He doth not rise by works, nor yet doth he descend.
"Then follow after this; who after this hath toiled,
"Will by his evil deed no more be stained and soiled."

"Therefore he who knows thus, is calm, subdued, resigned, "patient and collected; in his own Self only he beholds the "Self, he beholds all as the Self: evil doth not overcome "him, he overcomes all evil, evil doth not burn him, he burns "all evil; free from evil, free from passion, and free from "doubt, he becomes a *Brâhmaṇa*, he whose world is the *Brah-*"*man*!"—

"Thus spoke *Yâjñavalkya*. Then said the king: 'O holy "'man, I give thee my people in servitude and myself also.'"

It might be thought, Çañkara remarks on this section, that in it the individual soul is treated of, because towards the beginning and towards the end (under *a* and *f*) "that "among the life-organs which consists of knowledge" is spoken of (p. 330, 9); but we are rather to think of the highest soul all through, since in the passage concerning deep sleep and death it is distinguished from the individual soul, in the case of deep sleep, where it is said that the spirit is "embraced "by the Self of knowledge" (p. 331, 2), in the moment of death, where a burdening of the bodily self, that is, the individual soul, by the Self of knowledge, is spoken of (p. 331, 7). For that which is "of the nature of knowledge" (*prâjña*) is [in direct contrast with the terminology of the Vedântasâra, cf. note 82, p. 180] none other than the highest God, who is so called because he is eternally inseparable from omniscience (p. 331, 6). But with regard to the passage mentioned, at the beginning and the end, it is said there (under *a*): "it is as "though it meditated, it is as though it wavering moved," and (under *f*): "truly this great, unborn Self is that among the "life-organs which consists of knowledge," clearly proving that the individual soul is mentioned here solely in order to teach its identity with the highest soul (p. 332, 1—6). Also the conditions of waking and sleep are mentioned only in order to shew the soul's freedom from them; for it is said (under *b* and *c*), that the Spirit is not troubled by the images in waking and dreaming, and again, that it is not troubled by good and evil (p. 332, 12), as also the king repeatedly breaks out into the exclamation [omitted by us]: "say what "higher than this, makes for liberation" (p. 332, 11). Lastly, the passages (under *f*) "the Lord of the Universe" etc., and "he grows not higher through good works" etc., shew that we are to think, not of the individual, but of the highest soul (p. 333).

XIII. The Brahman as the highest Goal.

1. Brahman as Object of Meditation.

Sûtras 1, 3, 13.

THE Meditation on the Brahman can be more or less perfect and accordingly, as is known from the passages adduced in Chap. VI (above p. 102ff.), brings different fruit, namely, in part, earthly happiness, in part, heavenly though transitory felicity, in part, eternal union with Brahman. This thought is illustrated in the fifth section of the *Praçna-Upanishad* (p. 219ff.) by the doctrine that, in the word "*om*," the symbolical bearer of the meditation on the Brahman, the three metrical moments (*mâtrâ*), of which it is supposed to consist (*a-u-m*), are distinguished. The meditation is more perfect in proportion as it extends to one, two, or to all three elements of the word "*om*." The passage runs as follows:

"Verily, o Satyakâma, the sound '*om*' is the higher and the "lower Brahman. Therefore the wise, when he relies on it, "gains the one or the other."

"If he meditates on one element, enlightened by it, he "comes [after death] quickly to the state of the living. The "*Ṛig*-hymns lead him to the world of men; there he comes "to asceticism, pious life and faith and enjoys exaltation."

"When in his thought he attains two elements, then "[after death] he is borne by the *Yajus*-sentences upward into "the air to the Soma-world [to the moon]. After he has en-"joyed lordship in the Soma-world, he comes back again."

"But if, through all three elements of the sound '*om*,' "he meditates on the highest spirit, then, after he has entered "into the light, into the sun, as a serpent is freed from its "slough, so he is freed from evil; by the *Sâman*-songs he is "led upwards to the Brahman-world; then beholds he Him "who is higher than the highest complex of life, the spirit "who dwells in the city [the body] (*puri-çayam purusham*)."

It is a question, remarks Çañkara, which of the two Brahmans, mentioned in the opening passage, is to be understood in the last paragraph, the higher or the lower? The spatial reference, which lies in the leading upward to the world of Brahman, speaks for the latter, and does not suit the higher Brahman (p. 245, 7; above p. 109). Nevertheless we must think of the higher Brahman because it is said "he beholds," which can only refer to a reality, to the highest Brahman, as it is the object of perfect knowledge (*samyag-darçanam*) (p. 246, 6), while by the "highest complex of life" Brahman in the form of the individual soul[88] must be understood (p. 247, 1). In conformity with this also, in what has gone before, by the highest spirit, which is to be meditated on, the highest Brahman is to be understood (p. 247, 10), for meditation on it only brings the further mentioned deliverance from evil (p. 248, 4). But as to the reference to place, which lies in the leading upwards to the Brahman-world, it must be assumed that gradual liberation (*kramamukti*) is here taught, and that perfect knowledge is only communicated after the introduction into the Brahman-world (p. 248, 8),—though this last view is not quite in accordance with the doctrine of the system; as here the highest Brahman is to be understood, while on the contrary as we shall see later (Chap. XXXIX, 4), gradual liberation applies only to the worshipper of the lower Brahman.

---

[88] Somebody whose opinion is introduced very abruptly p. 247, 3 wishes to refer the "highest complex of life" to the Brahman-world, a view which is neither approved of nor opposed in what follows, and has probably been interpolated into the text, so that the *tasmât* p. 247, 7 was originally connected immediately with 247, 2 (cf. above p. 29).

2. Brahman as the Place of the Liberated.

Sûtras 1, 3, 1—7.

In the Muṇḍaka-Upanishad 2, 2, 5 it is said:

"The place in which the heavens, and earth, and mind,
"The sky with all the senses are entwined,
"That place as nought but Âtman shall ye know,
"All other turns of speech shall ye forego[89]
"He is the bridge of immortality."

Here, says Çañkara, we might think of something other than Brahman, perhaps primordial matter, or the wind, or the individual soul, which in a certain sense could be called the place of things (p. 225), for the bridge mentioned seems to presuppose another shore (something outside it), which is not true of Brahman (p. 224, 8). But the place, in which the whole world is woven, can only be Brahman (p. 225, 10), as is shewn by the word *Âtman*, which in its full sense is only valid for Brahman (p. 226, 1). The world is, of course, not related to it as the roots, trunk and branches to the tree (p. 226, 7), but is only a product of Ignorance (p. 226, 11); for the scripture warns us against accepting unreal plurality (p. 227, 3), when it is said (Kâṭh. 4, 10. Bṛih. 4, 4, 19):

"Their never ending death they weave,
"Who here a manifold perceive."

What is said of the bridge, only means that Brahman keeps things asunder (cf. above p. 133. 162), not that He has another shore (p. 227, 10). But that Brahman alone can be the place, follows from the fact that He is afterwards indicated as the place to which the liberated go. For just this illusion that the I consists in the bodily nature, is Ignorance; the esteem of this body is Passion (*râga*), the despising of it is Hate, thoughts of injury to it are Fear, and so on according to the names of the host of the unreal (p. 228, 10). Liberation from all these defects is a going to the place which is here spoken of; it is further said concerning it (Muṇḍ. 2, 2, 8):

---

[89] In the text the indicative stands: *jânatha, vimuñcatha.*

"He who this highest, deepest views,
"For him the heart's knots are untied,
"For him his doubts are all resolved,
"His works all pass to nothingness;"

and again (Muṇḍ. 3, 2, 8):

"As rivers run, and in the deep,
"Lose name and form, are lost to sight,
"The sage released, from name and form,
"Enters the highest spirit of light."

Here neither primordial matter nor the wind can be spoken of (p. 230), nor yet the individual soul (p. 231, 1), which, by the words: "This place alone you know the Âtman is," is distinguished as subject from the highest soul as object (p. 231, 8).

3. Brahman as Attainment of absolute Unity.

Sûtras 1, 3, 8–9.

All knowledge, which is different from its object, is limited and not free; that knowledge only is unlimited and free, which knows itself as identical with the known.—This is the fundamental thought of the *Bhûma-vidyâ*, the seventh section of the Chândogya-Upanishad (p. 473—527), whose chief contents are as follows.

Nârada prays *Sanatkumâra* to teach him; and, in answer to the question: what he already knows, enumerates the four Vedas and a long series of other sciences. In the consciousness of their insufficiency, he adds: "I know, O venerable one, "the *Mantras* [here the whole practical theology], not the "*Âtman* [metaphysics]; for I have heard from those who are "like thee, that he who knows the *Âtman* is above sorrow; "but I, O Master, am sorrowful; lead thou me away from "sorrow!"

Sanatkumâra, in his teaching, takes the following course. All, he says, that thou hast learnt, is name, greater (*bhûyas*) than name is speech, than speech, understanding, than this, resolve, than this, thought, than this, knowledge, than this, force, than this, food, than this, water, than this, fire, than this, space, than this, memory, than this, hope, than this the life (or the breath, *prâṇa*). "As the spokes are fastened in "the nave, so all this is fastened in the life. The life prospers "through the life (breath), the life (breath) gives life, gives it "to life. The life is father and mother, the life is brother "and sister, the life is teacher and Brahman. Therefore, "when anyone roughly uses a father or mother or brother or "sister or teacher or Brahman, it is said: Fie on thee! thou "art a parricide, matricide, fratricide, slayer of thy sister, "slayer of thy teacher, slayer of a Brahman [cf. I John III, "15 πᾶς ὁ μισῶν τὸν ἀδελφὸν αὐτοῦ ἀνθρωποκτόνος ἐστίν]; but if, "after the life has fled, he pokes the same persons with the "pike [on the funeral pile] and burns them up, it is not said: "thou art a parricide, matricide, fratricide, slayer of thy sister, "slayer of thy teacher, slayer of a Brahman: for the life only "is this all.—Verily, he who thus sees and thinks and knows, "he is a conqueror in speech (*ativâdin*); and if anyone should "say to him: thou art a conqueror in speech! he shall avow, "and not deny it."

By life (*prâṇa*) in this passage is to be understood, not as elsewhere frequently and also in the Châṇdogya-Upanishad itself (cf. above p. 147. 164. 177. 182) the highest Brahman, but (perhaps in intentional polemic against this view) empirically "the life-principle (*prâṇa*) shaped to the complex "of the subtle body, the *Prajñâtman* [*Brahman*, note 82] as "the central principle of the body, in which the highest god-"head [*Brahman*] enters to the end of evolution in name and "form as the living self (as the individual soul, *jîva âtman*), "like the image in the mirror."[90]—The result up to this is therefore only the highest point of the empirical view of the world, from which *Sanatkumâra* seeks to lift his pupil to the metaphysical view, proceeding as follows:

But he only is the true conqueror in speech, who conquers through the truth. The truth, therefore, must be investigated.

---

[90] Çaṅk. on Chând. p. 505, 15. Here should be distinguished 1. that which is imaged (*brahman, âtman*), 2. the image of the mirror (*jîva*), 3. the mirror (*prâṇa*), which however are all three at bottom one in Brahman. However the sense of the above scholion is in part obscure and the translation uncertain.

Now the truth is based on knowledge, knowledge on thought, thought on faith, faith on certainty, certainty on action, action on pleasure [the inclination to do something, as determining the will].

Now pleasure, [thus the speaker continues, the idea of a single satisfaction, such as is felt after an action, leading him on to that of an absolute, final satisfaction] consists only in illimitation (*bhûman*), not in the limited (*alpam*). Now what is illimitation?

"When one sees no other [outside himself], hears no other, "knows no other, that is illimitation; when he sees, hears, "knows another, that is the limited. Illimitation is the im- "mortal, the limited is mortal."—"But on what is it based "then, Master?"—"It is based on its own greatness, or, if you "will, not on greatness. For by greatness in this world one "understands many cows and horses, elephants and gold, "slaves and women, fields and lands. But this I mean not, "for here one is always based on the other."

"But it [the illimitation] is below and above, in the west "and in the east, the south and the north; it is this whole "world."

"Hence follows for the consciousness of "I" (*ahaṃkâra*): "I (*aham*) am below and above, in the west and the east, the "south and the north; I am this whole world."

"Hence follows for the soul (*âtman*): the soul is below and "above, in the west and the east, the north and the south, the "soul is this whole world."

"He who sees and thinks and knows thus, rejoicing in the "soul, playing with it, uniting and delighting with it, he is "autonomous (*svarâj*), and freedom (*kâmacâra*) is his in all "worlds; but they who regard it otherwise than thus, they are "heteronomous (*anyarâjan*), of transitory felicity, and unfree- "dom (*akâmacâra*) is theirs in all worlds."—

"Thus," it is said in conclusion, "he shewed him, whose "darkness was worn away, the shore beyond the darkness, he, "the holy *Sanatkumâra*."

Çañkara's efforts, in connection with this passage, are directed to proving that, by illimitation Brahman is to be understood, and not the previously mentioned life. For although nothing higher follows after life in the series (p. 235, 4), and who knows it is called a conqueror in speech (p. 235, 8), although the description, also, that one "sees no other outside himself," suits the life in the condition of deep sleep (p. 235, 14), as also the terms as pleasure, immortal, Âtman, could be understood of the life (p. 236), yet it is not the life; but only the highest Brahman which is to be understood by illimitation; for it is termed higher than deep sleep, that is, than the life in deep sleep (p. 237, 1) by the fact that from him who knows the life, we are directed to him "who through the truth conquers in speech" (p. 238, 10), while the first mentioned conquest is unjustified (p. 239, 8). And as the truth appears further illimitation, that is, the highest soul different from the life (p. 240, 3); for to Him alone can apply the passage concerning the destruction of sorrow (p. 240, 6), as also the phrase "the shore beyond the darkness," that is, Ignorance (p. 240, 10), and the immense greatness, which lies in the idea of illimitation, and is only applicable to the highest God as the cause of all (p. 240, 14). To it applies also the unity of subject and object, since the unity which arises in deep sleep is also to be reduced to it (p. 241, 6). Lastly, to it refers also the term pleasure, since by it no pleasure enduring for a time only (*sâmaya*) is to be understood (p. 241, 12); as also the expressions such as immortality, truth, being based on its own greatness, omnipresent, and all-animating (p. 241, 16).

XIV. Esoteric Theology.

Sûtras 3, 2, 11—37.

1. Preliminary Remark.

HOWEVER sublime are the ideas of the Brahman, which up to this we have gained from the Upanishads in pursuance of the selection made (not always quite happily) by Bâdarâyaṇa and Çañkara, yet, in their figurative character, they fall short of satisfactorily fathoming to the full the being of the Godhead. Because this was felt, to the theological part of the Brahmasûtras is added a supplement, which has as its subject the esoteric Brahman, and, along with two other (psychological) supplements, is found in the second Pâda of the third Adhyâya, that is, after the Cosmology, Psychology and doctrine of transmigration. Even if here and there a greater intelligibility is thereby gained, yet this gain is more than counterbalanced by the disadvantages inseparable from the treatment of the same subject in two widely severed passages; for this reason, we here, as frequently, in our arrangement depart from that of the original work.

The fundamental thought of the esoteric theology (cf. above p. 102ff. 115) is this, that Brahman strictly taken is without all differences (*viçesha*), attributes (*guṇa*), limitations (*upâdhi*) and forms (*âkâra*).—This undifferentiated Brahman, as we may briefly call it, has, however, two contraries: first the *forms of the phenomenal world*, as which Brahman, conditioned by Upâdhis, appears; then the imperfect *figurative ideas*, which we form of the Godhead, in order to bring it nearer to our understanding and our worship (*upâsanâ*). It is strange that between these two contraries of the undifferentiated Brahman, however wide apart they naturally are, Çankara draws no sharp distinction, and even if according to one passage (p. 807, 5) it seems as if he saw in the *phenomenal forms* the basis (*âlambanam*) of the *presentation-forms*, yet from the continual intermingling of the two, not only in the passage under consideration, but also in many other passages in the work [91] it follows that our author never became clearly conscious of the difference between them. Perhaps this was done more by other Commentators, who, of the one Adhikaraṇam 3, 2, 11—21, make two, of which the first (3, 2, 11—14) seems to have been directed against the manifoldness of phenomenal forms, and the second (3, 2, 15—21) against the plurality of the characteristics of Brahman, which Çankara (p. 812) discards as aimless (*vyartha*), without our having been able completely to gather the opinion of the Opponent from his words.

Here, therefore, we are limited to reproducing Çankara's view, and the shortcoming indicated compels us to consider only from a certain distance the two contraries of the undifferentiated Brahman, which he confuses; this makes a clear insight into all details impossible. In other respects our course is such that we do not unnecessarily depart from the line of thought as arranged by our author.

2. The differentiated and undifferentiated Brahman.

Sûtras 3, 2, 11—21.

Concerning Brahman there are, so Çankara expresses himself, passages of scripture of two kinds; the passages of one kind teach Brahman as possessing differences, for example, when it is said: "All-working is he, all-wishing, all-smelling, all-tasting" (above p. 153), the others as devoid of differences, as in the passage: "That is not coarse nor fine, nor short nor long" (above p. 133). Now the highest Brahman in itself

---

[91] Thus the same confusion is already found in the considerations which introduce the theological part (p. 110—114), and again very clearly p. 245, where in antithesis to the spaceless *param brahma* (p. 245, 7) appears as the *aparam brahma* the *prâṇa* which rules the body (p. 245, 10).

cannot be both, for it is not possible that one and the same thing in itself should be formed and formless (p. 803, 10). It is true that we might think that Brahman in itself is undifferentiated and becomes differentiated by Upâdhis (under which is to be understood everything which brings Brahman 1. to phenomenal existence, 2. to presentation in the mind). But one thing cannot become another, by the fact that it appears to be connected with limitations: the crystal remains clear, even when it is painted with red colour (p. 803, 14); as it is only an error if it is taken to be red in itself, so in the case of Brahman also the limitation rests only on Ignorance (p. 804, 1). Therefore it is to be firmly held, that Brahman is free from all differences and perfectly unchangeable and not the contrary (p. 804, 3).

How does it happen then, that, in many passages of scripture, manifold forms are attributed to Brahman, since He is called sometimes four-footed, sometimes of sixteen parts, sometimes dwarflike, sometimes having as body the three worlds, etc.? [p. 804, 9. Here and in what follows, the continual oscillation between phenomenal forms and forms of presentation should be noted.] Should we not perhaps admit that by the limitation a difference of form is actually brought about? For otherwise what is the purpose of the passages of scripture, which attribute differentiation to Brahman?—To this it is to be replied first, that every time that limitations appear, it is further said that Brahman is not affected by them [p. 805, 1: for this an isolated example is adduced; in reality it is most frequently not the case]; and that in many passages (Kâṭh. 4, 11. Bṛih. 4, 4, 19. Çvet. 1, 12) it is expressly asserted that there is no plurality, and that he who is predestined, what is predestined, and he who predestines are one in Brahman (p. 805, 13). At the same time it is to be noted that only the passages concerning the undifferentiated Brahman have as their aim, to teach the Being of God (p. 806, 7), while the passages concerning Brahman possessed of forms have another aim, namely worship (p. 806, 10).

A few similes may elucidate the relation of Brahman to His phenomenal forms. As the light of the sun or the moon, when it falls on the finger, shares in the finger's limitations, and in conformity with this, seems crooked when it is crooked, straight when it is straight, without in itself being crooked or straight, so also Brahman, when it is united with the limitation of the world of appearances, for example, of the earth, assumes its form, and on this is based (p. 807, 5) the apprehension of Brahman under different forms, as it is taught for the purpose of worship. It is therefore by no means purposeless; for all the words of the Upanishads have a purpose and are authoritative (p. 807, 8). But this does not prevent this view from resting on Ignorance all the same; for on inborn Ignorance depends worldly action as well as that prescribed by the Vedas (p. 807, 12).

Another simile is found in the *Moksha-çâstras*:

> "Like as this sun, whose being is the light,
> "Appears as manifold, in many streams,
> "By limitation multiplied in space,
> "E'en so it is with the unborn Âtman."

And the following:

> "One soul of beings dwells in every being,
> "One and yet many, like the moon in waves."

It is true, that the sun and the moon are formed and separated in space from their mirrored images, the Âtman, on the contrary, is not formed (read *mûrto* p. 810, 7) and not spatially separated from the limitations, but omnipresent and identical with all (p. 810, 8), but no simile can be applied any longer, if we abandon the *tertium comparationis* (*vivakshitam añçam*); for if it were identical with the thing compared, there would be no more comparison (p. 810, 13). It only affirms that Brahman, which is in the true sense unchanging and a unity, when it enters into limitation like the body and the rest, takes part, as it were, in the qualities of these limitations (p. 811, 6).

But if Brahman in itself is so perfectly devoid of differences, how are we to explain the passages of scripture concerning Brahman as possessing differences (p. 813, 12)?—Some think they also teach the undifferentiated Brahman, since the required annihilation of the phenomenal world must also be applied to the forms of Brahman taught by them (p. 814, 3). Yet this procedure is only permissible when they appear in a passage which treats of the esoteric teaching (*paravidyâ*), (p. 814, 4), but not where precepts of worship are spoken of (p. 814, 8). The passages which teach the nature of Brahman and those which prescribe worship of Brahman, must be kept separate throughout (p. 815, 6). The former aim at liberation, the latter have as their fruit, according to the object, purification from sins, attainment of lordship, or gradual liberation (p. 815, 5). And while the latter passages belong to the canon of precept, the former exclude all imperative elements, and aim only at the knowledge of the subject (p. 815, 10).

What should the precept prescribe in the case of knowledge of Brahman? Perhaps, to annihilate plurality, as one is ordered, by illuminating an object, to drive away the darkness (p. 816, 6)?—Then it must be asked: how is this annihilation of plurality to be thought of? Is it a real process, something like annihilating the hardness of butter, by putting it on the fire (p. 816, 10)?—But such an actual annihilation cannot be brought about by a mere man, and therefore cannot be ordered (p. 816, 15). Moreover in this case the whole plurality of earth etc. would have been annihilated by the first man who reached liberation, and the Universe would stand empty (p. 817, 2).

It must therefore be assumed, that the purpose is only to annihilate Ignorance which attributes to the one Brahman the plurality of appearances. But Ignorance is got rid of through teaching alone and without command (p. 817, 6), while a hundred commands without the teaching cannot remove it (p. 817, 9). Therefore, neither for the knowledge of Brahman nor for the annihilation of plurality are commands of any use; on the contrary both are accomplished by teaching alone (p. 817, 12).

And for whom should the command to annihilate plurality hold good? For the individual soul? But it is annihilated along with it! Or the highest soul? But it cannot be commanded (p. 818, 1—4).

It is true that it is said in the higher knowledge also: "this is to be seen!" (above p. 174). But the command here only means that it is to be brought before the eyes, and made the object of attention, not that it is to be known (p. 818, 7). Whether the latter happens or not, does not depend on a command, but on the quality of the object and the capacity for knowledge (p. 818, 12). If this were not so, if knowledge depended on will, it would be inexplicable that any one should go astray (p. 819, 1); but it depends not on the man, but on the object, and can, therefore, not be commanded (p. 819, 4).

If the scripture only commanded, then all in it that is not command, would have no meaning; it would, therefore, not explain (*avyâcakshîta*, optative with *a privativum*, p. 819, 8), that the knowledge of Brahman as soul cannot be commanded, but would command it to the man: but by this not only would one canon of commandments follow two opposite aims (works and teaching) and therefore be in contradiction with itself [it is difficult to see exactly why], but also liberation would be assigned to the sphere of meritorious works (*adrishṭa*) and therefore to something transitory (p. 820, 1). Finally, if the whole contents of the Veda were included under the idea of commandment, this commandment would be in contradiction with itself, since on the one hand it would enjoin annihilation of plurality, and on the other a partial maintenance of it. Therefore the imperative passages concerning differentiated Brahman and the non-imperative concerning undifferentiated Brahman must be kept separate from each other (p. 820).

3. Characteristics of the esoteric Brahman.

Sûtras 3, 2, 16. 17. 22.

When *Vâshkali* besought *Bâhva* to teach Brahman to him, the sage was silent. A second and third time this request was repeated. At last *Bâhva* said: "I am teaching it to thee, "but thou understandest it not; this Âtman is silent."

This narrative which Çañkara p. 808, 11 gives as *Çruti*, though its origin is unknown to us (cf. note 24, above p. 37), finds its elucidation in different passages of scripture quoted along with it (p. 808); thus when it is said (Taitt. 2, 4):

"From him all words turn back
"And thoughts, not finding him,"—

and in another passage (Kena 1, 3):

> "Other is it than all we know,
> "And higher than the unknown, too;"

as also when the *Smṛiti* (Bhag. G. 13, 12, echoing Ṛigv. 10, 129, 1) indicates Brahman as "neither the Existent, nor the non-Existent." But the full unknowableness of the original basis of things is most sharply expressed by the formula: "*Neti, neti!*"—"it is not thus, it is not thus",[92] which occurs in the Bṛihadâraṇyaka-Upanishad no less than five times (2, 3, 6. 3, 9, 26. 4, 2, 4. 4, 5, 15 and in a slightly different application 3, 2, 11). In the first of these passages it follows a statement of the two phenomenal forms (*rûpe*) of Brahman, of which one is called "formed, mortal, at rest, being," the other "formless, immortal, in motion, belonging to the Beyond." The latter comprises the wind and the atmosphere, breath and the space within the body, the former everything else in nature and man. Both, according to Çaṅkara (who subjects this passage to a lengthened consideration at 3, 2, 22 p. 821—826), are denied of Brahman by the formula "*neti, neti*"; the knowledge of its true form consists in this, that all forms are denied to it (p. 824, 12), whether we refer the repeated *na iti* to the two already adduced phenomenal forms (p. 825, 9) or to the phenomenal forms and the presentational forms (p. 825, 10) or in general to everything that can be perceived (p. 825, 11). Therefore all objective existence is negatived of Brahman and only its non-objective existence as the inner Soul remains (p. 825, 14). This negation of all distinctions in Brahman means, however, [as Brahman alone is true being] a negation of the whole phenomenal world falsely imposed on Brahman (p. 825, 15); therefore the formula *neti, neti* in Bṛih. 2, 3, 6 is explained by the words: "for outside him—therefore it is said 'it is not so'—there is no other beyond;" but he himself is not not (p. 826, 6).

Accordingly Existence remains as the sole characteristic of Brahman, and an Existence which is opposed to all empir-

---

[92] *itir idam-arthe*: "*idaṃ na, idaṃ na*" (Govindânanda p. 78, 21).

ical Existence, so that, in comparison with this, it can just as well be indicated as Non-existent (cf. above p. 129).

But what are the positive characteristics of this esoteric Brahman which presupposes the negation of all differences? The later Vedânta names three of them, which form the famous name of Brahman: *Sac-cid-ânanda*, that is "Existence, Intelligence, and Bliss;" this compound which, as far as I know, occurs first in the *Nṛisiṅha-tâpanîya-upanishad* (Ind. St. IX, 60. 84. 143. 147. 148. 154) is nowhere found in Çañkara's Commentary, and appears to be as yet unknown to our author. It is true that he repeatedly explains that, where Brahman is spoken of as Bliss, this limitation refers to the esoteric, attributeless Brahman (p. 127, 16. 868, 11), but here, in the strictly esoteric part, this is not spoken of, perhaps, because Çañkara counts it among the negative limitations as freedom from suffering; thus besides Existence, as the only positive quality of the esoteric Brahman, remains intelligence; p. 808, 2: "The scripture explains, that the undifferentiated Brahman is "pure intelligence and free from all that is different from it, "for it says (Bṛih. 4, 5, 13): 'as a block of salt has no [dis- " 'tinguishable] inside nor outside, but through and through " 'consists only of salt taste, so also this Âtman has no [dis- " 'tinguishable] inside and outside but consists throughout " 'altogether of intelligence.' That is: this Âtman is through- "out nothing but intelligence; intelligence is its exclusive "(*nirantara*) nature, as the salt taste is, of the lump of salt."

What relation have the only two remaining characteristics of Brahman, Existence and Intelligence (*bodha*), to each other?—The treatment of this question, expounded by other Commentators of the Brahmasûtras, Çañkara dismisses as purposeless (p. 812, 10) and on this point remarks as follows: (1) Brahman cannot be Existence without Intelligence, because this contradicts the passage of scripture (just quoted), and because otherwise he would not be the self of the individual soul, which is by nature intelligent; (2) not Intelligence without Existence either, because this is impossible; (3) and just as little Existence and Intelligence in their separate characters, because this would give rise to a plurality, which cannot exist in the case of Brahman; it therefore only remains that (4) Existence is the same as Intelligence, and Intelligence the same as Existence (*sattâ eva bodho, bodha' eva ca sattâ*, p. 813, 7), so that between the two there is no mutual exclusion. "Thus one might say," adds Çaṅkara, passing over, as secondary, this question which is so interesting for us.

We may, however, point out in connection with this, that both ideas in the End are resolvable into that of Force. All existence, in its essence, is nothing but a manifestation of Force and all Knowledge may be considered as a reaction against the crowd of impressions, and therefore as an activity of Force. That the Indian *caitanyam* comes very close to this idea, we have already remarked above (p. 59), and we shall encounter the proofs of it again in the course of the work.

4. On the Possibility of Knowing the esoteric Brahman.

Sûtras 3, 2, 23—30.

However much we may agree with the Vedânta, when it holds that a fathoming of Being-in-itself is only possible in our own "I", and, in its metaphysics, pushes aside everything objective, and relies on the Subject only, we can as little agree with it when, disregarding the objections of the opponent, which we became acquainted with above p. 135 ff. it finds the last basis of Being in the Subject of Knowledge. The consequence is, that the Vedânta denies itself an immediate insight into the essence of things; for the subject of knowledge can never become the object for us, precisely because in every cognition it must take the place of subject.—We shall see now how, notwithstanding this, the Indian was able to find a way of perceiving the subject, the spirit, Brahman.

At first our authors admit the objections thus raised as to the perceptibility of Brahman: Brahman is the Unmanifest (*avyaktam*), not perceptible, because in all perception it is assumed as the witness (*sâkshin*), that is, the knowing subject of knowledge (p. 827, 3). Yet there remains a possibility of knowing God: the *Yogin*, that is, here, he who has become one with God, sees him in the condition of *Saṃrâdhanam*, literally: perfect satisfaction, which Çañkara explains as a sinking oneself (*pra-ṇi-dhânam*) in pious meditation (p. 827, 10). This condition the scripture (Kâṭh. 4, 1) describes as follows:

> "The Self-existent pierced the openings
> "Of senses outwards, therefore a man looks
> "On outward things, not on the inner soul;—
> "A wise man saw, with backward-turned eye,
> "The inner Self, longing for deathlessness."

But does not the division of subject and object exist here also, between him who sinks himself, and that in which he sinks himself (p. 828, 6)?—Our authors answer this question with a negative, but, as the basis of their view, can only bring forward similes and passages of scripture. They begin by reminding us that this division only exists in virtue of the limitations (*upâdhi*) (p. 828, 11), and that these rest on Ignorance, after the dissipation of which the individual soul is identical with the highest soul (p. 829, 3); they compare this identity with that of the serpent and its coils (p. 830, 1), the sun and its light (p. 830, 5), they insist that the liberation, which consists in thus becoming one, would be impossible, if we held the separation to be in the strictest sense real (p. 830, 13) and conclude from the scripture, that, with the annihilation of plurality, only the knower in us, and therefore the Âtman, remains as the unit (p. 831, 7);—but an explanation of this unification of subject and object (as it actually takes place in the phenomena of æsthetic contemplation and religious devotion) cannot be obtained from their discussions.

5. On certain figurative Expressions used of Brahman.

For sake of completeness, we may here briefly touch on the section 3, 2, 31—37, in which, in the form of an appendix, are discussed certain expressions, which apparently do violence to the negation of all Being outside Brahman, and to Brahman's permeating all, and being omnipresent.

1. Brahman is called "the bridge which holds these worlds asunder," (above p. 162, cf. p. 133), and by a bridge is generally understood an aggregate of wood and earth, for the

purpose of crossing a continuous mass of water (p. 832, 2); even a traversing of this bridge is spoken of, and all this seems to presuppose something else outside Brahman (p. 832, 4).—To this it is to be answered, that Brahman is only compared to a bridge, because He holds asunder (p. 834, 12) the world and its boundaries (or orders, such as castes, Âçramas, etc., p. 258, 1), as the bridge does the banks [according to the primitive idea just quoted, however, it does not]; and the traversing of the bridge (above p. 162) means only the attainment of Brahman, as it is said: "he has gone through the grammar," in order to express the fact that he has gained mastery of it (p. 834, 15).

2. Further, Brahman has numbers and measures repeatedly applied to Him, such as "four-footed, eight-clawed, of sixteen parts," which seems to presuppose a limitation, for everything that can be measured is of limited size (p. 839, 9).—But this is only to bring it nearer to our [limited] understanding, as Bâdarâyaṇa says, our worship, as Çañkara adds in explanation (p. 835, 1. 4); for it is not possible for man to seize the unchanging, the endless (p. 835, 7).

3. A connection between the highest and the individual soul and again (in the passage discussed in Chap. IX, 6, above p. 140) a division (conditioned by it) within Brahman is repeatedly spoken of, in virtue of which two parts of it are defined along side of each other like the kingdoms of *Mâgadha* and *Vaideha* (p. 832—833).—But both exist only from the point of view of the *Upâdhis*, the relation of which to Brahman has already been discussed (p. 836, 7). The connection of the individual soul with Brahman is in reality an entering of the soul into its own Self (p. 836, 15), and the division within Brahman is no more real than that between cosmic space and the space within the body (p. 837, 5). Therefore it is proved that outside Brahman nothing is (p. 837, 10), that Brahman is in everything (p. 837, 16) and omnipresent (p. 838, 3).

THE SECOND PART OF THE VEDANTA SYSTEM:

COSMOLOGY

OR

THE DOCTRINE OF THE WORLD.

XV. Preliminary Remarks and Arrangement.

As before, our efforts will be directed, in the further course of our work, to the most faithful reproduction of the thoughts of Bâdarâyaṇa and Çaṅkara; we shall therefore abstain from all liberties with these thoughts and shall indicate unmistakeably as such our own incidental remarks. This fidelity extends to the whole material content of the work which we have to analyse, but not to its form as well; we take the thoughts as we find them, but in their arrangement and systematic connection, we allow ourselves to be guided only by the inner necessity which lies in the coordination of thought itself; this frequently compels us to deviate considerably from the arrangement of the original work.

That the latter does not in fact correspond to the nature of the subject, is due to several causes. To begin with, the tendency of the Brahmasûtras is chiefly polemical. The controversy with the opponents of the Vedânta teaching, which we, in following out our present aim, only introduce when it sheds new light on the system itself, is put in the foreground by our authors; while the most essential dogmas not seldom receive a subordinate treatment, just because they are not new and strange to Indian thought, as they are to us, but are matters of common currency and to a certain extent self-evident. Moreover it is the chief endeavour of the philosophers of the Vedânta to derive all their teachings directly from the Veda, and only in passing and as an appendix to show their rational basis although this is by no means lacking; thus what is really the fundamental idea often appears as a dependent thought. Besides this it is characteristic of Indian philosophers, that on the one hand they exhibit wonderfully profound conceptions reached by no other people of antiquity, and at the same time, on the other hand, a total lack of feeling for æsthetic form; in consequence of this they constantly allow themselves to drift without organising their material and are chiefly guided by the desire to find a *pro* and *contra* for every question, thus satisfying a highly developed taste for dialectic disputation, whether this leads to an explanation of the subject, or merely hinders and confuses it.[93] The consequence is, that the same fundamental thoughts are dealt with again and again to the point of weariness, without a true insight into their connection with the system as a whole, and thereby an insight into the thoughts themselves, being gained after all.

If while reproducing the content of the system of the Vedânta we did not at the same time refrain from reproducing its external form as it comes before us in the Brahmasûtras, it would be difficult to perceive the excellence of Indian thought; Colebrooke's praiseworthy study has had so little effect, for the sole reason that, apart from its brevity and the (very questionable) introduction of different commentaries, it confines itself to unmethodical extracts from the original work; by this course a full insight into the inner unity of the system is lost, not only by the reader, but even by the writer himself; the outline of the teaching according to the *Vedânta-sâra*, which was added as an appendix from a sense of this deficiency, cannot supply it, because it builds up the system on a basis essentially different from that of Çañkara.

The confusion in the treatment of the work on which we are engaged, is nowhere more noticeable than in the department of Cosmology, treated in 1, 4, 23—2, 3, 15, along with which are to be taken the conclusion of 2, 4 and 3, 2 (namely 2, 4, 20—22 and 3, 2, 38—41) and certain sections of the Division on Transmigration 3, 1 (e. g. 3, 1, 20—21. 3, 1, 24).

In Chapter VI and the translations from 4, 3, 14 which are

---

[93] Great as is the resemblance in this, to the Scholasticism of the Middle Ages, yet in other ways the contrast is as great: there we have the Bible, here the Veda (cf. note 52), there Aristotle, here original thought, there a compulsary belief, here a choice of the Vedic basis from free conviction.

added to it as an appendix, we have shown the existence of the antithesis between the exoteric and esoteric doctrine in all parts of the system. If this antithesis exists, it cannot of course fail to be decisive for the disposition of the materials. But this is not the case with our authors: in their Section on Cosmology they give a general sketch of the exoteric teaching as to Creation, thereby involving themselves in a series of contradictions, which they seek to explain by appeals to the esoteric teaching, and then go on quietly with their empirical picture of the universe, just as if nothing had happened, while the whole realism on which this picture rests has been again and again overthrown and exposed in all its inadequacy. Nowhere do we find sharp lines of demarcation; but rather we have a tendency (very pronounced in the passage above page 110) to explain the exoteric passages of Scripture in the sense of the esoteric, an attempt which, especially in the Section on Cosmology, has given rise to an enquiry, as difficult as it is unsatisfactory, into the idea of causality.

In order to bring clearness into the subject, and yet in no wise to do violence to our authors, we shall first of all treat of Brahman as Creator (Chap. XVI), and then (Chap. XVII) of the creation of nature, taking both in the exoteric sense, after which the few traces of natural science scattered here and there in the work can be gathered together. In another chapter (XVIII) we shall bring together all the problems that occur on our way, whose explanation our authors have reached by passing over to the esoteric teaching as to nature. Before we turn to the latter, we must deal further with our philosophers' conceptions of the idea of causality (Chap. XIX), for in it they find the justification of the esoteric teaching of the identity of the world with Brahman, apart from purely theological arguments. Only after explaining this doctrine of identity (Chap. XX), can the problems raised three chapters earlier find the solution dependent on this doctrine, according to the materials existing in the original work (Chap. XXI).

XVI. Brahman as Creator of the World.

1. The Motive of Creation.

Sûtras 2, 1, 32–33.

We have learnt to know Brahman as an intelligent being; as such, he seems to require a motive for his actions. For we see in life that an intelligent being, who thinks before he acts, for example a human being, prepares for no undertaking, whether great or small, unless a motive leads him to it (p. 488, 12). The application of this rule of experience to Brahman is, as it seems, confirmed by the scriptures, when they teach (above, p. 173) that the world is dear to him not for the world's sake, but for the sake of his own self (p. 489, 2).—If we ascribe to God a motive which determined him to create, this contradicts his all-sufficiency (*paritriptatvam*), but if we do not ascribe such a motive to him, creation becomes impossible (p. 489, 6). —Or shall we take it for granted that Brahman, like a thoughtless man, proceeded to create at random, and without a motive? This again would contradict his omniscience (*sarvajñatvam*).

We must then take it for granted that, as a prince or some great man who has all that he requires, undertakes something without a motive, purely for sport and pastime (p. 490, 1), or as outbreathing and inbreathing go on by themselves, without external motive (p. 490, 2), so too God created the world of himself and without a motive, purely for sport (*lîlâ*; cf. the παῖς παίζων of Heraclitus); for a further motive is not to be found by reflection or revelation of the scriptures[94]

[94] Such a motive is certainly to be found in the system, and our author does not find it only because he cannot separate the idea of a motive from that of personal (egoistic) interest. According to the Vedânta,

and it is impossible to ask God himself about it (p. 490, 6). Moreover it is only to us that the arrangement of this terrestrial disk appears such a difficult thing, for God, on the contrary, through the power of his immeasurable omnipotence, it is mere sport (p. 490, 8). And if in life a slight motive must be present even for sport, for God we need assume nothing of the sort, for the scripture forbids us to attribute any desire to him (p. 490, 9). That he could not for this reason proceed to act, is contrary to the teaching of the scripture concerning creation; that he acted without thought, and by chance, is contrary to the teaching concerning his omniscience (p. 490, 11).

Above all (thus Çañkara concludes this section), we must not forget that the whole teaching as to creation refers to this world of names and forms, founded on Ignorance, and it has really only the aim of teaching the identity of nature with Brahman (p. 491, 1);—an observation that will also hold good for what we have to put forward further, and which arises from the endeavour to hold fast to the exoteric teaching of of the scripture as completely valid.

2. Brahman is the efficient and at the same time the material Cause of the World.

Sûtras 1, 4, 23—27.

Brahman was defined at the outset of this work (1, 1, 2) as "*that by which the world originates, etc.* (subsists, and perishes)," (cf. the definitions above p. 123), and therefore as the cause of the world. The word "Cause", however, may mean two things, either the material cause (*prakṛiti, upâdânam*), or the efficient cause (*nimittam*); so the cause of the vessel is, on one hand, the clay, and on the other the potter, that of the golden ornament is on one hand the gold,

it is the inner destination of this world to become the stage for the reward of the deeds of an earlier existence, and the chain of these existences stretches back for each individual *ad infinitum*. According to these earlier deeds alone, God apportions weal and woe; and in them alone is to be sought the reason that he must create the world anew after each disappearance; for the fruit of deeds done outlasts that disappearance and requires each time a new creation for their explanation.

and on the other the goldsmith (p. 396, 10).—The question is, in which sense is Brahman to be regarded as the cause of the world?

It might be thought that Brahman can only be held to be the efficient cause of the world, because it is said of him, before he proceeds to create: "he intended" (above p. 135), and because he is called "the Lord" (*îçvara*); both these seem only to apply to an efficient cause (p. 397, 5, 8).—To this is added, that cause and effect must be of like nature; the world, however, is manifold, unspiritual, and unclean (p. 397, 10), which does not apply to Brahman and seems to require a material cause besides him, which shall possess these qualities.

The answer to these considerations is, that Brahman is both the efficient and material cause of the world (p. 398, 3).

The proof of this assertion, in the introductory passage of the Cosmology which we here treat of, is purely theological (based on references to passages of the Vedas) and, from the point of view which we now occupy, cannot be otherwise, because (quite apart from the consideration raised, as to the unlikeness of nature of the world and Brahman, which is here passed over by our author, and only taken up again, and brought under consideration, in a later discussion, cf. Chap. XVIII, 1, a) a solution of the idea of matter, from the empirical standpoint, which we have not yet transcended here, is impossible, for the only true consequence of this standpoint would be the eternal duration of matter.

Under these circumstances, it is comprehensible that Çañkara here contents himself with references to the scripture according to which, with the knowledge of Brahman, all is known, and in which Brahman is compared to the clay, all the transformations of which are also clay; as, for example, it is expressly said: Before the beginning of creation, there was one only, without a second, Brahman desired to become manifold, he himself made himself, he is the birthplace of beings, he limits them from himself, and reabsorbs them into himself, as the spider with her thread, etc. etc. (p. 398—403). In conclusion, our author disposes of the objections given above, and the appeals to experience, by the explanation (translated above

p. 93), that we need not here remain in accord with experience, for here we have not to do with an object of rational knowledge (*anumânam*), but with revelation (403, 7), and further refers to subsequent investigations.

3. Brahman creates without Instruments.

Sûtras 2, 1, 24—25.

Widely separated from the enquiry treated of above, although in fact standing in close relationship with it, and even in part coinciding with it, is the question of the instruments which Brahman uses. As the demonstration was reached there by quotations from the Veda, so it is here reached by examples from nature; if it is (from the cause stated above p. 224) no less inadequate on this account, it still possesses a certain interest, because it contributes to make clear the view of nature held by the Hindus; for this reason we give the Adhikaraṇam in question 2, 1, 24—25 (p. 475—479) almost word for word:

It might be objected that it is not feasible to assume the spiritual Brahman alone and without a second as the cause of the world, because in order to mould anything, all kinds of instruments are needed; thus in actual life the potters etc. when they wish to make vessels take all kinds of things, as the clay, the stick, the wheel, or thread as instruments, and thus we cannot assume that Brahman created the world without instruments. We reply to this, that creation takes place by the specific quality of the substance (*dravya-svabhâva-viçeshâd*, that is, Brahman) in much the same way that the change of milk into curds or water into ice takes place without exterior instruments. Certainly warmth assists in turning milk sour, still the milk follows nothing but the laws of change inherent in itself, and the process is only hastened by the warmth. Were the power to become sour not already in the milk, the warmth could not help it to change; since, for example, wind or ether cannot be changed to curds by warmth. The addition of the means only completes the process; but even such a completion is not needed in the case of Brahman.

for he possesses all the necessary powers (*çakti* of which immediately) perfect within himself.

It is true that milk etc. are unintelligent substances, and we see that beings with intelligence, like potters etc., call in the aid of instruments. Thus we may suppose it to be with Brahman, as he also is an intelligent being.—To this can be opposed the fact that gods also, and ancestors, and Rishis, who are certainly beings possessed of intelligence, through their own power, without external means, according to their innate sovereignty, and through meditation alone, creat many variously shaped bodies, palaces, carriages etc., as the Hymns and Brâhmaṇas as well as the epic and mythological works attest. Further, we must remember that the spider puts forth her thread from herself, that female cranes become fecundated without seed, and that lotus-flowers wander from one pond to another without outward means of transit. The applicability of these comparisons may be contested, because the gods accomplish their deeds only by taking bodily forms to aid them, and not by the spiritual Self alone, because the saliva of the spider, after it has been stiffened by eating smaller creatures, becomes threads, because the female cranes are fertilised[95] when they hear the voice of the thunder, because the lotus-flowers do not wander among the ponds by means of their unintelligent bodies, but precisely because they are endowed with intelligence, as climbing plants find their way to trees;—but to all this we can reply that the creatures named do not, like the potter, use external instruments in

---

[95] p. 477, 15: *balâkâ ca antareṇa eva çukram garbham dhatte*; p. 768, 6: *balâkâ api antareṇa eva retaḥ-sekam garbham dhatta', iti loke rûḍhiḥ*; p. 478, 8: *balâkâ ca stanayitnu-rava-çravaṇâd garbham dhatte.* These indications may serve to clear up the passage *Meghadûta* v. 9, which, as appears from Stenzler's note on page 29, has hitherto been understood differently:

garbha-âdhâna-kshaṇa-paricayân nûnam âbaddha-mâlâḥ
sevishyante nayana-subhagam khe bhavantam balâkâḥ

"Surely wilt thou [O Cloud], when thou floatest in the air, rejoicing the "eye, be honored by the female cranes in their serried ranks, because "they conclude (*colligunt*) [from thy arising] that the moment for receiv-"ing the fruits of the body [in the tempest] draws near."

their activity, and that, like them, Brahman does not, in creating, use any outward means to assist himself, which is what we wished to arrive at.

—The defective knowledge of nature, and the weakness of the arguments on this ground require no further comment, besides the examples we have given.

4. Brahman and the Powers of Nature.

Sûtras 2, 1, 30 and 1, 3, 30.

In all considerations of this section, it is well to keep in mind that the Indian idea of creation differs essentially from our own. For whilst by creation, we understand something done once for all, and therefore at a given time, the consciousness of the Vedântin is dominated by the concept that from eternity to eternity the world periodically emerges from and again returns to Brahman; and it emerges and returns times without number: "the past and future world-periods (*kalpa*) are measureless," as the Purâṇa passage quoted on p. 495, 10, declares.

But how comes it that the world, through all its new creations, remains the same in character?—This question compels us to seek the basis of this *uniformity* in Brahman himself.

Further: how can the manifold manifestations of the world arise from the uniform Brahman?—For this *multiplicity*, there must also be a sufficient reason in Brahman.

In these postulates we must seek for the motive of the manifold powers (*çakti*), which Brahman contains, the resemblance of which to the Platonic teaching of ideas we have already referred to, above pp. 69—70.

This valuable thought is unfortunately only slightly developed in our system; it only appears sporadically, and its position is uncertain; sometimes the powers of Brahman appear simply as the expression of his omnipotence, sometimes they mean the fructifying power of those things which, at the destruction of the world, enter as a germ into Brahman, to come forth again at the new creation. We will briefly gather together what is to be found scattered here and there, on this subject.

"That the uniform Brahman produces the diverse manifestation of the phenomenal world," so is stated on p. 486, 10, "is to be explained through His providing Himself with various powers." To prove this, certain Vedic passages are mentioned, which, however, do not appear to assert anything more than the omnipotence of Brahman ('all-working is he, all-wishing, all-smelling, all-tasting'): Brahman is furnished with all powers (p. 1125, 8), is connected with the unfolding of many powers (p. 445, 11), the Îçvara possesses innumerable powers (p. 490, 8), as appears from his being the cause of the origin, subsistence, and destruction of the world (p. 1126, 1); these powers without which Brahman could not create (p. 342, 6), are deduced from the multiplicity of their effects (p. 486, 2); as to their relation to Brahman, from the expression used on p. 476, 8, that Brahman "is filled with powers," (*paripûrṇaçaktikam*), we may conclude that these powers are believed to be immanent in Brahman.

The Scripture (Çvet. 1, 3) leads to the assumption of one power of the highest God, which orders and creates the whole world (p. 358, 5). It is this godlike power not unfolded in name and form, which is the original state (*prâg-avasthâ*) of names and forms (p. 358, 10); in this original state, the now manifested world existed before manifestation, in a state of seed-force (*vîja-çakti-avasthâ*, p 341, 9); "if" (it is said on p. 342, 2 in the polemic against the Sâñkhyas) "we acknow-"ledged a self-subsisting original state of the world as cause, "we should make room for the assumption of a material cause "(of the world); we assume though that this original state of "the world was not self-subsisting, but dependent on the highest "God. Such we must of necessity take it to be, and on good "grounds. For without it, the creative work of God is im-"possible, for an activity of God devoid of his powers is un-"thinkable... This unmanifested (*avyaktam*) seed-force, as "it is called, resting in the highest God, is in its inherent "character Ignorance (*avidyâ*), a deep sleep produced by "glamour (*mâyâ*) in which lie those wandering souls, who have "not awakened to the knowledge of their real nature [the "knowledge of their identity with Brahman]."

According to these passages, it appears that 1. the creative power of Brahman, 2. the seed-forces of things, and 3. individual souls existing by means of their subtle bodies, are all confused together in the indeterminate idea of the powers of Brahman. We have already seen (above p. 70) that these powers were not annihilated at each destruction of the world, but remained in existence as its root (p. 303, 1), and in such a way that their character remained unchanged (p. 303, 2). From this, it follows, that in spite of the continual destruction of the world, the same elements (earth, etc.), the classes of beings (gods, men, animals), and the worldly distinctions (castes and Âçramas), come forth anew (p. 303, 4).

The multiplicity of these powers does not contradict the unity of Brahman who contains them, since the p o w e r o f m u l t i p l y i n g (*vibhâga-çakti*), before and after the existence of the world, as well as the t e n d e n c y t o m u l t i p l i c i t y (*vibhâga-vyavahâra*), during the existence of the world, rest on false perception (*mithyâjñânam*) (p. 433, 13); as we shall see more in detail, in the esoteric cosmology.

XVII. The exoteric Picture of Creation.

1. General.

Two passages of the Upanishads, which we now give, are the main standards for the ideas of the creation of the world.[96]

1) *Taittirîya-Upanishad* 2, 1: "Truly from this Âtman the "Âkâça came forth; from the Âkâça, the wind; from the wind, "fire; from fire, water; from water, the earth; from the earth, "plants; from plants, nourishment; from nourishment, seed: "from seed, man."

2) *Chândogya-Upanishad* 6, 2, 2—3, 2: "Existent, alone, dear "one, was this in the beginning, one alone and without a second. "It conceived the idea (*aikshata*): 'I will become many, I will "'propagate myself'; so it created fire (*tejas*).—This fire conceived the idea: 'I will become many, I will propagate my- "'self'; so it created water. Therefore, when a man is hot "and sweats, from the heat arises water.—This water con- "ceived the idea: 'I will become many, I will propagate my- "'self'; so it created food. Therefore, when it rains, much "food arises, for from water arises the nourishment that man "eats.—In truth, these beings have three sorts of seeds (i. e., "origins), those born from the egg, those born alive, and those

---

96 A third important passage, *Aitareya-Up.* 1, 1, is only touched upon incidentally in 3, 3, 16—17, and plays no further part in the system. We give the beginning of this passage here, for the sake of comparison:

"Truly, this world was Âtman alone in the beginning; there was "naught else there to open the eyes. He conceived the idea: 'I will now "'create worlds.' Then he created these worlds; [they are:] the floods, "the rays, death, the waters [Çañkara reads p. 871, 8 *mara'*, *âpas*]. Yonder "is the flood, beyond the heavens; heaven is its support; the rays are the "atmosphere; death is the earth; underneath are the waters."

"born from the germ. That deity conceived the idea: 'Verily, "'I will enter into these three deities (fire, water, food), with "'this living Self [the individual soul], and spread forth into "'names and forms; and I will make each one of them three-"'fold.'—Then that deity entered into these three deities, with "this living Self, and spread forth names and forms; and each "one of them it made threefold" [of this, later].

As we see, in the first place five elements, Âkâça, air, fire, water, and earth, are mentioned, but in the second, only the last three. Our authors detailed discussion of the absence of contradiction in this, because in the second, Âkâça and air must be supplied from the first, may very well be omitted, since they are wholly exegetical in character. This, however, occasions a controversy of considerable interest, concerning the origin of Âkâça. For *Âkâça*, usually translated ether, is not so much this, as all-permeating, all-present space,—as may be understood from the popular expression, quoted for other purposes on p. 609, 7: *âkâçam kuru*, "make room," *âkâço jâtaḥ*, "room has been made"; but still it is space, as something corporeal, as an element;—a conception that is not far from the ideas of all those which take space to be something self-existent (that is, independent of our intellect) and therefore real. In this sense, the Indian thinkers make it the medium of sound (e. g. p. 557, 14), which therefore they did not recognise as a vibratory movement of the air, and, in consequence, the element of air receives a more concrete meaning, approaching the idea of wind. Of this material apprehension of space, Çankara (p. 558, 1) objects against the Buddhists, who define Âkâça as purely negative, as "the absence of hindrances" (*âvaraṇa-abhâva*), that, in that case, there could be no Âkâça in the space taken up by a body, a flying bird, for example; so that we must recognise in the Âkâça not the absence of hindrances, but that reality, through which the absence of hindrances is constituted, literally: characterised (*tad vastu-bhûtam, yena âvaraṇa-abhâvo viçishyate*),—all this in reality comes back to the verbal contention as to whether a negative can still be called real, and it clearly shows that the conception of the Âkâça wavers between that of space, and something material. It has the same character in the following controversy with *Kaṇâda*, who correctly recognizes the heterogeneity of Âkâça and the elements, and as a consequence, places Âkâça as a connecting link between corporeal nature and the power of nature manifesting itself therein (Brahman).

2. The Origin of Space (*Âkâça*).

Sûtras 2, 3, 1—7.

With unconcealed irony, Çañkara mentions those who follow in the footsteps of the illustrious *Kaṇabhuj*, (a nickname for *Kaṇâda*): "that we cannot conceive an origin of space" (p. 608, 6).—We will see how far this irony is well founded, by picking out from the chaos of discussion, the essential arguments and counter-arguments.

Space can have had no origin, says *Kaṇâda*, for the following reasons: (1) How can one conceive the causal relation between space as an effect, and its cause? The cause (*kâraṇam*), of an effect (for example, a textile fabric) has three moments, as *samavâyi-asamavâyi-nimitta-kâraṇam*, that is, inherent cause (the threads), non-inherent cause (the union of the threads), and efficient cause (weaver and loom). The inherent cause consists of a substance, which is (a) homogeneous (*ekajâtîyaka*), (b) manifold (*aneka*) [like the atoms of Kaṇâda]. "Now for "space, there is no homogeneous and manifold substance, from "which, as inherent cause, together with the union of the same "(that is, of its particles), as non-inherent cause, space could "originate. And if this does not exist, much less can we think "of an assisting efficient cause for space" (p. 608, 8ff.).

(2) In the case of created elements (for example, fire) we can picture to ourselves a difference between the time before, and the time after they had come into being. This difference we cannot conceive in the case of space [*na sambhâvayitum çakyate* p. 609, 4), that is, therefore, we cannot picture a condition in which space was not]. "For how can a man "assume that before the creation there was no place, no "vacuity, no opening?" (p. 609, 5).

(3) Space did not originate, for it is of a different nature

(*vidharma*) from the earth, &c., in so far as its distinctive character is, that it penetrates all things (*vibhutvam*) etc. (p. 609, 6).

(4) Lastly, in the scripture itself, space is called "undy-"ing, all-present, eternal" (p. 610, 3).

According to all this, we must assume that before the creation, when, as the scriptures say, there was "one only, "without a second," space must have formed an all-penetrating, formless unity with Brahman, like water mixed with milk; and this separated at the creation in such a way that space remained immovable, while Brahman exerted itself (*yatate*) to produce the world (p. 612, 3).

After Çañkara has pointed out that water and milk, although mixed, yet remain different essentially, whilst for the existent before the creation, an essential unity was required (p. 617, 15), he sets himself to refute Kaṇâda's arguments; first however he gives the following positive proof of the origination of space:

(p. 618, 13) "Whenever we see anything that has originated "through transformation, whether it be pitchers, pots, and "pails, or bracelets, clasps, and rings, or needles, iron arrow-"heads, and swords, we see division also in the world. On "the contrary, a thing without origin can never be thought "of as divided. The division of space is, however, shown by "the earth, etc. (that is in space); therefore space also must "be a transformation" (that is: all that has an origin is divisible; but space is divisible; *ergo*—!).

Probably from a perception of the weakness of this argument, our author at once passes from it to the domain of metaphysics, where he is more at home: Âtman, he says, is not divided by the earth, or anything else; for space (the principle of division) originates in Âtman; consequently Âtman is no transformation. With this thought, which takes its root in the profound perception that that which exists in itself is spaceless, Çañkara goes on to the fine statement of the Self-existence of Âtman, which we translated in Chapter VIII, 6 (above p. 127). He then turns to the arguments of Kaṇâda mentioned above, to refute them one after another.

(1) The cause need not necessarily be homogeneous and manifold; (a) not homogeneous: for the threads and their combinations need not be homogeneous, and still less the efficient cause, the loom (but no one ever maintained this).— Or is homogeneity to be asserted of the inherent cause only? That cannot be maintained unconditionally. For a single cord is twisted out of yarn and cow-hair; and many cloths are woven from thread and [unspun] wool. Or does the homogeneity of the cause only demand that it must be one being and one substance? That is self-evident, and the requirement is superfluous. (b) Further, the cause need not be manifold. For also the atoms of Kaṇâda work each for itself. It is not necessary that the cause should consist of several factors; for the effect can also be the result of transformation, since a substance passes into a different condition, and is then called the effect. The substance in this case may be manifold, as the earth and the seed that go to form plants, or uniform, as milk, which becomes curds. And so, according to the scripture, from the uniform Brahman, the manifold world, with space and all creatures, has sprung (p. 621, 5–623, 4).

(2) It is absurd to assert, with reference to space, that a difference cannot be imagined between the time before, and the time after creation; for that space, with all bodies, is there now, and that nothing was there before, is precisely the difference. [But here Kaṇâda is not even understood, much less disproved.] Besides, the scripture expressly declares (Bṛih. 3, 8, 8, translated above p. 133), that Brahman, amongst other things, is spaceless (*anâkâçam*, "not-ether," as we translated above p. 133) (p. 623, 5–12).

(3) It does not hold good, either, that space had no origin, because it is different in essence from the earth and the other elements. For, firstly, where the scripture contradicts this, a logical conclusion of the impossibility of its origin is fallacious, and, secondly, its origination follows even as a logical conclusion: for space is not everlasting, because it possesses qualities which are not everlasting (sound perhaps?—that would, however, under no circumstances be an essential

quality of space;) therefore we must postulate a beginning for it, as for vases, etc. Do you maintain that, in this, it is not distinguished from Âtman?—For of Âtman, no one has ever yet demonstrated to a follower of the Upanishads that he is the bearer of non-eternal qualities. Furthermore, it has never been proved that space is all-pervading *(vibhu)* (p. 624, 5; the same monstrous assertion p. 700, 4).

(4) When space is said by the scripture to be immortal, it is only in the (relative) sense in which the gods also are said to be immortal (on this, above p. 67). When, however, it is said of Brahman, that he is, "like space, omnipresent, eternal;" that is simply a simile, as when it is said: "the sun flies like an arrow," whereby it is not meant that it has only the same speed as an arrow; then also it is said of Brahman: "greater is he than space" (above p. 163) and "what is separate from him, is afflicted" (above p. 142).—Thus the origination of space is proved (p. 624, 6—625, 7).

3. The Origin of Air, Fire, Water, Earth.

Sûtras 2, 3, 8—13.

As Âkâça came forth from Âtman, so Vâyu (air or wind) came forth from Âkâça; its immortality and imperishability, as taught by the scripture (Chând. 4, 3, 1. Bṛih. 1, 5, 22) are to be taken as only relative *(âpekshika)*, that is, in comparison with the other elements, which all come forth from, and return to it, and only hold good in the lower doctrine (p. 626, 5), which seems to mean that, in the passage in question (Bṛih. 1, 5, 22), Vâyu is the representative of *aparam brahma.* As from Âkâça proceeds air, so from this proceeds fire (2, 3, 10), from fire water (2, 3, 11), and from water, earth (2, 3, 12), for this, and not rice or barley, is to be understood by "food" in the passage of the Chândogya at the beginning of this chapter, firstly, because the context requires this, and this is of more importance than the use of words (p. 634, 5) and also because "the food" is spoken of further on (Chând. 6, 4) as "black" and this refers to the earth which in some parts, it is true, is white like milk, and red, like [glowing] coals, (p. 633, 9), but as a rule is black, for which reason it is also called *Çarvarî* (night) in the Purâṇas (p. 633, 11). Plants, according to other passages, spring from the earth later and therefore the word "food" refers to the earth.

How are we to understand this emanation of the elements from each other? They are without intelligence (*acetana*), but (a weighty axiom of our system) without intelligence, no motion is possible (p. 635, 1; compare 528, 7). Therefore we must assume that God himself changes himself into the elements (p. 635, 3) and after he has become air, for example, he creates fire (p. 630, 10); his position in regard to the elements is this expressed by the passage of scripture (Bṛih. 3, 7, 3): "He who, dwelling in the earth, is different from the "earth, whom the earth does not know, whose body is the earth, "who inwardly governs the earth, He is thy soul, thy inward "guide, the immortal" (compare above p. 149 ff.). Consequently, in all elements, Brahman is the inner guide and overseer, and as such, brings about their motions (p. 635, 7).

It must, therefore, be borne in mind that the elementary creation, that is, the whole body of inorganic nature, as such, is inanimate, and therefore incapable of movement, like a cart without a horse (p. 507, 9. 727, 1) and that according to this, when, for example, water flows, not water, as such, but the Brahman in it, brings this about (p. 507, 12); and the contradiction is not important, if, in his stead, the nature-gods (created by him, and dependent on him) have the same functions assigned to them, of which we have spoken above p. 65 ff.

Further, the psychic organs (Buddhi, Manas, and the senses) of which we shall learn more in our psychological section, are, like the elements, emanations of Brahman; whether it be assumed that they are of like nature, and therefore of like duration, with these (p. 640, 1), or that they are different in kind from the natural elements and must be looked on as having emanated before or after them (p. 640, 3). In any case, they, as well as the elements, are, in themselves, lifeless, and both elements and organs are only created as means to an end, as we shall see further on.

4. Incidental Remark on the Destruction of the World.

Sûtram 2, 3, 14.

We must assume that, in the periodical re-absorption of the world in Brahman, the elements, in the same way as they have emerged from one another, are withdrawn again into one another in reverse order; for so experience teaches us, as, for example, in a staircase, coming down is the reverse of going up (p. 637, 5); therefore, as the vessel becomes clay again, and the ice, water (p. 637, 6), so also the dissolution of the elements takes place in such a manner that the less subtle goes back to that which is finer, the more remote effect returns everywhere into the nearer (p. 637, 9), for it is not right to assume that the effect continues when its cause is destroyed (p. 638, 4).

At the end of the Kalpa, therefore, the earth becomes water again; water, fire; fire, air; air becomes Âkâça, and Âkâça re-enters Brahman.—This view is likely to throw some light on the scientific motive of the teaching of the gradual evolution and absorption of the elements, as to which we have no other information: the observation that solids dissolve in water, that water turns into steam through heat, that the flames of fire flicker out into the air (Chând. 4, 3, 1: *yadâ vâ' agnir udvâyati, vâyum eva api-eti*), air, according to the altitude, rarifies more and more into empty space, might lead us to the gradual progression of the dissolution of the world, and by inversion to its opposite, the creation of the world.[97]

---

[97] A classification of the elements (with the omission of Âkâça), according to their greater or lesser density, and corresponding perceptibility, is indicated p. 536, 7: "the earth, as capable of being smelt, "tasted, seen, felt, is gross (*sthûla*); water, as being tasted, seen, and "felt, is subtle (*sûkshma*); fire, as being seen and felt, is more subtle "(*sûkshmatara*); the air, as only to be felt, is most subtle (*sûkshmatama*)." —As a rule, the Indians add to these a fifth, and still more subtle element, Âkâça, with the quality of audibility (also possessed by the other four). Cf. Aristotle, *de sensu* 2, p. 438 B. 17 ff.: φανερὸν ὡς δεῖ τοῦτον τὸν τρόπον ἀποδιδόναι καὶ προσάπτειν ἕκαστον τῶν αἰσθητηρίων ἑνὶ τῶν στοιχείων. τοῦ μὲν ὄμματος τὸ ὁρατικὸν ὕδατος ὑποληπτέον, ἀέρος δὲ τὸ τῶν ψόφων αἰσθητικόν, πυρὸς δὲ τὴν ὄσφρησιν,—τὸ δ'ἁπτικὸν γῆς, τὸ δὲ

5. Organic Nature.

Sûtras 3, 1, 24. 20–21.

The creation of the world, properly speaking, which, as it appears, is to be thought of as a disk,[98] concludes with the creation of inanimate nature. For in organic nature, quite a new principle comes before us: it is the soul, which is incarnate in all the thousand phenomena of life, in all forms of gods, men, animals, and plants. It is true that souls also are an emanation from Brahman, from whom they, according to the Upanishads (for example Muṇḍ. 2, 1, 1, translated above p. 131 ff.; Kaush. 3, 3. 4, 20. Bṛih. 2, 1, 20) have arisen as the sparks from the fire, and into which they return in the same manner; but neither their origination from Brahman, nor their return to him, is understood by our system in the strict sense of the word. For the soul exists together with its organs (*Prâṇas*) and the "subtle body," from eternity—and, unless liberation is reached, to eternity; its entrance into Brahman in deep sleep, death, and at the dissolution of the world, takes place in such a manner that its seed remains, from which it proceeds again unchanged, with its organs. Of this later.

By embodied souls, we are to understand all living beings (*bhûtâni,* more precisely [in contradistinction to the *mahâbhûtâni* or elements p. 140, 13] *prâṇinaḥ* p. 300, 5. 303, 4), therefore not only all gods, men, and animals, but also plants (therefore the expressions: *brahmâdi-sthâvarânta* p. 61, 11; *brahmâdi-stambaparyanta* p. 604, 2). Therefore plants (*sthâvara*) are also, as on p. 774, 5 it is expressly acknowledged, places of enjoyment (or suffering), they also have a living soul (*kshetrajña* p. 772, 5; *jîva* p. 773, 3), which has entered into

---

γευστικόν εἶδός τι ἁφῆς ἐστίν.—It should be noted that, while the Indians place fire between water and air, the Greeks, on the other hand, place air between water and fire.

[98] *jagad-vimbam* p. 488, 11. 489, 3. 490, 7.—The following expressions *nâkasya prishṭhe* (frequent in the Veda, for example, Muṇḍ. 1, 2, 10; cf. Plato, Phaedrus, p. 247, C: ἐπὶ τῷ τοῦ οὐρανοῦ νώτῳ, and *paro divo jyotir dîpyate viçvataḥ prishṭheshu* (Chând. 3, 13, 7, translated above p. 169) seem to point to the idea of a sphere or hemisphere.

them in consequence of impure deeds (p. 774, 6), and they are sensible of enjoyment and pain (p. 772, 4), in which, however, the souls that return from the moon and stay for a while in plants as guests take no part. If the plant is cut, crushed, or cooked, the plant-soul dwelling in it passes out (*pravasati*), like every soul, when its body is destroyed (p. 773, 13ff.). Plants must be in part endowed with perception, for, without it, the wandering of the lotus-flower from one pond to another, and the climbing of trees by creepers cannot be explained (p. 478, 9); for, as is often affirmed: without perception (*cetanâ*) there is no movement (*pravritti*).—It is true that the plant-world, as the immovable (*sthâvara*), is generally contrasted with the animal-world, as the movable (*jañgama*) (p. 769, 4. 113, 1. 118, 17. 178, 5. 642, 1. 687, 4); it may serve as characteristic of the latter, that the cow (p. 507, 14) is said to have perception of, and love for, its calf, as also the goose (*haṅsa*) can distinguish both components in a mixture of milk and water, while we cannot (p. 799, 3); for the rest, in regard to the difference between animal and human perception, we are confined to what the passages translated in note 34, p. 57 above offer us.—It seems strange that p. 491, 7 to the gods is assigned a condition of infinite enjoyment, to man a mixed state, and to the animals, "infinite suffering." For the rest, such a conception could only be formed where the height of pleasure is to be measured by the degree of intelligence, and where, consequently, intellectual enjoyments are esteemed as the highest.[99]

We find a classification of organic beings 3, 1, 20—21, where they (as in the Ait. Up. 3, 3 p. 243) are divided according to their origin into

(1) *udbhijja*, born from a germ (plants),

(2) *svedaja*, born of sweat (damp heat, *sveda*, for which Bâdarâyaṇa has the singular word *saṃçoka*), for example, vermin,

---

[99] The argument on p. 102, 13 also rests on this view: if the (unconscious) primordial substance of the Sâñkhyas were the place of the liberated, liberation would be a misfortune.

(3) *aṇḍaja*, born of the egg,

(4) *jarâyuja*, born of the womb[100] (literally, from the Chorion).

The two last classes originate by procreation, the two first, without it (p. 768, 10). The passage from the Châandogya-Upanishad, which we gave in the introduction to our chapter above p. 230, exhibits only three classes, for it joins the two first together, as if both came forth from germs, the one from earth, the other from water (p. 769, 3); yet the separation is justified, for the first class embraces immovable, the second movable beings (p. 769, 5).

6. Physiological Remarks.

Sûtras 2, 4, 20—22. 3, 1, 2.

In the passage from the Châandogya-Upanishad, the beginning of which we translated above, p. 230, it is shown further how all things are triply mixed from the three original elements, fire, water, and food. So, for example, in natural fire, in the sun, moon and lightning, the red comes from the fire-element, the white from the water-element, and the black from the food-element. A preponderance of one of the three elements over the two others, brings about the differences of fire, water, and the other elements, in nature (p. 737, 13; natural fire is *trivṛitkṛitaṃ tejas*, "the triply formed fire," p. 144, 1, in contradistinction with the *atrivṛitkṛitaṃ tejaḥ prathamajaṃ* p. 143, 7). The motive for this theory of commingling seems to be the wish to explain how the human body, although it only takes up single materials in nourishment, yet consists of all three original elements, of which the finer portion like the cream on the milk, rises, while the coarser descends. Thus the body is made up of the three original elements according to the following scheme:

	Gross:	Medium:	Fine:
Food:	Faeces	Flesh	Manas
Water:	Urine	Blood	Prâṇa
Heat:	Bones	Marrow	Speech.

[100] These four classes are to be understood by the *caturvidho bhûtagrâmaḥ* p. 357, 5. 406, 7. 431, 10. 768, 9, while, on the other hand, *bhûtacatushṭayam* p. 956, 3 means the four elements.

That which accomplishes this tripled mingling[101] in nature, and in the body, is, as is shown on page 733ff. not the individual soul, but Brahman.—That the body consists of the three elements, food, water, and heat, follows from the fact that their effects can be observed in it. On the other hand, it contains the three materials (*dhâtu*): wind, gall, and mucus (p. 743, 8). It is not said in what relation these stand to the elements. In the body, watery substances preponderate, fluids, blood, etc. (p. 743, 11); "in another respect, indeed, the earthy "preponderates" (p. 743, 12; in what respect, remains unsaid); that, however, the human body is essentially watery, can be observed from the fact that it originally springs from two liquids, the (male) seed, and the (female) blood (p. 743, 13; cf. Aristotle, Met. H, 4 p. 1044 A. 35 and Ait. âr. 2, 3, 7, 3).

7. The Controversy with the Buddhists concerning the Reality of the Outer World.

Sûtras 2, 2, 28—31.

Just as Kant, along with transcendental idealism, maintained the empirical reality of the external world, and defended it (against Berkeley), so the Vedântins are not prevented by their doctrine of Ignorance as the foundation of all Being expanded in name and form from maintaining the reality of the outer world against the Buddhists of idealistic tendencies. (In order to guard against misunderstanding, we must bear in mind the passage translated in note 31, above p. 55.) Because of the high importance of this question, and the difficulty of the section of our work which treats of it, we shall translate the passage here at length.[102]

---

[101] A *pañcîkaraṇam*, such as the Vedântasâra § 124 teaches, is already found in Govinda's Gloss, p. 139, 21. 733, 17; but not yet in Çañkara's Commentary to the Brahmasûtras.

[102] In what follows, we translate *vijñânam* presentation; *jñânam* knowledge; *anubhava* sensation, feeling; *pratyaya* perception; *upalabdhi*, *upalambha* apperception; *grahaṇam* comprehension; *avagamanam* apprehension; *saṃskâra* impression; *pratyaksham* observation;—the meaning of these terms is, however, not so much to be gathered from the modern terms which we have chosen (in default of others), but rather from the context.

Immediately before this, stands the discussion on Buddhist realism (2, 2, 18—27), to which the Buddhist idealist refers in the opening words.

The Buddhist speaks:

[p. 566, 12ff.] "Because the attraction of many scholars "towards external things has been noticed, this doctrine of "(the reality of) the outer world was put forward for their "sake. But this is not the Buddha's view; [p. 567] on the "contrary what he desired, is solely the doctrine of the sole "category (*skandha*) of presentation (*vijñânam*). According "to the doctrine of presentation, the outward form is only in "the intellect, (*buddhi*), and the whole worldly action of know-"ledge, what is known and [the enjoyment of] fruit is only "something interior; and even if there were exterior things, "yet without being in the intellect, this worldly action of "knowing etc. could not take place."

"How then can it be proved that the whole worldly action "is only something interior, and that beyond the presentation, "there are no external things?—For the reason that they are "impossible! For let it be taken for granted that there are "exterior objects, *e.g.*, solid bodies, they must be either in-"finitely small (*paramâṇu*) or an aggregate of the infinitely "small; now that of which our perception can trace the limit "as a solid body, etc., cannot be infinitely small, because the "infinitely small is not visible and knowable; so also no ag-"gregate of the infinitely small; for this can neither be thought "of, as different from the infinitely small, nor as identical with "it [p. 568] [not different, for it is made up of the infinitely "small, nor identical, for it would then escape observation in "all its parts]. The same is true of species [*jâti*, which exist "only in individuals]."

"Further: if knowledge (*jñânam*), which is in its nature "general, because it is produced by sensation (*anubhava*) alone, "varies according to objects, as knowledge of columns, know-"ledge of a wall, knowledge of a vessel, knowledge of a cloth, "this is possible only through the differentiation (*viçesha*) which "concerns the knowledge.—Therefore we must unquestionably "grant the identity (*sârûpyam*) of the knowledge with the ob-"ject. If we grant this, however, as the form of the object "is determined only by the knowledge of it, the hypothesis "(*kalpanâ*) of the existence of things is superfluous."

"Then too, as apperception (*upalambha*) of necessity com-"bines both, no division of the object from its presentation "(*vijñânam*) is possible; for it is impossible to apperceive the "one without apperceiving the other; and that would not be "so, if they were different in nature, for then nothing would "exist to prevent it. For this reason also, external objects "do not exist."

"In this it is, for example, like a dream. As in dreams "or hallucinations (*mâyâ*) there arise perceptions (*pratyaya*) "of water in a mirage, Gandharva cities, etc., without outward "objects in the form of apprehender and something to be "apprehended; just so [p. 569] in the state of waking, must be "the case with the perception of columns, etc., because we "cannot distinguish them from the former, in so far as they "are both perceptions."

"But if no external object exists, whence comes the variety "of perceptions?—We answer: from the variety of (subjective) "phenomena (*vâsanâ*). Because in the beginningless Saṃsâra, "the presentations and the phenomena, like seed and plant, "are in turn the cause and effect of each other, variety is "explained without contradiction. Also it is to be understood "that, for the rule (waking), as well as for the exception (sleep), "variety of knowledge has its ground solely in phenomena. "And we both agree that in dream, etc., without any outward "things, a variety of knowledge is produced by phenomena; "only that I admit no variety of knowledge caused by external "objects and not by phenomena. And therefore again there "are no external objects."

To this the Vedântin answers:

"It cannot be maintained that no external objects exist. "Why? Because we apperceive them. For we apperceive an "external object according to our perception of it as a column, "a wall, a vessel, a cloth; and what we apperceive, cannot

"not be. It is as though one who eats, while feeling completely satiated by what he is eating, should yet say: 'I am 'not eating, and I have not been satiated.' It is just the "same when a person directly apperceives outward objets by "touching them with the organs of sensation [p. 570] and at "the same time assures us: 'I do not apperceive them, and 'the objects are not there.'—How can we care for such talk?"

The Buddhist:

"But I do not say that I do not apperceive an object; I "only maintain that I apperceive nothing beyond the apperception."

The Vedântin:

"Yes indeed, you maintain that! But only because your "trunk is not goaded [elephants are guided by goads], and "not because you have reasons. For we are compelled to "admit objects outside our apperception, and this by our apperception itself. For no one apperceives a column or a "wall as a mere apperception, but everybody apperceives the "column and the wall as objects of apperception. And that "everybody thus apperceives, is shown by the fact that even "those who deny outward objects bear witness to this when "they say: 'The form perceived interiorly seems as if it were 'outside.' For they also call to their aid the consciousness "of an outside that everyone in the world has, when, in order "to deny the existence of outward objects with their 'as if it 'were outside,' they appeal to an assumed outside. For how "otherwise could they say 'as if it were outside?' No one "says: such a one looks as if he were the son of a barren "woman. Therefore, when we according to our feelings conceive the nature of anything that exists, we must say: 'It 'appears outside,' but not 'as if it were outside.'"

"But was not from the fact that no external things are "possible, the conclusion drawn that it only seems as if they "were outside?—[p. 571] Yes, but this conclusion is not justified. For we determine what is possible or impossible, from "what is proved or not proved; we do not, however, in the "opposite way, determine what is proved or not proved, from "what is possible or impossible. For what we apperceive "through one of the instruments of knowledge, perception, etc. "(above p. 88) is possible (or: real, *sambhavati*), and what we "do not apperceive, through any means of knowledge, is not "possible (real). External objects are, according to their "kind, apperceived by all means of knowledge; how then can "anyone, on the basis of such arbitrary reflections as those "concerning exceptions and non-exceptions [dream and waking], "maintain that they are not possible, since they are apper-"ceived!"

"And if knowledge has the same form as the object, this "is no reason to deny the object. For, were there no object, "there could not be a similarity of form; and, that the object "exists, follows from the fact that we apperceive it as external "(p. 572). Thus we are under the necessity of apperceiving "perception and object at the same time, on the ground that "they are related, as cause and effect, and not because they "are identical."

"Further: if we distinguish between the knowledge of a "pot, and the knowledge of a cloth, the difference lies in the "things which make different, the pot and the cloth, and not "in what is made different, knowledge. A white cow differs "from a black cow in whiteness and blackness, not in the fact "that they are cows. Therefore, through the two, we are able "to distinguish the one, and the one through the two. [They "could not be distinguished if they were not alike in being,—"or should we read: *naikasmâc ca* 'and not through the one?'] "Therefore object and knowledge are different, and we can "also appeal to the fact that we distinguish between seeing "the pot, and remembering it. For here also, the difference "lies in that which is distinguished, seeing and remembering, "and not in that which distinguishes the pot; just as in the "case of the words, smell of milk and taste of milk, the differ-"ence is in that which is distinguished, smell and taste, and "not in the milk, which distinguishes them."

"Also, between two [mere] presentations (*vijñânam*), which "are different in time, as they destroy each other by their "own coming to consciousness, no mutual [p. 573] relation of "comprehended (*grâhya*) and comprehender (*grâhaka*) can "exist [as if the subject were also a presentation, *vijñânam*!), "for thereby the theories which the Buddhists themselves have "maintained . . . [the statement of which we here pass over] "would fall through."

"And besides: you assume a series of presentations, then "why do you not also take outward things, such as columns "and walls for granted?—You say, because we are conscious "of the presentation?—But we are also conscious of external "things!—Or do you say that we are conscious of the pre-"sentations in themselves, because it is in their nature to "illumine, like a lamp, but not, on the other hand in the "nature of external things?—and so you take for granted that "which is in its nature an absolute contradiction, just as if "you said: 'Fire burns itself up;' but the general acceptation, "which does not contradict itself, that we are conscious of the "outward object, through the presentation which reaches beyond "itself [p. 574], you will not assume? Truly this is great wis-"dom that you display! The presentation, in so far as it "extends beyond the object, is certainly not felt, for that would "be contrary to its own being." [Here, as often before, the idea of the presentation changes into that of the presenting subject, and this is made easy by the use of the word *vijñânam*.]

"It may be objected that, if, from its nature, the present-"ation must be apprehended by something extending beyond it, "then this again by something beyond it, this, by something else "beyond it, and so *in infinitum*.—And further, if knowledge, "according to its nature, illumines like a lamp, and we assume "that this knowledge is known by another knowledge,—yet, "from the equality of these two, no relation of enlightener and "enlightened can exist, and the assumption becomes superfluous."

"But these two objections do not hold good. As only the "presentation is apprehended, and there is no need of the "apprehension of the subject (*sâkshin*) of the presentation, "therefore we are not face to face with a *regressus in infinitum*: "for subject and perception are in their nature contrary to "each other, and are related as the apperceiver, and the ap-"perceived; the subject, however, is, in itself, certain, and "cannot be denied [compare the discussion of this above "p. 127]. And if it be further maintained that the present-"ation, like the lamp, needs no other to illumine it, but makes "itself known by itself, then this means as much as a present-"ation which cannot be apprehended by any instrument of "knowledge, and which has no apprehender, which would no "more make itself known than would a thousand lamps if they "were set together in the middle of a block of stone.—But if "presentation is in its own nature sensation, have we not "[p. 575] in this granted the thesis of our opponents?—No; "but as the lamp, to illumine, requires yet another, to ap-"prehend, namely, the eye, in just the same way the present-"ation requires the power of making itself seen, and only, as "with the lamp, when another which apprehends it is present "does its light become visible.—But, the opponent might say, "if you explain the apprehending subject as self proved, that "is just what I maintain about the presentation making itself "known by itself, only expressed in other words.—But that is "not so, because the presentation has as its characteristics, "origin, perishability, and non-unity [accidentally, not as the "subject is a necessity; this further concerns its contents only, "not the form which is just what constitutes the nature of the "subject]. Thus we have proved that, like a lamp, the present-"ation also must be apprehended by something lying beyond it."

"When, further, those who deny external objects maintain "that, as in the case of perceptions in dream, so also per-"ceptions of pillars, etc., in waking, arise without an external "object, because the two cannot be separated, as both are "perceptions [p. 576], we answer: Perceptions in waking cannot "arise as do perceptions in dream. Why? Because they are "of a different nature. For between dream and waking, there "is a difference of nature. In what does this difference of "nature consist? In the refutability or irrefutability. For "that which is apperceived in dreams, refutes itself; for he "who is awakened, says: 'In error I apperceived a large "'assembly of people, for there is no large assembly, only my "'soul was confused by sleep, hence this error arose.' In the "same manner, all illusions of the senses are refuted, according to their character. On the other hand, there is no condition in which the existence of an object perceived in the "waking state, a pillar, for example, can be refuted. A dream-"face is only a remembrance, whilst seeing in the waking state "is apperception. The difference between remembrance and "apperception is evident, and is felt of itself; for it consists "in the fact that a person is either separated, or not separated, "from an object; when, for example, a beloved son is remem-"bered, he is not apperceived, but we wish to apperceive him. "[p. 577] As this is so, we cannot maintain that what is ap-"perceived in the waking state deceives, because, like apper-"ception in the dreaming state, it is [only] apperception. For "the difference between the two makes itself felt. And that "which is felt by pretended sages cannot be denied by them. "But just because their feelings protest, and they cannot "demonstrate to themselves the groundlessness of waking per-"ception, therefore they wish to prove it by its relation with "dreaming perception. But a quality that is not in a thing "in itself, will not be put there by relating it to another thing. "For when we feel that fire is hot, it does not become cold "because [as an element] it is related to water. And we have "demonstrated the difference between dream and waking."

"Finally we must answer the assertion that variety of know-"ledge can arise without objects, by a variety of [subjective] "appearances (*vâsanâ*). We reply: The existence of appearances "is not possible, if, as you take it, there is no apperception "of external objects. For the appearances in forms which "differ according to the object have their basis in the apper-"ception of the object [p. 578]; if, however, no objects are "apperceived, wherein have the various appearances their "foundation? If we accept the idea of beginninglessness, like "a row of blind people holding to each other, a *regressus in* "*infinitum* steps in, with no supporting basis, thus abolishing "the worldly action without proving your position. If, further, "he who denies the external world, appeals to the rule and "the exception [waking and dream] to prove that knowledge, "in order to come into being, has, as its ground, appearances, "and not objects, we must regard this also as refuted, if it is "as we said; for without the apperception of objects, appear-"ances cannot arise. And as, further, the apperception of "objects can exist without the appearance, while, on the other "hand, the appearances cannot exist without the apperception "of objects, the rule and the exception [under discussion] serve "but to affirm the reality of objects. For appearances are "only certain impressions (*saṃskâra*); and, as experience shows, "impressions can only be brought about by means of a sup-"porting basis; for you, however, there is no such basis of "impressions, because you follow as your guide the axiom that "apperception does not exist."

"[p. 579] If, finally, you set up a 'presentation of inwardness' "(*âlaya-vijñânam*) as the basis of appearances, this can no "more co-exist with your theory of non-duration than can the "'presentation of outwardness' (*pravṛitti-vijñânam*), and there-"fore cannot serve as the substratum of appearances. For "unless we either admit a Continuous Substance, which binds "past, present, and future together, or an overseer of all ob-"jects, an activity linking together remembrances--depending "upon appearances conditioned by space, time, and cause – is "impossible. If, however, the 'idea of inwardness,' implies a "continuum, you have thereby given up your principle (of non-"duration)."

XVIII. Cosmological Problems.

The doctrine of the empirical origin of the world from Brahman, set forth in the two preceding chapters, gives rise, in the course of the discussion, to a series of doubts; their solution is sought from the empirical standpoint, which can only partially solve them; their full solution is to be reached only by having recourse to the doctrine of Identity,—the special metaphysical teaching of the Vedânta. We shall now gather these various objections together, under three chief heads.

1. The Problem of Causality.

Sûtras 2, 1, 4. 5. 8.

a) The Difference of Essence (*vilakshaṇatvam*) between Brahman and the World.—Between two things which are different in essence, there can be no causal relation: the golden ornament can not have clay as its cause, and the earthen vessel cannot have gold as its cause (p. 419, 10); now, between Brahman and the world, there is a difference in essence, in so far as Brahman is pure and spiritual, and the world, on the contrary, is impure and unspiritual (p. 419, 8). For this world is impure, in that it consists, according to its essence, of desire, pain, and illusion (*moha*) from which joy, sorrow, and despair arise, and spread thoughout heaven and hell (p. 420, 4); it is unspiritual, first of all, because it is in the service of the enjoyer (the individual soul) and, according to its nature, it is only the means to produce the effects necessary for enjoyment, and such a relation of service can never exist between two spiritual beings: for where one spiritual being serves another, for instance, in the case of a slave and his master, he does not do this as a spiritual being, but in virtue of his unspiritual part, consisting of Buddhi [Intellect, which in itself is unspiritual, a mere instrument] etc. (p. 420, 7—14). And if we deny the unspirituality of the world, by regarding wood, earth, etc. as transformed spirit, whose spirituality is hidden out of sight, as is the real spiritual, in sleep and swoon (p. 421), the impurity of the world still remains, and proves its difference in essence from Brahman (p. 422, 1). Further, the scriptures maintain the unspirituality of the world, in so far as they separate knowledge from Ignorance, from which it follows that the unspiritual exists (p. 422, 6); and when the same scriptures sometimes ascribe spiritual functions to the unspiritual, in so far as they say: "the earth spoke" (Çatap. Br. 6, 1, 3, 4), "the waters conceived the idea" (Chând. 6, 2, 4, above p. 230) etc., we must understand here, not the elements, but the spiritual deities which are their representatives (p. 423, 5). —From this it is clear that the world differs in essence from Brahman and cannot therefore proceed from him (p. 424, 7).

b) The Contamination of Brahman by the World.— If the world proceeds from, and returns to, Brahman, then, on its return, through its qualities of materiality (*sthaulyam*) articulation, unspirituality, limitation, impurity, etc. it must defile Brahman; therefore it is absurd to regard Brahman as the cause of the world (p. 429, 15 ff.).

c) The Impossibility of a new Differentiation.— Further, it is absurd, because (p. 430, 6) after the world has been absorbed into the undifferentiated Brahman, no reason could exist for it to go forth again, differentiated into enjoyer and enjoyed [which is contradicted by the actual existence of these differences in each new world-period].

d) The Danger of a Return for the Liberated.—The basis of the ever repeated return of the world lies in the works performed in former lives which (apart from the liberated, whose works are annihilated) must be atoned for. In the case of a return of the world into Brahman, all works would disappear by absorption into unity. If, however, after this destruction of works, a return be possible, then we cannot perceive what should prevent the liberated also from being born again [p. 430, 9; whereby a doubt is cast on the most precious jewel of Indian faith—the certainty of liberation].

2. The Problem of the One and the Many.

Sûtras 2, 1, 26. 30. 31.

a) Total or partial Transformation.—In the transformation of Brahman into the world, we must of necessity assume one of two things: that either the whole, or only a part, of Brahman, changes into the world. In the first case, the root of Brahman would be destroyed, search after it would be aimless, for it would lie before our eyes as the world, beyond which there would be nothing, and the passages of scripture which declare that Brahman is unborn, etc., would be subverted (p. 480, 3).—If, on the contrary, we assume that only a part of Brahman becomes the world, then Brahman becomes subject to division, which is contradicted by the express words of the scriptures which forbid us to assume that Brahman has members, parts, or differences (p. 479, 9); and were Brahman divisible, the necessary consequence would be, that He is not eternal [p. 480, 8; that which is subject to the laws of space, is subject also to those of time; compare n. 43, above p. 68 69].

b) One Brahman with many Powers.—As we saw in Chap. XVI, 4 (above p. 227), in order to create the world, Brahman must unite with many powers. This assumption contradicts the teaching of the unity of Brahman, on the basis of which the scripture in the words: "it is not so, it is not so," negates in Brahman all and every difference (p. 487, 13). Compare with this, the characteristics of the esoteric Brahman in Chap. XIV, 3 (above p. 210ff.).

3. The Moral Problem.

Sûtras 2, 1, 34. 21.

a) The Creator of the World as the Author of Evil. —(p. 491, 5): "God cannot be the cause of the world, for then "he would be unjust and unmerciful. Some, like the gods, he "would have destined to the enjoyment of infinite pleasure; "others, like the animals, to the endurance of endless pain; "and still others, like mankind, to a mixed condition; according to this, God would have brought forth an unrighteous "creation, would be affected by love and hate, like an individual being, and the purity of his nature maintained by "Scripture and Tradition would suffer injury.[103] And therefore good men also (reading *akhala*, p. 491, 10) would be "afraid of his mercilessness and cruelty (which would be con-"trary to Bṛih. 4, 4, 15 *na tato vijugupsate*), because he in-"flicted pains on them, and swallowed up all beings. So, "because of the injustice and mercilessness which would be "attached to him, God cannot be the cause of the world."

b) The Creator of the World as the Cause of Evil. —The conception of sin which is so accentuated in the Hebrew world, from the very beginning (Genesis VI, 5. VIII. 21) is wanting in such a decided form, in Indian antiquity. Accordingly, the most effective argument against a divine creator of the world, namely, that he would be the (direct or indirect) cause of sin, is not brought clearly forward; the term "not good" (*ahitam*) in the passage 2, 1, 21, which we have under consideration here, rather holds the middle ground between the ideas of evil and of wickedness; it is more especially the first, with a tendency, however, to the latter, which becomes clearer from the answer to be brought forward later, to the objection which has its place here in the system, and substantially runs as follows: according to the Scriptures, God is not separated from the individual soul; by means of it he himself (above p. 231) has entered into nature (p. 471, 13). If he were the Creator of the world, then, as in his character of creator, he is free, he would have created good for himself, and not evil, such as birth, death, sickness, old age, etc. For no one who is free to do what he wishes, builds a prison, and then enters it himself (p. 472, 4). Again, as the absolutely pure, he would

---

[103] *çruti-smṛiti-avadhârita-svacchatva-âdi-îçvara-svabhâva-vilopaḥ prasajjyeta.* Or if we divide *svacchatvâd*: "and in the case of purity, "though Scripture and Tradition make (the contrary) certain, a contra-"diction would exist in the nature of God."

not enter the body, the absolutely impure, with his own self (p. 472, 5), and had he done so, he would leave it, remembering that he himself had made it. Without trouble the soul (in whose form God entered the world), would put an end to the world, just as the magician does to the glamour produced by himself. As this does not occur, it follows that the world cannot be created by a spiritual being who knows what is good for himself (p. 472, 6—13).

XIX. The Idea of Causality.

THE problems raised in the last chapter find their solution in the metaphysical teaching of the Vedânta concerning nature, according to which the world was perceived to be, not something different from Brahman, or existing apart from Brahman, but identical with Brahman, who appears in the form of existing nature. The identity of the two does not, therefore, mean that Brahman is like the world, but only that the world is like Brahman (p. 431, 13). Examined more closely, Brahman and the world stand to each other in the relation of cause and effect. But cause and effect are identical in their inner nature. Therefore our authors' teaching of identity is based upon an examination of the idea of causality; and this circumstance is not affected by the fact that in the work before us the doctrine of the identity of Brahman and the world 2, 1, 14, is first presented with mainly theological proofs, and then, as it were, as a corollary to this, 2, 1, 15--20, we find the logical evidence of the inner identity of cause and effect. The logical order is rather the reverse: from the identity of cause and effect, follows the identity of Brahman and the world, and not only does this follow of necessity, but it is plainly expressed at the end of the section p. 471, 2: "Therefore the effect is "identical with the cause, and consequently (*ataç ca*) as the "whole world is an effect of Brahman, they also are identical." —According to this, we shall first follow out the investigation of the idea of causality, and then the doctrine of identity which is based on this. But we have first to remark as follows:

However natural it may be to mankind, to conceive the

relationship between Being-in-itself and the phenomenal world from the point of view of causality, and so to regard God as cause and the world as effect,—nevertheless this view is false. For causality, which has its root in the organisation of our intellect, and nowhere else, is the bond which binds all the phenomena of the phenomenal world together, but it does not bind the phenomenal world with that which manifests itself through it. For between Being-in-itself and the phenomenal world there is no causality but identity: the world is the Thing-in-itself (das Ding an sich) as it displays itself in the forms of our intellect.—This truth has been correctly grasped by the Vedânta, which cannot free itself, however, from the old error of looking upon God as the cause of the world, and seeks to reconcile the two by interpreting the idea of causality as that of identity. To this end it forms too wide a concept of causality, in that it not only comprehends under this idea the bond of variations which only have to do with the qualities, forms, and conditions of substance, but also the bond between substance and qualities, and also between substance and substance. The continuity of substance forms the chief argument in these discussions, which we will now place before the reader in order, as we find them on pages 456—471.

1. The Cause persists in the Effect.

Only while the cause continues, can the effect be perceived, but not when it does not continue. Thus the clay continues in the vessel, the thread in the cloth. In things which are different, the perceptibility of the one is not conditioned by the persistence of the other: for example, a horse can be perceived without the presence of a cow. So cause and effect are not different (p. 456, 12).

2. The Effect exists before its manifestation, namely, as Cause.

When it is said: "This was Existent in the beginning" (above p. 230), the statement means that the world was already existent before its manifestation, in the form of the Existent, its cause. For where a thing is not already, according to its nature, it cannot arise: no oil can be pressed out of sand. But if the effect before manifestation was already identical with the cause, it remains so even after manifestation. As Brahman is never anything other than the Existent, so also the world is never anything other than the Existent. The Existent, however, is of like nature with itself (p. 459).

3. What is the difference between the effect before and after manifestation?

It is true that the Scripture also says: "This was in the "beginning non-Existent" (above p. 129). But this non-Existence is no absolute one but means only a difference of qualities (*dharma*). As the effect now consists in its quality as developed in name and form, so it existed before its manifestation in its quality of not being developed in name and form; it existed as the same but in the form of its cause (p. 460, 2).

4. The effect is prefigured in the cause.

Sour milk comes only from milk, never from clay; while jars come only from clay, not from milk. This could not be so, if the effect did not exist before its manifestation; rather, in that case, anything could arise out of anything. But there lies in the cause a certain extension beyond itself (*kaçcid atiçayaḥ*) towards the given effect—as of milk to sour milk, and of clay to the jar; and this forbids our regarding the effect as non-existent before its manifestation. For each cause has its peculiar power (*çakti*) and this power brings the given effect into manifestation, and no other. Therefore we may not regard cause and effect, substance and qualities, as different, like horses and oxen, but must regard them as of like nature (p. 461, 3—462, 5).

This is followed first by a criticism p. 462, 5—464, 8 of the apprehension of causality as an inherent relation, most probably directed against *Kaṇâda*, and, like most of the polemical expositions of the work, of more interest for the teachings controverted than for the Vedânta.

5. The Activity of becoming manifest must have a Subject.

If the effect did not exist before its manifestation, the activity of manifestation would be without an agent, and therefore without a subject (*nirâtmaka*). But every activity must necessarily have an agent. If the jar becomes manifest, who is the agent in this action, if not the jar itself?—The potter, perhaps? But then the potter would become manifest from his action, and not the jar. Or do you maintain that the effect originates and receives a self, after it has been previously connected with the Being of the cause?—But connection can only take place between two things which are, and not between what is and what is not.—And just as unthinkable is the limit which you set to the non-existence of the effect, by the moment of becoming manifest: for only what is, and not what is not, can have a limit.—And through no activity can the non-existence of the effect become existent, as little as the son of the barren woman can be made existent by any effort (p. 464, 8—466, 7).

6. The Activity of the agent is not superfluous.

If the effect was already existent before its becoming manifest as much as the cause, and was identical with it, surely it as little requires an agent as the cause itself, in order to become manifest?—Certainly not. The mission of the agent is to transform the cause into the form of the effect; though it is to be firmly maintained that also the form of the effect is already contained in the being of the cause; for that which has no self, cannot, as we saw, attain to one. —For the rest, a thing is not changed by difference in outward appearance: Devadatta remains Devadatta, whether he opens his arms or folds them (p. 466, 7—467, 7).

7. Generality of the Identity of Cause and Effect.

If you only admit the identity of cause and effect in that which is not altered by manifestation and dissolution, we dispute this: for does not milk change into sour milk before our eyes? When, too, manifestation, like the springing of plants from seeds, is only a becoming visible of what was already existent, conditioned by the accumulation of like particles; and, in exactly the same way, dissolution is only a becoming invisible, caused by the disappearance of these same particles. If we were to recognise a transition from non-Existence to Existence in them and from Existence to non-Existence, then the embryo would be other than the subsequently born man, the youth would be other than the greybeard he becomes, and the father of the one would not be the father of the other (p. 467, 7—468, 4).

8. The Activity of the agent must have an object.

If the effect were not in existence before its manifestation, the activity of the agent respecting it would be without an object, like sword-cuts through the air. Or is its object not the effect, but the inherent cause? Then the object would be different, and the result would also be different. Or is the effect an extension beyond itself of the cause which is inherent in it? Then the effect would be there already, and would not require to be first brought about (p. 468, 4—9).

9. Result.

"Then it comes to this, that the substances themselves "persist, *e.g.*, milk, through its existence as sour milk, etc.; "that they take the name of effect, and that we cannot think "of the effect as different from the cause, even if we tried "for a hundred years. And as it is the original cause which, "up to the last effect, appears in the form of this or that "effect, like an actor in all possible parts, it is thereby logic-"ally proved that the effect exists before its manifestation and "is identical with the cause" (p. 468, 10—469, 1).

Here follow other arguments of a theological character, p. 469.

10. Illustrative Examples.

1) So long as a cloth is rolled up, we cannot see whether it is a cloth or something else, and even if it be seen that it is a cloth, its real length and breadth are still unknown; if, however, it be unrolled, we perceive what it is, and how long

or broad it is; as the rolled up and unrolled cloth are identical, so are cause and effect (p. 470, 1—10; the words 470, 7—9 seem to be an interpolation).

2) As, when we hold our breath, in-haling and ex-haling only continue in the form of the cause (*prâṇa*, life, breath), and produce as effect, life only, but not the muscular movement of breathing; but if the breath be set free, besides life, movement of the muscles is produced; and as the so-called life-breaths are not different from life (*prâṇa*), of which they are branches, because the nature of both consists in animation (*samîraṇam*), so also effect is not different from cause (p. 470. 12—471, 2).

XX. The Doctrine of Identity.

1. Introductory.

There is a changeable element in things (their forms, qualities and conditions) which is subject to the law of causality, and an element of continuity (substance) which is not subject to this law. It was only by neglecting this difference, and by putting the whole complex of preceding and succeeding existence under the idea of cause and effect, that Çaṅkara was able to deduce, from the persistence of the inner nature of things, that cause and effect are fundamentally identical notwithstanding all differences of outer form.

In the beginning of the preceding Chapter (above p. 255) we saw how our author infers the identity of Brahman and the world from the identity of cause and effect. Yet this philosophical derivation of the chief position of the whole system of the Vedânta appears as a mere supplement. The same proposition has already been brought forward and explained on a theological basis (2, 1, 14); p. 443. 12: "The effect "is the manifested world, beginning with Âkâça; the cause is "the highest Brahman. With this cause, in the sense of the "highest reality (*paramârthataḥ*), the effect is identical, hav-"ing no existence beyond it. Why is this?—Because of the "word of the Scripture, as to change depending only on "words, etc."

The passage from which this inference is drawn, is the sixth Prapâṭhaka of the Chândogya-Upanishad, one of the most important portions of the Veda, which we shall give here in part translated, and in part in the form of an epitome, in order afterwards to analyse Çaṅkara's reflections on it.

2. *Tat tvam asi*--That art thou.

Chândogya-Upanishad VI.

1. "*Çvetaketu* was the son of [*Uddâlaka*] *Âruṇi.* His father "said to him: 'Çvetaketu, go forth to study Brahman, for one "'of our family, dear one, is not wont to remain unlearned, "'and [merely] an appendage of Brahmanhood.'—So he went "when he was twelve years old, to study, and at twenty-four "he had studied all the Vedas, and returned uplifted in mind, "fancying himself wise, and very proud. Then his father said "to him: 'Çvetaketu! since, dear one, thou art so uplifted in "'mind, fancying thyself so wise, and since thou art so proud, "'hast thou enquired concerning the teaching through which "'[even] the unheard is [already] heard, what is not understood "'is understood, and what is unknown becomes known?'— "'What then, venerable Sir, is this teaching?'—'Just as, dear "'one, by one lump of clay everything which consists of clay "'is known, and the change is dependent only on words, a "'mere name, it is only clay in reality;—just as, beloved, by "'one copper button everything made of copper is known, the "'change is dependent only on words, a mere name, and it is "'only copper in reality;—just as, dear one, by one pair of "'nail-scissors everything made of iron is known, the change "'is dependent only on words, a mere name, and it is only "'iron in reality;—so, dear one, is it with this teaching.'— "'Of a truth my venerable teachers did not know this them-"'selves, for if they had known it, why did they not tell it to "'me? But do thou, venerable one, now make it clear to "'me!'—'So be it, dear one!'—"

2—3. "Existent alone, dear one, was this in the beginning, "one only, and without a second. Some, it is true, say that "this was non-Existent in the beginning, one only, without a "second; that from this non-Existent was born the Existent. "But how could this be, dear one? how could the Existent "be born from non-Existent?"—Here follows the passage given above (p. 230ff.) in which Âruṇi explains to his son how the one Existent put forth from itself the three primordial elements: heat, water, and food, and entered into these with the living self (*jîva âtman*, that is, the individual soul).

4–7. This is followed by the teaching of the triplication of the elements. As the three primordial elements came forth from the one Existent, so all things in the world proceed anew from the three primordial elements: the red in things is radiance (*tejas*, the primal fire), the white is water, the black is food. This is exemplified in the natural phenomena of fire (*agni*), the sun, moon, and lightning, and it is said each time: "Vanished is the fire-being of the fire (the sun-being of the "sun, etc.), the change is dependent only on words, a mere "name, only the three forms are there in reality." Knowing this, the wise men of old said: "Henceforth can no one bring "forth anything which has not been heard, known, and under-"stood by us!" For they knew that what was unknown to them also could only be a combination of these three primordial elements; from them, like all else, the human body is built up, whereby, like the cream in milk, the finest part rises and forms the psychical organs, so that Manas is formed from food, breath from water, speech from heat. (For more on this subject, see Chap. XVII, 6, above p. 240ff.) For this reason the mind of mankind is weakened by continual fasting, and strengthened again by taking food, just as the glimmering ember which remains, can be rekindled by adding fresh fuel to it. [According to our system, *Manas*, *Prâṇa*, and *Vâc* did not come into being, but are the eternal companions of the soul. For solution of this contradiction see later on.]

8. On the conditions of a) Sleep, b) Hunger, c) Thirst, and d) Death.—

a) When a man sleeps, he enters into the Existent, for he then goes to himself (*svam apîta*), therefore it is said: he sleeps (*svapiti*). "As a bird bound by a cord flies hither and "thither, and after it has nowhere found a place of rest, settles "on the place where it is bound (*bandhanam* as in *nau-ban-"dhanam*) so, dear one, Manas flies hither and thither, and "after it has nowhere found a place of rest, it returns into "Life, for Life is the place where Manas is bound." (Cf. Chap. XII, 4, c, above p. 190ff.)

b) If a man is hungry and satiates himself, this is an effect (*çuñgam*) which as such must have a cause (*mûlam*). The satisfaction as effect has food as cause, food as effect, has water as cause, water as effect has heat as cause, heat as effect has the Existent as cause; all these creatures have the Existent as cause, the Existent as support, the Existent as basis.

c) If a man is thirsty and drinks, this effect is caused by water; water as effect has heat as cause, heat as effect has the Existent as cause; all these creatures have the Existent as cause, the Existent as support, the Existent as basis.

d) "When, dear one, a man departs hence, speech enters "to Manas, Manas to Life, Life to heat, heat to the highest "godhead: that which is that subtle (unknowable) essence, of "its being is the universe, that is the Real, that is the Soul, "that art thou, O Çvetaketu!"

9. "When, dear one, the bees prepare honey, they gather "the juices from many sorts of trees and unite the nectar in "one. As in these nectars, no difference is maintained between "the trees whose juice they are, so, of a truth, beloved, all "these creatures also, when (in deep sleep, and death) they "return into the Existent, have no consciousness that they "return into the Existent. Whether tiger, or lion, or wolf, or "boar, or worm, or bird, or fly, or gnat: whatever they may "be, to that form they return (*yad-yad bhavanti, tad* [or "with Çañkara p. 433, 12. 797, 16 *tad-tad*] *âbhavanti*).—That "which is that subtle essence, of its being is this universe, "that is the Real, that is the Soul, that art thou, O Çveta-"ketu!"

10. "These streams, dear one, flow eastward towards the "morning, and westward towards the evening; from the ocean "[they come] and to the ocean they return; in the ocean they "are born. As these [in the ocean whence they take their "rise] know not that they are this stream or that—so, of a "truth, beloved, all these creatures, when they again go forth "from the Existent, know not that they again go forth from "the Existent. Whether they are here tiger, or lion, or wolf, "or boar, or worm, or bird, or fly, or gnat: whatever they

"may be, to that form they return.[101]—That which is this "subtle essence, of its being is the universe, that is the Real, "that is the Soul, that art thou, O Çvetaketu!"

11. "If, dear one, a man cuts this great tree at the root, "it drips because it lives, if he cuts it in the middle, it drips "because it lives, if he cuts it at the top, it drips because it "lives; it stands penetrated through and through by the living "Self, exuberant and joyful. But if life leaves one bough, it "withers, if it leaves a second, it withers, if it leaves a third, "it withers, if it leaves the whole tree, the whole tree withers. "Thus also shalt thou know, dear one, said he: this [body] "certainly dies when the living one leaves it, but the living "one does not die. That which is this subtle essence, of its "being is the universe, that is the Real, that is the Soul, that "art thou, O Çvetaketu!"

12. "'Bring hither a fruit from yonder Nyagrodha tree.' "—'Here it is, venerable one.'—'Divide it.'—'It is divided, "'venerable one.'—'What seest thou therein?'—'I see here, "'venerable one, very small seeds.'—'Divide one of them.'— "'It is divided, venerable one.'—'What seest thou therein?'— "'Nothing at all, venerable one.'—Then said he: 'the subtle "'essence which thou canst not perceive, beloved, from that "'truly has this great Nyagrodha tree arisen. Believe me, "'dear one, that which is this subtle essence, of its being is "'the universe, that is the Real, that is the Soul, that art "'thou, O Çvetaketu!'"

13. "'Here, put this piece of salt into water, and come "'back to me to-morrow.' He did so. Then said he: 'Bring "'me the salt which you put in water yesterday.'—He looked "for it, but did not find it, for it had melted.—'Try on this

[101] According to the Commentary to Chând. (p. 447, 19: *samânam anyat*) the reading is here exactly the same as in the preceding paragraph; not as with Windischmann in the first passage (Sancara p. 180) *na ha* instead of the certainly strange *ta' iha* (we expect *tâ' iha*), nor in the second with Roer *sampadya* instead of *yad-yad*; and the latter's separation of *tadâ bhavanti* is to be rejected, not only because the Commentator (p. 445, 14: *punar âbhavanti*) is against it (for he often errs). but also because then it rather ought to be *tato bhavanti* in the first passage.

"'side!—How does it taste?'—'Salt!'—'Try in the middle!—"'How does it taste?'—'Salt!'—'Try on that side!—How does "'it taste?'—'Salt!'—'Leave it alone, and sit down near me.' "He did so (and he said): 'It exists still.'—Then said he: "'Truly so also thou canst not perceive the Existent here (in "'the body) but it is nevertheless in it. That which is this "'subtle essence, of its being is this universe, that is the Real, "'that is the Soul, that art thou, O Çvetaketu!'"

14. "Like as, dear one, a man whom they have led with "eyes bound from the land of the Gandhâras and then let "loose in the desert, wanders towards east, or north, or south, "because he was led there with eyes bound, and was set loose "with eyes bound; but after some one has taken off his ban-"dage, and said to him: 'That way dwell the Gandhâras, go "'that way,' he goes on asking his way from village to village, "with knowledge and intelligence, and returns home to the "Gandhâras, thus a man who has found a teacher here, con-"sciously says: 'I will only endure this [worldly action] until "'I have attained deliverance, then will I go home.'—That "which is this subtle essence, of its being is this universe, "that is the Real, that is the Soul, that art thou, O Çveta-"ketu!"

15. "Round a man who is sick unto death, sit his relations, "and ask him: 'Dost thou know me? Dost thou know me?'—"So long as his speech has not entered into Manas, his Manas "into Life, Life into heat, and heat into the highest godhead, "so long he recognises them; but after his speech has entered "into Manas, his Manas into Life, Life into heat, and heat "into the highest godhead, he knows them no more.—That "which is this subtle essence, of its being is this universe, "that is the Real, that is the Soul, that art thou, O Çveta-"ketu!"

16. "They bring a man with his hands bound, and cry: "'He is a robber, he has committed theft; heat the axe for "'him!'—If he is the doer, he makes himself untrue, speaking "untruth, he wraps himself in untruth, seizes the glowing axe, "is burned, and therefore executed; but if he is not the doer, "he makes himself true; telling the truth, he wraps himself in

"truth, seizes the glowing axe, is not burned, and therefore "is set free. [That is, as p. 103, 9. 447, 6 explains this simile: "from untruth come bonds, from truth comes freedom.] That "by which he did not burn himself [the truth], of its being "is the universe, that is the Real, that is the Soul, that art "thou, O Çvetaketu!"

"Thus was he taught by him."

3. The Doctrine of Identity in the Vedânta System.

Sûtram 2, 1, 14.

(a) The Extinction of plurality in Brahman.

For the Hellenic consciousness, the existence of the world has its purpose in itself. Christianity, inclining to the Old Testament, seeks to understand Creation through the love of God towards mankind, towards a thing to be created, though not yet existing. According to the Indian view, the creation of the world rests upon a moral necessity. The deeds done by the soul in an earlier existence must be atoned for. To be the place of this atonement, is the only purpose of this huge world. Its plurality originates solely from two factors, which are indicated by the two words *bhoktar* and *bhogyam*: on the one side, is the *bhoktar*, he who enjoys, that is, the (individual) soul, the subject of enjoyment and also of sorrow, and on the other side, the *bhogyam*, what is enjoyed, the fruit (*phalam*) of works done in an earlier existence, the object of the enjoyment and suffering of the soul. The world is this expansion of the Existent into the enjoying soul and the fruit to be enjoyed, and nothing else.

This division into enjoyer and fruit, so Çankara explains, is true so long as we remain on the empirical (literally: practical, *vyâvahârika*) standpoint; it is no longer true, when we rise to the metaphysical (literally: absolutely real: *pâramârthika*) point of view (p. 443, 9); for it, the whole worldly action is one with Brahman, its cause. This is confirmed by the passage of the *Chândogya-Upanishad*, which we have just given. The comparison with the lump of clay (Chând, 6, 1, above p. 262) teaches that, just as all transformation of the clay into vessels only depend upon words (we might say: upon presentations) while in reality it is nothing but clay, and clay only. So all the transformations of the world, are Brahman alone, and beyond this can have no being (p. 444). In this sense, the Scripture (Chând. 6, 4—7, above p. 263) reduces all phenomena in the world to the three primitive elements, and the three primitive elements (Chând. 6, 2—3, above p. 263. 230) back to the Existent, to Brahman (p. 444, 13). And the same thing is expressed by the formula at the end of the sections Chând. 6, 8—16, that the world, and (in the words: *tat tvam asi*, that art thou) that the soul, (*tvam*) is identical with Brahman (*tat*). [This also is the meaning of *etad vai tad*, in Kâṭh. 4, 3. 5. 6 etc., above p. 155.] Thereby all plurality is declared to be unreal, as is expressly taught in the verse (Bṛih. 4, 4, 19, above p. 195):

"In spirit musing shall they see:
"That here is no plurality.
"Their never-ending death they weave
"Who here a manifold perceive."

As the space in a vessel is identical with cosmic space, as the mirage is identical with the salt plain, so that it disappears when we examine it more closely, and in itself (*svarûpeṇa*) is not perceptible, so too, the world-extension of enjoyer and enjoyed has no existence beyond Brahman (p. 445, 7).

(b) The Relation of Unity to Plurality.

How are we to consider the relation between the unity of the Existent and the manifoldness of its developments? Is Brahman related to the many powers (above p. 227 ff.) as a tree is related to its branches, because, as a tree, it forms a unity, while, as it spreads into branches, it is manifold, or as an ocean to the manifoldness of its foam, waves, etc., or as the single clay to the plurality of vessels,—in such a manner that with the knowledge of unity, liberation is bound up, while worldly action and religious worship are connected with the knowledge of plurality?—By no means; rather, as in the simile of the lump of clay, only the clay is real, while all its transformations are only dependent on words, that is, unreal, so also in the world, the highest cause, that is, Brahman, is the one and only reality, and the embodied soul is no other than Brahman himself (p. 445, 10—446, 9).

This Brahmanhood of the soul does not require to be called into existence by effort, but is already existent, therefore only the inborn idea of the separateness of the soul requires to be refuted by the Scripture, as (in the well-known simile) by the knowledge that it is a piece of rope, the opinion that it was a snake is refuted.[105] But if the separate existence of the soul be refuted, the whole worldly action which depends on it, and on account of which a plurality was assumed for Brahman is refuted at the same time. And this non-existence of the worldly action is not only conditional (in deep sleep and death), but, as the words *tat tvam asi* show, it is to be accepted unconditionally, and without restriction to any given circumstances. The simile of the thief also, Chând. 6, 16, above p. 266), as it shows that bondage follows from false speech, while freedom follows from truth-speaking, teaches that only unity is true in the fullest sense, and that manifoldness, on the contrary, proceeds from false perception. Were both unity and manifoldness real, we could not say of one whose standpoint is that of worldly action, that he is caught in untruth, and "weaves a never-ending death;" it could not then be said: "from knowledge comes deliverance," [*jñânân mokshaḥ*, —a sentence also found in *Kapila* 3, 23, *jñânân muktiḥ* and which, in two words, gives food for much thought]; moreover, then the knowledge of manifoldness could not be annihilated by the knowledge of unity (p. 446, 9—447, 14).

---

105 The simile of a rope (Brahman) which is taken for a snake (the world), occurs on p. 268, 12. 432, 14. 446, 12. 817, 12. 822, 13 and with greater detail on p. 353, 7: "As in the dark, one takes a fallen rope for "a snake, and flees from it in fear and trembling, and another says to "him: 'Fear not; it is not a snake, it is only a cord;' and he, when he "has understood this, ceases to fear the snake, to tremble and flee, and "as there is not the slightest difference in the thing itself, at the time it "was taken for a snake, and at the time this opinion disappeared,—just "so is this also to be considered."

(c) How is the Knowledge of Unity possible, from the standpoint of plurality?

Only unity exists; plurality does not exist. This statement abolishes not only the empirical means of knowledge, perception etc., but also the Vedic canon of command and prohibition (compare above p. 56). But does it not also abolish the canon of liberation? For this certainly presupposes the duality of pupil and teacher, and thus rests upon untruth; and how can the teaching of unity from a false standpoint be true (p. 448, 5)?—

To this, it is to be replied that all empirical action, until knowledge comes, is just as true as are all dream faces, until awakening comes. For every being has forgotten its original identity with Brahman, and takes the empirical "I" and "mine" for the Self and its qualities. This is true until the knowledge of identity with Brahman arises.—True, but not beyond this! A rope snake cannot bite, a mirage does not really quench thirst; and so it is in dream: the poison of a dream-snake does not really kill, and dream water does not really wet!—Certainly not! But as (in dream) we perceive the cause, the water and the bite, in like manner we perceive the effect, death and wetness.—But this effect is still not real! [How can the real Brahman be known by means of unreal teaching?]—The effect is unreal, but the perception of it is real, and it is not removed by awakening. For when a person wakes, he perceives it to be untrue that the snake and the water were there, but not that he perceived them. In just the same way, what is perceived in dream is untrue, but the perception of it is true (therefore, as Çañkara remarks in passing, the opinion of the materialists, that the body is the Self, is refuted). It is also to be remembered that real events are often indicated beforehand by unreal dreams; does not the scripture say (Chând. 5, 2, 9), that love-adventures in dream betoken luck, and when we dream of a black man with black teeth, it signifies speedy death (according to Ait. âr. 3, 2, 4, 17). It is also well known that those who are acquainted with the rules and their exceptions (the interpreters of dreams) prophesy good and evil from dreams. Thus the true is known from the untrue, in the same way as from written signs which are soundless, the real sounds are perceived (p. 447, 14—451, 4).

From these discussions, we are to understand that in the non-reality of the world of appearances, the soul remains real. The teaching is directed to the soul, and thus it does not cease when the world of appearances ceases.

(d) The Value of the Doctrine of Unity.

The perception of unity is final, for, as it contains everything in itself, it does not leave anything beyond itself to be desired, as do the ritual precepts; it is attainable, as the Scripture shows by its examples and exhortations; it is not aimless, for its fruit is the cessation of Ignorance; and it is infallible, for there is no further knowledge which could remove it, for the Brahman unlike everything else, is not a mere transformation; He is the Highest, free from all change, and all qualities; only by the knowledge of Brahman, not by that of his transformations, can liberation be attained (p. 451, 4 to 454, 1).

(e) Criticism of Anthropomorphism.

The Vedânta maintains, on the one hand, the unity and non-duality of Brahman, which permits of no Being beyond itself, and, on the other hand, it calls Brahman "the Lord," and sets him up as ruler of the world. But the designations of Brahman as Ruler, Almighty, Omniscient, refer only to the extension in names and forms caused by Ignorance, and are not to be accepted in the highest sense. For we must distinguish between the two standpoints: the standpoint of worldly actions (*vyavahâra-avasthâ*) and the standpoint of the highest reality (*paramârtha-avasthâ*). From the latter standpoint, the Scripture teaches the non-existence of all worldly actions by sentences like: "But when all has become his own "Self for anyone, how could he see anyone else?" etc. (above p. 175). From the first standpoint, it admits the relation of ruler and ruled, etc.; as when it is said (above p. 195): "He is the Lord of the Universe, he is the Ruler of Beings, "he is the Guardian of Beings." And these are precisely the two points of view admitted by the author of the Sûtras. since on the one hand he teaches identity, while on the other hand he allows the concepts of Brahman as an ocean (in contradistinction to its waves, foam, bubbles, 2, 1, 13; the inadequacy of this picture is repeatedly brought into prominence. p. 445, 13. 446, 4. 456, 8, cf. 515, 11) and similar ideas, which presuppose the existence of the world, and are to be regarded as belonging to the adoration of Brahman possessed of attributes (p. 454, 1—456, 10) (above p. 102 ff.).

—Thus our authors confine the anthropomorphic ideas of God as a personality, which have their root in realism, to exoteric theology.

XXI. Solution of the Cosmological Problems.

The cosmological problems which we gathered together in Chapter XVIII, above p. 250ff., with their respective solutions, are found in the original work in part before, and in part after, the exposition of the doctrine of identity. Our rearrangement, and the division of the problems into two separate chapters, with the doctrine of identity between them, is justified by the fact that the raising of these problems is only possible from an empirical standpoint, and before the doctrine of identity is put forward, while their complete solution can only be given after this doctrine. If our authors follow a different course, it is because the difference between the empirical and metaphysical standpoints (*vyâvahârikî* and *pâramârthikî avasthâ*, above p. 106ff.), so distinctly made by them, is imperfectly carried out in their work. So far as this shortcoming can be supplied by a mere re-arrangement, we have believed ourselves justified in supplying it, and, in doing this, we in no case go further than a translator who adds to a work the improvements suggested by its author; when, however, as we shall see, the solution of the cosmological problems is first sought from an empirical standpoint, and only when this method fails is the metaphysical teaching of identity called in, we do not hold ourselves bound to remedy this; on the contrary, the fluctuations between the empirical and metaphysical standpoints, as we shall see further on, must remain untouched, as historical monuments of a stage through which the philosopher first struggled to fuller clearness, without entirely effacing from his work the traces of the intermediate stage he had passed through. It is also possible, and many indications speak for

18

it, (cf. above pp. 28ff. 139 and notes 17. 45. 21. 22), that the form of the Commentaries to the Brahmasûtras as we have them, bears the imprint of many hands; but these signs are too vague, and the whole work has too slight an individuality, for us to convert this possibility into a definite hypothesis.

We give the solutions in the same order as the problems, which can be referred to, point by point, in Chapter XVIII.

1. The Problem of Causality.

Sûtras 2, 1, 6. 7. 9.

(a) The Difference in Essence between Brahman and the World.—To the objection that Brahman could not be the cause of the world, because the two are different in essence, an empirical answer is first given, by adducing examples in which the effect is different from the cause; thus, from men, who are conscious, hair and nails which are unconscious, proceed; from dung which is unconscious, the conscious dung-beetle (*vṛiçcika* = *gomayakîṭa*) comes forth. But as here cause and effect, in spite of every difference of form, have this in common, that they have both sprung from the earth, so Brahman and the world have both this common characteristic,—Being (*sattâ*).—Of what nature is the difference in essence (*vilakshaṇatvam*) on the ground of which the opponent disputes the creation of the world by Brahman? Does it lie (1) in the fact that nature does not altogether harmonise with the being of Brahman? Without a certain reaching-forth beyond itself (*atiçaya*), in the cause, we nowhere find the relation of cause and effect. Or (2) is the difference between the two complete? That cannot be maintained; for the evidence teaches that the Being (*sattâ*), which is the essence of Brahman, is also to be found in the things which make up Nature. Or (3) is it impossible for Nature to have sprung from Brahman because Nature lacks consciousness (*caitanyam*)? The examples we have given above are opposed to this view; and not these examples only, but also the revelation of Scripture. But it is a mere [unjustified] postulate (*manoratha-mâtram*) that Brahman, because it is in fact existent (*parinish-*

pannam), must also be perceptible by worldly means of knowledge: for perception cannot comprehend Brahman, because Brahman is without form; inference also fails, because Brahman has no characteristic (*liñgam*); and if reflection is nevertheless recommended by the Scriptures, it is to be understood of reflection directed to the Scriptures, and not of reflection divorced from them.—Furthermore, we must not believe that because the world is an effect of Brahman, it did not exist before it was created. Even then, it already existed, in the form of its causal Self (*kâraṇa-âtmanâ*), just as now it only persists through the power of this causal Self (p. 424, 9 to 429, 13).

—The last phrase points plainly to the doctrine of identity, as it frees the causal relation from the form of sequence in time, and makes it simultaneous.

(b) The Contamination of Brahman by the World.—To the objection that, on re-absorbing the world, Brahman is polluted by it, it is to be replied that, according to our experience, a cause, when the effect returns into it, is not affected by the qualities of the latter; thus vessels return to clay; golden ornaments to gold; living beings, to the earth, without the latter being altered by their qualities. For it would certainly not be a true return, if the effect retained its qualities when withdrawn into its cause. Rather (and here our author passes to metaphysical explanations) the doctrine of the identity of cause and effect presupposes that the effect is identical with the cause, but not the cause with the effect. The above objection is taken in too narrow a sense; not only on its return, but also during its existence, would the world pollute Brahman; for in all time, past, present, and future, the world is identical with Brahman; but neither its existence nor its return pollutes Brahman, and this, because the world as effect, along with its qualities, is imputed only through the Ignorance [of the soul]. "As the magician is not affected by "the illusion (*mâyâ*) which he himself has created, because it "is without reality (*avastu*), so also *Paramâtman* is not affected "by the illusion of *Saṃsâra*. And as the dreamer is not "affected by the illusion of a dream, because (Bṛih. 4, 3, 15. 16, "above p. 190) the soul is not touched by sleep, or waking "[this appears to be an addition and not authentic]—so also "the one unchangeable witness of the three states [waking, "dreaming, deep sleep] is not touched by these three chang- "ing states. For the appearance of the highest soul in the "three states is only an illusion, like the appearance of the "rope as a snake. Therefore it is said by the teachers who "are learned in the Vedânta-tradition (*Gâuḍapâda ad Mâṇ- "ḍûkya-Up.* 1. 16, p. 384):

> "When from illusion's sleep that ne'er began,
> "The soul awaketh, then in her awakes
> "The unborn One, that never slumbereth."

"Consequently, it is false to hold that the cause is polluted "by the qualities, materiality, etc., of the effect, if they return "into that cause" (p. 431, 1—433, 4).

(c) The Impossibility of a new Differentiation.—To this objection, the reply is, that, as the soul, in deep sleep and meditation, returns (temporarily) to its original unity, but on waking from these states, because it is not free from Ignorance, it returns to its individual existence, so also is it with the return into Brahman. "For as at the time of the "duration of the world, in consequence of false knowledge, "the tendency to differentiate in the undifferentiated Para- "mâtman goes on unchecked like a dream, so we must also "take for granted that, after the return into Brahman, the "force of differentiation, conditioned by false knowledge, still "continues" (p. 433, 4—434, 2).

(d) The Danger of a Return for the Liberated.—From what has been said, it follows that the liberated cannot be born again, for the false knowledge which conditions individual existence, is taken away from them by perfect knowledge (p. 434, 1—2), since, as is said in another place (p. 342, 7), the seed-force (above p. 228) is burnt up, in their case, by the fire of wisdom.

2. The Problem of the One and the Many.

Sûtras 2, 1, 27. 28. 31.

(a) Total or partial transformation.—First, we must bear in mind that Brahman is not wholly changed into the world. For the Scripture, wherever it speaks of the transformation of Brahman, presupposes his continuance; as when it is said that "one part of him is all creatures, three parts "are immortal in the heaven" (Rigveda X, 90, 3, above p. 168); when it conceives deep sleep as a return to Brahman, where the transformed Brahman cannot be meant, for we are in Him already; when it is taught that Brahman cannot be reached by perception, which is not true of the transformed Brahman, etc. Moreover, the partial transformation of Brahman cannot be maintained, because the Scripture, which is the only authority here, most strongly insists on the indivisible unity of Brahman.[106]—But can the Scripture teach a plain contradiction? And that Brahman is neither wholly nor partially transformed into the world, is certainly one!—To this it is replied that the whole plurality of appearances rests on Ignorance. But a thing does not become divided because Ignorance takes it to be divided. The moon is not duplicated because people with defective vision see two moons. The whole empirical reality with its names and forms, which can neither be defined as Being nor as nothing (*tattva-anyatvâbhyâm anirvacanîya* p. 483, 9, a frequent formula, cf. p. 96, 6. 343, 1. 454, 10), rests upon Ignorance, while, in the sense of the highest reality, the

---

[106] The conception here repudiated, is further enforced by the simile of cosmic space and the space within vessels, which serves more frequently than any other to make clear the relation of Brahman to individual beings; p. 233, 3: "As the hollows of vessels, conceived "without the determinations (*upâdhi*)—the vessels—are nothing else than "cosmic space, so also living souls are not [apart from their *upâdhis*] "different from the highest soul." The same simile occurs: p. 121, 1. 173, 17. 198, 3. 199, 8. 443, 5. 445, 7. 455, 3. 473, 11. 645, 11. 1134, 2. (Space and the eye of a needle:) 175, 2. 836, 12. Its value lies in the fact that it admirably illustrates the fact that Brahman is not affected (*asañgatvam*) by the Upâdhis, to which p. 266, 8 refers; cf. p. 176, 5 (Space does not burn with bodies), 690, 2 (does not move with vessels).

Existent persists without change or transformation. A transformation resting merely on words (above p. 262) can alter nothing in the indivisibility of the Existent.—As the dreamer creates many forms, and yet remains one and undivided, as gods and magicians, without changing their nature, make horses, elephants, etc., appear, so the manifold creation arises in the uniform Brahman, without Brahman thereby undergoing the least change of nature (p. 480, 11—484, 14).

(b) One Brahman with many powers.—Further, the contradiction that Brahman, though without differences, has yet many powers, is solved by the fact that all diversity of form belongs only to the realm of Ignorance. The unfathomable depth of this subject cannot be reached by reflection, but only through revelation, through the Scripture which teaches that (Çvet. 3, 19):

"It feels without a hand, without a foot it runs,
"It sees without an eye and hears without an ear"

it uses no instruments, and yet can do all things (p. 488, 1—8).

3. The Moral Problem.

Sûtras 2, 1, 34—36. 22—23.

That empirical theism (for which the world is real and different from God) is untenable appears nowhere so clearly as in the region of morals. For however the matter be turned, in a real creation, which is seriously taken, the responsibility for evil, and for the sin of the world finally falls on God. This consequence does not trouble the morally undeveloped conscience. Therefore it is said in *Isaiah* XLV, 7: "I form the light, and create darkness: I make peace, and "create evil; I the LORD do all these things." And in the *Kaushîtaki-Up.* 3, 8: it is expressed even more strongly: "For "he makes those do good works whom he will guide out from "this world, and he makes those do evil, whom he will guide "downwards; he is the guardian of the world, he is the ruler "of the world, he is the lord of the world."—The Hebrews gained a solution of the question more apparent than real by adopting (or rather adapting) *Satan* from the mythology of

Persia, and thereby satisfying themselves. The Indians in a more philosophical spirit recognised the fact that there are only two ways out of this: either by referring the constitution (*essentia*), and also the creation (*existentia*) of the world not to God but to an immanent principle, or (idealistically) by denying the existence of the world altogether. We find Çañkara taking both ways, by bringing forward, as he always does, both empirical and metaphysical arguments for the solution of the problem.

(a) The Creator of the World as the Author of Evil.—To the argument that God, as Creator of the world, is responsible for the evil in it, the answer is first made that God, in the creation of creatures, does not act arbitrarily (*nirapeksha*), but is bound by a certain regard, namely, the regard for the good and evil works of each creature in an earlier birth (p. 492, 6). By this conception, for which, as we saw before (above p. 267), the world is nothing but the scene of atonement for the works of an earlier existence, the rôle of God as Creator sinks into a secondary, and purely instrumental one. The Body may be compared to a plant (p. 492, 10), which springs up from seed, grows, expands, and finally dies; yet not altogether, but so that something remains,—the seed, which, strewn in the kingdom of Ignorance, brings forth a new plant according to its kind. This seed of man (so far as individual determination is conditioned by it), is his works. In exact correspondence to their moral quality, is the form of the new life, because all happiness and unhappiness depend on it under an inflexible necessity, and also, as we shall see, all virtue and vice of the new existence. In this growth of the present out of the seed of works, the task of the Creator can only be a secondary one: he is to be compared to the rain (the chief condition of growth in India), which causes the plants to shoot. That they grow, is the work of outward circumstances (water, soil, air, light, or, as the Indians say, rain), but what they shall grow to be, does not depend upon those conditions which come from God, but upon the nature of the seed: only rice can come from rice, only barley from barley (p. 492, 9).—This concept requires as its unavoidable consequence, the assumption that *Saṃsâra* is without beginning, for, as far as we go back, each existence draws its conditions from some prior existence (p. **494**, 1).—This consequence is as yet absent from the older Upanishads; it contradicts their teaching, certainly intended seriously at first, of the Creation of the world from "the One without a Second" (above p. 230), and of the predestination which necessarily follows (above p. 278) from this. In the desire to do away with this contradiction, we must recognise the real motive of the periodicity of creation, already mentioned above (p. 227) the alternating evolution of the world from, and its re-absorption into Brahman, which is not mentioned in the older Upanishads. Çañkara certainly manages to indicate it as already in them, when (p. 495, 1) out of the words: "I will "enter into these three divinities with my living Self" (Chând. 6, 3, 2, see above p. 231) he drags the meaning that the "living Self" (the individual soul) must therefore have existed before the creation. But this argument is as little admissible as is his reference to the verse (Rigveda X, 190, 3):

Sûryâ-candramasau dhâtâ yathâpûrvam akalpayat,

which, according to the context, can only mean: "the creator created the sun and moon"—*yathâpûrvam*—"according to their order," not, as Çañkara says, "as before" (p. 495, 7).

(b) The Creator of the World as the Cause of Evil.—We have two answers to the arguments marshalled under this heading, an empirical answer, 2, 1, 23, and one which amounts to the doctrine of identity 2, 1, 22, and, remarkable to say, the former stands second. Even if these two parts were written down by the same hand, it is hardly thinkable that they were originated in the same head. We shall reverse their order, and examine the empirical answer first.—Just as, it is said, 2, 1, 23, the same earth brings forth many kinds of stones, the most costly jewels, as well as the most common stones of the fields; as the same earth produces plants which vary in leaves, flowers, fruits, smell and taste, or as in men from the same essence of food (*annarasa*) spring blood, hair, and nails, all quite different; in the same way, from the one Brahman proceeds the division into the individual and highest souls, and the variety of [good and evil] effects.—Quite another character than that of this empirical comparison is borne by the directly preceding section, 2, 1, 22. It is true that here also our author starts from the separation (only indicated by the Sûtram) of God and the soul, in order to transfer all moral guilt from the former to the latter. Brahman is omniscient and omnipotent, everlasting, pure, wise and free. Because he is free, he can do what he wills; for him, there is neither command nor prohibition, and therefore neither good nor evil.[107] The individual soul, on the contrary, is affected by good and evil (reading *ca* instead of *na*, p. 473, 4), and of it we do not at all maintain that it is the creator of the world.—Without committing himself to the question, unavoidable from this standpoint, "Whence then springs the individual soul, with its good and evil?" our author at once passes on to the metaphysical explanation: "But how is this? Are not "God and the soul the same, according to the words: *tat* "*tvam asi*?"—To this it is replied: "When, by the teaching "of non-separateness, through sentences like *tat tvam asi*, the "consciousness of non-separateness is awakened, then the "wanderings of the soul and the creative function of Brahman "cease; for the whole tendency of the world of division springs "from false knowledge, and is removed by perfect knowledge. "Whence, then, the creation? and whence the responsibility "for not having brought forth good only? For *Saṃsâra*, which "has as its characteristics the doing of good and evil, is an "illusion produced by non-discrimination of the determinations "(which, produced by Ignorance, consist in the aggregate of "the instruments of activity formed by names and forms), and "this illusion just as the error (*abhimâna*) of division and "separation by birth and death, does not exist in the sense "of the highest reality" (p. 472, 14—475, 4).

---

[107] For our author, every good thing (*hitam*) is a command (*kartavyam*) and every evil thing (*ahitam*) is a prohibition (*parihartavyam*); therefore the freedom of God excludes both. He knows, therefore, like the Old Testament, only a hypothetical imperative, not, like the philosophy of Kant, a categorical, which only becomes possible through freedom.

THE THIRD PART OF THE VEDÂNTA SYSTEM:

PSYCHOLOGY

OR

THE DOCTRINE OF THE SOUL.

XXII. Proofs of the Immortality of the Soul.

1. Preliminary Remarks on Psychology.

WITH Theology or the doctrine of the Existent, and Cosmology or the doctrine of its manifestation as the world, the foundations of the system are naturally completed; it is therefore only a further elaboration of what has already been expounded when in Psychology and the following sections we turn our attention specially to a particular side of the Universe, in order to consider more closely both in its own nature and in its two states of wandering and liberation that most important of cosmic phenomena, which is immediately present to the inner consciousness of every one, namely the soul.

There are two factors which constitute the Universe; one of them may be properly termed the stage in this drama of cosmic evolution, the other the players who appear on it; the first factor is inorganic Nature consisting of space, air, fire, water and earth; the second is organic Nature consisting of souls that have entered into the elements and wander as plants, animals, men, and gods. Both factors are ultimately resolvable into Brahman, into "the One without a second," who according to the exoteric view creates the elements anew at the beginning of each world-period and then enters into them (above p. 231) "with the living Self," *i. e.*, with the individual Soul; but both of them, the elements as well as the souls, are, from the higher, esoteric standpoint of the doctrine of identity, the one undivided Brahman Himself; for an existence in the highest sense real (*paramârthataḥ*) which passes beyond the one indivisible Brahman without a second cannot be predicated of the extension (*prapañca*) of the elements in names and forms as they are "laden on" the soul as "recompense of the deed on the doer" (*kriyâ-kâraka-phalam*, p. 273, 12. 291, 6. 447, 3. 987, 6), nor yet of the Brahman disguised by the Upâdhis whereby He represents a wandering, enjoying, acting soul.

This double fundamental view of the Vedânta: the esoteric doctrine according to which every soul is the whole indivisible Brahman, who admits of nothing outside Himself, and the exoteric doctrine according to which there has from eternity existed a plurality of souls wandering but nevertheless (illogically) conceived as emanating from the Brahman—this view must be clearly kept in mind in what follows, even when (on the supposition that the reader is now sufficiently familiar with the leading conceptions) we do not treat the exoteric and esoteric Psychology in two strictly sundered sections which would involve too great a dislocation of the sequence of thought of the original. In general, it may be noted, Çañkara in the Psychology takes the esoteric view, and leaves it to the opponent whose opinion is step by step developed in detail and then refuted, to represent the exoteric view; at the same time having regard to the doctrine of metempsychosis maintained by him for the "lower knowledge." Çañkara cannot avoid descending to the exoteric standpoint himself; in doing so he appropriates partially and conditionally the arguments which he himself combats, in order thereby to gain a foundation for the doctrine of *Samsâra*, *i. e.*, the "wandering" of the soul, which he then treats of.—The individual enquiries as found in the original work will be left as far as possible untouched; only in the order will certain changes demanded by the subject be made; therefore we shall first treat of the origin and nature of the soul (chap. XXIII), of its relation to God (chap. XXIV), to the body (chap. XXV) and to its own works (chap. XXVI), all this from the esoteric standpoint; this course, however, from the continual connection with the exoteric point of view opposed to it will disclose many aspects which are true for the other doctrine also; these will be further developed when passing to the exoteric standpoint we consider the soul in relation to its empirical organs (chap. XXVII) and states (chap. XXVIII) in detail; to these preliminaries in the following section will be readily joined the doctrine of transmigration.

However before we enter on these discussions, we must as an introduction produce the proofs of the immortality of the soul which are not found in the psychological part of the work (2, 3, 15—2, 4, 19, and 3, 2, 1—10) but 3, 3, 53—54 among the miscellaneous matter which forms the sections 3, 3 and 3, 4. Though Çañkara tries to justify artificially the interpolation of this episode at the place in question, it does not naturally belong there but to Psychology, and that as an introduction; for a *conditio sine qua non* of the doctrine of the soul is the proof that the soul exists, that there is in man a part which "reaches" beyond the body and is not affected by its dissolution.

The word "immortality" is here to be understood in its western sense as, used by us, of "indestructibility by death." The Indians as a rule understand by the corresponding *amṛitatvam* as has already been emphasised (above p. 149) something different, namely "the deliverance of the liberated soul from dying."[108] What we call immortality is commonly called by them *vyatireka* the "reaching" (beyond the body); and this idea is the subject of the following controversy between the materialists and Vedântins, which, for the high interest of the question discussed, we add in a unabbreviated translation.

2. Arguments of the Materialists against the Immortality of the Soul.

"Some, namely those materialists (*lokâyatika*) who see the "Self in the body only, believe that there is no Self which "persists beyond the body; they assume that consciousness "though indiscoverable in the external elements, earth, etc.,

---

[108] *Martyatvam* on the contrary means, p. 193, 7 "the necessity of dying again and again" of the individual soul.—However *amṛita* too is occasionally found in our sense; *e. g.*, p. 197, 12, where it means the soul "which cannot die" (because there still exist works to be atoned for); cf. also p. 241, 14.

"taken individually and collectively, is contained in them when "they take the form of the body; therefore they maintain that "consciousness proceeds from them in the form of intellect, "just as the power of intoxication [from fermenting matter], "and that man is only a body which is distinguished by this "consciousness. On the other hand they deny a Self which "persists beyond the body, by virtue of which consciousness "is in the body and which is capable of entering into heaven "or into salvation; on the contrary they assume that the body "alone is the conscious being and the Self, and cite as a "proof that this conscious being only continues as long as the "body. For when anything exists only as long as something "else exists, and ceases to exist with it, this is completely "expressed by terming it a quality of the other, just as heat "and light are qualities of fire. It is just the same with "breath, motion, spirit, memory, etc. which are considered qual-"ities of the soul by believers in the soul; for they too are per-"ceived only within the body and not without it, and as no "bearer of these qualities which reaches beyond the body can "be proved, therefore they can be nothing but qualities of the "body. Therefore the Self does not persist beyond the body" (p. 954, 5—955, 2).

3. Proofs of the Immortality of the Soul.

"To this we reply: it is not true that the soul does not "persist beyond the body; on the contrary its persistence "beyond the body must be assumed because its Existence "does not depend on the Existence (of the body). For "if from the fact that the qualities of the Self persist as long "as the body, the conclusion is drawn that they are qualities "of the body, then also from the fact that they do not persist "while the body persists must be concluded that they are not "qualities of the body because they differ essentially from the "qualities of the body. For what is a quality of the body, "*e.g.*, shape, etc., must persist as long as the body. Breath, "motion, etc. on the other hand do not persist though the "body does, namely in the state of death. Not only so but "the qualities of the body, as shape, etc., are perceived by "others, but this is not so with the qualities of the Self, Spirit, "Memory, etc."

"Further: it is true that from the existence of the body "in a living state can be proved the existence of those [qual-"ities of the Self], but from its non-existence the reverse "cannot be proved; for there is always the possibility that "whenever this body perishes the qualities of the Self persist "by entering into another body; the opponents' opinion there-"fore is excluded by its being a mere hypothesis (*saṃçaya*)."

"The opponent must further be asked how he imagines "consciousness if he assumes its origin from the elements; for "beyond the four elements the materialists of course admit "nothing existing. If he says: consciousness is the perception "of the elements and the products, consciousness has the latter "as its objects and consequently cannot be a quality of them, "for an activity directed towards one's own Self is a contra-"diction; for though fire is hot, it does not burn itself, and "however skilled a dancer is, he cannot climb on his own "shoulders; if consciousness is a quality of the elements and "their products, the elements and their products cannot be "objects of consciousness; for *e.g.* shapes cannot have their "own shape or another as object, while on the other hand "consciousness has as objects the elements and their products "whether without or within the Self. As the existence of the "elements and their products is concluded from the fact that "they are perceived, so the conclusion must also be drawn "that this perception is different from them [perception makes "the material world known, not *vice versa*]; and the proper "nature of perception is just what we call soul. Thus the "independence of the soul from the body and its eternity "follow from the unity of perception; and recollecting etc. "is possible through the recognition in a different condition "of a thing once perceived because the percipient is identical "[with himself]."

"Now if it be said that perception is a quality of the body "because it persists as long as the body, the method of reply-"ing has already been indicated; perception continues as long "as the means *e. g.* the lamp, exists, and continues no longer "when it does not exist; but from this cannot be concluded "that perception is only a quality of the lamp; just in the "same way because perception continues as long as the body "exists and ceases when it ceases, it does not need to be a "quality of the body; for the body like the lamp serves only "as a means. Moreover the help of the body is not un-"conditionally necessary in perception, for while the body lies "motionless in sleep we perceive many things.—Therefore the "existence of a soul persisting beyond the body is indisputable" (p. 955—957).

4. On the Doctrine of Immortality in general.

If human thought were what it is not and perhaps never will be—completely logical, there would probably be only two philosophical standpoints: Idealism which holds the world which surrounds us as not real in the strict sense, and Realism which regards it as real. If these standpoints are logically adhered to, there is place in neither system, as it seems to us, for the immortality of the soul. For it is essential to Idealism to reach by one of the ways indicated by us in chap. II, 1, above p. 47ff. the conviction of the unreality of all plurality as well as of all origination and dissolution and to grasp as the sole certainty the existence of the Self (*ego*): the logical consequence of this standpoint is the consciousness of the identity of the *Ego* with "Being-in-itself" and of the identification with it as soon as the dream of this existence is past—an identification which is not to be conceived so much as an absorption of the Self in the All, but rather (if we may speak spatially of the spaceless) as an absorption of the all into the Self, as a generalised realisation of what is in detail realised in every moral action. From this point of view the doctrine of immortality is superfluous; for it says us only what is self-evident. From the point of view of Realism on the other hand it is logically impossible. If nature is real, its dicta are real; and they tell us unmistakably that we arise out of nothing by procreation and at death return to nothing.—These considerations seem to show that the doctrine of immortality is a compromise between Idealism and Realism; it is an attempt to maintain from the realistic standpoint which is the natural one for the human intellect the idealistic certainty, rooted in self-consciousness, of the unchangeableness of the Self—a vain effort as the history of the doctrine of immortality sufficiently demonstrates.

In the Vedânta system Idealism is represented by the esoteric view of the doctrine of identity, Realism by the exoteric doctrine of the Creation of the world. For the esoteric view the soul is identical with the Brahman and to grasp this only the right knowledge of the Self is needed, and no proof of immortality. • The exoteric view makes us emerge from and return to Brahman; with this conception no doctrine of immortality can be reconciled but only the view of the Upanishads, expressed in the words (Muṇḍ. 2, 1, 1).

"Just as the sparks from out the glowing flame
"In thousand forms, all glowing skywards mount,
"All creatures from the changeless one emerge,
"And thus, dear friend, return unto their fount."

According to this doubtless original view the soul had an origin, and is as a necessary consequence, perishable. For what is so constituted that it can originate, is so constituted that it can perish. Τὸ μηδὲν εἰς οὐδὲν ῥέπει.—

But the soul is the point in the universe where the veil (woven of time, space, and causality) that covers "Being-in-itself" becomes so transparent that we perceive facts through it, which protest against the cosmic laws of Realism and oppose themselves to a logical elaboration of it. Such a fact is above all the metaphysical significance of human action, reaching as it does beyond the grave. When a human being dies and his body is scattered to the elements, there is something in him which does not leave him; that is his works, as the Veda (Bṛih. 3, 2, 13) says; and this conviction of the indestructibility of the moral part of man by death compels the Vedanta to maintain inconsistently instead of the absorption into Brahman demanded by the exoteric view a persistence of the soul in its individual character beyond the Brahman into whom it enters at death.

We shall return later to these questions of exoteric Psychology. The first question is not as to the empirical soul affected by Upâdhis and therefore wandering, acting and suffering, but as to the definition of the metaphysical nature of the soul free from all this; we shall however often enough have occasion to refer beforehand to this disguising of the soul by the Upâdhis.

XXIII. Origin and Nature of the Soul.

1. Origin of the Soul.

Sûtras 2, 3, 16—17.

ONE could imagine, says Çañkara, that the soul (*jîva*) also originates and perishes like all else, because experience shows how man is born and dies and even celebrates his birth by special ceremonies (p. 641, 6). But that idea is contradicted by the Scripture which accompanies its commands and prohibitions with promises and threats, and they are only accomplished in a future existence (641, 9). Therefore being born and dying refer only to the body; for the soul on the other hand they mean no more than the entering into the phenomenal world as body and passing out of it again (*prâdurbhâva* and *tirobhâva*, p. 642, 4); therefore birth is only to be regarded as the union of the soul with the body, death as the separation from it (642, 8). But by this only the independence of the soul from the gross (material) origin and dissolution is demonstrated; the question is, what is the relation of the soul to Brahman, does it originate from him or not (642, 11)?—

—It is clear that up to the present we have been speaking exoterically of the soul involved in transmigration. We might expect to find further the proof that it does not originate from Brahman on the ground that when in deep sleep and death and at the end of the world it enters into him, it persists in the form of seed-force (cf. above pp. 228 ff. 238. 276. 279). Instead of this in what follows Çañkara passes over to the esoteric doctrine in order to prove the non-origination of the soul from the fact of its identity with Brahman.

The origination of the soul from Brahman might he maintained on the following grounds: *Firstly*: If Brahman is recognised, it is said in Muṇḍ. 1, 1, 3, all is recognised. This passage forbids us to assume anything existent outside Brahman.—*Secondly*: Brahman and the soul are different in essence; Brahman is free from all evil [*e. g.* origination and dissolution] and the soul is not.—*Thirdly*: Everything divided and manifold in the world is transformed (not original); when the soul does good and evil and feels pleasure and pain, it is individualised according to the bodies and manifold; therefore it must have an origin (cf. note 43).—*Fourthly*: It is equally true of enjoyers (*bhoktar*) and of the things to be enjoyed (*bhogyam*), *i. e.*, the Prâṇas and Elements, that they proceed from Brahman as sparks spring from a fire (above p. 131ff.); by this passage other passages are to be supplemented and explained; thus the passage as to the entrance of Brahman into the elements (Taitt. 2, 6. Chând. 6, 3, 3; cf. above p. 280).—Therefore the soul has originated from Brahman (p. 643, 7 to 644, 11).

To the *fourth* assertion is to be replied first that in most passages an origination of the soul is not taught [as for the others, they will be treated immediately]; and then that an origination is impossible because in many passages (Çañkara cites no fewer than ten) the eternal nature of the soul is maintained.—To the *third* of the above assertions that the soul must have originated because it is manifold, it is to be replied, that the soul in itself (*svatas*) is by no means manifold (p. 645, 8), for it is said (Çvet. 6, 11):

"One God alone in every being hid,
"Pervadeth all, the inner soul of each."

The plurality of the soul is only phenomenal and is conditioned by the Upâdhis such as Buddhi etc., just as the plurality of space by the vessels (note 106) which bound it. In the same way we must take it as referring to the Upâdhis when the Scripture occasionally seems to speak of an origin and dissolution of the soul; this means only an origin and dissolution of the Upâdhis; *e. g.* in the passage (above p. 175) "after death there is no consciousness."[109]—By the identity of the soul with Brahman the *first* of the above assertions is met.—Lastly, as regards the *second* it is to be remarked that the difference in essence of the soul and Brahman refers only to the Upâdhis, as is to be seen by the passage Chap. XII, 4, in which all qualities of Saṃsâra are denied to the soul "consisting of knowledge." Thus it is proved that the soul[110] does not originate nor perish (p. 644, 12—647, 5).

2. Nature of the Soul.

Sûtram 2, 3, 18.

How is the nature of the soul to be imagined? Is it, as *Kaṇâda* maintains, in itself not intellectual, so that its intelligence is only accidental (*âgantuka*), or must we assume with the *Sâṅkhyas* that the Soul is in its essence an eternally intellectual being (p. 647, 7)?—

For the first eventuality, that the intelligence of the soul is accidental and produced by its association with the Manas, just as the heat of the pot is produced by its connection with the fire, we may adduce the fact that were the soul essentially intellectual it ought to be so in the case of sleepers, fainting persons, and madmen (*graha-âvishṭa*); but they affirm that in this condition they have had no consciousness. Therefore, since the intelligence of the soul is only temporary, we must assume that it is not essential but accidental (p. 647, 9 to 648, 2).

To this we reply: the soul is an eternally intellectual being; this follows from the fact that, as we have proved, it does not

---

[109] Here p. 646, 8 and 391, 3 an annihilation of the Upâdhis, *upâdhi-pralaya* is taught. But according to the system only the gross body is annihilated; the remaining Upâdhis (the subtle body and the Prâṇas) did not originate and (except in liberation) are imperishable; but by them the plurality of souls is conditioned, from which the opponent concluded their origination. His objection therefore remains unanswered.

[110] That is, as we must add, the soul which the esoteric doctrine recognises as identical with Brahman.—The indestructibility of the soul affected by Upâdhis follows on moral grounds as is developed *e. g.* above p. 112 ff.

originate but is the highest unchangeable Brahman itself, which when disguised by the Upâdhis appears as the individual soul. Now the highest Brahman is as we have proved (chap. IX, 4 above p. 134ff.) naturally intellectual; consequently to the soul also intellectuality is as essential as heat and light to fire. Yet the organs of perception are not for this reason superfluous; for they are the gates through which the intellect receives the specifically different sense-impressions, *e. g.* the perception of smells by the sense of smell etc.—If sleepers etc. do not perceive, this is to be explained by the passage: "If he then sees not, yet is he seeing, though he "does not see" etc. (above p. 191); *i. e.*, the soul does not then perceive, not because perception is wanting but because the objects are wanting; just as light does not become visible in space, as long as there are no objects to be illuminated (648, 2—649, 13).

XXIV. Relation of the Soul to God.

UNDER this heading, making a change in the arrangement of the Sûtras we treat the section 2, 3, 43—53, which, like the concluding sections in several other cases, makes the impression of a later addition, and in respect of its contents stands in close relationship to the thoughts of the preceding chapter; therefore we include it here; it is impossible in our presentation to avoid completely the numerous repetitions of the original if we wish to avoid too great a departure from the original line of thought.

1. Non-identity and Identity.

pp. 684, 13—688, 3.

The relation of the soul to God is presented by the Scripture in two ways, partly [exoteric] as the relation of a servant to his master and of the part to the whole, and partly [esoteric] as a relation of identity.

The position of the soul as servant with God as its master can be conceived in the following way: God (*îçvara*) by virtue of his connection with unsurpassable (*niratiçaya*) Upâdhis exercises authority over the soul which is affected only by imperfect (*nihîna*) Upâdhis (p. 688, 1; our author contents himself here with the remark that the whole relationship depends on the Upâdhis; for greater detail see chap. XX, 3, e, above p. 271).—The soul is further conceived as a part of God; *e.g.* by the simile of the Fire and the sparks (p. 685, 6; cf. above p. 131); further in the passage of the Ṛigveda X, 90, 3 (cf. chap. XI, 3):

"However great is nature's majesty,
"The spirit is yet higher raised by far
"Of it but one foot do all beings make
"Three feet are immortality in heaven."

where under one foot all animated beings, the immovable (plants) and the movable, are to be understood (p. 687, 3). The passage of *Bhagavadgîtâ* 15, 7 affirms the same (p. 687, 9).

However this view of the soul as a part of Brahman is not to be taken strictly, for Brahman has no parts (p. 685, 7); and the case is the same with the passages in which the soul appears as different from Brahman (p. 685, 9); for it is taught on the other hand that all souls, as they have entered "into "the complex of organs formed of names and shapes" (*nâma-rûpa-kṛita-kârya-karaṇa-sañghâta*, *i. e.* the body), are Brahman Himself (p. 686, 5). Not even the lowest creatures are to be excepted here, as a verse of the Brahman song of the *Âtharvaṇikas* (not found in our collection of Atharva songs) says:

"Brahman are fishers and slaves, and even the players are Brahman"

and another (Çvet. 4, 3 = Atharva-V. X, 8, 27):

"The woman art thou, and the man, the maiden and the boy,
"Thou art born, and growest in every form, thou totterest in old age."

Thus the soul is sometimes regarded as identical with Brahman, sometimes as a part of Him (p. 686).

The passages p. 1127, 14—1128, 14 (translated above p. 111) serve to complete what this passage leaves uncertain; it is there proved from the esoteric standpoint that the soul can be conceived neither a part nor a transformation of Brahman nor as different from him but only as identical with Brahman.—An explanation of this is offered by the image (used pp. 690, 3. 695, 1. 809, 12) of the sun and its reflections in the water (above p. 208) and that of cosmic space, whose local divisions depend only on the limitations of vessels which produce no change in its nature (note 106, above p. 277); cf. also p. 120, 13: "It is however forbidden, in the sense of the "highest reality (*paramârthatas*) to assume a seer or hearer "different from the highest God, when we read (Bṛih. 3, 7, 23): "'There is no seer besides him,' etc. (above p. 149); on the "contrary the highest God differs from the individual soul "created by Ignorance and termed *Vijñânâtman* (cf. note 82) "which acts and enjoys only in the same way as the magician, "who in reality remains upon the earth, is different from the "magician, who with sword and shield climbs up the rope."

2. Illusion of all Pain.

pp. 688, 3—691, 3.

One might imagine that, if the soul is a part of God, God must feel the pains of the soul also, just as when one member of the body suffers, the whole body suffers with it (p. 688, 3); nay the sufferings of God must be much greater than those of the individual soul, and it is better for us to remain as individual souls in the state of *Saṃsâra* than by the gaining of perfect knowledge to rise to a consciousness of identity with God (p. 688, 6).

To this is to be replied (in connection with what was brought forward above p. 154): only through Ignorance does the soul fall into the illusion of seeing the Self in the body, and upon this illusion (*abhimâna*) alone, from which God is free, depends the sensation of pain. Pain is consequently a delusion (*bhrama*) which arises from our not distinguishing the Self from the limitations, such as body, senses, etc. which have their origin in the realm of names and shapes created by Ignorance (p. 689, 1). Therefore pain depends only on a mistaken idea, as is proved by the fact that it persists even beyond the body. If for example a son or friend of ours dies, we feel pain from the mistaken idea that they belong to us. The *Parivrâjaka* (above p. 17) on the other hand, who has delivered himself from that illusion, feels no pain at it. In the same way he too feels no more bodily pain who has by perfect knowledge delivered himself from the illusion that his body belongs to him (p. 689, 9).

Just as sunlight falling on the finger appears straight when the finger is straight, and crooked when it is crooked but in reality is neither the one nor the other—just as space in vessels seems to move when they are moved but in reality remains motionless—just as the sun does not quiver when its reflections quiver in the water—so God does not suffer when the individual soul suffers, and even the suffering of the individual soul depends, as we saw, only on Ignorance. Such words of the Vedânta as *tat tvam asi*, "that art thou," serve to drive away this illusion of the existence of the individual soul and to produce the consciousness of the Brahmanhood of the soul (p. 689, 16—690, 9).

3. Subjection to and Freedom from Law.

pp. 691, 3—694, 3.

"If there is only one soul in all beings, how then are the "worldly and Vedic prohibitions possible?"

—So far as the individual soul is a part of God.

"But the Scripture teaches also that it is not simply a "part of him but also identical with him!"

—The difference and identity consists exactly in its being a part of Him.

"But where the Scripture speaks seriously, it surely teaches "the identity of God and the soul and reproves the natural "view of difference! It still remains therefore to be explained "how commands and prohibitions are possible."

—Let us take commands such as: a man shall visit his wife at a fit time—a man shall ask his consent of the sacrificial animal—a man shall stand by his friend; and prohibitions such as: thou shalt not commit adultery,—thou shalt not kill,—thou shalt avoid thy enemy, such commands and prohibitions are valid in spite of the unity of the Âtman, on account of the connection with the body. For on this connection with the body depends the mistaken opinion that we see the Self in the body, which is and remains common to all creatures with the exception of such as attain to perfect knowledge. The commands and prohibitions refer to this distinction [of the Ego from the non-Ego] though it depends on Ignorance and is caused by the connection with the body and the other Upâdhis; and only for him who has attained perfect knowledge do they cease to hold good; as he has no further object to aim at, he has also no further obligations. For him there is nothing to be toiled after or avoided because there is nothing that reaches beyond his own Self (*âtman*); but a duty towards one's own Self is meaningless (*na ca âtmâ âtmani eva niyojyaḥ syât*). It is true he has a body, but he knows that its structure (*saṃhatatvam*) is a mere illusion. Only for him who is still subject to the illusion of the body does the illusion of duty still persist: how should it persist for him who has recognised the unity of the soul?

"But if the sage has no duties, can he do what he will?"—

—Not at all! For it is only illusion that moves to action and it is just this illusion that exists no more for this sage.—But in spite of the unity of all existence, command and prohibition exist for him who has not attained knowledge. For as one shrinks from the fire which has burnt a corpse, though it is as much fire as any other—as one avoids sunlight in unclean places, though it comes just as much from the sun—as one flees from a human corpse though it consists of the same materials as the living body—so there are certain things to be avoided, though all things are one in the Âtman.

4. How are the individual Souls separated from each other?

Sûtras 2, 3, 49—50.

The works of souls are individually different, and so are the fruits (reward and punishment in the succeeding existence) which correspond to the works in each case. How is this possible if the soul is in reality only one?—How can it happen that works and fruits of different souls (which at death return to unity and proceed out of it again to a new existence Chând. 6, 10, above p. 264) do not mutually intermingle?

To this we have two replies:

1) The soul is, it is true, as a result of its unity with Brahman (as we shall soon see more in detail) omnipresent (*i. e.* spaceless); but this omnipresence does not mean that the acting and enjoying soul also pervades every thing and is thus connected with all bodies. For this individual soul is only

conditioned by the Upâdhis; as these Upâdhis are not all pervading, the individual soul is not so either, and no confusion of works and fruits happens (p. 694, 5—10).—Compare with this what has been said above pp. 228 ff. 276 as to the persistence of the power of differentiation after entrance into Brahman.

2) Individual souls are to be regarded only as phantoms (*âbhâsa*) of the highest soul, comparable to images of the sun in water. Just as when one of these reflected suns quivers, the others do not quiver too, the deeds and fruits of one soul do not concern the others. These phantoms and with them the whole of *Saṃsâra* with its deeds and fruits depend on Ignorance (*avidyâ*). Only when this is removed, is unity with Brahman attained (p. 694, 12—695, 5) and thereby, as we may add, a point of view, from which questions as to works and fruits and consequently as to their intermingling, have no meaning.

Of these two answers the one refers the plurality of souls to the *Upâdhis*, the others to *Avidyâ*. What is the relation of these two to each other? This question leads us to collect here the most important passages on the *Upâdhis*, a fundamental idea of the system, which is however nowhere treated connectedly by Çañkara.

5. Brahman and the Upâdhis.

In reality (*paramârthatas*) there is nothing else besides Brahman alone. If we imagine we perceive a transformation (*vikâra*) of Him into the world, a division (*bheda*) of Him into a plurality of individual souls, this depends on *Avidyâ*. But how does this happen? How do we manage to deceive ourselves into seeing a transformation and a plurality, where in reality Brahman alone is?—On this question our authors give no information.

Since Avidyâ is, as we saw above (p. 55) innate, and our birth depends on the works of a previous existence, one might imagine the innate obscuration of our knowledge was a result of previous offences reaching back *ad infinitum*. But the system gives no real ground for this assumption. *Avidyâ* cannot properly be a result of *Saṃsâra*, for on the contrary the reverse is the case and the whole of *Saṃsâra* depends on *Avidyâ*. Under these circumstances nothing remains but to recall the negative character of the idea of *Avidyâ*. It needs no explanation so far as it is not a positive defect, but only Ignorance, the absence of knowledge. It is true something very positive depends on Avidyâ; *viz.* the whole existence of the world and of the individual soul. It is however just the meaning of this reference of all empirical existence to Ignorance, that this whole world, the whole beginningless and endless *Saṃsâra*, is only for us something positive and real, but is in actuality non-Brahman and (as Brahman alone is the Existent) non-Existent, a mere mirage (*mâyâ, mṛigatṛishṇikâ*), a product of Ignorance.

The extension of the world and the plurality of wandering souls, this hybrid which is neither Being nor non-Being (*tattva-anyatvâbhyâm anirvacanîyam*) and comparable to an hallucination or to a dream. is produced by Ignorance by virtue of the *Upâdhis*, the limitations, literally "the ascription" (with the secondary idea of the unpermitted) by means of which we "ascribe" to Brahman what does not naturally belong to him, and through which, as we shall show in detail, he becomes 1) a personal God, 2) the world, 3) the individual soul. All this depends on the *Upâdhis*, and the *Upâdhis* on *Avidyâ*. *Avidyâ* alone is the cause of the origin of the Upâdhis (they are *avidyâ-kṛita* p. 1133, 12, *avidyâ-nimitta* p. 692, 14, *avidyâ-pratyupasthâpita* pp. 199, 5. 690, 5) and is the cause of their persistence so far as the essence of *Avidyâ* is the non-discrimination of Brahman from the Upâdhis (*upâdhi-aviveka* p. 473, 17. 689, 1. 98, 8, cf. 185, 10); Brahman himself on the other hand is not in the least affected or changed by the Upâdhis, just as little in fact as the crystal by the red colour with which it is painted p. 265, 7. 803, 14. It is in this sense that a contact of the Upâdhis (*upâdhi-samparka* p. 389, 2. 794, 7) and a contamination (p. 389, 2) by them is spoken of. Brahman is merged in the Upâdhis (*upâdhi-antarbhâva* p. 811, 5. 9) and thereby his nature is hidden (*svarûpa-tirobhâva*

p. 837, 2) and his natural omniscience (in his existential form as soul) suffers a limitation (the knowledge of the soul is *upâdhi-paricchinna* p. 231, 1).

On this connection of the Brahman with the Upâdhis depend, as we have said, three phenomena, and it is characteristic that all three are included under this conception without distinction: 1) Through the Upâdhis the higher Brahman becomes the lower, the object of worship p. 111, 3. 662, 13. 1142, 9; the Upâdhis of the *Îçvara* are however perfect (*niratiçaya*) in contrast with those of the individual soul which are imperfect (*nihîna*) (p. 688, 1); details of this distinction are not given. 2) The extension of nature too (*nâma-rûpa-prapañca*) which is commonly referred directly to *Avidyâ* (*e.g.* 1132, 10. 507, 1. 473, 17. 787, 13) seems occasionally to be reckoned among the Upâdhis of Brahman; this is the case p. 803, 12. 807, 4 (*prithivî-âdi-upâdhi-yoga*), 391, 2 (*upâdhi-âçraya-nâmarûpam*), 1133, 12 (*nâmarûpa-upâdhika*) just as external objects (*vishaya*) also appear among the Upâdhis of the soul (p. 265, 6, cf. 787, 10. 1056, 1. 739, 7). This description of nature however as Upâdhi of Brahman is uncertain and at any rate seldom. 3) But so much the more frequently is everything regarded as *Upâdhi*, which makes *Brahman* into a *Jîva* or *Çârîra*, *i.e.*, individual soul, whose existence as a being different from Brahman depends solely on the Upâdhis, p. 735, 3. 244, 13. 360, 2. 199, 8. 836, 8. 799, 5. 982, 5. 173, 16. 162, 16. The best explanation of this relationship is the comparison of the *Upâdhis* with vessels which limit cosmic space locally (cf. note 106 above p. 277). In this sense can be considered as Upâdhis firstly all psychic organs or *Prâṇas* (*Mukhya prâṇa*, *Manas*, and the *Indriyas*; for details see chap. XXVII) together with the subtle body and the moral determination of the soul (p. 1091, 9) which all share together in transmigration; further the gross body which only exists until death (*kârya-karaṇa-sañghâta* or *deha*, cf. 473, 17. 199, 5. 787, 13. 389, 2. 98, 4. 9. 692, 14. 811, 5. 9); and finally to these are added occasionally external objects and sensation (*vishaya-vedanâ* p. 265, 6. 787, 10. 1056, 1, where it must be taken as a Dvandva). In waking and dreaming contact with the Upâdhis (*upâdhi-samparka*) takes place, in deep sleep release (*upaçama*) from them (p. 794, 7. 836, 6). Frequently only such are to be understood as Upâdhis as share in transmigration; then for example p. 793, 14, where veins and pericardium are termed receptacles of the Upâdhis (*upâdhi-âdhâra*); thus the definition of the Upâdhis fluctuates and must in each case be settled by the context.

XXV. Relation of the Soul to the Body.

In the section 2, 3, 19—32, which we propose to analyse in the present chapter, the question raised by this heading is handled chiefly from the quantitative side, in so far as the enquiry into the size of the soul holds the foremost place. This leads however to discussions which are of considerable help to us in gaining in the sequel a clear idea (so far as this is possible) of the relation of the soul 1) to its organs (*Mukhya prâṇa*, *Manas*, and *Indriyas*), 2) to the subtle body which consists of the seed of the elements and shares in transmigration, 3) to the gross body which consists of the elements themselves.

A clear idea of the spacelessness of Being-in-itself is wanting in our system; in its place we find the doctrine of the infinite size (*vibhutvam*) or omnipresence (*sarvagatatvam*) of the soul; two other views are opposed to this; that according to which the soul is of minute size (*aṇu*), and the opinion of the *Jainas*, according to which the soul is of a certain, moderate size, *viz.* as large as the body. We begin with the discussion of the last view, which we take over from 2, 2, 34—36 to insert it here.

1. The opinion of the *Jainas* that the Soul is as large as the Body.

If the soul is, as the *Ârhatas* affirm, as large as the body it is limited and therefore, like all limited things, not eternal (cf. note 43, above p. 68 ff.). Moreover the size of the body changes. If, *e. g.* the human soul, as a fruit of works, enters into the body of an elephant, it cannot completely fill it; and if it enters the body of an ant, it has no room in it. The same objection may be raised in respect of the varying size of the body in youth and manhood (p. 587, 6).

Or does the soul consist of an infinite number of corpuscules (*avayava*) which in a small body close up, and in a large one open out? Then there is a question whether these corpuscules possess impenetrability (*pratighâta*) or not. If they are impenetrable there is no room in a limited space for an infinite number of corpuscules; if they are not, they take all together no more room than one corpuscule, they cannot produce the [necessary] extension and the whole soul is of minute size (p. 587, 12).

Or must we assume that with the increase and diminution of the body the soul gains new or loses old corpuscules? But then the soul is subject to change and perishable like the skin; and the doctrine [of the Jainas] of binding and liberation cannot hold good; the doctrine namely which asserts that the soul, clad in the eight kinds of its works and sunk in the ocean of Saṃsâra, rises like a gourd (*alâvu*) after the connection is broken (p. 588, 9). Moreover such changing corpuscules belong as little to the Self (*âtman*) as the body does; and if a part of him remain as soul, we cannot determine which (p. 588, 12).—And where do the new parts come from and the old go to? Not from the elements and not back into them; for the soul does not consist of the elements; and another common receptacle of soul-corpuscules is not demonstrable (p. 589, 5).

Or does the soul perhaps persist through all change of parts like a stream whose waters change? This is not admissible either; for if this continuity is not real, there is no soul at all; if it is real, the soul is subject to change (p. 590, 4).

If the dimensions of the soul remain for ever, as the *Jainas* maintain, as they were at the moment of liberation, this final state is to be regarded as its real dimensions; and therefore a given body and not every former body is to be taken as its measure; but then it is not discoverable why it should not have just as much right to remain in every former state as in that final state (p. 590, 9). We come therefore to the conclusion that the soul is unchangeable, whether it is minute (*aṇu*) or large (*mahant*), but it cannot be taken to be of the (changing) size of the body, as the Jainas assert (p. 591, 2).

2. The Opinion that the Soul is of minute (*aṇu*) size.

Sûtras 2, 3, 19–28.

1. That the soul is as large as the body has been refuted in the examination of the doctrine of the Jainas (p. 651, 2). Therefore it is only possible to regard it as either very large (*i.e.* infinite, *vibhu*) or as minute (*aṇu*). The infinitely large cannot move (p. 651, 1), and we must assume of the soul that it moves because a passing (out of the body), a going (to the moon) and a return (to a new incarnation) are ascribed to it by the Scriptures (p. 650, 9). And even if the passing, so far as we regard it as a cessation of lordship over the body, could possibly be reconciled with immovability (p. 651, 5) a going and return could not; but they must certainly be recognized as motion (p. 651, 7) and we are thus compelled to regard this passing as a real going away (p. 651, 9). Since the soul, being mobile, cannot therefore be infinitely large, nor yet, as shown, of middle size, we must assume (p. 651, 8) that it is minute (*aṇu*).

2. The soul is, it is true, termed by the Scripture large, omnipresent, infinite, but these expressions refer only to the highest, not the individual soul (p. 652, 9); and when we read Bṛih. 4, 4, 22 (above p. 195): "Truly this great, unborn Self, "is that among the life-organs which consists of knowledge" the individual soul is certainly termed "the great" but only so far as, in virtue of an innate power as seer, such as Vâmadeva had (Ṛigv. IV, 26, 1. 27, 1. Bṛih. 1, 4, 10. Ait. 2, 5; cf. above p. 180 and note 83) its identity with the highest soul is perceived (p. 653, 1). On the other hand in other passages the soul is expressly termed minute; *e.g.* Muṇḍ. 3, 1, 9 "the subtle Self" (*aṇur âtmâ*), Çvet. 5, 8 "large as the point of an awl," and Çvet. 5, 9 as large as the hundredth of a hundredth of the end of a hair.

3. But if the soul is minute, it can only be at one place in the body; how comes it thus that it perceives throughout the body? For after a bath in the Ganges one feels the cold, and in summer one feels the heat all over one's body (p. 653, 11).—We answer: just as a piece of sandalwood, even when it only touches the body at one spot, refreshes it all over (p. 654, 2) so the soul is only in one spot, *viz.*, as the Scripture teaches in many places, in the heart (p. 655, 5) and from here it feels throughout the body (p. 654, 3). This comes about by means of the sense of touch (*tvac*); the soul is connected with the sense of touch everywhere and the sense of touch pervades the whole body.[111] Or perhaps this power of the minute soul to feel throughout the body can be explained (p. 655, 10) from its spirituality (*caitanya-guṇa*) which here extends beyond the substance; just as we see in other cases in experience that the quality extends further than the substance, when *e.g.* the light of a jewel or of a lamp, which is only in one place in a room, extends from there through the whole room (p. 655, 11) or when we smell the scent of flowers without touching them (p. 656, 9). So too the Scripture teaches of the Soul, that though it is minute and dwells in the heart, by means of its quality of spirituality it penetrates the body (p. 658, 1) "to the hair and nails" (Kaush. 4, 20; cf. Bṛih. 1, 4, 7) and also in other passages (Kaush. 3, 6. Bṛih. 2, 1, 17) the soul is distinguished from the intellect (*prajñâ, vijñânam*) with which it pervades the body (p. 658, 4).

---

[111] p. 654, 5: *tvag-âtmanor hi sambandhaḥ kṛitsnâyâṃ tvaci vartate, tvak ca kṛitsna-çarîra-vyâpinî.* As the soul according to this view is minute and dwells in the heart, the outer skin cannot possibly be understood [if the passage really belongs to the context in which it stands; p. 654, 14—655, 1 *aṇutvam* seems to be opposed to *tvak-sambandha*; it is true that in this enquiry there is in places terrible confusion] but only the *Indriyam* termed *tvac*; for by this *Manas* and by Manas the soul feels cold, heat, pain, pleasure, etc. in the whole body. At Death this *tvac* or more accurately the *tvagvṛitti* enters into the *Manas* and like all the *Indriyas* shares in transmigration.

3. The Soul is infinitely great (*vibhu*).

Sûtram 2, 3, 29.

The soul has not originated (chap. XXIII, 1) but depends only on the entrance of the highest Brahman into the elements (above p. 231); from this the identity of both follows; the individual soul is nothing but the highest Brahman himself (p. 658, 11). If this is so, the soul must be as large as Brahman and therefore all pervading (p. 658, 13) as is expressly asserted in the passage Bṛih. 4, 4, 22: "truly this great unborn "Self is that among the organs of life which consists of know-"ledge" (p. 659, 1). To the arguments of the opponent we reply:

(To 3.) If the soul were minute, it could not feel throughout the whole body. The connection with the sense of touch (*tvac*) does not suffice to explain this; the thorn too, on which one has trodden, is connected with the whole sense of feeling (p. 659, 5) and yet one feels the pain from it only in the sole of the foot and not in the whole body (p. 659, 6). That the quality extends beyond the substance, we do not admit; the flame of the lamp and its light are not related as substance and quality; on the contrary both are fiery substances, but in the flame the corpuscules (*avayava*) are drawn closer together, and in the light which radiates they are more widely separated (p. 656, 5). Just in the same way the perception of smell depends on the subtle atoms (*paramâṇu*) streaming out in all directions from the objects without diminishing their volume (p. 657, 1) and penetrating into the nasal cavity (p. 657, 4). If this is not admitted, because atoms are not perceptible by the senses (p. 657, 5), because not the objects but their odours are smelt (p. 657, 6), or because what is perhaps true of the sense of sight may not be transferred to the sense of smell (p. 657, 8)—we must dispute the assertion that smell is only a quality; for if it were, it could only disseminate itself from its own substance and not from other substances to which it has been transferred (p. 659, 10). That this is so the sublime *Dvaipâyana* testifies when he (Mahâbhâratam 12, 8518) says:

"To water the unlearned folk ascribe,
"The odour which their senses show them there;
"But ever to the earth leads back its trace,
"And thence it goes to water and the air."

If it were true therefore that the spirituality of the soul pervaded the whole body, the soul could not be minute, for spirituality is not related to it as a quality to its substance but is its very essence, as warmth and light are of the fire (p. 660, 3); and we have proved that the soul is not of the same size as the body: therefore it is only possible that it is infinitely great (p. 660, 5).

(To 2.) But how can the soul be termed *aṇu* by the Scripture?—As answer to this serves the following: *because* in the state of Saṃsâra *it is the nucleus* (*sâra*) *of the qualities* of the Buddhi.[112] Such qualities of the Buddhi are: Love, hate, pleasure, pain, etc. (p. 660, 7). For we must distinguish the soul outside the state of Saṃsâra, which means that it is not acting, not suffering and eternally free, and the soul in the state of Saṃsâra, when it acts and suffers only through the qualities of the *Upâdhi* of *Buddhi* being transferred to it (p. 660, 10). In this state the soul has the dimensions of the Buddhi (p. 661, 1), is therefore (according to Çvet. 5, 9) as large as the ten thousandth part of the end of a hair, (p. 661, 4) or (according to Çvet. 5, 8) as large as the point of an awl (p. 661, 11) and dwells like the Buddhi in the heart (p. 662, 7). The minute size of the soul is therefore to be taken figuratively (*aupacârika*); from the point of view of the highest reality (*paramârtha*) it is infinitely great (p. 661, 7). We therefore find in the passages to which the opponent appeals (Çvet. 5, 8–9):

"Through qualities of Buddhi and the body,
"The other seems as large as an awl's point.

"Divide a hundred times a human hair, and take thereof the hundredth part,
"That know thou as dimension of the soul, and this enlarges to infinity."

---

[112] Under *Buddhi* (Intellect) *Manas* is to be understood from here to the end of the chapter, as will be evident further on.

When on the contrary Muṇḍ. 3, 1, 9 the epithet *aṇu* (minute) is applied to the soul, this either does not imply its smallness but the difficulty of perceiving it which is possible only by the grace of knowledge (p. 661, 13) not by sensual perception, or it refers here also to the *Upâdhis.*

(To 1.) So too the passing, going and return of the soul only refer to it so far as it is connected with the *Upâdhis* and therefore infinitely small (p. 662, 8); for in the same way for the purpose of worship the highest soul is represented in the *Saguṇâ vidyâḥ* as connected with *Upâdhis* and therefore (Chând. 3, 14, translated above p. 153) as "smaller than a "grain of rice or barley" (p. 662, 13).

—Our author's inconsistency in first disputing the possibility of a sense of feeling throughout the body for the minute soul, and then himself admitting the minute size of the soul in the state of Saṃsâra, is self-evident. An explanation of how the soul perceives the conditions of the body in the state of Saṃsâra can only be gathered from the arguments which he disputes. It is true he says on p. 715, 2: "The above mentioned "Prâṇas [the *Manas* and the ten *Indriyas*] must be assumed "to be minute (*aṇu*); but the minuteness in their case means "subtlety (*saukshmyam*) and limitation (*pariccheda*) not atomic "size (*paramâṇu-tulyatvam*) because [in that case] action that "pervades the whole body is impossible." But in the passage which we have considered he disputed the possibility of bodily sensation not for the soul of atomic size (*paramâṇu-tulya*) but for the minute (*aṇu*) soul.—The fact is, arguments and counter-arguments are thrown together in such confusion that the assumption of a fusion of different texts is in the highest degree probable.

4. Connection of the Soul with the Intellect (*buddhi*).

Sûtras 2, 3, 30—32.

The highest soul becomes the individual soul, as we have seen, by uniting itself with the *Upâdhis* (which depend on Ignorance) and especially with the Upâdhi of *Buddhi*; by this is to be understood here, as the sequel will show, on the one hand the intellect exclusive of the sense-organs (*Indriyas*) and on the other hand the "onlooking" soul (*Sâkshin*), that is to say exactly what the System calls *Manas*.

(a) Duration of this Connection.

What becomes of the soul when it separates itself from the Buddhi? Is this separation a passing over into non-Being or an escape from Saṃsâra (p. 663, 3)?—To this the reply is: as long as the state of Saṃsâra is not removed by perfect knowledge, the connection endures; and as long as the connection endures, the individual soul as such endures (p. 663, 8). But from the standpoint of the highest reality it does not exist at all; for beyond the eternal, free, omniscient God there is no other spiritual element (p. 663, 12) as is proved by the passages: "there is no other seer besides him" (Bṛih. 3, 8, 11), "that art thou" (Chând. 6, 8, 7), "I am Brahman" (Bṛih. 1, 4, 10). The continuance of the soul's connection with the Buddhi even after death and until liberation is taught firstly by the Scripture when it says (Bṛih. 4, 3, 7 translated above p. 189): "It is that among the organs of life which consists "of knowledge and is the spirit which shines in the heart "within. This spirit wanders unchanged through both worlds; "it is as though it reflected, as though it moved unsteadily;"— "consisting of knowledge" means here "consisting of Buddhi;" that it wanders unchanged through both worlds proves that at death no separation from the Buddhi takes place; its thinking and moving are conditioned by the thinking and moving of the Buddhi; therefore it is said: "it is as though it reflected —moved"; in itself (*svatas*) it does not reflect and does not move (p. 664, 13).—Moreover the persistence of the connection follows from its dependence on false knowledge (*mithyâ-jnânam*), for this can be removed by no other means than perfect knowledge (*samyag-jñânam*); therefore the connection must persist till the awakening of the consciousness of unity with Brahman (p. 664, 16), for only by this awakening can it be broken, as the Scripture also says (Çvet. 3, 8):

"The mighty spirit out beyond the gloom,
"My eyes have seen with sunlike radiance glow;
"Who seeth him escapes a mortal's doom;
"There is for us no other way to go."

(b) Potentiality and Actuality of the Connection.

But how is it with this connection in the states of deep sleep and death, in which according to the Scripture (Chând. 6, 8 translated above p. 263) an entrance into Brahman takes place?—It is in these states potentially (*çakti-âtmanâ*) present, and becomes manifest (actual) by awakening and birth, just as the power of procreation is present as a germ (*vîja-âtmanâ*) in the child, but only becomes manifest when he becomes a man (p. 665, 8). A potential continuance of this sort must be assumed because nothing can arise without a given cause, for otherwise everything would arise out of everything (p. 665, 13).

(c) Necessity of a connecting Organ of this Sort.

The *Upâdhi* in question of the soul,—"whether it be called "*Antaḥkaraṇam*, *Manas*, *Buddhi*, *Vijñânam*, *Cittam*, or whether, "as some do, a distinction be drawn between *Manas* and *Buddhi*, "and the function of doubt assigned to the former and that of "resolution to the latter" (p. 666, 7)—is indispensable as a connecting link between the soul and organs of sense; for without it, if soul and senses suffice for perception, there would be continuous perception, or, if they do not suffice, no perception at all; for the soul is unchangeable and in the senses there is no reason why they should at one time be active and then again become inactive. Therefore a connecting link must be assumed between the two, by whose attention (*avadhânam*) and inattention arise apperception and non-apperception; this connecting link is *Manas* (mind). Therefore the Scripture says: "My mind was elsewhere, so I did not see, did not hear" and "one sees with his mind, hears with his mind" (Bṛih. 1, 5, 3); and as functions of the *Manas* it mentions (*loc. cit.*): "Wish, resolution, doubt, belief, disbelief, constancy, incon- "stancy, shame, thought and fear" (p. 666, 5—668, 3).

XXVI. Relation of the Soul to its Actions.

1. Preliminary.

It may repeatedly be observed how psychological problems familiar to us reappear in a different form in Indian philosophy. The question as to the size of the soul gave us some informations as to the relation of the soul to the body; the question as to how the soul is related to its actions includes an enquiry into the will. Essential to the soul is as we saw (chap. XXIII, 2) intelligence; but this intelligence is at the bottom imaginary; for the Indians, as will be more exactly shown later, separate the whole apparatus of perception from the soul and unite it to the physical (*i.e.* dependent on *Avidyâ*) part of man, which indeed shares in transmigration but is extinguished by liberation. Now what is the position with regard to the will? Must we recognize in it perhaps an eternal absolutely inseparable determination of the soul?— The negation of this question which will appear in what follows, may at first seem strange to him who has accustomed himself to see in Will the final origin of Being. The denial however, as will be shown, comes to this, that besides the *Velle* another state of the soul is possible, *viz.* a *Nolle*; and it makes in the end no great difference whether this for us quite incomprehensible state is characterised in our fashion as a Negation of all volition, or in the Indian manner as an imaginary cognition, which, as may be seen by the sketch of the *Akâmayamâna* (chap. XII, 4, f, above p. 194), presupposes this Negation of all volition.

2. Reasons for Supposing the Soul to be essentially an Agent (*i.e.* exercising Volition).

Sûtras 2, 3, 33—39.

1. The canon of Scripture with its commands and prohibitions presupposes that the soul is an agent, for it prescribes for it a certain course of action. If the soul were not an agent, these prescriptions would be purposeless, which cannot be assumed to be the case (p. 668, 5).

2. Of the soul in the state of dreaming it is said (Bṛih. 4, 3, 12, above p. 190):

"Immortal soars the soul where'er it will."

This presupposes that the soul is an agent (p. 669, 4).

3. On the same presupposition depends the absorption ascribed to it in the passage (Bṛih. 2, 1, 17): "The soul absorbs [in deep sleep] by virtue of its intelligence the intelligence "of those vital spirits [into itself]" (p. 669, 8).

4. Taitt. 2, 5 says:

"Intelligence performs the sacrifice, and does the works"

By intelligence (*vijnânam*) the soul is here to be understood, not the Buddhi (p. 670, 5); for otherwise the word "intelligence" would have to be in the instrumental (p. 670, 7) and the passage would have to read: "it (the soul) by means of in- "telligence performs sacrifice and works."—Therefore the soul is an agent.

It might be objected: if the soul independently of the Buddhi [without the Upâdhi, and therefore as it really is] is an agent, why does it not, as it is in this state free (*svatantra*), bring about only what is pleasant and profitable to it? For experience shows that it often brings about the contrary of what is good for it (p. 670, 11).—Answer: the soul is free too with regard to perception and yet perceives what is pleasant and what is unpleasant. So it is too with action (p. 670, 16).—But in perception the soul is influenced by the causes of perception and is therefore not free (p. 671, 1)!—Answer: That is not so! The causes of perception only determine the objects of perception but not the act of perception, for the soul is in this by virtue of its spirituality free [! p. 671, 2; the difference between receptivity which is present in perception, and spontaneity which is present in thinking and acting, is here completely overlooked; in the same way empirical psychology asserts for both a common faculty, the *Manas*]. Besides in action the soul is not absolutely free but is determined by differences of time, space, and causality (*deça-kâla-nimitta* p. 671, 4; the same formula is found pp. 38, 3. 40, 2. 482, 1. 579, 5. 671, 4. 684, 9. 775, 2. 3. 4. 781, 3. 4. 1043. 6. 7. 10. 1075, 17. 1078, 9. 1129, 11); the soul is however all the same an agent, just as the cook remains a cook, though he makes use of fuel and water (p. 671, 5).

5. If you insist that not the soul but the Buddhi is the agent, you make the latter an agent instead of an organ; but in that case the Buddhi must also be an object of Self-consciousness (*ahampratyaya*) without which no action is possible; it takes the place of the agent, and therefore needs something else as its organ, and so the whole dispute is about a name (because you call Buddhi what we call soul); p. 671, 9 to 672, 7.

6. Moreover the meditation on the highest soul demanded by the Vedânta is impossible if the soul is not an agent (for that too is an action); p. 672, 12.

3. The Soul is naturally not an Agent (exercising Volition).

Sûtram 2, 3, 40.

The section in question—one of the most important in Çañkara's work—we translate literally:

(p. 673, 3:) "Activity cannot be the real nature of the soul, "because then no liberation would be possible. For if activity "were the real nature of the soul there would be no release from "it, just as fire cannot lose its heat;[113] but without release "from activity the attainment of the goal of man is impossible,

---

[113] The contradiction with the last sentence of p. 1130 (translated above p. 113) is resolved by the soul being spoken of there in an exoteric sense but here in an esoteric.

"for activity is naturally painful (*kartṛitvasya duḥkha-*"*rûpatvât*)."

"But cannot the goal of man be attained if one avoids the "effects by shunning the occasion of activity even when the "power of activity continues; just as with fire the effect of "burning does not follow if wood is withdrawn, though the "fire still possesses the power of burning?—By no means! "For it is impossible to avoid the occasions altogether because "they too are connected potentially[114] [with the soul]."

"But cannot liberation be attained by employing the means "(*sâdhanam*) necessary to it?—No! Because what depends on "means, is not eternal."

"Moreover the consummation of liberation is said to follow "from the teaching as to the eternal, pure, wise and free soul "[identical with Brahman]; but the teaching that the soul is "of this nature is not possible if activity is its proper nature."

"Therefore the activity of the soul depends only on the "qualities of the *Upâdhis* being ascribed to it (*upâdhi-dharma-*"*adhyâsena*) and not on its own nature."

"And so the Scripture teaches when it says (Bṛih. 4, 3, 7, "above p. 189): 'it is as though it reflected, as though it "'moved unsteadily' and in the passage (Kâṭh. 3, 4):

> "Bound up with Manas, senses, and the body,
> "The sages call it 'the enjoying one.'"

"where it asserts that the soul passes into the specific state "of enjoyment [and activity] only by the connection with the "*Upâdhis*. For in the opinion of competent persons there is "no agent and enjoyer different from the highest soul and "termed 'individual soul' (*Jîva*), because the Scripture says: "'besides him there is no other seer,' etc. (Bṛih. 3, 7, 23, trans-"lated above p. 149, cf. above pp. 133, 191)."

"But if besides the highest soul there is no individual soul "endowed with intelligence, which exists after the withdrawal "of the aggregate of Buddhi, etc., it follows that the highest

---

[114] p. 673, 9: *nimittânâm api çakti-lakshaṇena sambandhena sambaddhânâm atyanta-parihâra-asambhavât*; cf. note 65, above p. 113; the passage to which it refers must probably be understood in this sense.

"soul is itself a wanderer, agent, and enjoyer?—O no! For "enjoyment and activity are based on Ignorance. For so "teaches the Scripture (Bṛih. 4, 5, 15, translated above p. 175): "'For where a duplicity exists as it were, one sees the other;' "and after it has shown in these words that activity and en- "joyment exist for Ignorance, it denies the existence of the "activity and enjoyment for knowledge, continuing: 'but where "'all has become for a man as his own self, how should he "'see anyone?'—In the same way the Scripture shows (Bṛih. "4, 3, 19, translated above p. 190), how the soul in the states "of dreaming and waking in consequence of the contact (*sam-* "*parka*) with the *Upâdhis* grows weary like a hawk soaring "in the air, but in deep sleep on the other hand, where it is "embraced by the Self of knowledge there is no weariness: 'this "'indeed is that nature of his, in which his desire is satiated, "'in which he is himself his desire, without desire and free "'from sorrow;' and further (above p. 191) summarizing: 'this "'is his highest goal, this is his highest happiness, this is his "'highest world, this is his highest bliss.'—This is just what "the teacher [Bâdarâyaṇa in the Sûtram in question] says: "'*and as a carpenter in both ways*' where 'and' has the same "meaning as 'but' [a remark which possibly hints at fun- "damental differences between Bâdarâyaṇa and Çaṅkara]. *I.e.*, "we must not believe that activity is in the proper nature of "the soul, like heat in that of fire. On the contrary, as in "life a carpenter busies himself with the axe and other tools "in his hand, and feels pain, but afterwards goes home, lays "aside the axe and other tools and in his natural state "rejoicing and at ease feels pleasure, so too the soul, as long "as it is affected by the duality founded on Ignorance, is "busied in the states of dreaming and waking and feels pain; "but when it enters into itself, to throw off weariness, into the "highest self, it is freed from the complex of the organs of "work [the body], is not an agent and feels pleasure in the "state of deep sleep; it is the same in the state of liberation "where it is pure soul (*kevala*), reposes and is happy after "the gloom of Ignorance is driven away by the torch of know- "ledge. The simile of the carpenter is to be taken as follows:

"the carpenter is, in respect of various kinds of work such as "fitting, etc. with regard to certain tools such as his axe, etc., "an agent, but a non-agent so far as his body goes; so too "the soul in its exertions with regard to the organs, *Manas*, "etc. is an agent, but a non-agent in its own self. The soul "as opposed to the carpenter has not like him limbs with "which it could take up the organs, *Manas*, etc. or lay them "aside, as the carpenter with his hands takes up and lays "aside his tools [for all these organs belong to the *Upâdhis* "which are attributed to the soul only by Ignorance]."

Then follows a refutation of the arguments brought forward in the preceding section, so far as they maintain an activity of the soul dependent not on the *Upâdhis* but on its own nature (p. 673, 1). We go through these briefly in order, according to the numbers above on p. 316.

1. Certainly the Canon of Scripture presupposes an activity; it is not part of its real nature however but one which is founded on Ignorance (p. 676, 13).

2. If the soul is still an agent in the dream-state, this depends on its being in this state not yet [as in deep sleep] wholly free from the *Upâdhis*, in so far as the sense-organs are at rest in the dream-state while the *Manas* remains active. as the Smṛiti (Mahâbhâratam 12, 9897) says:

> "When senses rest, and understanding wakes,
> "And plays its part, this state is called a dream."

it is further to be noticed that action in dreams is a matter of appearance only (*vâsanâ*) and not real in the full sense (p. 678, 1).

3. When it is said that the soul by means of intelligence absorbs intelligence in itself, no activity of the soul delivered from its organs is to be recognised but only a phrase like "the king fights by means of his soldiers" where it is meant that only the soldiers fight (p. 678, 9). Further in the passage in question what is spoken of is only an entering into rest, not an activity properly so called.

4. In the passage Taitt. 2, 5 by "intelligence" not the soul but the Buddhi is to be understood, as is further proved pp. 679, 3—680, 1 from the context.—Çañkara does not here

return to the controversy as to the freedom of the soul in perception and action.

5. "There is in no sense a change of functions on the part "of the Buddhi if we ascribe activity to the organs; for all "organs are in respect of their functions necessarily agents; "but the activity of these organs demands in addition apper-"ception (*upalabdhi*) and this belongs to the soul; but activity "is not thereby ascribed to it; for its essence is eternal apper-"ception (*nitya-upalabdhi-svarûpatvât*). It is true self-conscious-"ness (*ahañkâra*) precedes activity, but it is not antecedent to "apperception, for it is itself apperceived." [Only the individual, active and enjoying soul is on the one hand *ahankartar* and *pratyayin*, on the other hand *aham-pratyaya-vishaya*, p. 73, 5; the *upâdhi*-less soul is neither the one nor the other but in its state of freedom is opposed to them as *sâkshin* or pure *upalabdhi*; cf. note 30, above p. 54].

6. Finally as to meditation (*samâdhi*), it certainly assumes an activity of the soul but only in the same sense as the other prescriptions of the canon discussed under no. 1, of which it is a part (p. 680, 8).

4. Freedom of the Will and Determinism.

Sûtras 2, 3, 41—42.

That the soul is metaphysically speaking identical with God and therefore like him "eternal, pure, wise, and free" we have already seen repeatedly. But how is it with the soul so far as it is an empirical being connected with the *Upâdhis*? Is it free or unfree in this state which is conditioned by Ignorance but has nevertheless existed from eternity?—This question in our system takes the following form (p. 680, 12): "Is the activity of the soul, which, from the standpoint of "Ignorance, is conditioned by the Upâdhis, dependent on God "(*îçvara*) or not?"

It is a fundamental principle of the original Brahman doctrine that everything existing, and therefore the soul also, is absolutely dependent on God; from this follows that He is on the one hand the necessary cause of the fate and sufferings of the soul, and on the other hand of its actions, whatever they are. The philosophical elaboration of the doctrine of the Vedânta has violated this principle in both directions by referring both the action and sufferings of man to a cause inherent in himself. It is true both are none the less dependent on God; but only in the same sense that the growth of plants depends on rain, which causes the seed to develop, but exercises no influence on its nature. We have already seen that the seed of the sufferings and destinies of this life is to be found in the works of the previous existence, which demand to be atoned for (above p. 279); and so too are the works of each existence necessarily determined by the works of the former existence—how this is possible is, as in the case of all moral questions, not plainly developed. According to p. 1131 (translated above p. 113) works are the product of the *nimittas* or motives and of the *çakti*, power, *i.e.*, character; and this consists generally speaking in the natural disposition (destructible only by perfect knowledge) to activity and enjoyment; however as it produces works that differ individually, character must be imagined as specially modified in the case of each individual. We must think of an innate character of this sort, conditioned by the works of the previous existence, when the soul, in what follows, is described as "connected with defects like love and hate" (*râga-dvesha-âdi-dosha-prayuktaḥ* p. 681, 3); and when as the seed from which works grow appears the "effort of the soul directed towards good and evil" (*kritaḥ prayatno jîvasya, dharma-adharma-lakshaṇaḥ*), which seems to be summed up just in that innate disposition of character.

One might think, says Çañkara, that we have no ground for assuming an influence of God on human action (p. 681, 2) so far as the soul alone, connected as it is with such defects as love and hate and equipped with the apparatus of the organs, suffices for activity (p. 681, 3); for it, like the ox at the plough, needs no further cause to move it to action (p. 681, 5). The actions of beings proceed only from their sense of justice and injustice; if the actions are referred to God, there happens *akṛita-abhyâgamaḥ* (p. 681, 11; cf. p. 798, 12) "the occurrence "of something that has not been incurred [by the actions of the previous life],"—an expression applicable to the motivation of suffering but not of actions, which seems to show that our thinker had not made clear to himself the difference between the two.

In reply to these objections Çankara (in the passage translated above p. 86) explains that the soul involved in Ignorance is dependent on God in respect of its action and sufferings (*kartṛitvam* and *bhoktṛitvam*) because by his permission (*anujñâ*) Saṃsâra results, and by his grace (*anugraha*) liberation (p. 682, 5). For even if the soul is connected with defects like love, etc., and equipped with the apparatus, yet in all activity God is the active cause, for thus says the Scripture (Kaush. 3, 8, above p. 179): "for he alone causes him to do good works, whom "he will raise out of these worlds, and he alone causes him to "do evil works, whom he will make to descend."—

(p. 683, 2:) "God causes the soul to act, but in so doing "he has regard to the efforts made by it towards good or "evil; hence the objections raised do not hold good. The good "and evil done by the soul is unequal; having regard to this "God divides the corresponding fruits unequally, for he like "the rain is only the efficient cause (*nimittam*). For as in "life the common cause of different bushes and shrubs, of rice, "barley, etc. that spring each from their own seed, which is "not common to all, is the rain, because without rain their "differences in respect of sap, blossom, fruit, leaf, etc. could "not develop any more than they could without the special "seed of each sort—so God, having regard to the efforts made "by the souls, apportions good and evil (*çubha-açubham*) among "them.—But can this regard to the efforts made by the "souls exist together with the dependence of all activity on "God?—Certainly! For though the activity depends on God, "it is only the soul that acts (*karoti*), while God causes it to "act (*kârayati*) when it acts; and as He now in causing it to "act pays regard to former efforts, so too He in causing it "to act formerly had regard to still earlier efforts; for Saṃ-"sâra is without beginning."

XXVII. The Organs of the Soul.

1. Preliminary Survey.

REGARDED from the standpoint of knowledge the soul is Brahman Himself and completely identical (*ananya*) with Him. The plurality of souls is illusory; each one of us is the whole, undivided Brahman; as such each is infinite, omnipresent, all-pervading, eternal and changeless, omnipotent and omniscient; without differences and without organs, neither agent nor enjoyer, neither sinning nor suffering, in his essence pure intelligence (*caitanyam*), an organless, objectless, painless, pure cognition. As such the soul is in us merely an onlooker (*sâkshin*) who in all cognition, present as its innermost nucleus looks on idly at worldly action and at its illusions without being in the least mixed up in it: *sa, yat tatra kiñcit paçyati, an-anvâgatas tena bhavati; asaṅgo hi ayam purushaḥ* (Bṛih. 4, 3, 16).

This is not so from the standpoint of Ignorance. For just as a man whose eyes are affected sees two moons where there is in reality only one—or as the sun is reflected in the water in a thousand images, each of which is not a part but the whole of the sun, though in truth a mere phantom without real existence, so the Ignorant sees instead of one Brahman without a second (which is his own Self) a plurality consisting of 1) a God (*îçvara*) whose office is that of dispensing retribution, 2) a world which is the scene of this retribution, and 3) a given number of souls subject to the limitations of individuality; they wander from eternity and in each new existence suffer retribution for the works of the previous life; for this purpose after each death a new body, corresponding exactly to the merits and faults of the previous life, arises out of the seed of the body with which the soul is inseparably connected; and this happens again and again without cessation during all eternity.—It is true these souls are in reality neither individual nor wandering; each one of them is on the contrary the *Âtman* (besides which nothing else exists), *i.e.*, the omniscient and omnipotent *Brahman* itself in his completeness. But the soul does not know that this is so, because it has not the proper knowledge of its own Self, in that its own nature is hidden from it. What prevents this self-knowledge, in which the soul is at once the perceiving subject and perceived object, is *Avidyâ*; Avidyâ puts itself between the soul as subject and the soul as object; and is sometimes characterised subjectively as defective intellectual force, sometimes objectively as defective perceptibility. The soul is from the subjective point of view compared to a blind man (above p. 87), whose lost sight can only be restored by the remedy of grace; objectively it is the *Upâdhis* by which the divine nature of the soul is disguised and as it were rendered latent like fire which slumbers hidden in the wood:

(p. 787, 9:) "The omniscience and omnipotence of the soul "is hidden *by its connection with the body*, *i.e.*, by the con-"nection with body, senses, Manas, Buddhi, external objects "and sensation. On this subject we have this simile: just as "fire has as properties burning and illuminating; but the heat "and light are hidden when the fire has entered into wood or "is covered with ashes, in the same way through the connection "of the soul with the *Upâdhis* such as body etc. which are "created of Ignorance and formed of name and shape, arises "the error of not distinguishing ourself from them [the Upâdhis] "and this produces the concealment of the omniscience and "omnipotence of the soul."

These Upâdhis which condition the individualisation of the soul, are, taking these all in all, the following:

I) The coarse body (*deha*, *sthûla-çarîram*) consisting of the elements; the soul casts it off at death.

II) Among what accompanies the soul on its migration we distinguish:

A) a changing part: *viz.* moral determination (*karma-âçraya*) which accompanies the soul into each life as a new moment, not previously (*apûrvam*) existent, and

B) an unchanging part with which the soul was invested from eternity and remains invested until liberation; this includes:

1) the subtle body (*sûkshma-çarîram, bhûta-âçraya*) consisting of the "subtle portions of the elements which compose the seed of the body" (*deha-vîjâni-bhûta-sûkshmâṇi*);

2) the life-organs, termed *Prâṇas* (in the more extended sense), *i.e.* vital breaths, spirits. These fall into two classes, the first includes the principles of the conscious, the second those of the unconscious life.

a) The system of the conscious life is formed by

α) five organs of sense (*buddhi-indriyâṇi*): sight, hearing, smell, taste, touch;

β) five organs of action (*karma-indriyâṇi*), including the functions of speech, of the hands, the feet, the organs of generation and evacuation;

γ) the *Manas*, the central organ of conscious life, directing the organs of perception and action.

b) The system of the unconscious life consists of the *Prâṇa* in the limited sense, more properly termed *Mukhya prâṇa, i.e.*, chief breath of life. This again is divided into five single Prâṇas, *viz.*, *prâṇa* (in the strictest sense), *apâna, vyâna, udâna* and *samâna*, on which depend the functions of respiration and nutrition as well as the act of dying.

We shall deal with the subtle body (*bhûta-âçraya*) and moral determination (*karma-âçraya*) when we consider transmigration; here we have more especially to consider according to the section 2, 4, 1—19 the psychic apparatus, consisting of the systems of the conscious and unconscious life, which the soul (like a snail with its horns) puts out during life and at death withdraws into itself; the special enquiry is preceded by the question as to the origin and nature of the *Prâṇas*, *i.e.*, of the whole psychic organism.

2. Origin and Nature of the Organs of Life (*prâṇa*).

By organs of life (*Prâṇas* in the more extended sense) are to be understood in the present case: the five organs of action, the five senses, the *Manas* and the *Mukhya Prâṇa* with its five branches.

Though this apparatus appears in strict and (except in liberation) inseparable connection with the soul, it does not belong to it all the same but to another non-spiritual part of nature. In the drama of world-development it does not belong to the player but the scenery; it is therefore in a similar position to the elements (earth, water, fire, air, ether) and appears in close connection with them; and if the metaphor is carried further one might say: the elements form the scenery (stage and wings) and the organs of life the costumes which the actors put on. For the rest, the idea of the Prâṇas is not clearly worked out; on the one hand they are the inseparable companions of the soul on its wanderings and therefore parcelled out individuals, on the other hand, as in what follows, they appear as a complex mass from which the soul draws its organs as it takes its body from the corresponding mass of the elements.

The question as to the nature and origin of the Prâṇas is twice treated, 2, 3, 15 and 2, 4, 1—4 without our arriving at settled ideas in the matter; in the first passage (as we saw above chap. XVII, 3 p. 236) Çaṅkara is undecided whether the Prâṇas are to be regarded as of the same nature as, or as different from the elements; in the former case, he thinks, they must have originated (in the creation at the beginning of each *Kalpa*) at the same time as the elements, in the latter before and after them; at any rate it is certain, he says, that they, like the elements, have arisen from Brahman.—The verbose treatment which he deals out to our question in the others passage, 2, 4, 1—4, does not bring us much further, for the essential content of his explanation is limited to the following: the question is whether the Prâṇas had an origin or not (p. 701, 6), for passages can be cited in support of both assumptions (p. 701, 7. 702, 1); one may not however therefore take the origin of the Prâṇas in a figurative (*gauṇa*) sense (p. 702, 7); on the contrary they are sprung from Brahman just as much as the rest of the world (p. 703, 11), for the Scripture teaches this expressly (p. 704, 7). If on the other hand the Scripture (Çatapathabr. 6, 1, 1, 1) makes them exist before the origin [of the world], they are for all that not absolutely primordial in their nature (*mûla-prakṛiti*) but only relatively so (*avântara-prakṛiti*) *viz.* with respect to what has originated in its turn from them (p. 706, 6). Whether their origin from the elements as taught Chând. 6, 6, 5 (above p. 263) is to be taken literally or figuratively (p. 708, 5), it follows in any case from it that they like all else have arisen from Brahman (p. 708, 9).

But this is in no way a satisfactory settlement of the question. For the Prâṇas exist, like the subtle body which carries them, as long as Saṃsâra endures (p. 1096, 11), and they accompany the soul inseparably even if it should enter a plant (p. 1096. 14), in which case Manas and Indriyas naturally cannot unfold themselves; now Saṃsâra exists, as we have seen many times already, from eternity; therefore the soul must have been equipped with the psychic organism of the Prâṇas from eternity too. Our author is everywhere only concerned to reconcile this eternal existence of the individual soul and its psychic apparatus with the entering into and origin from Brahman, taught by the Scripture of all that exists; this he does by making the soul continue in Brahman in the form of seed (*vîja-âtmanâ*) or potentially (*çakti-âtmanâ*) which makes its destruction and origin merely apparent;—but these Vedic apologetics have far less interest for us than the question as to the relation between the eyes and ears, hands and feet, etc., which wander forth with the soul and exist for ever, and the material parts of the body which bear these names and originate and perish with the body.—Çañkara gives a hint to guide us in solving the question when he, as we shall see, declares repeatedly that the function (*vritti*), not the organ wanders forth with the soul; that therefore even when the organs of sight, hearing, moving and grasping perish at death, the capability (we might say the will) to see, hear, move and grasp, etc. persists with the soul (cf. the passage from Chând. above p. 185 ff.). We find no further information, but a solution of the question in conformity with the system is not lacking. In this matter we must regard as fundamental the view that the body is related to the psychic complex as the developed plant to its seed. Since everything originates only from its seed, the wandering soul must necessarily, besides the Prâṇas, take with it the seed of the gross body in the form of the "subtle body" which we shall examine more closely in the section on transmigration. As the material body is the bearer of the material sense-organs, so this subtle body is the bearer (*âçraya*) of the psychic organs. They must like the body be conceived as germs which, on entering into material existence, by drawing homogeneous corpuscules from the whole mass of Prâṇa-materials, develop into material organs, just as the seed of the subtle body absorbs the materials of the elements and ripens into the gross body.

3. The System of the conscious Life: Organs of Relation.

In accordance with the anatomical theory which makes the brain, as the central organ of conscious life, branch out on the one hand as sensory nerves into the organs of sense and on the other hand as motor nerves into the muscles of voluntary movement, we find the Indians conceive the existence of a central function, *Manas,* and two systems dependent on it; *viz.* the five organs of perception (*buddhi-indriyas*) and the five organs of action (*karma-indriyas*). In these eleven organs according to Çankara the whole complex of conscious life is included.—How many Prâṇas, he asks (p. 709, 1), must we assume if we leave out of account the *Mukhya Prâṇa* (the principle of unconscious life)? Their number is variously stated and passages may be cited which make them seven, eight, nine, ten, eleven, twelve and thirteen in number (p. 709, 3—9). The right number is however eleven.

For there are in the first place five classes of perception (*buddhi-bheda*), according as their object is sound, the object touched, form, taste or smell [as to the order cf. note 97, above p. 237]; to these correspond the five organs of perception (p. 711, 7). There are further five classes of action (*karma-bheda*), speaking, grasping, going, evacuating, and procreating; these purposes are served by the five organs of action (p. 711, 9).

These external organs [which are limited to the present] have as correlative the inner organ (*antaḥkaraṇam*) or *Manas* (the two expressions are for Çañkara completely interchangeable cf. 711, 4. 21, 4. 666, 5) which extends (p. 711, 10) to past, present and future (p. 723, 9); "by division of the functions some "distinguish *Manas, Buddhi, Ahaṃkâra, Cittam*" (p. 711, 11); —"this inner organ which serves the soul as Upâdhi is here "and there variously termed *Manas, Buddhi, Vijnânam, Cittam*; "others even distinguish separate functions and term the "faculty of reflection (*saṃçaya*, p. 340, 6 *vikalpa*) *Manas*, that "of decision (*niçcaya*, p. 340, 7 *adhyavasâya*) *Buddhi*" (p. 666. 7). Çañkara mentions these different views without refuting them but also without making use of them; for him there is only one inner organ, the *Manas*; and even the *Buddhi* is for him not a distinct faculty but sometimes the activity of perception, sometimes the mind in general (though it occasionally in connection with Kâṭh. 3, 3 appears coordinate with the *Manas*. p. 638, 11; cf. 263, 8. 389, 2. 265, 6. 787, 10. 1056, 1).—So too *Ahaṃkâra* is in our system not a distinct organ but means in the first place "the word I" (p. 157, 5), then as a synonym of *Ahaṃpratyaya* "the idea of the Ego" "self-consciousness" (pp. 672, 1. 2. 680, 5. 6) whose object (*ahaṃpratyaya-vishaya*) is the individual soul (pp. 73, 5. 78, 6. 672, 1, while on the other hand p. 15, 2 *asmat-pratyaya-vishaya* refers to the highest soul); as subject of presentation of the Ego sometimes the individual soul (*ahaṃkartar* p. 73, 5) is mentioned, sometimes the *Manas* (*ahampratyayin* p. 21, 5); the highest soul on the other hand is not subject of the *Ahaṃkâra*, for that involves activity; on the contrary, like all else, the *Ahaṃkâra* (with its perceiving subject and perceived object) is for the Upâdhi-less Soul simply an object of perception (p. 680, 6). Cf. above p. 321.

As we have already seen (above p. 314) the necessity of the assumption of the *Manas* is deduced by Çañkara from the fact that while the soul is essentially an eternal cognition, there is no reason discoverable in the organs of sense for their different behaviour at different times; from this would result that we [in a waking state which alone comes in question here] should either not perceive at all or should perceive continuously, unless there were between the soul and the organs of sense the *Manas*, "by whose attention (*avadhânam*) and "non-attention apperception (*upalabdhi*) and non-apperception "[of the soul] results" (p. 667, 6).

As the central organ of the organs of perception and action *Manas* is on the one hand what we term understanding, on the other hand conscious volition. The ideas on these objects are not however further developed. Çañkara contents himself instead (p. 667, 7, cf. p. 21, 4) with a reference to the unsystematic information in Bṛih. 1, 5, 3: "My mind "was elsewhere (*anyatra-manas*), I did not see, my mind was "elsewhere, I did not hear, so we say; for only with the mind "does one see, only with the mind does one hear;[115] *kâma*, "*saṃkalpa*, *vicikitsâ*, *çraddhâ*, *açraddhâ*, *dhṛiti*, *adhṛiti*, *hrî*, "*dhî*, *bhî*,—all these are *Manas*; therefore when we are touched "from behind, we recognise the fact by the *Manas*."—The faculties mentioned are explained by Çañkara on Bṛih. *loc. cit.* as follows: "*kâma*, desire, the longing for sexual enjoyment, etc.; "*saṃkalpa*, decision, the determination of the character of a "presented object by differences such as white, black, etc.; "*vicikitsâ*, doubt; *çraddhâ*, belief, the perception of the existence "of invisible objects, *e.g.* the gods, by their effects; *açraddhâ*, "disbelief, the contrary; *dhṛiti*, steadiness, keeping oneself up-

---

[115] Cf. Epicharmos in Plut. Mor. p. 961 A:

Νοῦς ὁρῇ καὶ νοῦς ἀκούει, τἆλλα κωφὰ καὶ τυφλά.

"right when the body is tired; *adhṛiti,* the opposite; *hrî,* "shame; *dhî,* cognition; *bhî,* fear."

The *Prâṇas* mentioned (*Manas, Buddhi-indriyas,* and *Karma-indriyas*) are minute (*aṇu*) which means that they are 1) subtle (*sûkshma*), 2) limited (*paricchinna*), but not that they are of atomic size (*paramâṇu-tulya*), "because in this case the per-"vading of the whole body would be impossible."[116] Their subtlety is deducible from the fact that otherwise (if they were *sthûla,* coarse, material) they would necessarily be seen at the time of death, when the soul passes from the body, by the bystanders, just as a snake is seen which glides from its hole (p. 715, 6); and they must be limited and not (like the soul free from *Upâdhis*) infinitely great, because for the infinitely great no passing, going and return would be possible (p. 715, 7). "If you maintain that the infinitely great can by reason of "its function (*vṛitti*) be at a given spot in the body, we must "remark that the organs [of the soul] are altogether mere "functions; for the function or whatever it is, that brings about "perception we call an organ; the dispute is therefore only "about names and the assumption of omnipresence a purpose-"less one" [the Prâṇas enter into the question only in respect of what they are in the body, even if we call them here organs or functions, and assume as their bearers infinitely great organs]. Therefore the Prâṇas are to be regarded as the functions or faculties of seeing, hearing, feeling, grasping, going, etc. which, as they cleave to the soul, are not annihilated at death with the corresponding parts of the body but produce them again and again from themselves as seed produces plants.

---

116 p. 715, 4; above (p. 310 ff.) on the other hand the possibility of action throughout the body is disputed, not for the soul of atomic size, but for the minute soul (which in the state of Saṃsâra has the same size as the Buddhi, *i.e.,* the Manas). If we disregard this and ask what in the strict logic of our system is the nature of the reciprocal action of the minute soul, "large as the point of an awl," and the body, we have as answer that it is doubtless brought about by the *Prâṇas* which stand in the middle between soul and body; the nature of this connection however *e.g.* of the function or faculty of sight with Manas and soul on the one hand, and with the Ego on the other, is not cleared up.

4. The System of the unconscious Life: Organs of Nutrition.

The principle of the unconscious, vegetative life is the *Mukhya Prâṇa*, an expression which originally meant "Breath in the mouth" (thus Chând. 1, 2, 7 where Bṛih. in the parallel passage 1, 3, 7 reads *âsanyaḥ prâṇaḥ*; cf. Bṛih. 1, 3, 8); in our system however where respiration is only a part of its task it has taken the meaning of "chief breath of life." Its primacy over the other organs of life is a favourite theme of the Upanishads; *e.g.*, in the parable of the contest of the organs (Bṛih. 6, 1. Chând. 5, 1; cf. Kaush. 3, 3. Praçna-Up. 2) according to which the organs: speech, eye, ear, Manas, etc. go forth in order, and, when it is the turn of the (*Mukhya*) Prâṇa, become conscious of its indispensability and their own dependence on it. A variation of the same theme is the story of the quarrel of the gods (*i. e.*, the organs: smell, eye, ear, Manas, and Mukhya Prâṇa) with the demons, who visit evil on the other organs, but fly to dust on the Prâṇa like clods of earth on a stone (Bṛih. 1, 3. Chând. 1, 2).

With many references to these stories Çaṅkara sets forth (2, 4, 8—13) that though the *Mukhya Prâṇa* is also a creation of Brahman, it is still the oldest and noblest among all organs. It is true, he says, the *Nâsad-âsîya* song says (Ṛigv. X, 129, 2):

> "Death was not known nor immortality,
> "Night was not born, and day was not yet seen,
> "Airless, he breathed in primevality
> "The one beyond whom nought hath ever been;"

but that which "breathed" is not the Prâṇa in this case; on the contrary as the words "without air" proves, it is the highest cause (p. 716). Therefore the Prâṇa too [in the same sense as the other organs, *i. e.*, from its seed which has from eternity been connected with the soul] has originated, but is the oldest among the organs because its function begins from the moment the sperm is introduced, if it actually germinates in the Yoni (p. 717, 3), while the activity of the others is only possible after the auditory passage etc. have originated (p. 717, 5); so too the Prâṇa is the best, because the other organs in the parable of the quarrel of the organs confess to him: "of a "truth without thee we cannot live" (p. 717, 7).

What is then the constitution of this Prâṇa? It is in the first place not air alone, though one passage of Scripture (p. 717, 10) seems to assert this; for it is, Chând. 3, 18, 4, expressly distinguished from air (*Vâyu*); it seems rather to be a psychic analogue of the (cosmic) divinity of the air (*vâyur eva, adhyâtmam âpannaḥ*, p. 719, 8). Further, it is also not to be regarded simply as a combined function of the organs (*Manas* and *Indriyas*) as the *Tantrântarîyas* (p. 717, 12, *i.e.*, the *Sâṅkhyas*) maintain when they say:

"The working of the organs when combined
"Are the five airs with Prâṇa at their head;"[117]

for if it were no more than this it would not be specially mentioned Muṇḍ. 2, 1, 3 in addition to *Manas* and *Indriyas*. But could it not be the result of the united action of these eleven organs, which produce the life of the body in something the same way as eleven birds shut up in a cage raise it in the air, when they fly upwards?[118] To this is to be replied, that the organs cannot possibly produce the phenomenon of life, because it is absolutely heterogeneous from hearing, etc. (p. 719, 4). It is rather included in the primacy of the Prâṇa as taught by the Scripture, that the other organs are subordinated to it as qualities (*guṇa*) [p. 719, 6. 12; without prejudice to their original essential difference from it; of this below].

But the Prâṇa cannot therefore, like the individual soul, be termed the sovereign of the body (p. 719, 12); for even if it alone remains awake, while the organs sleep (Bṛih. 4, 3, 12, above p. 190) and does not fall into the grip of death (weariness)

---

[117] This verse, cited by Çankara (p. 718, 2) is found in the *Sâṅkhya-Kârikâ* v. 29 and in the *Sâṅkhya-sûtras* 2, 31, where it has manifestly been taken over from the *Kârikâ* as the artificial metrical form (it is a complete *Âryâ*-half-verse) sufficiently proves. Further examples in Hall, Sâṅkhya-Sâra, p. 12.

[118] p. 718, 13; this image too seems to belong to the *Sâṅkhyas*, at any rate it is found in a distorted form in *Gauḍapâda* on *Sâṅkhya-Kâr.* 29, ed. Wilson p. 26, 5.

like them (Bṛih. 1, 5, 21), even if it is called the "absorber" because in sleep it absorbs them into itself (Chând. 4, 3, 3, above p. 61) and guards them as a mother guards her children (Praçna 2, 13) still it is only the prime minister of the soul, just as eye, ear, etc. are its servants (p. 720, 7). For the rest, it is on the same level as the organs (p. 720, 9), is like them an aggregate [*saṃhata*, *i. e.*, produced from its seed by the depositing of corpuscules from the Prâṇa-material] and non-spiritual (p. 720, 11); it has not, however, as they have, an object (p. 721, 1) and cannot be reckoned with them as a twelfth organ; it rather supports, nourishes, and animates the whole body, as is further proved on p. 722 from the parable of the contest of the organs.—With this agrees the fact that the Mukhya Prâṇa is termed p. 161, 9 *prajñâ-sâdhana-prâṇa-antara-âçraya* "the support of the other Prâṇas which sub-"serve the purpose of perception" and that as its task *samî-raṇam* is mentioned p. 471, 2, and *parispanda* pp. 378, 6. 380, 12. 732, 6. 1090, 10, both of which seem to mean stimulation, animation.

As animating and supporting principle of life the *Mukhya Prâṇa* has five branches: *Prâṇa, Apâna, Vyâna, Udâna*, and *Samâna*, which are frequently enumerated (*e. g.*, Bṛih. 1, 5, 3. 3, 9, 26. Chând. 3, 13. 5, 18. Praçna 3; the three first only: Bṛih. 3, 1, 10. 5, 14, 3. Chând. 1, 3, 8; four: Bṛih. 3, 4, 1) and are sometimes very differently explained. According to Çañkara (p. 723, 1—4) *Prâṇa* is exhaling (*ucchvâsa*), *Apâna* inhaling (*niçvâsa*); *Vyâna* is a sort of combination of both, *viz.* what supports life when the breath is held for a great effort [119]

[119] This explanation of Çañkara of *Prâṇa, Apâna, Vyâna* rests on Chând. 1, 3, 3—5 and agrees with Çañkara's Commentary on this passage in which he expressly defines *Prâṇa* as exhaling (*vâyuṃ vahir niḥsâra-yati*), and *Apâna* as inhaling (*antar âkarshati vâyum*). On the other hand contradicting himself he explains *Apâna* in the Commentary on Chând. 3, 13, 3 and again on Praçna 3, 5 as *mûtra-purîsha-âdi-apanayan*, *i. e.* Secretion. The former view agrees with his explanation of Bṛih. 3, 2, 2, that smell is associated with *Apâna*; the latter, as it seems, with his Commentary on Bṛih. 3, 9, 26 as well as with the theory of the Vedântasâra § 95.—A reconciliation is perhaps attainable from the fact

[in Indian medicine *Vyâna* is the principle of the circulation of the juices and the blood, cf. the St. Petersb. Dict. *s. v.* as well as Praçna 3, 6]; *Samâna* is the principle of digestion; and finally *Udâna* is the faculty which at death brings about the passing of the soul from the body.—We see therefore that the Indians are not so far from our triple division of the regulative system into respiration, circulation, and digestion.

Quantitatively the *Mukhya Prâṇa* is of minute size (*aṇu*); here too this means, not that it is of atomic size; for by means of its five functions it pervades the whole body (p. 724, 3); but that it is 1) not coarse, for it is not perceived at the passing of the soul (p. 724, 4), and 2) not infinitely great, for otherwise passing, going, and return would not be possible (p. 724, 5); and when (Bṛih. 1, 3, 22) it is termed "as large as "a termite, as a midge, as an elephant, as these three worlds, "as this universe" this is to be understood in a cosmological sense of Hiraṇyagarbha (a mythological personification of Brahman, cf. note 41) and not in the psychological sense; for in this sense his dimensions are, as the words "as large as a termite" show, limited according to the size of each individual being (p. 724, 10; from the expression: the *prâṇa* is *pratiprâṇivartin* may be concluded that with its five branches it completely fills the body it happens to be in).

5. Mutual Relation of the Systems of the conscious and unconscious Life.

Sûtras 2, 4, 17—19.

There is a doubt whether the remaining *Prâṇas* (the *Manas* and the ten *Indriyas*) are mere functions of the *Mukhya Prâṇa* or are separate entities (p. 729, 3). The former opinion might be maintained, because we read (Bṛih. 1, 5, 21) "they all became part of its nature" and because they too bear the name *Prâṇa* (p. 729, 5). But this is not so; they are separate entities, as follows from their having the special name *Indriyam*;

---

that inhaling is of importance for the promotion of the movement of the contents of the intestines.

it is true the Çruti (Muṇḍ. 2, 1, 3) mentions the *Manas* as well as the *Indriyas*, but the Smṛiti (Manu 2, 89) enumerates eleven *Indriyas*, and includes the Manas among them, which is never done with the Prâṇa (p. 730). The difference is also exhibited in the fact that in the quarrel of the gods and demons (Bṛih. 1, 3. Chând. 1, 2) all except the Prâṇa are overcome (p. 730, 12).

The difference of the two consists in the following: 1) even if all others sleep, Prâṇa remains awake; 2) all except it are subject to death, Bṛih. 1, 5, 21, by which here weariness is to be understood (p. 732, 2); 3) the *Prâṇa*, not the Indriyas, conditions by its remaining the continuance, and by its removal the destruction of the body; 4) the activity of all *Indriyas* is directed to objects [they are organs of relation] but not that of the *Prâṇa*; 5) that "they became part of its nature" (Bṛih. 1, 5, 21) means that the *Indriyas* are dependent on the *Prâṇa*, so far as it brings about their stimulation (*parispanda*); and for this reason also bear its name (*prâṇa*) in a metaphorical sense (p. 731, 8—732, 11).

6. The Cooperation of the Gods.

Sûtras 2, 4, 14—16.

The general tendency of the Indians to draw parallels between cosmic and psychic potencies is also displayed in the relation in which the single organs of life are brought to the corresponding elements conceived as gods. Thus in Bṛih. 1, 3, 11 after the Prâṇa in the fight with the demons has warded off evil and death from the organs, the latter are "led beyond death;" speech becomes fire and illuminates, breath becomes wind and purifies, the eye becomes the sun and burns, the ear becomes the poles, and the Manas the moon and shines.— On the other hand Ait. 1, 2, 4 says of the gods who arose from the primitive man and, desiring a fixed abode, enter into human beings: "Fire entered as speech into the mouth, wind "as breath into the nose, the sun as sight into the eye, the "cardinal points as hearing into the ear, herbs and trees as "hair into the skin, the moon as Manas into the heart, death "as Apâna into the navel, and water as seed into the organs "of generation."—In agreement with this according to Bṛih. 3, 2, 13 at the death of man speech becomes fire, breath wind, the eye becomes the sun, the Manas the moon, the ear the cardinal points, the body the earth, the soul ether [in the heart], the hair on the body becomes herbs, the hair of the head trees, and blood and seed turn to water.

On these passages is based the Vedânta theory of the directorship (*adhishṭhâtṛitvam*) of the gods over the organs. The organs of life, so Çañkara sets forth p. 725—726 on the basis of the texts cited, can only act, so far as they are guided by the corresponding gods; of their own force they cannot do it though they are equipped with the strength requisite for their action (p. 726, 14); just as a waggon though it is strong (*çakta*) needs the oxen to move it (p. 727, 1). This last comparison points to the fact that the organs surrounding the soul are conceived as a mechanism in itself lifeless, which needs in addition a special principle of motion. The soul cannot be employed as such, because it is not an agent and only becomes an agent (*kartar*) through the Upâdhis (*i.e.*, the organs); therefore the activity of the organs is referred partly to the "inner ruler" (above p. 149), *i.e.*, the exoteric Brahman; and partly as here to the gods who are in other respects superannuated. Still their rôle is a purely subsidiary one; they do not share in enjoyment and suffering; this is wholly reserved for the individual soul affected by good and evil, pleasure and pain (p. 728, 3). At death the gods withdraw their assistance; this is all that is meant by the above mentioned return of speech into the fire, etc. (p. 745, 8); nevertheless the organs themselves, the *Prâṇa* as well as the *Manas* and *Indriyas* withdraw with the soul and accompany it on its wanderings (p. 728, 7).

7. Retrospect.

After the Indians had early attained the knowledge that the key to the enigma of the world is to be sought nowhere else than in the Self (*Âtman*), they asked themselves further which part of our Ego is to be regarded as the clearest expression of the thing-in-itself—unconscious life which in waking and sleeping goes tireless on its way, or conscious life in whose preponderance consists the advantage of man over other beings?—As it seems to us, both these paths were taken; in earlier times principally the first by the identification of the *Prâṇa* (breath, life) with *Brahman* and the corresponding theory of an entrance into Brahman in deep sleep (where according to Çatapathabr. 10, 3, 3, 6 all organs are absorbed into the life); later there was manifested an inclination to the Âtman rather in the subject of cognition within us, and to characterise it therefore as *drashṭar* (Bṛih. 3, 7, 23. 3. 8, 11), *prajñâ-âtman* (Kaush. 3), *prâjña âtman* (Bṛih. 4, 3, 21. 35), *prajñâna-ghana* (Bṛih. 4, 5, 13) etc., and to regard the entrance into Brahman in deep sleep rather as an unconscious because objectless Cognition (Bṛih. 4, 3, 23) or even as a fancifully elaborated ascent to the highest light (Chând. 8, 12, 3); Chând. 7 would there be a polemic of the younger school against the older and Kaush. 3 an attempt to reconcile the two; until finally the extreme intellectualism of the system of the Vedânta was reached, for which Brahman is pure intelligence (*caitanyam*), while the *Prâṇa* in the shape of the *Mukhya Prâṇa* sinks to a mere *Upâdhi* of the soul.

This view which can for the present only be presented as a hypothesis, would among other things explain the singular position of the *Mukhya Prâṇa* in the system, which on the one hand gives it the primacy over all other Upâdhis, and on the other hand connects the soul not so much with it as with the *Manas* (dependent on the Mukhya Prâṇa). For while the *Mukhya Prâṇa*, suiting itself to the size of the body whatever it is (above p. 336) pervades all parts of the body with its five branches, the soul in the state of Saṃsâra is "the nucleus "(quintessence) of the qualities of the Buddhi" (above p. 311), *i. e.*, of the *Manas*; it is like the Manas "large as the point of an awl" and dwells with it in the heart in quasi-identity; from there the *Manas* sends out the *Indriyas* as its feelers (organs of perception) and performers of its commands (organs of action) throughout the body. In deep sleep, as we shall see, the *Indriyas* creep into the veins, and these enter into the *Mukhya Prâṇa*, and, like the *Manas*, attain repose in it, while the soul, united with Brahman, sojourns in the ether of the heart. This liberation of the soul from the Upâdhis (*upâdhi-upaçama*) is conditioned by the cessation of the activity of the *Indriyas* and the *Manas*, but not of the *Mukhya Prâṇa*, whose activity continues in sleep as it does in the waking state; this makes clear how loose the connection between it and the soul is; its repose is not necessary for the repose of the soul, and its activity is without influence on the state of the soul. It appears rather as the antipodes of the soul in the life of the organism, as the gathering-place of the *Upâdhis* and therefore as the central point of all that individualises the soul and obscures its original divinity. True the *Mukhya Prâṇa* is not, like the *Manas* and *Indriyas*, servant of the soul but its prime minister (*mantrin* p. 720, 7); it is however a minister with whom the sovereign is not on the best of terms; the weal of the land is committed to his care, but his Highness prefers to reside in the castle of a favourite (the *Manas*) whom he prefers, but who is subject to the minister;—this is a position which may be reached in the course of political evolution, but it is certainly nowhere the original state of things.

The matter is somewhat different with regard to death; here, as we shall see, the *Indriyas* first of all enter into the *Manas*, and then in succession the *Manas* into the *Mukhya Prâṇa* [in which it already is, spatially considered], the *Mukhya Prâṇa* into the *Jîva* (individual soul), and therefore into the heart; finally the *Jîva* enters into the "subtle parts of the "elements which form the seed of the body," *i.e.*, into the subtle body, which is their bearer during the migration.

As this subtle body is related to the coarse body, so are the organs which pass out with it related to the material organs which perish with the body; they are their continuations *vîja-âtmanâ* or *çakti-âtmanâ* as seed or power; *i.e.*, while eye and ear, hand and foot perish at death, their function (*vṛitti*), the power of seeing, hearing, going, grasping, etc. connected with the soul, wanders out with it (in a latent state) and serves for a new incarnation as the seed from which the material organs proceed just as the coarse body arises from the subtle body. [A combination of the material of the subtle body from the three original elements, and of the material of the coarse body from their triply or quintuply mixed derivatives is not yet discoverable in Çaṅkara's commentary].

According to this the interaction of body and soul must be conceived as follows: the *Indriyas* are simply the powers or functions of the *Karaṇas, i.e.*, of the material organs; these they produce out of themselves and remain in the closest and most intimate connection with them; these *Indriyas* have their common centre in the *Manas*; the *Manas* is homogeneous with them and itself an *Indriyam*; it dwells, large as the point of an awl, in the heart; in the *Manas*, filling it completely and (except by liberation and temporarily in deep sleep) inseparably connected with it, is the Soul, which, by the mediation of the *Manas* and *Indriyas*, governs the movements of the *Karaṇas* and receives their impressions; while the *Mukhya Prâṇa* with its five branches pervades the whole body and provides for its nutrition on behalf of the soul; it is subject to the soul, but, leaving death out of the question, a connection between the two is not discoverable.

XXVIII. Special States of the Soul.

There are three states of the individual soul which sojourns in the body: they are: Waking, dream-sleep, and deep sleep (p. 799, 14), and these three are also to be understood when the highest soul is spoken of as "changeless onlooker "at the three changing states" (as *e.g.* 432, 12, above p. 276). A fourth state is dying consisting in a passing out of the body (p. 799, 15); we have further swooning, which is however not to be reckoned as a fifth state because it is only an occasional and exceptional phenomenon, which is in the sphere of the healing art (p. 802, 13).

We shall now consider these three states on the basis of the material afforded by the appendix 3, 2, 1—10 supplementary to the Psychology, prefixing a brief definition of them from p. 107, 12 ff.: "the soul is awake, when, in consequence of its "connection with the various *Upâdhis* [the ten *Indriyas*] which "proceed from the *Manas*, it apprehends sensuous objects and "examines their differences;—when, modified by the impress-"ions[120] of these, it sees dream-pictures, it is [occasionally, "*viz.* Chând. 6, 8, 2, above p. 263) described by the word *Manas* "[in the dream-state the senses repose, while the *Manas* remains "active, above p. 320]; in the state of deep sleep in which the "two kinds of *Upâdhis* [*Indriyas* and *Manas*, or, as Govinda "maintains: the coarse and fine] are in repose, and the differ-"ences conditioned by the *Upâdhis* cease to exist, the soul is "as it were dissolved (*pralîna*) in its own self and therefore

[120] The dream-pictures have as cause the impressions (*vâsanâ*) of the waking state; cf. p. 788, 11: *jâgarita-prabhava-vâsanâ-nimittatvât tu svapnasya*; p. 270, 8: *tad-vâsanâ-nimittâñç ca svapnân nâḍî-caro 'nubhûya.*

"it is said: it has entered into itself (Chând. 6, 8, 1, above "p. 263)."

1. Dream-Sleep.

Sûtras 3, 2, 1—6.

In the principal passage, Bṛih. 4, 3 (a knowledge of which from Chap. XII, 4, above p. 189 we shall in what follows assume in the reader) it is said: "there are no chariots, no "teams, no roads, but he creates for himself chariots, teams, "and roads." The question is (p. 778, 7) whether a real creation is here to be understood or one depending on illusion (*mâyâ*).

The first view might be taken, for it is said: "he creates;" and further: "for he is the creator" (p. 779, 6). Moreover another passage (Kâṭh. 5, 8) says of dream-sleep:

"The spirit that in the sleeper never tires
"And gives the form he will to his desires,
"He is the Brahman, he the stainless one,
"Immortal is his name.
"And all the spheres
"Repose in him; beyond him there is none."

It might be imagined that by wishes here as before (Kâṭh. 1, 23—24) real objects are to be understood, and that by the creating spirit (Kâṭh. 2, 14) the world-creating highest Soul (*prâjña*) is meant (p. 780, l. 5), so that the dream-creation is to be conceived as real just as much as the actual creation (p. 780, 10).

To this is to be replied: the dream-creation is a mere illusion, and not a reality (p. 780, 17) because it is not consistent with time, space, and causality and is refuted by them (p. 781, 3). 1) Not with space: for there is no room for chariots, etc. in the limited confines of the body (p. 781, 5). It might be imagined that the soul leaves the body in sleep because it is said (Bṛih. *loc. cit.*) "it soars from the nest and "hovers where it will" and because in dreaming, going and standing still are only possible on this supposition (p. 781, 6). But that is not so; for it is not possible to pass over the space of a hundred miles in a moment; besides a man who goes to sleep in the country of the *Kurus* and reaches in his dream the country of the *Pañcâlas*, ought to be able to wake up there too; but in reality he always wakes in the country of the *Kurus* (p. 781, 10, 14). Moreover objects in foreign countries are in reality not at all the same as they were in the dream (p. 782, 1). The above mentioned passage is therefore to be taken figuratively, and the going and standing still in dreams are an illusion (p. 782, 5. 7). The dream is just as unreconcilable with 2) the conditions of **time**; for one sleeps at night and believes it to be day, and often a dream that lasts an hour seems like a number of years (p. 782, 8); and the dream is in conflict 3) with **causality**; for one grasps chariots without hands, sees them without eyes, builds them without wood; besides their existence is refuted by the awakening (cf. above p. 247), and not by this alone but also by the course of the dream itself, for the chariot suddenly turns into a man, and a man into a tree (p. 782, 11).

True the dream is not completely illusory, for it is prophetic of good or ill luck. For thus says the Scripture (Chând. 5, 2, 9):

> "For him who dreams of happiness in love,
> "Good fortune when he wakes is near at hand;"

while (according to Ait. âr. 3, 2, 4, 17) a black man with black teeth indicates a speedy death (p. 783, 7). Again those skilled in dream-books (*svapna-adhyâya* p. 783, 10) explain the dream, when they for example teach that riding on an elephant is a foretoken of riches, and on a donkey of poverty. Here what is presaged is true, but what presages, the dream namely, is not true (p. 783, 14; cf. above p. 270).—Besides it is the purpose of dream-pictures to excite joy and fear, and that as a result of the good and evil that one has done (p. 784, 7).

Therefore the passage as to the creation of the chariot is to be understood figuratively (p. 784, 2) and serves to elucidate how far the spirit is its own light (p. 784, 9). The individual soul is in the first place to be regarded as the creator of dream-pictures (p. 785, 3); and if the context of the *Kâṭhaka*-passage we have cited indicates the highest soul, this depends on the two being properly speaking identical (p. 785, 6) in the sense of the words *tat tvam asi* [it would have been more appropriate to recall the words *etad vai tat* which we find not far from these cited]. God directs all things and therefore dreams too; but the dream-creation is not a real one in the same sense that nature is. "Further the creation of nature "is not an absolute reality (*âtyantikam satyatvam*); for on the "basis of the words of scripture referring to its depending on "words (above p. 262) we have proved its identity with Brah-"man (chap. XX), as well as that the whole extension of the "world is a mere illusion (*mâyâ*);[121] its difference from the "illusion of a dream consists only in the continuance of the "extension of the world until the soul is recognised as Brah-"man, while the extension of the dream is refuted daily" (p. 785, 10).

"But are not God and the soul related as fire and sparks; "and does not the soul therefore of necessity share in God's "omniscience and omnipotence, as sparks have their share of "light and heat; and cannot it therefore at will (*samkalpa*) "create in a dream?"

—Reply: the homogeneity of the soul and God is a fact, but is concealed by Ignorance, and only becomes manifest to him whose eyes are opened by the grace of God.

"But how does it come about that this homogeneity is "hidden from us?"

—It is, like fire under the ashes, hidden in consequence of the connection with the *Upâdhis*, to wit the body etc. which are produced by the world of names and forms dependent on Ignorance.

"But if the soul does not possess the omniscience and "omnipotence of God, it is essentially heterogeneous from "Him, and does not need to become so by the connection "with the body?"

---

121 The theory of the extension of the world as *mâyâ*, the occurrence of which in *Çañkara* is doubted hy Colebrooke, and in *Bâdarâyaṇa* by Cowell (Colebrooke, M. E.², p. 400) is quite clearly expressed in *Çvetâçvatara*-Up. 4, 9—10 which is accepted by both of them; from Çañkara's Commentary the following passages are applicable: pp. 120, 16. 269, 2. 342, 12. 406, 6. 432, 8—13. 472, 9. 484, 11. 785, 12; cf. above pp. 100, 187. 228, 254, 276, 277, 299.

—By the connection with the body it comes about, that the soul's (own) omniscience and omnipotence are concealed from it, and that is why it cannot create at will in a dream. If it could do so, no one would have an unpleasant dream, for no one creates what is not pleasing to himself (pp. 786 to 788).

2. Deep Sleep.

Sûtras 3, 2, 7—9.

In deep, *i.e.* dreamless sleep, the soul becomes temporarily one with Brahman. In course of time this doctrine, which, in our opinion, only expressed the extinction of conscious in unconscious life, that is perceived in sleep by simple observation, assumed an essentially different meaning. According as the soul came to be regarded as an essentially intellectual potency a separation of it from the *Mukhya Prâṇa* as principle of the unconscious life and a closer connection with the organs of conscious life, *viz. Manas* and *Indriyas,* became necessary. In deep sleep this connection is temporarily dissolved in such a way that *Manas* and *Indriyas* enter into the *Prâṇa,* and the soul on the other hand is submerged in the Brahman who sojourns in the ether of the heart. Çañkara's statements on this point are concerned with special questions and rest on assumptions which are nowhere clearly developed; we must therefore by putting things together attempt to lay down what these were.

In the w a k i n g s t a t e the soul, connected with the Manas, has its seat in the heart and from here by means of the *Indriyas* exercises its influence throughout the body.—In d r e a m - s l e e p the functions of the *Indriyas* are extinguished, for (Praçna 4. 2) they are absorbed into the Manas; and the soul surrounded by the still active *Manas* and the reposing *Indriyas* (above p. 320) passes through the whole body, as a prince surrounded by his vassals makes a progress through his kingdom. This view based on Bṛih. 2, 1, 18 seems to hover before Çañkara's mind when he says p. 270, 8, the soul enjoys the dream-pictures which are dependent on waking impressions *nâḍîcara,* "as it passes through the veins."—In deep sleep, as is said in the same passage (p. 270, 9), the two illusions of waking and dreaming are destroyed, and the soul, freed from all *Upâdhis* enters into Brahman in the ether of the heart. What becomes of *Manas* and *Indriyas* in this case? According to Chând. 4, 3, 3 the *Prâṇa* absorbs them and this view is adopted by Çañkara p. 720, 1. On the other hand it is said in the statement to be given below, the *Upâdhis* (*i.e.,* here *Manas* and *Indriyas*) sojourned in deep sleep in "the pericardium (*purîtat*) or the veins," which, 72 000 in number (according to Bṛih. 2, 1, 19) starting from the heart surround the *Purîtat* and thence (Çañkara on Bṛih. p. 367, 8) pass to all parts of the body, 101 of them subserving the withdrawal of the dying soul from the body. This information leads us to believe that the veins were taken to be the main seat of the *Mukhya Prâṇa*; with this agrees the statement that the *Vyâna* acts in them (Praçna 3, 6) and that the *Udâna* leads the soul from the body at death by the 101 principal veins.

After these preliminary remarks we turn to the statements of Çañkara, which we shall give in some detail on account of certain special difficulties.

On the question of the state of the soul in deep sleep (*sushuptam, supti, sushupti*), as we read in the Commentary on 3, 2, 7, the scripture seems to contradict itself; for there are passages according to which the soul in deep sleep "has crept into the veins" (Chând. 8, 6, 3), "lies in the pericardium" (Bṛih. 2, 1, 19), "has attained unity in the Prâṇa" (Kaush. 4, 19), "sojourns in the ether of the heart" (Bṛih. 4, 4, 22), "has entered into the Existent" (Chând. 6, 8, 1), "is embraced by the Self of knowledge" (Bṛih. 4, 3, 21).—One might think that different places are to be here understood, because they all subserve the same end and therefore cannot be dependent on each other (p. 789, 12). That is also the reason why they are mostly in the locative, and where this is not the case, as in the passage about "the Existent" (p. 790, 3) the locative meaning is made certain by the connection and context (p. 790, 8). As the essence of deep sleep consists in the suspension of individual cognition (*viçesha-vijñâna-upaçama*), and all the spots mentioned subserve this purpose, it seems that the soul in deep sleep can enter one or the other at choice (p. 790, 10).—To this is to be replied: not at choice (*vikalpena*) into one or the other, but at the same time (*samuccayena*) into all the places mentioned does the soul enter in deep sleep (p. 791, 1), because otherwise we should have a partial denial (*pakshe bâdhaḥ*) of the evidence of scripture. From the uniformity of case it does not follow that all (each for itself) fulfil the same purpose; they may fulfil different ends which require to be combined (p. 791, 7) and as a man can be at home and in bed at the same time, the soul too can be simultaneously in the veins, the pericardium, and the Brahman (p. 791, 8). Where (as in Chând. 8, 6, 3) the veins alone are mentioned, without excluding Brahman who dwells, as we know, in another spot [in the ether of the heart], an entrance into Brahman by means of the veins (*nâḍî-dvârena*) is to be understood (p. 791, 16); this is not in contradiction with the locative; for he who by means of the Ganges (*Gañgayâ*) journeys to the ocean, has journeyed on the Ganges (*Gañgâyâm*) (p. 792, 1). Moreover the passage in question is concerned with another matter, *viz.* the way through the veins and sunbeams into the Brahman-world [in heaven]; and in treating of this it is, to exalt the veins, mentioned that no evil touches him who has entered by them [into the heart], and that because, as Chând. 6. 8. 3 says, "he has thus become one with heat" (p. 792, 5). By heat (*tejas*) is here to be understood either the juice (*pittam*) in the veins that surrounds the organs of cognition (p. 792, 6) or Brahman; for (p. 792, 11) that it cannot be touched by evil agrees with the facts of the Brahman-world [in the heart, cf. above p. 164) while the complex of veins issues (*anugata*) in Brahman, as the place of deep sleep. So too the pericardium is in close relationship (*anuguṇa* p. 793, 4) with the place of deep sleep. For the envelope of the heart is termed pericardium, *purîtat*; what is in the heart is also in the *purîtat*, just as what is in a town is surrounded by the walls of the town (p. 793, 8). Of the three places of deep sleep, veins, pericardium and Brahman, the two first are therefore only to be regarded as entrances (p. 793, 13). "The "veins too, or the *Purîtat* are only the receptacle of the *Upâdhis* "of the soul; in them its organs sojourn [probably only the "*Indriyas*, and if a removal from its natural position be "assumed, the *Manas*]. For apart from the connection with "the *Upâdhis*, the soul in itself (*svatas*) needs no receptacle "but in its non-difference from Brahman reposes in its own "majesty" (Chând. 7, 24, 1), and thus identity (*tâdâtmyam*), not a relation of receptacle and contents, exists, between it and Brahman (p. 794, 2); "true the entrance of the soul into Brah-"man is never unrealised; it cannot give up its own nature; "but in dream and waking by virtue of its mingling with the "*Upâdhis* it is as though the soul had passed into a different "nature; therefore the release from the *Upâdhis* in deep sleep "is regarded as an entrance of the soul into its own nature" (p. 794, 7). The aim of deep sleep, the suspension of individual cognition, would not be attained by a mere entrance into veins and *Purîtat*, for (p. 794, 14) they involve plurality (*bheda-vishaya*); and "where a plurality as it were exists, one sees "the other," as the scripture (Bṛih. 4, 5, 15) says. True suspension of cognition can be effected by the great distance of the objects but only where the subject is limited, which is not the case with the soul, if the *Upâdhis* are left out of account (p. 795, 2); if however a removal of the *Upâdhis* is meant it is just this release from them of which we are speaking (p. 795, 5). We do not maintain either that veins, pericardium and Brahman are to be regarded as possessed of equal rights; for the two first do not come in question at all (p. 795, 8); the important thing is that Brahman is unchangeably the place of deep sleep, and that the Brahmanhood of the soul is adhered to, and a release in deep sleep from the activity of the waking and dream states (p. 795, 12).

Just as deep sleep is an entrance into Brahman, so awaking out of it is a withdrawal from him (p. 795, 15).

But, how is it possible, if deep sleep is a complete union with Brahman, that each soul on awaking finds its way back to its individuality? If a drop of water is poured into a body of water and a drop taken from it again, it can hardly be assumed that you get the same drop again![122] Just so, as it seems, must we assume that after its union with God in deep sleep the same soul cannot return to its individuality; that on the contrary it is another soul or even God himself who awakes in its place (p. 796, 8—797, 1).

But this is not so, as Çankara shows p. 797, 2ff.; he who awakes can neither be another soul nor God but must be the same who went to sleep and that for the following reasons which the words of the Sûtram also set forth:

1) *On account of works*; it cannot be assumed that a [religious] work begun in the evening and completed in the morning is divided between two different souls; and that *atiprasañgât* "because too much would follow from it;" to wit that then to every one could be apportioned the works of another and be imputed to him at the retribution.

2) *On account of remembrance*; for one remembers when one wakes: "I saw this and this yesterday" and "I am so and so." This continuity of the consciousness of external objects and the Self proves that the same soul awakes as went to sleep.

3) *On account of the text of scripture*; "then it hurries "back according to the entrance, according to the place, into "the waking state" (Bṛih. 4, 3, 34);—"all these creatures go day "by day into the Brahman-world and yet do not discover it" (Chând. 8, 3, 2);—"therefore of a truth, dear one, when all these

[122] The question raised above is explicable from the view that the soul as such is a completely indifferent principle, *i. e.* like God himself (chap. XIV, 3) *nirviçesha* without any difference, and that therefore all its individuality is to be sought in its empirical existential form. But wherein is this individuality to be found?—Not in the *Upâdhis* for they are only a mechanical apparatus, in themselves dead, which are alike an attribute of all. Therefore if the individual character can neither be found in the soul as such, nor in its *Upâdhis*, it must be discoverable in some tertium quid, and this is moral determination, which we here characterise by three expressions from Bṛih. 4, 4, 2: *vidyâ, karman, pûrvaprajñâ* (or as we preferred to say above p. 193 *apûrvaprajñâ*), knowledge, works, and previous (or newly acquired) experience. We return later (p. 374ff.) to this question; here we had to anticipate it to make what follows intelligible.

"creatures proceed out of the Existent again, do they not "know that they proceed out of the Existent again; whether "they are tigers here, or lions, or wolves, or boars, or worms, "or birds, or midges, or gnats, whatever they may be, that "they become again" (Chând. 6, 10, 2).

4) On account of the precepts as to knowledge and works, which in the absence of personal identity would become invalid; for otherwise deep sleep would mean complete liberation, and what would become then of the works that still remain and have to be atoned for, and of the (lower) knowledge? So too in the case of the other in whose person the soul would have to wake, the continuity of his actions would be destroyed. How can one even assume that any one goes to sleep in the person of A and wakes up in the person of B?— Finally the really liberated might also awake again in that case [for nothing distinguishes him from the others] and liberation would not be definitive. But this is, after Ignorance has once been destroyed, impossible; and from this it follows that God (*îçvara*), for whom Ignorance is eternally annihilated, cannot awake in the place of the soul.—That is; for the reason that otherwise man would suffer for what he has not committed, and not atone for what he has committed (p. 798, 12), it is impossible to assume that a different person from him who went to sleep wakes up. The comparison with the drop, which cannot be recovered from the body of water, does not agree with the facts; for the distinguishing cause is wanting in this case, but in the case of the soul it is present, namely in the shape of works and knowledge [in which therefore consists the individuality of the individual]. Moreover things which are hard to distinguish for such as we are, are still distinguishable; thus the goose (*haṅsa*, for a domestic animal must be meant here) is able to distinguish water and milk when they are mixed (p. 799, 3). "There does not exist an individual "soul different from Brahman, distinguishable from the Existent "like a drop of water from a body of water; but the Existent "itself is, in consequence of the connection with the *Upâdhis*, "termed individual soul in a metaphorical sense, as we have "often set forth; and therefore the matter stands thus: the "action of a given individual soul extends so far as the connection with a given *Upâdhi*[-complex] exists, and where "another *Upâdhi* is present, we have the action of another "individual soul; but one and the same *Upâdhi* is in deep "sleep and the waking state in the position of the seed and "the plant; therefore it is the same soul which wakes up "again."

—If in the course of these discussions it appears occasionally as if the exoteric theory could not be maintained throughout in the doctrine of deep sleep, the last remark shows that it is not so. The union with Brahman in deep sleep and death and at the destruction of the world is in every case merely a p p a r e n t, for the individualities continue to exist potentially and arise again from their seed unchanged; and this is at the bottom synonymous with a real continued existence of the soul.

3. Swooning.

Sûtram 3, 2, 10.

Besides the states of waking, dreaming, deep sleep, and death there is a special state, which is different from all, an intermediate condition between several of them, namely swooning (p. 799, 12). It is in the first place not the waking state; for in it the senses no longer perceive the objects. True the arrow maker perceives nothing beyond his work when he is buried in it; but he has all the same consciousness and control over his body, both of which are absent in the fainting person (p. 800, 7. 11). Further swooning is not dream-sleep on account of the accompanying unconsciousness, and not death because it is distinguished from it by bodily warmth and breath. That is why people look for warmth in the region of the heart, and breath in the nostrils to find out whether anyone is dead or only fainting; if both are absent people say he is dead and fetch wood to burn the body; if on the other hand warmth and breath are still present, he is cared for in order to restore him to consciousness (p. 800, 13). By his coming to himself again we see that he was not dead: for from *Yama*'s realm no return is possible [though *Naciketas* in the Kâṭhaka-Upanishad, like *Er*, the Armenian, in Plato Rep. 10, 13 p. 614 B, gains information as to the Beyond by sojourning in the kingdom of the dead]. Finally swooning is not deep sleep either; for while fainting is characterised by interrupted breathing, trembling of the body, a frightful expression on his face, and widely opened eyes, a person in deep sleep has a peaceful expression; he draws his breath regularly, and has his eyes closed, and his body does not tremble; moreover he is waked by merely stroking him with the hand, while not even blows with a hammer can rouse a fainting person. [Perhaps from observations during torture]. The causes of the two phenomena are different also; in the one case the blows of a club and the like produce it, in the other simple weariness (p. 801, 10). Therefore swooning is half deep sleep, not in the sense that it is a half union with Brahman, but in so far as it is intermediate between deep sleep and death. It is a gate of death (p. 802, 9): "if there remain works [that still have to be atoned "for] speech and consciousness return; if nothing remains "breath and warmth depart."

4. Metaphysical Significance of Death.

This last assertion is of importance because it shows how the strict predestination that governs life also controls its termination. The whole empirical reality is, as we know, nothing more than *kriyâ-kâraka-phalam* "the requital of works on the doer," and the whole bodily existence is *kârya-karaṇa-sanghâta* "a complex of the organs of work" intended to produce that requital in the form of action and suffering. True the possibility is not excluded, that the works of a single existence have to be atoned for in several succeeding existences (cf. p. 1129, 11 translated above p. 112); and in souls born as plants such an assumption is unavoidable; for the rest however the view is that life both in quality and quantity is in respect of the works of the previous existence an atonement exactly measured and completely fulfilling its aim. The atonement is brought about by *bhoktritvam* and *kartritvam* (the states of enjoyer and agent); the latter condition has as its unavoidable result works which have to be atoned for again in a following existence, so that the clockwork of atonement in running down always winds itself up again; and this goes on for ever,—unless perfect knowledge is gained which, as will be seen, does not depend on merit; it makes its appearance independently to dissolve the existence in its innermost essence, to consume the seed of works and thus for all time make a continuation of transmigration impossible. On the other hand, knowledge cannot put an end to the present existence because this is conditioned by the works of an earlier birth, whose seed has already germinated and cannot therefore be consumed but demands its full retribution. So long as a balance of works remains from a previous existence, death cannot occur; if they are however exhausted, life must go out, like a lamp when the oil is burnt up,—and lead the Ignorant on fancifully elaborated ways to a retribution in the Beyond, and then back to new forms of existence; while the sages who possess the higher knowledge are immediately swallowed up in identity with Brahman, and those who possess the lower knowledge indirectly by the Devayâna or way of the Gods.

It only remains for us to examine the Eschatology of our system, to follow the soul on its wanderings after death and to consider the two possible ways of its entrance into Brahman.

THE FOURTH PART OF THE VEDÂNTA SYSTEM:

SAṂSÂRA

OR

THE DOCTRINE OF THE TRANSMIGRATION OF THE SOUL.

XXIX. The Eschatology of the Vedânta.

1. The main Phases of Indian Eschatology.

In general we can distinguish three stages of development in the views of the Indians as to the condition of the Soul after death.

1. The oldest view, that which prevails in the hymns of the Ṛigveda, knows as yet of no transmigration of the soul. The souls of the good pass after death into Yama's heaven of light where they lead a blissful life in the company of the Fathers (*pitaraḥ*);[123] the wicked are shut out from it and pass (according to a less definite and perhaps already secondary view) into the "nether darkness."[124] A return either of the former or of the latter to a new earth-life does not occur.

2. According to the doctrine of transmigration in the Upanishads, as we shall become more closely acquainted with it in the next chapter, there are three Paths. The Wise, after death, will be carried ever higher and higher upon the *Devayâna* (sc. *panthâ*) that is the "Path of the Gods," on-

---

[123] Ṛigv. 10, 14, 10: *athâ pitṛînt suvidatrân upehi,*
Yamena ye sadhamâdaṃ madanti.
compare St. Matthew's Gospel viii, 11: πολλοὶ ἀπὸ ἀνατολῶν καὶ δυσμῶν ἥξουσι καὶ ἀνακλιθήσονται μετὰ Ἀβραὰμ καὶ Ἰσαὰκ καὶ Ἰακὼβ ἐν τῇ βασιλείᾳ τῶν οὐρανῶν.—26, 29: οὐ μὴ πίω ἀπάρτι ἐκ τούτου τοῦ γενήματος τῆς ἀμπέλου, ἕως τῆς ἡμέρας ἐκείνης, ὅταν αὐτὸ πίνω μεθ' ὑμῶν καινὸν ἐν τῇ βασιλείᾳ τοῦ πατρός μου.

[124] Ṛigv. 10, 152, 4: *yo asmân abhidâsati, adharaṃ gamayâ tamaḥ.*
Atharvav. 9, 2, 4: *nudasva Kâma, praṇudasva Kâma;*
avartiṃ (the downward way) *yantu, mama ye sapatnâḥ;*
teshâṃ nuttânâm adhamâ tamâṃsi
Agne vâstûni [anu-]nirdaha tvam!

wards into Brahman, whence there is no return. The doers of works go upwards by the *Pitṛiyâna*, the "Path of the Fathers," into the luminous realm on the moon, enjoy there the fruit of their works and then descend once more into a new incarnation, differing according to the moral character of the previous life. Finally, those who possess neither knowledge nor works come to the "third place," that is, they are reborn as lower animals or [Kâṭh. 5, 7] plants, without having tasted bliss on the moon.

3. According to the esoteric Vedânta doctrine, which already finds expression in the Upanishads, the soul is identical with Brahman and the entire existence of the manifold world is an illusion. For him who sees through this illusion, there is neither a migration of the soul nor an entering into Brahman, but "Brahman is he, and into Brahman he is resolved," as is said in Bṛih. 4, 4, 6 (translated above p. 194); compare with this, as also with what follows, the section of Çañkara's Commentary, p. 1132—1133, translated under the title of "Esoteric Eschatology" above p. 114 ff.

2. Exoteric and Esoteric Eschatology.

Our system is a combination of all the three views just stated. It retains, from the first stage of development, the doctrine of reward and punishment in the Beyond and unites this with the second theory in such a way as to assume a double retribution for the good and the evil: the one after death in the Beyond, the other through a descent to new incarnation following thereon and through the particular form of that incarnation. Opposed to the transmigration of the *Pitṛiyâna* is the liberation of the *Devayâna*; but both, the Path of the Fathers and the Path of the Gods, are valid only in the exoteric, lower knowledge. Only for him, to whom this whole world still appears as real, can the two Paths into the Beyond be real too: the *Pitṛiyâna,* which leads back again to earth-life, and the *Devayâna*, which, as reward for the lower exoteric knowledge and the accompanying worship (*upâsanâ*) of the lower (*aparam, saguṇam*) Brahman, leads the soul to him. In contradiction with the chief passage in the Upanishads on transmigration, the system regards this liberation attained through the *Devayâna* as being not yet complete. It becomes so only when those, who through the lower knowledge have entered into the *saguṇam brahma*, there obtain perfect knowledge, the *samyagdarçanam*. For only the latter, that is the knowledge of the identity of one's own Soul with Brahman, brings about absolute liberation, or rather is in itself already that liberation: hence, as soon as that knowledge dawns, even here on earth, liberation is accomplished and the persistence of corporeality till death is only an illusion of the senses, which when once true knowledge is attained, can no longer deceive us, even though we are unable to remove its appearance.—Thus a man suffering from a disease of the eyes sees the moon double and cannot prevent himself from doing so; but he knows that there is really only one moon there.

3. No Transmigration from the Esoteric Standpoint.

From what has been said it is clear that, in the Theory of Liberation to which our last part will be devoted, we shall again meet with the twofold doctrine that we have followed out in detail as the lower and higher knowledge in Theology, and as the empirical and metaphysical standpoint in Cosmology and Psychology; while in the present part, on the contrary, which deals with transmigration we shall encounter only the lower, exoteric, not the higher, esoteric doctrine which puts precisely in the place of this pilgrimage of the soul, the knowledge of the soul's identity with Brahman, through which liberation is gained at once, so that from the standpoint of the higher knowledge there can be no question of anything like transmigration. Accordingly the reality of the *Saṃsâra* stands or falls with the empirical reality of the world: as the latter is a mere illusion, so also are the ideas as to the former not so much, as with Plato, εἰκότες μῦθοι, but rather a continuation of that illusion into the domain of transcendent; the question remains open however how far our author's mind, deeply embued as it was with belief in transmigration according to the general views of his people, reached a clear, scientific consciousness of the mythical character of this doctrine of transmigration. It is true that he declares often enough, that neither the world, nor the individual wandering soul in truth exists; but this did not prevent him, as we have seen, from putting forward a detailed theory of world-creation; and with the same earnestness he treats of the doctrine of *Saṃsâra*, according to the Vedic revelation and in close connection with those passages of the Upanishads which treat of transmigration; amongst which we must specially single out the *Pañcâgnividyâ* from Bṛih. 6, 2 and Chând. 5, 3—10; then the *Paryañkavidyâ* in Kaush. 1; together with the *Upakosalavidyâ*, Chând. 4, 10—15 (translated above p. 164 ff.), the *Daharavidyâ*, Chând. 8, 1—6 (above p. 158 ff.); further Kâṭh. 5, 7, Praçna 5 (above p. 198 ff.), and other passages.

These and other passages we shall make use of according to the requirements of our present task; one only among them need be placed before the reader *in extenso*, because not only is it the most extensive monument from Vedic times of the doctrine which more than any other has dominated the entire thought of the Indians, but also because it underlies in general as well as in particular all the explanations of Bâdarâyaṇa and Çañkara in this and our last part: this is the *Pañca-agnividyâ*, that is "the Doctrine of the Five Fires," which is found in Bṛih. 6, 2 and Chând. 5, 3—10 in two recensions, which generally agree verbally, and yet again diverge materially from each other. Moreover, Bṛih. is simpler, more beautiful, more ancient, Chând. smoother, more modern, more detailed towards the end, so that the two stand to each other very much in the same relation as the many parallel passages in the Gospels according to *St. Matthew* and *St. Luke*. The additions in Chând. are such that, as we shall see, a further development of the doctrine is recognizable in them. For this reason and because our Vedânta authors take their stand chiefly on Chând., we shall take that version as our basis and make use of Bṛih. only when the latter is of special interest.

XXX. The Vedic Doctrine of the Five Fires.

Chândogya-Up. 5, 3—10 (Bṛihadâraṇyaka-Up. 6, 2).

1. Introduction.

Çvetaketu, the son of *Âruṇi* (cf. above p. 262), comes to the assembly of the *Pañcâlas*. There king *Pravâhaṇa*, son of *Jîbala*, asks him five questions:

1. "Knowest thou whither the creatures go from hence?"
2. "Knowest thou how they return hither again?"
3. "Knowest thou the parting of the two ways, the Path of the Gods and the Path of the Fathers?"
4. "Knowest thou why that world does not become full?"
5. "Knowest thou how at the fifth offering the waters speak with human voice?"

To all these questions *Çvetaketu* knows no answer. Downcast, he comes to his father and complains that he has been inadequately taught by him. The latter declares that he himself is unable to answer the questions asked. Both then set out and come to the king who grants *Âruṇi* a boon. As this boon *Âruṇi* chooses the solution of the questions asked, and after some resistance the king consents to impart the following instructions to him and says he is the first Brahman who had received them (cf. above p. 18).

2. The Five Sacrificial Offerings.

As in the sacrifice the offerings are thrown into the fire to come forth from it again in a spiritualised form, so too the fire, wherein the corpse is burnt, is a sacrificial fire, through which man passes to come forth out of it again "in a luminous form" (Bṛih.). This conception of the rising from the body as an offering, is also applied by the section under discussion to the descent of the soul into the body from the Beyond: this descent is a passing through five transformations, which are spoken of as five successive sacrificial acts and are described in detail.

The first sacrificial fire, through which man passes, is the other world; its elements (fuel, smoke, flame, coals, sparks) are the sun, its rays, the day, the moon, and the stars. In this fire the Gods offer Faith, and from this offering goes forth King Soma.

The second sacrificial fire, consisting of wind, vapour, thunderbolt, and hail, is Parjanya, that is, here: the storm cloud; in this fire the Gods offer king Soma, and from this offering goes forth Rain.

The third sacrificial fire, consisting of the year (that is time), space, night, and the cardinal points is the Earth (Bṛih.: this world); in this fire the Gods offer rain, and from this offering goes forth Food.

The fourth sacrificial fire, consisting of speech, breath, tongue, eye, ear, is Man; in this fire the Gods offer Food, and from this offering goes forth the Seed.

The fifth sacrificial fire, consisting of the generative organs and functions of woman, is Woman; in this fire the Gods offer the seed, and from this offering goes forth the Embryo.

"Thus it happens that at the fifth offering the waters [one "may understand by this either the subtle body or the "moral character; of this, later] speak with human voice. "Then when this embryo, surrounded by its chorion, has lain "for ten months or however long it may be, in the womb, it "is born. After it is born, it lives as long as may be. Then "when it dies, it is borne away to its destination in the fire. "even thither whence it came, whence it arose."

3. The Path of the God (*devayâna*).

"Those now who know this, and those others who practise "faith and penance (Bṛih.: Truth) in the forest, enter into the "flame, [of the funeral pyre] from the flame into the day, from "the day into the light half of the month, from the light half "of the month into the summer months [literally: into the six "months in which the sun journeys northwards], from the "months into the year, from the year into the sun (Bṛih.: the "world of the Gods), from the sun into the moon, from the "moon into the lightning—there indeed is a man, who is not "as a human being, he leads them to Brahman." (Addition in Bṛih.: "there in the world of Brahman they dwell far, far "away. For such there is no return.")

"This is the Path of the Gods."

4. The Path of the Fathers (*pitṛiyâna*).

"On the other hand, those who [only] practise sacrifices, "pious deeds, and alms-giving in the village (Bṛih.: who "through offerings, alms, and penance gain heaven), these "enter into the smoke [of the funeral pyre], from the smoke "into the night, from the night into the other [dark] half of "the month, from the other half of the month into the six "winter months [literally: the six months, in which the sun "journeys southwards]; these do not reach the year, but pass "from the months into the world of the Fathers, from the "world of the Fathers into the Âkâça, from the Âkâça into "the moon, who is King Soma, therefore he is the sustenance "of the Gods, him the Gods enjoy." (Otherwise Bṛih.: "When "they have attained to the moon, they become food; in that "place, just as one enjoys King Soma with the words: 'swell "'up and shrink,'[125] so also are they enjoyed by the Gods.")

[125] 1. The Soma-plant is placed in water which makes it swell; then it is pressed, which makes it shrink and the Soma-drink trickles out.— 2. To this earthly Soma corresponds as a heavenly Soma the moon, which decreases when the Gods drink it, and then increases again; Ṛigv. 10, 85, 5: *yat tvâ, deva, prapibanti, tata' âpyâyase punaḥ.* 3. The increase and decrease of the moon is however on the other side conditioned by the rising of the dead to the moon, where they enjoy the fruit of their works, and their subsequent re-descent to a new life upon earth.—4. A combination of these ideas gives us the concept, that the dead, in virtue of their works, rise to the moon, where they, that is, their works, are enjoyed by the Gods (according to Atharva-V. 3, 29, 1, the Gods take only $1/_{16}$ of the works as tribute), until they are consumed. The being-enjoyed by the Gods is on the other hand an enjoying of the fruit of

"—After they have dwelt there, so long as any residuum is "left, they return by the way they came, back again into the "Âkâça, from the Âkâça into the wind; after they have be-"come wind, they become smoke, after becoming smoke, vapour, "after becoming vapour, cloud, after becoming cloud, they "descend as rain; these same are born here below as rice "and barley, as herbs and trees, as sesame and beans. Thence "truly it is more difficult to escape; for only the man who "eats him as food, who emits him as seed, only his increase "(descendant) does he become.—(The following down to the "end only in Chând.) Now those whose conduct here was "fair, for them there is the prospect that they will come into "a fair womb, the womb of a Brahman, or a Kshatriya or a "Vaiçya;—those, however, whose conduct here was foul, for "them there is the prospect that they will come into a foul "womb, a dog's womb, a swine's womb, or (even) into the womb "of a Caṇḍâla,"

5. The third Place.

(Chândogya-Up.)

"But upon neither of these "two ways are to be found "those minute, ever-returning "beings, who originate and pass "away, as quickly as one says "it bites. This is the third "place.—

"Therefore that world "grows not full."

(Bṛihadâraṇyaka-Up.)

"But those who know not "these two paths, those are "the worms, birds, and what-"soever bites."

6. Epilogue (only in Chândogya-Up.).

"Therefore should one beware!—On this there is this "verse:

---

works on the part of the dead; just as, when a man enjoys a woman, so the woman on her side enjoys the man (Çaṅk. on Chând. p. 343, 10). The person and his works melt into one another in these fancies; more of this, later.

"The thief of gold and drinker of strong drinks,
"The slayer of a Brahman, and he who defiles his teacher's bed,
"These four perish and fifthly he who goes with them."

"But on the other hand, he who thus knows these five fires, "he verily consorts not with them and is not stained with their "evil, but remains pure and unspotted in the world of the "pure, he who knows this, who knows this."—

7. On the two Recensions of the Doctrine of the Five Fires.

The difference between these two passages cited from Bṛih. and Chând. is, in spite of all verbal agreement, very considerable. Penance (*tapas*) according to Bṛih. does not liberate but according to Chând. it does liberate; further the whole system of the three paths after death is essentially modified and much confused by the additions in Chând.:—their confusion is increased in the Vedânta-sûtras since they go back generally to Chând., but also to Bṛih., so that it is hardly possible to obtain a uniform and consistent view.

The conception in Bṛih. is perfectly clear: the wise by the *Devayâna* enter into liberation, the performers of pious works rise on the *Pitṛiyâṇa* to the moon, and thence descend, as it seems, only into human bodies. Those who possess neither knowledge nor works are shut out from both paths and enter as punishment into the bodies of animals.

It is otherwise in Chând.; here too the Path of the Fathers according to the opening words, is destined for those who have practised pious works. But this determination is quite lost sight of in the addition at the end, which distinguishes, among those who return upon the *Pitṛiyâna*, between those of fair conduct and those of foul conduct and accordingly destines the former to life in one of the three higher castes and the latter either to animal life or to existence in a lower caste. Through this "the third place" properly becomes superfluous and is left to low and short lived animals, which accordingly, as it seems, remain entirely shut out from ascent and descent in the transformation of the soul, quite contrary to the drift of the Vedânta system.—It is a further inconsistency, that Chând. recognises both reward and punishment for those who go by the *Pitṛiyâna* on their return to earth-life, but in the Beyond on the contrary reward only; this inconsistency our system removes by inserting, as contrast to the reward on the moon, the pains of hell in the Beyond also. How it further finds a way through the contradictions of its Vedic sources, we shall see further on.

We turn now to an examination of the single phases of transmigration; and in this we shall give the remaining Vedic texts in their proper places, assuming on the other hand that the main passage translated in the present chapter is always present in the reader's mind.

XXXI. The Passing of the Soul from the Body.

Sûtras 4, 2, 1—11. 17. 3, 1, 1—7.

1. The Vedic Basis.

THE doctrine of the passing of the soul, which is the same for all, except those who possess the *Samyagdarçanam*, (that is, for the ignorant and for the worshippers of Brahman possessed of attributes, who follow the lower knowledge), bases itself partly on the conceptions contained in the previous chapter of the Waters, which speak with human voice in the fifth offering, and of Faith, which the Gods offer in the first sacrificial fire, partly on the following passage from Chând. 6, 8, 6 (translated with the context above p. 264):

"When now, O dear one, man departs hence, speech "enters into Manas, Manas into life, life into heat, "heat into the highest God-head."

2. The Involution of the Organs.

Sûtras 4, 2, 1—5.

1. At death, according to the passage just quoted, speech first of all enters into *Manas* (p. 1087, 6); under speech here the remaining nine *Indriyas* (above p. 329) are included, for another passage says (Praçna 3, 9): "therefore, when his "splendour is extinguished, he passes to rebirth together with "his senses, which have entered into Manas" (p. 1089, 5). Are we now to understand by the senses, for example, speech, the sense itself or only its function (*vṛitti*) (p. 1087, 8)?—This question appears strange, after our author, as we saw above p. 332, has already stated p. 715, 10 that the organs (*karaṇam*)

are only functions (*vṛitti*), as indeed we can understand under the *Indriyas*, which depart hence with the soul, naturally not the material organs, but only functions conceived as independently existent potencies. In this sense it is a matter of course that only the function (*vṛitti*) of the Indriyas enters (*sampadyate*) into Manas, while the bodily organ perishes with the body. The question here raised on the other hand, as is apparent from the way it is answered, must be understood in the sense that by *vṛitti* are not to be understood these functions themselves, but only their activity, and by their *sampatti* not their entering into Manas, but their complete dissolution (*pravilaya* p. 1088, 1, *upaçama* p. 1088, 4). Accordingly we must interpret the question under discussion to be: whether at death the sense organ (the *vṛitti*, according to p. 715, 10) attached to the soul, when it enters (*sampadyate*) into Manas, is, on this entering in, dissolved (*sampadyate*) only in its functional activity (*vṛitti*) or in its very essence? The answer is that only the functional activity, not the Indriyam perishes (*vâg-vṛittir manasi sampadyate* p. 1088, 1), in the first place, because otherwise complete non-separateness (*avibhâga*) would ensue, and the condition of non-separateness, according to 4, 2, 16, belongs only to the liberated and not to others (p. 1088, 5); again, because the perception which shows how the activity of the senses dies out at death, while that of Manas (consciousness) persists for some time longer, only gives us the right to speak of an extinction of the functional activity, not of that of the agent (p. 1088, 10); finally, because a thing, according to its essence, can only enter into that from which it arose, as a pot into clay, but according to its functional activity, it can enter into something else, as for instance the functional activity of fire springs from fuel and is extinguished in water, although both are different from it (p. 1088, 14). If, notwithstanding, the passage says that speech enters into Manas, this depends on usage (*upacâra*), which does not distinguish between the action and the agent (p. 1089, 3).—The ambiguity displayed by the author in the use of these expressions *vṛitti* and *sampadyate* is to us unintelligible.

2. The second act at death, according to Chând. 6, 8, 6, is that *Manas* enters into *Prâṇa* (as the principle of unconscious life, above p. 333 ff.). Here the same question repeats itself. One might think that Manas as an organ enters into Prâṇa, because it is said, in Chând. 6, 6, 5 (above p. 263), that Manas is formed from food, and Prâṇa from water, while again it is said (above p. 235) that food, that is, the earth, arose from water (p. 1090, 4). But here too it seems rather to be the fact that only the function (functional activity) of Manas is to be understood as entering (dissolving into) Prâṇa; for it is only the function of Manas that we can observe coming to rest (p. 1090, 9) in Prâṇa in one who falls asleep and in one desirous of liberation (cf. Kâṭh. 3, 13); and again we cannot conclude from the mediate (*praṇâlika*, found only here as *adj.*) arising of Manas from Prâṇa that the former must re-enter into the latter, since otherwise it would also follow that Manas must dissolve itself in food, food in water, and Prâṇa in water (p. 1090, 13). Here too therefore we must understand by Manas only its functional activity, not the agent, since usage does not distinguish between them (p. 1091, 1).

3. When further it is said in Chând. 6, 8, 6 that Prâṇa merges into heat (*tejas*), we must note that, in the first place, it enters not into heat but *into the overseer* (*adhyaksha*) by which is to be understood "the overseer of the cage of the "body and the organs," that is, the individual soul (*jîva*) (p. 1091, 6); the latter (*jîva*) is defined on this occasion as "self of knowledge endowed with the limitations (*upâdhi*) of "knowledge, works and previous experience" (p. 1091, 9), by which, as we shall show immediately, the moral character is to be understood. With the latter the soul seems to be more closely united than with its organs; for while these must first enter into it, the moral character clings to the soul of itself.— Even though in the successive stages of the entering in the fundamental passage Chând. 6, 8, 6, does not mention the individual soul, yet its insertion between *Prâṇa* and *Tejas* is justified by another scriptural passage (Bṛih. 4, 3, 38, translated above p. 192) in which it is said that at death all the Prâṇas enter into the soul, and that, when the latter

departs, life and with it all the organs of life,[126] depart with it (p. 1091, 12).

4. Only after the Prâṇas have entered into the soul which is accompanied by the moral character, does the soul enter with them into heat, by which here, as will shortly be further shown, are to be understood the other elements also, as well as heat (*tejas*), in that sublimated form, in which they constitute the seed of the body (p. 1092, 2). This absorption of the Prâṇas into the soul, of the soul into heat, does not contradict the words of the fundamental passage, according to which the Prâṇas enter into heat; for if a man goes from *Çrughna* to *Mathurâ* and from *Mathurâ* to *Pâṭaliputram*, he has thereby gone from *Çrughna* to *Pâṭaliputram* (p. 1093, 2).

3. The subtle Body.

Sûtras 4, 2, 6--11. 3, 1, 1—6; cf. 1, 4, 1—7.

The soul with the organs of conscious and unconscious life (*Indriyas*, *Manas*, *Prâṇa*) which have entered into it, further needs in order to be able to withdraw from the body a vehicle (*âçraya*) of material nature, since without such, without a material basis, as experience shows, nothing living can move or stand (p. 744, 9). This basis is the subtle body, *sûkshmam çarîram* (p. 341, 3. 1097, 14), or, as Çañkara usually paraphrases it: *deha-vîjâni bhûta-sûkshmâṇi* (p. 740, 8. 741, 3. 744, 2; cf. 1095, 10. 1092, 10), that is, "the fine parts of the elements "which form the seed of the body."[127] In order hereafter

[126] That the soul takes the Prâṇas with it depends on the fact that without them the soul can neither move nor enjoy in the life after death (p. 745, 5); therefore when it is said (Bṛih. 3, 2, 13) that the Prâṇas at death go to the Gods, the eye to the sun, the breath to the wind, etc., this is only a metaphorical (*bhâkta*, *gauṇa*) expression (p. 745, 1), which means that at death the Gods withdraw (p. 745, 8) their assistance from the organs (above p. 337 ff.).

[127] Cf. *bhûta-sûkshmam* 206, 1. 207, 1. 341, 6. (plur.) 743, 1; and *bhûta-mâtrâḥ* 740, 13. 14; the expression *tanmâtrâṇi* is, so far as we know, not yet to be found in Çañkara's Commentary.—These fine parts of the elements, which form the seed of the body, are of like nature with the seed from which the world after its destruction comes forth anew each

to attain a body consisting of the different elements, the soul must take with it the seed of this body, and this seed, not of heat alone, but of all the elements, is to be understood, when in the fundamental passage, Chând. 6, 8, 6, it is said: Life enters into heat. For the scripture says (Bṛih. 4, 4, 5): "(this "soul is) of the nature of earth, water, air, ether, heat" (p. 1093, 12), and the Smṛiti (Manu 1, 27) declares:

> "The infinitely minute parts of the Five,
> "From which arises all in order."

Now these elementary germs of the future body, embraced by which the soul leaves the body (p. 741, 3), are also to be understood in the explanations in 3, 1, 1—6 by the term waters, which according to the doctrine of the Five Fires speak with human voice at the fifth offering, after having been offered five times in succession,—as Faith, Soma, Rain, Food, and Seed,—by the Gods in the Fires of Heaven, the Atmosphere, the Earth, Man, and Woman (p. 741, 6). True, only water is there spoken of (p. 742, 11), but under that name the germs of all the elements are to be understood (p. 744, 2) and these are called water, first, because according to p. 240 above water contains in itself (p. 743, 4) all elements (of which here, following Chând. 6, 2, three only are named; on this see p. 231 above), then because in the body, which likewise consists of them all (above p. 240ff.), water preponderates (p. 743, 9).

These waters then, representing the totality of the elementary germs, are thus what forms the bridge from one human existence to another by being offered successively as Faith, Soma, Rain, Food, and Seed. The description of the last four as water is readily explained from the preponderance of the water element in these materials (p. 746, 1); but by faith,

time (above p. 70. 228); they are both regarded as being alluded to by the *avyaktam* of Kâṭh. 3, 11 and the *aksharam* of Muṇḍ. 2, 1, 2; p. 341, 12 *jagad idam anabhivyakta-nâmarûpam, vîja-âtmakam. prâg-avastham avyakta-çabda-arham*—, *tad-âtmanâ ca çarirasya* (that is, of the subtle body) *api avyakta-çabda-arhatvam*; and p. 206, 1: the *aksharam* is *avyâkṛitam, nâmarûpa-vîjaçakti-rûpam bhûtasûkshmam, îçvara-âçrayam* (the material substratum in the creation of the world), *tasya eva upâdhi-bhûtam* (only an Upâdhi of the Îçvara, not a *pradhânam* independent of him).

which appears as the sacrificial element in the first offering, the same waters are equally to be understood (p. 746, 6), first because only in that way can question and answer harmonise with each other (p. 746, 10), then, because the first offering, being the cause of the subsequent ones as its effects, cannot be essentially different in nature from them (p. 746, 13). "Further "it is not possible, in so far as Faith, being an idea (*pratyaya*) "is a quality of Manas or the soul, to tear it away from the "substance in which it inheres, like the heart, etc. of a sacri-"ficial victim, to use it as an offering. By the word 'Faith' "therefore the waters are to be understood" (p. 747, 1—3). This designation corresponds to the usage of the Veda (Taitt saṃh. 1, 6, 8, 1: *çraddhâ vâ' âpaḥ*), and is explained by the fact, that the waters as seeds of the body assume a subtlety like that of faith (p. 747, 5), somewhat as one might call a hero of lion-like courage, a lion (p. 747, 6).—We shall see shortly, how our author brings himself into palpable contradiction with this express explanation of "faith" as the elementary seed of the body.

This "subtle body," forming the seed of the body,—subtle, because it departs through the veins (p. 1097, 7)—has, according to its essential nature, on one hand extension (*tanutvam*) and so the capacity of locomotion (p. 1097, 8), on the other, however, transparency (*svacchatvam*), in virtue of which it meets with no obstacle in departing and also is not seen by those standing round (p. 1097, 8). The bodily warmth proceeds from it (p. 1097, 14; otherwise Chând. 3, 13, 8, translated above p. 169); hence during life the body feels warm to the touch, after death on the contrary cold, while in other respects the body is yet unchanged (p. 1098, 1). Finally, it is owing to the subtle nature of this body, that it is not also injured when the (gross) body is injured: for example (p. 1097, 11) by burning (by which we must naturally not think of the burning of the corpse).

Sûtram 4, 2, 8: "*Until the entrance, because of the declaration as to Saṃsâra.*"—Commentary: "When further on in "the text (Chând. 6, 8, 6, above p. 367) it is said: 'the heat "'enters into the highest Godhead,' this means that the "above-mentioned heat [meaning the subtle body] accompanied "by the Onlooker, by Prâṇa, and the host of the organs and "united with the other elements, enters at death into the "highest Godhead. But of what kind is this entrance? this "is to be considered. One might think it to be a final dis-"solution of the own being in the highest Godhead, from "which it came forth; for the origin of all existence, of all "that has become bodily is, as we have established, the highest "Godhead; and thus also this entering into non-separateness "would be final.—To this we reply: *this* subtle body formed "out of heat, etc., as it is the bearer of the organs, ear, etc., "continues to exist *until the entrance*, until liberation from "Saṃsâra, as that liberation follows upon the perfect know-"ledge; *because of the declaration as to Saṃsâra*, as it is given "in the words (Kâṭh. 5, 7):

"The one attains a mother's womb and takes a human form,
"Another animates a plant, as deeds and knowledge fate."

"For otherwise mere dying would be for everyone a dissolution "of the Upâdhis and a final entrance into Brahman; but then "the Canon of Law would be purposeless, and equally so the "Canon of Knowledge. But bondage has its ground in false "knowledge and can therefore be loosed in no other way than "by perfect knowledge. Hence, in spite of its origin from it, "this entrance of the soul there into the Existent, like that in "deep sleep and at the dissolution of the world, is such that "a seed remains over and persists" (p. 1096, 3—1097, 3).

—In reality this entrance into Brahman, retained for the sake of the Vedic texts, is a mere passing through Brahman, and not even that: for the system, as such, knows nothing of it, but makes the souls pass immediately after death either by the *Pitṛiyâna* to the moon, or into hell, or finally by the *Devayâna* into the (lower) Brahman.

Upon all these Paths the soul is accompanied by the subtle body: for the latter, as we saw, continues to exist as long as *Saṃsâra*, but *Saṃsâra* has existed from Eternity (above p. 280) and endures until liberation, whence it follows that as the soul is clothed from all eternity with the organs (above p. 312) so also it is clothed with the subtle body and so it remains until it gains perfect knowledge, that is, esoteric knowledge. On the other hand, the exoteric knowledge, as it leads upwards into the lower Brahman by the *Devayâna*, does not free the soul from the subtle body. True, as this subtle body is a support of the soul by the elements, this support is for the purpose of rebirth, but rebirth no longer takes place in one who has (exoteric) knowledge, since according to the scripture he attains immortality (which means that he is no longer subject to death, above pp. 149. 287), for these reasons one might think that only the Ignorance (p. 1094, 12) departs (clothed with the subtle body); but this is not so: rather it is exactly the same in the case of the ignorant and of the possessor of (exoteric) knowledge except the difference of the Paths which they respectively take; the ignorant passes with the subtle body to new embodiment, the (exoteric) knower passes on his own special path to immortality (p. 1095, 10); true, immortality in the full sense of the word is not the sojourn in a given place and thus requires no going thither and therefore no material substratum (p. 1095, 13); but the immortality of the (exoteric) knower, with which we are here concerned, is only relative (*âpekshika*), since he has not yet burned up all Ignorance; hence for it a going, and, in order that this may be possible, a subtle body as material vehicle. are required, as without it no going can occur (p. 1096, 1).

4. Moral Determination of the transmigrating Soul.

(a) Prefatory Remark.

All the Upâdhis hitherto discussed, clothed with which the soul departs (namely, *indriyâṇi, manas, mukhya prâṇa, sûkshmam çarîram*), are purely neutral, not individually determined principles, and the soul itself is the same, as, according to its nature, it is identical with Brahman and is only apparently different from him through its being clothed with the said Upâdhis. Thus the soul with all its organs is entirely neutral. bearing in itself no moral distinction,—quite consistently with the Indian and, indeed, with every other standpoint, which. like it, places the essential nature of the soul in Knowing not in Willing.

But whence then the moral determinations, which condition the differences of character, the differences of Paths in the Beyond, the contrast of reward and punishment in the other world, and the form of the subsequent rebirth in this world?— .

We must assume for the departing soul, besides the just described elementary substratum (*bhûta-âçraya*) a second, *viz.* a moral substratum (*karma-âçraya*), and these two are expressly distinguished by Çañkara (p. 1094, 5) under these names.

Now in what does this moral substratum consist, which conditions all differences of character and of destiny?

Like all moral points, this important question is very inadequately dealt with by Çañkara (for reasons indicated above p. 59), and all that we find about it consists in occasional references to certain passages of scripture, which therefore we are to follow, according to the intentions of our author.

(b) The *Karma-âçraya.*

Sûtram 4, 2, 6, p. 1094.

In Brih. 3, 2, 13, the son of *Ritabhâga* questions *Yâjñavalkya*:
"'*Yâjñavalkya*,' he said: 'when after a man dies his speech "'enters into fire, his breath into the wind, his eye into the "'sun, his Manas into the moon, his ear into the cardinal "'points, his body into the earth, his Âtman into the Âkâça, "'the hair on his body into plants, the hair on his head into "'trees, his blood and seed into water,—where then does the "'man remain?'—Then spake *Yâjñavalkya*: 'Take me, *Ârta-*"'*bhâga*, dear one, by the hand; upon this we two must speak "'alone together, not here in the assembly.'—Then the two "went out and conversed together; and what they spoke of, "that was work, and what they praised, that was work.— "Verily, through good work one becomes good, through evil "work, evil."

"Then the son of *Ritabhâga* was silent."

Upon this remarkable passage, in which we seem to have the very birth of the doctrine of transmigration before our eyes, Çañkara merely remarks (p. 1094, 6), that it only lays stress upon works and does not thereby exclude the other, material-substratum of the soul, the *bhûta-âçraya*, that is, the subtle body, which is spoken of *loc. cit.* The contradiction that the organs, according to this passage, enter into the forces of nature, while in our system the soul withdraws them into itself, he puts aside in the manner indicated in note 126, above p. 370.—In another respect the circumstance that besides the *çarîram* the *âtman* also (according to Çañkara, it would be indeed the *âtma-adhishṭhânaṃ hṛidaya-âkâçam*) dissolves, while the *karman* persists, is very remarkable, in its bearing on Buddhism.

(c) *Vidyâ-karma-pûrvaprajñâ.*

Sûtram 3, 4, 11.

Of the soul after death it is said in Bṛih. 4, 4, 2 (translated above p. 193): "then their knowledge and their works "and their newly gained experience take them by the hand," —the last, as we read *apûrvaprajñâ* and find here already the conception of the *apûrvam*, which will be further spoken of shortly. Çañkara, indeed, reads (p. 740, 4. 1091, 9) *pûrva-prajñâ*, "previous experience" (which in the Com. on Bṛih. p. 843, he understands as *pûrva-anubhûta-vishayâ prajñâ*, "the "consciousness of what has been experienced before"). The contrast between knowledge and works he explains 3, 4, 11 at first following the Sûtram to mean that the former (those who go by the *Devayâna*) are taken by the hand by knowledge, the latter (those for whom the soul's transmigration continues by the *Pitṛiyâna*), are taken by the hand by works (p. 984, 4); but then he remembers that here it is not yet a question of liberation (to which the *Devayâna* also leads), but only of Saṃsâra, and explains, in harmony with his commentary on Bṛih. 4, 4, 2 that the question is only one of knowledge concerning *Saṃsâra*, that therefore by *Vidyâ* is to be understood here "ordained and forbidden knowledge" (Govinda cites as an example of the former the *Udgîtha*, of the latter *nagna-strî-darçanam*), as by *karman* the doing what is ordained and what is forbidden (p. 984, 9). By *Pûrvaprajñâ* in Bṛih. *l. c.* he understands, as already observed, "previous experience" and explains it as impressions (*vâsanâ*) which things leave behind in the soul, and upon which depend inborn gifts for artistic work (he gives as an example talent for painting) and perhaps also for moral conduct,[128]—the last if we may thus understand *vishaya-upabhogeshu* and *karmaṇi* (on Bṛih. p. 844, 5. 7) where however this idea, so important for us, of an inborn determination of the moral character is only touched on casually, not distinctly developed.

(d) The *Apûrvam*.

Sûtras 3, 2, 38—41. 3, 1, 6.

In the endless chain of transmigration, every new life is conditioned in its doing and suffering by the works of the preceding life; these therefore bring about the changes in the soul's destiny, and these changes interpose as a new moment, as "something which was not there before" (*apûrvam*), (although they too, consistently with the system, cf. above p. 322, are necessitated by the life preceding them). This conception of the *Apûrvam*[129] belongs to the *Karmamîmâṅsâ* school and is for it the metaphysical link between work and its retribution, that which persists when work has passed away and its fruit has not yet appeared. The opinion of *Jaimini* is thus summarised on p. 841, 6 of our work: "It is not possible that "previous work should bear within it the fruit as yet hidden "in the future, unless it causes a given *Apûrvam* to proceed "from itself. Therefore certain subtle persisting elements of "the work, or preparatory elements of its fruit, are termed "*Apûrvam.*" Now this conception of the *Apûrvam* is disputed

---

[128] On Bṛih. p. 844, 2—8: *Dṛiçyate ca keshâñcit kâsucit kriyâsu citra-karma-âdi-lakshaṇâsu vinâ eva iha-abhyâsena janmata' eva kauçalam; kâsucid atyanta-saukarya-yuktâsu api akauçalaṃ keshâñcit; tathâ vishaya-upabhogeshu svabhâvata' eva keshâñcit kauçala-akauçale dṛiçyete; tac ca etat sarvaṃ pûrvaprajñâ-udbhava-anudbhava-nimittaṃ. Tena pûrvaprajñayâ vinâ karmaṇi vâ phala-upabhoge vâ na kasyacit pravṛittir upapadyate.*

[129] Besides the passages cited above we find the *Apûrvam* only on p. 1139, 5 (on p. 1020, 6 it occurs in its etymological meaning). On the nearly allied conception of the *Adṛishṭam* compare pp. 697, 4. 9. 697, 12. 15. 698, 7. 699, 3. 7. 8. 703, 1. 2. 754, 10. 819, 10. 521, 2. 968, 8. 1074, 2.

by Çañkara in the passage cited, in so far as the Vedânta places retribution in the hand of God (cf. on this point above pp. 279, 323); the *Apûrvam* is something non-spiritual and cannot therefore act without being moved by something spiritual (p. 840, 2); hence the fruit cannot be explained by the mere *Apûrvam* (p. 842, 1); "whether therein God has regard to the "action, or to the *Apûrvam*, in either case the fruit comes "from Him" (p. 842, 2).

We must not see in this passage an unconditional rejection of the *Apûrvam*, if we do not wish to place ourselves in contradiction with 3, 1, 6, where the *Apûrvam* makes its appearance directly as a well known and admitted conception, in order to explain the Faith which, according to the doctrine of the Five Fires, is offered in the first fire, and this indeed in quite another way than that which we have considered in Chapter XXXI, 3, above p. 371.

(e) The *Çraddhâ*.

Sûtras 3, 1, 2. 5. 6.

The explanation of Faith (*çraddhâ*) given above p. 372 as "the waters, as these represent the subtle parts of the elements "which form the seed of the body," appears indeed very forced: first, because, so far as we can see, the conception of the subtle body accompanying the soul, has as yet no existence whatever in Bṛih., Chând. or any of the older Upanishads; then because the Indian *çraddhâ* (just as, though wrongly most probably, by Lactant. inst. 4, 28 the Latin *religio*) is etymologically traced back to the conception of knitting together and means the link between man and the Beyond, thus appearing to require a moral explanation. Such an explanation is offered without forcing the meaning: for it is quite natural to understand by *çraddhâ* (which Çañkara, on Praçna, p. 250, 6 defines as *çubha-karma-pravṛitti-hetu*) in Bṛih. and Chând. *loc. cit.*, the works of man produced by faith, as they condition his weal and woe in the Beyond; and this very explanation is also offered by Çañkara, whereby he brings himself into irreconcilable contradiction with himself. For after he has, on p. 747, given the explanation of Faith, quoted above on p. 372.

as the Waters, meaning the subtle body, he then immediately on p. 747, 7ff. explains Faith as the Waters, rising upwards in the sacrifice, they are the bearers of the works conditioned by Faith;—thus in the one case they were the garment of the dead, here they are the moral treasure, which the still living performers of the sacrifice lay up for themselves in heaven: "thus the Waters consisting of the sacrificial libations wherein "inheres the work conditioned by faith, these waters in the "form of the *Apûrvam* clothe the souls which bring the sacri-"fice and lead them, to receive their reward, into the other "world" (p. 748, 10); in the same manner Çankara explains *çraddhâ*, p. 743, 16 as the *karma-samavâyinya' âpas* and again two lines afterwards as the *deha-vîjâni bhûta-sûkshmâṇi.* By this all the explanations in 3, 1, 1—6 are rendered very far from clear and the impression is produced not so much that they originated from two different hands, as rather that a single hand had endeavoured to preserve two mutually irreconcilable interpretations and work them up into an apparent whole.

5. The Path into the Beyond.

Sûtram 4, 2, 7.

After the soul has drawn back into itself its perceptive powers, the organs, in the way just described, it then (according to Bṛih. 4, 4, 1) enters into the heart (in which, however, according to p. 311 above it already is): "thereupon the point of "the heart becomes luminous; from this, after it has become "luminous, the soul departs, either through the eye, or through "the skull, or through other parts of the body" (Bṛih. 4, 4, 2, above p. 192 f.); up to the moment when the point of the heart becomes luminous and thereby lights up the way (p. 1104, 9), everything is the same for the ignorant and for the (exoteric) knower; here, however, the way divides, in that the knowers depart through the head, the ignorant through other parts of the body (p. 1104, 10), for thus says the Scripture (Chând. 8, 6, 6 = Kâṭh. 6, 16):

"One hundred and one are the veins of the heart,
"Of these the one leads upward to the head,
"Who upward mounts by that, has conquered death;
"The others serve to lead the soul elsewhere."

While the knower thus mounts by the 101st vein [130] to tread the Path of the Gods, which, as the exoteric Path to Liberation, will occupy us further in the following part, the others depart through other veins (p. 1105, 3). The further stages of the *Pitṛiyâna*, upon which Bâdarâyaṇa and Çaṅkara give no further details, are according to the doctrine of the Five Fires, the following, in their order: (1) Smoke, while the Devayâna leads through Flame. Originally in both cases the smoke and flame of the funeral pyre seem to have been meant (although already in Chând. 4, 15, 5, translated above p. 166, the entrance into the *arcis*, ray or better flame, is made independent of the performance of the funeral ceremony); in our work, which makes the departure of the soul occur, not on the burning, but already on the growing cold of the corpse (p. 402). Çaṅkara explains the "flame" (*arcis*), as we shall see here after, as "the Godhead presiding over the flame," and in accordance with this, in the Commentaries on Bṛih. 1059, 11. Chând. p. 341, 13, "Smoke" is also taken to mean the Godhead of the smoke.—The following stages also are referred to the Gods presiding over these phenomena: (2) Night, (3) the halves of the month wherein the moon decreases, (4) the halves of the years wherein the days decrease. We must here think of these not as phases of time, but spatially as planes one above another, through which the soul mounts upward, in order to reach the following stages; these are: (5) the world of the Fathers, (6) (only Chând.) the Ether, (7) the Moon, upon which retribution takes place, subject to the limitations, of which we have now to treat.

---

130 This artery is called *sushumnâ* Maitri-Up. 6, 21; as also in the Commentaries on Bṛih. p. 877, 8, on Praçna p. 190, 8, on Taitt. p. 25, 14, on Kâṭh. p. 157, 5 and in the gloss to Çaṅkara's Commentary on the Brahmasûtras p. 1104, 24. In the latter itself, on the other hand, we do not yet find this name but in place of it paraphrases such as that also employed on Chând. 529, 7. 563, 6. 570, 5,—: *mûrdhanyâ nâḍî* (cf. especially p. 1105, 1).

XXXII. The Destinies of the Soul in the Beyond.

1. Contradictions of the Vedic Texts.

1. According to Bṛih. 6, 2 those who have obtained knowledge pass by the *Devayâna* into Brahman, the performers of works ascend by the *Pitṛiyâna* to the moon and, having received their reward, descend, and become men (Bṛih. 6, 2, 16, p. 1062, 1); those who have neither knowledge nor works become worms, birds and "whatever bites;" by the last expression seem originally to have been understood not "gnats and flies," as the scholiast has it, but, correspoding to the ascending scale indicated in the first-named classes of animals, higher, in particular perhaps fierce animals, or snakes etc.

2. These plain and clear facts are entirely distorted in the parallel passage, Chând. 5, 3—10, as was remarked above (Chap. XXX, 7), by an addition distinguishing, among those who return by the *Pitṛiyâna*, between those of fair conduct who are reborn in one of the three higher castes, and those of foul conduct and who go into the bodies of animals or Caṇḍâlas. Thus on the one hand there arises the question, quite overlooked by Chând.: since reward upon the moon is the lot of those of fair conduct only, what is the fate in the other world of those whose conduct is foul? Moreover, if the wicked also go along the *Pitṛiyâna*, then the "third place" (first so named by Chând.) becomes superfluous; and accordingly suppressing the words in Bṛih.: "those who know not "these two Paths," this "third place" is abandoned to the lowest animals, who quickly come into existence and as quickly perish, while the problem whether any transition between them and human existence is possible, remains undiscussed.

3. To increase the confusion, a passage from the Kaushîtaki-Up. 1, 2, is cited (p. 763, 2) which expressly says: "all "who depart from this world, all go together to the moon," and teaches a return thence to all kinds of human and animal bodies.

4. This last difficulty our work gets rid of very easily, by interpreting the passage of the Kaushîtaki, without regard to its context, in the sense that only "all who are called thereto "(*adhikṛita*)" are to be understood. The difficulty previously mentioned. however. is disposed of on the one hand by means of a passage dragged in from the Kâṭhaka-Upanishad (2, 6) in which, as a contrast to the reward of the good upon the moon, the pains of hell are added in the other world for the evil, while on the other hand the "third place" is pointed to as the place of punishment. These two are not, however, connected by coordinating the pains of hell and the third place, but remain unconnected beside each other (p. 62, 7, too gives no help), so that it is difficult here to escape from the impression that different hands have worked at the Sûtras as well as on the Commentary.

To elucidate what has been said, we will lay before the reader the leading thoughts of the section which treats of the punishments of hell and the third place (3, 1, 12—21), in the sequence in which we find them in Çankara.

2. The Punishments of Hell.

Do not those also, who have not performed sacrifice and other works, go to the moon (p. 762, 11)?—Since it is said in Kaush. 1, 2 that all go to the moon (p. 763, 2), and since the fivefold sacrifice through which the new body is attained, implies the going to the moon (p. 763, 4), one might think that both, the performers of works and the non-performers, went to the moon, the latter however without enjoying reward (p. 763, 7).

But that is not so. For the ascent to the moon occurs for the purpose of enjoyment, not without a purpose or merely in order to re-descend, as one climbs a tree to pick its blossoms and fruits, not aimlessly or merely to fall down again (p. 763, 11). Now for those who do not perform works there is no enjoyment on the moon (p. 763, 13); consequently only those who have performed works such as sacrifice ascend to the moon, not the others (p. 763, 15). "But the others enter into *Saṃyamanam* (that is, constraint) the dwelling of *Yama*, suffer "there the *Yama*-tortures corresponding to their evil deeds "and then descend once more to this world. Of this nature "are for them the ascent, and the descent [p. 764, 2, *âroha* and "*avaroha*, both expressions are found in the Sûtram also].— "For thus teaches the scripture by the mouth of *Yama* him-"self (Kâṭh. 2, 6):

> "The other world[131] is hidden from the fool,
> "Who blind with riches staggers on his way;
> "'This is the world,' he raves 'there is nought else,'
> "And then he falls again beneath my sway."

In these words then, according to Bâdarâyaṇa and Çaṅkara, are meant the punishments of hell (p. 764, 2), while according to the context of the passage and also according to Çaṅkara's Commentary on it they refer only to a continual succession of births and deaths. The Smṛiti authors also, Manu, Vyâsa etc. mention the city of *Yama*, *Saṃyamanam*, in which foul deeds come to fruition (p. 764, 10), and the *Purâṇa* poets speak of seven hells, *Raurava* ("the roaring," to be understood like Arist. anal. post. 2, 11, p. 94b 33, or like St. Matthew xxiv, 51) etc. as the places of retribution for evil deeds (p. 764, 13); and if, as the rulers thereof, not *Yama* but *Citragupta* and others are named, it must be remarked that these latter are in the service of *Yama* (p. 765, 3).

3. The Third Place.

Immediately after these reflections our author passes on in 3, 1, 17, to a discussion of the "third place," wherein he

131 Instead of *sâmparâya* we have on p. 764, 5 *sâmparâpa*, which also Govinda faithfully explains as such: *samyak parastât prâpyata', iti samparâpaḥ paralokas; tad-upâyaḥ sâmparâpaḥ.*

seems to have completely forgotten his theory of the punishments of hell.—There is, so he develops his thought p. 765, fusing together the accounts of Bṛih. and Chând. (Chapter XXX, 5, above p. 364), first the Path of the Gods for knowledge, secondly the Path of the Fathers for (religious) works; "but those, who neither in virtue of knowledge are called to "the Path of the Gods, nor in virtue of works to that of the "Fathers, for them there exists this third Path which embraces "minute creatures and leads back to earth again and again: "therefore also (hence: because they have nothing to do "on the moon, and because the third place is destined for "them) those who do not perform works do not go to the "moon" (p. 766, 3). One must not think that they first ascend to the moon's disk and then pass down among minute creatures, "because the ascent (*âroha*) would be purposeless" (p. 766, 6;—but above p. 383 an *âroha* and an *avaroha* were also taught for those fated to suffer the punishments of hell). Hence therefore that world is not overfilled (p. 766, 7), not because they constantly descend again, although this in itself would be possible (p. 766, 10), but because they go, as the Scripture teaches, to the third place (p. 766, 11). Were they (the evil) not different from the performers of works in this respect, that they descend again, the doctrine of the third place would be superfluous (p. 766, 13).

The punishments of hell are quite left out of sight in these discussions as they are in the following, where the author passing them over entirely goes back to what was stated at the beginning of Chapter XXXII, 2 (above p. 382) in order to dispose of the doubts there noted. He continues: when it is said, Kaush. 1, 2, that all go to the moon, we must understand thereby all who are called (p. 767, 1); and when, for the attainment of a new body, the passing through the five fires and with it the journey to the moon have been maintained to be necessary (p. 767, 3, cf. 763, 4), it is to be remarked that the process of the five fires takes place only in the case of human rebirths and not in the case of rebirths as a worm, a bird, etc. (p. 767, 11); as it is also said that at the fifth offering the waters speak with human voice (not with the voice of an animal) (p. 767, 12); hence only those who ascend and descend go through the process of the five fires (p. 767, 14), the others, without the fivefold offering. receive a new body by the mingling of the water with the other elements (p. 767, 16). Moreover the possibility of becoming man even without the five fires is not excluded (p. 767, 13); thus, for instance, *Droṇa* is said to have come into existence without the fire of woman, *Dhṛishṭadyumna* and others even without the fire of man and of woman (p. 768, 3); and other such elusions of separate fires also occur. as for instances female cranes conceive without seed (p. 768, 6, cf. note 95 above p. 226), and of the four classes of beings (born alive, egg-born, born from sweat, and born from germs, above p. 239f.) the two last are said to be produced without sexual intercourse (p. 768, 10).— Only just previously our author had restricted the process of the five fires to those coming from the moon; here he extends, in part at least, even to the animals. A consistent view cannot be gained from his words.

4. Felicity on the Moon.

The Indian belief, which regards the moon's peaceful realm of light as the abiding place of the pious dead, and associates her waxing and waning with the ascent and the descent of their souls, is a lovely poetical thought.

But if this temporacy felicity is a reward, how then can it be said, Bṛih. and Chând. *l. c.*, that the pious on the moon are the nourishment of the Gods? Surely there can be no enjoyment in being devoured by the Gods, as if by tigers! (p. 749, 10).

The answer to this is that being the food of the Gods is to be taken metaphorically not literally (p. 749, 13), since otherwise it would be unintelligible that a man should merit the sojourn on the moon through arduous works (p. 750, 2). If the Gods are said to eat this does not mean chewing and swallowing, but signifies the enjoyable intercourse which they hold with the pious, just as one finds enjoyment in intercourse with virtuous women, sons and friends (p. 750, 5); moreover "the Gods neither eat nor drink," as is said in Chând. 3, 6, 1 (p. 750, 7). But that nevertheless the Gods enjoy the pious and thereby derive benefit from them, depends on the fact, that the pious do not possess the highest knowledge, namely that of Âtman, and hence are as serviceable to the Gods in the other world as in this, in reference to which it is said (Bṛih. 1, 4, 10): "He who worships another Godhead [than the Self, "the Âtman] and says 'he is one and I am another,' he is "not wise, but is like unto a domestic animal of the Gods" (p. 750, 12). Thus the being enjoyed by the Gods indicates the inadequacy of the whole *Pañcâgnividyâ* (p. 751, 3). That this being enjoyed is at the same time an enjoying on the part of the pious, we have already seen in note 125, above p. 363, from a passage of the Commentary on Chând. p. 343, 10.

XXXIII. The Cause of the Return to Earthly Existence.

1. Prefatory Remark.

Our System teaches a twofold retribution for good and evil works: once in the Beyond, and then through a rebirth on earth. We have already pointed out (above p. 358), as the ground of this double retribution, the endeavour to hold fast at the same time both to the older view of a retribution in the Beyond and to the later one of a retribution through rebirth. But by this the system now becomes inconsistent with itself: for if good and evil receive their due reward in the other world, one fails to see why penance should be done for them over again in a new existence upon earth; or *vice versâ*, if the retribution consists in the particular form of this earthly existence, then no sound reason is forthcoming for the assumption of rewards and punishments in the other world. We shall see how the Indian theologians deal with this inconsistency (into which, moreover, Plato also fell), by reproducing in brief the contents of 3, 1, 8-11, p. 751—762 in the present Chapter.

2. In Retribution a Residue remains (*anuçaya*).

The question arises whether in the retribution of works in the other world a residue[132] is left or not (p. 752, 2).—One

[132] *anuçaya*, literally *residuum*, "heel taps," whereby Bâdarâyaṇa, as it seems, alludes to the corresponding *sampâta*, "the sediment of any liquid, which runs together at the bottom of the vessel," in Chând. 5, 10, 5. In the Commentary to Chând. p. 344, 8, *sampâta* is indeed taken

might think that no residue was left, because in Chând. 5, 10, 5 (above p. 364) it is said: "they remain there so long as any "sediment (*sampâta*) exists" and in Bṛih. 6, 2, 16: they descend "when this is consumed (*pari-ava-eti*)," as further another passage of Scripture says (Bṛih. 4, 4, 6, translated above p. 194):

> "After he has received reward
> "For all, that he has here performed,
> "He comes back from that other world,
> "Into this world of deeds, below;"

and if the meaning of death consists in its being the revealer of the fruit of works (p. 752, 13), then it must be the revealer of all the fruit of works, for the same cause cannot bring forth dissimilar effects (p. 752, 16); and if the lamp makes the pot visible, it must also make the dress visible at a like distance (p. 753, 1).

In contradiction to these arguments we maintain, that a residue of works is certainly left over. For while on the moon works are gradually consumed by enjoyment, the water-form of these works (*am-mayam-çarîram*, that is, the *karma-âçraya*, above p. 375 which is thus distinguished here from the *karman* itself) melts away, through the fire of pain at the dwindling away of works, like hoar-frost in the sun, or like the hardness of butter in the fire, and the descent takes place, while a residue is still left (p. 753, 8). This follows, in the first place, from the fact that the Scripture (Chând. 5, 10, 7) makes a difference as regards those who descend between fair and foul conduct; here we are to understand by conduct (*caraṇam*) this very residue of works (p. 753, 14); and moreover the various allotment of earthly goods from birth onwards compels us, since nothing is without a cause, to admit such a residue (p. 753, 15). Thus too teaches the Smṛiti (cf. *Âpastamba, dharmasûtra* 2, 1, 2, 3), that, after the retribution for works has taken place in detail, it is through a residue (*çesha*) that difference of re-birth in respect of country, caste, family, form,

---

to mean *karmaṇaḥ kshayaḥ* ("until the destruction of works results"), in our work on the contrary, p. 752, 5 to mean *karma-âçaya* ("so long as an accumulation of works remains"). As to this meaning of *karma-âçaya* cf. p. 909, 12. 915, 3. 916, 5. 7. 1081, 1. 1086, 6.

duration of life, Vedic study, destiny, wealth, desire and intelligence is conditioned (p. 754, 4).

3. How is this Residue to be conceived?

But how are we to conceive this residue of works, by which the course of the new life is conditioned? (p. 754, 6).—

Some think of it as a viscous fluid, which clings to the vessel (p. 754, 7); this, they think, does not contradict the law of effect [which must operate completely] (p. 754, 10); for even if the purpose of the ascent to the moon is the enjoyment of the fruit without exception, yet a continuance there becomes impossible when the residue of works has become very small indeed (p. 754, 13), just as a wandering knight who has come well provided to the king's court, can no longer maintain himself when his outfit has dwindled down to an umbrella and shoes (p. 755, 1).

But this explanation is not attractive (*peçala*). For in the case of the vessel and that of the knight one understands that a residue can be left, but not here (p. 755, 10); on the contrary such a residue is contradicted by the canon of scripture as to the reward in heaven (that is, in the realm of the moon), which takes place without diminution (p. 755, 11); further such a remainder of good works would only explain rebirth in a fair form, and not a rebirth which serves as punishment (p. 756, 1).

We must rather distinguish two classes of works, the first bearing fruit in the other world, the second in this; the former are recompensed in the Beyond, the latter through the rebirth here (p. 756, 3). In accordance with this, one must take the verse quoted above (p. 388): "for all, that he has done," as referring only to those works which bear fruit in the other world (p. 756, 8), and the same limitation must be made when death is conceived as the revealer of works (p. 756, 9). For why, we ask, is death the revealer of works? Because, no doubt, this life is demanded for the manifestation of other works. Now it is just that which prevents those works which death reveals from being revealed previously, which makes it impossible that works, bearing an opposite kind of fruit, should be revealed at the same time after death (p. 757, 3). That all works cannot receive retribution at once, may be readily seen from the fact that, in the following birth, all accumulated works do not always work themselves out, because each one of them demands its own special retribution (p. 757, 9); and a remission, with the exception of those actions which have been atoned for by penance (*prâyaçcittam*), does not take place (p. 757, 11). If all (religious) works were recompensed in one birth, then, for those who have passed into heaven[133] or hell or the bodies of animals [and plants], since in this state they perform no ritual works, there would be no cause for a subsequent existence which thus would be impossible (p. 758, 5); for we have no other authority for the doctrine of retribution except the Canon of Works (p. 758, 8).—It is thus unconditionally true that death is the revealer of works: crimes like the murder of a Brahman require, according to the Smṛiti, more than one life for their atonement (p. 758, 6), and on the other hand works like the rain-sacrifice (*kârîrî*) bring their fruit in the present life already (p. 758, 9).—The example of the lamp (above p. 388) does not apply; rather, just as the lamp at the same distance renders coarse things visible, but not subtle things, so by death the "stronger" works are revealed but not the "weaker" (p. 759, 5). Finally if anyone should object that, if some residue of works is always left, there can be no liberation, he must be reminded that through perfect knowledge all works without exception are dissolved (p. 759, 8).

4. Ritual and Moral Work.

As the foregoing shows, our author seeks to solve the question of the basis of double retribution by drawing a distinction between those works which bear fruit in the Beyond and those which bear fruit here. But he makes no effort to

[133] Meaning here not the realm of the moon, but heaven as the place of rebirth, which may take place in heaven, in the world, or in hell: the *saṃsâra* is *brahma-âdi-sthâvara-anta* p. 61, 11, *nâraka-sthâvara-anta* 62. 7 cf. pp. 300, 7. 303, 4. 420, 6. 604, 2.

determine what works belong to the one or the other category, and he only allows it to appear incidentally that the difference is quantitative, in so far as the stronger works reveal themselves first, and therefore in the Beyond, while the weaker remain behind as a residue and condition the rebirth. We have already encountered a similar struggle for existence among works above p. 112; in contradiction to the passage there translated, as also to various statements in the section we have just analysed, is the remark to which we called attention above p. 353 according to which death means just the moment when the store of works conditioning life has been completely exhausted.

Now it would be very easy to make the twofold retribution follow from the difference between ritual and moral works, the former being recompensed in the Beyond, the latter in the new career on earth; and it seems as if some such distinction had been attempted by the Vedânta school, but rejected by the authorities, but yet without the latter being able to come to a complete agreement on this point. We shall endeavour to gain an insight into these interesting but somewhat obscure circumstances, by translating here word for word the section bearing upon them, 3, 1, 9—11.

(3, 1, 9:) "'*Because of conduct? No! because it denotes it* "'*as well; thus Kârshṇâjini.*'—That may be so; but the passage "of Scripture, which was quoted in proof of the existence of "a residue of works (*anuçaya*): 'who now are of a fair con- "'duct,' (Chând. 5, 10, 7, above p. 364), teaches that entering "into the womb results from conduct (*caraṇam*) and not from the "remainder of works; for conduct is one thing, and the residue "of works another. For conduct can mean nothing but "behaviour (*câritram*), manner of life (*âcâra*), character (*çîlam*); "by residue of works, on the other hand, is meant a balance "remaining over from the works which have received retribution; "and the scripture too distinguishes work and conduct, for it "is written (Bṛih. 4, 4, 5, translated above p. 193): 'according "'as he acts, according as he walks, according to this is he "'born,' and (Taitt. 1, 11, 2): 'the works which are blameless, "'those shalt thou perform, no others; what among us is

" 'accounted good conduct, that shalt thou follow!' Therefore "the passage of Scripture which makes entering into the womb "follow *on account of the conduct*, proves nothing as to a "balance of works.—To this we answer: *No! because* this "passage of Scripture concerning conduct *denotes also* the "remainder of works, *thus* thinks the teacher *Kârshṇâjini*."

(3, 1, 10:) " '*Purposelessness, you think? No! because it is* " '*thereby conditioned!*'—Good, one might say, but why must "one abandon the Vedic meaning of 'character,' for the word "*caraṇam* and accept the metaphorical one of 'balance of "works?' Should not the character rather receive the entrance "into a fair or a foul womb as retribution for the good com-"manded and for the evil forbidden by the scripture? For "of course one must assume a reward of some kind for the "character. For otherwise there would be *purposelessness* of "character.—*If you think* so, then we answer: *no!* Why? "*Because it is thereby conditioned*; that is, the work done, such "as sacrifice etc., is conditioned by conduct; for no one who "does not lead a good life is admitted thereto:

"The Veda cleanseth not immoral men."

"as the Smṛiti says. Further there is no *purposelessness* of "character, because it also belongs to the goal of man. For "when the work performed, such as sacrifice etc., reaps its "fruit, then too conduct, *because it is thereby conditioned*, will "also receive a certain surplus (*atiçaya*); and work accomplishes "all purposes, as both scripture and tradition admit. There-"fore work alone, because it indicates the character as well. "is, in the form of the residue of works, the cause of entering "into the womb; such is the opinion of Kârshṇâjini. For as "the work is there, an entering into the womb on account of "the character cannot properly be assumed; for he who is "able to run upon his feet, does not need the crawl upon his "knees."

(3, 1, 11:) " '*Only good and evil work on the contrary, says* " '*Bâdari.*'—*On the contrary* the teacher *Bâdari* holds, that "by the word 'conduct' *only good and evil works* are to be "understood. For, as is seen, the word 'conduct' is used of "a mere work. For of him who performs holy (*puṇya*) works, "such as sacrifice etc, people say: 'this noble man walks in "'the path of duty (*dharmaṃ carati*).'—Moreover manner of life "itself is only a kind of duty, and the distinction between "work and conduct is only the same as that between Brâh-"maṇa and Parivrâjaka [that is, *genus* and *species*, cf. 382, 2. "640, 3]. Thus those of fair conduct are those whose works "are of good repute, and those of foul conduct those whose "works are of ill repute; this is certain."

—However far the foregoing thoughts of Çaṅkara fall short of clearness, it is evident from them, that a tendency showed itself to distinguish between ritual and moral conduct or character, and to regard the retribution in the Beyond as conditioned by the former, and the shaping of the succeeding existence by the latter; and further that this tendency did not prevail in the Vedânta-school.—Such an attitude may seem strange to our consciousness which has been well schooled in this very question (the corner-stone of difference between the morality of the Old and New Testaments). We must remember however that we are here concerned with the doings of men only in so far as they call for reward and punishment aud thus serve egotistic purposes. And in so far as they are in the service of Egotism, the value of all human deeds lies not in themselves, but in what they aim at; and it is in fact quite a matter of indifference whether this object is attained by ritual or by moral acts.

XXXIV. The Descent of the Soul for a new Embodiment.

Sûtras 3, 1, 22—27.

1. The Stages on the Way.

THE road by which the soul descends is like that by which it ascended (p. 759, 10. 769, 9). But it reminds us more of the manner in which the individual elements came forth from Brahman (cf. above p. 230 ff.). As the elements: Âkâça, Air, Fire, Water, Earth, there emanated one after the other in order from the Âtman in progressively increasing density, so the descending soul passes first into the Âkâça, from the Âkâça into the Air, from the Air into Smoke (which here takes the place of the Fire), from smoke—or vapour—it is condensed into Cloud, from which it pours down as Rain, as such nourishes Plants and passes over in the form of plant food into the male body as Seed, whence it comes into a womb corresponding to the merit of its works, to emerge thence in a new embodiment.

2. Duration of the Descent.

Scripture gives no definite information as to the duration of the stay in these various stages (p. 771, 4); still one may assume that the stay is not very protracted (p. 771, 5); for after the entrance of the soul into plants the Scripture says (Chând. 5. 10, 6): "from thence truly it is more difficult to escape" (*durnishprapataram*, according to Çañk. p. 771, 9, cf. on Chând. p. 351, 13 for *durnishprapata-taram* = *durnishkrama-taram*) whence it may be inferred that the remaining stages are more easily escaped from (p. 771, 11). The endeavour to escape which in these words is ascribed to the Soul, depends on the fact that it desires enjoyment which it does not attain in these intermediate stages but only after entrance into its new body (p. 771, 13).

3. The Soul sojourns in the various Stages only as a Guest.

How must we conceive the relation of the Soul to the elements through which it passes? Does it actually become Âkâça, Plant, Seed etc.?—That is not so, but rather the soul on its descent only enjoys the passing hospitality of the elements and souls, through which its road leads, as is proved in detail by our authors.

When on the moon the watery body, which has been allotted to the soul for its enjoyment (above pp. 371, 378), disappears through the consumption of the enjoyment (p. 770, 5), the Soul passes over into a subtle condition resembling the Âkâça (p. 770, 6), and this the scripture expresses by saying that the Soul becomes Âkâça. That this is not to be taken literally follows from the fact that a thing cannot be transformed into the being of another thing (p. 770, 8), and that in this case an escaping from the Âkâça to the Air etc. would not be possible, since the soul in virtue of the omnipresence of the Âkâça would have to remain eternally united to it (p. 770. 10; that is, probably: from what is everywhere one cannot escape to anywhere else). Thus the Soul does not pass over into the Âkâça, but only into a condition like it; and the same applies to the passing into Air, Smoke, Cloud and Rain.

The entrance of the Soul into the plant, too, is not to be regarded as a transformation into the soul of that particular plant; for on the contrary each plant has its special soul (*jîva* p. 773, 3; which, like every embodied soul, is atoning for the deeds of a former existence, and therefore necessarily possesses s e n s a t i o n); the Soul descending from the moon is only received by the plant and takes no part in its pleasure and pain (p. 773, 5, cf. above p. 238 ff.), since enjoying or suffering is only possible as retribution for works done (p. 773, 9).

Further if the soul entered the plant as its own proper soul it would have to depart at the cutting, shelling, breaking up, cooking and chewing of the plant, for every soul departs as soon as its body is destroyed (p. 774, 1). By this we do not deny that plants also [according to Kâṭh. 5, 7, translated above p. 373] are places of expiation for souls, which by reason of impure works have sunk down into plant life (p. 774, 6), but we deny that the souls which come from the moon become plant-souls on entering into the plants (p. 774, 8). Further it is not to be admitted that this entering into the plant serves as a punishment for the killing of animals in connection with the work of sacrifice (p. 774, 10); for the privilege (*anugraha*, p. 775, 6) of killing for the purpose of sacrifice, rests on the injunction of the canon of Scripture, which is the sole authority in reference to good and evil works, because these relate to the Beyond (p. 775, 1); and if the prohibition of killing animals forms the rule, then the injunction to kill them in sacrifice is an exception to it (p. 775, 9).

In the father's body also, as his own soul has long been there, the soul, which enters into him through food, sojourns as a guest (p. 776, 7), to pass as seed from him into a womb corresponding to its works, whence it comes forth in new embodiment for the retribution of its previous works (p. 776, 13).

4. Retrospect.

However full of contradictions in detail the doctrine of the Soul's transmigration has become through the endeavour to uphold the different accounts in the Veda, as also through a certain carelessness in the handling of secondary matters, peculiar to the Indians, yet in its main outlines this fundamental dogma of Indian religion lies quite clearly before our eyes.

For perfect knowledge, there is no world and therefore also no transmigration of the Soul. According to the highest truth the Soul cannot wander, because it is the omnipresent, that is, spaceless, Brahman itself. But this the Soul does not know: what prevents its knowing is the *Upâdhis* which veil from the Soul its own proper nature; these Upâdhis it regards as belonging naturally to its own Self, while in truth they are to be referred to the non-Ego and therefore, like the whole world of plurality are non-existent and without reality.

We saw how to these Upâdhis, apart from the gross body which is laid aside at each death, belongs in the first place the complicated psychic organism, consisting of the organs of cognition, the organs of action, the Manas, the Prâṇa, and the subtle body, which accompanies the Soul on its wanderings; the Soul has been connected with this unchanging apparatus from eternity, and remains so, liberation apart, for eternity.

With this is further associated, conditioning its re-embodiment, a variable element: namely works, whether ritual or moral, performed by the Soul in the course of each life. The system declines to make any difference between these two, and not wrongly, in so far as we here find ourselves not in the sphere of morality but in that of Egotism; all works have value and meaning only in so far as they condition the weal and woe of the Soul in the Beyond and in the coming existence. —True, it is God, who assigns this weal and woe to the soul; but he is bound, or binds himself, in this by the works of the previous existence; from these result not only the enjoyment and suffering of the Soul in the following birth; but also the works of the new existence depend on moral determination, that is, on the works of the previous life, with just the same necessity as a plant depends on its seed; and thus one life determines another throughout all world-periods,—for even during the periodical absorptions of the world in Brahman the Soul with its organs, *bhûta-âçraya*, and *karma-âçraya* continues to exist like a seed,—and so without cessation *ad infinitum*.

To what extent in this the works of one life exert their influence not only upon the next in succession, but upon several lives to come, is a question that cannot be made clear from the statements of our author. Similarly we remain in the dark as to the possibility of a gradual moral purification of the character; true, reference is made p. 1045, 7 to the verse of the Bhagavadgîtâ (6, 45):

> "By many a new birth made pure
> "He treads at last the highest path,"

but how this purification is to be understood in accordance with the system, is hard to say; for the Soul, and equally the organism with which it is clothed, are unchanging in their nature; the moral does not lie in any *esse* whatever, but in the *operari* on each case; the latter can raise the soul step by step, but always remains external to it; whence also it does not lead to liberation. Rather it is just these works. which continually reproduce themselves from the works of the previous existence, which hold the Soul emprisoned in the eternal cycle of birth and death (*saṃsâra*), which embraces everything that has life (*jîva*), all Gods, men, animals, and plants, in which an ascent to the divine, a descent to plant life can occur, but from which no escape is possible.,

One thing alone is possible: the awakening to perfect knowledge, in consequence of which the Soul recognises itself as identical with Brahman, and Brahman as the only Being; and thus recognises the whole empirical reality, the *Saṃsâra* included, as an illusion.

He who has reached this esoteric knowledge of the attributeless Brahman, is at his goal; he knows all that is manifold, the world as well as his own body with all its organs as non-Ego, non-Âtman, non-Existent,—for him death means only the cessation of an illusion, which has already been recognised as illusory, and as unreal, as nothing.

With the exoteric knowledge it is otherwise: he who has by this recognised Brahman as having attributes, as a personal God and has worshipped him according to this theological form of knowledge, after death mounts upwards on the *Devayâna* to the lower Brahman and there at last gains the perfect knowledge and therewith liberation. This mediate liberation by the Path of *Devayâna* is called *Kramamukti*, "progressive liberation" because it is attained by progress towards Brahman or "liberation by steps" because it is attained by the intermediate step of the exoteric felicity.

We now turn to describe liberation first in its pure, esoteric form, and then we shall depict the attainment of the same goal by the indirect way of the exoteric *Kramamukti*.

THE FIFTH

AND LAST PART OF THE VEDÂNTA SYSTEM:

MOKSHA

OR

THE TEACHING OF LIBERATION.

XXXV. The Path of Liberation.

1. Definition of Liberation.

(p. 64, 7:) "That [entity] in the absolute sense real, highest "of all, eternal, all-penetrating like the ether, exempt from "all change, all-sufficing, undivided, whose nature is to be its "own light, in which neither good nor evil has any place, nor "effect, nor past, nor present, nor future,—this incorporeal "[entity] is called Lib'eration."

As may be seen from this passage, the conception of Liberation contains the same characteristics as serve as a rule to define Brahman; and indeed Brahman and the state of liberation are identical terms (p. 1046, 4: *brahma eva hi mukti-avasthâ*); for liberation is nothing else than the becoming one with Brahman, or rather, since the identity of the Soul with Brahman has always subsisted and has only been hidden from it by an illusion, liberation is nothing else but the awakening of the consciousness that our own Self is identical with Brahman. Accordingly, in liberation there is no question of becoming something which does not already exist, but only of the attainment of the knowledge of what has existed from all eternity. It is because of this, that liberation is not accomplished through any sort of work, nor through moral improvement, but by knowledge alone (as the Christian redemption is by faith alone, *sola fide*, which comes very near to the metaphysical knowledge here spoken of).

We shall now consider more closely Çañkara's explanations of these points.

2. Liberation impossible through Works.

All works, good as well as evil, demand their retribution in the following existence. Hence no performance of works, of whatever kind it may be, ever leads to liberation, but only back again ever to Saṃsâra.—But granted, thus Çañkara proceeds in the passage translated on above p. 112 ff., that a person abstains from all works, then there would be no material left for a new life for him, and thus after death liberation would be attained?—Not so! For in the first place one is never certain that there may not be works demanding for their atonement several lives (a conception analogous to that of Exodus xx, 5); and even if one were successful in getting rid of the evil works by ceremonies, yet the good works would still be left, and even these same ceremonies may possibly also bring with them not only this annihilation but in addition positive fruits to be enjoyed in a future life. And, further, it is practically impossible to avoid all works throughout an entire existence, so long as the natural disposition of the soul to action and enjoyment persists; for actions continually come forth afresh from this inborn nature, through causes which are always potentially inherent in the soul, just as much as its natural disposition to action. So long, therefore, as this natural disposition is not removed through perfect knowledge (on which see above p. 317 ff.), there is no hope of liberation.

The discussions of this same question go still deeper in 1, 1, 4. Here Cañkara first explains (p. 61, 5 ff.) that works are of two kinds: ordained and prohibited, good and evil, and accordingly bear also two kinds of fruit, namely, pleasure and pain, which, in order to be experienced, demand a body ("the place of the enjoyment of the fruit of the various kinds of works," p. 501, 3), which body, according to the quality of the works, may be that of a god, man, animal, plant. But then our author recalls (p. 63, 6) the passage, Chând. 8, 12, 1 (translated above p. 184) according to which pleasure and pain pertain only to corporeal and not to incorporeal Being, and shews that, as Liberation is such an incorporeal Being, and is thus untouched by pleasure and pain, it cannot be produced by works which demand these as their atonement (p. 64, 3). Further, he urges the fact, that liberation, if it were dependent upon works, would necessarily be: (1) transitory (owing to the consumption of the works), (2) graduated (because of their different value), both of which contradict the conception of liberation as an eternal and paramount condition (admitting neither less nor more) (p. 65).

3. Liberation impossible through moral Improvement.

(p. 71, 9:) "But also for this reason is liberation not conditioned by any action, that it is not attainable by [moral] purification (*saṃskâra*). For all improvement takes place in him who is to be purified by the addition of virtues or the diminution of faults. Liberation does not come about by the addition of virtues: for it consists in identity (*svarûpatvam*) with Brahman, who is incapable of any augmentation of perfection; and just as little by the diminution of faults: for Brahman, in identity with whom liberation consists, is eternally pure.—But if, according to this, liberation is a quality (*dharma*) of our own Self, which however remains hidden from us, can it not then be made visible by the purification of the Self through our own efforts, just as brightness, as a quality of the mirror, becomes visible through the action of cleaning? —That cannot be so, since the Self (*âtman*) is no object of action. For an action cannot realise itself otherwise than by altering the object to which it relates. If now the Self, the Âtman, were altered through any action, it could not be eternal and phrases such as 'changeless is he called' would be incorrect, which is not admissible. Consequently there can be no activity which relates to the Self as object; but if it relates to some other object, then the Self is not touched thereby and consequently also not improved."

Observation. Christianity sees the essence of man in Will, Brahmanism in Knowledge; therefore, for the former, salvation consists in a transformation of the Will, a new birth whereby the old becomes the new man; for the latter in a transformation of Knowledge, in the dawning of the consciousness that one is not an individual but Brahman, the totality of all Being.—In this respect, we think the Christian view the more profound, but for that very reason the more incomprehensible; for a transformation of the Will (of that which is fundamental in us and in all being) is totally beyond our understanding. It we desire to understand it, we can do so only as it manifests itself as phenomenon, that is, upon the superficies of our intellect (on which the entire phenomenal world is based). Now the innate fundamental form of the intellect, to which an understanding is fettered, is Causality; and in it all human action without exception appears as the product of an Egotism which is determined by motives. While the intellect forces even moral action into this form of intuition, morality also seems to result from Egotism, which, however, enlarging its natural boundaries as the result of a new mode of knowledge (*Vidyâ*), draws the not-Ego within the sphere of the Ego and treats it accordingly: even the good man (according to the law of Causality) loves only his Ego, and yet he loves "his neighbour as himself," just because he has recognised him as his own Self. This is the direct consequence of the Indian doctrine that the world is Brahman, and Brahman is the Soul; and we do in fact find this conclusion drawn, though not in Çañkara and indeed nowhere to the extent we should have expected; compare the verse of the Bhagavatgîtâ translated in note 36, above p. 59. This is, we believe, the deepest explanation of the essence of morality, which can be reached with the plummet of the intellect (bound to causality). Yet even this remains inadequate; for in truth morality lies beyond Egotism, but therefore also beyond causality and consequently beyond comprehension. Thus it is in Christianity: therefore Christianity demands, not like Brahmanism Self-knowledge (destruction of error), but Self-denial (destruction of Egotism). This is verified by experience and felt by us to be the highest attainable; but regarded from the standpoint of the intellect, it remains something unintelligible, unthinkable, impossible: βλέπομεν γὰρ ἄρτι δι' ἐσόπτρου ἐν αἰνίγματι.

Hence there would remain to Christianity the merit of

having more profoundly grasped morality, to Brahmanism, on the other hand, that of having set forth the highest attainable explanation of it.

4. Knowledge without Works liberates.

Sûtras 3, 4, 1—17. 25. 1, 1, 4.

The goal of man, liberation, is to be gained through **Knowledge of Âtman**, attainable by the Vedânta (that is, by the Upanishads). This knowledge is independent (*svatantra*) of performance of works and in itself alone (*kevala*) suffices for liberation (p. 973—974). — When on the contrary *Jaimini* maintains that this knowledge is an Appendix to works (p. 974, 12) and only serves the purpose of proving the immortality (*vyatireka*) of the Soul, because without this proof the theory of retribution would not hold good (p. 976, 5), the answer is this: if the Vedânta had only the purpose of proving the continuance beyond this bodily existence of the transmigrating, individual, acting, and enjoying soul, then it most certainly would (as *Jaimini* contends) be subordinate to the doctrine of works (p. 980, 7); but in fact it goes further and teaches us to know the highest Soul, which stands above the individual, is God (*îçvara*, here used in the esoteric sense) and remains freed from all the qualities of Saṃsâra, such as activity etc., as well as untouched by all evil; and this knowledge does not impel to works, but rather abolishes them (p. 981, 1).—If it is further objected, that even the knowers of Brahman, as for instance *Açvapati* (above p. 156) who makes known the *Vaiçvânara-vidyâ* (Chând. 5, 11—24), still perform works and that they would not do this if the goal of man could be reached through knowledge alone (p. 978, 1), then one can oppose to them as of equal weight (*tulya*, p. 982, 9) the conduct of those in whose case knowledge makes its appearance unconnected with works; for thus says a passage of scripture (Ait. âr. 3, 2, 6, 8): "Knowing this of a truth the Ṛishis of "the family of Kavasha spoke: 'What good is it for us to "'read the Vedas, what good is it for us to sacrifice!' know- "ing this of a truth the ancients did not offer the fire-sacri-

"fice." And Bṛih. 3, 5, 1 (above p. 142): "Verily, after they "have found this Soul (*viditvâ* in the sense of *vittvâ*), the "Brahmans cease from desiring children, from desiring possess-"ions, from desiring the world, and wander about as beggars." Further it is to be remembered that the *Vaiçvânaravidyâ*, in which knowledge appears accompanied by works, is an exoteric passage (*sa-upâdhikâ brahmavidyâ*), (p. 983, 7).—Finally, to pass over the other objections, when in Îçâ-Up. 2 it is said:

"Let him perform whatever works he will,
"And wish to live a hundred years below,"

yet the following proves in what sense this is meant:

"If he knows Brahman works are of no weight,
"To him there cleaves no stain of earthly woe;"

that is, even though thou performest works all thy life long, yet in so far as thou hast knowledge, they cannot stain thee (p. 986, 6).—Whether the knower shall perform works rests with himself to choose (p. 986, 8); no necessity for so doing, for example, for begetting offspring, exists (p. 986, 10), hence it is written (Bṛih. 4, 4, 22, above p. 195): "This our fore-"fathers knew, when they did not desire offspring and said: "'Wherefore do we need offspring, we whose soul is this "'universe'" (p. 986, 12). For the fruit of knowledge does not, like the fruit of works, consist in something future, but is *anubhava-ârûḍha*, based upon immediate (inner) perception (p. 987, 1; cf. 66, 7).—To this must be added that this whole extension of the world which as the requital of works on the doer, is the cause of the duties of works, is based only upon Ignorance and for the Knower has been annihilated in its very essence (p. 987, 6); even as also, by those who live under the vow of chastity (*ûrdhvaretas* = *parivrâjaka*, according to Ânandagiri on p. 989, 13), Wisdom indeed is sought, but no longer the works prescribed by the Vedas (p. 988, 3).

But is not the knowledge itself, which conditions liberation, a work in so far as it is still an action of the intellect (*manas*) (p. 74, 6)?—By no means! For an action is always dependent upon the will of the agent, by whom it can be done, be left undone, or be done otherwise; every sacrificial work is such an action, such too is meditation (p. 75, 2). Knowledge on the contrary cannot like a work be done in one way or another, indeed it entirely depends not upon any human action, but upon the quality of the object to be known (p. 75, 4). When therefore it is said, for instance in the *Pañca-agni-vidyâ* (Chapter XXX): "man is a fire," "woman is a fire" (above p. 362), this is an invitation to conceive of man, or woman as a fire and its realisation depends upon the choice of the conceiver; on the contrary the knowledge of actual fire as such depends not upon any invitation or action of man, but only upon the object which lies before the eyes, and thus it is knowledge and not action (p. 75). Similarly the cognition of Brahman is dependent upon the nature of Brahman, but not upon any invitation (p. 76, 1). "Hence, all imperatives, even "those found in the Scripture, when they refer to the know- "ledge of Brahman, which is not the object of any command, "become blunt, as the edge of a razor when applied to a "stone" (p. 76, 2).—But then what meaning have such expressions as: "Âtman truly is to be seen, to be heard, to be sought "for, to be known" (Bṛih. 2, 4, 5, above p. 174), which at any rate appear to contain a command?—Their purpose is only to divert man from the natural drift of his thoughts. For everyone is by nature turned to external things and anxious to attain the objects of his desire and to avoid the objects of his aversion. In this way he can never reach the highest aim of man. In order to attain it, the stream of his thoughts must be diverted from natural objects and turned towards the inner soul, and to this end serve such commands as those quoted. To him who has turned to the investigation of Âtman on account of them the true nature of Âtman, which can neither be sought after nor avoided, is pointed out in such phrases as: "this whole universe is what that Soul is" (Bṛih. 2, 4, 6). Thus the knowledge of Âtman is neither an object to be sought for nor avoided, as also its purpose is liberation from all that is to be done; "for that is our orna- "ment and our pride, that after having recognised the soul "as Brahman all obligation of action ceases, and the goal "(*kṛita-kṛityatâ*) is reached" (p. 76—77).

5. How is this saving Knowledge brought about?

Liberation as the fruit of knowledge is distinguishable from the fruit of works in that the former is not, like the latter, produced only in the future, but is produced at once and simultaneously with the knowledge (p. 987, 1). In this sense it is said (Muṇḍ. 3, 2, 9): "He who knows Brahman, becomes "Brahman," as also (Muṇḍ. 2, 2, 8):

"In him who sees the One both high and low,
"His heart's strong fetters bursting, fall apart;
"For him all doubts are solved,
"All works are naught,"

and (Bṛih. 1, 4, 10): "That knew itself and said: 'I am Brah-"'man'; thereby it became this universe,"—these and like passages of Scripture imply that simultaneously with *Brahmavidyâ*, and without any other effect intervening between the two, liberation results (p. 66, 5); to behold Brahman and to become the Soul of the Universe occur simultaneously (p. 66, 7); for liberation is nothing else but our true Self, existent from all eternity, but it is hidden from us through Ignorance; whence also the knowledge of Âtman has not to produce anything new whatever as its fruit, but only to remove the obstacles of liberation (p. 67, 5).

This knowledge of Âtman is thus not a becoming anything, not doing anything, not occupying oneself with any work (p. 68), is altogether independent of human activity, and like the knowledge of every other object, it also is dependent upon the object itself (p. 69, 8; cf. 819, 4). Therefore it cannot be brought about by the action of investigating (p. 69, 10) or of adoring (p. 70, 3), and even Scripture produces the knowledge only so far as it removes the obstacles to it, that is, the division into knower, knowledge and thing known, which springs from Ignorance (p. 70, 9). Therefore also the Scripture says (Kena-Up. 11):

"He only understands who understands it not,
"From him who understands, 'tis evermore concealed,
"For it is not disclosed to him who knowledge hath
"But unto him who hath it not the secret is revealed,"

and teaches (Bṛih. 3, 4, 2), that one cannot see the Seer of seeing, nor hear the Hearer of hearing, nor know the Knower of knowing (p. 71, 1).

We here perceive most clearly the impossibility of attaining liberation by any effort on our part. True, liberation consists only in Knowledge, but in Knowledge of a special kind, in that there is no question of an object which investigation could discover and contemplate, but only of that which can never be an object, because in every cognition it is the subject of cognition: everything can be seen, but not "the Seer of seeing." Since in all empirical knowledge the Âtman is the subject and for that very reason unknowable, the first condition of its attainment is, that all empirical knowledge separating subject and object, should cease: "he "who knows not, alone doth know it." For all empirical knowledge is from its very nature directed to external things, therefore turned away from the inner Soul and consequently, where it is a question of comprehending the latter, is actually an obstacle. To destroy this obstacle is the object of the teaching of scripture; it turns the stream of thoughts away from external things and towards Âtman; but to impart the knowledge of Âtman, that even scripture is not able to accomplish unconditionally; therefore it is written (Kâṭh. 2, 23):—

> "Not by instruction can he be attained,
> "Not yet by understanding, nor the word:
> "Whom he elects, by him will he be gained;
> "To him reveals himself the eternal Lord."

According to this, the knowledge of Âtman is attainable neither by thinking, nor by investigating the scripture, nor by any effort whatsoever of our will: for the latter, that is, "the acting and enjoying soul," belongs only to our phenomenal form, the removal of which is what is required, in order that knowledge may arise:—and yet again, on the other hand, the attainment of knowledge must depend solely and entirely upon ourselves: for the knowledge of Brahman can be conditioned by nothing else except that which in it is at once object and subject, by the Âtman, the Self; and this is our own real, metaphysical Ego. This metaphysical Ego appears in the exoteric doctrine personified as God (*îçvara*, *saguṇam brahma*), and corresponding to it this knowledge, which depends upon him, appears as Grace of God, concerning which we have already collected together the leading passages in Chapter IV, 4. What corresponds to this "Grace of God" in the esoteric system it is difficult to say, and we look in vain for a satisfactory solution. We may compare what was said in Chapter XIV, 4. on the knowledge of the esoteric Brahman. The metaphysical knowledge, in which the Self comes back to itself from its absorption in the contemplation of the external world and thereby comprehends all else as non-Self, non-Ego, non-Being, this knowledge does arise as a matter of fact; but we cannot enquire into its cause because, as already clearly appears in the Vedânta, it is not within the sphere of causality; the Âtman lies beyond Cause and Effect (*anyatra asmât, kṛita-akṛitât*, Kâṭh. 2, 14), and therefore into the knowledge of it, a knowledge of which the Âtman would be the cause, no further enquiry is possible: it arises, when it does arise; how, why, whereby it arises, remains an insoluble problem.

As we saw above p. 318, the impossibility of bringing about liberation by any means whatever has been expressly emphasised; under these circumstances we must regard it as a deviation from the logical structure of the system and a concession to practical demands when we treat of the means (*sâdhanam*) of knowing of Brahman, and these means refer not only to the exoteric, but also to the esoteric Brahman, which two are in general not separated in respect of this question. Of these means there are two, with which we may compare the requirements of those who are called to this knowledge, Chapter IV, 2, namely, first Works, and secondly devout Meditation. We have now to examine according to our sources these two kinds of means of attaining the saving knowledge.

6. Works as Means to Knowledge.

Sûtras 3, 4, 25—27. 32—35. 36—39. 51—52.

Although, as is once more repeated in 3, 4, 25, the goal of man is to be reached only through knowledge, not through works (p. 1007, 2), yet religious works, such as Sacrifice etc., are very far from being without significance in this connection (1008, 3); true, when once that knowledge is realised they have no further importance, but they are nevertheless auxiliary to its attainment (p. 1008, 5). For thus says the scripture (Bṛih. 4, 4, 22, above p. 195): "Him the Brahmans seek to "know by Vedic study, by sacrifice, by alms, by penance, by "fasting," from which it may be gathered that pious works are a means to the attainment of that knowledge (p. 1008, 8). The works named cease when knowledge is attained; certain other obligations, however, still persist for the knower; for the scripture says (Bṛih. 4, 4, 23, above p. 196): "Therefore he who "knows this, he is calm, subdued, resigned, patient, and collect-"ed;" the former (Vedic study, sacrifice, alms, penance, fasting) are the more outward (*vâhya*), the latter (tranquillity, self-restraint, renunciation, patience, concentration, cf. above p. 81) are the "closer" (*pratyâsanna*) means to knowledge (p. 1012, 4). [The concentration (*samâdhi*) here mentioned must be distinguished from the Meditation (*dhyânam, upâsanam*) of which we shall presently have to speak; for Meditation ceases, as we shall see, after the attainment of knowledge, while concentration still continues even in one who has attained knowledge.]

Still the works named do not, strictly speaking, produce knowledge as their fruit, because knowledge is subject to no prescribed rule, and because its fruit (liberation) cannot be brought about by any means (p. 1018, 8). These works are only auxiliaries (*sahakârin*) to the attainment of knowledge, in as much as the man who leads a life of holy works is not overpowered by affections (*kleça*) such as Passion, etc. (p. 1021, 2). According to this their rôle in the scheme of salvation would be not so much meritorious as ascetic; cf. 1082, 12.[134]

However works are not indispensably necessary as a condition of wisdom, since scripture shows by the examples of *Raikva* (note 37, above p. 61) and others, how knowledge may come even to such as from poverty (p. 1021, 8) cannot perform the works of the *Âçramas* (above p. 16); in consequence of common human actions, such as the muttering of prayers, fasting, worship of the Gods, or perhaps in consequence of works performed in some former existence by them the grace of knowledge is vouchsafed to them (p. 1023, 1. 6); yet a life in the *Âçramas* is to be preferred as a means of knowledge (p. 1024, 2).

Knowledge as the fruit of these means ensues either here and now or in the succeeding birth; here, if no hindrance exists, that is, if no other works with greater supersensuous power come to ripeness (p. 1044, 1); for even the hearing of the Veda, by which knowledge arises, is only effective in so far as it succeeds in overcoming those obstacles (p. 1044, 4), which according to Kâṭh. 2, 7, is not always possible (p. 1044, 5);—otherwise knowledge ensues as the fruit of these means in the following life, when it may occasionally, as in the case of *Vâmadeva*, exist from birth onwards (p. 1045, 1); and the Smṛiti too teaches a gradual ascent to perfection, when it says (Bhagavadgîtâ 6, 45):—

"By many a new birth made pure,
"He treads at last the highest Path."

---

[134] The question of the value of pious works for liberation is again ventilated in an Appendix to 4, 1 (4, 1, 16—18), which is perhaps a later addition, with the tendency to reconcile *Jaimini* and *Bâdarâyaṇa* (cf. p. 1083, 7). Works, it is there stated, are auxiliary to liberation, just as even poison may serve as medicine (p. 1082, 5); they may further liberation from a distance (p. 1082, 7), by bringing about knowledge and, through the latter, liberation (p. 1082, 8). In the *nirguṇâ vidyâ* they cease with the attainment of knowledge, in *saguṇâ vidyâḥ*, which are not yet exempt from activity, they continue (p 1082, 11). This effect belongs to works whether connected with knowledge or not; only that in the former case the effect according to Chând. 1, 1, 10 is *vîryavattara*, more powerful, whence it follows that even works without knowledge must be to a certain extent powerful (p. 1085, 6).

Of course such a gradual progress, is only admissible for the exoteric branches of knowledge (p. 1047, 9), not for the esoteric, which knows no differences, no "more" or "less," and brings forth as its fruit the liberation which is an absolutely uniform state and nothing else than the undifferentiated Brahman Himself (p. 1046, 4).

7. Devout Meditation (*upâsanam*) as Means to Knowledge.

Sûtras 4, 1, 1—12.

When it it said: "Âtman verily is to be beheld, is to be "heard, is to be tought upon, is to be meditated upon" (Bṛih. 2, 4, 5),—"him shall ye investigate, him shall ye seek to know" (Chând. 8, 7, 1), then the question arises: is the conception (*pratyaya*) with which worship is concerned, to be called forth once only or repeatedly?—To this is to be answered, as the accumulation of expressions shows, this meditative conception is to be made repeatedly (p. 1050, 8), that is, until intuition occurs (p. 1051, 2), just as one must go on threshing until the grain is freed from the husk (p. 1051, 3). Here, search and worship have to alternate; sometimes worship follows search, and sometimes search worship, as the examples of scripture show (p. 1051, 8).

One might object: Such a repetition of the conception is thinkable, where we are concerned with a result which is capable of being increased (p. 1052, 9); but what end can this repetition serve in the case of the highest Brahman, who is eternal, pure, wise, and free? If this Brahman is not comprehended at the first hearing of scripture then no repetition can be of any use (p. 1053, 1); and how can he who does not understand the first time, the words: *tat tvam asi* (that art thou) grasp it through repetition? And the case is just the same, if we are concerned, not with a single notion, but with a combination of notions (p. 1053, 6). Or is one perhaps to assume, that through once hearing, knowledge in abstract form (*sâmânya-vishaya*) is attained, like that of the sufferings of another, while through repetition knowledge in intuitive form (*viçesha-vishaya*), is gained like that of one's own sufferings (p. 1053, 7)?—This cannot be so either: for if the intuitive knowledge is not brought about through a single hearing, then one fails to see how it can be brought into existence even by hundredfold repetition (p. 1053, 13). Such repetition may be serviceable in respect of a worldly object, which consists of many parts and comprises abstract and intuitive characteristics (p. 1054, 4) or again in the study of a longer treatise, but not in respect of the undifferentiated Brahman, who is free from abstract (general, common to others) characteristics and consists of pure spirit (p. 1054, 6).

To this is to be answered: Only for such as grasp the identity of the Soul and Brahman from once hearing the *tat tvam asi*, is the repetition superfluous, but not for those who are unable to do this and in whom first one doubt and then another must be removed (p. 1054, 8). Here a repetition is most certainly suitable, as is proved by experience with scholars of slow understanding (p. 1055, 2). Further, the sentence *tat tvam asi* consists of two concepts (*padârtha*): (1) *tat*, the Existent, the Brahman who is called the ruler and the cause of the world and is described by the scripture as seeing, not seen, knowing, not known, unborn, not aging, immortal, neither coarse nor fine, neither short nor long; and (2) *tvam*, the inner Self, that which sees and hears in us, which with the body [the outer Self] as a starting-point is grasped as the inner Self and retained as purely spiritual. Now to understand the words *tat tvam asi*, it is necessary for many first to lay hold on the two concepts of which it consists.—Further: The Self which is to be grasped is indeed without parts; but the false knowledge of it as though it consisted of Body, Senses, Manas, Buddhi [which here, as is often the case, is inconsistently named along with Manas] has many parts and requires for its gradual dissipation repeated devout contemplation, so that for many, even in this knowledge, a gradual advance takes place (p. 1055). Others again, whose minds are quicker and have not to battle against Ignorance, doubt and contradiction, can grasp the *tat tvam asi* on hearing it once only.

But can it really be possible that anyone ever completely

grasped this doctrine? Granting even, that he came to the consciousness that all else outside Brahman is not real, yet he must take as real the pain which he feels (p. 1056, 10)?— "By no means! For the feeling of pain like the entire body, "is based on illusion. For the feeling that, when my body is "cut or burnt, I myself am cut and burnt, is a delusion, like "the delusion that I myself suffer, when other persons, for "instance my children or friends, suffer. The case is just the "same with the delusion of feeling pain: for like the body, "all feeling of pain lies outside the spirit; wherefore also it "ceases in deep sleep, while the activity of the spirit is not "interrupted; for 'when he does not see then, yet he is see-"'ing, though he sees not,' as the Scripture says (Bṛih. 4, 3, 25, "above p. 191). Thus the knowledge of the Self consists in "this that I am conscious of myself as pure painless spiritual-"ity; and he who possesses this knowledge for him there "remains nothing more to do; therefore the scripture says "(Bṛih. 4, 4, 22, above p. 195): 'What shall we do with off-"'spring, we, whose soul is this world,' and the Smṛiti says:—

"The man who in the Self hath his delight,
"Who in the Self contentment finds, and peace,
"For him no duty more hath binding force."

But how are we to understand the identity of God and the soul which is taught by the Vedânta, since the two are different? For God is free from evil, but the soul is entangled in it. Now if God is the transmigrating soul, then he cannot be God; if on the contrary the soul is God, then the duty imposed upon the soul by the canon of scripture is superfluous; moreover this view is contradicted by perception (p. 1058, 10).—To this is to be replied: One must conceive of the soul as God; for thus it is said in a passage of the *Jâbâlas* (which is not found in our Jâbâla-Upanishad): "Verily, "I am Thou, O holy Godhead, and Thou art I;" further Bṛih. 1, 4, 10: "I am Brahman;" Bṛih. 3, 7, 3: "He is thy "soul, thy inner Ruler, thy Immortal;" Chând. 6, 8, 7: "That "is the real, that is the soul, that art thou," etc.; and again it is written Bṛih. 1, 4, 10: "But he who worships the God-"head as another, and says: 'that Godhead is one and I am "'another,' he knows it not;" Bṛih. 4, 4, 19: "His never-ending "death he weaves, who here plurality perceives;" Bṛih. 2, 4, 6: "The universe shuts out him, who regards the Universe as "outside the Self," etc.—Thus God and the soul are not different, since their difference rests only on illusion; if the soul is stripped of its Saṃsâra state, it is God and hence free from evil, and what contradicts this is mere illusion. But as regards the duties of the canon of scripture and perception, they both continue to exist as long as Saṃsâra, that is, until awakening. This being attained perception becomes naught; and if you base on the objection, that with it the Veda is also annihilated, then it is to be noted that according to our own teaching, "then the father is not father, the Veda not "Veda" (above p. 191):

"But who then is the not-awakened?"

—Thou, who askest.

"But I am God, according to the teaching of scripture!"

—When thou knowest that, then art thou awakened, and then there exists no unawakened more (*na asti kasyacid aprabodhaḥ*).[135]

So much concerning the inner nature of devout meditation. As regards outward attitude, the position of the body is a

---

[135] Compare with this logical consequence of the System my "Elements of Metaphysics," § 292, p. 305: "The saint to whom true know-"ledge has arisen, knows himself as the entire Will to life. Accordingly "he is filled with the consciousness that he removes the sufferings of the "whole world in removing his ego which he knows is the bearer of these. "And this consciousness indeed does not lie, for the saint, in removing "and delivering the Will in himself, has removed and delivered this "whole world. For him, who is enlightened by transcendental knowledge, "there remains of it nothing but an unsubstantial phantom, a shadow-"play without reality. To us alone it will not seem so, just because we "are still on the empirical standpoint of affirmation, and only so far as "transcendental knowledge awakes in us, can we take part in his deliver-"ance."—§ 174, p. 131: "Thus the regenerate saves himself and the groan-"ing creation: and yet affirmation still continues, even after he has found "the way out of its circle; also this world for ever and aye will exist, "will affirm, will suffer,—but again all time in the light of denial is no-"thing, and all that it contains fades away as the shadow-play on the "wall for the Will, when it has turned."

matter of indifference both in those meditations which are undertaken for the purpose of attaining perfect knowledge, as well as in those meditations which are connected with the service of works (p. 1070, 14). In the remaining kinds of worship (that is, presumably, in those used in the exoteric knowledge) one should not walk, run or stand, because this distracts, nor lie down either, because one might then be overtaken by sleep, but sit (p. 1071, 7). Moreover in regard to direction, place and time, one need only be careful about them, so far as they promote the undivided concentration of the mind as much as possible (p. 1072, 9). The forms of worship which lead to perfect knowledge come to an end with the attainment of this knowledge (p. 1073, 8); those on the contrary, whose fruit is felicity (as it seems not only those of the *Pitṛiyâna*, but also those of the *Devayâna*), must be continued until death, since the attainment of their fruit in the other world is dependent on the thoughts at the moment of death (p. 1074, 2; cf. 112, 8). For the scripture says (Çatapathabr. 10, 6, 3, 1): "with whatever mind a man departs from "this world, with the same mind he enters into the other "world, after death," and the Smṛiti declares (Bhagavadgitâ 8, 6):—

> "The nature that he thinks upon, when he departs this life,
> "E'en this he will put on whene'er he reaches the Beyond."

In the exposition of these means no distinction is maintained between the esoteric and the exoteric doctrine; so much the more, however, does this distinction dominate the liberation which appears as their result. We turn next to consider the man who has fully and unconditionally reached the goal of humanity, the man of esoteric knowledge, the Sage possessing *Samyagdarçanam*, to study his condition in Life, Death, and in the Beyond. After we have come to know in him the essence of liberation in its purity and completeness, we shall in conclusion have to consider the Path, upon which the Devotee, the man who has recognised and adored Brahman in his exoteric form, is led to the same goal by means of *Kramamukti*.

XXXVI. Condition of the Sage in this Life.

1. Characteristics of the Sage.

In contrast to the Devotee, who knows and worships Brahman in the exoteric, theological form, we understand in this and in what follows by the term Sage, him to whom has come *Samyagdarçanam*, perfect knowledge, that is, esoteric knowledge of the higher, attributeless (*param, nirguṇam*) Brahman, and who in consequence of this possesses an immediate consciousness [136] on the one hand of the identity of his own Self with Brahman, on the other of the illusory character of all that is different (*nânâ*) from the Soul, from Brahman, therefore of the whole extended world (*prapañca*), his own body and the other Upâdhis of the Soul (*indriyas, manas, mukhya prâṇa, sûkshmam çarîram, karman*) included. For such a one there is no longer any world to be perceived nor any perception, and even his own suffering, since it depends upon perception, is no longer felt by him as pain; on which point compare the fuller treatment above p. 299 and p. 415. Further since all works have only the purpose of attaining pleasure and avoiding pain, while pain and pleasure concern not bodiless, but only embodied Being based upon illusion (above p. 402), for him who has seen through this illusion, all

---

136 *anubhava*; p. 917, 5: "The fruit of Knowledge depends upon immediate consciousness; for the scripture says (Bṛih. 3, 4, 1, translated "above p. 141): 'the immanent, not transcendent Brahman;' and the "words 'That art thou' (Chând. 6, 8, 7) denote something already existing and must not be understood as if they meant only: 'That wilt thou "'become after death;'... consequently for the knower of Brahman "liberation is absolutely accomplished." Cf. p. 987, 1. 66, 7. 1055, 10. "1057, 2.

works (Vedic study, sacrifice, alms, asceticism, fasting) are abolished, as also all the injunction of the Veda which command them. And not only does the Part of Works become superfluous, but also that Part of the Veda which treats of knowledgo, above p. 21; for this is also only a means to an end: "Thinking and meditating have like hearing (only) "attainment as their purpose;" when that purpose is attained, the scripture has fulfilled its object; as there exists for the awakened neither perception, nor pain, nor action, so there exists for him no Veda either; to him "the Veda is not Veda" as the scripture says (above p. 416). In a word: everything outside Brahman, that is the Self, the Soul, has no more reality for him and can no longer disturb him, just as little as the rope which he mistakenly held to be a snake (note 105, above p. 269) or the trunk, in which in the darkness of his ignorance, he thought he saw a man (p. 86, 12).

(p. 84, 5:) "And yet experience shows how, even for one "who knows Brahman, Saṃsâra still persists, so that he has "not attained his goal, as in the simile of the rope?—To this "we reply: It must not be maintained that for him who has "recognised that the Soul is Brahman, Saṃsâra persists as "before, because the knowledge of the Self (the Soul) as "Brahman contradicts this. For so long as he held the body "etc. to be the Self, so long was he affected by pain and "fear, but after that delusion has been destroyed by means of "the knowledge (produced by the Veda), of the Self as Brah-"man, then it can no longer be maintained that he is affected "by pain and fear since that depended upon erroneous know-"ledge. For so long as for instance, a rich householder has "the consciousness of his wealth, pain arises for him from its "loss; but after he has gone away as a hermit into the forest "(above p. 16) and has freed himself from the conciousness of "his wealth, then there can arise for him no more pain from "the loss of it. And so long as one wears ear-rings, pleasure "arises from the consciousness of wearing them; but after "one has laid them aside and freed oneself from the conscious-"ness of wearing ear-rings, then the pleasure in wearing them "no longer exists for him. Therefore the scripture says

"(Chând. 8, 12, 1): 'Verily, the bodiless is not touched by pain "'and pleasure.' If you maintain that bodilessness is only "attained after the dissolution of the body, not during life, "then we do not admit this, because being clothed with the "body depends (only) upon false cognition. For the circum-"stance of the Self's being connected with a body can be "understood in no other way, than by conceiving it as erron-"eous knowledge, consisting in the delusion of the body be-"ing the Self. For we have seen that [for the Self] the "condition of bodilessness is an eternal one, and this because "it is not conditioned by action [only what belongs to the "fruit of works is perishable]. If however you maintain that "being embodied is the consequence of good and evil works "done by it [the bodiless Âtman], then we deny this; for "since its union with the body is untrue, therefore the assertion "is also untrue that the Âtman has done good and evil. For "the assertions that it is clothed with a body and has done "good and evil works are always supported by each other and "therefore lead to the assumption of a *regressus in infinitum*; "and this is comparable to a chain altogether of blind "persons each holding the other, since it is impossible for the "Âtman to be affected by works, the Âtman being no acting "principle."---(p. 87, 5:) "Consequently being clothed with a "body depends only upon a false conception, and thus it is "proved that the knower of Brahman is, in his life time, "already bodiless. Therefore the scripture says (Bṛih. 4, 4, 7, "translated above p. 194): 'As the slough of a snake dead "'and cast off lies upon an anthill, thus lies this body then, "'but the bodiless, the immortal, the life is pure Brahman, is "'pure Light;' and [where is unknown to me]: 'with eyes as "'if without eyes, with ears as if without ears, with speech "'as if without speech, with Manas as if without Manas, with "'life as if without life,' and the Smṛiti shows in the passage: "'What is the essence of him who is firm in knowledge?' etc. "(Bhagavadgîtâ 2, 54) where it enumerates the characteristics "of one who is firm in knowledge and reckons as such that "he is set free from all work.—Thus for one who has recognised "the Brahmanhood of the Soul, Saṃsâra does not continue "as before, and he for whom it still continues, has in truth "not yet recognised that the Soul is Brahman; that is certain."

2. The Destruction of Sin.

Sûtram 4, 1, 3.

Existence without works is, as we have seen repeatedly, (above pp. 112. 390. 402) impossible. But it lies in the nature of works to have as purpose the production of a definite fruit, and without its having brought forth this fruit—one might think—no work can be annihilated, provided that the authority of the scripture is to be maintained (p. 1075, 9). That liberation thereby becomes impossible, need not be admitted; only one would have to incorporate liberation, like the fruit of works in the chain of Space, Time, and Causality (p. 1075, 17; that is, regard it equally as a fruit of works).—But that is not so! On the contrary, when once Brahman is known, sin committed is annihilated, and future sins cannot cleave to such a one (p. 1076, 2). For the scripture says (Chând. 4, 14, 3, translated above p. 165): "As water does not cling to the lotus "leaf, so no evil deed clings to one who thus knows;" and (Chând. 5, 24, 3; translated above p. 157) "as burns the leaflet "of the bulrush when thrust into the fire, so are burnt up all "his sins;" and yet again (Muṇḍ. 2, 2, 8):

> "For him who sees the One, both high and low
> "His heart's strong fetters, bursting, fall apart,
> "For him all doubts are solved, all works are naught."

We do not thereby deny the fruit-producing power of works; such a power certainly exists; but we assert that it is checked in its development by a cause of another kind, namely, by knowledge (p. 1076, 14). For the canon of the doctrine of works holds good only on the assumption, that the power of the works exists; where the power is checked, the canon then loses its validity (p. 1076, 15). When then the Smṛiti says: "no work can be lost," this remains the rule and implies that no work, without having borne its fruit, can be annihilated, and even the penance (*prâyaçcittam*) prescribed for certain deeds forms no exception, in that it is itself a kind of retribution (p. 1077, 1). The case is otherwise, on the contrary, with knowledge. If one takes exception to the fact that this (knowledge) is not, like penance, prescribed as a means of purification from sin (p. 1077, 6) then it is to be noted that the attribute-ascribing forms of knowledge (*saguṇâ vidyâḥ*) do likewise also belong to the doctrine of works and in consequence are also accompanied by promises of heavenly lordship and release from evil (p. 1077, 9); in the attributeless knowledge, on the contrary, the prescription does not hold good, and yet the "burning up" of works is accomplished by it, and this by the knowledge that the Âtman is not an acting principle (p. 1077, 12). This knowledge that the soul is by nature a non-agent brings about in the first place the result that future works no longer cleave to the knower of Brahman who is no longer an agent, and further, that the former works which he performed under the false delusion of being an agent are annihilated through the dissipation of this delusion by the power of knowledge (p. 1078, 1). For the knower of Brahman says: "That Brahman the nature of which "is opposed to the nature of formerly held to be true, being "an agent and enjoyer, that Brahman which is in its very "nature in all time past, present and future not-agent, not-"enjoyer, that Brahman am I, and therefore I never was "either agent or enjoyer, nor am I such now, nor shall I ever "be one" (p. 1078, 4).—Only thus can liberation take place; in any other way the destruction of the works which have been taking their course from eternity in the past, and therefore liberation itself also, becomes impossible. "Hence liber-"ation cannot, like the fruit of works, be conditioned by Space, "Time, and Causality, for then the fruit of knowledge would "be transitory and would lose its transcendent character "(*parokshatvam*)" (p. 1078, 10).

3. Destruction of Good Works also.

Sûtram 4, 1, 14.

When knowledge arises, past sins, as we have seen, are annihilated, and future sins can no longer cleave to the Soul. But how about the good works? For these indeed are commanded by the same scripture which is the source of knowledge and it cannot contradict itself. Must not good works therefore be excepted from annihilation?—We reply: annihilation and non-cleaving apply equally to good works and evil, for the following reasons: 1) good works also bring their own fruit and thereby hinder the fruit of knowledge; 2) the scripture teaches that both, the good and the evil works, disappear at the appearance of knowledge (Bṛih. 4, 4, 22, translated above p: 196): "[Who thus knows] him both overcome not whether "he therefore [because he was in the body] has done evil or "has done good; but he overcomes both; him neither what he "has done nor what he has not done burns;" 3) in the destruction of works resulting from the knowledge that the Soul is not an agent, good and evil deeds are of equal value (*tulya*); of both it is said indifferently (Muṇḍ. 2, 2, 8) "and his works are "naught;" 4) where evil works only are mentioned. good works must be understood as well, because their fruit, in comparison with that of knowledge, is inferior; 5) when the scripture says (Chând. 8, 4; translated above p. 162): "this bridge day and "night traverse not, nor old age, nor death, nor pain, nor "good, nor evil works, and from it all sins turn back," then in the words "all sins" both the good and evil works just mentioned are included (p. 1079).

—We may compare with this, the explanations of the Apostle Paul in the Epistles to the Romans and Galatians as to the impossibility of a redemption through the law. According to Paul the law, if fulfilled, would set us free; but, in consequence of the sinfulness of our nature, it cannot be fulfilled; according to *Çañkara* the law can he fulfilled, but its fulfilment does not bring liberation, but only reward on the path of transmigration. The former has the deeper consciousness of the sinfulness of our nature, the latter the more correct estimate of the value of the works of the law;—both combined give the philosophical truth. The law (for instance the Vedic or Mosaic) can unquestionably be fulfilled, but, in consequence of our innate egotism can be fulfilled only from selfish motives; hence its fulfilment has no moral value; lawful and unlawful actions both depend upon egotism, and are therefore, morally considered, both equally valueless and do not lead to liberation. This is only accomplished through that transformation of our Ego, which according to the Christian view proceeds from Faith, according to the Hindu view consists in Knowledge.—Both, Faith and Knowledge, are at the bottom one and the same,—that metaphysical consciousness which lifts us above the world and raises us above all possibility of sin. Whether this consciousness, assuming its genuineness, leads over into Quietism as among the Indians, or, as among us, is realised in deeds of love, touches only its form of appearance and establishes no difference in the value of what appears here.

4. Why the Body, in spite of Liberation, still continues to exist.

Sûtras 4, 1, 15. 19.

Knowledge burns up works, but only works whose retribution has not yet begun, whether they originate from this life as led before the awakening (*prabodha*), or consist in a balance from some previous life which could not come to realisation in the present existence (above pp. 112. 390). But knowledge does not destroy those works whose seed has already germinated, that is, those from which the present life, serving as basis for dawning knowledge, has been fashioned (p. 1080, 9; the same predestination of the course of life as we find in Plato's Republic 10, 15, p. 617E). For if this were not so, if all works without exception were annihilated by knowledge, then quiescence (*kshema*) would not arise only after death, but immediately upon the attainment of knowledge, since there would be no further cause for the continuance of life [no further work to be atoned for] (p. 1080, 12). For this fact certainly startling in our system, that in spite of liberation the body still continues to exist for a while, Çañkara gives two explanations, of which the one is more realistic, the other more idealistic. (1) As the vessel which is being formed requires the potter's wheel to support it, so liberation requires a life as a substratum; and as the potter's wheel continues for a time to revolve, even after the vessel has been completed, so also life continues after liberation, since it contains no cause to check the impetus already gained (p. 1081, 2); hence only after works, like the velocity of the flying arrow, have expended themselves, does liberation become an accomplished fact for all who possess knowledge; therefore it is said (Chând. 6, 14, 2; translated above p. 266): "To this "[worldly action] I shall belong only until I am liberated, "then shall I go home" (p. 916, 8). (2) As when a man suffering from eye disease, continues to see two moons even after he has attained the conviction that there is only one moon there, owing to the force of the impression (*saṃskâra-vaçât*), so too the impression of the sense-world persists, after a man has attained the knowledge of its non-existence (p. 1081, 5).—In view of the questionable character of these explanations, our author falls back upon the inner certainty of liberation: "Here, he remarks, no discussion at all is admissible; for how could anyone who is convinced in his heart that he is Brahman, be refuted by another, even when he is in the body?"

Truly there are venerable, holy words, which prove how profoundly the Indian was convinced of what he lays before us!—But the condition here described (to which, as the highest goal of existence, humanity will ever return, whatever else man may undertake)—this condition must have been nothing very rare in India, as is proved by the fact that later ages had a technical expression for it, namely *jîvan-mukti* (liberation during life) and *jîvan-mukta* (the living liberated), although we do not yet meet with these expressions in Çañkara.

Thus after works, whose retribution has not yet begun, have been destroyed by knowledge, while those whose seed had already germinated, have been consumed through continuance of life, death comes, as the outward sign of this consumption (above p. 353), and with death comes definitive and eternal union with Brahman; for the works on whose account one had to live are exhausted, while the balance, and in them the seed of a further existence, has been burnt up, through the destruction of false knowledge, on which they depend, by perfect knowledge (p. 1086).

XXXVII. The dying Sage.

1. His Soul does not depart.

THE *Utkrânti*, that is, the "withdrawal" of the Soul from the body described in Adhyâya 4, 2, which as we saw (above p. 379) was common both to the ignorant and the possessor of exoteric knowledge, is interrupted (4, 2, 12—16) by an episode pertaining to the higher knowledge (*prâsaṅgikî para-vidyâ-gatâ cintâ*, p. 1103, 12), which treats of the death of him who possesses esoteric knowledge and is consequently free from desire (*akâmayamâna*). Of such it is said in Bṛih. 4, 4, 6 (translated above p. 194):—

"And now of him who desires not.—He who is "without desire, free from desire, whose desires are "stilled, whose desire is the Self, his vital breaths "do not depart, but Brahman is he and into Brah-"man is he resolved."

One might think, says Çaṅkara, since instead of "his "(*tasya*) vital breaths do not depart" we read in the other (Mâdhyandina-)recension: "out of him (*tasmâd*) the vital breaths "do not depart"—that what is denied in this passage is not the departure of the Soul from the body (*deha*, *çarîram*), but that of the organs from the individual Soul (*dehin*, *çârîra*); that one who is liberated departs from the body is, it might be believed, self-evident; what is taught here being that from him (that is, from the Âtman) his vital organs do not depart, but remain united with him (p. 1099, 2).

But this is not the case; this passage rather teaches that the *Akâmayamâna*, he "who does not desire," that is, the completely liberated sage, does not, at death, like others (the pious worshipper and the performer of works) depart from his body. This is proved by the passage (Bṛih. 3, 2, 11) where the son of *Ṛitabhâga* asks *Yâjñavalkya*: "Yâjñavalkya! so "said he, when such a man dies, do then the vital breaths "depart from him or not?—No, said Yâjñavalkya, even at that "very spot they are dissolved;[137] he swells, is bloated, bloated "lies the dead."—Here it is evidently the departure from the body, which is denied, and the above passage must also be explained in accordance with this, whether we read *tasmâd* (that is, out of the body) or *tasya* (that is, of the sage) in the passage in question (p. 1100, 4). This explanation is further supported by the fact that in the passage in question, after the description of the departure from the body, it is said: "So much for him who desires.—Now we have to speak "of him who does not desire" (above p. 194). This contrast would be meaningless if a departure of the Soul from the body were to be assumed in the case of one who does not desire (p. 1100, 12). Such a departure, finally, cannot be admitted in the case of the knower of Brahman who has conquered desire and works for this reason also, that there is no cause for it, since he who is liberated becomes Brahman at death, and Brahman is all-pervading (p. 1101, 2). In this sense the Smṛiti also says (Mahâbhâratam XII, 9657):—

> "Who of all nature has become the Self,
> "Whose vision fully pierces nature through,
> "His path is found not by the gods themselves,
> "Who trace the track of him who leaves no trace."

2. The Dissolution of the Psychic Apparatus.

As we have already frequently seen, the individual Soul is surrounded by a complicated apparatus of *Upâdhis*, which in part dwell with it in the heart (above p. 311), in part are concentrated in it at death (above p. 379), in order to depart

---

137 Çaṅkara reads instead of *samavanîyante*, p. 1099, 12, *samavalîyante*, and instead of *ucchvayati*, p. 1099, 13. 14, *ucchayati*, *ucchayana*, which the Gloss explains as *vâhya-vâyu-pûraṇâd vardhate*.

along with the Soul. To this complex of *Upâdhis* which accompanies the Soul in all its wanderings, there belong: *Indriyas*, *Manas*, *Prâṇa*, and *Sûkshmam Çarîram*, which are as it were knit together into a knot that death cannot loose. This knot of the heart (if we may take *hṛidaya-granthi*, Muṇḍ. 2, 2, 8; cf. Kâṭh. 6, 15, in this concrete sense, which however is unsupported by any authority) is cut for the Sage, and while at death others do indeed enter into the highest Godhead, yet they do so in such a way that a germ remains over for the new existence, which consists in this very apparatus, folded up and charged with the works of each particular life (above pp. 340. 373), thus while in them the seed-powers just named remain over as a residue (p. 1103, 3), the resolution of the dying sage into Brahman, on the contrary, takes place without residue (*niravaçesha*) and he enters into indivisibility with all his parts (p. 1103, 4). For thus says the scripture (Praçna 6, 5):

"Just as those flowing rivers, which take their course to "the ocean, when they have reached the ocean, come to rest,— "their names and forms perish and they are now called ocean "only—just so too the sixteen parts of the all-beholder [of "him who possesses the *Samyagdarçanam*] which take their "course to the Spirit (*purusha*), after they have reached the "Spirit, come to rest, their names and forms perish, and they "are then called Spirit only; this is that partless, immortal "one."

By the "sixteen parts" Çañkara here understands "the *In-*"*driyas* called *Prâṇa* and the Elements" (p. 1102, 4), of which, however, according to his system there are seventeen. In the passage of the Praçna the following parts are originally meant: 1. *Prâṇa*, 2. *Çraddhâ*, 3. Ether, 4. Air, 5. Fire, 6. Water, 7. Earth, 8. the ten *Indriyas*, 9. *Manas*, 10. Food, 11. Force (*vîryam*), 12. Asceticism, 13. the *Mantras* of the Veda, 14. Works. 15. the Worlds, 16. the Name.

3. Can the Liberated assume a new Body?

An episode in 3, 3, 32, deals with the question, whether the Sage, after his body has turned to dust, can again assume a new body (p. 913, 2)?—True it is that from knowledge (and we must here understand *Samyagdarçanam* p. 915, 1) proceeds absoluteness (*kaivalyam*) yet the Itihâsas and Purâṇas relate how some knowers of Brahman have yet come again to embodiment (p. 913, 7); thus *Apântaratamas*, *Vasishṭha*, *Bhṛigu*, *Sanatkumâra*, *Daksha*, *Nârada* and others (p. 913), as too *Sulabhâ* during her life temporarily left her body (p. 915, 8), and others again inhabited several bodies at the same time (p. 914, 2). Hence one might conclude that the knowledge of Brahman sometimes leads to liberation and sometimes not (p. 914, 5); but that is not so; for if those whom we have named returned to bodily existence, it was in fulfilment of a mission (*adhikâra*), *e.g.* to promote the spread of the Veda for the good of the world (p. 914, 6). "As yonder holy *Savitar* "(the sun), after having fulfilled his earthly mission through a "thousand world-periods, at length neither rises nor sets, but "enjoys absoluteness—as the scripture (Chând. 3, 11, 1) says: "'but then after he has risen up, he will no longer rise nor "'set, but stand alone in the centre' [a prophesy fulfilled since "Copernicus],—and as also the living knowers of Brahman. "after the fruit of actions already entered on has been ex-"hausted, enjoy absoluteness, as it is said (Chând. 6, 14, 2. "translated above p. 266): 'to this [world of action] I shall "'only belong until I am liberated, then shall I return home.' "—as we must assume that those glorious ones also, *Apân-"taratamas* and others entrusted by the Most Glorious with "this or that mission, in spite of the fact that they possessed "full knowledge which is the condition of perfection, continued. "their works not [yet] disappearing, so long as the mission "lasted, and [only] after its completion were they dispensed "therefrom" (p. 914, 8—915, 2). Wherein, we must assume, that, besides the work committed to them, no further work came into existence which could have served as the seed of a new life, as otherwise their liberation would have become illusory (p. 915, 11). But that liberation should come to an end, is unthinkable after the works, which are the seed of future existence, have been burnt up by the fire of knowledge; as the Smṛiti says (the first verse in Bhagavadgîtâ 4, 37):—

"As fiery heat to ashes turns the wood
"By knowledge are all works to ashes turned—
"As seed when it is burnt can grow no more,
"So the Soul's sufferings, by knowledge burnt."

XXXVIII. Condition of the Sage after Death.

1. Entrance into the highest Light.

In the passage Chând. 8, 7—12 (discussed chap. XII, 3 above p. 183 ff.), with reference to the Soul that has become one with Brahman, whether temporarily, in deep sleep, or —which is the case here—in the final condition of liberation after death, it is said (8, 12. 1—3):

"Of a truth this body is mortal, O mighty one, and subject "to death; it is the dwelling place for that immortal bodiless "Self. The embodied is subject to pleasure and pain; for "because he is embodied no warding off of pleasure and of "pain is possible. But pleasure and pain touch not the bodi-"less. Bodiless is the wind; the cloud, the lightning, the "thunder are bodiless. Now as these arise from cosmic space "[in which they, like the soul in the body, are fettered], enter "into the highest light and thereby stand forth in their proper "forms, so also arises this perfect peace [that is, the "soul, properly in deep slumber, here in liberation] out of "this body, enters into the highest light and thereby "stands forth in its own proper form; that is the supreme "spirit."

One might think, so Çaṅkara develops the thought 4, 4, 1—3 that by this "standing forth in its own proper form" something new is added to the Soul, because after all liberation is also a fruit (reward), because this standing forth means a becoming something, and because its own proper form too was already proper to it in its former conditions (waking, dream and deep sleep), from which its present condition is however different (p. 1137, 7).—But that is not so; the new condition consists rather in this, that the Soul, in its mere Self, without any other quality, becomes manifest; for "its own proper form" denotes not a form which accidentally (*âgantuka*) belongs to the Self, but that form which the Self is, according to its own nature (p. 1138, 6). Liberation is a fruit only in this negative sense, that bondage is annihilated, not as if it had reference to the appendage of an *Apûrvam* (above p. 377) (p. 1139, 5); further the standing forth is only a becoming in the sense that it is a cessation of the former state, as becoming healthy is only a cessation of sickness (p. 1139, 6); and the difference from its previous existence consists in this, that the Soul up to that time as the Chândogya passage describes it above, is affected with blindness grief, and mortality, whilst now, liberated from its former blindness, it abides in its pure Self (p. 1138, 10). Accordingly the light, into which the Soul enters, is no created light (p. 1139, 12), for such light, like all created things would be afflicted; "what is different from "him is afflicted," as the scripture says (Bṛih. 3, 4, 2, above p. 142); rather that light is the very Self, the Âtman, of which it is said (Bṛih. 4, 4, 16, above p. 195):

"Him 'neath whose feet time's rolling stream of days and year rolls past,
"In whom all beings' fivefold host, with Space itself stands fast.
"Whom Gods as Light of Lights adore as Immortality,
"The Brahman know I as my deathless Self, for I am he."

2. Characteristics of him who has obtained absoluteness.

From the passage quoted we also learn the characteristics of the liberated, as is said (Chând. 8, 7, 1, above p. 183):—

"The Self, the sinless, free from death and free from suffer-"ing, without hunger and without thirst, whose wishes are "true, whose decree is true, that Self is to be sought out, "that Self one must seek to know."

In these predicates, to which are added omniscience and omnipotence, consist according to *Jaimini*, the characteristics of the liberated (p. 1141).

On the other hand, *Auḍulomi* takes exception to the plurality of these predicates and thinks they can denote only negatively the freedom from all evil, while to the Âtman as its only positive quality, belongs spirituality (*caitanyam*) (p. 1142, 5). Further, the attributes "of true wish and of true "decree" cannot, he thinks, be conceived, apart from connection with the *Upâdhis*, and can only serve, like the succeeding passage in Chând. *loc. cit.*, wherein even laughing and playing are spoken of, to indicate freedom from all evil (p. 1142, 12). Hence the entire passage must mean that the Âtman, "after "having cast off without exception the world of plurality, "stands forth in the unspeakable Self of Knowledge."

Thus think *Jaimini* and *Auḍulomi*, while *Bâdarâyaṇa* finds no contradiction between these two conceptions, since he regards as reconcilable (p. 1143, 5) (though in what sense it is not explained) the pure spirituality ascribed to the Âtman, in the sense of the highest reality (*pâramârthika*), and the lordship in Brahman predicated of it in the empirical sense (*vyavahâra-apekshayâ*) [in other words the esoteric and exoteric doctrines] (p. 1143, 5).

3. The *Unio mystica.*

All that is changeable ultimately leads back to an unchangeable, to discover and learn to know which is the whole problem of metaphysics; wherefore in the domain of metaphysics there can be no becoming. For this reason too it cannot admit any union in the proper sense of the word: that which in its very nature is two, can never become one; that only can become one, which was one already, the comprehension of which as two before, depended on an error. After knowledge has removed this error, and after the dissolution of the body, connected with it, has taken away the last semblance of it, then the eternally existent unity comes forth. In pointing to this unity the last word of Metaphysics has been spoken, a word which, from the very nature of the topic, is brief.

One must not imagine, says Çañkara p. 1140, because in the last mentioned passage from the Chândogya an entering into, a circulating, etc. is spoken of, that the Soul therefore still exists separate from the highest Âtman. The condition of the liberated is rather that of indivisibility; for thus teach the words of the scripture: (Chând. 6, 8, 7) "That art thou;" (Bṛih. 1, 4, 10) "I am Brahman;" (Bṛih. 4, 3, 23) "there is no second there, no other, different from him;" and for the elucidation of this state of indivisibility serve the similes, Kâṭh. 4, 15:

> "As water still remaineth pure,
> "When into water pure 'tis poured,
> "E'en so 'tis with the Sage's soul."

and Muṇḍ. 3, 2, 8 (cf. Chând. 6, 10, 1. Praçna 6, 5, above pp. 264. 429):—

> "As rivers run and in the deep
> "Lose name and form, are lost to sight,
> "The Sage released from name and form,
> "Enters the highest spirit of light."

The separation between the supreme and the individual Soul, which here seems to find expression, is not to be taken as such; this also the scripture indicates, when it is said (Chând. 7, 24, 1, above p. 203): "Wherein, O holy one, does "he stand?—He stands in his own majesty."

XXXIX. The Passing of the Pious to Brahman.

1. The Characteristics of the Pious.

In the Doctrine of the Five Fires (chapter XXX), a distinction is drawn between those who perform pious works and thereby are led along the *Pitṛiyâna* to their reward in the beyond and then to a new life upon earth, and those "who "know this, and those others who in the forest practise Faith "and Penance (Bṛih.: Truth);" these latter ascend upward upon the *Devayâna* and enter into Brahman, whence there is no return (above p. 363). — Obviously, in the belief of the original authors of the doctrine entering into Brahman was the highest goal of man. This it could no longer remain when once on the basis of passages like Bṛih. 4, 4, 6 (above p. 427) which from their position appear older and from their stage of development more recent than the doctrine of the five fires, the esoteric doctrine had been reached, according to which Brahman is without attributes (*nirguṇam*), empirical reality together with *Saṃsâra* an illusion, and the individual soul is completely identical with the highest. From this standpoint there could no longer be any question of a passing of the soul into Brahman, but only a knowledge of its identity therewith, in which knowledge, as we saw, liberation consists. In contrast with this liberation in the strict esoteric sense of the word, there now appeared, as a lower form, the exoteric union with the attribute-possessing (*saguṇam*) Brahman, attainable upon the *Devayâna* by entering into Brahman, and it was therefore termed *Kramamukti*, that is, "progressive liberation" or "gradual liberation" (above p. 398); as the former, esoteric liberation is the fruit of the *Paravidyâ*, that is, of

Samyagdarçanam, so *Kramamukti* forms the reward of the *Aparavidyâ*, that is, of the knowledge of *saguṇam brahma*, of Brahman as, clothed with attributes, it usually appears personified as God (*îçvara*) and is accordingly the object of worship (*upâsanâ*) for the pious.

"The passing [to Brahman]," says Çañkara, p. 909, 7, "has "a purpose only in the worship through attributes, as for "instance in the teaching concerning the throne (Kaush. 1), "in which the ascent to the throne, the conversation with "Brahman seated on the throne, the attainment of various "sweet odours etc., is described, in short, various rewards, "which imply motion in space. Here a passing is in place; "but no such goal can be admitted in the case of *Samyag-* "*darçanam.* For there is nothing more to expect for those "who, knowing their unity with Âtman, have already obtained "their desire here and have burnt up the seed of all troubles "without leaving a residue, except the consumption of the "sum of works whose retribution has already begun, and thus "a passing is purposeless, just as in life the traveller, on "arriving in a village, enquires about his further journey [but "not one who has reached his journey's end, and as the sick "man has recourse to medicine] but not he who has attained "health. And so a passing has its purpose in the *Saguṇâ* "*Vidyâḥ*, but none in the *Nirguṇâ Paramâtma-vidyâ.*" It is true, it is said further, that the *Devayâna* is only mentioned in certain *Saguṇâ Vidyâḥ*, as in the *Paryañkavidyâ* (Kaush. 1), *Pañcâgnividyâ* (Bṛih. 6, 2. Chând. 5, 3—10, above p. 362), *Upakosalavidyâ* (Chând. 4, 10—15, above p. 166), *Daharavidyâ* (Chând. 8, 1—6, above p. 162); in others again not, as in the *Madhuvidyâ* (Bṛih. 2, 5 or Chând. 3, 1—11), *Çâṇḍilyavidyâ* (Chând. 3, 14, above p. 152), *Shoḍaçakalavidyâ* (Praçna 6, above p. 429), *Vaiçvânaravidyâ* (Chând. 5, 11—24, above p. 156); "yet "the path named *Devayâna* is equally valid in all the *Saguṇâ* *Vidyâḥ*, as they have as their fruit the attainment of ascent.[138]

---

[138] *abhyudaya*, which therefore here (p. 911, 3) denotes the *Kramamukti* on the *Devayâna* path, while in all other passages where the word occurs (p. 26, 2. 112, 5. 203, 5. 352, 4. 396, 7. 754, 1. 858, 4. 7. 1073, 11.

If we look at the connection of our system as a whole, without letting ourselves be misled by isolated contradictions, we have, as is well known, in the first place two doctrines of Brahman, the esoteric, philosophical (*paravidyâ*) and the exoteric, theological (*aparavidyâ*); and, corresponding to these, two paths to liberation; the one, upon which the Sage, possessing *Samyagdarçanam*, attains the goal, we have already become acquainted with; it consists in the consciousness of identity with Brahman and of the unreality of all plurality; the other, exoteric path of *Kramamukti* is for all such as, while they do not cling to the service of works belonging to the old Vedic gods but to the doctrine of Brahman, are yet unable to see through this unreality of the phenomenal world; and consequently know Brahman, not as the Self within themselves, but as the Godhead opposed to themselves and accordingly worship Brahman in pious meditation. (By worship is in general to be understood "that which produces an "increase of faith accompanied by awe;" p. 1071, 4. 10: *upâsanam nâma sa-mâna-pratyaya-pravâha-karaṇam*). Still all worship of the conditioned Brahman has not *Kramamukti* as its fruit, but according to p. 112, 5 part *Kramamukti* part *Abhyudaya* (note 138), part the success of sacrifice; according to p. 815, 5 part *Kramamukti*, part *Aiçvaryam* (note 138), part annihilation of sins; according to 4, 1, 4, p. 1061, the

---

1099, 1), the temporary felicity of the Pitṛiyâna is to be understood by it, either with certainty or probability in all.—With similar inconsistency it is maintained on p. 148, 5, that the fruit of the *Saguṇâ Vidyâḥ* is limited to *Saṃsâra*; and similarly on p. 1133, 14 that *Aiçvaryam* (Chând. 8, 2, 1) is a *saṃsâragocaram eva phalam*, just as on p. 815, 5 this very *Aiçvaryam* is opposed to the *Kramamukti*, of which, as we shall see in chapter XL, it forms an integral part.—The same inconsistency, depending upon imperfect revision, of the entire *Kramamukti* of the *Devayâna* expresses itself finally in the fact that exoteric knowledge is sometimes reckoned as *Vidyâ*, and sometimes as *Avidyâ*. Thus the exoteric knower is repeatedly called, in the description of the *Devayâna*, "*vidvân*" (p. 1095, 11. 1134, 11), while on p. 1095, 15 it is said of him, that he has not completely burnt up *Avidyâ*; p. 1133, 15: *anivartitatvâd avidyâyâḥ*; p. 804, 1: the *Upâdhis* through which Brahman becomes *saguṇam brahma* are said to be *avidyâ-pratyupasthâpita*.

worship of Brahman under any symbol (*pratîkam*), for example, as Manas, Âkâça, Sun, Name, etc., does not lead to the knowledge of Âtman, and according to 4, 3, 15—16 these worshippers of symbols do not attain the world of Brahman (p. 1135, 1), but receive as recompense the reward attributed to each symbol in Chând. 7, 2, 14. With the exception of these worshippers of symbols, all worshippers of the lower Brahman enter into Him upon the *Devayâna*, according to Bâdarâyaṇa, whose authority is here expressly invoked (p. 1134, 9. 1135, 1).

Besides these exoteric possessors of knowledge and worshippers occupy a middle position between the possessors of perfect knowledge and the performers of works; according to p. 1082, 11 they have not as yet passed beyond the sphere of actions and are therefore further bound to works; according to p. 1047, 10 their worship admits of a more and a less and thereby conditions various fruits; according to p. 1077, 8 the law (*vidhânam*) still subsists for them, and as reward for its fulfilment, lordship [of the world of Brahman] awaits them and freedom from evil.—

A more sharply defined conception of the nature of the worshipper of the lower Brahman is not to be obtained from the available materials. We now turn to the consideration of the fate which awaits him after death.

2. The Departure of the Soul of the Pious.

Just as in the case of the performer of works, so too in that of the pious, when he dies, the *Indriyas* enter into *Manas*, *Manas* into *Prâṇa*, *Prâṇa* into the individual Soul, which, clothed in the subtle body, withdraws itself into the heart, the point of which becomes luminous, to light up the road. But now comes the parting of the ways; of the 101 chief arteries of the body, 100 serve to lead forth the souls of the performers of works from the body in all directions and to cause them to enter upon the *Pitṛiyâna*; the (exoteric) knower, on the contrary, rises by the 101st artery (note 130) to the head, whence he enters upon the *Devayâna*. (For details see above chapter XXXI, 2, 3, 5.)

For this artery and the Sun are according to Chând. 8, 6, 2, (above p. 162), constantly connected by a ray (*raçmi*), "as "two villages are by a road" and by this the knower ascends (p. 1105, 12). Whether it is day or night when he dies, is all the same, since this connection of the artery with the ray persists as long as the body (p. 1106, 7). And that this ray is present even at night, can be perceived by the fact that in summer it is warm at night also; at other seasons it is less noticeable because the rays are too weak (p. 1106, 12). Were the ray not present at night one would have to assume either that the knower can ascend even without a ray,—in that case the ray would be altogether superfluous,—or that some of the knowers, those, namely, who die at night time, do not ascend at all, whereby the fruit of knowledge would become conditional (*pâkshika*); which cannot be admitted (p. 1107, l. 4). And further it cannot be assumed that he who dies at night awaits the return of day, because by then, as the body is burnt in the meanwhile, there may no longer be any body capable of connection with the ray (p. 1107, 6; whence it seems to follow that the burning of bodies followed quickly upon the occurrence of death; cf. the note above p. 352).

On the same grounds (because waiting is impossible, because the fruit of knowledge cannot be conditional, and because the time of death is not determined) we must assume, that the knower, even if he dies during the period when the days are decreasing, reaches the goal; and when the Smṛiti (Bhagavadgîtâ 8, 23 ff.) teaches that only those who die in the daytime and in the half-year in which the days increase, do not return, it is to be noted that this refers only to the followers of *Yoga* (above p. 19), and, since it rests only on the Smṛiti, this has no validity in a doctrine founded on the Çruti (p. 1108, 13).

3. The Stages on the Path of the Gods.

The *Devayâna*, which leads the pious after death to Brahman, has a series of stages, which are differently given in the different accounts. Thus in Chând. 8, 6, 5 (above p. 162) all that is said is that the Soul ascends from the artery to the sun by a ray (*raçmi*), while on the other hand Chând. 5, 10, 1 (above p. 362) as also previously Chând. 4, 15, 5 (above p. 166) the following stages are given: 1. Flame (*arcis*), 2. the Day, 3. the half-month in which the moon increases, 4. the half-year in which the days increase, 5. the Year, 6. the Sun, 7. the Moon, 8. Lightning, 9. Brahman.—With this agrees the parallel passage Bṛih. 6, 2, 15 (above p. 363), only that no. 5 is not "the year" but "the world of the Gods," and no. 7 "the moon" is wanting.—On the other hand we find Kaush. 1, 3, as stages of the Devayâna quite different ones named: 1. *Agniloka*, 2. *Vâyuloka*, 3. *Varuṇaloka*, 4. *Indraloka*, 5. *Prajâpatiloka*, 6. *Brahmaloka*.

In view of these condradictions Çankara (p. 1110 ff.) insists on the fact that there is only one *Devayâna*, and consequently that one must combine the different accounts. How in so doing he pictures the relation between the "ray," which in Chând. 8, 6, 5 connects the artery and the sun, and the stages 1—5, which according to Chând. 5, 10, 1 lead to the sun, is not clear from his remark p. 1112, 7, that both are not mutually exclusive; he further identifies "the Flame" Chând. 5, 10, 1 with *Agniloka* Kaush. 1, 3, inserts *Vâyuloka* Kaush. 1, 3 between "Year" and "Sun" Chând. 5, 10, 1, and then again *Devaloka* Bṛih. 6, 2, 15 between "Year" and *Vâyuloka*, and likewise finally *Varuṇaloka*, *Indraloka*, *Prajâpatiloka* from Kaush. 1, 3 between "Lightning" and "Brahman" Chând. 5, 10 (p. 1113 ff.). We thus get the following order of the stages of the *Devayâna*: 1. The Flame = *Agniloka*, 2. the Day, 3. the Fortnight in which the moon increases, 4. the Half-year in which the days increase, 5. the Year, 6. the World of the Gods, 7. *Vâyuloka*, 8. the Sun, 9. the Moon, 10. Lightning, 11. *Varuṇaloka*, 12. *Indraloka*, 13. *Prajâpatiloka*, 14. *Brahman*.

Now what meaning have these stages for the ascending Soul? Are they sign-posts or places of enjoyment? To this must be answered: they are neither one nor the other, but guides who conduct the Soul to Brahman. For after the Soul has reached the Lightning, it is said (above pp. 166. 363) "there indeed is a man (spirit), who is not as a human being, "he leads it to Brahman;" whence it is to be inferred that the preceding spirits: Flame etc. are of human nature (p. 1117, 6). For the Soul, in this condition, when all its organs are drawn in, is in need of guidance, somewhat like a drunken man or one whose senses are confused; this guidance is undertaken by the Flame, the Day etc.; wherefore we must understand by them not the natural phenomena which serve as signposts, for they would be incapable of leading him, but the Gods presiding over them; and also for the reason that Flame, Day, etc., are not always present, and waiting is impossible, as we saw (above p. 440). For the same reason too the stages named are not places of enjoyment for the Soul, as the designation *Loka* (world, place of enjoyment) might seem to indicate; to other Souls which dwell in them, they may serve as such places of enjoyment, but the Soul which is ascending through them is deprived of its organs and hence not capable of enjoying (p. 1118). After the Soul has come to the Lightning, it is led onwards by the "man who is not like a human "being" into Brahman, through *Varuṇaloka, Indraloka, Prajâpatiloka*; these are in some way or other helpful, either by removing obstacles, or by some other assistance (p. 1119).

4. Brahman as Goal of the Path.

After the description of the *Devayâna* in Bṛih. 6, 2, it is said in conclusion: "there in the worlds of Brahman they "dwell far away; for such there is no return."— Which Brahman are we to understand here, the real uncreated, highest Brahman as such, or the created (*kâryam*), lower, attribute-possessing Brahman (p. 1119, 10)?

To this *Bâdari* replies that the highest Brahman cannot be meant, because an entering into it is impossible, since it is omnipresent and is the inner Soul of him who goes (p. 1120, 1), because the plural "the worlds of Brahman" indicates plurality, which does not pertain to the highest Brahman, and because the expression "World" (*loka*) denotes a place of enjoyment, into which one enters, and therefore something changeable (p. 1120, 7). But this place is termed Brahman because of its near relationship to Brahman; "for the highest "Brahman becomes the lower Brahman (p. 1121, 2), through "association with pure determinations (*viçuddha-upâdhi-sambandhât*), when one conceives of it, for the purpose of worship, "as connected with certain qualities of the created Brahman "as 'Manas is its substance'" (Chând. 3, 14, 2, above p. 152) etc. (p. 1121, 2). Like all that is created, the world of the lower Brahman perishes at last, but by then its inhabitants have attained *Samyagdarçanam*, and thus they then enter, together with *Hiranyagarbha*, the ruler of the world of Brahman, into the highest, perfectly pure (*pariçuddha*) Brahman, "that highest seat of *Vishnu*" (Kâth. 3, 9); this is the *Kramamukti*, of which the Smriti says:—

> "After the world's deliverance has come,
> "And with it God's; in union with him,
> "All pious folk, attaining Selfhood go
> "With him into the fields of perfect bliss."

With this interpretation of *Bâdari* is contrasted, in what follows (p. 4, 3, 12—14) that of *Jaimini*, who insists that not the lower, but the higher Brahman is to be understood, whence it seems to follow that he did not go beyond the doctrine of the Five Fires and hence did not recognise at all the esoteric metaphysics of the Vedânta. "Several" adhered according to p. 1124, 9 to this view of *Jaimini*, among them probably the compiler of the Brahmasûtras (above p. 24) as he otherwise would probably not have left to *Jaimini* the last word on a question so vitally important for the system. This deviation on the fact of a portion of the Vedânta school gives Çankara occasion for the beautiful digression p. 1124—1134, which we have translated in full above p. 109—115 and in which the esoteric metaphysics of the Vedânta find clearer expression than anywhere else.

XL. Heavenly Lordship and Final Liberation of the Pious.

Sûtras 4, 4, 8–22.

1. Lordship (*aiçvaryam*).

The condition of those who have entered into Brahman by the Path of the Gods is indicated by the word, derived from *îçvara* (Lord), viz. *aiçvaryam*: that is, being Lord or God. As a description of this condition may be taken among others the passage Chând. 8, 2 (above p. 161), where is described how he who has attained freedom (*kâmacâra*) enjoys the fulfilment of all wishes. Should he desire intercourse with the departed, with fathers, mothers, brothers, sisters, friends, should his mind desire after sweet odours and garlands, food and drink, song and music, or women,—"whatsoever goal he "may desire, whatsoever he may wish, that ariseth for him at "his wish, and that he obtaineth; therefore is he glad."

If it be asked whether the mere wish alone suffices for the fulfilment of the wish, or whether, besides that, some other special means are needed, it is to be noted that the scripture mentions the wish only and no other means besides for its fulfilment (p. 1144, 10); if however such other means cooperate, then it is certainly without any trouble, and without its being possible for the wish to be frustrated; moreover, in contrast with earthly wishes, the fulfilment is here not a passing one. but endures as long as its purpose (the satisfaction of the wisher) demands it (p. 1144, 14). Upon this fact, that the wishes of the liberated are not in vain, depends also their freedom, since no one, if he can avoid it, chooses to remain under a ruler (p. 1145, 3).

2. The Existence of those who have obtained Lordship.

The power of wishing possessed by the Blessed presupposes that they also possess *Manas*, the organ of wishing. Whether they are besides provided with a body and with senses, is doubtful. *Bâdari* disputes it, because otherwise it ought not to be said by way of exclusion: "with *Manas* he beholds "those wishes and rejoices in the world of Brahman;" *Jaimini* on the other hand maintains it, appealing to the passage: "he is one, he is threefold," etc. (Chând. 7, 26, 2); being threefold presupposes a bodily existence; and even if the passage quoted is taken from the *Bhûmavidyâ*, that is, from a *nirguṇâ vidyâ*, yet the *aiçvaryam* to which it refers belongs to the fruit of the *saguṇâ vidyâḥ* (p. 1146, 5). *Bâdarâyaṇa*, finally, assumes, that, because the scripture teaches both, those possessed of lordship can subsist at pleasure either in bodily or in bodiless form (p. 1146, 10); in the latter case the enjoyment of wishes must be conceived as taking place as in dreaming, in the former as in the waking state (p. 1146, 15. 1147, 4).—But how are we to conceive existence in three or more bodies at once? Are they to be conceived as being all animated, or rather, since the Soul cannot multiply itself, as all soul-less except one, like automata (wooden machines, *dâruyantram*)? The answer to this is: as one light can divide itself into several lights, so he who has attained lordship can be in different bodies simultaneously, as without this their moving would be impossible; his Âtman rules them, entering into them by means of a division of the *Upâdhis*; just as indeed the books of *Yoga* teach such a connection of the *Yogin* with several bodies (p. 1148, 10; cf. above p. 68). —We must not bring forward here the passages which teach the "unity without a second" of the Âtman (above p. 435) for the lordship here described is only the ripened fruit of the branches of knowledge that ascribe attributes (p. 1149, 13).

3. Limits of Lordship.

The lordship of the pious in the beyond extends without restriction to everything, with the exception of the government of the world. They thus possess the prefections[139] connected with *aiçvaryam*, and only the ruling of the world, that is, its creation, guidance and destruction, is reserved to the eternally perfect *Îçvara* because he is once for all appointed for it, and because the *aiçvaryam* of the others has not subsisted from eternity, but has a beginning in time. Otherwise, too, unpleasantnesses might occur, in that, for instance, one might wish the continued existence of the world and another its destruction; so that there belongs to the highest *Îçvara* a supremacy over the others, in that he has to bring their wishes into harmony (p. 1151, 1). Their Freedom (*svârâjyam*) "rests" upon that of the highest *Îçvara*; into him, who in this sense is named "the Lord of wishes" (*manasaspati*) (Taitt. 1, 6, 2), the pious enter, so that his lordship is conditioned by that of the highest *Îçvara* (p. 1151, 14).

When, in Ṛigv. X, 90, 3 (above p. 168), it is said:—

> "However great is nature's majesty,
> "The Spirit is yet higher raised by far,
> "Of it but one foot do all beings make,
> "Three feet of him are immortality in heaven,"

two forms of the highest God are here spoken of, the one changeable, belonging only to the realm of change (*vikâra-mâtra-gocara*) and one unchangeable, to which all changes return (*vikâra-âvartin*), of which it is written (Kâṭh. 5, 15): "after him, the Shining, shine all things, from his light shines "this whole world." From these two forms of existence, the changeless and the changing (*avikṛitam* and *kâryam*

---

[139] As an example of these, Çaṅkara names, on p. 1150, 8 as also p. 314, 7, *aṇiman.* According to Gauḍapâda on Sâṅkhyakârikâ v. 23 there are the following eight: 1. *aṇiman*, 2. [*gariman* and] *laghiman* 3. *mahiman*, 4. *prâpti*, 5. *prâkâmyam*, 6. *vaçitvam*, 7. *îçitvam*, 8. *yatra-kâma-avasâyitvam*; for the explanation of these expressions see above p. 39.

brahma, p. 1119, 11), which for Çaṅkara coincide with the attributeless and attribute-possessing conceptions,[140] the pious, because they have looked only to the attribute-possessing Brahman, attain to that conditioned Brahman only (p. 1152, 6), because their insight (*kratu*) reaches only to it. And as they have not attained the higher, attributeless, but only the lower, attribute-possessing Brahman, therefore even within the latter their power is not boundless, but limited (p. 1152, 8), and only in respect of enjoyment does their lordships equal that of the highest *Îçvara* (p. 1153, 2).

4. Final Liberation of the Pious.

But if this is so, if the lordship of the pious is not unsurpassable (*sa-atiçaya*), must it not then also be finite, so that its possessors at last return to earth-life? — To this answers "the venerable Bâdarâyaṇa" in the last Sûtram of the work: "*No return according to Scripture, no return according to Scripture.*" And the meaning of this is: "Those who "through artery and ray attain to the world of Brahman "described in the scripture, by the stages of the Flame etc., "upon the Path of the Gods, where are the lakes *Ara-* and "*-nyam*, in the world of Brahman, in the third heaven from "here, where is the lake *Airammadîyam* and the fig-tree "*Somavasana*, and the stronghold of Brahman *Aparâjitâ*, and "the golden palace *Prabhuvimitam* (Chând. 8, 5, 3). as it is "described in many hymns and explanations (cf. Kaush. 1, "3—5),—those who have attained to it, do not return like "those in the world of the moon, on the expiration of enjoy-"ment: 'Immortality attains he who ascends by it' (Chând. "8, 6, 6),—'for them there is no return' (Bṛih. 6, 2, 15),— "'those who enter thereupon, return not again to this world' "(Chând. 4, 15, 6),—'he goes to the world of Brahman and "'returns not again' (Chând. 8, 15, 1),—as the scripture says. "But rather, even when their lordship comes to an end, they

[140] Upon this confusion of the phenomenal forms and the forms of presentation of Brahman compare above p. 206.

"do not return, but go, as shown (above p. 442), when the "transformed [Brahman] ceases to exist, pass with the ruler "thereof into the highest Brahman. Namely, after the dark-"ness [of their Ignorance] has melted away in *Samyagdar-"çanam*, then, as the highest goal there opens before them "the eternal, perfect *Nirvâṇam*; in this they take their refuge "and therefore for such also as place themselves under the "protection of the attribute-possessing Brahman, there is "verily no return."

Concordance.

On the left are the numbers of the pages in Çañkara's work, on the right those of our work; n. = note; * translated.

*5, 1—12, 1 = 53

12, 1—14, 5 = 54

*14, 5—16, 1 = 54 n.

*16, 1–4 = 55

16, 4—17, 1 = 56

*17, 2—18, 4 = 56 n.

*18, 4—20, 5 = 57 n.

*20, 5—8 = 56 n.

*20, 8—21, 7 = 54 n.

*21, 7—22, 3 = 58

24 = 78

25—28 = 82

28, 3 = 79—82

*32, 4—36, 1 = 126

*38, 2—5 = 123

40—45 = 95 ff.

47—48 = 94

61—65 = 402

*64, 7 ff. = 401

66—71 = 408

69—71 = 85

*71, 9—72, 9 = 403

74—77 = 406

76, 2—77, 8 = 82 ff.

*78, 6—79, 5 = 127

*84, 5—88, 1 = 419

*90, 2—3 = 123

90—110 = 134 ff.

*107, 12 ff. = 337

111—114 = 120 n.

*111, 2—3 = 102

*112, 2—8 = 104

114—129 = 137 ff.

129—134 = 140 ff.

*133, 7—12 = 103

134—138 = 145

138—142 = 147

142—154 = 168

*148, 2—6 = 104

154—166 = 177 ff.

166—177 = 153 ff.

177—179 = 150

179—185 = 171

186—194 = 164 ff.

194—199 = 149

200—209 = 131

209—223 = 156 ff.

224—233 = 200

233—242 = 201 ff.

242—244 = 134

244—248 = 198 ff.

249—260 = 158 ff.

260—271 = 183 ff.

271—275 = 130

275—279 = 155

280, 1—286, 6 = 67–69

*286, 7—287, 2 = 69

288—289, 9 = 71

*289, 10–297, 7 = 72–76

297, 9—298, 3 = 71

*301, 6 = 94 n.

*303, 1—304, 2 = 70. 229

*307, 3—8 = 65 n.

*309, 11—310, 8 = 65 ff.

*313, 8–314, 8 = 38–39

315, 6–323, 2 = 60–64

323—326 = 148

326—328 = 188

328—330 = 146

330—333 = 188 ff.

334—354 = 370 ff.

*342, 2—10 = 228

370—377 = 129

378—385 = 181 ff.

385—396 = 172

396—403 = 223 ff.

*403, 6—9 = 93

418-434 = 250 ff. 274 ff.

435, 11—436, 5 = 91

436, 5—437, 10 = 91

*437, 11—438, 1 = 92

438—439 = 92

443—456 = 267 ff.

*443, 12 = 261

*448, 6—12 = 55 n.

456—471 = 256 ff.

471—475 = 253. 280

*473, 13—14 = 106

475—479 = 225

479—486 = 252. 277

*481, 13—482, 5 = 93

486—487 = 227 ff.

487—488 = 252. 278

488—491 = 222

*490, 11—491, 2 = 106

491—495 = 252. 279

*500, 3–502, 5 = 125
507 = 236
*536, 7–9 = 237 n.
557–558 = 231
*566–579 = 242 ff.
586–591 = 307
*595, 8–11 = 93
605–625 = 232 ff.
*619, 8–621, 3 = 127
625–636 = 235
*627, 4–628, 10 = 124
636–638 = 237
638–641 = 236. 327
641–647 = 293 ff.
647–649 = 295
650–668 = 308 ff. 330
668–672 = 316
*673–676 = 317 ff.
676–680 = 320
680–684 = 321 ff.
*682, 3–7 = 86
*683, 2–684, 1 = 323
684–695 = 297 ff.
701–708 = 328
708–715 = 329
716–724 = 333 ff.
725–728 = 338. 66
729–732 = 336
732–738 = 240
739–749 = 370 ff. 379
743 = 241
749–751 = 385
751–762 = 387
*760–762 = 391 ff.
762–769 = 382 ff.
768–769 = 239
769–777 = 394 ff.
772–774 = 238
778–802 = 337
*786, 7–787, 5 = 86
*787, 9 ff. = 325
803–838 = 205 ff.
*803, 3–804, 5 = 102
*806, 9–11 = 103 n.
*815, 5–7 = 104 n.
838–842 = 377
*843, 4–844, 5 = 95
866–868 = 137
*867, 12–868, 8 = 103
*909, 7 ff. = 437
913–917 = 430
*917, 5 ff. = 418 n.
922–924 = 141 ff.
*953 = 25 n.
*954–957 = 287 ff.
973–988 = 405 ff.
984 = 376
1006–1012 = 411
*1007, 1–3 = 83 n.
*1008, 5–9 = 83
*1009, 4 = 84
1010–1021 = 84
1017–1024 = 411
1021–1024 = 85
1034–1041 = 143
1042–1045 = 84
1042–1048 = 412
*1047, 7–1048, 1 = 104 n.
1049–1075 = 413 ff.
*1064, 5–8 = 95
1075–1078 = 421
1078–1079 = 423
1080–1081 = 424
1081–1085 = 412 n.
1085–1086 = 426
1087–1093 = 367 ff.
1093–1098 = 370 ff. 375
1098–1103 = 427 ff.
1103–1105 = 379
1105–1109 = 440
1110–1119 = 441
1119–1124 = 442
*1121, 1–4 = 103
*1124, 10–1134, 3 = 109 ff.
1134–1136 = 439
1137–1139 = 432
1140 = 434
1141–1143 = 433
1143–1153 = 444 ff.
*1153–1155 = 447

APPENDIX.

I. Short Survey of the Vedânta System.
II. Index of all Quotations in Çañkara's Commentary on the Brahma-sûtras.
III. Index of proper Names in Çañkara's Commentary.
IV. Terminology of the Vedânta, etc.

I. Short Survey of the Vedânta System.

1. Introductory.

§ 1. The fundamental thought of the Vedânta, most briefly expressed by the Vedic words: *tat tvam asi*, "that art thou" (Chând. 6, 8, 7) and *aham brahma asmi*, "I am Brahman" (Bṛih. 4, 10), is THE IDENTITY OF BRAHMAN AND THE SOUL; this means that *Brahman*, *i. e.*, the eternal principle of all Being, the power which creates, sustains and again absorbs into itself all worlds, is identical with the *Âtman*, the Self or the Soul, *i. e.*, that in us which we recognise, when we see things rightly, as our very self and true essence. This soul of each one of us is not a part, an emanation of Brahman, but wholly and absolutely the eternal, indivisible Brahman Himself. **Fundamental thought of the Vedânta.**

§ 2. The statement contradicts experience (*vyavahâra*), which shows us not that unity, but a plurality (*nânâtvam*), an extension (*prapañca*) of names and forms (*nâma-rûpe*, *i. e.*, impressions of ear and eye, sense-impressions) and as a part of them our own Self in the form of our created and perishable body. **Contradiction by experience.**

§ 3. But the fundamental dogma of the Vedânta is equally in contradiction with the canon of Vedic ritual; this it is true teaches the continued existence (*vyatireka*) of the soul after the body, but it assumes a plurality of individual souls different from Brahman; they are entangled in unceasing transmigration (*saṃsâra*) and at the death of each body pass into a new **Contradiction by the law of works.**

body; in this process the works (*karman*) of anyone life condition inexorably the succeeding life and its nature.

Ignorance and Knowledge.

§ 4. Both experience, as a result of worldly means of cognition (*pramâṇam*)—perception (*pratyaksham*), inference (*anumânam*) etc.—, and the canon of the Vedic ritual with its commands and prohibitions, promises and threats rest on false knowledge (*mithyâ-jñânam*), an innate illusion (*bhrânti*), which is called *Avidyâ*, Ignorance; what it tells us is, like the pictures of a dream, only true till the awakening comes. This innate *Avidyâ* is more accurately described by saying that the *Âtman*, the Soul, the Self is unable to distinguish itself from the *Upâdhis* or limitations (*i. e.*, the body, the psychic organs and works) with which the Soul is clad, and of which only a part—the body—is annihilated in death, the rest accompanying the Soul on its migrations.—This *Avidyâ* is the contrary of *Vidyâ*, knowledge, also called perfect knowledge (*samyagdarçanam*), by virtue of which the *Âtman* distinguishes itself from the *Upâdhis*, and recognises that they are dependent on *Avidyâ*, a glamour (*mâyâ*) or an illusion (*abhimâna*); while it is itself identical with the one Brahman, without a second who comprehends all things in Himself.

Source of Knowledge

§ 5. *Samyagdarçanam*, perfect knowledge can neither be produced by worldly means of knowledge (*pratyaksham, anumânam*, etc.), nor commanded by the canon of the Veda as a duty, because both are rooted in *Avidyâ* and do not lead beyond it. The only source of *Vidyâ* is revelation, *Çruti* (which we, not quite correctly, generally term "Scripture"), *i. e.*, the Veda, and of this in particular the part of knowledge (*jñâna-kâṇḍa*) which exists side by side with the part of works (*karma-kâṇḍa*); and contains certain texts scattered through the *Mantras* and *Brâhmaṇas*; but more especially formed in the concluding chapter of the latter, the *Vedânta* (end of the Veda), known as the *Upanishads*.—The whole of the Veda without distinction, that is the whole body of *Mantras* (Hymns and formulas) and *Brâhmaṇas* (theological explanations) together with the *Upanishads* is of divine origin; it was "breathed out" by Brahman and only "beheld" by the human authors (*rishis*). The world and the Gods with it pass away but the Veda is eternal; it outlasts the destruction of the world and continues to exist in the spirit of Brahman; in accordance with the words of the Veda, which contain the eternal archetypes of things, gods, men, animals, etc. are created by Brahman at the beginning of each world period; thereupon the Veda is revealed to them by "Expiration"—the part of works as a canon of actions which have happiness (*abhyudaya*) as their object, the part of knowledge as the source of *Samyagdarçanam*, the only fruit of which is bliss (*nihçreyasam*) *i. e.*, liberation.—Perfect knowledge is not attainable by reflection (*tarka*), and just as little by tradition or *Smriti* (including the Vedic Sûtras, Kapila, Manu, the Mahâbhâratam, etc.); both of these, reflection and Smriti, can only in a secondary sense be considered a source of truth, so far as they are directed to the Veda and serve to clear up and complete its revelation.

2. Theology.

§ 6. The aim of man (*purusha-artha*) is liberation (*moksha*) *i. e.*, the cessation of transmigration (*samsâra*); and the release of the soul from its wanderings is brought about by man's own Self (*âtman*) being recognised as identical with the highest Self (*parama-âtman*), *i. e.*, the *Brahman*. The whole content of *Vidyâ* is therefore knowledge of the *Âtman* or *Brahman* (they are interchangeable ideas).—But there are two sorts of knowledge of Brahman—the higher knowledge (*parâ vidyâ*); its aim is *Samyagdarçanam* and its one and only fruit is liberation; and the lower knowledge (*aparâ vidyâ*) which does not aim at the knowledge but at the worship (*upâsanâ*) of Brahman; it brings as its fruit, according to the steps of this worship, in part the prospering of works (*karma-samriddhi*), in part happiness (*abhyudaya*, heavenly, perhaps also in the following birth), and finally in part *kramamukti*, *i. e.*, gradual liberation.—The object of the higher knowledge is the **higher Brahman** (*param brahma*) and of the lower the **lower Brahman** (*aparam brahma*).

Higher and lower Knowledge.

Higher and lower Brahman.

§ 7. For the Scripture distinguishes two forms (*rûpe*) of Brahman; the higher, attributeless (*param, nirguṇam*) and the lower attribute-possessing (*aparam, saguṇam*) Brahman. In the former case it is taught that Brahman is without any attributes (*guṇa*), differences (*viçesha*), forms (*âkâra*), and limitations (*upâdhi*)—in the latter, for the purpose of worship many attributes, differences, forms, and limitations are ascribed to him.

Difference between them.

§ 8. One and the same object cannot be at the same time with and without attributes, and with and without form; in Himself (*svatas*) Brahman is therefore without attributes, forms, differences, and limitations; and this higher Brahman becomes the lower when Ignorance (*avidyâ*) for the purpose of worship ascribes to him the limitations or *Upâdhis.* That Brahman is subject to *Upâdhis* is only an illusion (*bhrama*), just as much as it is an illusion to hold a crystal for red in itself because it is painted red. As the clearness of the crystal is not changed by the red colour, so the essence of Brahman is not altered by the limitations ascribed by Ignorance.

The higher Brahman cannot be perceived.

§ 9. The higher Brahman is in his own nature attributeless (*nirguṇam*), formless (*nirâkâram*), and without differences (*nirviçesham*) and limitations (*nirupâdhikam*). It is "not "coarse, and not fine, not short, and not long," etc. (Bṛih. 3, 8, 8); "not to be heard, not to be felt, not formed, imperish-"able" (Kâṭh. 3, 15); it is "not thus and not thus" (*neti, neti,* Bṛih. 2, 3, 6); *i.e.*, no shape and no idea corresponds to its real being. Therefore it is "different from what we know, "and from what we do not know" (Kena 1, 3); "the words "and thoughts turn back from it and find it not" (Taitt. 2, 4); and the sage *Bâhva* met the question as to its essence by silence (above p. 210).

Essence of the higher Brahman

§ 10. The only assertion that can be made of the attributeless Brahman is that it is not not. In this sense it is "the Existent" (*sat*); but if this conception is taken in its empirical sense, Brahman is rather "the non-Existent."—The

Scripture further defines the essence of Brahman as through and through pure **spirituality** (intelligence, *caitanyam*) just as the lump of salt tastes salt through and through. But by this two characteristics (plurality) are not ascribed to Brahman, because both are identical, so far as the essence of Being consists in spirituality, and of spirituality in Being. **Bliss**, *ânanda* [attributed to Brahman as a third predicate by the later Vedânta in the name *Sac-cid-ânanda*] is occasionally recognised as a limitation of the attributeless Brahman; it remains unmentioned however in the discussion of his being, perhaps because it can be regarded as a merely negative quality, as painlessness, which is ascribed to Brahman alone, for "what is different from him is afflicted" (*ato 'nyad ârtam*) as the Scripture (Bṛih. 3, 4, 2) says.

§ 11. That the attributeless Brahman cannot be perceived depends on the fact that he is the inner Self (*antar-âtman*) of all; as such he is on the one hand the greatest certainty of all and cannot be denied by anyone; on the other hand He is not to be perceived because in all perception He is the Subject (*sâkshin*), and can therefore never become the object. —He is however beheld by the sages in the state of *Saṃrâdhanam* (perfect satisfaction), which consists in a withdrawal of the organs from all external things, and a concentration on their own inner nature. On the consciousness of being this attributeless Brahman and on the accompanying conviction of the unreality of all plurality of names and forms depends salvation. Brahman is the soul.

§ 12. The **higher Brahman** becomes the **lower Brahman** by being connected with pure (*viçuddha*) or perfect (*niratiçaya*) limitations. The lower Brahman is to be recognised wherever the Scripture ascribes limitations, attributes, forms or differences of any sort to Brahman. This happens when the aim is not knowledge but worship (*upâsanâ*), and the fruit of this worship is, like that of works, which are to be placed in the same category, not liberation (*moksha, niḥçreyasam*) but happiness; this is, as it seems, mainly heavenly; it is however The lower Brahman.

limited to the *Saṃsâra* (p. 148, 5) though the heavenly lordship (*aiçvaryam*) attained after death by the path of the gods (*devayâna*) as a result of the worship of the lower Brahman leads by means of *Kramamukti* or gradual liberation to perfect knowledge and therefore complete liberation. This result however does not follow immediately, because the worshippers of the lower Brahman have not completely "burnt up" Ignorance; for it is this which ascribes the limitations to the higher Brahman and transforms it into the lower Brahman. The nature of Brahman is as little changed by these limitations as (in the already mentioned simile) the clearness of the crystal by the colour with which it is painted—as the sun by its images swaying in the water—as space by bodies moving or burning in it.—The richly developed ideas of the lower Brahman may be divided into three groups, according to whether they regard Brahman pantheistically as world soul, psychologically as principle of the individual soul, or theistically as a personal God.

The lower Brahman as world soul.

§ 13. The most important passages of the first group are Chând. 3, 14 which terms Brahman "all-working, all-wishing. "all-smelling, all-tasting [the principle of all action and sen- "suous perception], embracing the All, silent, ungrieved" (above p. 153); and Muṇḍ. 2, 1, 1 according to which sun and moon are his eyes, the cardinal points his ears, the wind his breath etc. (above p. 132). We bring under the same head Brahman as source of all light (p. 130); as the light beyond the sky and in the heart (p. 169); as the ether from which all things proceed (p. 145), and which holds asunder names and forms (p. 146); as the life from which go forth all beings (p. 146). in which the whole world trembling moves (p. 148); as the inner ruler (p. 149) as the principle of the world-order; the bridge, which holds these worlds asunder that they do not blend (p. 162), by which sun and moon, heaven and earth, minutes, hours, days and years are kept apart (p. 133); finally as destroyer of the world, who swallows up all created things (p. 151).

§ 14. With the dimensions expressed by these ideas is often contrasted the smallness which belongs to Brahman as psychic principle; as such he dwells in the stronghold of the body (p. 199), in the lotus of the heart (p. 160), as a dwarf (p. 50), a span large (p. 156), an inch high (p. 155), smaller than a grain of millet (p. 153), large as the point of an awl (p. 311), as principle of life (pp. 177, 182) as onlooker (p. 171); also as the man in the eye (pp. 140, 165) etc. The lower Brahman as individual Soul.

§ 15.* These ideas which assign attributes to Brahman culminate in the conception of Him as *Îçvara, i. e.*, personal God. In the Upanishads this idea is relatively rare and little developed (*e. g.*, Îça 1; Bṛih. 4, 4, 22 above p. 195; Kaush. 3, 8; Kâṭh. 4, 12); in the system of the Vedânta on the other hand it plays an important part; it is *Îçvara* by whose permission Saṃsâra, and by whose grace (*prasâda, anugraha*) the saving knowledge is conditioned; He decrees for the soul its works and sufferings, taking into consideration in this the works of the previous life, and causing the fate in the new life to proceed from them as the rain produces the plant from the seed after its nature. The personification of Brahman as *Îçvara*, Lord, Ruler, to whom is opposed the world as that which is to be ruled, is expressly limited to the standpoint rooted in Ignorance of worldly action, which has no reality in the highest sense (above p. 272). The lower Brahman as personal God.

3. Cosmology.

§ 16. The dual knowledge (*aparâ* and *parâ vidyâ*) of Theology (and as we shall see of Eschatology) has as its counterpart in the spheres of Cosmology and Psychology the dual standpoint:—the empirical (*vyavahâra-avasthâ*, literally, standpoint of worldly action) which teaches a creation of the world by Brahman and a wandering of the soul rendered individual by the Upâdhis; and the metaphysical (*paramârtha-avasthâ*, literally, standpoint of the highest reality) which maintains the identity of the soul with Brahman, and denies all plurality, and therefore the validity of the ideas of the creation and existence of the world, as well as the individuality and The empirical and metaphysical standpoint.

wanderings of the soul.—To the detriment of clearness and logic this dual standpoint in Psychology and Cosmology is not always strictly adhered to. The system takes up the metaphysical standpoint as a rule and neglects the empirical, without however denying or being able to deny its relative right of existence, it being the indispensable presupposition for the *aparâ vidyâ* of Eschatology. This *aparâ vidyâ* treats the creation in the Cosmology very fully and regards it as real, at the same time we meet with the assertion again and again that this scriptural doctrine of the creation has only the purpose of teaching the Brahmanhood of the world; to support this view the idea of causality is transformed into that of identity; in Psychology the metaphysical doctrine of the identity of Brahman and the world is always in the foreground, and is defended against an opponent who generally speaking upholds the empirical standpoint indispensable for the Eschatology of the system, but also (*e. g.*, in maintaining the creation of the soul) deviates from it, so that the relative recognition and appropriation of his arguments only concerns a part of them, and a complete theory of the empirical psychology is thus wanting. Still by bringing together occasional and scattered assertions a reliable picture of this part of the system too may be obtained.

Relation of the two kinds of knowledge to the two points of view.

§ 17. The coherence of the system may prove to us that the *parâ vidyâ* in Theology and Eschatology forms with the *paramârtha-avasthâ* in Cosmology and Psychology an inseparable unity of metaphysical doctrine; and that on the other hand the *aparâ vidyâ* of Theology and Eschatology with the *vyavahâra-avasthâ* of Cosmology and Psychology a connected picture of metaphysics viewed from the empirical standpoint of *Avidyâ* (*i. e.,* innate realism) and forms a system of popular religion for all those who cannot raise themselves to the standpoint of the doctrine of identity.—And it is clear that only a lower, not a higher Brahman can be conceived as creator of the world, firstly because the act of creation, as has been repeatedly insisted on, requires a plurality of powers (above p. 227), which can only be ascribed to the *aparam brahma*;

and further, because the passage by which this plurality of creative powers is proved: "all-working is he, all-wishing, all-"smelling, all-tasting" (Chând. 3, 14, 2) receives the preference as a proof of the doctrine of the lower Brahman.

§ 18. According to the Upanishads Brahman creates the world and then as individual soul (*anena jîvena âtmanâ*) enters into it (Chând. 6, 3, 2. Taitt. 2, 6. Bṛih. 1, 4, 7. Kaush. 4, 20). There is no question either of an existence of individual souls before the creation, or of a periodically repeated creation.— In this view the germs of the empirical and metaphysical doctrine of the Vedânta are present in an undeveloped form side by side; the metaphysical part is the identity of the soul with Brahman, the empirical the extension of the world of sense. In the Vedânta system the two are separated; metaphysically we have the identity of the soul with Brahman but neither origin, persistence, nor destruction of the world; empirically on the other hand we have a creation of the world but no identity of Brahman and the soul; on the contrary the individual soul with the Upâdhis, which cause its individuality, has existed from all eternity and migrates (except in the case of liberation) from one body to another to all eternity; and the dogma of the creation of the world is transformed into that of a periodically alternating emanation of the world from Brahman and reabsorption in it; these processes repeat themselves not once only but countless times throughout eternity. Souls, like the elements, continue to exist, at the reabsorption of the world, potentially and as seed in Brahman, and at each new creation go forth from Him unchanged. The original sense of the doctrine of creation is thus completely abandoned; it is adhered to, in the modified form in question, simply because the Veda teaches it; in the system there is a motive not for a creation of the world, but rather for its eternal duration; in place of this (to save the authority of Scripture) we have the periodical creation and reabsorption, which however must incessantly be repeated, and are not permitted to alter the order of the world; this is to satisfy the condition of eternal existence demanded by

World-periods.

the system, and is as we shall see, dependent on a moral necessity.

The world has no beginning.

§ 19. The fundamental idea of the empirical Cosmology and Psychology is that Saṃsâra (transmigration) has no beginning. There exists from eternity a plurality of individual souls different from Brahman. What distinguishes them from Brahman (with whom they are in the metaphysical sense identical) is the *Upâdhis* in which they are clothed; by Upâdhis are understood, in addition to the works, which accompany the soul, the psychic organs (*indriyas, manas, mukhya prâṇa*), the subtle body (*sûkshmaṃ çarîram*) which bears them, and, in a more extended sense, occasionally the gross body together with external objects. Only the gross body is annihilated by death; the subtle body on the other hand with the psychic organs has existed from eternity as the vestment of the soul and accompanies it on all its wanderings. And the wandering soul is further accompanied by the works (ritual and moral) performed by it during life; and it is just these which prevent Saṃsâra from coming to a standstill. For every deed, good and evil, demands retribution, and therefore reward and punishment, not only in the Beyond but, besides that, in the form of another existence. Without works no human life is conceivable; and therefore also no life that is not followed by another as its retribution. Very good works result in existence as a god; very bad in existence as an animal or plant; even if the soul does no works in these lives, this does not protect it from rebirth, for works of special goodness or badness demand for their retribution several successive existences. On this depends the fact that Saṃsâra through all spheres of existence from the gods down to plants is without beginning and (if the seed of works is not "burnt up" by knowledge) without end.

Moral necessity of the creation of the world.

§ 20. The spatial extension of the sense-world (*nâmarûpa-prapañca*) is essentially nothing more than the fruit of works which is imposed as a burden (*adhyâropita*, p. 1056, l. 1132, 10) on the soul; the world is, as the common formula runs, *kriyâ-*

kâraka-phalam (pp. 273, 12. 291, 6. 447, 3. 987, 6), "requital of the deed on the doer;" it is *bhogyam* (what is to be enjoyed) while the soul in it is *bhoktar* (enjoyer) and on the other hand *kartar* (doer); both of these of necessity and in exact agreement with its *kartritvam* (activity) in the preceding existence. The intermediator between the works and their fruit (which includes the deeds and suffering of the succeeding existence) is not an *adrishtam* (invisible power of the works reaching beyond life) or at least not this alone but rather the *Îçvara*, a personification of Brahman, which is valid for the empirical standpoint alone (§ 15); the Îçvara decrees action and suffering for the soul in the new birth in exact correspondence to the works of the former existence. Moreover each new creation of the world after its absorption into Brahman depends on the same necessity as the rebirth; for even when the souls are absorbed in Brahman, they still continue to exist in the form of seed together with their works, and the latter require for their retribution another creation of the world, *i. e.*, the emanation of the elements from Brahman; this process we shall now consider more closely.

§ 21. At the creation, *srishti*, which according to this word is to be conceived as an "outpouring," *i. e.*, emanation, there goes forth from Brahman first of all the *Âkâça*, ether, or more properly all-penetrating space conceived as a very subtle form of matter; from *Âkâça* goes forth air (*vâyu*), from this fire (*agni, tejas*), from this water (*âpas*), from this earth (*prithivî, annam*); and in this process each successive element is produced not by the elements themselves but by Brahman in the form of the elements. In reverse order at the end of the world earth first becomes water, this fire, this air, this ether, and this Brahman.—Ether is perceived by the sense of hearing, air by hearing and touch, fire by hearing, touch and sight, water by hearing, touch, sight and taste; and earth by hearing, touch, sight, taste and smell. These elements occurring in nature, however, are not the pure, original elements but a mixture of all with preponderance of some one of them. [There is no systematic account of the theory of

Inorganic nature (the elements).

mixture in Çañkara's Commentary on the Brahmasûtras; we do not find one before the Vedântasâra.]

Organic nature (souls). § 22. After Brahman has created the Elements, he enters them, according to the Upanishads, as the individual soul; *i.e.*, in our system the wandering souls, which continue to exist potentially (*çakti-âtmanâ*) in Brahman even after the destruction of the world, awake from this state, itself a part of the glamour [of empirical reality], of very deep sleep (*mâyâmayî mahâsushuptiḥ*, p. 342, 9) and assume divine, human, animal or plant bodies according to their works in the previous existence. This comes about by the seed of the elements, carried by the soul with it on its wanderings in the form of the subtle body, becoming the gross body by the addition of homogeneous particles from the coarse elements which surround it (above p. 259); at the same time it unfolds the psychic organs (*mukhya prâṇa, manas, indriyas*) which during the wandering were rolled together (*sampiṇḍita*). (What becomes in the case of the organs of plant souls remains undiscussed; it may be assumed that they remain rolled up.) The body is *nâmarûpakṛita-kârya-karaṇa-sañghâta* (pp. 473, 17. 455, 4. 686, 5), "the complex of "the organs of work formed of names and shapes"* [*i.e.*, from the elements], and the soul is lord (*svâmin*) of this complex. The growth of the body takes places from the elements, in which gross, middle and fine are distinguished; correspondingly faeces, flesh, and Manas are developed from earth; urine, blood, and Prâṇa from water; and bones, marrow, and speech from fire;—as however according to the system the soul already has with it its psychic organs, and among them Manas, Prâṇa, and speech, we must either see a contradiction here, or assume that the growing Manas, Prâṇa and speech are

* According to Chând. 6, 3, 2 Brahman enters into the elements by means of the individual soul and by this means expands Himself as names and shapes; Çañkara on the other hand speaks, p. 507, 1, of a *nâmarûpa-mâyâ-âveça*, an entrance into the illusion of names and shapes and in this sense the above formula is probably to be translated; for p. 787, 13 the expression *kârya-karaṇa-sañghâta* is replaced by *deha* in this formula.

related to the similarly named organs which the soul always has with it, as the coarse body is to the subtle. The absorption of this material from food is rendered possible by the fact that (v. § 21) every natural body contains all the original elements.—According to their origin organisms are divided into those born from germs (plants), those born from moisture (vermin), the oviparous, and the viviparous; procreation consists in the soul of the child, which has entered into the father as food and sojourned in him as a guest, passing by means of the sperm into the body of the mother and from her blood developing the subtle into the coarse body. Death is the separation of the soul (with its organs and the subtle body) from the material body; if the organism is destroyed the soul wanders forth. The duration of life is not accidental but is predestined exactly according to the quantum of works to be atoned for, just as the nature of the life is by their quality. On the other hand again we find works, which cease to be, not all at once, but only after repeated rebirths; only in this way can we explain why *e. g.* transmigration does not come to a standstill when the soul enters into a plant. As every plant is an embodied soul, and every incarnation only serves the end of atonement, the system is quite logical (pp. 772, 4. 774, 5) in attributing sensation to plants also.—While the duration of life of plant, animal, and human souls is short, those souls which, in consequence of exceptional performances in the previous life, are born as gods, are immortal, *i. e.*, they continue to exist till the next destruction of the world; then they again enter the cycle of Saṃsâra; and the places of Indra etc. can be occupied by another soul in the next period (above p. 69).

§ 23. Just as all clay vessels are in reality only clay, since the conversion of the clay into vessels is "a mere name, dependent on words" (*vâcârambhaṇaṃ vikâro, nâmadheyam,* Chând. 6, 1, 4 cf. Parmenides' saying: "τῷ πάντ' ὄνομ' ἐστίν, ὅσσα βροτοὶ κατέθεντο, πεποιθότες εἶναι ἀληθῆ), so also the whole world is in reality only Brahman and has no existence beyond Brahman (*brahma-vyatirekena*); there is nothing different from

No world from the metaphysical point of view.

Brahman (*na iha nânâ asti kiñcana*, Bṛih. 4, 4, 19). But here our system goes further than the Veda. The whole extension of names and forms (*nâmarûpa-prapañca*), the whole plurality of phenomena (*rûpa-bheda*) is, from the standpoint of highest reality, caused, produced and laid as a burden [upon the soul] by Ignorance (*avidyâ-kalpita, avidyâ-pratyupasthâpita, avidyâ-adhyâropita*), arises from false knowledge (*mithyâjñâna-vijrimbhita*), is a mere illusion (*abhimâna*), which is refuted by perfect knowledge (*Samyagdarçanam*);—just as the illusion that there is a snake, where there is only a rope, a man where there is only a tree trunk, or a sheet of water where there is only a mirage, is refuted by closer examination and deceives no longer. The whole world is only an illusion (*mâyâ*) which Brahman projects (*prasârayati*) from himself like a magician (*mâyâvin*), and by which he is not affected any more than the magician is by the magic he creates; or, to change the image, Brahman owing to Ignorance appears as multiplex (*vibhâvyate*) just as the magician does owing to the illusion; he is the cause of the continued existence (*sthiti-kâraṇam*) of the world, as the magician is of the magical scene he projects, and of the absorption of the world into his own Self (*sva-âtmani eva upasaṃhâra-kâraṇam*), just as the earth withdraws living beings into itself; the action of plurality (*bheda-vyavahâra*) during the existence of the world and the force of plurality (*bheda-çakti*) before and after both depend on Ignorance or false knowledge. As to this idea of *avidyâ, mithyâjñânam*, all further enquiry is at a loss; of the origin of this Ignorance, innate in all of us, we learn nothing; we penetrate deepest by the repeatedly employed image of the person with diseased eyes, who sees two moons, where in reality there is only one.*

* Guilt reaching back *ad infinitum* is in this case not to be thought of; cf. what has been said above p. 302 and as confirmation the important passage p. 85, 4: *tat-kṛita-dharma-adharma-nimittam saçarîratvam, iti cet? na! çarîra-sambandhasya asiddhatvâd dharma-adharmayor âtma-kṛitatva-asiddheḥ; çarîra-sambandhasya dharma-adharmayos tat-kṛitatvasya ca itara-itara-âçrayatva-prasañgâd andha-paramparâ eva eshâ anâditva-kalpanâ kriyâ-samavâya-abhâvâc ca âtmanaḥ kartṛitva-anupapatteḥ* (translated above p. 420).

However the non-existence of the world is only relative: the plurality of phenomena, names and forms, and Mâyâ are *tattva-anyatvâbhyâm anirvacanîya, i. e.,* "one cannot say that they "are Brahman (*tat*), nor yet that they are different from Him." They are, like the figures in a dream, true (*satya*) so long as the dream lasts, and are so no longer when the awakening (*prabodha*) comes.—This idealism, of which we see the dawn only in the Upanishads, the Vedânta tries to bring into unison with the Vedic doctrine of creation by maintaining that by creation is only meant the identity (*ananyatvam, tâdâtmyam*) of the world and Brahman; the world is the effect, Brahman is the cause; and effect and cause are identical; for the proof of this proposition the persistence of matter through changing states serves as the main argument.

4. Psychology.

§ 24. While we recognise in all Being around us, in all the names and forms, of which the world consists, a deception, a mere illusion dependent on Ignorance and comparable to a dream, there is one point in the Universe when these considerations have no application; this point is our soul, *i. e.*, our own Self (*âtman*). This Self cannot be demonstrated because it is the basis of every proof, but it cannot be denied either, because anyone who denies it presupposes its existence (above p. 127). Of what nature is there this sole foundation of all certainty, the soul or inner Self? How is it related to Brahman, who includes all Being in Himself? **The soul alone is real.**

§ 25. The soul can (1) not be different from Brahman because there is nothing "Existent" outside Brahman; but it is (2) not to be regarded as a transformation of Brahman either, for Brahman is unchanging; it is (3) just as little a part of Brahman, for He has no parts.—Therefore it only remains that the soul is identical with Brahman, and that each of us is the whole, indivisible, changeless Brahman who comprehends all Being in Himself. **Identity of the soul with Brahman.**

The soul from the metaphysical standpoint.

§ 26. From this follows that all that is established of the Brahman who is without differences, is also true of the soul; like Brahman the Soul is essentially pure spirituality (*caitanyam*), and to it are applicable all those negative characteristics whose purpose is to secure the conception of Brahman from all ideas by which His Being might seem to be limited. Therefore the soul is, like Brahman (1) omnipresent (*vibhu, sarvagata*), or, as we should say, spaceless, (2) omniscient and omnipotent, (3) neither agent (*kartar*) nor enjoyer (or sufferer as the case may be, *bhoktar*).

The soul from the empirical standpoint.

§ 27. If the true nature of the soul lies in these characteristics, it follows that all which contradicts them is "ascribed" to it only by Ignorance. These ascribed limitations or *Upâdhis* have their foundation only in false knowledge and to them as we saw all which conditions bodily existence belongs; on them depends the fact that the soul in the state of Saṃsâra is (1) not all-pervading and omnipresent but dwells in the heart, its size being limited to that of the *Manas*, (2) is also not omniscient and omnipotent; for its natural omniscience and omnipotence become latent through the *Upâdhis*, just as the light and heat of fire in wood in which it is hidden and slumbers; (3) finally the soul by its connection with the *Upâdhis* becomes an agent and enjoyer (*kartar* and *bhoktar*) and by these latter qualities its entanglement in Saṃsâra is conditioned; for the works of one life must be recompensed by enjoyment and works in the following existence; the works however which form one part of the requital demand a further requital and so on *ad infinitum.*

The *Upâdhis.*

§ 28. This beginningless and endless Saṃsâra depends only on the soul's true nature being hidden from it by the *Upâdhis* due to *Avidyâ.* They make Brahman the individual, active and enjoying soul; in addition to all outward things and relations and including the "gross body" which belongs to them and at death returns into the elements, they are the following: (1) the *Manas* and *Indriyas*; (2) the *Mukhya Prâṇa*; (3) the *Sûkshmaṃ Çarîram*; and with this unchanging psychic apparatus, with which the soul has been clothed from eternity and remains clothed till liberation, is associated (4) a changeable element which we shall term moral determination. We have now to consider these *Upâdhis* individually.

Manas and Indriyas.

§ 29. While the gross body (*deha, kârya-karaṇa-saṅghâta*) and its organs (*karaṇam*), such as eye, ear, hands, feet etc. perish at death, their functions (*vritti*) regarded as separate entities remain united with the soul for all time. These organs are the *Indriyas* (the powerful ones) which the soul puts forth like feelers and withdraws at death. On these depend the two sides of conscious life, perception on the one hand and action on the other. Answering to this the soul has five faculties of perception (*jñâna-indriyas*)—sight, hearing, smell, taste, and touch, and five faculties of action (*karma-indriyas*)—grasping, moving, speaking, procreating, and evacuating. These ten *Indriyas* commonly named after the corresponding organs of the gross body, are directed by a central organ, the *Manas*, which on the one hand works up the data of perception into ideas (*manasâ hi eva paçyati, manasâ çriṇoti*, Bṛih. 1, 5, 3), and on the other by the faculties of action causes what is willed to be executed; it is therefore at once what we call understanding and conscious volition. While the *Indriyas* pervade the whole body, the *Manas* "large as the point of an awl" dwells in the heart, and in the *Manas*, filling it completely, dwells the soul in the closest connection with it, broken only by liberation; only by the organs to which Ignorance chains it does the soul become an agent and enjoyer; it is itself as regards the activity of the organs a passive onlooker (*sâkshin*), pure apperception (*upalabdhi*) so that in spite of its immersion in worldly action it remains in its essence untouched (*asaṅga, ananvâgata*) by it.

Mukhya Prâna.

§ 30. With the *Mukhya Prâṇa* the soul seems to be less intimately connected than with *Manas* and the *Indriyas*; this term still has in the Upanishads the meaning of "breath in the mouth," but in the system it has come to denote "chief breath of life." Just as *Manas* and the *Indriyas* are the functions of perception and action hypostatised into separate entities, the *Mukhya Prâṇa* on which they all depend is a hypostasis of empirical life itself, which its five branches—*Prâṇa, Apâna, Vyâna, Samâna,* and *Udâna* condition. Of these *Prâṇa* causes exhalation, *Apâna* inhalation; *Vyâna* is what supports life when breathing is momentarily suspended; *Samâna* is the principle of digestion; just as these four sustain life, *Udâna* brings about its termination, leading the soul out of the body at death by one of the 101 principal arteries. By the same road withdraw *Manas,* the *Indriyas* and *Mukhya Prâṇa*; just as during life they are the forces that rule the organs of the body, they are after the death of the body the seed from which at each rebirth the bodily organs arise.

Sûkshmam Çarîram

§ 31. Just as the soul carries with it the seed of the bodily organs in the *Indriyas*, it bears with it the seed of the body itself in the form of the "subtle body" *sûkshmaṃ çarîram*, or as it is paraphrased repeatedly by Çañkara, *deha-vîjâni bhûta-sûkshmâṇi, i. e.*, "the subtle parts of the elements which form the seed of the body" [and, according to Çañkara, as is demonstrable from p. 743, 4, the impure elements; cf. for a contrary view Vedântasâra § 77]. How these subtle parts are related to the coarse elements is not further explained. The subtle body formed of them is material (*tanutvam*) but transparent (*svacchatvam*); therefore it is not seen at the withdrawal of the soul. On it depends animal heat; the corpse grows cold because the subtle body has left it to accompany the soul on its wanderings along with the other organs.

Moral determination.

§ 32. With this psychic organism (*manas, indriyas, mukhya prâṇa, sûkshmaṃ çarîram*) which is attached to the soul in life and death at all times, and appears completely unchanging, is associated further as a companion in the migrations a changing Upâdhi; this is moral determination, consisting in the treasure of works (*karma-âçaya*) collected during life; side by side with the physical substratum (*bhûta-âçraya*) *i. e.*, the subtle body, it departs with the soul as a moral substratum (*karma-âçraya*) and inexorably determines the nature of the future existence in respect of enjoyment and suffering as well as of works.

§ 33. There are four states of the wandering soul—waking, dreaming, deep sleep, and death. In the waking state the soul sojourning in the heart in association with *Manas* rules over the whole body, perceiving and working through *Manas* and the *Indriyas*. In dream sleep the *Indriyas* enter into rest while the *Manas* remains active; and the soul, surrounded by *Manas* into which have withdrawn the *Indriyas*, pervades the body in the veins and in doing so beholds the dreams "fitted together" from waking impressions (*vâsanâ*). In deep sleep the union of the soul with the *Manas* is dissolved; *Manas* and the *Indriyas*, entering into rest, go into the veins or the pericardium and then into *Mukhya Prâṇa*, whose activity continues in deep sleep also; meanwhile the soul, temporarily freed from all the Upâdhis, enters into Brahman in the ether of the heart; as the soul without the Upâdhis is Brahman, this entrance into Brahman is only another way of expressing the complete deliverance from the Upâdhis. From this temporary identification with Brahman the soul on waking issues with all its individual characteristics, the same that it was before. **Special state of the soul.**

5. Transmigration.

§ 34. At death the *Indriyas* first of all enter into the *Manas*, this into the *Mukhya Prâṇa*, this into the soul affected by moral determination, and lastly the soul into the *Sukshmam Çarîram*. After all these are assembled in the heart, its tip glows to illuminate the way and the *Udâna* leads the soul, together with the Upâdhis mentioned, out of the body. The soul of him who has acquired (lower) knowledge passes by the artery of the head (*mûrdhanyâ nâḍî*, later termed *sushumnâ*); those who have not knowledge depart by the 100 remaining main arteries of the body. (He who has acquired the higher knowledge does not, as we shall see later, depart at all.) From this point the roads branch; the Ignorant who has performed works follows the *Pitṛiyâna* or way of the fathers; he **The passing of the soul from the body.**

who has the lower knowledge the *Devayâna* or way of the gods; he who has neither knowledge nor works, *i. e.*, the wicked man, is excluded from both these roads.

Fate of the doers of works (*Pitriyâna*) § 35. The *Pitriyâna*, intended for those who have neither the higher nor the lower knowledge of Brahman but have performed good works, leads the soul up to the moon to be recompensed. The stages on this road are the following—(1) smoke, (2) night, (3) the half of the month in which the moon wanes, (4) the half of the year in which the days grow shorter, (5) the world of the fathers, (6) the ether, and (7) the moon. In the luminous realm of the moon the souls enjoy converse with the gods as a reward for their works, and that until no more works remain. Only a part of the works however is recompensed on the moon. Another part forms a residue (*anuçaya*) and finds its recompense in the next birth. Which works are to be understood in each case is a question that is not cleared up. After the works which find their reward on the moon are consumed the soul descends again; on the return journey the stages are—(1) the ether, (2) the air, (3) smoke, (4) the cloud, (5) rain, (6) the plant, (7) the male semen, and (8) the mother's womb. In all the soul sojourns merely as a guest and is to be distinguished from the elements and souls it traverses. After it has finally reached a womb corresponding to the merit of its works it again passes out to another life on earth.

Fate of the wicked (Hell and the third place). § 36. The wicked who have neither knowledge nor works do not ascend to the moon; their fate is not clearly developed, for Çañkara refers on the one hand to punishment in the seven hells of *Yama*, and on the other to the "third place," in which they are born again as lower animals, but the connection between the two is not made clear. Though the wicked remain excluded from life on the moon, among those who return from the moon there is a further difference made between those of good conduct who are reborn in one of the three higher castes and those of evil conduct who enter the bodies of Caṇḍâlas or animals. A combination of these ideas to a connected whole, easily possible by the distinction of various steps in the good and evil works to be atoned for, is not found in the work from which we draw our facts.

Fate of the pious worshippers of Brahman (*Devayâna*).

§ 37. From those who do good works (§ 35) and adhere to the old Vedic cult of sacrifice are to be distinguished those who retain the Brahman doctrine but are unable to rise to the perfect knowledge of the doctrine of identity; and who therefore regard Brahman not as the soul in themselves but as God outside themselves and worship him accordingly. These possessors of the lower knowledge (*aparâ vidyâ*), *i. e.*, the worshippers of the lower, attribute-possessing (*aparam. saguṇam*) Brahman, all enter, (with the exception of such as have worshipped Brahman under a symbol, *pratîkam*), after death by the *Devayâna* into the lower Brahman. The stages of this road are variously given in the different accounts, and Çaṅkara weaves them into a whole. According to Chând. [Bṛih., Kaush.] the soul of him who possesses the lower knowledge, after leaving the body by the artery of the head, traverses the following regions—(1) Flame [= *Agniloka*], (2) the day, (3) the half of the month when the moon waxes, (4) the half of the year when the days grow longer, (5) the year, [(6) *Devaloka*, (7) *Vâyuloka*], (8) the sun, (9) the moon. and (10) lightning. These stages are neither to be regarded as signposts, nor as places of enjoyment for the soul, but as guides which it needs, because it cannot use its own organs as they are rolled up. While therefore by those already mentioned we are to understand divine, quasi-human guides of the soul, the soul after its entrance into the lightning is received by a "man, who is not as a human being" (*purusho 'mânavaḥ*), and conducted to Brahman [through (11) *Varuṇaloka*, (12) *Indraloka*, and (13) *Prajâpatiloka*]. By Brahman however the lower, attribute-possessing Brahman is here to be understood, who has himself originated (*kâryam*) and therefore perishes at the destruction of the world. In the world of this Brahman the souls enjoy *aiçvaryam*, lordship, which consists in a quasi-divine but limited omnipotence and includes the fulfilment of all wishes. The *Manas* serves as organ of enjoyment; whether the soul can also make use of the accompanying *Indriyas* is doubtful. Among other powers of the soul is that of animating several bodies at once, among which the soul distributes itself by dividing its Upâdhis.—Though this *aiçvaryam* of those who have entered into the lower Brahman by the *Devayâna* has an end and only lasts till the destruction of the world, the scripture says of them: "For such there is no return." We must therefore assume that the higher knowledge of *Samyagdarçanam* is communicated to them in the Brahman-world, and that thus at the destruction of the world, when the lower Brahman also perishes, they enter with Him into the "eternal, perfect *Nirvâṇa.*" This way of entering Brahman is termed *Kramamukti* "progressive liberation" because it is conditioned by a progression, or "liberation by steps" because it is brought about by the intermediate step of heavenly lordship. To be distinguished from it is the immediate liberation of those who possess knowledge and this we shall now consider.

6. Liberation.

"From knowledge comes release." § 38. The question of the possibility of a release from individual existence which forms the cornerstone of the Vedânta as of other Indian systems presupposes the pessimistic view that all individual existence is a misery. This view is occasionally put forward both in the Veda (Bṛih. 3, 4, 2. *ato 'nyad ârtam*, "what is different from him is afflicted;" Bṛih. 4, 4, 11, *anandâ nâma te lôkaḥ*, "yea joyless are these worlds" above p. 194; cf. Kâṭh. 1, 3. Îça 3) and in the system (above pp. 318, 433, cf. p. 1139, 12); but is not emphasised to anything like the extent we should expect.—How is liberation (*moksha*) from the bond (*bandha*) of existence possible?—Not by works; for they, good and evil alike, demand their recompense, condition a new existence and are the cause of the continuance of *Saṃsâra*; but not by a (moral) purification (*saṃskâra*) either; for this can only take place in an object capable of change; but the Âtman, the soul, whose liberation is in question, is unchangeable. Therefore liberation cannot consist in a process either of becoming or of doing something but only in the knowledge of something, already present, that is hidden by Ignorance: "from knowledge liberation" (*jñânân mokshaḥ*). After the Brahmanhood of the soul is recognised liberation follows at once ("that thou art" is the phrase· not "that thou wilt be," p. 917, 7); simultaneously with the attainment of the knowledge of the identity with Brahman the soul becomes the Soul of the universe (p. 66, 7).

§ 39. The Âtman, in the knowledge of which consists liberation, is nought else than the subject of knowledge in us. For this reason it is not recognisable by natural means: "thou canst not see the seer of seeing" etc. (Bṛih 3, 4, 2); it cannot be sought for and looked at as an object; knowledge of it cannot be obtained at will, and even research in the scriptures does not produce a knowledge of it at once; this only serves to clear away the obstacles in the way. Whether the Âtman is known depends like the knowledge of every object on whether it shows itself to us, and therefore on itself. For this reason in the lower knowledge, which contrasts the Âtman to ourselves and worships him as a personal God, knowledge appears as dependent on the grace of God; but in the higher knowledge, as the Âtman is in reality not an object, we cannot enquire further after the cause which makes it known to us.

Knowledge brought about by the grace of God.

§ 40. Religious practice however knows certain means (*sâdhanam*), by which the acquisition of knowledge of the Âtman is furthered. Thus from those who are called to knowledge is demanded the study of the Veda and the four requirements ((1) Discrimination between eternal and non-eternal substance, (2) Renunciation of the enjoyment of reward here and in the other world, (3) the attainment of the six means–tranquillity, self-restraint, renunciation, resignation, concentration, belief, (4) desire for release).—In a more general sense and apart from this enumeration customary in instruction there are two means of furthering knowledge—works and meditation. (1) Works cannot, it is true, produce knowledge but are auxiliary (*sahakârin*) to the attainment of it,

Auxiliary means of acquiring knowledge.

and that by destroying the obstacles that stand in the way; as obstacles are reckoned the affections (*kleça*) such as (passionate) love, hate, etc. (Works have therefore in the plan of salvation not a meritorious but an ascetic rôle; cf. 1082, 12 *nirabhisandhin*). Works which serve as a means of knowledge are auxiliary in part "outside" (*vâhya*) in part "closer" (*pratyâsanna*). As these "outside" means are reckoned—"the study "of the Veda, sacrifice, alms, penance, fasting" (Bṛih. 4, 4, 22); these are to be employed only till knowledge is gained. In contrast to these the "closer" means continue to exist even when knowledge is attained; they are "tranquillity, restraint, "renunciation, resignation, concentration" (Bṛih. 4, 4, 23).—(2) Side by side with works pious meditation (*upâsanâ*) serves as a means of knowledge. It consists in the devout consideration of the words of scripture, *e. g.*, the saying *tat tvam asi*, and is, like threshing, to be repeated till knowledge appears as its fruit; this requires a longer or shorter time according as a person is mentally limited or afflicted by doubts. With the attainment of the higher knowledge meditation becomes unnecessary, for it has served its purpose. (The meditation on the other hand which is a part of the service of works, and that which is usual in the lower knowledge are to be practised till death, for the thoughts in the hour of death are of importance in determining the fate in the life beyond.) The posture is indifferent in the case of meditation serving the purpose of the higher knowledge. (So too for meditation as part of the service of works; the meditation necessary for the lower knowledge must be practised sitting, not standing or lying down.)

Destruction of works. § 41. Knowledge consists in the immediate intuition (*anubhava*) of the identity of the soul with Brahman. The works of Him who has attained this and with it the conviction of the unreality of the world of plurality and transmigration, are annihilated and in the future cleave to him no more. This annihilation refers just as much to good as to evil works, for both demand retribution and therefore do not lead beyond Saṃsâra. He on the other hand who has attained knowledge has won this conviction—"that Brahman the nature of which "is opposed to the nature, previously considered by me to be "true, of agent and enjoyer, which is in its own nature in all "time past, present and future non-agent and non-enjoyer, "that Brahman am I; therefore I never was agent and en-"joyer, and I am not one now, nor shall I ever be" (p. 1078, 4). With the unreality of activity the unreality of the body which exists as the fruit of works is recognised; therefore he who has attained knowledge is as little affected by the sufferings of his own body as by the sufferings of another; and he who still feels pain, has verily not yet attained full knowledge.

Abolition of all duties.

§ 42. Even as for the man who has attained knowledge there is no longer a world, a body, or suffering, there is also no longer prescribed action. But he will not therefore do evil; for that which is the presupposition of all action, good and evil,—illusion—has been annihilated. It is a matter of indifference if he does works or not; whether he does them or not they are not his works and cleave to him no more. (However natural it would have been to desire from the described position of him who knows himself as soul of the world a positive moral disposition which shows itself in works of justice and love, this consequence is not drawn in Çaṅkara but only in the Bhagavadgîtâ, cf. above p. 59, note 36).

Why the body of the liberated continue to exist.

§ 43. Knowledge burns the seed of works so that no material is at hand to cause a rebirth. On the other hand knowledge cannot annihilate works, the seed of which has already germinated, *i. e.*, those from which the present life is put together. This is why the body, even after the awakening (*prabodha*) is complete, continues to exist for a while, just as the potter's wheel goes on revolving even when the vessel which it supported is completed. This continuance is however a mere appearance; the possessor of knowledge cannot destroy it, but it cannot deceive him any more either; just so the man with diseased eyes sees two moons but knows that in reality there is only one there.

Absorption of the possessor of knowledge in Brahman.

§ 44. After the works whose fruit has not yet begun to appear have been destroyed by knowledge, and after those, the fruit of which is the present existence, have by completion of this present life come to an end, with the moment of death full and eternal liberation comes to him who possesses knowledge; "his vital spirits withdraw not; Brahman is he, and into "Brahman he is resolved."

"As rivers run and in the deep
"Lose name and form and disappear
"So goes, from name and form released,
"The wise man to the Deity."

II. Index of all Quotations in Çaṅkara's Commentary on the Brahmasûtras.

Explanation of the Abbreviations.

Aâ = Aitareya-âranyakam
Ab = Aitareya-brâhmaṇam
Âçvçr = Âçvalâyana-çrautasûtram
Âpdh = Âpastamba-dharmasûtram
Ârsh = Ârsheya-brâhmaṇam
Au = Aitareya-upanishad
AV = Atharvaveda-saṃhitâ
BhG = Bhagavadgîtâ
Bs = Brahmasûtram
Bu = Bṛihadâraṇyaka-upanishad
Cb = Chândogya-brâhmaṇam
Çb = Çatapatha-brâhmaṇam
Ch = Chândogya-upanishad
Çv = Çvetâçvatara-upanishad
GdpK = Gauḍapâda's Kârikâ on the Mâṇḍûkya-upanishad
Jâb = Jâbâla-upanishad
Js = Jaimini-sûtram
ISpr = Indische Sprüche[2] (Boehtlingk)
Îçâ = Îçâ-upanishad
Kap = Kapila-sâñkhyasûtram
Kâtyçr = Kâtyâyana-çrautasûtram
Kauç = Kauçikasûtram
Kaushb = Kaushîtaki-brâhmaṇam
Kb = Kâṭhaka-brâhmaṇam
Kena = Kena-upanishad
Kshu = Kaushîtaki-upanishad
Ku = Kâṭhaka-upanishad
MaitrS = Maitrâyaṇi-saṃhitâ
Manu = Mânava-dharmaçâstram
MârkP = Mârkaṇḍeya-purâṇam
Mbh = Mahâbhâratam
Mu = Muṇḍaka-upanishad
Ns = Nyâyasûtram
Pañc = Pancaviñça-brâhmaṇam
Pâṇ = Pâṇini
Pârgṛ = Pâraskara-gṛihyasûtram
Pu = Praçna-upanishad
Râmây = Râmâyaṇam
ṚV = Ṛigveda-saṃhitâ
Sâṅkhyak = Sâṅkhya-kârikâ
Shaḍv = Shaḍviñça-brâhmaṇam
Tâ = Taittirîya-âraṇyakam
Tb = Taittirîya-brâhmaṇam
Ts = Taittirîya-saṃhitâ
Tu = Taittirîya-upanishad
Ys = Yogasûtram
Ysk = Yâska (ed. Roth)
Vaiç = Vaiçeshikasûtram
Vs = Vâjasaneyi-saṃhitâ

I, 1.

29, 1 = Ch 8, 1, 6
—, 3 = Tu 2, 1
31, 6 = Tu 3, 1
37, 2 = Tu 3, 1
39, 2 = Ysk 31, 15
41, 4 = Bu 2, 4, 5
42, 1 = Ch 6, 14, 2
43, 1 = ?[1]
—, 2 = Ab 5, 31, 1
45, 5 = Tu 3, 1
46, 1 = Tu 3, 6
48, 6 = Bu 2, 4, 10
49, 3 = Tu 3, 1
50, 5 = Js 1, 2, 1
51, 5 = Ts 1, 5, 1, 1
52, 1 = Js 1, 2, 7
—, 3 = Ts 1, 1, 1, 1
54, 1 = Ch 6, 2, 1
—, 2 = Au 1, 1, 1
—, 3 = Bu 2, 5, 19
55, 1 = Mu 2, 2, 11
—, 4 = Bu 2, 4, 14
—, 6 = Ch 6, 8, 7
58, 2 = ?[2]
—, 4 = Js 1, 1, 25
—, 4 = Js 1, 2, 1
59, 10 = Bu 2, 4, 5
60, 1 ~ Ch 8, 7, 1
—, 1 = Bu 1, 4, 7
—, 2 = Bu 1, 4, 15
—, 2 cf Mu 3, 2, 9
—, 6 = Bu 3, 9, 28
61, 1 = Bu 2, 4, 5
—, 7 = Js 1, 1, 1
—, 8 Quotation?
62, 6 = Ch 5, 10, 5
63, 6 = Ch 8, 12, 1
64, 1 = Ku 2, 22
—, 2 = Mu 2, 1, 2
64, 2 = Bu 4, 3, 15
—, 10 = Ku 2, 14
65, 5 = Mu 3, 2, 9
66, 1 = Mu 2, 2, 8
—, 2 = Tu 2, 9
—, 2 = Bu 4, 2, 4
—, 3 = Bu 1, 4, 10
—, 4 = Îçâ 7
—, 6 = Bu 1, 4, 10
67, 1 = Pu 6, 8
—, 1 = Ch 7, 1, 3
—, 3 = Ch 7, 26, 2
—, 6 = Ns 1, 1, 2
68, 2 = Bu 3, 1, 9
—, 4 = Ch 3, 18, 1
—, 4 = Ch 3, 19, 1
—, 6 = Ch 4, 3, 1
—, 6 = Ch 4, 3, 2
69, 1 = Ch 6, 8, 7
—, 1 = Bu 1, 4, 10
—, 2 = Bu 2, 5, 19
—, 3 = Mu 2, 2, 8
—, 5 = Mu 3, 2, 9
70, 1 = Kena 1, 3
—, 2 = Bu 2, 4, 14
—, 4 = Kena 1, 4
—, 10 = Kena 2, 11
71, 1 ~ Bu 3, 4, 2
72, 6 = ?[3]
73, 7 = Mu 3, 1, 1
—, 8 = Ku 3, 4
—, 9 = Çv 6, 11
74, 1 = Îçâ 8
—, 8 = Ab 3, 8, 1
75, 1 = ?[4]
—, 7 = Ch 5, 7, 1
—, 7 = Ch 5, 8, 1
76, 4 = Bu 2, 4, 5
77, 1 = Bu 2, 4, 5
—, 3 = Bu 2, 4, 6
—, 3 = Bu 4, 5, 15
77, 5 = Bu 2, 5, 19
—, 9 = Bu 4, 4, 12
—, 12 = BhG 15, 20
—, 14 = ?[5]
78, 3 = Bu 3, 9, 26
79, 5 = Ku 2, 11
—, 6 = Bu 3, 9, 26
—, 9 = 58, 2
80, 1 = Js 1, 2, 1
81, 8 = ?[4]
83, 4 = ?[6]
84, 16 = Ch 8, 12, 1
87, 7 = Bu 4, 4, 7
—, 9 = ?[7]
—, 11 = BhG 2, 54
89, 2 = Js 1, 1, 1
—, 6 = Bu 1, 4, 10
—, 10 ?[8]
92, 5 = BhG 14, 17
93, 11 = Ch 6, 2, 1
—, 12 = Ch 6, 2, 3
—, 16 ~ Au 1, 1, 1—2
94, 3 = Pu 6, 3
—, 4 = Mu 1, 1, 9
97, 5 = Çv 6, 8
—, 9 = Çv 3, 19
98, 2 = Bu 3, 7, 23
99, 10 = Ch 6, 2, 3
100, 3 = Ch 6, 2, 3. 4
—, 5 ~ Js 2, 2, 12
—, 9 = Ch 6, 2, 1
—, 10 = Ch 6, 3, 1
—, 12 = Ch 6, 3, 2
101, 3 = Ch 6, 8, 7
102, 10 = Ch 6, 8, 7
—, 11 ~ Ch 6, 14, 2
103, 7 = Ch 6, 8, 7
—, 9 cf Ch 6, 16
—, 10 = Aâ 2, 1, 2, 6
105, 5 = Ch 6, 8, 7
106, 4 = Ch 6, 1, 3. 6

[1] = 370, 1 = 483, 1 = 849, 13 cf Pañcav. 21, 9, 9.—[2] = 79, 9 *çâstratâtparyavidaḥ* (*bhâshyakrit* gloss.).—[3] = 427, 5 = 827, 7 *smṛiti*.—[4] brâhmaṇa-like.—[5] *Prâbhâkara* gloss.—[6] "*na îksheta udyantam âdityam*" gloss.—[7] upanishad-like.—[8] *brahmavidâṃ gâthâm udâharati* gloss.

107, 6 = Ch 6, 8, 1
108, 5 = Ch 8, 3, 3
—, 7 = Ch 6, 8, 3
—, 8 = Ch 6, 8, 5
—, 12 ~ Bu 4, 3, 21
109, 9 = Kshu 3, 3[9]
—, 12 = Tu 2, 1
—, 12 ~ Ch 7, 26, 1
—, 13 = Pu 3, 3
110, 5 = Çv 6, 9
111, 4 = Bu 4, 5, 15
—, 6 = Ch 7, 24, 1
—, 8 = Tâ 3, 12, 7[10]
—, 9 = Çv 6, 19
—, 10 = Bu 2, 3, 6
112, 1 = Bu 3, 8, 8
—, 1 = ?[11]
—, 8 = ?[12]
—, 9 = Ch 3, 14, 1
—, 11 = BhG 8, 6
113, 3 = ?[13]
—, 5 = BhG 10, 41
—, 8 cf Ch 1, 6, 6. 7
114, 1 = Bs 1, 1, 22
—, 5 = Bs 1, 1, 12
—, 8 = Bs 1, 1, 10
—, 12 = Tu 2, 1—4
—, 13 = Tu 2, 5
115, 1 = Tu 2, 1
—, 7 = Tu 2, 5
—, 8 = Tu 2, 5
116, 1 = Tu 2, 7
—, 3 = Tu 2, 8
—, 4 = Tu 2, 9
—, 5 = Tu 3, 6
—, 6 = Bu 3, 9, 28
118, 3 cf Tu 2, 8
Bu 4, 3, 33
—, 8 = Tu 2, 7
118, 14 = Tu 2, 1
—, 17 cf Tu 2, 6
119, 2 = Tu 2, 5
—, 6 = Tu 3, 6
—, 11 = Tu 2, 6
120, 5 = Tu 2, 7
—, 7 cf Ku 3, 11
—, 14 = Bu 3, 7, 23
121, 5 = Tu 2, 6
—, 7 = Bs 1, 1, 5
122, 2 = Tu 2, 7
—, 9 = Tu 2, 1—4
123, 7 = Tu 2, 5
—, 9 = Tu 2, 1
124, 9 = Tu 2, 6
125, 3 = Bu 4, 3, 32
—, 7 = Tu 2, 9
—, 10 = Ch 7, 24
126, 1 = Tu 2, 1
—, 2 = Çv 6, 11
—, 4 = Tu 2, 7
—, 6 = Tu 2, 8
—, 7 = Tu 2, 9
—, 7 = Tu 3, 6
—, 11 = Bu 3, 9, 28
—, 12 = Tu 2, 7
—, 14 = Tu 2, 8
127, 5 = Tu 2, 9
—, 6 = Tu 2, 6
—, 7 = Tu 2, 5
—, 9 = Tu 2, 7
—, 10 = Tu 2, 6
—, 11 = Tu 2, 1
—, 13 = Tu 3, 6
128, 1 cf Tu 2, 9
—, 5 = Bs 1, 1, 12
—, 7 = Tu 2, 6
—, 8 = Bs 1, 1. 13
—, 15 = Bs 1, 1, 14
129, 2 = Tu 2, 6
—, 7 = Ch 1, 6, 6—7
130, 2 = Ch 1, 7, 5
—, 7 = Ch 1, 7, 5
—, 9 = Ku 3, 15
—, 10 = Ch 1, 6, 6
—, 10 = Ch 1, 7, 5
—, 11 = Ch 7, 24, 1
—, 12 = ?[14]
131, 1 = Ch 1, 6, 8
—, 2 = Ch 1, 7, 6
—, 4 = Bu 4, 4, 22
—, 9 = Ch 1, 6, 7
—, 12 = Ch 1, 7, 5
—, 13 = Ch 8, 7, 1
132, 1 = Ch 1, 7, 5
—, 4 ~ Ch 1, 6, 8
—, 5 ~ Ch 1, 7, 5
—, 6 ~ Ch 1, 7, 6
—, 9 = BhG 10, 41
133, 5 = Mbh 12, 12909
—, 8 = Ku 3. 15
—, 10 = Ch 3, 14, 2
134, 3 = Bu 3, 7, 9
—, 11 ~ Ch 1, 9, 1
135, 6 = Tu 2, 7
—, 7 = Ch 8, 14
—, 15 = Ch 1, 9. 1
—, 17 = Tu 2, 1
136, 2 cf Ch 1, 9, 1
—, 5 = Ch 1, 9, 1
—, 12 = Ch 3, 14, 3
—, 15 = Bu 3, 9, 28[15]
—, 16 cf Ch 1, 8, 8
137, 2 = Ch 1, 9, 2
—, 6 = Ch 8, 14
138, 1 = RV 1, 164, 39
—, 2 = Tu 3, 6
—, 3 ~ Bu 5, 1, 1[16]

[9] or Kaush. 4, 20, in both cases both recensions without *sarve*; likewise 299, 12.—[10] = 390, 6 = 454, 14 = 686, 9.—[11] brâhmaṇa-like.—[12] = 1047, 12 = 1135, 6 upanishad-like.—[13] upanishad-like.—[14] = 172, 5 = 610, 3 = 624, 8 = 652, 7 = 838, 9 = 1124, 12, according to the comment. to Chând. p. 409 *kâṭhake*, but improbably.—[15] with the reading *râter* (Mâdhy.).—[16] confounded with Chând. 4, 10, 5.

138, 5 = ?[17]
—, 8 Ch 1, 10, 9
—, 9 Ch 1, 11, 4—5
—, 12 Ch 6, 8, 2
—, 12 Bu 4, 4 18
139, 8 Çb 10, 3, 3, 6
—, 13 cf Ch 1, 11, 6—9
140, 5 = Ch 1, 11, 5
—, 12 = Ch 1, 11, 5
—, 15 = Kshu 3, 3[18]
141, 7 = Bu 4, 4, 18
—, 8 = Ch 6, 8, 2
—, 15 = ?[19]
—, 16 = Ch 6, 8, 2
142, 5 = Ch 3, 13, 7
143, 10 = Ch 6, 3, 3
144, 5 = Ch 3, 13, 7
—, 6 = Ch 3, 13, 7
—, 9 = Bu 5, 5, 3
—, 10 = Ch 3, 13, 7. 8
—, 11 = Ch 3, 13, 8
—, 12 cf Ch 3, 13, 8
—, 15 = Ch 3, 12, 1
145, 2 = Ch 3, 12, 6
—, 3 = Ch 3, 13, 7
—, 6 = Ch 3, 12, 6
146, 5 cf Ch 3, 14
—, 6 = Ch 3, 13, 7
—, 9 = Tb 3, 12, 9, 7[20]
—, 11 = Bu 4, 3. 5
—, 12 = Ts 1, 6, 3, 3
147, 3 = Ku 5, 15
—, 4 = Bu 4, 4, 16
—, 14 = Ch 3, 13, 8
148, 6 = Bu 4, 4, 24
—, 11 = Ch 3, 13, 7
149, 3 = Ch 3, 12, 1
—, 6 = Ch 3, 12, 6
—, 9 = Ch 3, 12, 5—6
149, 12 ~ Ch 3, 12, 7
—, 13 = Ch 3, 11, 3
150, 1 = Ch 3, 12, 1
—, 4 = Ch 3, 14, 1
—, 5 = Bs 2, 1, 14
—, 6 = Aâ 3, 2, 3, 12[21]
151, 2 = Ch 4, 3, 8
—, 9 = Ch 3, 12, 5
—, 11 = Ch 3, 12, 6
—, 13 = ṚV 10, 90
152, 2 = BhG 10, 42
—, 3 ~ Ch 3, 12, 7
—, 4 = Ch 3, 13, 6
—, 9 = Ch 3, 12, 6
—, 10 = Ch 3, 13, 7
154, 5 = Kshu 3, 1
—, 7 = Kshu 3, 2[22]
—, 9 = Kshu 3, 3[23]
—, 10 = Kshu 3, 8
—, 11 = Kshu 3, 8
155, 2 = Bs 1, 1, 23
—, 3 = Kshu 3, 8
—, 6 = Kshu 3, 1
—, 7 = Kshu 3, 3
—, 7 = Kshu 3, 8
—, 12 = Kshu 3, 1[23]
155, 1 = Kshu 3, 1
—, 4 = Çv 3, 8 [= 6, 15]
—, 5 = Kshu 3, 1[23]
—, 7 = Mu 2, 2, 8
—, 10-15 = Kshu 3, 8[24]
157, 4 = Kshu 3, 1
—, 5 = Kshu 3, 2[22]
—, 7 ~ Bu 3, 8, 8
—, 8 = Kshu 3, 1
—, 10 Quotation?
158, 4 = Kshu 3, 2[25]
—, 7 = Kshu 3, 2[25]
—, 8 = Kshu 3, 3
158, 9 = Kshu 3, 8[25]
159, 4 = Bu 2, 5, 19
—, 9 = Kshu 3, 1
—, 10 = Bu 1, 4, 10
—, 11 = Bu 1, 4, 10 .
—, 12 = Kshu 3, 1
160, 1 = Kshu 3, 1[25]
—, 6 = Kshu 3, 2[22]
—, 10 cf. Bs 1, 1, 29
—, 12 = Kshu 3, 8
161, 2 = Kshu 3, 3[23]
—, 4 = Pu 2, 3
—, 6 = Kshu 3, 3[25]
—, 11 = Kshu 3, 3[25]
—, 12 = Kshu 3, 4
162, 2 = Kshu 3, 1
—, 2 = Kshu 3, 2[22]
—, 3 = Kshu 3, 8
—, 6 cf Kshu 3, 8
—, 10 = Kshu 3, 3
—, 11 = Ku 5, 5
—, 13 = Kshu 3, 8
—, 15 = Ch 6, 8, 7
—, 15 = Bu 1, 4, 10
163, 2 = Kshu 3, 8
—, 3 = Kena 1, 4
—, 6 = Kshu 3, 4
—, 14 = Kshu 3, 2[23]
—, 15 = Kshu 3, 3
—, 15 = Kshu 3, 3
164, 1 = Kshu 3, 4[25]
—, 3 = Kshu 3, 6
—, 4 = Kshu 3, 8[25]
165, 5 = Ch 3, 14, 2

I, 2.

166, 13 = Ch 3, 14, 1
167, 6 = Mu 2, 1, 2
—, 7 = Ch 3, 14, 1

[17] here *agni* is said to be = *mâṇavaka*.—[18] in contradiction to both recensions; likewise 299, 7.—[19] cf. schol. Kâty. 7, 1, 4 p. 625, 23.—[20] "mantravarṇa".—[21] gloss.: "*Taittirîyake*".—[22] according to the second rec. by Cowell.—[23] according to the first rec. by Cowell.—[24] in contradiction to both rec., but possibly free according to the first.—[25] in contradiction to both rec. by Cowell.

167, 9 = Ch 3, 14, 1
—, 14 = Ch 3, 14, 1
168, 1 = Ch 3, 14, 2
—, 3 = Ch 3, 14, 2
—, 4 = Ch 3, 14, 3
—, 5 cf. Çv 5, 8
—, 6 = Ch 3, 14, 3
—, 11 = Ch 3, 14, 4
169, 1 = Ch 3, 14, 1
170, 10 = Ch 8, 7, 1
—, 11 = Ch 8, 7, 1
—, 11 = Ch 3, 14, 2
—, 13 = Ch 3, 14, 3
—, 17 = Ch 3, 14, 2
171, 4 ~ Çv 4, 3
—, 5 = BhG 3, 13 [Çv 3, 16]
—, 7 = Mu 2, 1, 2
—, 8 = Ch 3, 14, 2
172, 1 = Ch 3, 14, 2
—, 1 ~ Ch 3, 14, 2
—, 2 = Ch 3, 14, 3
—, 5 = Ch 3, 14, 3
—, 5 = 130, 12
—, 10 = Ch 3, 14, 4
173, 3 = Çb 10, 6, 3, 2
—, 9 = BhG 18, 61
—, 12 = Bs 1, 2, 3
—, 13 = Bu 3, 7 23
—, 14 = BhG 13, 2
174, 1 = Ch 6, 8, 7
—, 5 ~ Ch 3, 14, 4
—, 6 = Ch 3, 14, 3
175, 12 = Bu 3, 7, 23
176, 9 = Ch 6, 8, 7
—, 9 = Bu 1, 4, 10
—, 9 = Bu 3, 7, 23
177, 8 = Ku 2, 25
178, 1 = Bu 1, 4, 6
—, 2 = Mu 3, 1, 1
—, 3 = Mu 3, 1, 1
178, 12 = Mu 3, 1, 1
179, 3 = Ku 2, 18
—, 4 = Ku 2, 25
—, 7 = Ku 3, 1
—, 13 = Ku 1, 20
180, 3 = Ku 2, 14
—, 10 = Mu 3, 1, 1
181, 9 ~ Bu 4, 4 23
182, 6 = Ku 2, 12
—, 6 = Tu 2, 1
—, 7 = ?[7]
183, 1 ~ Ku 3, 3
—, 3 = Ku 3, 9
—, 4 = Ku 2, 12
—, 8 = Ku 3, 1
—, 10-12 = Mu 3, 1, 1
—, 14 = Mu 3, 1, 2
184, 3 = ?[26]
—, 7 = ?[26]
185, 2 = Ch 6, 8, 7
—, 2 = BhG 13, 2
—, 4 = ?[26]
—, 13 = Bu 4, 5, 15
—, 15 ibidem[27]
186, 2 = Ch 4, 15, 1
—, 7 = Ch 4, 15, 1
187, 2 = Bu 5, 5, 2
—, 7 = Ch 6, 8, 7
—, 11 = Ch 4, 15, 1
—, 13 = Ch 4, 15, 2
—, 14 = Ch 4, 15, 3
—, 15 = Ch 4, 15, 4
188, 5 = Bu 3, 7, 3
—, 6 = Bu 3, 7, 18
—, 9 = Ch 1, 6, 6. 5
—, 17 = Ch 4, 10, 5
189, 1 = Ch 4, 11, 1
—, 3 = Ch 4, 10, 5
—, 4 ~ Ch 4, 10, 5
—, 5 = Ch 4, 10, 5
190, 6 = Ch 4, 14, 1
190, 9 = Ch 4, 14, 3
191, 4 = Ch 4, 15, 1
—, 8 = Pu 1, 10
192, 1 = BhG 8, 24
—, 3 = Ch 4, 15, 5
—, 14 = Ch 4, 15, 1
—, 18 = Ch 8, 9, 1
193, 9 = Bu 5, 5, 2
—, 13 = Tu 2, 8
194, 2 = Ch 4, 15, 1
—, 5 = Bu 3, 7, 1
—, 6 = Bu 3, 7, 3
195, 5 = Bu 3, 9, 10
196, 1 = Bu 3, 7, 3
—, 2 = Bu 3, 7, 3
—, 5 = Bu 3, 7, 23
—, 13 = Manu 1, 5[28]
197, 2 = Bs 1, 1, 5
—, 7 = Bu 3, 7, 23
—, 14 ~ Bu 3, 4, 2
198, 7 = Bu 3, 7, 22
—, 8 = Çb 14, 6, 7, 30
199, 1 = Bu 3, 7, 23[29]
—, 11 = Bu 4, 5, 15[29]
200, 2 = Mu 1, 1, 5—6
—, 8 ~ Mu 1, 1, 7
201, 2 = Mu 1, 1, 9
—, 4 = Mu 1, 1, 5—6
—, 6 = Mu 2, 1, 2
—, 13 = Mu 1, 1, 9
202, 2 = Mu 1, 1, 7
—, 5 = Mu 1, 1, 9
—, 8 = Mu 2, 1, 2
—, 10 = Mu 1, 2, 13
—, 13 = Mu 2, 1, 2
203, 2 = Mu 1, 1, 5
—, 9 = Mu 1, 1, 3
204, 1 ~ Mu 1, 1, 1
—, 6 ~ Mu 1, 2, 7
—, 9 ~ Mu 1, 2, 12
205, 8 = Mu 2, 1, 2

---

[26] from the Paiṅgirahasyabrâhmaṇam = Paiṅgi-Upanishad (232, 12), cf. Ṛ V. 1, 164, 20.—[27] according to the Mâdhyandinas; otherwise (111, 4. 393, 3. 199, 12) according to the Kâṇvas.—[28] quoted directly as *Sâṅkhya-smṛiti*.—[29] Kâṇvas not Mâdhyandinas.

205, 13 = Mu 2, 1, 2
207, 5 = Mu 2, 1, 3
—, 8 = Mu 2, 1, 4
—, 15 = Mu 2, 1, 3
—, 15 = Mu 2, 1, 4
208, 3 = Tu 3, 10, 6
—, 5 = Mu 2, 1, 3
—, 7 = Mu 2, 1, 4
—, 8 = Mu 2, 1, 9
—, 11 = Mu 2, 1, 10
—, 13 = Ṛ V 10, 121, 1
—, 15 = MârkP 45, 64
209, 3 = Mu 2, 1, 10
—, 7 = Ch 5, 11, 1
—, 7 = Ch 5, 11, 6
210, 3 = Ch 5, 18, 1—2
211, 9 = Bu 5, 9, 1
—, 11 = Ṛ V 10, 88, 12
—, 13 = Ṛ V 1, 98, 1
212, 3 ~ Ch 5, 11, 1
—, 12 = Ch 5, 18, 2
213, 4 = Ch 5, 18, 1
—, 6 = Ch 5, 24, 3
—, 7 ~ Ch 5, 11, 1[30]
—, 12 = Mbh 12, 1656
214, 3 = ?[31]
—, 12 = Çb 10, 6, 1, 11
—, 13 cf Ch 5, 18, 2
—, 14 = Ch 5, 19, 1
—, 16 = Çb 10, 6, 1, 11
215, 1 = Ch 5, 18, 2
—, 6 = Ṛ V 10, 88, 3
—, 12 = Ch 3, 18, 1
—, 14 = Ch 3, 14, 2
216, 2 = Ch 5, 18, 2
—, 6 ~ Çb 10, 6, 1, 11
—, 12 = Çb 10, 6, 1, 11
—, 14 cf Ch 5, 18, 2
—, 15 cf Çb 10, 6, 1, 11[32]
217, 1 = Ch 5, 18, 2
218, 5 = Çb 10, 6, 1, 11
—, 8 = Çb 10, 6, 1, 11
218, 11 = Çb 10, 6, 1, 11
219, 6 cf Ch 5, 18, 1
Çb 10, 6, 1, 10
221, 3 ~ Çb 10, 6, 1, 10-11
—, 12 cf Çb 10, 6, 1, 9
222, 1 cf Çb 10, 6, 1, 8
—, 1 cf Ch 5, 12, 1
—, 2 cf Ch 5, 13, 1
—, 8 ~ Jâb 2 p. 438
223, 1 ~ Jâb 2 p. 440
—, 3 cf Ch 5, 18, 1

I, 3.

224, 3 = Mu 2, 2, 5
225, 1 = Bu 2, 4, 12
—, 3 = Bu 3, 7, 2
—, 6 cf Bu 3, 3, 2?
—, 12 = Mu 2, 2, 5
226, 2 = Ch 6, 8, 4
—, 4 = Mu 2, 1, 10
—, 5 ~ Mu 2, 2, 11
227, 3 = Ku 4, 10
—, 5 = Bu 4, 5, 13
229, 1 = Mu 2, 2, 8
—, 3 = Mu 3, 2, 8
—, 5 ~ Bu 4, 4, 7
—, 8 = Mu 2, 2, 5
—, 11 ~ Bu 4, 4, 21
230, 10 = Mu 1, 1, 9
231, 7 = Mu 2, 2, 5
—, 12 = Mu 1, 1, 3
—, 17 = Mu 3, 1, 1
232, 10 = Bs 1, 2, 11
—, 12 cf p. 184, 3
233, 7 = Bs 1, 2, 21
—, 8 = Mu 2, 2, 5
—, 11 ~ Ch 7, 23—24
234, 3 = Pâṇ 6, 4, 158
—, 5 = Ch 7, 15, 1
—, 6 = Ch 7, 1, 3
235, 1 = Ch 7, 1, 5
—, 2 = Ch 7, 2, 1
235, 2 = Ch 7, 2, 2
—, 3 = Ch 7, 3, 1
—, 7 = Ch 7, 15, 1
—, 8 = Ch 7, 15, 4
—, 9 ~ Ch 7, 16, 1[33]
—, 12 = Ch 7, 24, 1
236, 1 = Ch 7, 24, 1
—, 2 = Pu 4, 2. 3
—, 6 = Ch 7, 23, 1
—, 6 ~ Pu 4, 6
—, 8 = Ch 7, 24, 1
—, 9 cf Kshu 3, 2
—, 10 = Ch 7, 1, 3
—, 12 = Ch 7, 15, 1
—, 14 = Ch 7, 15, 1
237, 4 cf Bu 4, 3, 12
Pu 4, 3
—, 8 = Ch 7, 2, 1
—, 14 ~ Ch 7, 16, 1[33]
238, 3 = Ch 7, 16, 1
—, 4 Quotation?
—, 13 ~ Ch 7, 16, 1[33]
—, 14 Ch 7, 16, 1
239, 8 = Ch 7, 16, 1
—, 9 = Tu 2, 1
—, 11 ~ Ch 7, 16, 1
240, 6 = Çv 6, 15
—, 7 = Ch 7, 1, 3
—, 8 = Ch 7, 26, 2
—, 11 = Ch 7, 26, 1
—, 12 = Ch 7, 24, 1
241, 3 = Ch 7, 24, 1
—, 5 = Bu 4, 5, 15
—, 7 cf Bu 4, 3, 16
—, 10 = Bu 4, 3, 32
—, 11 = Ch 7, 23, 1
—, 13 = Ch 7, 24, 1
—, 15 = Bu 3, 4, 2
242, 4 = Bu 3, 8, 7—8
—, 8 = Ch 2, 23, 4
—, 13 = Bu 3, 8, 7
243, 1 = Bu 3, 8, 11

[30] inaccurate as 212, 3, accurate 209, 7.—[31] Smṛiti, probably Mahâbhâratam.—[32] 216, 14, 15 both recensions confounded.—[33] *vâ* is wanting in Chând. 7, 16, 1.

243, 3 = Ch 2, 23, 4
—, 10 = Bu 3, 8, 9
244, 7 = Bu 3, 8, 11
—, 10 = Bu 3, 8, 11
—, 12 = Bu 3, 8, 8
—, 16 = Pu 5, 2
245, 1 ~ Pu 5, 5
—, 4 cf Pu 5, 2
—, 5 = Pu 5, 5
—, 6 = Pu 5, 5
246, 2 = Pu 5, 5[34]
247, 10 cf Çv 3, 9
—, 11 = Ku 3, 11
248, 3 ~ Pu 5, 5
249, 2 = Ch 8, 1, 1
250, 1 = Ch 8, 1, 2
—, 10 cf Çv 5, 8
251, 3 ~ Ch 8, 1, 2
—, 5 = Ch 8, 1, 3
252, 4 = Çb 10, 6, 3, 2
—, 9 = Ch 8, 1, 5
253, 9 = Pu 5, 5
—, 10 = Bu 2, 5, 18
254, 1 ~ Ch 8, 1, 6
—, 3 = Ch 8, 1, 6
—, 8 = Ch 8, 1, 3
—, 11 ~ Ch 8, 1, 2
255, 2 = Ch 8, 1, 5
—, 4 = Ch 8, 1, 6
256, 1 = Ch 8, 3, 2
—, 5 = Ch 6, 8, 1
257, 5 = Ch 8, 1, 1
—, 8 = Ch 8, 4, 1
258, 3 ~ Bu 3, 8, 9
—, 5 ~ Bu 4, 4, 22
—, 11 = Ch 8, 14
—, 12 = Ch 1, 9, 1
259, 3 = Ch 8, 3, 4
—, 8 cf Ch 8, 12, 2
—, 10 = Ch 8, 14
260, 5 = Bs 1, 3, 20
—, 10 = Ch 8, 7, 1
261, 1 = Ch 8, 7, 4
—, 2 = Ch 8, 9, 3. 10, 4. 11, 3
—, 4 = Ch 8, 10, 1
—, 4 = Ch 8, 11, 1
—, 6 = Ch 8, 11, 1
—, 7 = Ch 8, 11, 1
—, 9 ~ Ch 8, 11, 3[35]
262, 1 ~ Ch 8, 12, 3
—, 5 = Ch 8. 1, 1
—, 12 = Ch 8, 9, 3
—, 13 = Ch 8, 12, 3
263, 4 = Ch 6, 8, 7
—, 7 = Bu 1, 4, 10
—, 10 = Ch 6, 8, 7
264, 2 = Mu 3, 2, 9
266, 3 = Ku 2, 22
—, 3 = BhG 13, 31
—, 9 = Ch 8, 7, 4
—, 14 = Ch 8, 10, 1
267, 1 = Ch 8, 9, 3
—, 5 = Ch 8, 11, 3
—, 8 = Ch 8, 11, 1
—, 9 = Bu 4, 3, 30
—, 11 = Ch 8, 11, 3
—, 12 = Ch 8, 12, 1
—, 14 = Ch 8, 12, 3
269, 4 = Bs 1, 3, 18
—, 13 = Bs 1, 1, 30
270, 2 = Ch 8, 3, 4
—, 15 = Ch 8, 1, 1
—, 16 cf Çv 5, 8
271, 2 = Bs 1, 2, 7
—, 5 = Ch 8, 1, 3
—, 8 = Mu 2, 2, 10
= Ku 5, 15
272, 9 = Ch 3, 14, 2
273, 7 = Bu 4, 4, 16
274, 2 = Mu 2, 2, 5
—, 3 = Mu 2, 2, 9
275, 1 = Bu 4, 3, 6
—, 2 = Bu 4, 2, 4
275, 5 = BhG 15, 6
—, 7 = BhG 15, 12
—, 10 = Ku 4, 12
—, 11 = Ku 4, 13
276, 7 = Mbh 3, 16763
—, 12 = Ku 4, 13
277, 1 ~ Ku 2, 14
278, 3 cf Js 6, 1, 25 sq
—, 8 = Ch 6, 8, 7
279, 6 = Ku 6, 17
281, 4 = Ch 8, 11, 3
—, 5 = Tu 3, 1
283, 2 = Bu 3, 9, 1
—, 6 = Bu 3, 9, 9
—, 9 = Mbh 12, 11062
285, 3 cf Js 1, 1, 5
—, 11 = Bs 1, 1, 2
288, 1 = ?[36]
—, 3 = Bu 1, 2, 4
—, 6 = Mbh 12, 8534
—, 10 = Mbh 12, 8535
289, 1 = Manu 1, 21
—, 6 = Tb 2, 2, 4, 2
298, 3 = ṚV 10, 71, 3
—, 5 = Mbh 12, 7660
299, 7 = Kshu 3, 3[25]
301, 4 = Çv 6, 18
—, 6 Quotation?
—, 8 = Ârsh p. 3
302, 7 = Mbh 12, 8525
304, 4 = ṚV 10, 190, 3
—, 7 = Tb 3, 1, 4, 1
—, 12 = Mbh 12, 8535
305, 1 = Mbh 12, 8550
—, 3 = ?[31]
—, 11 = Ch 3, 1, 1
306, 3 = Ch 3, 6, 3
—, 7 = Ch 3, 18, 2
—, 8 = Ch 4, 3, 1
—, 9 = Ch 3, 19, 1
—, 10 = Bu 2, 2, 4
309, 6 = Bu 1, 4, 10

[34] inaccurate, another version 253, 9.—[35] inaccurate, 267, 11 accurate. —[36] from a Chandoga-brâhmaṇam gloss. cf. ṚV. 9, 62, 1.

309, 7 ~ Ch 8, 7, 2
—, 10 = ?[37]
—, 11 = Bs 1, 3, 32
310, 2 = Shaḍv 1, 1[38]
—, 4 cf Mbh 1, 4397
—, 5 = Çb 6, 1, 3, 2. 4
311, 5 = ?[39]
—, 12 ~ Ts 2, 1, 1, 1
312, 1 = Ts 3, 4, 3, 2
313, 2 = Ab 3, 8, 1
314, 6 = Ys 2, 44
—, 9 = Çv 2, 12
315, 11 = Ts 7, 1, 1, 6
316, 4 cf Ch 4, 1—3
—, 5 = Ch 4, 2, 3
317, 6 = Ts 7, 1, 1, 6
318, 4 = Ch 4, 1, 3
319, 6 = Ch 4, 3, 5
—, 9 = Pañc 20, 12, 5
—, 10 ~ Pañc 20, 12, 5
320, 7 = Çb 11, 5, 3, 13
—, 7 = Ch 7, 1, 1
—, 8 = Pu 1, 1
321, 1 = Ch 5, 11, 7
—, 2 cf Manu 10, 4
—, 3 = Manu 10, 126
—, 8 = Ch 4, 4, 5
322, 5 = ?[40]
—, 6 = ?[40]
—, 9 = ?[40]
—, 10 = Manu 4, 80
—, 11 = ?[40]
—, 14 = Mbh 12, 12360
323, 5 = Ku 6, 1
324, 4 = Bu 3, 3, 2
—, 10 = Ku 6, 1
325, 1 = Bu 4, 4, 18
—, 3 = Ku 5, 5
—, 6 = Ku 6, 3
—, 16 = Tu 2, 8
326, 2 = Çv 6, 15
326, 3 cf Bu 3, 3, 2
—, 5 = Bu 3, 4, 2
—, 7 = Ku 2, 14
—, 11 = Ch 8, 12, 3
327, 2 = Bs 1, 1, 24
—, 5 = Ch 8, 6, 5
—, 9 = Ch 8, 7, 1
328, 1 = Ch 8, 11, 3
—, 2 = Ch 8, 12, 1
—, 4 = Ch 8, 12, 3
—, 9 = Ch 8, 14
329, 9 = Ch 6, 3, 2
330, 1 = Ch 8, 14
—, 2 = Bs 1, 1, 22
—, 4 = Bu 4, 3, 7
—, 9 = Bu 4, 3, 7
—, 10 = Bu 4, 4, 22
331, 2 = Bu 4, 3, 21
—, 7 ~ Bu 4, 3, 35
—, 13 = Bu 4, 3, 7
332, 2 = Bu 4, 3, 7
—, 4 = Bu 4, 4, 22
—, 11 = Bu 4, 3, 14-16
—, 12 = Bu, 4, 3, 15. 16
—, 13 = Bu 4, 3, 22
333, 6 = Bu 4, 4, 22
—, 8 = Bu 4, 4, 22

I, 4.

334, 4 = Bs 1, 1, 2
—, 6 = Bs 1, 1, 5
335, 6 = Ku 3, 11
337, 3 = Ku 3, 3—4
—, 7 cf Ku 3, 7—9
—, 12 = Ku 3, 10—11
338, 6 cf Bu 3, 2
—, 12 ~ Mbh 13, 1011
339, 1 = Çv 6, 18
—, 15 = Ku 3, 12
340, 3 = Ku 3, 13
341, 7 = Ṛ V 9, 46, 4
341, 7 = Bu 1, 4, 7
342, 11 = Bu 3, 8, 11
—, 12 = Mu 2, 1, 2
—, 13 = Çv 4, 10
343, 2 = Ku 3, 11
—, 11 = Bs 3, 3, 1
345, 10 = ?[41]
346, 1 = ?[41]
—, 9 = Bs 1, 4, 5
—, 11 = Ku 3, 15
347, 6 = Ku 3, 11
—, 8 = Ku 3, 12
—, 9 = Ku 3, 13
348, 3 = Ku 1, 13
—, 5 = Ku 1, 20
—, 8 = Ku 2, 14
—, 11 = Ku 1, 15
—, 13 = Ku 5, 6—7
349, 3 = Ku 2, 18
—, 6 = Ku 1, 20
350, 4 = Ku 1, 20
—, 5 = Ku 2, 14
351, 2 = Ch 6, 8, 7
—, 3 = Ku 2, 18
—, 8 = Ku 4, 4
—, 13 = Ku 4, 10
352, 2 = Ku 1, 21
—, 4 cf Ku 2, 1
—, 5 = Ku 2, 4
—, 7 = Ku 2, 12
—, 12 = Ku 1, 20
353, 1 = Ku 2, 14
—, 6 = Ch 6, 8, 7
—, 12 = Ku 2, 18
354, 7 = Ku 3, 10
—, 8 = Ku 2, 22
—, 8 = Çv 3, 8
355, 4 = Çv 4, 5
—, 12 = Sâñkhyak 3
356, 10 = Bu 2, 2, 3
357, 1 = Bu 2, 2, 3

[37] gloss.: *mokshadharmeshu*, so probably Mahâbh. XII.—[38] *indro* is wanting in Shaḍv. br.—[39] according to p. 1016, 11, where the same quotation, *Kathânâṃ saṃhitâyâm*.—[40] probably from a *Dharmasûtram*.—[41] a *Sâñkhya*-quotation?

357, 9 = Ch 6, 4, 1
358, 3 = Çv 1, 1
—, 4 = Çv 1, 3
—, 7 = Çv 4, 10
—, 8 = Çv 4, 11
360, 4 = Çv 6, 11
—, 5 cf Ch 3, 1
—, 6 cf Bu 5, 8
—, 6 cf Bu 6, 2, 9
—, 11 = Bu 4, 4, 17
361, 4 ~ Sâṅkhyak 3
362, 7 = ?[42]
—, 11 = Ts 1, 6, 1, 2
365, 1 = Bu 4, 4, 17
—, 5 = Bu 4, 4, 17
366, 1 = Pâṇ 2, 1, 50
—, 8 = Bu 4, 4, 17
—, 9 = Çb 14, 7, 2, 21[43]
367, 6 = Ch 3, 13, 6
—, 7 ~ Ch 7, 15, 1
—, 9 Quotation?
369, 7 = Bu 4, 4, 16
—, 9 Quotation?
370, 1 cf p. 43, 1
—, 11 = Tu 2, 1
—, 12 = Ch 6, 2, 3
—, 13 = Pu 6, 4
371, 1 ~ Au 1, 1, 2
—, 3 = Tu 2, 7
—, 4 = Ch 3, 19, 1
—, 6 ~ Ch 6, 2, 1. 2
372, 1 = Bu 1, 4, 7
—, 9 = Tu 2, 1
—, 10 cf Tu 2, 6
373, 2 cf Tu 2, 2—5
—, 3 = Tu 2, 6
—, 5 — Tu 2, 6
—, 8 = Ch 6, 2, 2—3
—, 9 ~ Au 1, 1, 1
374, 4 = Bs 2, 3, 1
374, 10 = Ch 6, 8, 4
—, 12 cf Ch 6, 1, 4—6
375, 3 = GḍpK 3, 15
—, 5 = Tu 2, 1
—, 6 = Ch 7, 1, 3
—, 6 = Çv 3, 8
—, 7 = Ch 6, 8, 7
—, 9 = Tu 2, 7
—, 12 = Tu 2, 7
—, 13 ~ Tu 2, 6
376, 2 = Tu 2, 6
—, 3 = Tu 2, 6
—, 4 = Tu 2, 7
—, 9 = Ch 3, 19, 1
—, 11 = Ch 6, 2, 1
—, 15 = Bu 1, 4, 7
377, 6 = Bu 1, 4, 7
—, 9 = Ch 6, 3, 2
378, 2 = Kshu 4, 19[44]
—, 7 = Kshu 4, 20
379, 1 ~ Bu 3, 9, 9
—, 3 = Kshu 4, 19
—, 9 = Kshu 4, 20[23]
380, 5 = Kshu 4, 1
—, 7 = Kshu 1, 19[25]
382, 8 = Bs 1, 1, 31
—, 13 = Kshu 4, 20[23]
383, 5 = Ch 6, 8, 1
—, 12 = Kshu 4, 19[25]
—, 14 = Kshu 4, 19
384, 1 = Kshu 4, 20[25]
—, 11 ~ Bu, 2, 1, 16
385, 1 = Bu 2, 1, 17
—, 2 = Ch 8, 1, 1
—, 3 = Çb 14, 5, 1, 23[45]
—, 8 = Bu 2, 4, 5[46]
—, 9 = Bu 2, 4, 5[47]
386, 7 = Bu 2, 4, 12[49]
—, 11 = Bu 2, 4, 14[46]
387, 2 = Bu 2, 4, 2[46]
387, 3 = Bu 2, 4, 3[49]
—, 9 = Bu 2, 4, 6[46]
—, 13 = Bu 2, 4, 6[46]
—, 15 ~ Bu 2, 4, 10[46]
388, 1 cf Bu 4, 5, 11[48]
—, 4 cf Bu 4, 5, 13[50]
—, 9 ~ Bu 2, 4, 5
—, 10 = Bu 2, 4, 6[46]
389, 5 = Ch 8, 12, 3
—, 9 = Mu 3, 2, 8
390, 4 = Ch 6, 3, 2
—, 6 = Tâ 3, 12, 7
—, 15 = Ch 6, 8, 7
391, 3 cf Mu 2, 1, 1
—, 7 = Bs 1, 4, 20
—, 8 ~ Bu 2, 4, 5
—, 14 = Bs 1, 4, 21
392, 2 = Bs 1, 4, 22
—, 5 = Bu 2, 4, 12[46]
—, 8 = Bu 2, 4, 13[47]
—, 10 = Bu 4, 5, 14[51]
—, 15 = Bu 2, 4, 14[46]
393, 3-5 = Bu 2, 4, 14[52]
—, 8 = Bu 2, 4, 14[46]
394, 3 = Ch 6, 2, 1
—, 4 = Ch 7, 25, 2
—, 4 ~ Mu 2, 2, 11
—, 4 = Bu 2, 4, 6
—, 5 = Bu 3, 7, 23
—, 5 = Bu 3, 8, 11
—, 6 ~ BhG 7, 19
—, 6 = BhG 13, 2
—, 7 = BhG 13, 27
—, 8 = Bu 1, 4, 10
—, 9 = Bu 4, 4, 19
—, 10 = Bu 4, 4, 25
395, 4 = Mu 3, 2, 6
—, 5 = Îça 7
—, 5 = BhG 2, 54
—, 10 = Tu 2, 1

[42] epic quotation.—[43] *i. e.*, Brihadâr. 4, 4, 18 according to the Mâdhyandinas.—[44] quoted as Kaushîtaki-brâhmaṇam.—[45] *i. e.*, Bṛih. 2, 1, 20 according to the Mâdhyandinas.—[46] conform in 2, 4 and 4, 5.—[47] only in 2, 4.—[48] only in 4, 5.—[49] in 4, 5 only Mâdhy.—[50] only in 4, 5 Kâṇva.—[51] only in 4, 5 Mâdhy.—[52] in 2, 4 only Mâdhy., in 4, 5 only Kâṇva!

396, 2 = Tu 2, 6
—, 8 = Bs 1, 1, 2
397, 4 = Pu 6, 3—4
—, 12 = Çv 6, 19
398, 6 = Ch 6, 1, 3
—, 12 = Ch 6, 1, 4
—, 14 = Ch 6, 1, 5
399, 1 = Ch 6, 1, 6
—, 2 = Mu 1, 1, 3
—, 3 = Mu 1, 1, 7
—, 4 = Bu 4, 5, 6[53]
—, 5 = Bu 2, 4, 7[46]
—, 9 = Tu 3, 1
—, 10 = Pâṇ 1, 4, 30
400, 2 = Ch 6, 2, 1
—, 10 = Tu 2, 6
—, 11 = Ch 6, 2, 3
401, 3 = Ch 1, 9, 1
—, 10 = Tu 2, 7
402, 7 = Tu 2, 6
—, 10 = Mu 3, 1, 3
—, 10 = Mu 1, 1, 6
403, 2 = ṚV 1, 104, 1
—, 3 = Mu 1, 1, 7
—, 12 = Bs 1, 1, 5

II, 1.

408, 8 Çv 5, 2
409, 6 = Mbh 12, 13679
—, 9 ~ Mbh 12, 12895
410, 1 = ?[54]
—, 5 = BhG 7, 6
—, 6 = Âpdh 1, 8, 23, 2
411, 2 = Js 1, 3, 3
412, 6 cf Mbh 3, 8831 sq
12, 10613 sq
—, 8 = Ts 2, 2, 10, 2
—, 10 = Manu 12, 91
413, 1 = Mbh 12, 13713
—, 2 = Mbh 12, 13714
—, 4 = Mbh 12, 13715
413, 7 = Mbh 12, 13743
414, 1 = Îçâ 7
415, 3 = Bs 1, 4, 1
—, 5 = Bs 2, 1, 4
—, 13 = Bu 2, 4, 5
—, 14 = Çv 2, 8
416, 2 = Ku 6, 11
—, 3 = Ku 6, 18
—, 4 = Ys[55]
—, 6 means Pâṇini
—, 12 ~ Çv 6, 13[56]
417, 3 = Çv 3, 8
—, 6 ~ Çv 6, 13[56]
—, 9 = Bu 4, 3, 16[57]
—, 11 = Jâb 5 p. 452
418, 1 = Tb 3, 12, 9, 7
—, 2 = Bu 3, 9, 26
419, 4 = Bu 2, 4, 5
420, 13 Quotation?[58]
422, 6 = Tu 2, 6
—, 9 = Çb 6, 1, 3, 2. 4
—, 10 = Ch 6, 2, 3. 4
—, 11 = Bu 6, 1, 7
—, 12 = Bu 1, 3, 2
423, 10 = Kshu 2, 14
—, 11 = Kshu 2, 14
—, 14 = Au 1, 2, 4
424, 1 = Ch 5, 1, 5
—, 3 cf Bu 6, 1, 13
—, 5 = Ch 6, 2, 3
426, 11 = Ku 2, 9
—, 12 ~ ṚV 10, 129, 6. 7
427, 3 = ?[59]
—, 5 = p. 72, 6
—, 7 = BhG 10, 2
428, 1 = Bs 2, 1, 11
—, 3 = Tu 2, 6
—, 7 ~ Tu 2, 6
429, 7 = Bu 2, 4, 6
—, 12 cf Bs 2, 1, 14
431, 14 = Bs 2, 1, 14
432, 3 = Bu 2, 4, 6
—, 3 = Ch 7, 25, 2
—, 3 = Mu 2, 2, 11
—, 4 = Ch 3, 14, 1
433, 1 = GḍpK 1, 16
—, 9 ~ Ch 6, 9, 2—3[60]
437, 3 = Manu 12, 105
443, 3 = Tu 2, 6
444, 3 ~ Ch 6, 1, 4
445, 1 = Ch 6, 4, 1
—, 3 = Ch 6, 8, 7
—, 3 = Bu 2, 4, 6
—, 4 ~ Mu 2, 2, 11
—, 4 = Ch 7, 25, 2
—, 4 = Bu 4, 4, 19
446, 4 = Ch 6, 1, 4
—, 7 = Ch 6, 8, 7
—, 8 = Ch 6, 8, 7
447, 1 = Bu 2, 4, 14[61]
—, 5 = Ch 6, 8, 7
—, 6 cf 103, 9 (Ch 6, 16)
—, 9 = Bu 4, 4, 19
—, 11 cf Kap 3, 23
450, 4 = Ch 5, 2, 9
—, 7 = Aâ 3, 2, 4, 7
—, 8 = Aâ 3, 2, 4, 17
451, 6 = Ch 6, 8, 7
—, 10 = Ch 6, 16, 3
452, 7 = Bu 4, 4, 25
—, 8 = Bu 3, 9, 26
—, 9 = Bu 3, 8, 8
453, 7 = Bu 3, 9, 26
—, 7 = Bu 4, 2, 4
454, 3 = Tu 2, 1
—, 7 = Bs 1, 1, 2
—, 12 = Ch 8, 14, 1
—, 13 = Ch 6, 3, 2
—, 14 = Tâ 3, 12, 7
455, 1 = Çv 6, 12
—, 9 = Ch 7, 24, 1
—, 10 = Bu 2, 4, 14[61]

[53] only in 4, 5 Mâdhy.—[54] from a *Purâṇam.*—[55] not in our Yoga-sûtras.—[56] 416, 12. 417, 6 the same reading.—[57] cf. Kapila 1, 15.—[58] *"nirâtiçayâ hi akartâraç cetanâḥ" iti Sâṅkhyâ manyante.*—[59] according to 482, 6 from a Purâṇam.—[60] or Chând. 6, 10, 2?—[61] in 2, 4 only Mâdhy., in 4, 5 both.

455, 13 = BhG 5, 14–15
456, 2 = Bu 4, 4, 22
—, 5 = BhG 18, 61
—, 7 = Bs 2, 1, 14
—, 8 = Bs 2, 1, 13
458, 8 cf Ch 6, 4
—, 8 cf Ch 4, 3
—, 9 cf Ch 1, 9
459, 3 = Ch 6, 2, 1
—, 4 = Au 1, 1, 1
—, 13 = Ch 3, 19, 1
—, 13 = Tu 2, 7
460, 7. 9 = Ch 3, 19, 1
—, 10 = Tu 2, 7
469, 3 = Ch 6, 2, 1
—, 6 = Ch 6, 2, 2
—, 10 = Ch 6, 1, 3
471, 4 = Ch 6, 1, 3
—, 10 = Ch 6, 8, 7
—, 11 = Tu 2, 6
—, 13 = Ch 6, 3, 2
473, 6 = Bu 2, 4, 5
—, 7 = Ch 8, 7, 1
—, 7 = Ch 6, 8, 1
—, 8 = Bu 4, 3, 35
—, 10 = Ch 6, 8, 7
474, 3 = Ch 8, 7, 1
476, 11 = Çv 6, 8
479, 12 = Çv 6, 19
—, 13 = Mu 2, 1, 2
480, 1 = Bu 2, 4, 12
—, 1 = Bu 3, 9, 26
—, 2 = Bu 3, 8, 8
481, 3 = Ch 6, 3, 2
—, 4 = Ch 3, 12, 6[62]
—, 6 cf Ch 8, 3, 3
—, 6 cf Ch 6, 8, 1
—, 8 = Ch 6, 8, 1
482, 6 = 427, 3[59]
483, 1 = 43, 1
484, 4 = Bu 4, 2, 4
—, 10 = Bu 4, 3, 10
485, 7 cf Kap 1, 61
487, 4 = Ch 3, 14, 2
—, 5 = Ch 8, 7, 1
—, 5 = Mu 1, 1, 9
—, 5 = Bu 3, 8, 9
—, 9 = Bu 3, 8, 8
—, 13 = Bu 2, 3, 6
488, 6 = Çv 3, 19
489, 1 = Bu 2, 4, 5
490, 10 cf Ch 8, 7, 1
493, 2 = Kshu 3, 8[25]
—, 4 = Bu 3, 2, 13
—, 6 = BhG 4, 11
—, 9 = Ch 6, 2, 1
495, 1 = Ch 6, 3, 2
—, 7 = ṚV 10, 190, 3
—, 9 = BhG 15, 3
—, 10 = ?[54]

II, 2.

498, 5 = Bs 1, 1, 5
—, 6 = Bs 1, 1, 18
—, 6 = Bs 1, 4, 28
507, 10 ~ Bu 3, 7, 4
—, 11 = Bu 3, 8, 9
508, 3 = Bs 2, 1, 24
524, 1 ~ Vaiç 7, 1, 9
—, 2 ~ Vaiç 7, 1, 10
—, 2 = Vaiç 7, 1, 17
525, 1 ~ Vaiç 4, 2, 2
—, 6 = Bs 2, 1, 6
—, 9 = Bs 2, 1, 12
534, 5 = Vaiç 4, 1, 1
—, 7 = Vaiç 4, 1, 4
535, 2 = Vaiç 4, 1, 5
539, 13 = Vaiç 1, 1, 10
555, 6 = ?[63]
557, 12 = Tu 2, 1
558, 7 = ?[63]
563, 4 = ?[63]
580, 1 = Bs 2, 2, 20
594, 1 = Ns 1, 1, 18
601, 3 = ?[64]
—, 5 = Ch 7, 26, 2
602, 1 = Bs 2, 3, 17
—, 6 = ?[64]
—, 14 = ?[64]
604, 6 = ?[64]
—, 8 = ?[64]

II, 3.

606, 4 = Ch 6, 2, 1
—, 5 = Ch 6, 2, 3
607, 1 = Tu 2, 1
—, 11 = Tu 2, 1
608, 1 = Tu 2, 1
609, 10 = Çb 13, 5, 1, 15
610, 2 = Bu 2, 3, 3
—, 3 = 130, 12
—, 6 = ?[65]
—, 7 = ?[65]
—, 13 = Tu 2, 1
611, 3 = Tu 3, 2
—, 7 = Ch 6, 2, 1
612, 4 = 610, 7
613, 2 = Ch 6, 1, 2
—, 2 = Bu 4, 5, 6[50]
—, 3 = Mu 1, 1, 3
—, 4 = ?[66]
—, 11 = Ch 6, 1, 2
614, 2 = Ch 6, 2, 1
—, 3 = Ch 6, 2, 3
—, 4 = Ch 6, 8, 7
—, 9 = Bu 2, 4, 6
—, 9 = Mu 2, 2, 11
—, 12 = Tu 2, 1
—, 13 = Ch 6, 2, 3
615, 3 = Tu 2. 1
616, 2 = Ch 3, 14, 1
—, 7 = Ch 3, 14, 1
—, 9 = Ch 6, 2, 3
617, 1 = Ch 6, 2, 3
—, 2 = Tu 2, 1
—, 5 = Ch 6, 1, 2

[62] assimilated to ṚV. 10, 90, 3 (*pûrusha*, *viçvâ*).—[63] buddhistic quotation?—[64] Bhâgavata-quotation.—[65] upanishad-like.—[66] upanishad-like; cf. the Parmenideic: οὐ γὰρ ἄνευ τοῦ ἐόντος—εὑρήσεις τὸ νοεῖν.

617, 10 = Ch 6, 2, 1
618, 2 = Ch 6, 2, 1
—, 6 = Ch 6, 1, 2
619, 7 = Tu 2, 1
623, 4 = Bs 2, 1, 24
—, 10 = Bu 3, 8, 8
—, 11 = Bu 3, 8, 8
624, 8 = 130, 12
625, 2 = Çh 10, 6, 3, 2
—, 3 = Çv 4, 19
—, 4 = Bu 2, 4, 2
—, 12 = Tu 2, 1
626, 3 = Bu 1, 5, 22
627, 1 cf Ch 4, 1—3
628, 4 = Ch 6, 2, 2
—, 5 = Çv 6, 9
629, 4 = Ch 6, 2, 3
—, 6 = Ch 3, 14, 1
—, 6 = Mu 2, 1, 3
—, 8 = Tu 2, 6
—, 9 = Tu 2, 1
—, 11 = Tu 2, 1
630, 1 = Tu 2, 1
—, 9 = Ch 6, 2, 3
631, 3 = Tu 2, 7
—, 4 = BhG 10, 4, 5
632, 1 = Ch 6, 2, 3
—, 1 = Tu 2, 1
—, 5 = Ch 6, 2, 4
—, 9 = Ch 6, 2, 4
633, 4 = Ch 6, 2, 3
—, 7 = Ch 6, 4, 1
—, 12 = ?[54]
634, 1 = Tu 2, 1
—, 2 = Bu 1, 2, 2
—, 3 = Tu 2, 1
—, 13 = Tu 2, 1
635, 2 — Ch 6, 2, 3. 4
—, 5 = Bu 3, 7, 3
636, 1 = Tu 2, 6
—, 2 = Tu 2, 7
—, 3 = Bu 3, 7, 23
—, 5 = Ch 6, 2, 3

636, 10 = Tu 3, 1
638, 1 = Mbh 12, 12893
—, 12 = Ku 3, 3
639, 4 = Mu 2, 1, 3
640, 1 = Ch 6, 6, 5
—, 8 = ?[67]
641, 10 = Ch 6, 11, 3
642, 6 = Bu 4, 3, 8
643, 8 cf Mu 1, 1, 3
Ch 6, 1, 3. 4, 5
644, 1 = Bu 2, 1, 20
—, 4 = Mu 2, 1, 1
—, 10 = Tu 2, 7
645, 1 = Ch 6, 11, 3
—, 1 = Bu 4, 4, 25
—, 2 = Ku 2, 18
—, 3 = Ku 2, 18
—, 3 = Tu 2, 6
—, 4 = Ch 6, 3, 2
—, 5 = Bu 1, 4, 7
—, 5 = Ch 6, 8, 7
—, 5 = Bu 1, 4, 10
—, 6 = Bu 2, 5, 19
—, 9 = Çv 6, 11
646, 1 = Bu 4, 4, 5
—, 7 = Bu 4, 5, 13
—, 9 = Bu 4, 5, 14[68]
647, 3 = Bu 4, 3, 14
648, 5 = Bu 3, 9, 28
—, 5 = Tu 2, 1
—, 6 = Bu 4, 5, 13[69]
—, 9 = Bu 4, 3, 11
—, 9 = Bu 4, 3, 14
—, 10 = Bu 4, 3, 30
649, 1 = Ch 8, 12, 4
—, 4 = Ch 8, 12, 4
—, 6 Bu 4, 3, 23
650, 11 = Kshu 3, 3[23]
—, 12 = Kshu 1, 2
—, 13 = Bu 4, 4, 6
651, 11 = Bu 4, 4, 2
652, 1 = Bu 4, 4, 1
—, 2 = Bu 4, 3, 11

—, 6 = Bu 4, 4, 22
—, 7 = 130, 12
—, 7 = Tu 2, 1
—, 11 = Bu 4, 4, 20
—, 12 = Bu 4, 4, 22
653, 6 = Mu 3, 1, 9
—, 8 ~ Çv 5, 9
—, 9 ~ Çv 5, 8
655, 5 = Pu 3, 6
—, 5 = Ch 8, 3, 3
—, 5 = Bu 4, 3, 7
658, 1 = Ch 8, 8, 1[70]
—, 1 = Bu 1, 4, 7
—, 4 = Kshu 3, 6
—, 6 = Bu 2, 1, 17
—, 11 cf Tu 2, 6
Ch 6, 8, 7
—, 14 = Bu 4, 4, 22
660, 1 = Mbh 12, 8518
—, 7 cf Çv 5, 8
661, 4 ~ Çv 5, 9
—, 10 = Çv 5, 8
—, 12 = Mu 3, 1, 9
662, 3 = Kshu 3, 6
—, 8—10 = Pu 6, 3
—, 14 = Ch 3, 14, 3. 2
—, 15 = Ch 8, 7, 1
663, 13 ~ Bu 3, 7, 23
—, 13 ~ Bu 3, 8, 11
—, 14 = Ch 6, 8, 7
—, 14 = Bu 1, 4, 10
664, 2 = Bu 4, 3, 7
—, 6 = Bu 4, 4, 5
—, 9 = Bu 4, 3, 7
—, 12 = Bu 4, 3, 7
665, 1 = Çv 3, 8
—, 3 = Ch 6, 8, 1
—, 15 = Ch 6, 9, 2
666, 1 = Ch 6, 9, 3
667, 7 = Bu 1, 5, 3
—, 9 = Bu 1, 5, 3
669, 1 ~ Pu 1, 4, 9
—, 5 = Bu 4, 3, 12

[67] *âmnâyate*; brâhmaṇa-like; cf. Bṛih. 1, 2, 1, 4.—[68] Mâdhy., only instead of *idam imam* (Kâṇva).—[69] only Kâṇva.—[70] or Kaush. 4, 20.

669, 5 = Bu 2, 1, 18
—, 9 = Bu 2, 1, 17
—, 10 = Bu 2, 1, 18
670, 3 = Tu 2, 5
—, 8 = Bu 2, 1, 17
—, 9 = Tu 2, 5
672, 10 = Bu 2, 4, 5
—, 11 = Ch 8, 7, 1
—, 11 = Mu 2, 2, 6
674, 2 = Bu 4, 3, 7
—, 3 = Ku 3, 4
—, 6 = Bu 3, 7, 23
—, 9 = Bu 4, 5, 15 [69]
675, 5 = Bu 4, 3, 21
—, 7 = Bu 4, 3, 32
676, 13 = Pu 4, 9
677, 2 = Bu 2, 1, 18
—, 4 = Bu 2, 1, 17
—, 7 = Çb 14, 7, 1, 7 [71]
—, 9 = Mbh 12, 9897
—, 11 cf Bu 1, 5, 3
678, 3 = Bu 4, 3, 13
679, 3 = Tu 2, 5
—, 5 = Tu 2, 4
—, 7 = Tu 2, 5
—, 8 = ? [72]
681, 8 = Bs 2, 1, 34
682, 10 = Kshu 3, 8[24]
—, 12 = Çb 14, 6, 7, 30 [73]
685, 9 = Ch 8, 7, 1
—, 9 = Bu 4, 4, 22
—, 10 = Çb 14, 6, 7, 30 [73]
686, 2 = ? [74]
—, 7 = Çv 4, 3
—, 9 = Tâ 3, 12, 7
—, 10 = Bu 3, 7, 23
687, 2 = Ch 3, 12, 6
—, 5 = Ch 8, 15
687, 9 = BhG 15, 7
690, 8 = Ch 6, 8, 7
—, 13 = Mbh 12, 13754
691, 1 = Mu 3, 1, 1
—, 2 = Ku 5, 11
—, 8 = Tu 2, 6
—, 8 = Bu 3, 7, 23
—, 9 = Bu 4, 4, 19
—, 10 = Ch 6, 8, 7
—, 10 = Bu 1, 4, 10
692, 4 = ? [75]
—, 4 = ? [75]
—, 5 = ? [76]
—, 5 ~ Mbh 12, 9971

II, 4.

701, 4 = Ch 6, 2, 3
—, 5 = Tu 2, 1
—, 7 = Çb 6, 1, 1, 1
702, 1 ~ Bu 2, 1, 20
—, 3 = Mu 2, 1, 3
—, 3 = Mu 2, 1, 8
—, 4 = Pu 6, 4
703, 9 ~ Bu 2, 1, 20
704, 1 = Mu 2, 1, 3
—, 3 cf Ts 2, 3, 2, 6
705, 5 = Mu 1, 1, 3
—, 7 = Mu 2, 1, 3
—, 11 ~ Mu 2, 1, 10
—, 11 = Mu 2, 2, 11
706, 1 = Bu 2, 4, 5
—, 4 = Mu 2, 1, 2
—, 9 = Bs 2, 3, 3
707, 4 = Mu 2, 1, 3
—, 9 = Pu 6, 4
—, 12 = Bu 2, 1, 20
—, 15 = Ch 6, 2, 3
708, 4 = Ch 6, 5, 3
708, 7 = Ch 6, 1, 3
—, 8 = Ch 6, 8, 7
709, 3 = Mu 2, 1, 8
—, 5 = Bu 3, 2, 1
—, 5 = Ts 5, 3, 2, 5
—, 6 = Ts 5, 3, 2, 3
—, 7 = Bu 3, 9, 4
—, 8 = Bu 2, 4, 11
—, 9 = Pu 4, 8
—, 11 = Mu 2, 1, 8
—, 12 = Ts 5, 3, 2, 5
—, 13 = Mu 2, 1, 8
710, 9 ~ Bu 3, 2, 8
711, 3 = Bu 3, 9, 4
—, 13 = Bu 1, 5, 3
—, 15 cf Ts 5, 3, 2, 5 [77]
712, 3 = Ts 5, 3, 2, 3
—, 12 = Bu 4, 4, 2
713, 1 = Bu 4, 4, 1
—, 6 cf Bu 4, 4, 2
—, 10 ~ Bu 3, 2, 8
—, 14 ? [78]
714, 1 = Pu 4, 8
—, 2 = Pu 4, 8
—, 4 = Bu 3, 9, 4
716, 3 = Mu 2, 1, 3
—, 5 = Pu 6, 4
—, 7 = ṚV 10, 129, 2
—, 13 = Mu 2, 1, 2
717, 2 = Ch 5, 1, 1
—, 7 = Bu 6, 1, 13
—, 10 = ? [79]
718, 2 = Sâṅkhyak 29 [80]
—, 4 = Ch 3, 18, 4
—, 9 = Mu 2, 1, 3
719, 8 = 717, 10
—, 14 cf Ku 5, 8
720, 1 cf Bu 1, 5, 21

[71] *i. e.*, Bṛih. 4, 3, 7 according to the Mâdhy.—[72] cf. Çatap. br. 10, 4, 1, 4.—[73] *i. e.*, Bṛih. 3, 7, 23 according to the Mâdhy.—[74] *âtharvaṇikâ brahmasûkte* (not in A. V.).—[75] dharmasûtra-like.—[76] çrautasûtra-like.—[77] the words *dve çrotre* etc. seem to contain no quotation, but only Çaṅkara's explanation of the passage.—[78] "smṛiti", perhaps from a Purâṇam.—[79] in this form unknown to me; cf. Bṛih. 1, 5, 3. 22.—[80] or Sâṅkhyasûtra 2, 31; in every case inaccurate.

720, 1 cf Ch 4, 3, 3
—, 2 cf Pu 2, 13
721, 12 ~ Ch 5, 1, 6
—, 13 ~ Ch 5, 1, 7
722, 4 = Pu 2, 3
—, 6 = Bu 4, 3, 12
—, 7 = Bu 1, 3, 19
—, 8 = Ch 1, 2, 9
—, 10 = Pu 6, 3
—, 16 = Bu 1, 5, 3
723, 7 = Bu 1, 5, 3
—, 12 = Ys 1, 6
724, 6 = Bu 1, 3, 22
725, 12 = Au 1, 2, 4
726, 2 = Au 1, 2, 4
—, 4 = Ch 3, 18, 3
—, 6 = Bu 1, 3, 12
—, 11 = ?[81]
727, 9 = Ch 8, 12, 4
728, 5 = Bu 1, 5, 20
—, 7 = Bu 4, 4, 2
729, 6 = Bu 1, 5, 21
730, 1 = Mu 2, 1, 3
—, 5 = Manu 2, 89
—, 12 = Bu 1, 3, 2
731, 2 = Bu 1, 3, 7
—, 3 = Bu 1, 5, 3
—, 13 = Bu 1, 5, 21
732, 1 = Bu 1, 5, 21
—, 3 = Bu 1, 5, 21
—, 5 = Bu 1, 5, 21
—, 8 = Bu 1, 5, 21
—, 13 = Ch 6, 3, 2—3
735, 6 = Ch 8, 14
—, 11 = Ch 6, 4, 1
736, 3 = Ch 6, 3, 4
—, 5 = Ch 6, 4, 6
—, 5 = Ch 6, 4, 7
—, 8 = Ch 6, 4, 7
736, 13 = Ch 6, 5, 1
737, 3 cf Ch 6, 5, 2—3
—, 5 = Ch 6, 3, 4

III, 1.

740, 3 = Ch 5, 10, 8
—, 6 = Bu 4, 4, 1
—, 6 = Bu 4, 4, 4
—, 11 = Bu 4, 4, 1
741, 5 = Ch 5, 3, 3
—, 10 = ?[82]
742, 1 = Bu 4, 4, 3
744, 5 = Bu 4, 4, 2
—, 14 = Bu 3, 2, 13
745, 2 = Bu 3, 2, 13
—, 14 = Ch 5, 4, 1
—, 15 = Ch 5, 4, 2
747, 4 = Ts 1, 6, 8, 1
—, 8 = ?[83]
748, 1 = Ch 5, 10, 3
—, 3 = Ch 5, 10, 4
—, 4 = Ch 5, 4, 2
749, 1 = Çb 11, 6, 2, 6
—, 6 = Ch 5, 10, 4
—, 7 ~ Bu 6, 2, 16
750, 7 = Ch 3, 6, 1
—, 12 = Bu 1, 4, 10
751, 6 = Pu 5, 4
—, 7 ~ Bu 4, 3, 33[84]
—, 15 = Ch 5, 10, 5
752, 7 = Bu 6, 2, 16
—, 10 = Bu 4, 4, 6
753, 10 = Ch 5, 10, 7
754, 3 cf Âpdh 2, 1, 2, 3
756, 2 = Ch 5, 10, 7
—, 5 = Bu 4, 4, 6
758, 1 = Mbh 12, 10713
760, 3 = Ch 5, 10, 7
—, 7 = Bu 4, 4, 5
760, 8 = Tu 1, 11
761, 5 = ?[85]
763, 2 = Kshu 1, 2
764, 5 = Ku 2, 6[86]
—, 7 = ṚV 10, 14, 1
—, 11 cf Ku 1[87]
765, 6 = Ch 5, 3, 3
—, 7 = Ch 5, 10, 8
—, 12 = Ch 5, 10, 1
—, 14 = Ch 5, 10, 8
766, 11 = Ch 5, 10, 8
767, 1 cf Kshu 1, 2
—, 8 = Ch 5, 10, 8
—, 9 = Ch 5, 3, 3
768, 11 = Ch 6, 3, 1
769, 2 = Ch 6, 6, 1
—, 7 = Ch 5, 10, 5
—, 9 = Ch 5, 10, 5. 6
770, 2 = Ch 5, 10, 5
—, 7 = Ch 5, 10, 5
771, 8 = Ch 5, 10, 6
772, 2 = Ch 5, 10, 6
773, 12 cf Ch 5, 10, 7
775, 7 = Mbh 12, 9971
776, 5 = Ch 5, 10, 6
777, 1 = Ch 5, 10, 7

III, 2.

778, 5 = Bu 4, 3, 9. 10
779, 3 = Bu 4, 3, 9
—, 6 = Bu 4, 3, 10
—, 10 = Ku 5, 8
780, 3 = Ku 1, 23
—, 3 = Ku 1, 24
—, 6 = Ku 2, 14
—, 8 = Ku 5, 8
—, 11 = Bu 4, 3, 14
781, 8 = Bu 4, 3, 12
782, 3 = Bu 2, 1, 18

[81] Smṛiti, perhaps Mahâbh. 12.—[82] çruti; cf. Bṛih. 4, 4, 3. Brahma-upanishad p. 245.—[83] çruti; *asmai = yajamânâya* gloss.—[84] according to the Mâdhyandinas.—[85] smṛiti.—[86] with the reading *sâmparâpaḥ* (for *sâmparâyaḥ*), which the gloss. explains: *samyak parastât prâpyata', iti samparâpaḥ paralokaḥ, tadupâyaḥ sâmparâpaḥ*. [87] *smaranti*; a Smṛiti-tale of Naciketas is not know to me.

783, 2 = Bu 4, 3, 10
—, 7 = Ch 5, 2, 9
—, 9 = Aâ 3, 2, 4, 17
—, 11 = ?[88]
784, 2 = Bs 3, 2, 1
785, 2 = Bu 4, 3, 9
—, 4 = Ku 5, 8
—, 5 = Ku 5, 8
—, 6 = Ch 6, 8, 7
—, 11 = Bs 2, 1, 14
787, 3 = Çv 1, 11
788, 2 = Ch 6, 3, 2
—, 4 = Ch 6, 8, 7
789, 1 = Ch 8, 6, 3
—, 3 = Bu 2, 1, 19
—, 4 = Kshu 4, 19—20
—, 6 = Bu 4, 4, 22
—, 7 = Ch 6, 8, 1
—, 8 = Bu 4, 3, 21
790, 4 = Ch 6, 8, 1
—, 6 = Ch 6, 8, 2
—, 9 = Ch 6, 9, 2
791, 10 = Kshu 4, 19–20
—, 13 = Bs 1, 1, 28
—, 14 = Ch 8, 6, 3
792, 1 = Ch 8, 6, 3
—, 5 = Ch 8, 6, 3
—, 8 = Bu 4, 4, 7
—, 10 = Ch 8, 6, 3
—, 11 = Ch 8, 4, 2
793, 4 = Bu 4, 4, 22
—, 5 = Bu 2, 1, 19
—, 9 = Bs 1, 3, 14
—, 10 = Bu 2, 1, 19
794, 3 = Ch 6, 8, 1
—, 12 = Bu 4, 5, 15
—, 14 = Bu 4, 5, 15[51]
795, 16 = Bu 2, 1, 16
796, 1 = Bu 2, 1, 20
—, 2 = Ch 6, 10, 2
797, 12 = Bu 4, 3, 16
797, 13 = Ch 8, 3, 2
—, 14 = Ch 6, 10, 2
801, 14 = Ch 6, 8, 1
—, 15 = Bu 4, 3, 22
—, 15 = Ch 8, 4, 2
803, 4 = Ch 3, 14, 2
—, 5 = Bu 3, 8, 8
804, 4 = Ku 3, 15
—, 9 cf Ch 3, 18, 2
—, 10 cf Pu 6, 1
—, 10 cf Ku 5, 3
—, 10 cf Bu 1, 3, 22
—, 11 cf Ch 5, 11, 2
805, 2 = Bu 2, 5, 1
—, 10 ~ Bu 4, 4, 19[84]
—, 12 = Çv 1, 12
806, 3 = Bu 3, 8, 8
—, 3 = Ku 3, 15
—, 4 = Ch 8, 14, 1
—, 5 = Mu 2, 1, 2
—, 6 = Bu 2, 5, 19
—, 8 = Bs 1, 1, 4
808, 3 = Bu 4, 5, 13
—, 9 = Bu 2, 3, 6
—, 10 = Kena 1, 3
—, 11 Tu 2, 9
—, 11 = ?[89]
809, 3 = BhG 13, 12
—, 6 Mbh 12, 12909
—, 14 = ?[90]
810, 1 = ?[91]
811, 11 = Bu 2, 5, 18
—, 13 = Ch 6, 3, 2
812, 9 cf Bs 3, 2, 11—14
—, 10 cf Bs 3, 2, 15—21
—, 11 = Bu 2, 4, 12
813, 1 = Ku 6, 13
814, 5 = Bu 2, 5, 19
—, 7 = Bu 2, 5, 19
—, 9 = Ch 3, 11, 2
—, 10 = Ch 3, 14, 1
815, 3 = Bs 3, 2, 14
—, 11 = Bs 1, 1, 4
817, 5 = Ch 6, 2, 1
—, 5 = Ch 6, 8, 7
821, 3 ~ Bu 2, 3, 1
—, 6 = Bu 2, 3, 6
823, 4 = Bu 2, 1, 1 (?)
—, 4 = Tu 2, 6
—, 5 = Ku 6, 13
—, 8 = Tu 2, 1
—, 10 = ISpr^2 3117
—, 12 = Tu 2, 4
824, 11 = Bu 2, 3, 6
825, 5 = ISpr^2 3117
826, 2 = Bu 2, 3, 6
827, 4 = Mu 3, 1, 8
—, 5 = Bu 3, 9, 26
—, 6 = Mu 1, 1, 6
—, 6 = Tu 2, 7
—, 7 = 72, 6
—, 14 = Ku 4, 1
828, 1 = Mu 3, 1, 8
—, 3 = Mbh 12, 1642
—, 5 = ?[81]
829, 4 = Mu 3, 2, 9
—, 5 = Bu 4, 4, 6
—, 8 = Mu 3, 1, 8
—, 10 = Mu 3, 2, 8
—, 10 = Bu 3, 7, 15
—, 12 = Ch 6, 8, 7
—, 12 = Bu 1, 4, 10
—, 12 = Bu 3, 4, 1
—, 13 = Bu 3, 7, 15
831, 5 = Bu 3, 7, 23
—, 5 = Bu 2, 3, 6
—, 6 = Bu 2, 5, 19
—, 16 = Ch 8, 4, 1
832, 4 = Ch 8, 4, 2
—, 7 cf Ch 3, 18, 2
—, 8 cf ?[92]
—, 8 cf Pu 6, 1

---

[88] "*âcakshate svapnâdhyâyavidaḥ*". — [89] an entirely unknown, very remarkable Upanishad-quotation. — [90] "*mokshaçâstreshu*", perhaps Mahâbh. 12 ? — [91] found in Brahmavindûp. 12; but more probably taken from the Mahâbh. — [92] *ashṭâçapham* (sc. brahma).

832, 11 = Ch 6, 8, 1
—, 12 cf Bu 4, 3, 21. 35
833, 1 = Ch 1, 6, 6
—, 3 = Ch 1, 7, 5
—, 4 = Ch 1, 7, 5
—, 6 = Ch 1, 6, 5
—, 7 = Ch 1, 7, 6
834, 1 = Ch 6, 2, 1
—, 14 = Ch 8, 4, 2
835, 8 cf Ch 3, 18
836, 15 = Ch 6, 8, 1
837, 2 = Ch 6, 8, 1
—, 5 = Ch 3, 12, 7
—, 6 = Ch 3, 12, 8
—, 6 = Ch 3, 12, 9
—, 11 cf Ch 7, 25, 1—2
—, 12 = Bu 2, 4, 6
—, 13 ~ Mu 2, 2, 11
—, 13 = Ch 7, 25, 2
—, 13 = Bu 4, 4, 19
—, 13 Çv 3, 9
—, 14 = Bu 2, 5, 19
—, 16 cf Bu 3, 4, 1
838, 8 = Ch 8, 1, 3
—, 9 = 130, 12
—, 9 = Çb 10, 6, 3, 2
—, 10 = BhG 2, 24
840, 8 = Bu 4, 4, 24
842, 4 = Kshu 3, 8[23]
—, 8 = BhG 7, 21—22

III, 3.

844, 8 = Bs 1, 1, 4
846, 2 = ?[93]
847. 1 cf Mu 3, 2, 10
—, 9 = Bu 6, 1, 1
—, 11 = Bu 6, 1, 1
848. 6 = Js 2, 4, 10
849. 1 = Bu 6, 2, 14
—, 2 = Ch 5, 10, 10
—, 6 cf Ch 5, 1, 8—11
—, 7 = Bu 6, 1, 6
—, 13 cf 43, 1
849, 14 = Ch 5, 9, 2
850, 2 = Bu 6, 2, 14
851, 4 = Mu 3, 2, 11
—, 6 ~ Mu 3, 2, 10
—, 11 cf AV 10, 9 Kauç 64 sq.
852, 3 = Ku 2, 15
—, 3 = Aâ 3, 2, 3, 12
—, 5 = Ku 6, 2
—, 7 = Tu 2, 7
—, 8 cf Çb 10, 6, 1, 10
—, 9 = Ch 5, 18, 1
853, 12 = Bs 3, 3, 10
854, 2 = Bu 1, 3, 1. 2
—, 5 = Bu 1, 3, 7
—, 6 = Ch 1, 2, 1
—, 8 = Ch 1, 2, 7
855, 4 = Bu 1, 3, 2
—, 5 = Ch 1, 2, 7
—, 11 = Bu 1, 3, 23
856, 4 = Ch 1, 1, 1
—, 6 Ch 1, 1, 10
857, 2 = Bu 1, 3, 7
858, 2 = Bu 1, 3, 24
—, 5 = Ts 2, 5, 5, 2
—, 6 = Ts 2, 5, 5, 2
—, 10 = Ch 1, 9, 1
859, 7 = Bs 3, 3, 7
860, 4 = Ch 1, 1, 1
—, 15 = Ch 6, 8, 7
861, 14 = Ch 1, 1, 7
863, 10 = Bu 6, 1, 14 ~ Ch 5, 1, 13
864, 1 = Kshu 2, 14
—, 6 = Kshu 2, 14
867, 2 = Tu 2, 5
—, 10 = Ch 6, 2, 1
—, 12 = Bs 1, 1, 12
868, 3 cf Mu 3, 2, 1
—, 3 cf Ch 8, 7, 1
869, 2 = Ku 3, 10—11
870, 2 = Ku 3, 15
—, 9 = Ku 3, 12
870, 13 = Ku 3, 13
—, 14 = Bs 1, 4, 1
871, 1 = Ku 3, 9
—, 6 = Au 1, 1, 1
872, 4 = Au 1, 1, 2
—, 6 = Bu 1, 4, 1
—, 8 = MârkP 45, 6
—, 10 = Aâ 2, 1, 3, 1
—, 12 = Bu 1, 4, 1
873, 1 = Au 1, 2, 2—3
—, 5 = Tu 2, 1
—, 8 = Bu 1, 4, 1
—, 11 = Au 1, 1, 1
874, 4 = Ch 6, 2, 3
—, 7 = Au 1, 2, 2
—, 12 = Au 1, 3, 11
—, 13 = Au 1, 3, 12
—, 14 = Au 1, 3, 11
875, 2 = Au 1, 3, 11
—, 2 = Au 1, 3, 13
—, 4 = Au 3, 3
—, 5 = Au 3, 3
—, 9 = Bu 4, 3, 7
—, 11 = Bu 4, 4, 25
—, 12 = Ch 6, 2, 1
—, 14 = Ch 6, 8, 7
876, 6 = Ch 6, 2, 1
—, 7 = Bu 4, 3, 7
—, 12 = Ch 6, 1, 3
—, 14 = Ch 6, 2, 1
877, 3 = Ch 6, 8, 7
878, 4 = Ch 5, 2, 2
—, 5 = Bu 6, 1, 14[94]
880, 1 = Bu 6, 1, 14
—, 9 ~ Bu 6, 1, 14[95]
881, 7 = Bu 6, 1, 14
882, 5 = Çb 10, 6, 3, 2
—, 7 = Bu 5, 6, 1
884, 9 = Bu 5, 5, 1. 2
—, 13 = Bu 5, 5, 3. 4
886, 1 = Bu 5, 5, 3
—, 2 = Bu 5, 5, 4
887, 1 = Ch 1, 7, 5

[93] ritual quotation; the supplement in gloss. p. 845, 11.—[94] according to the Mâdhyandinas.—[95] confounded with Chând. 5, 2, 1.

887, 8 = ?[96]
888, 1 ~ Ch 3, 14, 2
—, 2 ~ Ch 8, 1, 1
—, 4 = Ch 4, 15, 1
—, 7 = Ch 3, 14, 3
—, 8 = Ch 4, 15, 4
—, 9 = Ch 8, 1, 3
889, 10 cf Ch 3, 16
—, 12 cf Ch 3, 17, 1
890, 2 = Tâ 10, 64
—, 11 cf Ch 3, 16, 1—5
—, 13 cf Ch 3, 17, 5
Tâ 10, 64
891, 1 = Tâ 10, 64
—, 5 = Tâ 10, 64
—, 6 = Tâ 10, 64
—, 10 = Tâ 10, 64
892, 1 = Tâ 10, 64
—, 3 = Ch 3, 16, 7
—, 7 = ?[97]
—, 9 = Cb 1, 1[98]
893, 1 = ?[99]
—, 1 = Kb[100]
—, 1 = Tu 1, 1
—, 3 = Çb 14, 1, 1, 1
—, 4 = Kaushb[101]
894, 8 = Ch 3, 15, 3
—, 10 cf Âçvçr 9, 9, 19
897, 1 = Js 3, 3, 14
—, 5 = Âçvçr 9, 9, 19
899, 3 = Ch 8, 13, 1
—, 5 = Mu 3, 1, 3
—, 7 = ?[99]
—, 8 = Kshu 1, 4
900, 8 cf Kshu 1, 4
901, 6 = Ch 2, 10, 5
—, 8 = Çb 6, 2, 2, 3
—, 9 = Ab 1, 4, 11
902, 1 ~ Tb 1, 7, 9, 2
—, 9 = ?[102]
—, 10 = ?[99]
903, 2 = ?[103]
—, 4 = ? Ârcâbhin
—, 9 = Js[104]
906, 2 = Ch 8, 13, 1
—, 3 = Js[105]
—, 8 = Kshu 1, 3—4
907, 8 = Ch 8, 13, 1
—, 8 = 899, 7
—, 12 cf Manu 4, 204
908, 14 = Mu 3, 1, 3
911, 7 = Ch 5, 10, 1
—, 14 = Çb 10, 5, 4, 16
912, 1 = Bu 6, 2, 15
—, 5 = Bu 6, 2, 16
—, 10 = BhG 8, 26
914, 9 = Ch 3, 11, 1
—, 12 = Ch 6, 14, 2
915, 8 cf Mbh 12, 11854 sq
—, 15 = Mu 2, 2, 8
—, 17 = Ch 7, 26, 2
916, 1 = BhG 4, 37
—, 3 = ?[106]
—, 8 = Ch 6, 14, 2
—, 11 = Bu 1, 4, 10
917, 1 = ?[106]
—, 5 = Bu 3, 4, 1
—, 6 = Ch 6, 8, 7
—, 8 = Bu 1, 4, 10
—, 13 ~ Bu 3, 8, 8
918, 1 = Mu 1, 1, 5, 6
919, 1 = Bs 3, 3, 11
—, 5 ~ Pañc 21, 10, 11
—, 10 = Js 3, 3, 9
920, 2 = Mu 3, 3, 1
= Çv 4, 6
920, 6 = Ku 3, 1
921, 5 = Mu 3, 1, 2
= Çv 4, 7
—, 8 = Ku 2, 14
—, 9 = Ku 3, 2
—, 10 = Bs 1, 2, 11
922, 2 = Bu 3, 4, 1
—, 2 = Bu 3, 5, 1
923, 1 = Çv 6, 11
—, 8 = Ch 6, 8, 7
—, 11 = Ch 6, 8, 7
—, 14 = Bu 3, 4, 2
—, 14 = Bu 3, 5, 1
—, 16 = Bu 3, 5, 1
924, 6 = Aâ 2, 2, 4, 6
—, 7 = Jâb[107]
926, 2 = Bu 5, 4, 1
—, 4 = Bu 5, 5, 2
—, 7 = Bu 5, 4, 1
—, 7 = Bu 5, 5, 3
—, 9 = Bu 5, 5, 2
927, 12 = Ch 1, 6, 6
—, 13 = Ch 1, 7, 5
928, 5 = Ch 1, 6, 1
—, 5 = Ch 1, 6, 8
—, 6 = Ch 1, 7, 7
—, 10 = Ch 8, 1, 1
—, 11 = Ch 8, 1, 5
—, 13 = Bu 4, 4, 22
929, 6 = Bu 4, 4, 22
—, 8 = Ch 8, 1, 5
—, 13 = Bs 1, 3, 14
—, 15 = Ch 8, 1, 6
930, 2 = Bu 4, 3, 14
—, 2 = Bu 4, 3, 15
—, 5 = Bu 4, 5, 15[50]
—, 9 = Ch 5, 19, 1
—, 12 = Ch 5, 24, 2

96 "*Râṇâyanîyânâṃ khileshu*". —97 *âtharvaṇikânâm upanishad-ârambhe.* —98 the beginning of the "Chândogya-brâhmaṇam", cf. Râj. M., Chând. introd. p. 17 n. —99 "Çâṭyâyaninâm". —100 Kâṭhakam, or another recension of the Kâṭhaka-Up.—101 Kaushîtakinâm agni-shṭoma-brâhmaṇam.—102 "Bhâllavinâm".—103 "Paiñgi-âmnâya".—104 "*dvâdaçalakshaṇyâm*".—105 "Jaiminisûtram" gloss.—106 smṛiti, perhaps Mahâbh. 12.—107 not in our Jâbâla-Up.

930, 14 = Ch 5, 24, 5
931, 4 = Jâb. [107]
—, 11 cf Kâṭyçr 24,4,24
932, 4 = Ch 5, 19, 1
—, 8 = Kâṭyçr 24,4,24
933, 4 = 931, 4
—, 6 = Ch 5, 18, 2
934, 8 = Ch 1, 1, 1
935, 2 = Ch 1, 1, 7
—, 4 ~ Ts 3, 5, 7, 2
—, 8 cf Ch 1, 1, 3. 6. 7
1,2, 7 1, 3, 1
936, 1 = Ch 1, 1, 10
—, 3 = Ch 1,10,9.10.11
—, 8 = Ch 1, 1, 10
937, 4 = Ch 2, 2, 3
938, 9 = Bu 1, 5, 21
—, 11 = Ch 4, 3, 1
—, 12 = Ch 4, 3, 2
939, 3 = Au 1, 2, 4
—, 4 = Bu 1, 5, 13
—, 7 = 717, 10
—, 8 = Bu 1, 5, 23
—, 9 = Bu 1, 5, 23
—, 10 = Bu 1, 5, 23
940, 1 = Ch 4, 3, 6
—, 9 = Bu 1, 5, 22
—, 11 = Bu 1, 5, 23
—, 13 = Bu 1, 5, 21
—, 14 = Bu 1, 5, 21
941, 2 = Bu 1, 5, 23
—, 5 = Bu 1, 5, 22
—, 6 = Ch 4, 3, 4
—, 7 = Ch 4, 3, 8
—, 9 = Ts 2, 3, 6, 1
942, 1 = Ts 2, 3, 6, 2
—, 5 = Js [108]
943, 2 ~ Çb 10, 5, 3, 1
—, 3 = Çb 10, 5, 3, 3
—, 4 = Çb 10,5,3,4–11

944, 1 = Çb 10, 5, 3, 3
—, 2 = Çb 10, 5, 3, 12
—, 4 = Js 3, 3, 14
946, 2 = Çb 10, 5, 3, 11
—, 10 = Çb 10, 5, 3, 12
—, 13 = Bs 3, 3, 44
947, 5–8 = Çb 10,5,3,12
—, 17 = Kshu 2, 6, 5
948, 9 = Çb 10, 5, 3, 4
—, 16 ~ Çb 10, 5, 3, 3
949, 11 = Çb 10, 5, 3, 11
951, 3 = Js 11 [109]
—, 11 = Çb 10, 5, 2, 3
—, 12 ~ Ts 5, 1,10,3 [110]
—, 13 ~ Ch 5, 4, 1
952, 4 = Çb 10. 5, 4, 1
—, 7 = Çb 10, 5, 4, 16
—, 10 = Çb 10, 5, 1, 1
—, 11 = Çb 10, 5, 2, 23
953, 5 cf ad Js 1, 1, 5
—, 8 ad Js 1, 1, 5
—, 10 = ? [111]
958, 3 = Ch 1, 1, 1
—, 3 = Ch 2, 2, 1
—, 4 = Aâ 2, 1, 2, 1
—, 5 = Çb 10, 5, 4, 1
959, 14 = MaitrS 1, 1, 6
960, 1 = VâjS 1, 16
—, 3 = ? [112]
—, 4 = ? [113]
—, 5 ~ Vs 21, 41
—, 7 ~ Pañc 21, 10, 11
—, 8 = ṚV 2, 12, 1
—, 9 = Ts 7, 5, 5, 2
961, 3 = Ch 5, 11, 1
—, 4 = Ch 5, 12, 1
—, 7 = Ch 5, 18, 2
—, 12 = Ch 5, 12, 1
962, 8 ~ Ch 5, 11, 4
—, 10 = Ch 5, 12, 2

862, 11 = Ch 5, 12, 2
—, 14 = Ch 5, 18, 1
963, 6 = Ch 5, 12, 2
964, 1 = Ch 3, 14, 1
—, 1 = Ch 4, 10, 5
—, 1 = Ch 8, 7, 3
—, 2 = ? [114]
—, 2 = Ch 4, 3, 3
—, 2 = Ch 5, 1, 1
—, 3 = Ch 7, 15, 1
—, 8 = Ch 3, 14, 1
966, 4 = Bs 3, 3, 1
967, 3 = Ch 3, 14, 1
—, 3 = Ch 4, 10, 5
—, 4 = Ch 8, 7, 3
—, 12 = Ch 3, 14, 4
—, 13 = Bu 4, 1, 3
—, 13 = BhG 8, 6
968, 5 = Bs 3, 3, 59
—, 6 = Ch 3, 15, 2
—, 7 = Ch 7, 1, 5
969, 8 = Ch 1, 5, 5
970, 5 = Ch 1, 1, 9
971, 4 cf Ts 3, 1, 2, 4
—, 10 = Bs 3, 3, 42
972, 5 = Ch 4, 17, 10 [115]

III, 4.

974, 2 = Ch 7, 1, 3
—, 3 = Mu 3, 2, 9
—, 3 = Tu 2, 1
—, 4 = Ch 7, 14, 2
—, 5 = Ch 8, 7, 1
—, 7 = Bu 4, 5, 6, 15 [54]
975, 2 = Ts 3, 5, 7, 2
—, 3 = Ts 6, 1, 1, 5
—, 4 = Ts 2, 6, 1, 5
976, 8 cf Bu 2, 4, 5
977, 8 = Bu 3, 1, 1
—, 8 = Ch 5, 11, 5

[108] "*sañkarshe*" (= *devatya-kâṇḍe* gloss.).—[109] *ekâdaçe* gloss.—[110] or rather from Çatap. Br. 10?—[111] from the commentary of Upavarsha to the Jaiminisûtras.—[112] "*Maitrâyaṇîyânâm*" gloss.—[113] "*Yajurvedinâm agnîshomîyaḥ paçuḥ çruto, na 'aja' iti jâtiviçeshaḥ*" gloss.—[114] related to 717, 10.—[115] 972, 7 is no quotation.

978, 3 = ?[116]
—, 6 = Ch 1, 1, 10
—, 10 = Bu 4, 4, 2
979, 2 = Ch 8, 15, 1
—, 9 = Îçâ 2
980, 1 = Çb 12, 4, 1, 1
cf Tâ 10, 64
—, 5 = Bs 3, 4, 2
981, 2 = Bs 3, 4, 16
—, 3 = Bs 3, 4, 1
—, 7 = Mu 1, 1, 9
—, 7 = Tu 2, 8
—, 8 = Ku 6, 2
—, 8 = Bu 3, 8, 9
—, 9 = Ch 6, 2, 3
—, 11 = Bu 2, 4, 5
—, 12 = Bu 3, 4, 1
—, 12 = Ch 8, 7, 4
—, 13 = Ch 8, 9, 3
—, 14 = Bu 2, 4, 10
982, 1 = Bu 3, 5, 1
—, 2 = Ch 8, 12, 3
—, 6 = Ch 6, 8, 7
—, 6 = Bu 3, 7, 23
—, 11 = ?[117]
983, 1 = Bu 3, 5, 1
—, 4 = Bu 4, 5, 15[51]
—, 6 = Ch 5, 11, 5
—, 9 = Bs 3, 4, 4
—, 11 = Ch 1, 1, 10
—, 12 = Ch 1, 1, 1
984, 2 = Bu 4, 4, 2
—, 7 = Bu 4, 4, 6
—, 8 = Bu 4, 4, 6
—, 12 = Bs 3, 4, 6
985, 2 = Ch 8, 15, 1
—, 9 = Bs 3, 4, 7
—, 12 = Îçâ 2
986, 2 = Îçâ 2
986, 11 = Bu 4, 4, 22
987, 8 = Bu 4, 5, 15
988, 6 = Ch 2, 23, 1
—, 6 = Ch 5, 10, 1
—, 7 = Mu 1, 2, 11
—, 7 = Bu 4, 4, 22
—, 8 = Jâb. p. 445
989, 2 = Ch 2, 23, 1
—, 7 = Ch 2, 23, 2
—, 11 = Ch 2, 23, 2
990, 4 = Ch 2, 23, 1
—, 8 = Ts 1, 5, 2, 1
—, 9 = Tu 1, 11, 1
—, 10 = Ab 7, 13, 12
—, 11 = Ch 5, 10, 1
—, 11 = Mu 1, 2, 11
991, 2 = Ch 2, 23, 2
—, 3 = Bu 4, 4, 22
—, 4 = Jâb. p. 445
992, 3 = Ch 2, 23, 1
—, 5 cf Ts 2, 5, 11, 1
—, 7 = Bu 4, 4, 22
—, 8 = Ch 5, 10, 1
—, 9 = Ch 2, 23, 2
993, 1 = Ch 2, 23, 1
—, 6 = Ch 5, 10, 1
994, 6 = ?[118]
995, 1 ~ Js 3, 4, 3
998, 2–4 = Tâ 10, 62
—, 4 = Tâ 10, 10, 3
—, 6 = BhG 5, 17
999, 6 = Jâb. p. 444
1000, 1 = Jâb. p. 445
—, 3 = Jâb. p. 452
—, 8 = Ch 1, 1, 3
—, 9 = Ch 1, 6, 1
—, 9 = Çb 10, 1, 2, 2
—, 9 = Aâ 2, 1, 2, 1
1001, 4 = ?[119]
1002, 3 = Js 1, 2, 7
—, 9 = Ch 1, 1, 1
—, 9 = Ch 2, 2, 1
—, 9 = Aâ 2, 1, 2, 6
1003, 1 = ?[120]
—, 4 = Ch 1, 1, 7
—, 5 = Ch 1, 7, 9
—, 5 = Ch 2, 2, 3
1004, 2 = Bu 4, 5, 1
—, 3 = Kshu 3, 1
—, 4 = Ch 4, 1, 4
1005, 4 = Çb 13, 4, 3, 3
1006, 6 = Bu 2, 4, 5
—, 7 = Kshu 3, 2[22]
—, 8 = Ch 4, 3, 1
—, 8 = Ts 2, 1, 1, 4
—, 12 = Bs 3, 4, 1
1007, 6 cf Bs 3, 4, 25
1008, 7 = Bu 4, 4, 22
—, 10 = Ch 8, 5, 1
1009, 2 = Ku 2, 15
—, 6 = ?[121]
1010, 9 = Bu 4, 4, 23
1011, 10 = Ts 2, 6, 8, 5
—, 12 = Js 3, 3, 34
—, 13 = Bs 3, 4, 20
1012, 4 cf Bu 4, 4, 23
—, 8 ~ Ch 5, 2, 1
—, 9 = Bu 6, 1, 14[122]
1013, 6 = Ch 2, 13, 2
—, 11 = Ch 5, 2, 1
1014, 3 ~ Ch 5, 2, 1
—, 11 = Ch 1, 10, 1
1015, 1 = Ch 1, 10, 4
—, 7 = Ch 5, 2, 1
1016, 4 ~ Manu 10, 101
—, 6 = ?[123]
—, 11 = ?[124]
—, 12 = Ch 5, 2, 1

116 proverbial.—117 fine and remarkable Upanishad-quotation; I am indebted to Weber for the conjecture *Kâṇveyâḥ* instead of *Kârayeyâḥ*.—118 *mahâ-pitṛiyajñe dishṭaṃ gata-agnihotre ca çrutaṃ vâkyam udâharati*, gloss.—119 Brâhmaṇa-quotation, taittirîya-like.—120 "*nyâyavidâṃ smaraṇam*".—121 "smṛiti", perhaps Mahâbh. 12.—122 Mâdhy.—123 "*smaryate*" dharmasûtra-like.—124 "*Kaṭhânâṃ saṃhitâyâm*".

1017, 2 = Bs 3, 4, 26
—, 5 = Bu 4, 4, 22
—, 10 = ?[125]
1018, 4 = Bu 4, 4, 22
—, 5 = Bs 3, 4, 26
—, 10 = Bs 3, 4, 25
1019, 4 = Bu 4, 4, 22
1020, 1 = Kâty 24, 4, 24
—, 3 = Bu 4, 4, 22
—, 6 = BhG 6, 1
1021, 3 = Ch 8, 5, 3
1022, 2 cf Ch 4, 1
Bu 3, 6. 3, 8
—, 5 cf Mbh 14, 137 sq.
1023, 3 = Manu 2, 87
—, 8 = BhG 6, 45
1024, 3 = Bu 4, 4, 9
—, 4 = ?[126]
1025, 3 = Ch 2, 23, 2
—, 4 quotation?
—, 5 = Mbh 12, 8578
—, 8 = Jâb. p. 444
—, 11 = BhG 3, 35
1026, 7 cf Âpdh 1, 9, 26, 8
Pârgṛ 3, 12, 2
1027, 1 = Js 6, 8, 22
—, 3 = ?[126]
1028, 10 = Js 1, 3, 8. 9
1030, 1 = ?[128]
—, 6 = 1027, 3
1031, 1 = ?[126]
1032, 1 = Ch 2, 3, 2
—, 6 = Bu 1, 3, 28
1033 4 = Ch 1, 2, 13
—, 10 ~ Çb 1, 3, 1, 26
—, 11 = Ch 1, 7, 8
1034, 5 = Bu 3, 5, 1
1036, 3 = BhG 10, 37
—, 4 = Âpdh 2, 9, 21, 1
—, 5 = Râmây 1, 1, 1
1037, 2 ~ Bu 3, 5, 1
1038, 1 = Ch 8, 15, 1

1038, 12 = Ch 2, 23, 2
1039, 5 = Bu 3, 5, 1
1041, 8 = ?[127]
—, 12 = ?[127]
1042, 2 = Bs 3, 4, 26
1044, 6 = Ku 2, 7
—, 10 cf Au 2, 4, 5
1045, 3 = BhG 6, 37
—, 4 = BhG 6, 40
—, 6 = BhG 6, 43
—, 7 = BhG 6, 45
1046, 5 = Bu 3, 8, 8
—, 5 = Bu 3, 9, 26
—, 6 = Ch 7, 24, 1
—, 6 = Mu 2, 2, 11
—, 6 = Bu 2, 4, 6
—, 7 = Bu 4, 4, 25
—, 8 = Bu 4, 5, 15
1047, 9 = Ch 3, 14, 2
—, 12 = 112, 8
1048, 1 = Mbh 12, 7125

IV, 1.

1049, 6 = Bu 2, 4, 5
—, 7 = Bu 4, 4, 21
—, 8 = Ch 8, 7, 1
1050, 4 = Bu 2, 4, 5
—, 8 = Bu 2, 4, 5
1051, 9 = Ch 4, 1, 4
—, 10 = Ch 4, 2, 2
—, 12 = Ch 3, 18, 1
—, 12 = Ch 3, 18, 3
1052, 5 = Ch 1, 5, 1
—, 6 = Ch 1, 5, 3
1053, 1 = Ch 6, 8, 7
1054, 10 = Ch 6, 8, 7
—, 13 = Bu 2, 4, 5
1055, 5 = Tu 2, 1
—, 5 = Bu 3, 9, 28
—, 6 ~ Bu 3, 8, 11
—, 6 = Mu 2, 1, 2

1055, 6 = Bu 3, 8, 8[129]
—, 6 = Bu 3, 8, 8
1057, 1 = Bu 4, 3, 23
—, 4 = Bu 4, 4, 22
—, 6 = ?[130]
1059, 1 = 924, 7
—, 3 = Bu 1, 4, 10
—, 4 = Bu 3, 4, 1
—, 5 = Bu 3, 7, 3
—, 5 = Ch 6, 8, 7
—, 9 = Ch 3, 18, 1
—, 9 = Ch 3, 19, 1
—, 11 = Bu 1, 4, 10
—, 12 = Bu 4, 4, 19
—, 13 = Bu 2, 4, 6
1060, 8 = Bu 4. 5, 15
—, 10 = Bu 4, 3, 22
1061, 4 = Ch 3, 18, 1
—, 5 = Ch 3, 19, 1
—, 6 = Ch 7, 1, 5
1063, 1 = Ch 3, 19, 1
—, 2 = Kshu 2, 2
—, 2 = Bu 5, 7, 1
—, 9 cf Kâ 1, 7
1065, 5 = Ch 3, 19, 4
—, 6 = Ch 7, 2, 2
—, 6 = Ch 7, 4, 3
—, 10 = Bs 3, 2, 38
—, 14 = Ch 1, 2, 1
—, 14 = Ch 2, 2, 1
—, 15 = Ch 2, 8, 1
1066, 1 = Ch 1, 6, 1
—, 12 = Ch 1, 6, 1
1067, 3 = Ch 2, 2, 1
—, 4 = Ch 2, 11, 1
—, 6 = Ch 3, 19, 1
—, 8 = Ch 2, 2, 1
—, 13 = Ch 1, 1, 10
1068, 2 = Ch 2, 2, 3
—, 6 = Ch 1, 1, 1
—, 7 = Ch 1, 1, 10
—, 12 = Ch 1, 6, 1

---

[125] Çruti; *yâvajjîva-çruteḥ* gloss.—[126] smṛiti, dharmaçâstra-like.—[127] "*tathâca uktaṃ smṛitikâraiḥ*".—[128] Upanishad-quotation.—[129] Mâdhy.—[130] smṛiti, probably Mahâbh. 12.

1069, 6 = Ch 1, 6, 1
—, 8 = Ch 1, 7, 9
—, 10 = Ch 2, 2, 1
1070, 3 = Ch 2, 11, 1
—, 5 = Ch 2, 9, 1
—, 7 = Ch 2, 7, 2
—, 7 = Ch 2, 8, 1
—, 9 = Ch 2, 2, 1
1071, 15 = Ch 7, 6, 1
1072, 2 = BhG 6, 11
—, 3 cf ad Ys 2, 46 [131]
—, 13 = Çv 2, 10
1073, 7 cf Bs 4, 1, 1
1074, 4 = Bu 4, 4, 2
—, 5 = ? [128]
—, 7 cf Bu 4, 4, 3
—, 10 ~ Çb 10, 6, 3, 1
—, 12 = BhG 8, 6
1075, 1 = BhG 8, 10
—, 1 = Ch 3, 17, 6
—, 11 = ? [130]
1076, 5 = Ch 4, 14, 3
—, 7 = Ch 5, 24, 2
—, 10 = Mu 2, 2, 8
1077, 2 = Ts 5, 3, 12, 1
1079, 5 = Bu 4, 4, 22 [132]
—, 8 = Mu 2, 2, 8
—, 11 = Ch 8, 4, 2
1080, 4 = Bu 4, 4, 22
—, 10 = Ch 6, 14, 2
1081, 9 cf BhG 2, 55
1082, 2 = Bu 4, 4, 22
—, 15 = 899, 7
1083, 4 = 899, 7
—, 15 = Ch 4, 17, 1
—, 15 = Ch 1, 1, 10
1084, 1 ~ Bu 4, 4, 22
—, 5 = Bu 1, 5, 2
—, 7 = BhG 2, 39
—, 8 = BhG 2, 49
—, 9 = Ch 1, 1, 10
—, 13 ~ Bu 4, 4, 22
1085, 3 = Ch 1, 1, 10
1086, 1 = Ch 6, 14, 2
—, 2 = Bu 4, 4, 6

IV, 2.

1087, 6 = Ch 6, 8, 6
1088, 3 = Bs 4, 2, 16
1089, 1 = Ch 6, 8, 6
—, 5 = Pu 3, 9
—, 10 = Ch 6, 8, 6
—, 14 = Ch 6, 8, 6
1090, 3 = Ch 6, 6, 5
—, 5 cf Ch 6, 2, 4
1091, 5 = Ch 6, 8, 6
—, 11 = Bu 4, 3, 38
—, 14 = Bu 4, 4, 2
1092, 2 = Bu 4, 4, 2
—, 2 = Bu 4, 4, 2
—, 4 = Ch 6, 8, 6
—, 7 = Ch 6, 8, 6
—, 11 = Ch 6, 8, 6
1093, 10 = Ch 5, 3, 3
—, 10 = Bs 3, 1, 2
—, 12 = Bu 4, 4, 5
—, 14 = Manu 1, 27
1094, 1 = Bu 3, 2, 13
—, 13 quotation?
1095, 1 = Ch 6, 8, 1. 3. 5
—, 6 = Ch 6, 8, 7
1096, 4 = Ch 6, 8, 6
—, 13 = Ku 5, 7
1098, 3 = Çb 8, 7, 2, 11
—, 6 = Bs 4, 2, 7
—, 8 = Bu 4, 4, 6
—, 13 = Çb 14, 7, 2, 8
1099, 9 ~ Bu 3, 2, 11
1100, 7 = Bu 4, 4, 2 [129]
—, 10 = Bu 4, 4, 6
1101, 3 = Bu 4, 4, 7
—, 6 = Mbh 12, 9657
—, 9 = ? [133]
—, 15 = ? [133]
1102, 6 = Pu 6, 5
—, 7 = Mu 3, 2, 7
1103, 5 = Pu 6, 5
1104, 2 = Bu 4, 4, 1
—, 4 = Bu 4, 4, 2 [129]
1105, 4 = Ch 8, 6, 6
—, 7 = Ch 8, 1, 1
—, 9 = Ch 8, 6, 1
—, 10 = Ch 8, 6, 5
—, 11 = Ch 8, 6, 6
1106, 9 = Ch 8, 6, 2
—, 13 cf Ch 8, 4, 2
1107, 7 = Ch 8, 6, 5
—, 14 cf Mbh 6,5672
—, 14 = Ch 5, 10, 1
1108, 4 = Bs 4, 3, 4
—, 5 = BhG 8, 23
1109, 1 = BhG 8, 24
—, 2 = BhG 8, 25
—, 4 = BhG 8, 23

IV, 3.

1110, 4 = Ch 8, 6, 5
—, 5 = Ch 5, 10, 3
—, 6 = Kshu 1, 3
—, 7 = Bu 5, 10, 1
—, 8 = Mu 1, 2, 11
1111, 1 = Ch 8, 6, 5
—, 2 = Ch 8, 6, 5
—, 7 = Bu 6, 2, 15
1112, 2 = Bu 6, 2, 15
—, 2 = Bu 5, 10, 1
—, 3 = Kshu 1, 7
—, 4 = Ch 8, 4, 3
—, 6 = Ch 8, 6, 5
—, 11 = Ch 5, 10, 8
1113, 3 = Kshu 1, 3
—, 9 = Ch 5, 10, 1
—, 14 = Bu 5, 10, 1
1114, 6 = Kshu 1, 3
—, 12 = Bu 6, 2, 15
1115, 4 = Ch 5, 10, 2
—, 5 = Kshu 1, 3
—, 6 = ? [134]
1116, 7 = Ch 5, 10, 1

[131] cf. Yogaçikhâ 2.—[132] Kâṇva.—[133] *smaryate.*—[134] with the addition, customary otherwise only in Chând. Up.: "*iti* (*tathâ*) *brâhmaṇam*".

1116, 9 = Kshu 1, 3
—, 11 = Çatap. br. 10, 2, 6, 8[134]
1117, 1 = Ch 5, 10, 2
1118, 1 = Ch 5, 10, 1
—, 6 = Ch 5, 10, 1
—, 7 = Ch 5, 10, 2
1119, 4 ~ Bu 6, 2, 15
—, 10 = Ch 5, 10, 2
1120, 4 = Bu 6, 2, 15
—, 9 = Bu 4, 4, 23
1121, 7 = Ch 4, 15, 6
—, 8 = Bu 6, 2, 15[129]
—, 8 = Ch 8, 6, 6
1122, 1 = 917, 1
—, 7 = Ch 5, 10, 2
—, 9 cf Paribhâshâ to Pâṇ 8, 3, 82
—, 12 = Ch 8, 6, 6
—, 14 ~ Ch 7, 24, 1
1123, 1 = Ku 2, 14
—, 4 = Ch 8, 14, 1
—, 5 = Ch 8, 14, 1
—, 6 = Ch 8, 14, 1
—, 7 = Vs 32, 3
—, 10 = Ch 8, 5, 3
—, 13 cf Bs 4, 3, 7–11 4, 3, 11–14
1124, 4 = Ch 8, 6, 6
—, 5 = Ch 8, 14, 1
—, 7 = Ch 3, 14, 2
—, 12 = 130, 12
1125, 1 = Bu 3, 4, 1
—, 2 = Ch 7, 25, 2
—, 2 ~ Mu 2, 2, 11
—, 9 = Çv 6, 19
—, 10 ~ Bu 3, 8, 8
—, 11 = Mu 2, 1, 2
—, 11 = Bu 4, 4, 25
—, 12 = Bu 3, 9, 26
1126, 10 = Îça 7
—, 11 = Bu 4, 2, 4
—, 11 = Tu 2, 9
—, 12 = Tu 2, 9
1127, 2 = Bu 4, 4, 19
1127, 6 = Ch 6, 8, 3
—, 8 = Tu 3, 1
—, 12 = Bu 4, 4, 6
—, 14 = Bs 4, 2, 13
1128, 9 = Ch 6, 8, 7
1129, 14 = Ch 5, 10, 7
1130, 9 = Âpdh 1,7,20,3
1131, 8 = Çv 3, 8
—, 11 = Bu 2, 4, 14^{5}_{2}
1132, 3 = Ch 4, 10, 5
—, 4 = Ch 8, 1, 1
—, 7 = Bu 4, 4, 6
—, 8 = Tu 2, 1
—, 11 = Bu 4, 4, 6
1133, 6 = Pu 5, 2
—, 9 = Bu 3, 8, 8
—, 10 = Ch 3, 14, 2
—, 13 = Ch 8, 2, 1
1134, 3 = Bs 2, 3, 29
—, 3 = Bs 4, 3, 7
—, 4 = Bs 4, 3, 12
—, 12 = Bs 3, 3, 31
1135, 6 = 112, 8
—, 9 = Ch 5, 10, 2
—, 14 = Ch 7, 1, 5
1136, 1 = Ch 7, 2, 1. 2
—, 2 = Ch 7, 3, 1

IV, 4.

1137, 3 = Ch 8, 12, 3
1138, 11 = Ch 8, 9, 1 8, 10, 2 8, 11, 1
1139, 1 = Ch 8, 12, 1. 3
—, 3 = Ch 8, 7, 1
—, 13 = Ch 8, 7, 1
—, 16 = Bu 4, 4, 16
—, 17 = Bs 1, 3, 40
1140, 4 = Ch 8, 12, 3
—, 7 = Ch 6, 8, 7
—, 7 = Bu 1, 4, 10
—, 8 = Ch 7, 24, 1
—, 8 = Bu 4, 3, 23
—, 10 cf Bs 4, 3, 15
—, 11 = Ku 4, 15
1140, 13 cf Mu 3, 2, 8
—, 14 = Ch 7, 24, 1
—, 15 = Ch 7, 25, 2
1141, 5 cf Ch 8, 7, 1
—, 8 = Ch 8, 7, 1
—, 10 = Ch 8, 12, 3
—, 11 = Ch 8, 1, 6
1142, 6 = Bu 4, 5, 13[135]
—, 11 = Bs 3, 2, 11
—, 13 = Ch 7, 25, 2
1143, 7 = Ch 8, 2, 1
1144, 9 = Ch 8, 2, 1
1145, 5 = Ch 8, 1, 6
—, 8 = Ch 8, 2, 1
—, 12 = ?[136]
1146, 1 = Ch 7, 26, 2
1147, 7 = Bs 4, 4, 11
1148, 3 = Ch 7, 26, 2
1149, 1 = Bu 2, 4, 14
—, 2 = Bu 4, 3, 30
—, 3 = Bu 4, 3, 32
—, 6 = Ch 6, 8, 1
—, 7 = Bu 4, 4, 6
—, 10 = Bu 2, 4, 12
—, 11 = Bu 4, 5, 15
—, 12 = Bu 4, 3, 19
1150, 4 = Tu 1, 6, 2
—, 5 = Tu 1, 5, 3
—, 5 = Ch 8, 1, 6
1151, 6 = Tu 1, 6, 2
—, 11 = Tu 1, 6, 2
—, 13 = Tu 1, 6, 2
1152, 4 = Ch 3, 12, 6
—, 11 = Mu 2, 2, 10
—, 13 = BhG 15, 6
1153, 3 ~ Kshu 1, 7
—, 4 = Bu 1, 5, 20
—, 5 = Bu 1, 5, 23
—, 12 = Ch 8, 5, 3
1154, 1 = Ch 8, 5, 3
—, 5 = Ch 8, 6, 6
—, 5 = Bu 6, 2, 15
—, 6 = Ch 4, 15, 6
—, 7 = Ch 8, 15, 1
—, 9 = Bs 4, 3, 10

[135] Kâṇva.—[136] "*evaṃ hi âha âmnâyaḥ*".

III. Index

of the proper Names in Çañkara's Commentary on the Brahma-sûtras, with the exception of those, which appear in the Upanishad passages and Sûtras treated.

Agnirahasya 882, 4, 10. 883, 13. 943, 2.
Aniruddha 600, 12. 14. 601, 11. 602, 8. 603, 11.
Apântaratamas 913, 8. 914, 6. 13.
Ayodhyâ 174, 12.
Arundhatî 105, 8.
Ardha-vainâçika 546, 6.
Âtharvaṇa (Muṇḍ. Up.) 639, 3; 640, 6. 851, 12; (Praçna-Up.) 714, 1.
Âtharvaṇika (brahma-sûkte) 686, 2; (Muṇḍ.) 847, 1. 850, 13. 899, 5. 920, 2. 851, 3. 13; (upanishadârambhe) 892, 7.
Âditya 286, 2.
Âdhvaryava means Taitt. Saṃh. 960, 9.
Âpastamba 410, 6. 1130, 9.
Âyurveda 802, 14.
Ârcâbhin 903, 5.
Ârya 546, 2.
Ârhata 586, 6. 14. 591, 3. 651, 2.
îçvarâḥ (inferior gods) 300, 3. 6. 301, 1. 303, 9. 397, 8 (Vaivaçvata-âdi).
îçvaragîtâḥ (*i. e.*, Bhag. G.) 455, 13. 687, 9
Udgâtriveda 919, 6.
Uddâlaka 977, 10.
Upanishad, "secret name", 884, 13. 14. 885, 7. 886, 5. 8. 13. 887, 6.
Upavarsha 291, 7. 953, 9.
Ushasti (Brih.-*sta*) 922, 3.
Ṛigveda 47, 2.
Aitareyaka (Ait. Up.) 871, 6.
Aitareyin (Ait. âr.) 872, 10. 924, 6.
Aupanishada (= Vedântin) 515, 3. 624, 4.
aupanishadam darçanam 976, 8.
Kaṭha (-*ânâm saṃhitâ*) 1016, 11; (not Kaṭhop.) 893, 1; (Kaṭhop.) 920, 6.
Kaṭhavallîshu 177, 8. 179, 7. 350, 2. 1122, 15.
Kaṇabhuj (= *Kaṇâda*) 436, 4. 526, 10. 608, 7.
Kapila 334, 11. 408, 7. 411, 5. 412, 3. 5. 6. 13. 436, 2. 4.
Kamalâsana 256, 9.
Kalpasûtra 938, 6.
Kâṭhaka (the Up.) 335, 6. 852, 5. 869, 2; (the Kâṭhakam) 859, 12.
Kâṇabhuja (sûtra) 524, 3. 647, 7.
Kâṇâda 91, 5. 527, 6. 696, 5. 13. 697, 11.
Kâṇva 198, 5. 369, 1. 5. 12. 881, 7.
Kâpila 356, 5. 407, 9. 412, 4. 12. 414, 3.
Kâryabrahman 257, 2. 1120, 5.
Kuṇḍapâyinâm ayane 932, 8. 1020, 1.
Kuru 781, 12. 15.
Krishṇagupta 1118, 5.
Krishṇa-dvaipâyana 913, 9.
Kauṇḍapâyinâm ayane 931, 11.
Kauthumakam 846, 1
Kauçîtakam (sic) 846, 1.
Kaushîtakibrâhmaṇa (Kaush. Up.) 378, 2. 865, 3.
Kaushîtakibrâhmaṇo-panishad 154, 5.
Kaushîtakinaḥ (Kaush. Up.) 423, 8, 763, 2. 864, 1. 906, 7. 1113, 3;

-âm agnishṭomabrâhmaṇam 893, 4
Kaushîtakirahasyam (Kaush. Up.) 900, 8.
Gaṅgâ 792, 1. 2.
Gautama 321, 7.
Citragupta 764, 17. 765, 3.
Caitraratha 319, 1. 3 8. 9.
Caitrarathi 319, 5. 7. 10.
Chandoga 625, 11. 849, 1. 6. 14. 850, 4. 855, 5. 863, 8. 876, 4. 7. 878, 2. 3. 928, 2. 11. 1012, 8.
[*Chandogabrâhmaṇam* Gov. to 288, 1.]
Chândogya 134, 11. 222, 1, 606, 3. 11. 615, 5. 617, 5. 629, 2. 852, 9. 854, 6. 855, 13. 856, 4. 875, 12. 876, 3. 927, 12. 928, 3. 929, 5. 8. 12. 14. 15. 930, 9. 938, 11. 940, 1. 1038, 1. 1054, 10. 1114, 14. 15.
Janaka 915, 8.
Jayasiṅha 1118, 5.
Jânaka 915, 9.
Jâbâla 321, 7. 924, 7. 931, 4. 991, 5. 1059, 1.
Jâhnavî (= Gaṅgâ) 653, 11.
Jaina 590, 7.
Jaimini 1083, 7. — The Jaimini - sûtram is quoted by the names: prathame tantre 897, 1. 953, 9. 1011, 12; prathame kâṇḍe 919, 9. 951, 3; pûrvasmin kâṇḍe 944, 4; çâstra-pramukha' eva prathame pâde 953, 5; adhikâralakshaṇe 1027, 1.
ḍittha ḍavittha 733, 10.
Tantrântarîya (= Sâṅkhya) 718, 2.
Tarkasamaya 78, 7.
Tâṇḍin (Chând. Up.) 889, 10. 890, 8. 899, 3. 907, 7. 908, 5; (*-âm upanishadi shashthe prapâṭhake*) (= Chând. Up. VI) 923, 8; (Chând. br.) 892, 9.
Târkika 91, 6.
Târkikasamaya 109, 5.
Taittirîya 625, 12.
Taittirîyaka 890, 1. 4. 8; *-am* 114, 12. 607, 9. 615, 2. 617, 7. 629, 7. 852, 6. 867, 2. 890, 14. 892, 5.
Tvâshṭra 159, 13. 14. 16.
Daksha 913, 14.
Devadatta 227, 1. 2. 286, 5. 290, 2. 292, 5. 441, 9. 463, 12. 464, 2. 467, 3. 538, 11. 542, 2. 602, 5. 641, 5. 664, 8. 699, 3. 6. 865, 10. 12. 866, 10. 929, 4. 997, 1. 2.
Devala 404, 4.
Droṇa 768, 2. 3
Draupadî 768, 2.
Dvaipâyana 660, 1.
Dhṛishṭadyumna 768, 2, 4.
Nakshatreshṭi-vidhi 304, 9.
Nâciketa 764, 11.
Nârada 809, 5. 913, 14.
Nârâyaṇa 601, 3. 809, 5.
Nâsadâsîya 716, 6.
Nimi 913, 10.
Nishâda 368, 5.
Nyâyavit-samaya 594, 1.
Pañcajanyâ Viç 368, 6.
Pañcarâtra 603, 13.
Pañcâla 781, 13. 14.
Paçupati 592, 5.
Pâṭaliputra 463, 12. 464, 2. 1093, 2.
Pâṇini 48, 2.
Purâṇa 410, 5. 495, 10.
Purushasûkta 151, 13.
Pûrṇavarman 465, 14.
Paiṅginaḥ 890, 8. 903, 3.
Paiṅginâṃ rahasyabrâhmaṇam 899, 10.
Paiṅgi - Upanishad 232, 12 (= the following).
Paiṅgi - rahasyabrâhmaṇam 184, 2.
Paurâṇika 482, 6. 633, 11. 764, 14.
Prajâpati 266, 14. 288, 1. 289, 5.
Pradyumna 600, 12. 14. 601, 10. 602, 7. 603, 10.
Prâjâpatya 260, 9.
Balavarman 703, 1. 1118, 5.
Bâdarâyaṇa 1083, 7. 1153, 8.
Bâhva 808, 12.
Bṛihadâraṇyaka 237, 2; (shashthe prapâṭhake = Bṛih. IV) 330, 4; 385, 8. 882, 6. 10. 883, 13. 884, 9. 1031, 7.
Bṛihaspati 894, 10. 897, 5.
Bauddha 566, 12.
Brahmán 913, 10. 11. 12. 13. 917, 1.
brâhmaṇa (means Chând. Up.) 143, 6 (Ch. 3, 13, 7). 240, 11 (7, 26, 1). 262, 12 (8, 9, 3). 367, 7 (7, 15, 1). 390, 4 (6, 3, 2). 906, 2 (8, 13, 1). 1014, 11 (1, 10, 1); (unknown passage) 1115, 6; (Çat. Br. 10, 2, 6, 8) 1116, 11.

Bhagavadgîtâḥ 132, 9. 275, 4. 410, 5. 842, 8. 1012, 1; cf. *îçvara-gîtâḥ.*
Bhagavant 601, 1. 3. 7. 14. 603, 7. 8. 604, 2. 3.
Bhadrasena 102, 2. 103, 14.
Bhâgavata 600, 10. 602, 6.
Bhârata Varsha 782, 9.
Bhâllavin 902, 9. 903, 6.
Bhîshma 1107, 14. 1108, 2.
Bhṛigu 913, 11.
Mathurâ 1093, 2.
Madhucchandas 301, 6.
Manu 407, 4. 412, 8. 9. 414, 4. 437, 3. 440, 6. 537, 11. 546, 1. 764, 10.
Marutaḥ 286, 2.
Mahâbhârata 1101, 6.
Mâgadha 833, 8.
Mâdhyandina 198, 6. 369, 1. 10. 881, 8. 1011, 4.
Mâheçvara 592, 4.
Mitrâvaruṇau 913, 11.
Maitreyîbrâhmaṇa (Bṛih. Up. 2, 4) 385, 8. 1006, 5.
[*Moksha-dharma* (plur.) Gov. to 309, 10.]
Mokshaçâstra 448, 3. 5; (plur.) 809, 14.
Yajñadatta 286, 5. 290, 2. 292, 5. 464, 2. 699, 5. 6. 997, 1. 2.
Yama 763, 15. 764, 3. 4. 10. 15. 765, 2. 3. 801, 3.
Yama-niyama-vidyâ 907, 12.
Yâma 764, 1.
Yâmadagnye'hîne (= Jâmad.) 919, 4.
Yâska 39, 2.
Yoga 415, 13. 416, 4. 5. 417, 2. 5. 11. 816, 3; (not nom. pr.) 997, 5.
Yogaçâstra 96, 8. 416, 4; (Yogas. 1, 6) 723, 11; (plur.) 1072, 3. 1148, 9.
Yoga-sâṅkhye 1108, 12 (cf. *Sâṅkhya-yogau*).
Yogasmṛiti 415, 8.
Yogin (sing.) 194, 11. 195, 8. 283, 10.
Yoginaḥ 92, 6. 95, 4. 96, 7. 827, 11. 828, 5.
Râṇâyanîyânâṃ khileshu 887, 9; — *upanishadi* (Chând. Up.) 887, 10.
Rudra 286, 2. 913, 13.
Raurava 764, 13. 16.
Lokâyatika 34, 4. 505, 6. 506, 1. 954, 6. 956. 3.
Vasishṭha 913, 10.
Vasu 286, 2.
Vâjasaneyaka 221, 12. 846, 1. 852, 8. 854, 2. 855, 11. 856, 12. 875, 8. 876, 2. 917. 13. 926, 3. 927, 11. 928, 7. 929, 6. 7. 12. 930, 1. 4. 938, 9. 1114, 15.
Vâjasaneyibrâhmaṇa (Çat. Br.) 220, 13; (Bṛih. Up.) 865, 4. 5. 939, 8.
Vâjasaneyin 216, 6. 12. 384, 9. 847, 10. 848, 10. 849, 6. 850, 1. 855, 3. 4. 863, 8. 876, 8. 878, 2. 5. 882, 4. 912, 1. 922, 3. 928, 2. 13. 943, 2. 986, 11. 1012, 9. 1114, 12; V—âm upanishad-ârambhe (Ç. Br. 14, 1. 1) 893, 3.
Vâmadeva 159, 10. 653, 1. 1044, 10.
Vâmadevyavidyâ (Chând. 2, 13, 2) 1013, 7.
Vâruṇa yajña 913, 12.
Vâshkali 808, 11.
Vâsudeva 412, 6. 600, 10. 12. 13. 601, 1. 10. 11. 602, 14. 603, 5. 7. 9. 13. 604, 1. 7. 1045, 4.
Vidura 316, 6. 322, 12.
Vidhikâṇḍa 78, 7.
Vivasana - samaya 581, 6.
Viçve devâḥ 286, 2.
Vishṇu 860, 10. 1058, 13. 1059, 6. 1065, 12.
Vishṇumitra 570, 12. 795, 3. 997, 2.
Visic (= Digambara) 590, 2.
Veda-vyâsa 298, 5 (cf. *Vyâsa*).
Vedântârtha - sampradâyavidaḥ (means Gauḍapâda) 433, 1 (vgl. 375. 1).
Vaideha 833, 9.
Vainâçika (Buddhists) 546, 6. 555, 6. 559, 2. 560, 1. 4. 7. 565, 11. 580, 2.
Vainâçika tantra 580, 10.
Vainâçika-samaya 562, 9. 563, 2. 580, 8.
Vaivaçvata 397, 8. 764, 7.
Vaiçeshika 520, 4. 525, 8. 10. 533, 5. 538, 2. 543, 6. 546, 5. 551, 1. 592, 7. 649, 11. 696, 3. 698, 9.
Vyâsa 313, 9. 440, 6. 690, 11. 764, 10 (cf. *Vedavyâsa*).
Çatakratu 362, 7.
Çabarasvâmin 953, 8.
Çâtyâyanakam 846, 1.

Çâṭyâyaninaḥ 898, 1. 899, 7. 902, 10. 907, 7. 908, 5.
Çâṇḍilya 604, 8 (882, 4).
Çuka Vaiyâsaki 1101, 9. 15.
Çaunaka 301, 6.
Çrughna 463, 12. 464, 2. 1093, 2.
Çvetâçvatarâḥ (means Çvet. Up.) 920, 2.
Çvetâçvatarâṇâṃ mantropanishad 110, 5.
Çvetâçvataropanishad 416, 1.
shashṭha-prapâṭhaka 106, 1 (means Chând. VI).
Saṃyamana 763, 16. 764, 10.
Saṃvarta 1022, 5.
Sagaraputra 412, 6.
Sañkarsha 942, 5.
Saṃkarshaṇa 600, 12. 13. 601, 1. 10. 12. 602, 7. 12. 603, 10.
Satyaloka 257, 2.
Sanatkumâra 913, 13.
Sampradâyavidaḥ (means Gauḍapâda) 375, 3 (cf. *Vedântârthasampr.*).
Sarvavainâçika 546, 7.
Savitar 914, 8.
Sâñkhya 64, 6. 90, 4. 91, 4. 10. 93, 9. 121, 6. 345, 10. 346, 9. 347, 12. 354, 6. 356, 6. 360, 10. 361, 3. 417, 5. 10. 420, 14. 497, 6. 498, 1, 8. 499, 1. 5. 508, 7. 514, 13. 515, 3. 519, 8. 525, 7. 528, 8. 539, 1. 647, 8. 695, 9. 696, 5. 697, 9.
Sâñkhya-Yogau 416, 10. 417, 7. 8. 592, 2. 596, 1 (cf. *Yoga-sâñkhye*).
Sâñkhya-smṛiti (means Manu!) 196, 12; (doubtful) 280, 4. 415, 8. 417, 1.
Sîtâ 768, 2.
Sugata 566, 14. 581, 1.
Sugata samaya 581, 3. 6.
Subrahmaṇya 310, 2.
Sulabhâ 915, 8.
Saugata 591, 3.
Saugataṃ matam 554, 7.
Saugata samaya 550, 2. 558, 7.
Skanda 913, 14.
Hari 174, 16.
Hiraṇyagarbha 247, 6. 300, 4. 6. 300, 9. 301, 1. 339, 3. 1121, 13.
Hairaṇyagarbha 724, 8.

IV. Terms of the Vedânta.

P. page of the present work, n. note, p. page of the commentary on the Brahmasûtras.

abhimâna delusion (of empirical knowledge) P. 56. 281. 299.

abhyudaya felicity (in the hereafter; perhaps also that in the following incarnation) P. 104. 437 n.

âcâra custom, manner of life P. 12. 90 n. 391.

âçrama brahmanical stage of life P. 16.

âçraya base, support P. 128.

adhidaivatam in cosmological respect (cf. *adhyâtmam*) P. 140. p. 726, 9. 12.

adhikaranam section in works, chapter P. 39.

adhikrita called to cf. P. 60. 382.

adhvaryu priest of the Sâmaveda P. 5 ff.

adhyaksha overseer (1) of the body: individual soul P. 369. p. 161, 1. 270, 7; (2) in the lower Brahman-world P. 65 n.; creator p. 377, 1. 2. 3. 7. 10.

adhyâtmam adv. in psychological respect (cf. *adhidaivatam*) P. 140. 158. p. 726, 9. 11.

adhyâtmam n. = *pratyagâtman* p. 158, 3.

adhyâsa the (wrong) transference P. 53. 318.

adhyâya main section in works, lection P. 4. 30. 39.

adrishtam the invisible result of works, the moral merit P. 377 n. 210.

âgama the (sacred) tradition P. 91. p. 418, 7. 8. 426, 5. 6. 9. 435, 11. 437, 13. 439, 7.

agni fire, god of fire P. 156.

agnihotram fire-sacrifice P. 156.

agniloka region of the Devayâna P. 441.

aham brahma asmi "I am Brahman" Bṛih. 1, 4, 10.

ahampratyaya selfconsciousness P. 330. 54 n. 317. 321.

ahampratyayin the subject presenting the "I" = Manas P. 53 n. 54 n. 330.

ahañkâra selfconsciousness P. 330. 203. 321.

ahañkartar the individual soul P. 321. 330. 53 n.

aiçvaryam ruling power, lordship (1) of the gods P. 66. 67. (2) of the pious, who have entered by the Devayâna P. 444 ff.

akâmayamâna he who desires not (more), the liberated P. 194. 80. 315. 427.

âkâça ether, space, understood as a material element P. 231.

âkâra form P. 205.

âkriti form, εἶδος, species P. 69.

aksharam the Imperishable (1) Brahman P. 133, (2) the seed of the world P. 133. 371 n.

amritatvam immortality, the deliverance from dying P. 149. 287.

ânanda Bliss P. 139. 212.

ananya, ananyatvam identical, identity cf. P. 267.

anavasthâ the regressus in infinitum P. 125.

andaja P. 240.

andha-paramparâ p. 85, 6. 578, 3. 593, 6.

antahkaranam the inner organ = Manas P. 330.

antar-âtman the inner self, the soul P. 214.

antaryâmin the inner ruler, Brahman P. 149.

anu fine, subtle, minute P. 308. 311. 332. 336.

anubhava sensation, feeling, the (inner) perception P. 90 n. 96. 241 n. 406. 418 n.

anuçaya residue of works cf. P. 387 ff.

anugraha grace P. 86.

anukalpa the following period of the world p. 300, 10.

anumânam inference P. 88, cf. P. 23.

anuvâda p. 312, 6. 676, 14. 677, 1. 785, 4. 850, 3. 884, 4. 1010, 7. 1035, 2.

aparam brahma the lower Brahman P. 102 ff.

aparâ vidyâ the teaching of the lower Brahman P. 102. 105.

apâna the inhaling P. 335.

âpas (nom. plur.) water P. 235. 240. 371.

apavâda p. 227, 3. 860, 12.

apavarga end p. 102, 3. 356, 4; liberation p. 816, 4. 954, 10.

âptavacanam P. 89.

apûrvam the moral merit P. 377.

âranyakam section of a Brâhmanam, destined for the study in the woods (Çañk. ad Brih. p. 3, 2) P. 8. cf. p. 898, 6.

arcis flame P. 380. 441.

arddhajaratîya P. 139 n.

arthavâda P. 7; p. 280, 9. 287, 3. 307, 9. 423, 13. 308, 2; 477, 14; 309, 13. 310, 7. 8. 313, 4. 441, 4. 914, 1. 1154, 3; 975, 1. 6. 980, 8. 1014, 6. 1016, 12. 13; 948, 3. 5. 1015, 7; 312, 6. 9; 937, 6.

ârya belonging to the friends (*arya*); Aryans P. 15.

asangatvam the fact that the soul is not affected by the terrestrial P. 277 n. cf. 324.

asmatpratyaya P. 54 n. 330.

âtman the Âtman, the self, the soul, god P. 17. 49. 120.

âtmavidyâ the teaching of the Âtman P. 3 n.

ato 'nyad ârtam "what is different from him is afflicted" (Brih. 3, 4, 2); cf. p. 1139, 12: *vikârasya ârtatva-prasiddheh.*

aupanishada âtman p. 672, 9; *purusha* 205, 11; *jñânam* 439, 6; *darçanam* 496, 8; 976, 8; = Vedântin 515, 3. 624, 4.

avadhânam attention (function of Manas) P. 331.

avagamanam P. 241 n.

avayava part, corpuscule P. 307.

avidyâ ignorance (the empirical knowledge) P. 55 ff. 58 n. 302.

avidyâ-avasthâ the empirical point of view p. 680, 12. 682, 3 (cf. *prapañca-avasthâ* 817, 14, *vibhâga-avasthâ* 838, 13).

avyaktam the Unmanifest (1) Brahman P. 213, (2) the seed of the world P. 228. 371 n.; cf. p. 343, 1.

âyurveda p. 802, 14.

balâkâ P. 226 n.

bâlyam childlike simplicity P. 143.

bandha attachment p. 830, 10.

bandhyâputra P. 70 n.

bhikshu beggar = *saṃnyâsin* P. 16 ff.
bhogyam what is to be enjoyed, the fruit of works, the world P. 267. 294.
bhoktar the enjoyer (and sufferer), the soul P. 267. 175. 294.
bhoktṛitvam to be the enjoyer P. 323.
bhrama the error (of empirical knowledge) P. 53. 102. 299.
bhrânti = *bhrama* p. 474, 1.
bhûman illimitation P. 203.
bhûta-âçraya the subtle body P. 376.
bhûtam (1) element (2) living being P. 238.
brahmacârin Brahman student P. 16. 164. 68 n.
brahmacâryam life as such a student, renunciation P. 162.
brahmaloka (1) the world of Brahmân P. 162. 441. (2) Bráhman as the world P. 164. (3) he whose world is the Brahman P. 196.
brahma-mîmâṅsâ research of Brahman, doctrine of the Vedânta cf. P. 20.
bráhman (neutr.) (1) the prayer (2) the Bráhman P. 17. 49. 119.
brahmán (masc.) (1) he who prays, the priest P. 5 ff., (2) Brahmán as a popular deity P. 119 n.
brâhmaṇa he who prays, the Brahman P. 13 (in its exact meaning P. 62. 143. 133. 196, the opposite: *brahma-bandhu* P. 262.
brâhmaṇam species of Vedic literature P. 7 ff.
brahmaṇaspati the lord of prayer, a mythological personification of prayer, forerunner of the Brahman-conception P. 17.
brahma-vidyâ the teaching about the Brahman P. 3 n. 162. 408.
bṛihaspati = *brahmaṇaspati.*
buddhi (1) the perception, (2) the intellect in general; not a distinct psychic faculty P. 330, though it is occasionally counted as that P. 414.
buddhi-indriya's the (five) organs of perception P. 329.
çabda the revelation, Çruti P. 93.
çaçavishâṇam P. 70 n.
çâkhâ branch (of the Veda), Vedaschool P. 5. 9 ff.
çakti power P. 70. 227 ff.; 113 n. 318 n.
çakti - âtmanâ δυνάμει potentially P. 314.
çâlagrâma p. 174, 16. 188, 12. 253, 12.
caṇḍâla, câṇḍâla variation of the Çûdras, lowest human class P. 157. 191. 364.
caraka a wandering scholar P. 15.
caraṇam the (moral) conduct P. 391.
çârîra the individual soul cf. p. 171, 11 ff. 461.
çarîram the body; cf. P. 177 n. 427.
caitanyam spirituality P. 58. 135. 212. 295. 309. 324.
çata-adhikâ nâḍî cf. *sushumnâ.*
citragupta P. 383.
cittam P. 330.
çraddhâ faith P. 372. 378.
çruti revelation, holy scripture P. 23. 90. 90 n.
çûdra member of the fourth caste P. 13. 60 ff.
çuktikâ mother of pearl p. 14, 4. 86, 13.
dakshiṇâ reward of sacrifice P. 14.
darçanam conception of the world, philosophical system cf. P. 19.
deça-kâla-nimitta P. 317.
deha the (coarse) body P. 325. 427.
dehavîjâni bhûtasûkshmâṇi = *sûkshmaṃ çarîram* P. 370.
dehin individual soul P. 427.
deva old Vedic god P. 65 ff. (whereas Brahman is *îçvara*).
devaloka world of the gods, region of the Devayâna P. 441.
devayâna path of the gods P. 362. 440.

dharma (1) quality P. 53. 527,
(2) duty P. 82. 393.
dharma-sûtra's species of vedic literature P. 12.
dharmavyâda p. 322, 12.
drishṭânta example of experience P. 93.
drishṭi p. 856, 12. 880, 12. 14. 1062, 4. P. 27 n.
dvija the twice born, reborn through the Upanayanam, member of the three upper castes P. 14. 16 n. 60.
etad vai tad "Verily, this is that" P. 148. 155.
gauṇa figurative P. 328.
gâyatrî P. 168.
grahaṇam P. 241 n.
graha-âvishṭa madman P. 295.
grihastha P. 16. 419.
guṇa attribute P. 104.
guṇavâda p. 312, 7. 8. 937, 6. 751, 3. 945, 2. 994, 5.
Hiraṇyagarbha a mythological personification of the creative power P. 65 n. 119 n. 336.
hrid, hridayam heart P. 162.
hridaya-granthi the knot of the heart P. 429.
hotar the caller, priest of the Ṛigveda P. 5.
îçvara lord, god, Brahman considered personally P. 65. 119. 271.
îçvarâḥ inferior gods P. 65 n.; probably personifications of the powers (P. 227 ff.) of Brahman.
Indra old Vedic god P. 65. 69.
indraloka region of the Devayâna P. 441.
indriyas organs of perception and will of which there are ten besides Manas P. 329 ff.
itihâsa epic poem P. 430; p. 308, 1. 280, 9. 307, 9. 423, 13. 477, 14. 313, 6. 322, 14. 913, 7.
jagat world, especially the ensouled; defined p. 38, 2.
jagad-vimbam world-disk P. 238 n.
jaṅgamam the movable P. 239.
jarâyuja P. 240.
jîva, jîva âtman the individual soul (defined p. 100, 16) P. 120. 318.
[*jîvan-mukta, jîvan-mukti*] P. 425.
jñâna-kâṇḍa Part of Knowledge in the Veda P. 21. 19 n.
jñânam P. 241 n.
jñânân mokshaḥ "from knowledge comes deliverance" P. 269; cf. p. 916, 11. 438, 2.
ka p. 377, 4.
kaivalyam absoluteness, liberation p. 913, 3. 914, 9. 11. 915, 1. 916, 14. 917, 10. 1086, 9. 1129, 2. 1130, 15. 1149, 7. 9.
kalpa world-period, lasting from the creation to the dissolution of the world P. 70 ff. 237. 227; *atîta-kalpa, vartamâna-kalpa, kalpa-antaram* p. 301, 1 ff. 299, 6.
kâma desire P. 152 n.
kamalâsana P. 164
kâmayamâna he who desires P. 194.
karaṇam organ, physical and psychic P. 136. 341. 367.
kâraṇam cause P. 232. 256 ff. 275.
karma-âçaya store of works P. 388 n.
karma-âçraya the moral substratum P. 375.
karma-indriyas the (five) organs of action P. 329.
karma-kâṇḍa the Part of Works in the Veda P. 20. 19 n.
karma-mîmâṅsâ cf. *mîmâṅsâ*.
karman work P. 152 n. 315 ff. 353. 402. 411. 421 ff. 388; is threefold: *çârîram, vâcikam, mânasam* p. 61, 6. 10. 71, 4.
kartar the doer, individual soul P. 175. 316 ff. 338. 423.
kartritvam to be the doer P. 318. 323. 422.
kârya-karaṇas the organs of action p. 161, 1. 167, 5. 199, 5.

kârya-karaṇa-sañghâta the complex of the organs of action, *i. e.*, the body P. 298. 353, p. 473, 17. 455, 4. 686, 5 (synonymous word *deha* p. 787, 13); 76, 9. 197, 15. 675, 15. 682, 3. 727, 6. 179, 12.

kâryam effect P. 237. 256 ff.

kâryam brahma the lower Brahman p. 1119, 9. 10. 1120, 5. 1121, 10. 12. 1154, 8.

kleça affection (for example love, hate) P. 84. 411.

koça p. 123, 11. 867, 11, P. 137.

kramamukti progressive liberation (or liberation by steps) P. 398. 436 ff.

kratu insight P. 447, opinion, will P. 152. 193.

kriyâ-kâraka-phalam retribution to the doer of the deed p. 273, 12. 291, 6. 987, 6. 447, 3.

kshatriya warrior, member of the second caste P. 13.

kshema cessation of wandering, liberation P. 424.

kshetrajña individual soul p. 180, 7. 15. 181, 4. 6. 11. 772, 5.

liñgam characteristic P. 90 n. 92. 275.

lokâyatika materialist P. 126. 287.

manas central organ of imagination and conscious will P. 330 ff.

mañca p. 747, 7 (cf. ad *Praçna* p. 192, 4).

maṇḍalam section of the Ṛigveda P. 13. 15.

mantra hymns and sacrificial formulas of the Veda P. 6. 90.

mâyâ the illusion (of empirical reality) P. 100. 187. 228. 254. 275. 278. 299. 345.

mâyâmayî mahâsushuptiḥ p. 342, 9. P. 228.

mâyâvin magician P. 100. 187. 254. 275. 278. 299.

mîmâñsâ (1) research, (2) the system of *Jaimini* P. 20.

mithyâjñânam the false (empirical) knowledge P. 53. 55. 313 (the opposite: *samyagjñânam, samyagdarçanam*).

mṛigatṛishṇikâ fata morgana, phantasmagoria p. 445, 7.

mukhya âtman Brahman P. 120, p. 104, 4. 105, 7.

mukhya prâṇa central organ of unconscious life P. 333 ff. 339 ff.

mukti = ***moksha***.

muni an inspired one, ascetic (especially a silent one) P. 142 (etymology p. 1036, 2).

mûrdhanyâ nâḍî cf. ***sushumnâ***.

moksha liberation (the opposite: *bandha*).

nâḍî the vein P. 347 ff.

naishṭhika P. 16.

nâma-rûpam (name and form, *i. e.*, impressions of ear and eye, sense-impressions) the sense-world p. 93, 13. 96, 6. 111, 3; 816, 8. 12. 817, 7; 376, 7; 205, 10; 1133, 12; 391, 2; 473, 17.

nânâtvam diversity (of the soul from Brahman) P. 52.

naraka, nâraka hell P. 382. 390 n. p. 420, 6. 758, 4.

neti, neti! P. 211.

nigamanam p. 128, 7.

niḥçreyasam the summum bonum, liberation p. 27, 1. 203, 5. 352, 4. 396, 7. 1099, 1; 417, 2. 3. 1133, 2.

nimittam the causa efficiens P. 223. 323, the motive P. 113 n. 318 n.

nirguṇam brahma the attribute-free (higher) Brahman P. 102 ff. 205 ff.

nirguṇâ vidyâ the doctrine of the higher Brahman P. 102.

nirvâṇam extinction, bliss, only p. 1154, 10 (P. 448).

nirviçesham brahma the undifferentiated (higher) Brahman P. 102 ff. 205 ff.

nyâya the system of Gotama P. 20.

om P. 198 ff. 8 n. 133.
pâda the foot, the quarter P. 39.
padârtha the conception P. 414.
pañcâgnividyâ the doctrine of the five fires P. 361 ff.
[*pañcîkaraṇam*] P. 241.
pâṇḍityam erudition P. 143.
parabrahmavid the wise one, the knower of the higher Brahman p. 1098, 11. 1099, 6. 1102, 1. 4. 12. 1131, 15.
paramâṇu atom P. 310. 332.
paramârtha-avasthâ, pâramârthikî avasthâ the standpoint of the highest reality, the metaphysical standpoint P. 106. 271.
paramâtman the highest soul, Brahman P. 120. 275.
param brahma the higher Brahman P. 102 ff.
parâ vidyâ the higher doctrine of the *param brahma* P. 102.
parispanda animation P. 335.
parivrâjaka = *saṃnyâsin* P. 16 ff. 393.
paulkasa variation of the Çûdra P. 191.
phalam the fruit (of works), retribution P. 323.
pitriyâna the path of the fathers P. 363. 380.
prabodha the (spiritual) awakening P. 85. 416.
pradhânam primitive matter of the Sâṅkhyas P. 23.
Prajâpati mythological personification of the creative power P. 183.
prajâpatiloka region of the Devayâna P. 441.
prajñâ knowledge P. 178 ff.
prâjña, prâjña âtman, prajñâ âtman P. 180 n.
prakrita-hâna-aprakrita-prakriyâ, μετάβασις εἰς ἄλλο γένος p. 119, 4. 123, 4, 11. 146, 3. 169, 2. 338, 2. 344, 9. 1139, 15.
pramâṇam canon of knowledge P. 88 ff.
prâṇa breath, life; especially (1) the metaphysical life-principle, Brahman P. 147. 148. 164. 177. 180; (2) the physical life-principle (a) the whole complex of the subtle body and of its organs, only P. 202; (b) more limited: the psychic organs (*manas, indriyas, mukhya prâṇa*) P. 327 ff.; (c) still more limited: the *mukhya prâṇa* alone P. 333 ff.; (d) most limited: the exhaling, as a branch of the *mukhya prâṇa* P. 335.
prapañca the spatial extension (of the sense-world) P. 418. 462.
prapâṭhaka section of a work = *adhyâya* P. 30.
pratîkam the symbol P. 8 n. 439, p. 147, 14. 189, 8. 217, 10. 835, 9. 1059, 6.
pratyaksham observation, sense-perception P. 23. 88. 241; not to be confounded with the *anubhava*, the object (Brahman) of which is *paroksha* P. 211. 408. 422; contradictory P. 54.
pratyavâya descent (in transmigration) p. 754, 1, contrary to *abhyudaya*; cf. p. 997, 9. 10. 998, 2. 1128, 15. 1130, 7 (degradation p. 1064, 3. 5).
pratyaya perception P. 241 n., conception P. 8 n.
prasâda = *anugraha*.
prâyaçcittam penance P. 390. 421.
prithivî the earth P. 235. 237 n.
purâṇam a species of mythological literature P. 61. 236. 34.
purîtat (masc.) pericardium P. 347.
purohita family chaplain of a prince P. 6.
purusha man, spirit P. 119.
purusha-artha the aim of man (liberation) P. 95 n.

urusha puriçaya P. 199. 163.
ûrva-mîmâṅsâ cf. *mîmâṅsâ*.
ûrvapaksha the (generally premised) argumentation of the opponent (the opposite: *siddhânta*).
ûrvaprajñâ P. 193. 376.
rakshas, râkshasa goblin P. 158.
raurava P. 383.
ṛic verse P. 5. 140; therefrom *ṛig-veda*.
ṛitvij sacrificer P. 5.
ṛishi the human composers of the Vedas (Mantras and Brâhmaṇas) P. 38. 94 n. 405.
rûpam form, phenomenal form, appearance P. 103. 179. 211.
[*sac-cid-ânanda*] P. 212.
sâdhanam the means P. 99. 411 ff. 19.
saguṇam brahma the attribute-possessing, lower Brahman P. 102 ff.
saguṇâ avasthâ p. 1116, 4.
saguṇâ vidyâḥ (plur.) the doctrines (conceptions) of the attribute-possessing Brahman p. 910, 2. 1132, 1. 911, 4. 1017, 9. 1077, 7. 1082, 11. 1149, 13.
sâkshin the witness, spectator, soul P. 51 n. 58. 321. 324. 127.
samâdhi concentration, meditation (1) P. 411, (2) 321. 81.
sâman hymn P. 5. 140; therefrom *sâmaveda*.
samâna P. 336.
saṃhitâ collection (vedic) P. 6.
samîraṇam P. 260. 335.
saṃkalpa function of Manas (1) imagination P. 331, (2) decision, desire P. 345.
saṃnyâsa p. 891, 9.
saṃnyâsin one who (in the fourth Âçrama) has cast off everything P. 17.
sâmparâpa, sâmparâpa P. 383 n.
samparâya death; *sâmparâya* the life after death P. 383.
samprasâda deep sleep, soul in deep sleep, soul (*avasthâvant* for *avasthâ* p. 259, 6) P. 162. 164. 184. 432.
saṃrâdhanam ecstasy P. 214.
saṃsâra cycle, migration (of the soul) P. 357 ff.
saṃsârin the wandering (individual) soul p. 98, 1.
saṃskâra (1) impression P. 72. 241 n. 425, (2) moral purification P. 86 n. 403.
samyagdarçanam "universal knowledge" (referring everything to one point); perhaps better translated: "perfect knowledge" (τὸ τέλειον 1. Cor. 13, 10).
samyagjñânam = *samyagdarçanam*.
saṃyamanam P. 383.
sâṅkhyam the system of Kapila P. 19.
sarvagatatvam P. 306.
saṅgati p. 908, 5. 1082, 13.
sat the existing, Brahman P. 124. 129. 230. 264.
sattvam P. 171.
satya P. 161.
saviçesham brahma the differentiated (lower) Brahman p. 125, 5. 127, 16.
shashṭha-indriya-vishaya P. 70 n.
siddhânta the final opinion P. 71 n.
smṛiti (1) the tradition P. 12, (2) species of literature P. 24. 90.
sphoṭa P. 72 ff.
sṛishṭi the outpouring, creation P. 463.
stamba the plant-world P. 238.
sthaulyam materiality P. 251.
sthâvara = *stamba* P. 238.
sthûla material; *sthûla-çarîram* the coarse body P. 325.
sûkshmam çarîram the subtle body P. 370 ff.
[*sushumnâ*] the vein of the head, by which the soul of the devout departs, circumscribed in the Comm. to the Brahmas. by *mûr-*

dhanyâ nâḍî, çatâdhikâ nâḍî (p. 1105, 12); cf. P. 10 n., 380 n.
sushupti (*sushuptam, supti*) the deep sleep P. 346 ff.
sûtram (1) Vedic P. 11, (2) philosophical P. 25.
svapna dream-sleep, dream P. 343 ff.
svedaja P. 239.
tâdâtmyam identity P. 349.
[*tanmâtram*] P. 370 n.
tapas penance, asceticism P. 365.
tapya, tâpaka p. 515, 4.
tarka reflexion P. 91.
tat Brahman, *tat-tvam* to be Brahman P. 303. 467.
tat tvam asi "that art thou" P. 262 ff. 414.
tejas heat, fire P. 230. 369.
trailokhyam p. 298, 12 (cf. *bhûr-âdi-lokâḥ* p. 303, 4).
trishṇâ thirst, desire P. 159.
tvac (1) skin, (2) sense of touch P. 309 n.
udâna P. 336, 347.
udbhijja P. 239.
udgâtar priest of the Sâmaveda P. 5.
udgîtha song of the Sâman, transformed P. 8 n. 140. 145.
ukthum hymn P. 8 n. 178.
upâdânam matter P. 71. 223.
upâdhi limitation P. 302 ff.
upalabdhi, upalambha apperception P. 241 n. 321.
upanayanam P. 14. 60. 67.
upanishad (intimate) session, secret doctrine P. 3; secret name p. 884, 13. 14. 885, 7. 886, 5. 8. 13. 887, 6.
upâsanâ, upâsanam the devout meditation, worship P. 411. 413 ff. 438.
upasamhâra absorption (of the world in Brahman), cf. P. 237.
utkrânti passing of the soul from the body P. 367 ff.
uttara-mîmâṅsâ the doctrine of the Vedânta P. 20.
vairâgyam renunciation P. 173.
vaiçeshikam the philosophical system of Kaṇâda P. 20.
vaiçvânara (1) epithet of Agni, which he owes to the extraordinary circumstance, that he dwells not only in those that worship him faithfully, but "in all men" (The Hebrew world found what is emphasized in Matth. 5, 45 also strange). (2) epithet of Âtman P. 156 ff., where a double controversy is to be noticed, against sacrificial rites and against the castesystem.
vaiçya member of the third caste P. 13.
vânaprastha hermit (in the third *Âçrama*) P. 16. 173.
Varuṇa old Vedic god.
varuṇaloka region of the Devayâna P. 441.
vâsanâ (subjective) appearance P. 248; (in dreams) P. 320. 342.
vayas, vâyasa (as synonyms) P. 158.
Vâyu air, wind P. 231. 235. 237 n.; god of the wind P. 17.
vâyuloka region of the Devayâna P. 441.
vedânta (1) (closing chapter of the Veda) the Upanishads, (2) (final aim of the Veda) the doctrine of the Upanishads, (3) the system of Bâdarâyaṇa P. 3 ff. 20.
vibhutvam character of penetrating all things (as a quality of space, of Brahman, of the soul) P. 233. 310.
viç tribe, district P. 12.
viçesha difference P. 102. 104. 205.
vidhi order, constituent part of the Brâhmaṇas P. 7.
vidvant the knower (used in reference to the knower of the lower as well as the higher Brahman) P. 438 n.

vidyâ knowledge P. 55. 405 n.
vigraha, vigrahattvam individuality (as a quality of the gods in contrast to Brahman) p. 157, 3. 7. 159, 4. 13. 281, 1. 282, 4.
vîja-âtmanâ seed-like, potential P. 314.
vîja-çakti the seed-force of things P. 228. 371 n.
vijñânam (individual) knowledge P. 241 n. 314. 330.
vijñâna-âtman individual soul P. 180 n.
vishaya object P. 53.
vishayin subject P. 53.
Vishṇoḥ paramam padam originally: the highest step (point of culmination) of the sun; symbolical for the highest attainment, liberation Kâṭh. 3, 9; cf. p. 1121, 14. P. 443.
vritti function P. 332. 368.
vyakti individual P. 69.
vyatireka reaching beyond the body, immortality (of the soul) P. 287.
vyâna P. 336. 347.
vyâpti p. 861; *vyâpyam* p. 246, 1.
vyavahâra-avasthâ, vyâvaharikî avasthâ the practical (empirical) standpoint P. 106. 267. 271.

Yama god of death P. 383.
yama-niyama-vidyâ p. 907, 12.
yajus sacrificial formula P. 5. 198.
yoga (1) preparation (for union with the world's spirit) P. 18. 39. 138. (2) the system of Patañjali that leads to this P. 19. 440.
yogakâṇḍa certain Upanishads, that are in the service of Yoga P. 19 n.
yogin (1) who practices Yoga P. 213, who possesses supernatural powers P. 68. 39. 445, (2) follower of the Yogasystem P. 22.

Published by

Facsimile Publisher
Ashok Vihar, Delhi-110052 (India)
Website: www.facsimilepublisher.com

Distributed by

Gyan Books Pvt. Ltd.
5, Ansari Road, Daryaganj, New Delhi-110002 (India)
E-mail: books@gyanbooks.com, Website: www.gyanbooks.com

8 888007 040715